D1685247

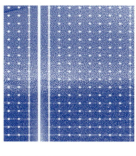
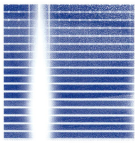
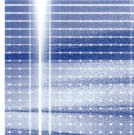

Strategy: Analysis and Practice

John McGee
Howard Thomas
David Wilson
Warwick Business School
University of Warwick, UK

The **McGraw·Hill** Companies

London   Boston   Burr Ridge, IL   Dubuque, IA   Madison, WI   New York   San Francisco   St. Louis   Bangkok   Bogotá   Caracas   Kuala Lumpur   Lisbon   Madrid   Mexico City   Milan   Montreal   New Delhi   Santiago   Seoul   Singapore   Sydney   Taipei   Toronto

Published by McGraw-Hill Education
Shoppenhangers Road
Maidenhead
Berkshire
SL6 2QL
Telephone: 44 (0) 1628 502 500
Fax: 44 (0) 1628 770 224
Website: www.mcgraw-hill.co.uk

British Library Cataloguing in Publication Data
A catalogue record for this book is available from the British Library

Library of Congress Cataloging in Publication Data
The Library of Congress data for this book has been applied for from the Library of Congress

Publishing Director: Catriona King
Acquisitions Editor: Kate Mason
Senior Development Editor: Caroline Howell
Sales and Marketing Director: John Donovan
Marketing Manager: Marca Wosoba

Text Design by Fakenham Photosetting Limited, Fakenham, Norfolk
Cover design by Fielding Design
Printed and bound in the UK by Ashford Colour Press Ltd, Gosport, Hampshire

ISBN 0-07-7119363
ISBN 13 978-0-07-711936-2

Detailed Table of Contents

Case Study Section

A Guide to Using the Case Studies

The main text of our book contains sixty case boxes within the chapters and twenty-one short case studies at the end of the chapters. These have been chosen to exemplify and enlarge upon the concepts and issues raised in each chapter. They are practical examples of how strategy concepts and ideas are manifested in the real world of making strategic decisions. Together with the Recap Questions at the end of each chapter these represent a practical study content that is further developed in the Online Learning Centre that accompanies this book at www.mcgraw-hill.co.uk/textbooks/mcgee.

The case studies that appear in this section take your learning onto a different level. These case studies are written around real, practical problems but in using them you should recognize that they are not intended as illustrations of either effective or ineffective management practice. In reading the previous chapters we hope to have persuaded you that the world of strategy and practice is messy and complicated. It follows usually that it is not easy or indeed sensible to attempt to categorize management practice as good or bad. These case studies are intended to provide a basis for analyzing and discussing a range of different situations in which the decisions to be taken are either not obvious or their implementation carries risks and complexities. These cases are typically quite long and contain considerable detail. Whereas the earlier case boxes and end of chapter cases are designed to be short so as to highlight the learning of concepts, the case studies in this section show the application of strategy theory and concepts in the real world of complex detail that is characteristic of companies and other organizations. The learning objective of analyzing long case studies is to bring together your ability to think conceptually with your ability to collect, select, analyze and interpret considerable amounts of data. Taken together these abilities are the basis for being able to understand and make strategic decisions.

This general and overarching objective can be broken down into specific learning experiences.

1   The first step is to gain practice in identifying key problems. The strategist's usual questions are where are we going? How are we going to get there? How do we expect to be able to succeed? These questions need to be fully articulated so that the context of the case is properly captured in the questions. For example, it is not enough to simply make a distinction between a growth strategy and a share retention strategy. The alternatives have to be expressed in terms of the detail of the situation so that the nature of the required judgments can be understood.

2   The cases are also designed to give practice in specifying what is meant by key concepts such as competitive advantage and core competence in real terms. As intellectual constructs these are powerful ideas but only gain real meaning when placed within the specific context of the individual company.

3   Case studies also allow the analyst to gain practice in how to shape an implementation plan. This should be expressed in terms of the business model, the key functional strategies and tactics, the key decisions to be taken and the risks involved.

4   The complexity of the real worlds of these cases allows you to explore larger issues such as mergers and acquisitions, technical innovation and R&D, performance assessment, corporate governance, and ethics and social responsibility. These represent significant 'strategic issues' that have concepts and content of their own and attract significant debate and controversy.

The summary table that follows displays how the cases relate to the chapters. There is an indication of the main focus of each case and also an indication of the minor focus. Each case may apply to more than one chapter and may cover a variety of concepts. The country location of each case is also shown so that you can choose to focus or diversify your use of cases as you wish.

In using cases you should be aware that before going onto the main theme of the case you will need to carry out a strategy analysis such as that shown in chapters 5, 6 and 7 (where the basic idea of competitive strategy is explained). Thus, a question posed in the case might be: 'Should Unilever buy cosmetics company X?' In order to address this question properly it is first necessary to undertake

Guide to the main focus of cases

Page	Companies/Industries Featured:	Ch 1 and 2 — Introduction: basic concepts	Ch 3 and 4 — Economics of Strategy	Ch 5 — Industry Analysis & Competitive Strategy	Ch 6 — Competitive Position: competitive advantage	Ch 7 — Strategic Capability: core competence	Ch 8 — Life cycles, turnarounds, entrepreneurs	Ch 9 — Corporate Strategy: parenting advantage	Ch 10 — M&A and Alliances	Ch 11 — Global Strategies	Ch 12 — New Economy	Ch 13 — Strategic Decision Making	Ch 14 — Risk & Uncertainty	Ch 15 — Strategic Change	Ch 16 — Learning	Ch 17 — Corporate Governance	Ch 18 — Performance Assessment: balanced score card	Ch 19 — Knowledge, Information, Innovation	Ch 20 — Total quality, process improvement	Ch 21 — Business value as a system	Country location of case study
C407	Abrakebabra						◆◆										◆				Ireland
C357	British Airways									◆◆				◆◆							UK
C337	Blue Circle								◆◆												UK
C258	BSkyB				◆						◆◆		◆								UK
C106	Canon				◆	◆◆						◆									Japan
C195	Cola Wars in China			◆	◆◆		◆			◆			◆								China
C471	Consulting Industry				◆◆																Global
C418	Creyf in the Euro Temping Industry	◆			◆			◆◆	◆◆				◆								Belgium
C437	DSM - Performance Management							◆◆									◆◆			◆	The Netherlands
C079	easyJet			◆	◆◆	◆															UK
C237	Ferrari												◆	◆	◆◆			◆◆			Italy
C059	Finland & Nokia		◆◆								◆							◆			Scandinavia
C224	Formula 1 Constructors			◆														◆			UK/Europe
C458	Gatetrade: Nordic B2B Marketplace				◆				◆		◆◆		◆								Scandinavia
C324	Grand Metropolitan to Diageo							◆◆	◆					◆							UK

Key: ◆◆ = major focus   ◆ = important subsidiary focus

Page	Companies/Industries Featured:	Ch 1 and 2: Introduction: basic concepts	Ch 3 and 4: Economics of Strategy	Ch 5: Industry Analysis & Competitive Strategy	Ch 6: Competitive Position: competitive advantage	Ch 7: Strategic Capability: core competence	Ch 8: Life cycles, turnarounds, entrepreneurs	Ch 9: Corporate Strategy: parenting advantage	Ch 10: M&A and Alliances	Ch 11: Global Strategies	Ch 12: New Economy	Ch 13: Strategic Decision Making	Ch 14: Risk & Uncertainty	Ch 15: Strategic Change	Ch 16: Learning	Ch 17: Corporate Governance	Ch 18: Performance Assessment: balanced score card	Ch 19: Knowledge, Information, Innovation	Ch 20: Total quality, process improvement	Ch 21: Business value as a system	Country location of case study
C027	Honda A & B	◆◆	◆◆	◆	◆◆								◆								Japan/USA
C376	House of Townend			◆	◆◆							◆◆									UK
C097	Hewlett-Packard			◆◆								◆							◆◆		Global
C143	HSBC							◆		◆◆			◆								China
C245	IKEA			◆	◆					◆◆		◆◆									Sweden
C210	Leo Burnett					◆				◆◆		◆◆									Canada
C310	Low-Cost Airlines Industry		◆	◆◆																	UK
C123	LVMH				◆			◆◆		◆					◆						France
C290	Mobile Telecoms Industry in the UK			◆							◆◆										UK
C005	NEC and GTE				◆	◆◆															Japan
C043	Nike	◆										◆◆		◆							USA
C174	Rank Xerox A,B,C															◆◆	◆◆		◆◆		Europe
C477	Rockware			◆			◆◆														UK
C391	Shell															◆◆					The Netherlands/UK
C152	Virgin						◆◆	◆													UK

Key: ◆◆ = major focus   ◆ = important subsidiary focus

a preliminary strategy analysis in order to understand the major strategic objectives, the nature of the competitive advantage and the degree of success of the implementation of the current strategy. This places the 'buy/not buy' decision in proper context.

The cases are intended to be used as they stand without recourse to more recent information such as financial reports or websites. You may find it helpful to review your recommendations against these data sources but you should bear in mind that the future, as it actually took place, is *not* necessarily the best answer!

亞洲商業案例中心
Centre for Asian Business Cases
School of Business, The University of Hong Kong

Case 1 **Core competence at NEC and GTE**

In 1990, a *Harvard Business Review* article touted NEC Corporation of Japan's 'core competence' and its focus on 'computers and communications'.[1] The same article heavily criticised GTE Corporation of the United States for focusing its attention on 'businesses' rather than 'competencies'. The authors proceeded to predict a bright future for NEC and other 'competence-based' companies, and potential obsolescence for GTE and other 'business-based' companies. The article, 'The Core Competence of the Corporation', which went on to become the best-selling HER reprint in history, ushered in a wave of consulting and academic work that said that 'core competence' was the key to company performance. NEC, with its 'C&C' strategy, became the darling of consultants and business academics around the world and the veritable 'poster child' for strategies

Professor Michael J. Enright prepared this case for class discussion. This case is not intended to show effective or ineffective handling of decision or business processes. This case is best used with Prahalad, C.K. & Hamel, G., 'The Core Competence of the Corporation', Harvard Business Review. Vol. 68, No. 3, pp.79–91 (reprints available from Harvard Business School Publishing, reprint no. 90311).

[1] Prahalad, C.K. & Hamel, G., (1990), 'The Core Competence of the Corporation', *Harvard Business Review*, Vol. 68, No. 3, pp.79–91.

based on core competencies. By mid-1999, however, NEC was in the midst of unprecedented upheaval. New CEO Koji Nishigaki promised to shake up the company by eliminating unprofitable businesses and by turning the manufacturer of computers, semiconductors, electronic devices, and communications equipment into an Internet-based company. Meanwhile, GTE appeared to be moving from strength to strength and to be well situated in the burgeoning international market for telecommunications.

NEC, GTE, and 'The Core Competence of the Corporation'

In the opening of 'The Core Competence of the Corporation,' authors C. K. Prahalad and Gary Hamel motivated the notion of 'core competence' by comparing NEC and GTE.

> *Consider the last ten years of GTE and NEC. In the early 1980s, GTE was well positioned to become a major player in the evolving information technology industry. It was active in telecommunications. Its operations spanned a variety of businesses including telephones, switching and transmission systems, digital PABX, semiconductors, packet switching, satellites, defense systems, and lighting products. And GTE's Entertainment Products Group, which produced Sylvania color TVs, had a position in related display technologies. In 1980, GTE's sales were $9.98 billion and net cash flow was $1.73 billion. NEC, in contrast, was much smaller, at $3.8 billion in sales. It had a comparable technological base and computer business, but it had no experience as an operating telecommunications company.*
>
> *Yet look at the positions of GTE and NEC in 1988. GTE's 1988 sales were $16.46 billion, and NEC's sales were considerably higher at $21.89 billion. GTE has, in effect, become a telephone operating company with a position in defense and lighting products. GTE's other businesses are small in global terms. GTE has divested Sylvania TV and Telenet, put switching, transmission, and digital PABX into joint ventures, and closed down semiconductors. As a result, the international position of GTE has eroded.*

Non-US revenue as a percent of total revenue dropped from 20% to 15% between 1980 and 1988.

NEC has emerged as the world leader in semiconductors and as a first-tier player in telecommunications products and computers. It has consolidated its position in mainframe computers. It has moved beyond public switching and transmission to include such lifestyle products as mobile telephones, facsimile machines, and laptop computers – bridging the gap between telecommunications and office automation. NEC is the only company in the world to be in the top five in revenue in telecommunications, semiconductors, and mainframes. Why did these two companies, starting with comparable business portfolios, perform so differently? Largely because NEC conceived of itself in terms of 'core competencies', and GTE did not.[2]

NEC to 1990

NEC (Nippon Electric Corporation) was founded in Tokyo on 17 July 1899, by a group of Japanese investors, led by Kunihiko Iwardare, as a joint venture with the US-based Western Electric Company, the manufacturing subsidiary of AT&T. Two years later, the company built its first manufacturing plant and in 1908 established its first foreign sales office in Seoul, Korea. NEC's initial products were telephone lines and equipment made primarily with Western Electric's technology. In 1918, the company successfully completed the installation of its own telephone lines and equipment in Hankow and Wuchang in China. During the rebuilding of Tokyo after the 1923 Kanto earthquake, NEC was chosen to modify automatic telephone exchange equipment from European and US manufacturers. NEC soon began to manufacture its own systems and in 1925 it began to produce vacuum tubes and phototelegraphy equipment, a forerunner of the modern facsimile machine.

---

2 Prahalad, C.K. & Hamel, G., (1990), 'The Core Competence of the Corporation', *Harvard Business Review,* Vol. 68, No. 3, pp.79–80. Reprinted by permission *of Harvard Business Review.* Copyright © 1990 by the Harvard Business School Publishing Corporation; all rights reserved.

The Japanese Government's desire for technological self-sufficiency in the 1930s pushed NEC to develop more and more of its own products. It began manufacturing radio broadcast equipment in 1930 and began research on microwave communications technology in 1935. It extended its business in cables and related technologies, and made history in 1939 by laying one of the world's longest telephone cable lines; 3,000 kilometres from Tokyo, through Korea, and into China. NEC also made efforts to develop technologies related to television relay and broadcasting, aiming at covering the Tokyo Olympic Games scheduled to be held in Tokyo in 1940. However, the Games were cancelled due to Sino-Japanese hostilities, and the research was further interrupted by the outbreak of World War II. By the late 1930s, some 40 per cent of the company's sales were to the Japanese military, a figure that increased to nearly 97 per cent by the end of the war in 1945.

Post World War II product developments

The years after the war heralded a new era in NEC's operations. NEC was able to take advantage of post-war rebuilding in Japan, rapid technological change, and the globalisation of business. In 1949, its shares were listed on the Tokyo and Osaka stock exchanges.

NEC became one of four principal suppliers to Nippon Telegraph and Telephone (NTT), the government-owned company that was formed in 1952 to control Japan's telephone industry. The post-WWII need to repair Japan's telephone systems and the country's continuing economic recovery resulted in strong demand from NTT for NEC's products. In the late 1950s and in the 1960s, NTT business represented over 50 per cent of NEC's sales. NTT provided a firm, protected source of demand for NEC and other Japanese suppliers for decades. NTT, for example, decided to press ahead with microwave communications links for the national telephone system, a decision that provided substantial demand for NEC microwave technology. The 1950 Radio Waves Law, which made radio waves available for use by the private sector, also created a large private-sector demand for radio and television receivers, as well as microwave links. NEC soon became a leading producer of microwave equipment.

The company also began to supply radios, television sets, and other consumer electronics products.

The development of the transistor in 1947 at the Bell Telephone Laboratories in the United States provided the forerunner of modern semiconductor integrated circuits (ICs), which in turn were to form the basis of modern communications and computer technologies. NEC signed a technology licensing agreement with GE from the United States in 1958 (five years after Sony had signed a similar agreement with Western Electric). The company established its Integrated Circuits Division in 1960 and became the first Japanese company to manufacture integrated circuits. The company eventually moved into large-scale integrated circuits (LSIs) in the mid-1960s and very large-scale integrated circuits (VLSIs) in 1967. NEC made its first foray into the computer industry in the 1950s. It demonstrated the world's first working transistorised computer in 1959, made the first Japanese microprocessor in 1974, and developed its first personal computer in 1979. By the end of the 1970s, NEC had established itself as a leader in its three main lines of business: communications equipment, computers, and semiconductors.

International operations

NEC had been cut off from international markets during the Second World War. The company began to expand internationally in the 1950s with the export of communications equipment to Asia. By the late 1950s, NEC was exporting large-scale communications equipment for public telephone networks to the Middle and Near East. It established its first marketing subsidiary for communications equipment in North America in 1963, and later developed a number of local manufacturing subsidiaries there, with product lines ranging from communications systems and computer peripherals to semiconductors. NEC's operations in Latin America began in the 1960s with the sale of microwave communications systems, and it entered the European market in the same period by shipping satellite communications earth stations and microwave communications systems. It continued to expand its European operations and concentrated on building a marketing network throughout Europe.

NEC began operations in Africa in the 1970s, with an emphasis on building communications networks to promote economic development. NEC introduced its first digital switching system for the overseas market in 1977, although Japanese telephone networks were based on analog technology at the time. In the early 1980s, NEC delivered and installed digital optical communication networks in Argentina using optical fire cables manufactured by Sumitomo and digital switching equipment supplied by NEC. Meanwhile, NEC consumer electronics products were exported throughout the world, with substantial increases in foreign sales in the 1980s.

C & C – computers and communications

In 1964, Koji Kobayshi was appointed NEC president, and in 1976 he became chairman and CEO, a position he held for the next 12 years. In 1977 he articulated his vision of NEC's future as an integrator of computers and communications through semiconductor technology. Kobayashi believed that the integration of computers and communications was inevitable. He refocused the company on equipment to process and transmit information, thus forming the vision of NEC in terms of 'computers and communications', or 'C&C'. The company built on its past experience to focus on developing its capabilities in the technologies that were common to the different products that would emerge from this vision.

At the time, NEC has four separate divisions for its main businesses – communications, computers and industrial electronic systems, electron devices, and consumer electronics. It set up project teams that spanned different divisions. Marketing and sales had a team devoted to the promotion of C&C products, such as office and factory automation equipment and switching technology. Increasingly, however, the company organised itself around its core technologies rather than lines of business.

By the late 1980s, NEC was the largest of Japan's four major telecommunications equipment companies (in many other countries, telecommunications equipment was dominated by a single national champion or monopoly supplier).[3] NTT, which was partially privatised in 1985, still provided

---

[3] The other three companies were Fujitsu, Hitachi and Oki.

an important, though less dominant, market for Japanese companies. NTT accounted for roughly 50 per cent of NEC's sales in 1967, but only 13 per cent in 1985. NEC sold its digital public telephone exchange equipment in 28 countries (but never achieved much success in the United States), and was the world's largest supplier of satellite earth stations and microwave communications equipment. Although numerous competitors, first from Japan and then from Korea, had entered the cyclical and price-sensitive memory chip portion of the semiconductor industry, NEC was the world leader in semiconductor sales (mostly memory chips) and boasted the largest factory for standardised memory chips in the world.

NEC held the third-largest market share for computers within Japan and dominated the Japanese personal computer market, a market it had helped pioneer in the late 1970s and early 1980s. NEC's proprietary operating system helped it to dominate the Japanese PC market and shielded it from the cut-throat competition that broke out among producers in the United States, but also limited its presence in international markets, where systems based on Intel microprocessors and Microsoft operating systems became the norm. In 1987, in an attempt to extend its position in the hotly contested mainframe computer market, where it faced companies such as IBM and Fujitsu among others, NEC formed a partnership with Honeywell (United States) and France's Groupe Bull.

NEC was also a significant player in the home electronics business, an industry that had come to be dominated by several highly competitive Japanese firms, including Matsushita and Sony, and from which many United States and European firms had exited. NEC's home electronics division, which was responsible for about 10 per cent of sales, included televisions, video recorders and hi-fis.

Other firms that tried to carry out 'C&C' strategies, such as AT&T and IBM in the United States and Olivetti and Siemens in Europe, however, had found it impossible to compete in the three areas (or even two out of the three areas) profitably. NEC's foreign sales peaked at 35 per cent of total sales in 1984 and declined to 25 per cent of sales by 1989. As **Exhibit 2** shows, NEC was unique in appearing among the world's top five in its three core

technologies: computers, telecommunications, and semiconductor devices. It was this position that Prahalad and Hamel wrote about in 1990.

GTE to 1990

GTE got its start in 1918 when three entrepreneurs, John O'Connell, Sigrid Odegard, and John Pratt, bought the Richland Center Telephone Company. The name was changed to Commonwealth Telephone Company two years later, and by 1935, the company was reorganised as the General Telephone Corporation. The company entered a period of rapid growth in the early post-World War II period, as US demand for telephone services exploded.

General Telephone's initial line of business was the provision of local telephone services. At the time, local telephone service in each area in the United States was provided by a local monopoly supplier. General Telephone created a subsidiary to produce telephone directories in 1926 and acquired a communications equipment-manufacturing company in 1950. In 1955, General Telephone acquired Theodore Gary and Company. Gary's subsidiary Automatic Electric would become General Telephone's main communications equipment-manufacturing operation. Along with the Gary purchase came companies that served 600,000 telephone customers in the United States, the Dominican Republic, and Canada, as well as a minority interest in the Philippines Long Distance Telephone Company. The acquisition of Peninsular Telephone of Florida added another 300,000 customers. By 1957, General Telephone was providing telephone service to 2.8 million customers in the United States, Canada, and the Dominican Republic.

Merger and expansion

In 1959, General Telephone merged with Sylvania Electric Products, and the name of the parent company was changed to General Telephone & Electronics Corporation (GTE). At the time, Sylvania, whose roots went back to 1901, was a major electronics supplier. Its products included light bulbs, fluorescent lamps, flash bulbs for photography, vacuum tubes, speciality chemical products, and metallurgical products for the electronics industry.

The merger with Sylvania, which had 45 plants and sales exceeding US$333 million (making it roughly comparable in size to General Telephone) created a diversified electronics and communications group.

The merger also marked the beginning of a period of tremendous expansion. In the 1960s, GTE expanded its telephone operations by acquiring phone companies in British Columbia, Quebec, Hawaii, and several Western and Midwestern US states, while selling off its Philippine stake. In 1969, GTE installed its ten-millionth telephone. The company expanded its product offerings in other areas in the 1960s and 1970s. It set up a data services subsidiary, acquired a communications company, obtained the name and distribution rights for Philco consumer electronics products in the United States and Canada, and introduced new technologies, such as the world's first fibre-optic communications system to provide a regular telephone service (between Long Beach and Artesia, California, in 1977).

The 1970s also saw GTE consolidating and reorganising its management. Corporate headquarters was relocated to Stamford, Connecticut, from New York City. The GTE Products Group was formed to bring worldwide manufacturing and marketing under a single entity. Foreign manufacturing subsidiaries, which had been under a single international division, were reassigned to their respective global divisions headquartered in the United States. Thomas A. Vanderslice, formerly of GE, was named President and Chief Operating Officer in 1979 with a mandate from Chairman and CEO Theodore F. Brophy to change the company into a leaner and more aggressive operation.

Liberalisation in the US telecommunications industry

The US telecommunications industry experienced dramatic change in the 1980s. In 1984, an anti-trust case resulted in the break-up of AT&T and an end to its virtual monopoly of telephone service in the United States. At the time, telephone service in most countries was provided by a single monopoly supplier. AT&T had been granted a virtual monopoly over telephone service in the United States in 1918, and by 1984 AT&T served the vast majority of the United States with local (80 percent), long-distance

(100 per cent), and international (100 per cent) telephone service, telephone directories, and telephone equipment, including everything from simple handsets to the most complicated central-office switching equipment.

Under the 1984 settlement, AT&T's local telephone companies were formed into seven regional Bell operating companies (RBOCs). Each RBOC was granted a monopoly on local fixed-line services within its region, but was denied the right to manufacture equipment and could not sell inter-regional or international long-distance services. Eventually, the local fixed-line companies were given one of two cellular phone licences granted in each region. AT&T retained its manufacturing, laboratories, and the right to sell interstate and international long-distance call services. The settlement created a totally open market for telecommunications equipment of all types, by separating manufacturing from the provision of local telephone service, as the RBOCs were now free to purchase equipment from any vendor. It left local monopolies in fixed-line local service, but created competition in long-distance and international services by opening these services up to new competitors.

GTE in the 1980s

The AT&T settlement left GTE as the only company in the United States with its own manufacturing arm, local operating companies, long-distance service, and mobile or cellular phone activities. GTE's local telephone companies pre-dated the granting of monopoly status or had been set up in relatively remote areas before AT&T could supply service (sometimes with the latter's blessing). As a result, by 1984, GTE served rural and suburban markets in some 28 states. In its areas, GTE traditionally operated like a mini-AT&T, supplying local telephone service, telephone directories, and telephone equipment, though AT&T provided long-distance and international phone service to GTE customers. By 1984, GTE provided approximately 10 per cent of US local connections, compared to 80 per cent for AT&T and 10 per cent for a host of other small independent companies. GTE's relatively small share meant that there was no effort by the US Government to break up the company. However, the AT&T decision came at an unsettled time for GTE, as President Vanderslice had resigned in December 1983 amid some controversy before he could completely implement his plans for GTE.

GTE decided to realign its business portfolio, announcing in 1984 that it would focus on three 'core' businesses: telecommunications, lighting, and precision materials. The company had already entered new communications businesses. In 1982, GTE Mobilnet® was formed. The following year, GTE acquired a long-distance telephone services company (renamed GTE Sprint), and satellite communications companies (renamed GTE Spacenet), and began offering mobile phone service and developing satellite communications services in 1984. Airphone, a company that provided telephone services from commercial aircraft, was acquired in 1986. By 1989, GTE was the first cellular phone provider to offer service nationally in the United States. The company's research focused on the telecommunications business, by developing advanced ISDN capabilities, beginning the development of advanced network systems (such as video on demand), and creating new military communications systems.

The firm also sold or exited several businesses. Television- and radio-manufacturing operations were sold (many other US and European firms had already exited these businesses), as was the company's cable television equipment, electrical equipment, and structural support (for construction) businesses. In communications equipment, GTE's communications transmission and central-office switch-manufacturing activities were transferred to a joint venture 80 per cent controlled by the German company Siemens in 1986, and its US business systems and PABX businesses were transferred to a joint venture 80 per cent owned by Fujitsu of Japan in 1987. In 1989, its consumer communications products business was divested. GTE also gradually divested its stake in GTE Sprint, which had incurred huge investment costs and substantial operating losses in what had become a fiercely competitive long-distance telephone market.

The end of the decade saw GTE in the midst of restructuring. It announced major job cuts, sold off various businesses, and reorganised the company into six operating groups. Previously the company had had just two units: telephone and communications products/services. Following the reorganisation, the six operating groups were: Telephone Operations, Electrical Products, Government Systems, Information Services, Mobile Communications, and Spacenet.

The 'Core Competence' take on NEC and GTE

Prahalad and Hamel characterised the evolution of the two companies until 1990 as follows;

NEC versus GTE, again, is instructive and only one of many such comparative cases we analysed to understand the changing basis for global leadership. Early in the 1970s, NEC articulated a strategic intent to exploit the convergence of computing and communications, what it called 'C&C'. Success, top management reckoned, would hinge on acquiring competencies, particularly in semiconductors. Management adopted an appropriate 'strategic architecture', summarized by C&C, and then communicated its intent to the whole organisation and the outside world during the mid-1970s.

NEC constituted a 'C&C Committee' of top managers to oversee the development of core products and core competencies. NEC put in place coordination groups and committees that cut across the interests of individual businesses. Consistent with its strategic architecture, NEC shifted enormous resources to strengthen its position in components and central processors. By using collaborative arrangements to multiply internal resources, NEC was able to accumulate a broad array of core competencies.

NEC carefully identified three interrelated streams of technological and market evolution. Top management determined that computing would evolve from large mainframes to distributed processing, components from simple ICs to VLSI, and communications from mechanical cross-bar exchange to complex digital systems we now call ISDN. As things evolved further, NEC reasoned, the computing, communications, and components businesses would so overlap that it would be very hard to distinguish among them, and that there would be enormous opportunities for any company that had built the competencies needed to serve all three markets.

NEC top management determined that semi-conductors would be the company's most important 'core product'. It entered into myriad strategic alliances – over 100 as of 1987 – aimed at building competencies rapidly and at low cost. In mainframe computers, its most noted relationship was with Honeywell and Bull. Almost all the collaborative arrangements in the semiconductor-component field were oriented toward technology access. As they entered collaborative arrangements, NEC's operating managers understood the rationale for these alliances and the goal of internalizing partner skills. NEC's director of research summed up its competence acquisition during the 1970s and 1980s this way: 'From an investment standpoint, it was much quicker and cheaper to use foreign technology. There wasn't a need for us to develop new ideas.'

No such clarity of strategic architecture appeared to exist at GTE. Although senior executives discussed the implications of the evolving information technology industry, no commonly accepted view of which competencies would be required to compete in that industry were communicated widely. While significant staff work was done to identify key technologies, senior line managers continued to act as if they were managing independent business units. Decentralization made it difficult to focus on core competencies. Instead, individual businesses became increasingly dependent on outsiders for critical skills, and collaboration became a route to staged exits. Today, with a new management team in place, GTE has repositioned itself to apply its competencies to emerging markets in telecommunications services.[4]

NEC in the 1990s

NEC, which entered the 1990s as one of the world's most admired corporations, soon faced new challenges. The Japanese economy, which accounted for most of NEC's sales, stalled as asset values collapsed. This in turn exacerbated a banking crisis that had been hidden during the prior decade's growth. Japan's economy slowed for most of the decade and the Nikkei index, which stood at nearly 39,000 at the end of 1989, was just under 19,000 at the end of 1999. The 'Big Bang' reforms in Japan's financial markets in the late 1990s saw a heightened interest in profitability and returns on the part of shareholders. Many Japanese firms found their competitive positions under threat as North American and European firms regained their footing and as production from Newly Industrialised Economies such as Korea, Taiwan, Hong Kong, Singapore, and other Asian economies grew.

NEC lost its status as the world's largest semiconductor maker to Intel (which concentrated on the microprocessors that ran most of the world's personal computers) in the early 1990s. By 1998, market research indicated that NEC had slipped to third place in memory chips behind the Korean companies Samsung Electronics Company and Hyundai Electronics Industries.[5] The memory portion of the semiconductor industry continued to be cyclical, with firms losing as much money in downturns as they made in upturns, if not more, and continued to see governments (in places such as Korea, Malaysia, and Taiwan, among others) supporting new entry into the business.

Competition in the telecommunications equipment industry had changed substantially from the days in which cosy monopolies and oligopolies dominated national markets. The darlings of the industry had become fast-moving specialist companies such as Nokia, Ericsson, and Motorola, rather than slower-moving, broad-line companies such as NEC. Several foreign players made significant inroads into the Japanese market, particularly in newer and more

[4] Prahalad, C.K. & Hamel, G., (1990), 'The Core Competence of the Corporation', *Harvard Business Review*, Vol. 68, No. 3, pp.80–81. Reprinted by permission *of Harvard Business Review*. Copyright © 1990 by the Harvard Business School Publishing Corporation; all rights reserved.

[5] MacLellan, A., 'Japan revamps strategies', *Electronic Buyers News*, 5 April, 1999.

advanced applications such as mobile telephony and data transmission and handling equipment.

In October 1992, Compaq Computer Corporation of the United States stunned the Japanese PC market when it introduced its Prolinea series into Japan. The standardisation around the 'Wintel' combination of Microsoft operating systems and Intel microprocessors had made the personal computer industry in the United States a commodity business. NEC's proprietary system based on internal competencies had limited direct price competition in Japan. With the Prolinea, which undercut Japanese rivals by more than 50 per cent in price, Compaq initiated price competition that had not been seen formerly in the Japanese PC market. When NEC's PC operations began to suffer, it responded in 1994 by allowing licensing of PCs based on its operating system for the first time. However, the days of the proprietary NEC system were numbered as even NEC began making 'Wintel' computers in earnest. By June 1995, NEC's share of Japan's personal computer market had fallen to below 50 per cent. It would fall to 27 per cent by 1998.

In the late 1990s, NEC entered into a number of joint ventures and alliances covering its whole range of operations. In 1995, NEC and Packard Bell Electronics, the leader in US retail PC market share, formed Packard Bell-NEC. In 1998, NEC raised its stake in Packard Bell from 20 per cent to 80 per cent. In 1996, in an attempt to improve the yield on the chip production lines of both companies, NEC and Samsung Electronics agreed to jointly research improving production efficiency and to swap sensitive information on manufacturing yields and processing techniques. This was viewed as an attempt to shore up the situation in a commodity business. In the same year, NEC created US subsidiary Holon Net Corp. to make hardware and software for Internet and intranet markets.

In spite of these efforts, by 1998 NEC was in crisis. Tadahiro Sekimoto resigned as chairman in October 1998, taking responsibility for NEC's activities in a defence procurement scandal, in which several NEC officials were indicted on charges of overcharging the Japanese military in procurement contracts. Despite president Hishashi Kaneko's assurances that he would remain in his position, he was forced to resign in February 1999 in the wake of massive losses forecast for the year.

On March 26 1999, Koji Nishigaki was appointed president of NEC. Nishigaki soon announced a plan to eliminate unprofitable business and concentrate on those tied to the Internet. More radical was his intention to create cost-of-capital measurements for individual businesses, set targets for return on that capital, and allocate funds to high-return operations. This move was in stark contrast to traditional Japanese measures of business performance, which were commonly market share and top-line sales growth, regardless of the amount of money invested. It also was in stark contrast to the 'core competence' model of organisation that the company had followed. Mr. Nishigaki was clear that NEC would focus on shareholder value, and even more radically, that each division would have a separate profit and loss account, which would be made public.

We will promote decentralisation by transferring a significant amount of authority to NEC's business groups through the balanced implementation of in-house divisional companies. These in-house companies will develop and execute business plans as well as take responsibility for business results independently of each other.

– Koji Nishigaki.[6]

In September, Nishigaki announced a business plan that put the Internet at the centre of each division's mission statement and positioned NEC as a 'solutions provider' for businesses trying to cash in on e-commerce. The restructuring was to break the company into three separate entities – NEC Solutions, NEC Networks, and NEC Electron Devices. Each company was to be responsible for its own operations, from production to sales, in a business-unit structure. Nishigaki also announced an alliance with Intel, which planned to open 12 worldwide Internet hosting centres, offering systems for service providers, by the end of 2000. Intel planned to establish the first centre in Japan with NEC. Customers of Biglobe (NEC's flagship Internet service provider) were to be able to use Intel's standard e-business application and hosting services once the centre was up and running. Nishigaki also announced a joint venture with Hitachi

---

[6] Nishigaki, K., 'The Path Towards Corporate Excellence', January 2000.

to consolidate their money-losing memory chip operations, the restructuring of Packard Bell-NEC (which laid off 80 per cent of its employees and exited the US retail market), and entered an agreement with Hewlett-Packard to develop a next-generation Internet network for Japan.

GTE in the 1990s

GTE developed substantially in the 1990s. The United States, where GTE had the bulk of its sales, saw substantial economic growth in the decade. Asset prices rose dramatically, with the S&P 500 average going from 353 at the end of 1989 to 1,455 at the end of 1999. The decade also saw dramatic expansion of most communication services in the United States, with data applications and then the emerging Internet driving growing demand.

GTE began the decade with the announcement of what was (at that time) the largest merger in telecommunications history. The merger with Contel Corporation, a major local telephone and cellular service provider, created the fifth-largest domestic telephone company in the United States and, together with the acquisition of additional cellular properties, the nation's second-largest cellular phone service provider. GTE closed the decade with an agreement to merge with one of the RBOCs, Bell Atlantic (1998), the acquisition of cellular phone assets from Ameritech (1999), and the announcement of an alliance with Vodaphone Airtouch (1999) to form the largest wireless communications company in the United States.

Throughout the 1990s, GTE's focused its efforts on new and enhanced communications businesses. By 1992, GTE was launching large-scale market trials of two-way personal communications services. It introduced new advanced switching modes, the first wide-area multimedia communications network in the United States, interactive video services, wireless data and personal communications services, international roaming services for cellular phones, Internet access services, online services, and others. In order to position itself for the Internet revolution and related data communication markets, GTE purchased BBN, along with its national IP network, in 1997. GTE also reached agreements with Lycos (online services), Qwest (fibre optic networks), and Cisco (internetworking capabilities) to enhance its position in Internet-related businesses.

GTE also expanded in foreign markets in the 1990s. In 1991, it announced a joint venture with SOVINTEL to provide instantaneous, high-quality telephone service from the Soviet Union to the West and Asia. In the same year, it led the consortium that acquired a 40 per cent share in the Venezuelan telephone company CANTV. GTE also began activities in Argentina (cellular phone services), Belgium (directory services), Mexico (alliance to provide communications services), China (research and development, installation of cellular phone equipment on China Southern Boeing 777s, and helping set up a wireless paging network), Japan (cellular phone service), Taiwan (cellular phone service), and Puerto Rico (local telephone services). In several instances, GTE obtained local monopoly or oligopoly positions in its new markets.

Continuing its focus on specific businesses rather than competencies, GTE divested its worldwide lighting, electrical products, space-based communications, and aircraft cellular phone businesses, and its remaining stake in long-distance company Sprint. It also announced that it would sell its Government Systems operation (mostly communications systems for the military). Each of the businesses was described as either under-performing or non-core. The divestitures would free up resources for high-growth initiatives in the company's core businesses.

In the United States, the Telecommunications Act of 1996 had forced the RBOCs to open up their facilities so that competitors could connect to them, but also allowed the RBOCs to sell long-distance services once they met a 14-point 'Competitive Checklist' to ensure they had opened their networks to competition. On December 22, 1999, Bell Atlantic became the first RBOC to be granted the right to sell long-distance services. The Act, increased competition, data and voice network convergence, and the emergence of the Internet all contributed to unprecedented growth and transformation in the US telecommunications industry. The barriers that had created separate worlds of wireless, wireline, voice, data, local, and long-distance services were eroding, and a new communications network was being constructed in its place. Local exchange carriers had gained ground by introducing new services at lower prices using alternative technology, and cable operators who had recognised their capability of transferring voice and data had also entered the market. GTE had positioned itself right in the middle of this communications revolution.

According to GTE management, the company was well positioned in its core businesses, and was confident that these businesses would allow it to compete successfully in the future:

> We understood that, within the first few years of the next century, 80 to 90 per cent of our total traffic would be data, and the kinds of services high-value customers would demand could only be delivered via an IP infrastructure.... To ensure our status as a Tier One company, GTE is establishing itself in three key areas of the data market – transport, access, and value-added services.[7]

The new millennium

For nearly 20 years, NEC had focused on its 'core competencies', while GTE had focused on its 'core businesses'. The two strategies left the firms in very different positions as they faced the start of the new millennium. GTE seemed to remain confident in its business-based approach, whereas NEC had decided that it had to promote decentralisation, a business-unit focus, and individual business group accountability. Senior executives from the two companies adopted very different tones:

> We enter the 21st century with strong core businesses that performed very well in 1999 and provide a solid foundation for future growth.
> – Charles R. Lee, Chairman and CEO of GTE.[8]

> Our short-term target is returning to profitability, our mid-term goal is recreating NEC into a highly valued corporation that sets standards in global excellence.
> – Koji Nishigaki, President, NEC Corporation.[9]

[7] GTE, 'Investor Information', January 2000.

[8] GTE, January 2000.
[9] Nishigaki, K., January 2000

APPENDIX 1: What are core competencies?

According to Prahalad and Hamel,

Core competencies are the collective learning in the organization, especially how to coordinate diverse production skills and integrate multiple streams of technologies.[10]

The authors claim that the recognition and development of core competencies rely on communication and co-operation across traditional organisational boundaries, and that this communication and co-operation can make disparate businesses coherent and position a company to take advantage of opportunities for future growth. In addition, they see a core competence as not diminishing with use or deteriorating over time. Instead they conclude the more it is used, the more valuable it becomes.

The authors provide three tests to identify a core competence:

- It must have the potential to form the basis for entry into new product markets.

- The competence must make a significant contribution to customer perceived value.

- It should be difficult for competitors to imitate.

They state that while a company's short-term competitiveness derives from the price and performance of its current products, its long-term competitiveness derives from an ability to build core competencies that generate the products of the future. Therefore, 'the real sources of advantage are to be found in management's ability to consolidate corporate wide technologies and production skills into competencies that empower individual businesses to adapt quickly to changing opportunities.'[11]

Core competencies versus business units

Prahalad and Hamel claim that the 'traditional' corporate focus on business units and industries makes the issue of putting competitive products on today's shelves the most significant one. In their view however, corporations should be seeking to maximise their world manufacturing share of core products, which they define as the link between core competencies and end products, rather than the end products themselves.

According to the authors, there are three dangers in the 'traditional' approach:

- If the organisation focuses on business units, no single unit may feel responsible for maintaining a viable position in core products or competencies, and the company may find itself dependent on external sources for critical components.

- Competencies developed within a business unit become 'imprisoned' within that unit, denying the corporation the necessary harmonisation and communication across those boundaries necessary to fully exploit all opportunities.

- Opportunities for growth will be missed if the potential for these products crosses SBU (strategic business unit) parameters.

Thus, according to Prahalad and Hamel, in order to prevent the fragmentation of core competencies, which is inevitable for any corporation organised in business units and focused on positioning within 'industries', a corporation needs to establish a corporate-wide strategic architecture for competence-building. They claim that successful organisations of the future will be those that have shifted their focus from that of SBUs to the core competencies of their organisation, as these form the foundations of future growth.

---

[10] Prahalad, C.K. & Hamel, G., (1990), 'The Core Competence of the Corporation', *Harvard Business Review,* Vol. 68, No. 3, p.82. Reprinted by permission *of Harvard Business Review.* Copyright © 1990 by the Harvard Business School Publishing Corporation; all rights reserved.

[11] Prahalad, C.K. & Hamel, G., (1990), 'The Core Competence of the Corporation', *Harvard Business Review,* Vol. 68, No. 3, p.81. Reprinted by permission *of Harvard Business Review.* Copyright © 1990 by the Harvard Business School Publishing Corporation; all rights reserved.

EXHIBIT 1 NEC and GTE, sales, 1980–1990

NEC		GTE	
Fiscal Year Ending	**Sales (USD millions)**	**Fiscal Year Ending**	**Sales (USD millions)**
March 1981	4,711	Dec 1980	9,979
March 1982	4,872	Dec 1981	11,026
March 1983	6,013	Dec 1982	12,066
March 1984	7,830	Dec 1983	12,944
March 1985	8,998	Dec 1984	14,547
March 1986	13,116	Dec 1985	15,732
March 1987	16,779	Dec 1986	15,111
March 1988	21,893	Dec 1987	15,421
March 1989	23,178	Dec 1988	16,460
March 1990	21,798	Dec 1989	17,424

Source: Compustat

EXHIBIT 2 Worldwide electronic supplier ranking

	Computers Sales in US$ billions		Telecommunications Sales in US$ billions		Semiconductors Sales in US$ billions	
1	IBM	49.6	AT&T	17.3	NEC	2.6
2	Unisys	9.4	Alcatel-ITT	7.6	Hitachi	2.3
3	DEC	8.4	Northern Telecom	4.1	Toshiba	2.3
4	Fujitsu	6.6	NEC	3.6	Motorola	2.3
5	NEC	6.3	Siemens	3.2	Texas Instruments	1.8

Source: 'NEC Sets Global Strategy for Medium Term', *PR Newswire*, 19 October 1987.

EXHIBIT 3 NEC Corporation, financial results, 1981–1990 (in USD millions)

Fiscal Year Ending	Sales	Operating Income Before Depreciation	Income Before Tax	Net Income	Total Assets	Shareholders' Equity
March 1981	4,711	579	206	99	5,174	782
March 1982	4,872	590	225	109	5,405	812
March 1983	6,013	794	299	138	6,880	1,194
March 1984	7,830	1,040	417	198	9,243	1,818
March 1985	8,998	1,374	596	267	10,801	1,901
March 1986	13,116	1,732	714	153	14,529	2,798
March 1987	16,779	1,701	420	103	18,944	3,522
March 1988	21,893	2,220	630	205	23,427	4,784
March 1989	23,178	2,682	1,085	485	25,161	5,183
March 1990	21,798	2,737	1,179	539	23,316	5,096

Source: Compustat
Note: Results are reported in accordance with US Generally Accepted Accounting Principles, and are converted at the prevailing exchange rate at the end of the fiscal year.

EXHIBIT 4 GTE Corporation, financial results, 1980–1989 (in USD millions)

Fiscal Year Ending	Sales	Operating Income Before Depreciation	Income Before Tax	Net Income	Total Assets	Shareholders' Equity
Dec 1980	9,979	3,105	1,218	478	19,720	4,851
Dec 1981	11,026	3,518	1,376	722	21,113	5,289
Dec 1982	12,066	3,790	1,469	836	22,294	6,025
Dec 1983	12,944	4,253	1,698	956	24,223	6,785
Dec 1984	14,547	4,708	1,900	1,125	26,364	7,811
Dec 1985	15,732	4,988	(72)	(161)	26,558	7,235
Dec 1986	15,111	5,381	2,182	1,184	27,402	8,017
Dec 1987	15,421	5,489	1,845	1,119	28,745	8,429
Dec 1988	16,460	5,464	1,944	1,225	31,104	8,752
Dec 1989	17,424	5,620	2,193	1,417	31,986	8,518

Source: Compustat

EXHIBIT 5 NEC and GTE, share price, and dividend history, 1979–1989

Year End	NEC Corporation				GTE Corporation		
	Share Price at Year End (USD)	Per Share Div./Year (USD)	Nikkei 225 Average Price Index (Yen)	Nikkei 225 Average Price Index (USD)	Share Price at Year End (USD)	Per Share Div./Year (USD)	S&P Composite Price Index (USD)
1979	7.19		6,569.73		9.42		107.94
1980	11.21	2.763	7,063.13	31.15	9.08	2.72	135.76
1981	15.05	3.153	7,681.84	34.83	10.67	2.75	122.55
1982	17.86	2.712	8,016.67	32.19	13.58	2.86	138.34
1983	28.41	0.624	9,893.82	41.66	14.58	2.94	164.93
1984	24.25	0.690	11,542.60	48.59	13.54	3.02	167.24
1985	32.88	0.850	13,083.18	54.85	15.33	3.10	211.28
1986	63.88	1.168	18,820.64	111.69	19.46	3.18	242.17
1987	73.50	1.414	21,564.00	149.11	17.69*	2.46*	247.08
1988	78.50	1.484	30,159.00	235.34	22.25	2.56	277.72
1989	65.50	0.660	38,915.87	282.08	35.00	2.74	353.40

Source: Datastream, Sequencer, CEIC and Annual Reports.
Note: * In 1987, GTE stock was split three-for-two. The price indicated is the post-split price per share. The dividend is the total annual dividend per post-split share.

EXHIBIT 6 NEC corporation, financial results, 1991–1999 (in USD millions)

Fiscal Year Ending	Sales	Operating Income Before Depreciation	Income Before Tax	Net Income	Total Assets	Shareholders' Equity
March 1991	26,233	3,161	992	386	27,869	6,248
March 1992	28,375	2,685	445	115	30,686	6,604
March 1993	30,565	2,205	(260)	(393)	34,599	7,007
March 1994	35,096	2,852	314	65	39,606	7,667
March 1995	43,326	4,351	995	406	47,716	9,089
March 1996	41,095	4,748	1,473	721	43,767	8,214
March 1997	39,907	3,683	980	739	38,703	8,092
March 1998	36,851	3,581	693	311	37,397	8,051
March 1999	40,334	2,624	(1,958)	(1,339)	42,174	7,230

Source: Compustat
Note: Results are reported in accordance with US Generally Accepted Accounting Principles, and are converted at the prevailing exchange rate at the end of the fiscal year.

EXHIBIT 7 GTE Corporation, financial results, 1990–1998 (in USD millions)

Fiscal Year Ending	Sales	Operating Income Before Depreciation	Income Before Tax	Net Income	Total Assets	Shareholders' Equity
Dec 1990	18,374	6,042	2,365	1,541	33,769	9,210
Dec 1991	19,621	7,194	2,319	1,580	42,437	11,417
Dec 1992	19,984	7,326	2,889	(754)	42,144	10,171
Dec 1993	19,748	7,694	1,692	882	41,575	9,677
Dec 1994	19,944	8,072	4,141	2,441	42,500	10,556
Dec 1995	19,957	8,731	4,253	(2,144)	37,019	6,871
Dec 1996	21,339	9,258	4,668	2,798	38,422	7,336
Dec 1997	23,260	9,497	4,675	2,794	42,142	8,038
Dec 1998	25,473	9,911	4,335	2,172	43,615	8,766

Source: Compustat

EXHIBIT 8 NEC and GTE, share price and dividend history, 1990–1999

Year End	NEC Corporation				GTE Corporation		
	Share Price at Year End (USD)	Per Share Div./Year (USD)	Nikkei 225 Average Price Index (Yen)	Nikkei 225 Average Price Index (USD)	Share Price at Year End (USD)	Per Share Div./Year (USD)	S&P Composite Price Index (USD)
1990	47.50	2.140	23,848.71	164.70	29.13*	1.49*	330.22
1991	48.25	2.290	22,983.77	170.83	34.63	1.61	417.09
1992	26.88	1.705	16,924.95	133.64	34.63	1.73	435.71
1993	38.13	1.955	17,417.24	156.65	34.50	1.83	465.44
1994	57.00	2.123	19,723.06	192.93	30.38	1.88	459.27
1995	61.00	2.298	19,868.15	211.22	43.88	1.88	615.93
1996	60.75	2.187	19,361.35	177.97	45.38	1.88	740.74
1997	53.63	1.919	15,258.74	126.11	52.25	1.88	970.43
1998	45.25	1.807	13,842.17	105.75	65.00	1.88	1,229.23
1999	114.50	1.049	18,934.34	164.75	73.00	1.88	1,455.22

Source: Datastream, Sequencer, CEIC and Annual Reports.
Note: * In 1990, GTE stock was split two-for-one. The price indicated is the post-split price per share. The dividend is the total annual dividend per post-split share.

EXHIBIT 9 NEC, business results, selected years

	1999	1998	1997	1996	1995	1994	1993	1990	1989	1988	1985	1984	1983	1980
Information & Communications Systems														
• Communication Systems & Equipment (% of Total Sales)	31.35	35.03	34.09	27.90	27.25	27.07	27.34	25.41	26.02	27.92	29.22	32.52	36.31	37.59
• Computers & Industrial Electronic Devices (% of Total Sales)	46.02	40.34	42.00	44.19	47.47	49.75	50.90	43.76	43.25	41.62	31.93	30.53	27.72	24.24
• Operating margin (%)	3.18	5.55	5.39											
Electron Devices														
• % of Total Sales	18.39	20.18	19.46	23.49	20.56	18.32	16.87	17.59	18.36	17.05	26.39	24.12	21.76	21.46
• Operating margin (%)	(5.96)	5.36	5.61											
Other														
• % of Total Sales	4.24	4.45	4.45	4.41	4.72	4.83	4.89	13.27	12.36	13.41	12.44	12.83	14.14	16.71
• Operating margin (%)	(1.98)	(0.46)	(1.82)											

Source: Annual Reports.

EXHIBIT 10 GTE, business unit results, 1980–1990

	1990	1989	1988	1987	1986	1985	1984	1983	1982	1981	1980
Telephone Operations											
• % of Total Sales	69.46	71.50	71.00	72.35	71.14	63.44	62.32	64.65	64.74	61.34	59.32
• Operating margin (%)	23.97	22.79	23.26	25.80	27.27	29.34	28.72	27.17	27.66	29.73	28.87
Communication Products & Services											
• % of Total Sales	18.45	16.29	15.78	14.33	16.79						
• Operating margin (%)	4.57	4.51	4.08	2.35	4.97						
Communications Products											
• % of Total Sales						16.66	17.15	19.71	20.34	19.94	20.75
• Operating margin (%)						3.74	0.96	5.64	6.23	5.14	6.28
Communications Services *											
• % of Total Sales						8.54	8.56	4.86	0.89	0.73	0.45
• Operating margin (%)						(18.21)	5.38	14.19	(25.23)	(30.00)	(62.22)
Electrical Products											
• % of Total Sales	12.39	12.53	13.59	13.81	17.72	12.07	12.74	11.43	11.78	14.45	16.83
• Operating margin (%)	10.46	10.16	10.19	10.43	9.36	10.27	11.44	7.16	10.27	12.81	14.40

Note: GTE changed the way it reported results in 1986.
* Communication services consisted mostly of long-distance services
Source: Annual Reports.

EXHIBIT 11 GTE, business unit results, 1991–1998

	1998	1997	1996	1994	1993	1992	1991
Telephone Operations							
• % of Total Sales				79.75	80.15	79.37	79.77
• Operating margin (%)				26.65	17.02	25.43	24.32
Telecommunication Products & Services							
• % of Total Sales				20.25	19.85	20.63	20.23
• Operating margin (%)				15.05	(1.45)	4.42	0.81
National Operations							
Network Services							
• % of Total Sales	59.86	62.44	63.52				
• Operating margin (%)	31.59	32.54	28.69				
Wireless Products & Services							
• % of Total Sales	12.05	12.56	12.34				
• Operating margin (%)	21.07	14.95	18.30				
Data Products & Services							
• % of Total Sales	3.08	1.20					
• Operating margin (%)	(67.09)	(128.31)					
Other National Sales							
• % of Total Sales	12.32	11.38	11.30				
• Operating margin (%)	(13.96)	(1.62)	14.14				
International Operations							
• % of Total Sales	12.69	12.42	12.83				
• Operating margin (%)	22.70	24.65	26.22				

Note: GTE changed the way it reported results in 1995.
Source: Annual Reports.

EXHIBIT 12 NEC selected products, 1999

Computers and Industrial Electronic Systems
Auto electronic
Automated fingerprint
identification systems
CD-ROM drives
Colour plasma display panels
Hard disk drives
Laser equipment
Mainframe computers
Monitors
Optical disc players
Personal computers
Postal automation systems
Printers
Recognition control equipment
Semiconductor manufacturing equipment
Servers
Software
Supercomputers
Test and measurement systems
Video projectors
Workstations

Electronic Devices
Capacitors
Colour display and other tubes
Diodes
Electrical connectors
Gate arrays
Integrated circuits
Memory
Microcontrollers
Microprocessors

Optical semiconductor devices
Relays
Transistors

Communications Systems and Equipment
CATV systems
Cellular phones
Defence electronics systems
Digital switching equipment
Fibre-optic submarine cable systems
Fibre-optic transmission systems
Hubs
ISDN terminal adapters
Microwave communications systems
Mobile communications systems
Modems
Network management systems
Pagers
Radio navigation and radar equipment
Rocket guidance and control equipment
Routers
Satellite communications systems
Satellites
Teleconferencing systems
Television and radio broadcast
equipment
Video and studio equipment

Other
Lighting
Receivers
Televisions

Source: NEC 1999 Annual Report.

EXHIBIT 13 GTE selected products and services, 1999

Home and Family
Additional phone lines
Answering devices
Call waiting
Caller ID devices (displays)
Caller ID displays
Caller ID services
Calling services
Corded phones and accessories
Cordless phones
Digital subscriber lines
GTE calling card services
GTE DSL solutions
GTE easy savings plan
GTE international calling plan
GTE in-touch 800
GTE nationwide saver
GTE total call
GTE unlimited packages
Home and family
Internet services
Integrated services digital network
Long distance
Multi-line corded phones
Multi-line cordless phones
Novelty phones
Phone books
Phone lines
Phones and accessories
Prepaid calling cards
Send a text message
Single phone line
Single-line ISDN
Telephone answering devices
Telephone products for the hearing impaired

Video services/digital cable services
Voice mail
Wireless data
Wireless service

Business
Additional business lines
Business voice messaging
Cable TV advertising opportunities
Caller ID services
Calling services
CentraNet
Custom Networks
Dial-up access
DSL
Frame Relay
Full range of business phones and accessories
ISDN
LAN (ISDN) access
Long distance
Manage my account
Other Internet services
Outsourced e-mail
Platinum value plan
Single business lines
SmartPark services
SuperPages.com
Yellow pages advertising

Wireless
Coverage maps
Store locator
Wireless
Wireless data services
Wireless voice services

Source: GTE 1999 Annual Report

EXHIBIT 14 Worldwide electronic supplier ranking

	Computers* (1996) Sales in US$ billions		Telecommunications Equipment (1998) Sales in US$ billions		Semiconductors (1998) Sales in US$ billions	
1	IBM	36.0	Lucent	26.8	Intel	22.8
2	HP	19.0	Ericsson	23.2	NEC	8.1
3	Fujitsu	18.5	Motorola	20.6	Motorola	7.1
4	NEC	14.1	Alcatel	19.9	Toshiba	5.9
5	Compaq	13.5	Nortel	17.3	Texas Instruments	5.8
6	Toshiba	11.4	Siemens	16.3	Hitachi	4.6
7	Hitachi	11.3	Nokia	13.7	Samsung	4.6
8	Apple	10.2	NEC	11.7	Philips	4.4
9	DEC	6.1	Cisco	8.5	STM	3.8
10	Sun	5.3	IBM	6.1	Fujitsu	3.7

Note: * sales of personal computers, servers, large computers, and computer peripherals
Sources: Datamation, Dataquest, IDATE.

EXHIBIT 15 1997 Results, selected companies

	Sales (USD mil.)	Operating Income Before Dep'n (USD mil.)	Net Income (USD mil.)	Operating Margin Before Dep'n (%)	Pretax Profit Margin (%)	Net Profit Margin (%)	Return on Assets (%)	Return on Equity (%)
NEC	39,907	3,683	739	9.23	2.46	1.85	1.91	9.13
Toshiba	43,979	3,304	541	7.51	2.57	1.23	1.15	5.30
Fujitsu	36,318	4,037	372	11.12	3.26	1.02	0.98	3.91
Hitachi	68,735	6,780	735	9.86	3.09	1.04	0.89	2.69
GTE	23,260	9,497	2,794	40.83	20.10	12.01	6.63	34.76
AT&T	51,319	10,795	4,638	21.04	14.04	8.71	7.63	19.75
Ameritech	15,998	6,181	2,296	38.64	23.03	14.35	9.06	27.64
Bell Atlantic	30,368	12,889	2,455	42.44	13.12	8.08	4.55	19.20
Bellsouth	20,633	9,412	3,261	45.62	26.44	15.85	9.01	21.56
Bellsouth Tel.	15,418	7,592	2,314	49.24	23.97	15.07	10.00	27.24
PAC Bell	9,938	3,926	350	39.50	0.54	0.08	0.05	0.24
US West	11,479	2,776	1,374	24.18	21.16	11.97	7.75	31.46

Note: In addition to GTE and AT&T, the other US companies are RBOCs.
Source: Compustat.

EXHIBIT 16 Country data

Year Ended	USA		JAPAN			
	GDP Current Prices (USD billions)	GDP per capita in Current Prices (USD)	GDP Current Prices (Yen billions)	Average Annual Exchange Rate (Yen to USD)	GDP Current Prices (USD billions)	GDP per capita in Current Prices (USD)
1980	2,795	12,303	240,176	226.74	1,059	7,559
1981	3,131	13,646	257,963	220.54	1,170	8,287
1982	3,259	14,069	270,600	249.08	1,086	7,643
1983	3,535	15,120	281,767	237.51	1,186	8,289
1984	3,933	16,676	300,543	237.52	1,265	8,783
1985	4,213	17,707	320,419	238.54	1,343	9,266
1986	4,453	18,543	335,457	168.51	1,991	13,660
1987	4,742	19,574	349,759	144.62	2,418	16,516
1988	5,108	20,893	373,973	128.152	2,918	19,844
1989	5,489	21,989	399,998	137.96	2,899	19,639
1990	5,803	22,980	430,040	144.80	2,970	20,050
1991	5,986	23,420	458,299	134.54	3,406	22,906
1992	6,319	24,451	471,020	126.65	3,719	24,920
1993	6,642	25,410	475,381	111.18	4,276	28,557
1994	7,054	27,069	479,260	102.23	4,688	31,225
1995	7,400	28,135	483,219	94.06	5,137	34,129
1996	7,813	29,434	500,309	108.79	4,599	30,484
1997	8,301	30,984	507,851	121.00	4,197	27,755
1998	8,760	32,409	495,327	130.90	3,784	24,955
1999	9,222	33,800	499,042	114.93	4,342	28,524

Sources: Datastream, CEIC.

Harvard Business School

Case 2 Honda A and B

Honda A

The two decades from 1960 to 1980 witnessed a strategic reversal in the world motorcycle industry. By the end of that period, previously well-financed American competitors with seemingly impregnable market positions were faced with extinction. Although most consumers had an initial preference to purchase from them, these U.S. manufacturers had been dislodged by Japanese competitors and lost position despite technological shifts that could have been emulated as competition intensified.

The Japanese invasion of the world motorcycle market was spearheaded by the Honda Motor Company. Its founder, Sochiro Honda, a visionary inventor and industrialist, had been involved peripherally in the automotive industry prior to World War II. However, Japan's postwar devastation resulted in the downsizing of Honda's ambitions; motorcycles were a more technologically manageable and

Dr. Richard T. Pascale of Stanford Graduate School of Business prepared this case with the collaboration of Professor E. Tatum Christiansen of Harvard Business School as a basis for class discussion rather than to illustrate either effective or ineffective handling of an administrative situation.

Note: This case is based largely on the Harvard Business School's 'Note on the Motorcycle Industry – 1975' (No. 9-587-210) and on a published report of the Boston Consulting Group ('Strategy Alternatives for the British Motorcycle Industry'), 1975.

economically affordable product for the average Japanese. Reflecting Honda's commitment to a technologically based strategy, the Honda Technical Research Institute was established in 1946. This institute, dedicated to improvements in internal combustion engines, represented Honda's opening move in the motorcycle field. In 1947, Honda introduced its first A-type, 2-stroke engine.

As of 1948, Honda's Japanese competition consisted of 247 Japanese participants in a loosely defined motorcycle industry. Most competitors operated in ill-equipped job shops, adapting clip-on engines for bicycles. A few larger manufacturers endeavored to copy European motorcycles but were hampered by inferior technology and materials that resulted in unreliable products.

Honda expanded its presence in the fall of 1949, introducing a lightweight 50cc, 2-stroke, D-type motorcycle. Honda's engine at 3 hp was more reliable than most of its contemporaries' engines and had a superior stamped metal frame. This introduction coincided closely, however, with the introduction of a 4-stroke engine by several larger competitors. These engines were both quieter and more powerful than Honda's. Responding to this threat, Honda followed in 1951 with a superior 4-stroke design that doubled horsepower with no additional weight. Embarking on a bold campaign to exploit this advantage, Honda acquired a plant, and over the next two years it developed enough manufacturing expertise to become a fully integrated producer of engines, frames, chains, sprockets, and other ancillary parts crucial to motorcycle performance.

Motorcycle manufacturers in the Japanese industry tended to minimize risk by investing in one winning design and milking that product until it became technologically obsolete. Beginning in the 1950s, Honda began to depart from this pattern – seeking simultaneously to (1) offer a multiproduct line, (2) take leadership in product innovation, and (3) exploit opportunities for economies of mass production by gearing designs to production objectives. Most notably, in 1958 Honda's market research identified a large, untapped market segment seeking a small, unintimidating motorcycle that could be used by small-motorcycle businesses for local deliveries. Honda designed a product specifically for this application: a step-through frame, automatic transmission, and one-hand controls that enabled drivers to handle the machine with one hand while carrying a package in the other. The 50cc Honda was an explosive success. Unit sales reached 3,000 per month after six months on the market. Deciding to make this the product of the future, Honda gambled, investing in a highly automated 30,000-unit-per-month manufacturing plant – a capacity 10 times in excess of demand at the time of construction.

Honda's bold moves set the stage for a yet bolder decision – to invade the U.S. market. The following section depicts the sequence of events as taken from a Harvard Business School case on the motorcycle industry.[1]

In 1959 ... Honda Motor Company ... entered the American market. The Japanese motorcycle industry had expanded rapidly since World War II to meet the need for cheap transportation. In 1959, Honda, Suzuki, Yamaha, and Kawasaki together produced some 450,000 motorcycles. With sales of $55 million in that year, Honda was already the world's largest motorcycle producer ...

In contrast to other foreign producers who relied on distributors, Honda established a U.S. subsidiary, American Honda Motor Company, and began its push in the U.S. market by offering very small lightweight motorcycles. The Honda machine had a three-speed transmission, an automatic clutch, five horsepower (compared with two and a half for the lightweight motorcycle then sold by Sears, Roebuck), an electric starter, and a step-through frame for female riders. Generally superior to the Sears lightweight and easier to handle, the Honda machines sold for less than $250 retail, compared with $1,000–$1,500 for the bigger American or British machines.

---

[1] D. Purkayastha and R. Buzzell, 'Note on the Motorcycle Industry – 1975,' HBS No. 9–578–210, pp. 5–7.

Honda followed a policy of developing the market region by region, beginning on the West Coast and moving eastward over a period of four to five years. In 1961 it lined up 125 dealers and spent $150,000 on regional advertising. Honda advertising represented a concerted effort to overcome the unsavory image of motorcyclists that had developed since the 1940s, given special prominence by the 1953 movie *The Wild Ones,* which starred Marlon Brando as the surly, destructive leader of a motorcycle gang. In contrast, Honda addressed its appeal primarily to middle-class consumers and claimed, 'You meet the nicest people on a Honda.' This marketing effort was backed by heavy advertising, and the other Japanese exporters also invested substantial sums: $1.5 million for Yamaha and $0.7 million for Suzuki.

Honda's strategy was phenomenally successful. Its U.S. sales rose from $500,000 in 1960 to $77 million in 1965. By 1966, Honda, Yamaha, and Suzuki together had 85% of the U.S. market. From a negligible position in 1960, lightweight motorcycles had come to dominate the market.

The transformation and expansion of the motorcycle market during the early 1960s benefited British and American producers as well as the Japanese. British exports doubled between 1960 and 1966, while Harley-Davidson's sales increased from $16.6 million in 1959 to $29.6 million in 1965. Two press reports of the mid 1960s illustrate these traditional manufacturers' interpretation of the Japanese success:

'The success of Honda, Suzuki, and Yamaha in the States has been jolly good for us,' Eric Turner, chairman of the board of BSA Ltd., told Advertising Age. 'People here start out by buying one of the low-priced Japanese jobs. They get to enjoy the fun and exhilaration of the open road and frequently end up buying one of our more powerful and expensive machines.' The British insist that they're not really in competition with the Japanese (they're on the lighter end). The Japanese have other ideas. Just two months ago Honda introduced a 444cc model to compete, at a lower price, with the Triumph 500cc. [Advertising Age, December 27, 1965]

'Basically we do not believe in the lightweight

market,' says William H. Davidson, son of one of the founders and currently president of the company (Harley-Davidson). 'We believe that motorcycles are sports vehicles, not transportation vehicles. Even if a man says he bought a motorcycle for transportation, it's generally for leisure time use. The lightweight motorcycle is only supplemental. Back around World War I, a number of companies came out with lightweight bikes. We came out with one ourselves. We came out with another one in 1947 and it just did not go anywhere. We have seen what happens to these small sizes.' [Forbes, *September 15, 1966*]

Meanwhile, the Japanese producers continued to grow in other export markets. In 1965, domestic sales represented only 59% of Honda's total of $316 million, down from 98% in 1959. Over the same period, production volume had increased almost five-fold, from 285,000 to 1.4 million units. In Europe, where the Japanese did not begin their thrust until the late 1960s, they had captured a commanding share of key markets by 1974.

In short, by the mid–1970s the Japanese producers had come to dominate a market shared by European and American producers 20 years earlier ...

It was often said that Honda created the market for the recreational uses of motorcycles through its extensive advertising and promotional effort.

The company achieved a significant product advantage through a heavy commitment to R&D and advanced manufacturing techniques. Honda used its productivity-based cost advantage and R&D capability to introduce new models at prices below those of competitive machines. New products could be brought to market very quickly; the interval between conception and production was estimated to be only 18 months. Honda was also reported to have a 'cold storage' of designs that could be introduced if the market developed. ...

Since 1960, Honda had consistently outspent its competitors in advertising. It had also established the largest dealership network in the U.S. On average, Honda dealers were larger than their competitors. In new markets, Honda had been willing to take short-term losses in order to build up an adequate selling and distribution network.

In 1975, the Boston Consulting Group was retained by the British government to diagnose the British motorcycle industry and the factors contributing to its decline. The remainder of this case, reflecting on Honda's strategy, consists of excerpts from that report:[2]

The market approach of [Honda] has certain common features which, taken together, may be described as a 'marketing philosophy.' The fundamental feature of this philosophy is the emphasis it places on market share and sales volume. Objectives set in these terms are regarded as critical, and defended at all costs.

The whole thrust of the marketing program ... is towards maintaining or improving market share position. ... We have seen some ways in which this goal is pursued. It is worth adding, as an example of how pervasive this objective is ... that in an interview with a Honda personnel director, we were told that the first question a prospective Honda dealer is asked is the level of his market share in his local area. 'I don't know why, but this company places an awful lot of emphasis on market share' was the comment. ... We shall return to the reasons why market shares are critical for commercial success in the industry.

We were also told by representatives of [Honda] that their primary objectives are set in terms of sales volume rather than short-term profitability. Annual sales targets – based on market share penetration assumptions and market growth prospects – are set, and the main task of the sales company is to achieve these targets. The essence of this strategy is to grow sales volume at least as fast or faster than any of your competitors.

A number of more specific policies follow from this general philosophy, and our descriptions of each of the Japanese competitors provide ample examples of these policies:

1 Products are updated or redesigned whenever a market threat or opportunity is perceived.

2 Prices are set at levels designed to achieve market share targets and will be cut if necessary.

2 Boston Consulting Group, 'Strategy Alternatives for the British Motorcycle Industry,' Her Majesty's Stationery Office, London, 30 July 1975, pp. 16–17, 23, 39–43, 54–55.

3 Effective marketing systems are set up in all markets where serious competition is intended, regardless of short-term cost.

4 Plans and objectives look to long-term payoff.

The results of these policies for the Japanese competitors have, of course, been spectacularly successful. Over the last fifteen years, the rates of growth of the four major Japanese companies have been as shown in [Table A].

Table A Growth of Japanese production

	Production in 1959 (000 units)	Production in 1974 (000 units)	Average Annual Growth Rate (% p.a.)
Honda	285	2,133	14
Yamaha	64	1,165	21
Kawasaki	10	355	27
Suzuki	96	840	16

Source: Japan Automobile Industry Association

Selling and distribution systems. We have so far discussed market share as a function of the product features and prices of particular models. Market share across all cc classes is also influenced by what we shall call the selling and distribution system (s and d system). Within the s and d system we include all the activities of the marketing companies (or importers) in each national market:

◆ Sales representation at the dealer level

◆ Physical distribution of parts and machines

◆ Warranty and service support

◆ Dealer support

◆ Advertising and promotion

◆ Market planning and control.

We also include the effects of the dealer network established by the marketing companies:

◆ Numbers and quality of dealers

◆ Floor space devoted to the manufacturers' products

◆ Sales support by dealers.

The s and d system supports sales of the manufacturer across the whole model range, and its quality affects market shares in each cc class where the manufacturer is represented. **Table B** compares the s and d systems of the four full-line Japanese manufacturers in the USA, and shows that high market shares both overall *and* in each cc class go with high levels of expenditure on s and d and with extensive dealer networks.

The interaction between product-related variables and s- and d-related variables is complex. The better the product range in terms of comprehensiveness, features, and price, and the more sophisticated the s and d system of the sales company, the easier it will be to attract good dealers. This is because good products, which are well supported at the marketing company level, lead to good retail sales. Equally, good dealers themselves improve retail sales, and active competition between dealers can lead to retail discounting which acts as a volume-boosting price cut to the public. The manufacturers' products and s and d system therefore influence sales both directly, at retail, and proximately, through their effect on the dealer network.

In particular cc categories, each manufacturer's position is substantially influenced by its specific product offerings. For example, Kawasaki are strong in the 750cc-and over class due to the Z-1, and Yamaha have been weak due to its poor 750cc model. Outstanding products obtain market shares that are unusually high for a manufacturer, and weak products lead to atypically low market shares. For products of average attraction, however, market shares seem to move towards some equilibrium level. For each manufacturer, this level in the USA appears to be:

Honda	*40–50%*
Yamaha	*15–25%*
Kawasaki	*10–15%*
Suzuki	*9–12%*

As overall market leaders, the Japanese have dominated pricing in the motorcycle industry. It is therefore appropriate to begin this analysis by examining the extent to which the experience curve concept appears to explain the performance of the Japanese. Unfortunately, it is impossible directly to determine unit cost performance data for competitors, since the data are not publicly available. Sources can be found, however, for unit price and production volume data. Over the long term, price behavior is a useful guide to movements in the underlying costs, and so an experience curve analysis on prices can be extremely revealing.

Japanese price performance. In **Figure A**, price experience curves are drawn for the Japanese motorcycle industry as a whole, based on aggregate data collected by MITI. These curves show price reduction performance of a consistent nature for

each of the size ranges of motorcycle considered, the rate of price reduction being most rapid of all in the largest range, 126–250cc, which is following an experience curve slope of 76%. The other slopes are more shallow, at 81% and 88%, but there is no mistaking the fact that real prices are descending smoothly over time. These experience-based price reductions clearly go a long way towards explaining the historical competitive effectiveness of the Japanese in the marketplace in small and medium motorcycles.

For the purposes of strategy development … it is

Table B The selling and distribution systems of Japanese companies in the U.S.A.

	Estimated Total S&D Expenditure by Sales Company 1974 ($m)	Advertising Expenditure 1972 ($m)	Dealers 1974 Numbers	Units Sold per Dealer	1974 % Share Total Market (units)	Lowest % Share of any cc Class	Highest % Share of any cc Class
Honda	90–100	8.1	1,974	220	43	34	61
Yamaha	40–45	4.2	1,515	135	20	4	34
Kawasaki	30–35	2.2	1,018	127	13	9	19
Suzuki	25–30	3.0	1,103	98	11	5	16

Source: R.L.. Rolk, Motorcycle Dealer News, Ziff-Davis Market Research Dept., BCG estimates.

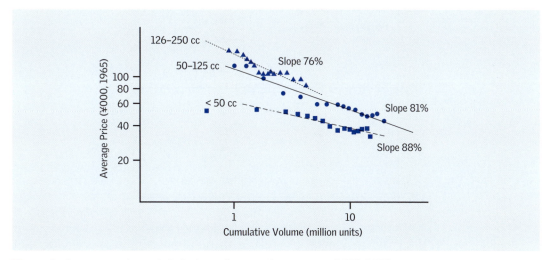

Figure A Japanese motorcycle industry: price experience curves, 1959–1974
Source: MITI

[helpful] to look more closely at price performance in the larger bike models. The Honda CB 750 has been the pacesetter in superbikes in terms of both market penetration and pricing. In **Figure B**, price experience curves are plotted for this product and for two other large Honda bikes. The prices of other Japanese manufacturers have been broadly comparable to Honda's in the equivalent size range (they usually tend if anything to price at a slight premium relative to Honda), so that we may use Honda as a good 'benchmark' for the Japanese competition in big bikes in general.

It is clear from **Figure B** that price performance in the large bikes has been consistent with that in small: real prices have declined along experience curve slopes in the region of 85%–87%. This has also been true of the price in the United States, when converted into yen terms.

An interesting feature of the curves is that the prices in the United States are so much higher than [those] of the same products in Japan. As shown in **Table C**, the premiums are high across almost the entire range of bikes and are far larger than seems necessary, even allowing for the extra costs incurred for duty, freight, and packing in shipping bikes from Japan to the United States. This certainly suggests that there is no possibility that the Japanese are 'dumping' their products in the U.S. market: quite the reverse. Furthermore, it may well indicate that competitive though the Japanese have been in the United States, based on the downward trends in their real price levels over time, there may well be plenty of

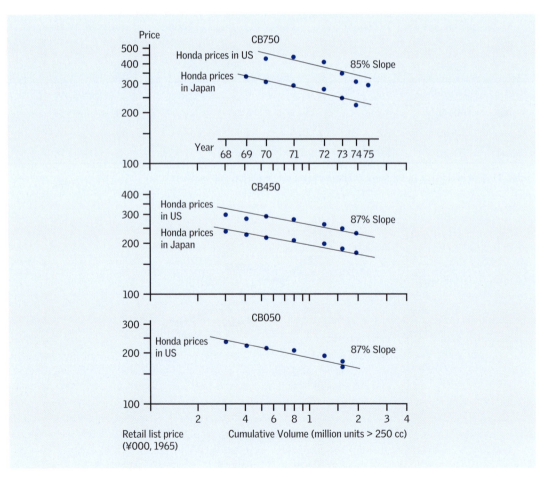

Figure B Honda large bikes: price experience curves

Table C Honda price premium, USA vs Japan

Premium on retail list prices, 1974				
Model	Japan Price		U.S. Price ($)	Premium
	¥000	$ Equiv.		
CB 750	395	1411	2024	43%
CB 550	355	1268	1732	37%
CB 450	303	1082	1471	36%
CB 360	253	904	1150	26%
CB 350	275	982	1363	39%
MT 250	218	779	965	24%
MT 125	158	564	743	32%
CB 125	166	593	640	8%

Premium allowing for freight, duty and packing

CB 750, U.S. retail price 1975 = $2112
   Price to dealer $1584 (75% of 2112)
   Price to distributor $1373 (65%)

   Japan list price   ¥440,000 or
                        $1517 (equivalent)
   Price to distributor $ 986 (65%)
   Ocean freight to LA   60
   Duty   63 (3% U.S. Retail Price)
   Packaging costs   40
                       $ 163

Thus, indicated price to U.S. distributor for equal manufacturer's margin to that on bikes sold in Japan
                    = $ 986 + 163
                    $1149

Thus, premium in U.S.A. even after allowing for freight, duty and packing
                    = $(1373/1149 - 1) \times 100$
                    = 20%

Note: The versions of the smaller bike models shipped to the States may be slightly more expensive than their Japanese equivalents (extra lighting, etc.). The versions of the larger bikes are, however, reported to be identical in both markets.

scope for them to be even more competitive in the future if seriously challenged in that market. They could simply reduce their margins on exports to the United States to levels more in line with those enjoyed in their domestic business.

Japanese cost performance. The implication of the downward trends in real prices for the Japanese is, of course, that there have been underlying experience-based cost reductions: that the decline has not

been accounted for simply by a reduction in margins. ... However, the major Japanese manufacturers have been continuously profitable, and this suggests that cost reductions have indeed taken place in parallel with real price reductions. On the other hand, all the Japanese motorcycle manufacturers also make a significant proportion of products other than motorcycles (in 1974 about 35% of Honda's turnover, and about 40% of Suzuki's, was accounted for by cars; of Yamaha Motor's turnover about 40% was in products such as boats and snowmobiles). It is, perhaps, reasonable to question whether these products are sufficiently profitable to 'subsidize' the motorcycle business.

... It seems clear that ... none of [the three major Japanese] manufacturers is subsidizing the motorcycle business from other businesses. Indeed, Honda was actually losing money in its car business in 1974, which suggests that their motorcycle business that year may have shown returns of the order of 20% (BIT) compared with the 12.4% return earned by the company overall. The overall inference from this profit performance must be that each manufacturer has indeed achieved an experience curve effect on costs in parallel with those achieved on price. The existence of this experience curve effect in the motorcycle industry has important strategy implications.

Competitive strategy implications

As we have discussed, failure to achieve a cost position – and hence cost reductions over time–equivalent to your competitors' will result in commercial vulnerability. At some point your competitors will start setting prices which you cannot match profitably, and losses will ensue. The strategic importance of the experience curve is that it explains clearly the two possible long-term causes of uncompetitive costs:

♦   Relative growth: failure to grow as rapidly as competitors, thereby progressing more slowly than them along the experience curve.

♦   Relative slopes: failure to bring costs down the characteristic experience curve slope achieved by competitors. ...

Summary

From the perspective of the writers of the BCG study, a fundamental cause for the Japanese success was their high productivity. The motorcycle industry was exhibiting the effects that differences in growth rates, volume, and level of capital investment among competitors can have on relative costs. The high rates of growth and levels of production achieved by the Japanese manufacturers resulted in their superior productivity. In terms of value added per employee, Honda outperformed Western competitors by as much as four times. Even the smaller Japanese competitors were able to out perform their Western counterparts by a factor of two or three.

The BCG report also countered the common argument that the relatively inexpensive Japanese labor was the primary source of competitive advantage. The Japanese competitors in fact had higher labor costs than companies in the West. Their relative high growth and scale caused total costs to drop quickly enough to support regular pay increases and price decreases at the same time.

Essentially the argument presented by BCG was that the Japanese emphasis on market share as the primary objective led to high production volume, improved productivity, low costs, and in the long term to higher profitability than their competitors.

Harvard Business School

Honda (B)

Sochiro Honda, an inventive genius with a legendary ego, founded the Honda Motor Co., Ltd., in 1948. His exploits have received wide coverage in the Japanese press. Known for his mercurial temperament and bouts of 'philandering,'[1] he is variously reported to have tossed a geisha out a second-story window,[2] climbed inside a septic tank to retrieve a visiting supplier's false teeth (and subsequently placed the teeth in his own mouth),[3] appeared inebriated and in costume before a formal presentation to Honda's bankers requesting financing vital to the firm's survival (the loan was denied),[4] hit a worker on the head with a wrench,[5] and stripped naked before his engineers to assemble a motorcycle engine.[6]

....

Dr. Richard T. Pascale of Stanford Graduate School of Business wrote this case with the collaboration of Professor E. Tatum Christiansen of Harvard Business School as the basis for class discussion rather than to illustrate either effective or ineffective handling of an administrative situation. It is based largely on internal Honda sources and interviews with founders of Honda Motor Co., Ltd., and the Japanese management team that founded Honda of America.

....

1. Sakiya, Tetsuo. 'The Story of Honda's Founders,' *Asahi Evening News,* June 1–August 29, 1979, Series #2 and #3.
2. Interviews with Honda executives, Tokyo, Japan, July 1980.
3. Sakiya, Tetsuo. *Honda Motor: The Men, The Management, The Machines,* Kadonsha International. Tokyo, Japan, 1982, p 69; also Sakiya, 'Honda's Founders,' Series #4.
4. Sakiya, 'Honda's Founders,' Series #7 and #8.
5. Sakiya, *Honda Motor,* p. 72.
6. Sakiya, 'Honda's Founders,' Series #2.

Company background

Postwar Japan was in desperate need of transportation. Motorcycle manufacturers proliferated, producing clip-on engines that converted bicycles into makeshift 'mopeds.' Sochiro Honda was among these, but his prior experience as an automotive repairman provided neither the financial, managerial, nor technical basis for a viable enterprise.

Sochiro Honda viewed 'technology' as the vehicle through which Japanese society could be restored and the world made a better place in which to live. Reflecting the intensity of this commitment, he established the Honda Technical Research Institute in 1946. The term institute was somewhat misleading, since the organization was composed of himself and a few associates and had no practical means of support. Under this organizational umbrella, he began to tinker, and, as a means of livelihood, he purchased 500 war surplus engines and retrofitted them for bicycle use. Lacking marketing know-how, he entered into an exclusive arrangement with a distributor, who packaged a motorcycle conversion kit for bicycles. The Honda Motor Company was formed. Further tinkering led, in turn, to the introduction of the 'A-design' – a 2-stroke, 50cc engine. The engine had numerous defects, and sales did not materialize. Scraping by on occasional orders, the company lost money in 1947 and grossed $55,000 in 1948.

In 1949, Sochiro Honda turned to friends. Raising $3,800, he developed and introduced the 2-stroke, D-type engine. This engine, generating 3 hp, was more reliable than most on the market and enjoyed a brief spurt of popularity. Recruiting a work force of 70 employees, Honda produced engines one at a time and approached an annualized production rate of 100 units per month by the end of 1949.

Success was short-lived, however. Honda's exclusive distributor elected to artificially limit sales to 80 units per month in order to maintain high margins. Sochiro Honda was irate and vowed to avoid such dependencies in the future. In late 1949 he set out to raise additional financing but suffered a second setback when competitors leapfrogged the 2-stroke design and introduced quieter and more powerful 4-stroke engines.

A classic dilemma now faced the struggling enterprise. Honda's engine was obsolete, and his distribution system held him at ransom. Without additional financing he could not correct these deficiencies, and banks and investors did not regard him as a sound management risk.

In late 1949, an intermediary urged him to accept a partner – Takeo Fujisawa. Fujisawa was prepared to invest 2 million yen (about $7,500). More important, Fujisawa brought financial expertise and marketing strengths.

Despite Fujisawa's presence, the firm continued to falter. No further capital could be raised in 1950. Fujisawa pressed his partner to quit tinkering with his noisy 2-stroke engine and join the industry leaders with a 4-stroke design, since it was clear that competition had threatened Honda with extinction. At first too proud to accept this counsel, in 1951 he unexpectedly unveiled a breakthrough design that doubled horsepower over competitive 4-stroke engines. With this innovation, the firm was off and putting, and by 1952 demand was brisk.[7]

Honda's superior 4-stroke engine enabled Fujisawa to raise $88,000 in 1952. With these funds, Fujisawa committed to reduce dependency on suppliers and distributors by becoming a full-scale motorcycle manufacturer. To forestall technological obsolescence, he encouraged Honda to stay abreast of technological developments. He also sought more flexible channels of distribution. Unfortunately, Honda was a relatively late entrant; the best Fujisawa could do was to arrange for several distributors to carry Honda as a secondary line. He compensated for weak product positioning by going directly to the consumer with advertising.

In late 1952 a sewing machine plant was purchased and converted to a crude motorcycle factory. Neither partner had managerial or manufacturing experience, and there was no real plan other than to work as long as necessary each day to keep up with

orders. Honda's more powerful engine and superior stamped motorcycle frame created considerable interest, and demand remained strong. Employment leaped from 150 in 1951 to 1,337 by the end of 1952. Honda integrated into the production of chains, sprockets, and motorcycle frames. Altogether, these factors greatly complicated the management task. There were no standardized drawings, procedures, or tools. For several years the plant was, in effect, a collection of semi-independent 'activities' sharing the same roof. Nonetheless, by the beginning of 1959 Honda had become a significant participant in the industry, with 23% market share (see **Exhibit 1**).

Honda's successful 4-stroke engine eased the pressures on Fujisawa by increasing sales and providing easier access to financing. For Sochiro Honda, the higher-horsepower engine opened the possibility of pursuing one of his central ambitions in life: to build and to race a high-performance, special-purpose motorcycle – and win. Winning provided the ultimate confirmation of his design abilities. Racing success in Japan came quickly. As a result, in 1959 he raised his sights to the international arena and committed the firm to winning at Great Britain's Isle of Man – the 'Olympics' of motorcycle racing.[8] Again, Honda's inventive genius was called into play. Shifting most of the firm's resources into this racing effort, he embarked on studies of combustion that resulted in a new configuration of the combustion chamber, which doubled horsepower and halved weight. Honda leapfrogged past European and American competitors – winning in one class, then another, winning the Isle of Man manufacturer's prize in 1959, and sweeping the first five positions by 1961.[9]

Throughout the 1950s, Fujisawa sought to turn his partner's attention from enthusiasm with racing to the more mundane requirements of running an enterprise. By 1956, as the innovations gained from racing had begun to pay off in vastly more efficient engines, Fujisawa pressed Honda to adapt this technology for a commercial motorcycle.[10] He had a particular segment in mind. Most motorcyclists in Japan were male, and the machines were used

---

[7] Sakiya, *Honda Motor,* pp. 71–72.

[8] Sakiya, 'Honda's Founders,' Series #11.

[9] Ibid.

[10] Ibid., Series #13; also Sakiya, *Honda Motor,* p. 117.

primarily as an alternative form of transportation to trains and buses. However, a vast number of small commercial establishments in Japan still delivered goods and ran errands on bicycles. Trains and buses were inconvenient for these activities. The purse strings of these small enterprises were controlled by the Japanese wife – who resisted buying conventional motorcycles because they were expensive, dangerous, and hard to handle. Fujisawa challenged his partner: Can you use what you've learned from racing to come up with an inexpensive, safe-looking motorcycle that can be driven with one hand (to enable carrying packages)?[11]

The first breakthrough

In 1958 the Honda 50cc Supercub was introduced – with an automatic clutch, 3-speed transmission, automatic starter, and the safe, friendly look of a bicycle (without the stigma of the outmoded mopeds). As a rule of thumb, a 50cc engine is 50% cheaper to make than a 100cc engine. Achieving high horsepower with a small engine thereby reaps automatic cost savings – making the new bike affordable. Innovative design provided a cost advantage without requiring Honda to manufacture more efficiently than its competitors. (This was fortunate since the firm, having expanded into three plants in the 1950s, had still not achieved a well-integrated production process.)

Overnight, Honda was overwhelmed with Supercub orders. Demand was met through makeshift, high-cost, company-owned assembly and farmed-out assembly through subcontractors.[12] By the end of 1959 Honda had skyrocketed into first place among Japanese motorcycle manufacturers. Of its total sales that year of 285,000 units, 168,000 were Supercubs.[13] The time seemed appropriate to build an automated plant with a 30,000-unit-per-month capacity. 'It wasn't a speculative investment,' recalls one executive. 'We had the proprietary technology, we had the market, and the

demand was enormous.'[14] The plant was completed in mid-1960.

Distribution channels

Fujisawa utilized the Supercub to restructure Honda's channels of distribution. For many years, Honda had rankled under the two-tier distribution system that prevailed in the industry. As noted earlier, these problems had been exacerbated by Honda's being carried as a secondary line by distributors whose loyalties lay with older, established manufacturers. Further weakening Honda's leverage, all manufacturer sales were on a consignment basis.

Fujisawa had characterized the Supercub to Honda's distributors as 'something much more like a bicycle than a motorcycle.' The traditional channels, to their later regret, agreed. Under amicable terms, Fujisawa began selling the Supercub directly to retailers – and primarily through bicycle shops. Since these shops were small and numerous (approximately 12,000 in Japan), sales on consignment were unthinkable. A cash-on-delivery system was installed – giving Honda significantly more leverage over its dealerships than the other motorcycle manufacturers enjoyed.[15]

Honda enters U.S. market

Sochiro Honda's racing conquests in the late 1950s had given substance to his convictions about his abilities. Success fueled his appetite for new and different challenges. Explosive sales of the Supercub in Japan provided the financial base for new quests. The stage was now set for the exploration of the U.S. market.

From the Japanese vantage point, the American market was vast, untapped, and affluent. 'We turned toward the United States by a process of deduction,' states one executive. 'Our experiments with local Southeast Asian markets in 1957 and 1958 had little success. With little disposable income and poor roads, total Asian exports had reached a meager 1,000 units in 1958.[16] The European market,

[11] Sakiya, 'Honda's Founders,' Series #11.
[12] Pascale, Richard T., Interviews with Honda executives, Tokyo, Japan, September 10, 1982.
[13] Data provided by Honda Motor Company.
[14] Pascale interviews.
[15] Ibid.
[16] Ibid.

while larger, was heavily dominated by its own name-brand manufacturers, and the popular mopeds dominated the low-price, low-horsepower end.'

Two Honda executives – the designated president of American Honda Motor Company, Kihachiro Kawashima, and his assistant – arrived in the United States in late 1958. Their itinerary: San Francisco, Los Angeles, Dallas, New York, and Columbus. Kihachiro Kawashima recounts his impressions:[17]

My first reaction after traveling across the United States was 'How could we have been so stupid to start a war with such a vast and wealthy country!' My second reaction was discomfort. I spoke poor English. We dropped in on motorcycle dealers who treated us discourteously and, in addition, gave the general impression of being motorcycle enthusiasts who, secondarily, were in business. There were only 3,000 motorcycle dealers in the United States at the time, and only 1,000 of them were open five days a week. The remainder were open on nights and on weekends. Inventory was poor, manufacturers sold motorcycles to dealers on consignment, the retailers provided consumer financing, and after-sale service was poor. It was discouraging.

My other impression was that everyone in the United States drove an automobile – making it doubtful that motorcycles could ever do very well in the market. However, with 450,000 motorcycle registrations in the United States and 60,000 motorcycles imported from Europe each year it didn't seem unreasonable to shoot for 10% of the import market. I returned to Japan with that report.

In truth, we had no strategy other than the idea of seeing if we could sell something in the United States. It was a new frontier, a new challenge, and it fit the 'success against all odds' culture that Mr. Honda had cultivated: I reported my impressions to Fujisawa – including the seat-of-the-pants target of trying, over several years, to attain a 10% share of the U.S. imports. He didn't probe that target quantitatively. We did not discuss profits or deadlines for breakeven. Fujisawa told me if anyone could

succeed, I could, and authorized $1 million for the venture.

The next hurdle was to obtain a currency allocation from the Ministry of Finance. They were extraordinarily skeptical. Toyota had launched the Toyopet in the United States in 1958 and had failed miserably. 'How could Honda succeed?' they asked. Months went by. We put the project on hold. Suddenly, five months after our application, we were given the go-ahead – but at only a fraction of our expected level of commitment. 'You can invest $250,000 in the U.S. market,' they said, 'but only $110,000 in cash.' The remainder of our assets had to be in parts and motorcycle inventory.

We moved into frantic activity as the government, hoping we would give up on the idea, continued to hold us to the July 1959 start-up timetable. Our focus, as mentioned earlier, was to compete with the European exports. We knew our products at the time were good, but not far superior. Mr. Honda was especially confident of the 250cc and the 305cc machines. The shape of the handlebar on these larger machines looked like the eyebrow of Buddha, which he felt was a strong selling point. Thus, after some discussion and with no compelling criteria for selection, we configured our start-up inventory with 25% of each of our four products – the 50cc Supercub and the 125cc, 250cc, and 305cc machines. In dollar-value terms, of course, the inventory was heavily weighted toward the larger bikes.

The stringent monetary controls of the Japanese government together with the unfriendly reception we had received during our 1958 visit caused us to start small. We chose Los Angeles where there was a large second- and third-generation Japanese community, a climate suitable for motorcycle use, and a growing population. We were so strapped for cash that the three of us shared a furnished apartment that rented for $80 per month. Two of us slept on the floor. We obtained a warehouse in a run-down section of the city and waited for the ship to arrive. Not daring to spare our funds for equipment, the three of us stacked the motorcycle crates three-high, by hand; swept the floor; and built and maintained the parts bin.

[17] Ibid.

We were entirely in the dark the first year. We were not aware that the motorcycle business in the United States occurs during a seasonal April-to-August window – and that our timing coincided with the closing of the 1959 season. Our hard-learned experiences with distributorship in Japan convinced us to try to go to the retailers direct. We ran ads in the motorcycle trade magazine for dealers. A few responded. By spring 1960, we had 40 dealers and some of our inventory in their stores – mostly larger bikes. A few of the 250cc and 305cc bikes began to sell. Then disaster struck.

By the first week of April 1960, reports were coming in that our machines were leaking oil and encountering clutch failure. This was our lowest moment. Honda's fragile reputation was being destroyed before it could be established. As it turned out, motorcycles in the United States are driven much farther and much faster than in Japan. We dug deeply into our precious cash reserves to air freight our motorcycles to the Honda testing lab in Japan. Throughout the dark month of April, Pan Am was the only enterprise in the United States that was nice to us. Our testing lab worked 24-hour days bench testing the bikes to try to replicate the failure. Within a month, a redesigned head gasket and clutch spring solved the problem. In the meantime, events had taken a surprising turn.

Throughout our first eight months, following Mr. Honda's and our own instincts, we had not attempted to move the 50cc Supercubs. While they were a smash success in Japan (and manufacturing couldn't keep up with demand there), they seemed wholly unsuitable for the U.S. market where everything was bigger and more luxurious. As a clincher, we had our sights on the import market – and the Europeans, like the American manufacturers, emphasized the larger machines.

We used the Honda 50s ourselves to ride around Los Angeles on errands. They attracted a lot of attention. One day we had a call from a Sears buyer. While persisting in our refusal to sell through an intermediary, we took note of Sears's interest. But we still hesitated to push the 50cc bikes out of fear they might harm our image in a heavily macho market. But when the larger bikes started breaking, we had no choice. We let the 50cc bikes move. And surprisingly, the retailers who wanted to sell them weren't motorcycle dealers; they were sporting goods stores.

The excitement created by Honda Supercub began to gain momentum. Under restrictions from the Japanese government, we were still on a cash basis. Working with our initial cash and inventory, we sold machines, reinvested in inventory, and sunk the profits into additional inventory and advertising. Our advertising tried to straddle the market. While retailers continued to inform us that our Supercub customers were normal everyday Americans, we hesitated to target toward this segment out of fear of alienating the high-margin end of our business – sold through the traditional motorcycle dealers to a more traditional 'black leather jacket' customer.

An advertising twist

As late as 1963, Honda was still working with its original Los Angeles advertising agency, its ad campaigns straddling all customers so as not to antagonize one market in pursuit of another.

In the spring of 1963, while fulfilling a routine class assignment, an undergraduate advertising major at UCLA submitted an ad campaign for Honda. Its theme was 'You Meet the Nicest People On a Honda.' Encouraged by his instructor, the student passed his work on to a friend at Grey Advertising. Grey had been soliciting the Honda account – which, with a $5-million-a-year budget, was becoming an attractive potential client. Grey purchased the student's idea – on a tightly kept nondisclosure basis. Grey attempted to sell the idea to Honda.[18]

Interestingly, the Honda management team, which by 1963 had grown to five Japanese executives, was badly split on this advertising decision. The president and treasurer favored another proposal from another agency. The director of sales, however, felt strongly that the Nicest People campaign was the right one – and his commitment eventually held sway. Thus, in 1963, Honda adopted a strategy that

[18] Ibid.

directly identified and targeted that large, untapped segment of the marketplace that was to become inseparable from the Honda legend.[19]

The Nicest People campaign drove Honda's U.S. sales at an even greater rate. By 1964 nearly one out of every two motorcycles sold was a Honda. As a result of the influx of medium-income leisure-class consumers, banks and other consumer credit companies began to finance motorcycles – shifting away from dealer credit, which had been the traditional purchasing mechanism available. Honda, seizing the opportunity of soaring demand for its products, took a courageous and seemingly risky position. Late in 1964 it announced that thereafter, it would cease to ship on a consignment basis but would require cash on delivery. Honda braced itself for a revolt that never materialized. While nearly every dealer questioned, appealed, or complained, none relinquished the Honda franchise. In one fell swoop, Honda shifted the power relationship from the dealer to the manufacturer. Within three years, C.O.D. sales would become the pattern for the industry.[20]

Honda's growth on several dimensions is shown in Exhibit 2. Automobiles were introduced into the product line in 1963, shifting resources and management attention heavily in that direction in the ensuing years.

25 years later

In late 1972, anticipating the company's twenty-fifth anniversary, Fujisawa, 62, raised the issue of retirement. 'We are strong dominating individuals,' he said. 'I must step aside and let the younger men lead our company.' Sochiro Honda, 66, also conceded to retire. In September 1973, the two stepped down. States one source: 'Fujisawa retired early to provide Mr. Honda with an opportunity to retire, also. It is a reflection of Fujisawa's genuine personal friendship with Mr. Honda.'[21]

---

[19] Ibid.

[20] Ibid.

[21] Sakiya, Tetsuo. 'The Story of Honda's Founders,' *Asahi Evening News,* August 29, 1979.

Exhibit 1 Motorcycle production in Japan by Japanese makers

Calendar Year	Honda	Yamaha	Suzuki	Kawasaki	Other	Total
1950	531	–	–	–	6,960	7,491
1951	2,380	–	–	–	21,773	24,153
1952	9,659	–	–	–	69,586	79,245
1953	29,797	–	–	–	131,632	161,429
1954	30,344	–	–	200	133,929	164,473
1955	42,557	2,272	9,079	–	205,487	259,395
1956	55,031	8,743	18,444	5,083	245,459	332,760
1957	77,509	15,811	29,132	6,793	280,819	410,064
1958	117,375	27,184	66,363	7,018	283,392	501,332
1959	285,218	63,657	95,862	10,104	425,788	880,629
1960	649,243	138,153	155,445	9,261	520,982	1,473,084
1961	935,859	129,079	186,392	22,038	531,003	1,804,371
1962	1,009,787	117,908	173,121	31,718	342,391	1,674,925
1963	1,224,695	167,370	271,438	34,954	229,513	1,927,970
1964	1,353,594	221,655	373,871	33,040	128,175	2,110,335
1965	1,465,762	244,058	341,367	48,745	112,852	2,212,784
1966	1,422,949	389,756	448,128	67,959	118,599	2,447,391
1967	1,276,226	406,579	402,438	79,194	77,410	2,241,847
1968	1,349,896	423,039	365,330	78,124	34,946	2,251,335
1969	1,534,882	519,710	398,784	102,406	21,091	2,576,873
1970	1,795,828	574,100	407,538	149,480	20,726	2,947,672
1971	1,927,186	750,510	491,064	208,904	22,838	3,400,502
1972	1,873,893	853,317	594,922	218,058	25,056	3,565,246
1973	1,835,527	1,012,810	641,779	250,099	22,912	3,763,127
1974	2,132,902	1,164,886	839,741	354,615	17,276	4,509,420
1975	1,782,448	1,030,541	686,666	274,022	28,870	3,802,547
1976	1,928,576	1,169,175	831,941	284,478	20,942	4,235,112
1977	2,378,867	1,824,152	1,031,753	335,112	7,475	5,577,359
1978	2,639,588	1,887,311	1,144,488	326,317	2,225	5,999,929
1979	2,437,057	1,653,891	1,100,778	308,191	79	5,499,996
1980	3,087,471	2,241,959	1,551,127	521,846	–	7,402,403
1981	3,587,957	2,792,817	1,764,120	521,333	–	8,666,227

Source: Japan Automobile Manufacturers Association, Inc.
Note: KD sets and scooters are included.

Exhibit 2 Honda's financial performance and U.S. motorcycle sales

Calendar Year	Gross Sales (million yen)	Honda U.S. Motorcycle Sales (units)	Outside Financing (million yen)	Employees
1948	14.3	–	1	20
1949	34.6	–	2	70
1950	82.8	–	–	90
1951	330.3	–	–	150
1952	2,438	–	15	1,337
1953	7,729	–	60	2,185
1954	5,979	–	–	2,494
1955	5,525	–	120	2,459
1956	7,882	–	–	2,377
1957	9,786	–	360	2,438
1958	14,188	–	720	2,705
1959	26,165	–	1,440	3,355
1960	49,128	1,315	4,320	4,053
1961	57,912	6,052	8,640	5,406
1962	64,552	27,840	9,090	5,798
1963	83,206	65,869	–	6,816
1964	97,936	110,470	–	7,696
1965	123,746	227,308	–	8,481
1966	106,845	272,900	–	9,069
1967	141,179	181,200	–	11,283
1968	193,871	174,706	18,180	13,165
1969	244,895	272,600	–	16,614
1970	316,331	441,200	–	17,511
1971	332,931	656,800	–	18,079
1972	327,702	707,800	–	18,297
1973	366,777	556,300	19,480	18,287
1974	519,897	628,500	24,350	18,455
1975	563,805	343,900	–	18,505
1976	668,677	444,624	25,500	19,069
1977	849,635	439,822	29,600	19,968
1978	922,280	401,114	–	21,316

Note: Above figures are related solely to Honda Motor Co.. Ltd., and are not consolidated with those of its subsidiaries.

Harvard Business School

Case 3 Phil Knight Managing NIKE's Transformation

Woodell as president

After appointing Woodell as president, Knight worked on manufacturing projects in China, and was effectively incommunicado; thereafter he continued to be absent for long periods of time. Typically, Woodell spoke to him about once every two weeks. Woodell tried to run the company as he thought Knight had intended and 'to get done the things that needed to get done.' In his first six months, he focused on NIKE's brand softness, the inventory problem, making sure he had the right people in areas like marketing and sales, and 'dealing with the fact that our founder and our leader was not present. It would have been a real trap to try to copy Phil. Historically, we've had a tendency to go to Knight for decisions. My style is to build the organization so people out there make the decisions.'

Woodell continued to work with the old NIKE management team, and relied extensively on the two other Gang of Four members: Rob Strasser for

This case, prepared as the basis for class discussion rather than to illustrate either effective or ineffective handling of an administrative situation, is based on NIKE in Transition (A) and (B) (392–105 and 392–106) by Research Associate Robert W. Lightfoot under the supervision of Professor Christopher A. Bartlett.

marketing and Del Hayes for manufacturing operations. Woodell recalled:

> My approach was to try to identify the issues and get them under control one piece at a time. There may be been other approaches. Knight's approach, quite often, might have been more to 'shake things up.' As founder and CEO, he could do that. A new president and COO couldn't do it that way.

Woodell added that the difficulty of this transition from peer to leader was compounded by the tough business environment, as he, Strasser, and Hayes began to realize that the company's business problems were larger and more deeply rooted than the management team had recognized before Woodell's appointment.

Changing market forces

During fiscal year 1984, growth slowed in the running shoe market, NIKE's core business. As the decade-long running boom diminished, a general fitness boom arose to include other sports. Niche segments like aerobics began to mushroom in 1982. Reebok expanded the market by designing and styling two aerobics shoes specifically for women. Launched in 1982, the 'Energizer' (made of nylon and suede) and the 'Freestyle' (made of garment leather) lifted Reebok's sales from $13 million in 1983 to $66 million in 1984. While the soft garment leather was comfortable and required no break-in period, it also wore out quickly. Still, many consumers preferred comfortable Reeboks – with holes – to durable NIKES.

At Knight's urging, NIKE had produced a prototype aerobics shoe in 1983. The factories in Korea felt, however, that the leather was too thin and would wear out too quickly; it was 'simply unsuitable' for a NIKE product. Furthermore, women employees – who had urged the company to produce an aerobics shoe – thought the prototype profoundly ugly. They did not even want to try it on. And while NIKE shoes were still selling well, even without an aerobics line, Harry Carsh, a senior executive who had joined the company in 1983, suggested another reason behind NIKE's delay – arrogance:

We could still be purists and talk about shoes that were for runners and athletes. And anybody who didn't make it the way we made it was a fool. We also had the idea that everything we sold, even though we were selling a lot of garbage, was used by an athlete to perform, which was absolute bull.

Reebok's sales exploded as the first-mover into the aerobics segment. By the end of 1983, Nike management realized that Reebok posed a serious threat, but they could not push the company to get a good product to market fast enough to prevent the upstart from reaching a critical mass. Woodell had Hayes visit Exeter to expedite product development. By that time, the Exeter facility had grown into a fairly complex operation. Hayes targeted 10 of the more than 300 shoes that were under development there and introduced 'critical path' procedures for getting select shoes to market quickly.

Inventory problems

The shoe inventory buildup that had first attracted management's attention in late 1982 began to snowball in 1983 and 1984. Just months after receiving its largest Futures order in August 1982 for November 1982 delivery, the market changed. The problem became apparent in March 1983, and by the end of the fiscal year on May 31, 1983, inventories had reached 21 million pairs.

Director of production, Ron Nelson, who coordinated Futures orders with orders to factories, was reluctant to cut factory orders at that time for two reasons. First, he wanted to protect the relationships that NIKE had carefully cultivated with new shoe suppliers so as to reduce its dependence on increasingly expensive Korean sources. He estimated that through the end of calendar year 1982, NIKE ordered about 6 million pairs of shoes for which it had no orders, simply to build up capacity with non-Korean factories. 'We knew we were ordering extras,' said Nelson, 'so we ordered models that we *thought* were safe. Second, Nelson was optimistic

that the product really was still popular, and he anticipated fill-in orders from international operations to take up some of the slack. International orders had grown more than 115% between 1982 and 1983, and seemed a better prospect for growth than domestic orders. Indeed, although international accounted for only 20% of sales, international Futures orders for delivery during the first half of 1983 had grown 1.1 million pairs over the same period in 1982, while domestic Futures orders had grown only 0.6 million pairs. In anticipation of these international orders, NIKE over-built about 2 million pairs per month between January and March 1983 (for delivery three months later).

Woodell saw the growing inventory as 'a cancer that was going to eat us alive,' but was constrained because much of it was tough-to-sell 'athleisure' shoes and apparel. He was also aware that many people within NIKE – including Knight – had strong personal ties to manufacturers in Asia and were reluctant to cut factory orders. Woodell found it frustrating to steer the course between building up even more inventory and 'pissing too many people off:'

My approach was, let's do what we can and work with what we've got, and that's the best we can do. And that's what we were doing for six months. But every time you told people you had to cut these orders back more, somebody would say, we can't do that because we've worked with these people and Knight's got these personal relationships. My frustration was, we're having trouble doing this crap [cutting factory orders] because everybody has got a reason why we can't do it and the only guy that can do it [Knight] is tough to get a hold of.

Restoring the brand magic

Woodell and his management team decided to focus on restoring some of the 'magic' to NIKE's brand image by asking Rob Strasser to develop and implement a new strategy and implement it. In 1983, Strasser and a small group targeted the 1984 summer Olympics in Los Angeles for a major publicity blitz 'to light the second stage of NIKE's rocket.' Woodell and Strasser believed that a successful advertising campaign would breathe some life into the NIKE brand and give the company some of the time it needed to develop a new product line, requiring about 18 months.

The campaign that began in Los Angeles with a slew of visual advertisements was expanded to include 10 major metropolitan areas. This 'Cities Campaign' featured colorful, oversized, 'outrageous' murals and billboards of well known athletes – some in sweaty contemplation, some performing great athletic feats. John McEnroe, many times the U.S. Open and Wimbledon tennis champion, appeared on the side of New York buildings wearing street clothes and looking like a hometown boy – wearing NIKEs. The murals contained no text, nor did they attempt to sell specific shoes; instead, they simply established a link in the consumer's mind between the athletes and NIKE. The campaign included promotions for Olympic athletes.

In the games themselves, 58 NIKE-supported athletes won 65 medals. One senior marketing manager, who had been working on the Olympics promotions and the Cities Campaign at the time, said:

> When you asked who the host of this Olympic Games was, people said NIKE. Converse had paid $5 million for the right to be the official shoe of the Olympics. Well, nobody wore Converse. I don't think we saw one pair of Converse out there [in track and field events].

The campaign received critical acclaim for its creativity, and the marketing department saw it as a great success. The finance department was less impressed, however, seeing no improvement in the inventory situation following the effort. The marketing manager acknowledged, 'We recognized after the '84 Olympics that having the most gold medals was great for our image, but did nothing for our shoe sales, which kept going down. We thought we were missing something.' (See **Exhibit 1** for quarterly financial data.)

'Loading the wagon' with apparel

Woodell, who had been in charge of NIKE's apparel division from 1980 to 1982, thought apparel could potentially keep the company's sales from declining in fiscal year 1984. Sales of the broad product line of athletic performance clothing (including running shorts, warm-ups, soccer jerseys; and tennis outfits)

and comfortable athleisure cloths (shirts, sweaters, jackets, and pants), had grown dramatically from $2 million in 1979 to $107 million in 1983, and sales representatives described demand as 'smoking.'

Woodell believed there were competitive and strategic reasons, too, for continuing emphasis on the apparel business. The shoe company, for example, might 'run out of feet.' Meanwhile, larger competitors, such as Adidas, relied on apparel for as much as 40% of sales. Margins in the apparel business, however, were lower than those in shoes.

In an off-site meeting in December 1983, Woodell and Hayes proposed to Knight, and later the rest of the management team, that NIKE 'aggressively grow apparel' for the Fall 1984 season. By investing an additional $15 to 20 million in inventories, and budgeting another $25 million in sourcing, sales, advertising, promotion and other operating expenses, Woodell thought apparel could boost sales by $100 million over the next fiscal year (ending May 1985), and by $200 million within the next two years. Said Hayes:

> We couldn't convince vendors – the mills and people that we would buy from – that we were really in the business. It seemed ridiculous that if you were in the business that you weren't able to buy the apparel [with short lead times] you wanted to sell. So we 'loaded the wagon.' We committed to buy as much apparel [in advance] as our marketing and sales people said we could sell.

With Woodell's backing, NIKE committed to the apparel business with a vengeance. The program quickly established the company's credibility with vendors and retailers.

Organizational developments

One of Woodell's early changes was to reconstitute the old Friday Club's membership and redefine its role to improve decision-making. Woodell thought the old Friday Club meetings had lost much of their focus, and he wanted to run the meetings differently. He told the group: 'Bring up as subject matter only those issues that you think other members of the group *must* be informed about, or important issues where you need their collective counsel.' 'I tried to get answers about a few specific issues in each meeting,' recalled Woodell. 'But I had to get to those answers in a different way than Knight did. I had to use the power of the whole management group.' He explained his view of the new group, which colleagues immediately dubbed 'The Wednesday Club:'

> My purpose is to reinforce the NIKE process of debating the issue, collaborating, making decisions, and getting counsel from each other. I don't want to put people out on a limb too quickly, but I'm trying to get people to take more responsibility.

A Policy and Procedures Committee was established to formalize some of the company's key practices that for years had been managed informally. For example, it established subcommittees to consider holidays, sick leave, education reimbursement, leave of absence, termination, and compensation. In July 1983 – his second month as president – Woodell approved PPC recommendations on sick leave, leave of absence, and educational reimbursement policies, and charged the group with addressing NIKE's most difficult personnel problem: how to formalize NIKE's widely divergent compensation practices. Although for years, many managers believed that a more formal salary administration system was needed – any action to develop one had always foundered on the shoal of a deep dislike for 'systems.'

George Porter, who chaired the PPC, said:

> Everybody has heard stories illustrating the inconsistencies faced by employees. And most managers can recount the dilemmas they've faced in trying to balance a human responsibility to the company. We shouldn't have to fight this battle each time a situation comes up. There should be a policy that's right for us, that captures what the company is. It can probably deal with about 90% of the cases.

A PPC subcommittee eventually suggested adopting a formal system developed by Hay Associates, a compensation consulting firm. The system rated each job on the basis of three factors required for all jobs: know-how, problem-solving, and accountability. 'Job points' were assigned to each job, and because these were determined by Hay's objective national standards, NIKE's pay system could be compared to 4,000 other U.S. companies; moreover, NIKE could correlate each person's pay with job points.

Phil Knight returns

'By the Spring of 1984, things were going to hell, and Woodell and I didn't have the communication to stop the bleeding. The more I got into this, I saw I had lost touch and had to step back in,' said Phil Knight, who in September 1984 decided to return full-time as president. Woodell was appointed head of a New Business unit charged with finding new, entrepreneurial business ventures.

Inventory and cost control

Knight's first priority was to reduce swollen inventories and to bring operating costs under control. By March 1984, inventories had reached 22 million pairs of shoes, including unsuccessful experiments in boots and punk-fashion athleisure shoes. On his return, Knight ordered prices slashed, then worked closely with the company's larger national accounts, such as J.C. Penney, to reduce inventory further. He even authorized bartering $12 million worth of surplus inventory for office furniture and airline tickets. By November 1984, the inventory stockpile had fallen to 15 million pairs, and by May 1985, to a manageable 9.8 million pairs.

This experience provoked a change in thinking about inventory within NIKE. Before, the focus on Futures ordering and demand forecasting allowed factories to run at optimal levels, but had masked short-term market changes. Said George Porter:

> As a result, we couldn't see the downturn fast enough in our own factories. We wanted to keep them filled. Until that time, the problem had been one of production, not of sales. We could sell everything that we could produce. That attitude eventually catches up with you, and it did at that time.

In 1985, apparel sales were $160 million rather than the $235 million Woodell had projected. Apparel inventory remained high, not only because of the sales shortfall, but also because the company did not have a shippable mix of sizes, tops, and bottoms, and color-coordinated apparel. More inventory-reduction efforts eventually brought results, though at negative gross margins.

Knight planned to adopt stricter controls. He cautioned, however, 'Certainly there's a need to have more formalized procedures, but that doesn't mean a sledgehammer approach. With a 5% increase in sales and a 5% cut in operating expenses, you restore margins and have a very, very healthy performance.' Nevertheless, over the 12 months following his return, Knight discharged 400 people, or about 10% of NIKE's work force. Yielding to financial pressures, he also made the difficult move to close 5 of 30 supplier-owned plants.

Research and development

In December 1984, Phil Knight asked Tom Clarke to relocate the Research and Development Center from Exeter, New Hampshire to Beaverton, Oregon. The decision was controversial within NIKE because it cut about 75 of the Exeter facility's 125 employees. The move was received positively in the business press, which construed it as a cost-cutting measure. Knight's main motivation, however, was to improve communication and eventually collaboration between design and marketing. This was a major reversal of his early philosophy, which held that R&D should be kept away from corporate headquarters to protect designers from pressures that might limit their creativity. However, the old logic was eroding, as Tom Clarke explained:

> The R&D center had been set up in Exeter because of its proximity to some of the East Coast manufacturing. We continued to make our high-tech running shoes there through 1984. Because of that proximity, the R&D center's focus had been on running shoes. As court shoes started to be made in Asia, it became clear that the R&D center was not involved enough in non-running product categories. It was really separated from the decisions being made about the Asian factories. There was a need to unite marketing and design and development.

Organization

As he undertook these early initiatives, Knight stuck with his old management team. At the same time, however, he began to invite a wider circle of people

to meetings. By February 1985, Knight was ready to modify the organization. He wanted to fix two major organizational shortcomings: to get NIKE back in touch with the market so it would no longer miss major market trends; and to improve its ability to implement a coordinated response. The reorganization created divisions around the major product categories to supplement the previous function- and geography-based structure. As a consequence, he had 12 vice presidents reporting directly to him.

Knight also used this occasion to shuffle his senior management group again. Among the many changes, Rob Strasser headed up the newly formed New Products Division with a mandate to develop ideas and products and bring them quickly to the marketplace. Knight also made an effort 'to get some I.Q. around here,' and hired several outsiders with MBA degrees and experience in footwear or athletic products. The management style of these new marketing- and production-oriented managers was more formal than NIKE veterans were used to, and some within the company resisted being 'professionalized.' Old-timers did not understand 'how wearing a tie makes us any more professional.'

A proliferation of teams (variously described as 'speed groups,' 'SWAT teams,' and, when organized around product launches, 'launch groups') began to tackle NIKE's problems. Some speed groups were formed as a means of 'getting together the product and marketing concepts.' Others were less product-oriented; for example, the 'Big Fitness' speed group addressed the issue of how to organize and position the shoe company as a fitness enterprise that provided all kinds of fitness products. Generally, speed groups were seen within the company as effective, even if some were overly exuberant (see **Exhibit 2**).

Rob Strasser, a strong advocate of the groups and leader of many of them, saw them as an effective way to implement his management 'principles' (see **Exhibit 3**). Mark Parker, who had worked in marketing, research and development, and design, recalled:

> Strasser wanted to make decisions quickly and keep moving ahead. That's what he really brought to the group. He forced progress. He really forced decisions to be made, and I think

we were able to cut through a lot of bureaucracy that had developed in the company at that time.

Recognizing the power of the team concept and the need to become more responsive to the market, in October 1985, Knight reorganized the New Products group around Launch Teams. Led by product line managers (PLMs), launch teams brought together individuals from all three departments to bring a specific new product to market. It aimed to do so by altering the product development process. Teams were responsible for all stages of developing new products – from the design stage through product development, marketing, production, and sales. After the reorganization, PLMs were designated team leaders of groups including a marketing manager, information manager, and a designer (in most instances). According to Carsh, PLMs formerly had been dedicated to 'getting products built and delivered, not getting products marketed.' Responsibility for new products was divided into three areas, product direction under Strasser, product management under Carsh, and production under Nelson. All three men reported directly to Knight.

Product-market strategy

Knight initiated a strategy review, and concluded that by copying Reebok's strategy, NIKE had let itself stray too far into the athleisure market segment and away from its core business of performance athletic products. Early in 1985, he explained to shareholders his intention to refocus NIKE's strategy: 'NIKE is a sports company,' he contended. 'Our innovation, our technology, and our talents are best suited for providing for the demands of athletes.' Knight pinned NIKE's hopes for restoring high profitability on diversifying into other fitness and sports shoes, especially medium- to high-end products.

As a result of this decision, management decided to review NIKE's 'Air' technology, which incorporated sealed gas bladders in the soles of the shoes to add cushioning and reduce weight. Air technology, patented in 1974, and developed since then, required specialized manufacturing techniques unavailable to NIKE's competitors. Although running enthusiasts recognized that Air technology improved performance and gave the innovative and successful 1979 Tailwind shoe high marks, the general public did not understand the concept or believed that Air soles enhanced performance. Consequently, NIKE had not exploited the technology more widely in the early 1980s. The management review led to a decision to revive this potential asset.

One of the first products that Rob Strasser drove through the New Products group was the best-selling basketball shoe ever marketed. The shoe was built around Michael Jordan of the Chicago Bulls, the National Basketball Association (NBA) Rookie of the Year, and represented a departure from NIKE's promotion and marketing strategy. First Jordan's agent asked for a million dollars per year to sign a contract with the up-and-coming superstar. This was in contrast to existing practices of promoting 'grass roots athletes' or local stars at maybe one-tenth Jordan's price. To justify paying that price, NIKE 'had to do something special' with Jordan. Second, Jordan's personality and high profile made him a bona fide national star. Signing him gave NIKE the impetus to create a major new product line.

A launch team led by Strasser designed a distinctive red, black, and white shoe for Jordan, gave it its own logo, and called it the 'Air Jordan by NIKE.' They built on the color scheme and the styling to offer a coordinated line of clothing – NIKE's first experiment with collection selling. The coordinated Air Jordan apparel line rekindled the interest of retailers, who had been disappointed by NIKE's previous clothing offerings.

Strasser hired a new advertising agency which created exciting new commercials. After Jordan first appeared in the shoe, the NBA banned it from games, not because of the shoe's structure or technology, but because its red and black color scheme violated NBA dress regulations. NIKE fully exploited the controversy in a follow-up advertisement offering the public the shoe that the NBA banned because of its 'revolutionary design.'

Although Air Jordan was a huge marketing success with fiscal 1986 sales of $88 million – an achievement many credited to Strasser's speed group – the company had problems with logistics. Product quality was questionable, and late supply required expensive air shipment from Korea. When NIKE could not meet demand for the product, the company developed a new distribution strategy, called the 'allocation method.' Basically, those who provided the best distribution got the shoes. That meant targeting the important markets (such as Los Angeles, Chicago, Atlanta, and New York) and the large athletic specialty distributors (such as Foot Locker). A small athletic shoe retailer complained:

NIKE built the company on our backs. We took their product back in 1976 and said this is the best thing out there, and worked real hard to sell it. But when NIKE got hot, it went to the big guys. We little guys weren't treated well. It made us buy six months in advance; it didn't service us well; its sales force was arrogant. The big guys always got the product first. Also, NIKE's product line turned over very fast. We would book our orders six months in advance, and sometimes, before we even got them, they were closing out that line.

Del Hayes explained:

We gave the second tier of accounts some shoes, but we couldn't give them very much. They became very upset with us, but we learned they would come back if you had something that was really hot in the marketplace. Our strategy was to pull all products through the system as opposed to push them. If we convince the consumer with our promotional activities that he has to have that shoe, the hell with the retailer. He doesn't have any choice. This was NIKE's arrogance – using that pyramid theory together with the idea that we'll pull our product right through the marketplace, right through the chain by hitting that consumer. And it was very effective.

Following two years of falling earnings, NIKE rallied in fiscal 1986 to earn a record $59 million, despite $11 million in charges from plant closings and from the sale of its Japanese subsidiary. Unit sales were up 15% over the previous year and the average price per pair rose 12%. The gain reflected strong sales of Air Jordan products. By managing inventory levels and product lines better, and by selling higher-margin shoes, NIKE was able to improve its gross margin from 26.3% in 1985 to 32.4% in 1986. The effects of NIKE's cost-cutting efforts showed up in lower SG&A expenses, which fell from 21.6% to 19.6% of sales, and lower interest expenses, which fell because of reduced interest rates and lower borrowing. Yet, market share declined again as Reebok overtook NIKE. (See **Exhibits 4 and 5** for financial and market share data.)

NIKE's mid-life crisis

By Fall 1986, it was clear that fiscal 1987 was not going to be as profitable as fiscal 1986. Despite initial shortages of the Air Jordan, by the end of the season, NIKE had clogged up its distribution channels with excess inventory. The Air Jordan II was not the profit engine that the first model had been after the product's fadishness cooled, and injuries forced Michael Jordan to withdraw from the Chicago Bulls for the season. In December of 1986, Phil Knight announced a second round of layoffs, displacing 280 of NIKE's 2,150 employees.

Organizational tensions

Over time, speed groups created resentment in the company because of the resources at their disposal and the credit they often received for efforts that represented a larger group's contributions. One manager who worked in some of the speed groups with Strasser, described 1986-1987 as a time of two separate NIKEs, the 'mainstream NIKE' and the 'one running around it.' Often, speed groups duplicated other efforts within the company, and individuals in the mainstream complained of receiving conflicting directions. Moreover, noted Tom Clarke, who also worked in a speed group with Strasser and Parker:

There were people in those groups who were very good, but there was a tendency to jump from project to project, rather than to dive into each one and see the worth of stability, defining roles, defining how the groups would interact with the other divisions.

Harry Carsh, vice president of the Footwear Division, reflected on the difficulties with the organization:

I ran around firing people. It was a nightmare and 1986 was just a horrible, horrible year.

Finally, in early 1987, it came to a head. Brendan Foster, who had been brought over from Europe two years earlier to run marketing, had some really good ideas, but he was an egomaniac, and he took on Phil. He said, 'Hey, Phil, you run a lousy company.' And we were a lousy company. There was nothing wrong with what he was saying, but he was saying it to the wrong person. It wasn't Knight running the company. The rest of us were really doing a horrible job. And basically, Foster blamed it on Knight.

Foster departed, increasing tension between Knight and Strasser, who looked upon Foster as his protege. Meanwhile, Knight was concerned that Strasser was getting too involved in others' activities. Ron Nelson described the tension:

Trying to get Strasser to work on creative things and keep him out of the operations was kind of a balancing act that Knight had for a couple years. In all that time, Strasser didn't truly understand how much you needed the operations. You needed the base in there to make things happen. To go from 2 million to 5 million pairs a month – we could do that because we had all the systems, all of the operations, and the people all set up.

Finally, Strasser decided to take a five-month leave of absence. When he returned, Knight told him that he 'could not micro-manage from the corner office.' Just a few weeks later, Strasser quit. He was the eighth of the founding group of vice presidents to leave in a two-year period. Meanwhile, it became increasingly clear that the outside group of 'professional managers' Knight had hired in 1985 would not be able to fill the gap created. Indeed, all seven of the MBA's recruited 'to get some I.Q. around here' eventually left the company.

Developing people: reorganizing around the matrix

Although Strasser and Foster had been an immensely successful marketing team and had contributed greatly to the success of the Air Jordan and other products, Knight thought their dominance had not allowed others to really perform. He felt that Strasser's strong personal control, combined with his fleeting zeal for different projects, led to confusion about management direction. Said Parker:

Strasser had difficulty focusing for a very long period of time on any one thing. He zoomed in on something and wanted to play with it for a while, and when something else caught his eye, he'd run over and play with that. What that meant in terms of NIKE was that he'd jump on an idea and stay with it for a little while. He would get everybody moving in that direction, get a little frustrated with it, and eventually shift to another area. The rest of the company was sitting back, trying to figure out what this small cadre of upper management was doing and where they were going.

During Strasser's five-month absence, Knight realized a need to develop other people and decided to reconceptualize the organization to achieve this objective. Harry Carsh recalled the ensuing period of searching as a tense one in which he literally 'got midnight phone calls from Knight asking me who could perform.' There were many people who had been in middle management for a decade or more and who really knew the company. Because many were athletes, they knew the product as well. 'So we started picking these guys out,' he said. 'A lot of them had been on the verge of being fired under the Strasser regime. Some of them had already quit; others were just about to go.'

But many felt that this new generation of internally developed managers could only be effective if NIKE broke out of its old organizational approaches. As he considered what to do, Knight talked to Tom Paine, a board member and consultant who had spent much time doing organizational design within the aerospace industry. Paine felt a matrix organization might fit NIKE's needs, and spent a lot of time educating the management team about the ways in which such organizations worked. Other key managers became persuaded by Paine's arguments. Dick Donahue, another board member with whom Knight communicated closely at the time believed:

You have natural competition for voice [in a company], so you have to try to devise an organization that allows not only competition, but also communication and collaboration. A matrix not only gets people talking; it also reassures them. In other words, if you interrelate with a couple of departments on your decision over sales, design, marketing, or something of that nature, it almost guarantees you're not going to make a colossal mistake. And it does make you consider all the factors.

Key managers such as Mark Parker thought the matrix would coordinate activities without stifling NIKE's entrepreneurial culture:

We were concerned about losing some of the emotional fire within NIKE, some of the risk-taking, some of the spirit of adventure that made NIKE special. The matrix was an attempt to move away from an emotionally driven, dicta-torial situation to one where there's more collaboration on the future of the company.

The matrix helped us look more in depth, not only at the product and marketing aspects of NIKE, but also the operational and business side. It helped us look at the total picture – what it takes to make a business successful – not just the marketing and design aspects. It was also sensitive to the NIKE irreverence, the need to take risks, to punch it out, and to make sure we were not turning into a dry, predictable company.

Rather than developing a classic formal matrix, the managers preferred to create a looser, less formal set of relationships. Yet, despite the need for increased communication and shared responsibility, the management team still wanted Knight very much in charge. So much so that Del Hayes quipped, 'I didn't realize it was a very good matrix organiz-ation. I thought it was more like a wheel with a hub in the middle.'

The essence of the matrix was coordination among four key functional areas, each headed by a divisional vice president reporting directly to Knight. (See **Exhibit 6**, which shows NIKE's organization in late 1987.) Strong personal friendships and the common experience of growing up together as NIKE managers had created a strong bond among these 'matrix heads' and kept communication at the top of the matrix strong. Matrix heads met every week as a group and also communicated informally.

Across these functional divisions, two corporate vice presidents took on what were described as general management roles. One major task was 'to check that the business plans of the divisions were connected.' Contact between the matrix heads and the general managers occurred in staff meetings, which were collaborative, not directional. The two general managers acted as facilitators, who 'made sure decisions were made, but did not actually make the decisions.' The general managers dealt mostly with administrative issues (such as compensation or new company-wide guidelines). Because the people in the matrix reported up to the divisional vice pres-idents, the general managers had less formal power than the divisional vice presidents. However, the div-ision vice presidents clearly valued the general managers' coordinating role, and respected the fact that they, too, reported directly to Knight.

The matrix heads collectively chose the members of cross-functional teams organized to accomplish product launches. Referred to internally as 'P.T. boats,' these intrapreneurial teams were composed of members who were two or three levels below the matrix heads. Typically, teams consisted of a mar-keting manager, a designer, and a development manager. The teams would meet with the matrix heads two or three times per six-month season. The matrix heads, who walked around the departments regularly, were familiar with the goings-on of the P.T. boats.

Changes in style

Within this overall structure, the new generation of managers began to exert a different organizational approach and management style than their prede-cessors. For example, in 1987, Clarke felt that the marketing department had to develop a more disci-plined approach: 'My belief has always been that you have to be organized to be creative. The former mar-keting regime didn't believe in organization. They felt that was stifling creativity.' Under Clarke, the mar-keting department began to write formal marketing plans. At first descriptive in nature, they grew pro-gressively more strategic and market-focused. Also, in 1987, for the first time the marketing department subscribed to independent color services, which tracked the colors and color schemes that were popular in different parts of the country.

Finally, Clarke required employees to focus more on individual projects, rather than bouncing from one to another as they had under Strasser:

We started to stress that there are these individual teams that have a certain amount of autonomy under a central direction. They're going to spend their whole day working on basketball, or a whole day on running, as opposed to before, when we had people jumping from category to category, kind of wild-catting on various projects. That [old style] just wasn't yielding the best results given the size and scope of the business that we were trying to drive.

With the new organization came more job stability. George Porter recalled the 1984–1986 period, 'I had four jobs in two years. It was impossible in these circumstances to learn the job and to develop relationships.' He believed that organizational stability and job continuity enabled people to really learn their jobs. Clarke concurred:

It sounds incredibly mundane, but you win in business just by putting some emphasis on the fact that people aren't totally interchangeable, that they have skills, that they need job descriptions.

In 1987, the new managers had confidence in the cohesion of the management team and the clarity of purpose this leant the business. Mark Parker reflected:

The chemistry among the people in the matrix was really exceptional. People finished each other's sentences and had a sixth-sense of what others were thinking. That chemistry within the group and with the other people around the company appeared in 1987. We had a real shared vision, a sense of what we were and what we needed to do.

New products

One of the new products developed was the cross-training shoe. First introduced in 1986, this was a multiple-use shoe that could be used for running, tennis, basketball, and other sports activities as well. Cross-training shoes were backed by a well-coordinated marketing, advertising, and sales distribution program that was built around multi-sport star athlete, Bo Jackson, and the theme: 'Bo Knows.' In the late 1980s, this cross-training shoe category really took off.

Although NIKE's Air Jordan Shoe had been phenomenally successful, design and marketing people believed that even by 1987, the public did not understand air technology. Management saw the opportunity to change that in a new product line of twelve 'Visible Air' shoes. In 1985, a speed group composed of designers and marketers had started working on this new group of products, the 'Air Pack.' Air Pack shoes contained translucent, gas-filled plastic bladders in their midsoles that were visible through windows in the sides of the shoes. This revolutionary design not only helped the public understand that there really was something structurally different about NIKE's products, but it also enhanced the shoes' performance by increasing the volume of air in the midsole and cutting the shoe's weight.

The 'Air Pack' range of products reflected a more coordinated effort between product design and marketing than had occurred previously. Never had the design of the shoes been pushed so far in order to make that technology marketable. Furthermore, the concept was executed in a range of twelve shoes from running to tennis to basketball. And it was launched in 1987 with a $20 million advertising campaign based on the Beatles' song, 'Revolution.' In 1992, Knight commented[1]:

Today, when people talk about NIKE, the television ads are practically all they want to talk about. But we became a billion dollar company without television. For years, we just got the shoes out there on the athletes and ran a limited number of print ads in specialized magazines like Runner's World. We didn't complete the advertising spectrum until 1987, when we used television for the first time.

Our first television campaign was for Visible Air shoes. Having gone thorough the painful experience of laying people off and cutting overhead in

---

[1] *Harvard Business Review*, July–August 1992, 'High-Performance Marketing: An Interview with NIKE's Phil Knight.'

the mid-1980s, we wanted the message about our new line of shoes to hit with a punch, and that really dictated television advertising.

The Visible Air launch was a critical moment for a couple of reasons. Until then, we really didn't know if we could be a big company and still have people work closely together. Visible Air was a hugely complex product whose components were made in three different countries, and nobody knew if it would come together. Production, marketing, and sales were all fighting with each other, and we were using television advertising for the first time. There was tension all the way around.

We launched the product with the Revolution campaign, using the Beatles' song. We wanted to communicate not just a radical departure in shoes, but a revolution in the way Americans felt about fitness, exercise, and wellness. The ads were a tremendous hit, and Nike Air became the standard for the industry immediately thereafter.

Back to the future

Fiscal 1987 was NIKE's last year of declining sales, profits and marketshare. Thereafter, sales and profits skyrocketed and NIKE regained market leadership. (See **Exhibit 4**.) In 1989, Knight named 63-year-old Richard Donahue – an 11-year veteran of NIKE's board – as COO. At that time, the matrix heads described the company's organization as a collection of distinct silos rather than a matrix. The vertical chains of command in the functional divisions had remained intact or been strengthened, but the general management roles that sought to promote coordination across functions had atrophied. Cross-functional teams still operated in much the same way as before, but all were now devoted exclusively to one product segment (e.g., basketball) rather than two or three. Communications among the former matrix heads remained strong, and all these divisional vice presidents had been made corporate vice presidents.

In a 1992 interview,[2] Knight commented:

For years, we thought of ourselves as a production-oriented company, meaning we put all our emphasis on designing and manufacturing the product. But now we understand that the most important thing we do is market the product. We've come around to saying that NIKE is a marketing-oriented company, and the product is our most important marketing tool. What I mean is that marketing knits the whole organization together. The design elements and functional characteristics of the product itself are just part of the overall marketing process.

We used to think that everything started in the lab. Now we realize that everything spins off the consumer. And while technology is still important, the consumer has to lead innovation. We have to innovate for a specific reason, and that reason comes from the market. Otherwise, we'll end up making museum pieces.

When the formulas that got NIKE up to $1 billion in sales – being good at innovation and production and being able to sign great athletes – stopped working, we faced a series of problems. For one thing, Reebok came out of nowhere to dominate the aerobics market, which we completely miscalculated. We made an aerobics shoe that was functionally superior to Reeboks', but we missed the styling. Reebok's shoe was sleek and attractive, while ours was sturdy and clunky. We also decided against using garment leather, as Reebok had done, because it wasn't durable. By the time we developed a leather that was both strong and soft, Reebok had established a brand, won a huge chunk of sales, and gained the momentum to go right by us.

We were also having management problems at that time because we really hadn't adjusted to being a big company.

We understood our 'core consumers,' the athletes who were performing at the highest level of the sport. We saw them as being at the top of a pyramid, with weekend jocks in the middle of the pyramid, and everybody else who wore athletic hoses at the bottom. Even though about 60% of our product is bought by people who don't use it for the actual sport, everything we did was aimed at the top. We said, if we get the people

² Ibid.

at the top, we'll get the others because they'll know that the shoe can perform.

But that was an oversimplification. Sure, it's important to get the top of the pyramid, but you've also got to speak to the people all the way down. Just take something simple like the color of the shoe. We used to say we don't care what the color is. If a top player like Michael Jordan liked some kind of yellow and orange jobbie, that's what we made – even if nobody else really wanted yellow and orange. One of our great racing shoes, the Sock Racer, failed for exactly that reason: we made it bright bumble-bee yellow, and it turned everybody off.

Whether you're talking about the core consumer or the person on the street, the principle is the same: you have to come up with what the consumer wants, and you need a vehicle to understand it. To understand the rest of the pyramid, we do a lot of work at the grass roots level. We go to amateur sports events and spend time at gyms and tennis courts talking to people.

We make sure that the product is the same functionally whether it's for Michael Jordan or Joe American Public. We don't just say Michael Jordan is going to wear it so therefore, Joe American Public is going to wear it. We have people who tell us what colors are going to be in for 1993, for instance, and we incorporate them.

Beyond that, we do some fairly typical kinds of market research, but lots of it – spending time in stores and watching what happens across the counter, getting reports from dealers, doing focus groups, tracking responses to our ads. We just sort of factor all that information into the computer between the ears and come up with conclusions.

We've created lots of new categories under the NIKE brand, everything from cross-training and water sports to outdoors and walking.

But what's interesting is that we've sliced up some of the categories themselves.

We've always believed that to succeed with the consumer, you have to wake him up. He's not going to walk in and buy the same stuff he always has, or listen to the same thing he's always heard. There are 50 different competitors in the athletic shoe business. If you do the same thing you've done before or that somebody else is doing, you won't last more than one or two seasons.

And from the beginning, we've tried to create an emotional tie with the consumer. Why do people get married – or do anything? Because of emotional ties. That's what builds long-term relationships with the consumer, and that's what our campaigns are about. That approach distinguishes us from a lot of other companies, including Reebok. Our advertising tries to link consumers to the NIKE brand through the emotions of sports and fitness. We show competition, determination, achievement, fun, and even the spiritual rewards of participating in those activities. People at NIKE believe in the power of emotion because we feel it ourselves.

In mid-1993, the CEO of one of NIKE's competitors commented:

I believe that NIKE is the class act of the industry. NIKE has a clear point of view on who they are which is incorporated into all of their marketing and product. They sell an attitude and a benefit (performance) which greatly lessens their dependence on a 'hot' shoe or a 'hot' feature.

They have built a high quality, professional organization which is extremely loyal to NIKE. An attitude of investing in their people and business is, in my opinion, widening the gap between NIKE and the rest of the industry.

Exhibit 1 NIKE quarterly statements (fiscal year ending May 31)

		Sales ($million)	Gross Margin	S,G&A	Net Income	RoA	Inventory (Turnover)
II	1983	188.4	32.2%	16.0%	6.4%		
III	1983	199.2	29.3	16.9	4.7	7.3%	2.0
IV	1983	222.9	33.2	15.9	6.7	11.8	2.1
I	1984	270.2	33.4	14.7	8.4	18.6	2.7
II	1984	168.9	28.9	20.7	3.3	4.9	1.9
III	1984	224.0	26.7	19.4	2.9	4.8	2.5
IV	1984	256.7	24.3	17.7	2.3	4.3	2.8
I	1985	284.6	27.5	20.0	2.7	5.4	3.0

Source: Standard & Poors' Compustat.

Exhibit 2 NIKE Inc., cartoon from NIKE's in-house newspaper, 1985
Source: *The Nike Times*, 1985.

<u>Principles</u>

1. Our business is change.

2. We're on offense. All the time.

3. Perfect results count – not a perfect process. Break the rules; fight the law.

4. This is as much about battle as about business.

5. Assume nothing. Make sure people keep their promises. Push yourselves, push others. Stretch the possible.

6. Live off the land.

7. Your job isn't done until *the* job is done.

8. Dangers:

    Bureaucracy
    Personal ambition
    Energy takers versus energy givers
    Knowing our weaknesses
    Getting too many things on the platter

9. It won't be pretty.

10. If we do the right things, we'll make money damn near automatic.

Exhibit 3 NIKE Inc., The principles that Rob Strasser distributed to his marketing team.
Source: Company records.

Exhibit 4 NIKE financial information (fiscal year ending May 31)

	Sales ($million)	% Foreign	Gross Margin	S,G&A	Net Income	RoA	Inventory (Turns)
1983	867.2	10.8%	32.0%	15.3%	6.6%	11.2%	2.4
1984	919.8	17.2	28.4	17.8	4.4	7.3	2.3
1985	946.4	22.9	26.3	21.6	1.1	2.0	3.0
1986	1,069.2	23.6	32.4	19.6	5.5	12.4	3.9
1987	877.4	26.9	32.0	23.3	4.1	7.0	4.0
1988	1,203.4	25.2	33.2	20.5	8.5	14.3	5.0
1989	1,710.8	20.4	37.2	20.7	9.8	20.2	5.1
1990	2,235.2	21.5	38.1	20.3	10.9	22.2	5.2
1991	3,003.6	28.7	38.4	22.1	9.6	16.8	4.1
1992	3,405.2	33.3	38.7	22.4	9.7	17.6	3.9
1993	3,931.0	35.7	39.3	23.5	9.3	16.7	4.5

Source: NIKE Annual Reports, 1983-1992. NIKE's fiscal year ended in May.
Note: Total assets grew from $512 million in 1987 to $2,187 million in 1993. Long term debt decreased from $40 million to $15 million during this period, while shareholders' equity rose from $338 million to $1,646 million (of which retained earnings rose from $254 million to $1,542 million).

Exhibit 5 Athletic footwear market (Branded)

	Market Size ($ million)	NIKE's Share	Reebok's Share
1980	1,700	14.4%	–
1981	1,800	22.2	–
1982	1,900	30.5	–
1983	1,960	34.0	1.1%
1984	1,962	32.6	3.4
1985	2,086	27.2	14.3
1986	2,642	24.6	31.8
1987	3,189	16.0	32.5
1988	3,831	19.8	30.0
1989	4,476	23.5	25.7
1990	5,003	27.3	23.4
1991	5,353	31.3	23.9
1992	5,700	31.7	23.4
1993	6,100	32.0	22.0
1994 (est.)	6,300	33.0	23.0

Source: Company estimates.

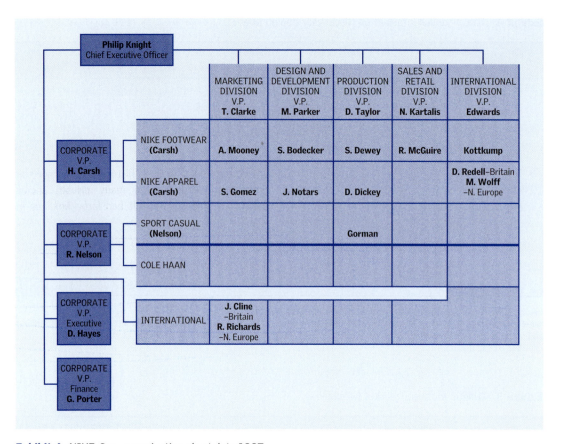

Exhibit 6 NIKE, Inc., organization chart, late 1987

Explanation: Individuals in the matrix (e.g., Mooney, Bodecker, Gomez, etc.) reported up to division vice presidents. Matrix heads (Clarke, Parker, Taylor, Kartalis) established and managed cross-divisional teams. Those on the left side of the matrix were of equal rank to matrix heads and filled a general management role: they provided checks to ensure that cross-divisional coordination was effective, and addressed corporate issues. The company was in the process of acquiring Cole Haan Holdings Inc., which marketed footwear and accessories under the brand name 'Cole Haan'.

Source: Company records.

HARVARD | BUSINESS | SCHOOL

Case 4 **Finland and Nokia**

Örjan Sölvell
Michael E. Porter

When an inventor in Silicon Valley opens his garage door to show off his latest idea, he has 50% of the world market in front of him. When an inventor in Finland opens his garage door, he faces three feet of snow.
— J.O. Nieminen, CEO of Nokia Mobira, 1984

Until the 1990s, Finland was considered a remote and sleepy country in the northeastern corner of Europe, lying in the shadow of its large neighbor Russia. Finland had been part of Sweden for six centuries until 1809, when it was ceded to Russia. The Bolshevik revolution in 1917 and the collapse of the Romanov dynasty led Finland to unilaterally declare independence on December 6, 1917 (still the national day). After difficult years during World War II, Finland remained somewhat isolated, and its economy remained highly dependent on the Soviet Union. Following the model of its Nordic neighbors in

Professor Örjan Sölvell and Professor Michael E. Porter, Institute for Strategy and Competitiveness at Harvard Business School, prepared this case from published sources with the assistance of Pekka Yla-Anttila, Laura Paija, and Christian Ketels. HBS cases are developed solely as the basis for class discussion. Cases are not intended to serve as endorsements, sources of primary data, or illustrations of effective or ineffective management.

the post-war years, Finland was characterized by heavy investments in social welfare and public infrastructure. There was a history of reliance on government leadership in many private sector companies. The government had large holdings in many top Finnish companies (see **Exhibit 1**), and through its active involvement in major mergers and acquisitions transactions, influenced the ownership structures of key industries. Finland's prosperity level caught up to the OECD average only slowly. With few exceptions, notably in pulp and paper and specialty shipbuilding, Finnish companies were absent from international business rankings.

By 2001, Finland had become one of the fastest growing and most competitive economies in the world. A member of the European Union, it was known for fiscal stability and was the only Nordic country introducing the Euro in the first wave. In the Competitiveness Rankings of the Global Competitiveness Report, Finland won the top spot from the United States in 2000. One Finnish company, Nokia, had outpaced others to cast a long shadow on the entire economy. Its emergence as the market leader in global mobile telecommunication equipment had made the company the leading influence on Finnish exports, R&D expenditures, and market capitalization.

With the slowdown of the global telecommunication market, however, both Nokia and the Finnish economy were facing challenges, raising questions about the company and the country's recent achievements.

Country background

Finland was a sparsely populated European country, surrounded by the Baltic Sea in the South and the West, a 1,000-mile plus border with Russia in the East, and Sweden and Norway in the Northwest. The country's capital Helsinki was located at the same latitude as southern Alaska and Greenland.

Finland's population of 5.3 million in 2001 was spread thinly across the country's 130,000 square miles. Only the region of the southern cities of Helsinki, Espoo, and Vantaa was more heavily populated accounting for about 20% of the total population.

Finland was one of the world's most homogenous societies with a very low proportion of immigrants. Finns shared one culture, although about 6% of its population belonged to the Swedish minority. Finland had close cultural ties to its Nordic neighbors but had followed a separate path in many other respects. The Finnish language was part of the Finno-Ugrian language group and was related only to Estonian, Hungarian, and to the Inuit language spoken in the far north. Apart from Finnish and Swedish, the two official languages, most of the population also spoke English. With the establishment of the common Nordic labor market in 1954, large numbers of Finnish women moved to Sweden to work in the textile factories, making Finns the largest immigrant group in Sweden. Very few Swedes, however, had moved to Finland.

Beginning in 1919, the Finnish constitution had enshrined a so-called 'semi-presidential' form of government. The president, directly elected by the people for a 6-year term, had significant policy making powers, especially in foreign relations, and the right to dissolve parliament and call elections. He or she (Tarja Halonen was elected the first female Finnish president in February 2000) also nominated government ministers that had to be confirmed by parliament. The 200 members of the one-chamber parliament were elected for four years. Legislative proposals were usually initiated by the government, but could also come from any member of the parliament. On March 1, 2000, Finland adopted a new constitution that integrated four previously separate constitutional acts but did not change the substance of the political system.

The country's vulnerable geopolitical position vis-à-vis the Soviet Union, plus the constitution had allowed President Urho Kekkonen to dominate the country's political agenda during his 26 years of office from 1956 to 1982. The parliament was controlled by coalitions often encompassing the whole spectrum of left- to right-wing parties. Kekkonen had forced these broad coalitions which were accepted out of desire to avoid divergent views on domestic policies that would destabilize Finland's external relations. This logic lived on in the government that had been elected in 1999. Only one party, the rural Center party, was not included in the government coalition.

The Finnish economy prior to 1990

The Finnish economy was historically driven by the wealth of the country's natural resource endowment and its long coastline. The economy was dominated by manufacturing industries and had a service sector smaller than in many comparable European countries. The three largest clusters were pulp and paper, wood products, and engineered metal products. Pulp and paper accounted for 40% of exports, wood products for 16%, and engineered metal (including shipbuilding) for 23% in 1970.

The pulp and paper cluster had grown, based on the large forests and woodland covering 76% of the country's total land area. It achieved a leading role in the world industry, however, despite slower growing forests and higher energy costs than in competing regions of the world. A shipbuilding cluster was focused on specialized ships such as icebreakers and ferries. Domestic demand, for example by ferry lines connecting Finland to Sweden and to continental Europe, was an important initial market for the cluster.

Finland's post-war economic performance was characterized by slow catch-up to more advanced western economies from an initially low level. In 1950, Finland's GDP per hour worked was at 46% of the U.S. level, in between its Nordic neighbors and war-torn Germany and Austria. GDP per hour had reached 69% of the United States in 1970, closing some of the gap to its neighbors but falling behind Germany and Austria. GDP growth rates stayed between 3 and 5% per year, investment rates were high, and total factor productivity growth outperformed many other European countries from the 1960s through the 1980s. Wage dispersion in the Finnish economy was low. Company profitability in Finland was also historically low compared to other OECD countries.

Finland's trade was dominated by the Soviet Union. Having joined forces with Germany during World War II, Finland was made to pay substantial war indemnities in the form of steel, ships, textiles and machinery to the Soviet Union. This created important business linkages in the east. Some 20% of all Finnish exports were sent east between the 1950s and the 1980s; Finland became an important supplier of manufactured products to the Soviet Union. Payments for these exports were usually made in natural resources, often oil. Other important export markets were in Europe, primarily Sweden and Germany. The United States, accounted for only 3% of Finnish exports in the early 1980s. The country had joined the European Free Trade Association (EFTA) as an associate member in 1961. Finland's economic policy in the 1970s and 80s followed Western European and Nordic patterns. Finland had traditionally been a country with a large public sector and strong welfare aspirations. Taxes were high after an era of active interventionism by government in the 1960s and 1970s. Transfer payments and public spending on services were high. Macroeconomic policy featured a fixed nominal exchange rate, centralized wage bargaining, and an increasing fiscal budget through the 1980s. After World War II, Finland experienced at least one large devaluation every decade; 30.7% in 1949, 28.1% in 1957, 23.8% in 1967, and over 20% in a series of devaluations in the 1970s.

Finland had developed a sophisticated public education and university system. Education between the ages of 7 and 16 was compulsory and most students stayed on for three to four more years in upper secondary or vocational schools. Public spending on education relative to GDP was traditionally above the level in many other European countries, and had increased at a steady growth rate. Quality of education was considered good, and Finnish students generally performed well in international school performance tests. Nearly 60% of the population had completed a secondary education or beyond.

Finland also was home to 20 universities and other institutions of higher education, with a student population of approximately 270,000. A number of universities had a long tradition; the University of Åbo was founded in 1640 but moved to Helsinki in 1828. Nearly 13% of the population had a university degree or the equivalent.

Finland's financial markets were characterized by strong ties between companies and their banks, not unlike the system prevalent in the Germanic countries. Financial regulation was tight, making credit approval restrictive. Finnish competition policy, not unlike other Nordic countries, had a history of lax enforcement. Mergers and acquisitions were decided and negotiated by a small elite group of managers and owners (the so called 'bergsråd'), together with the large banks and government officials.

The Finnish corporate sector had traditionally been dominated by large, often highly diversified groups, such as Valmet, Nokia, and Ahlström, with roots back to the nineteenth century. Valmet was a world leader in sophisticated machinery for the pulp and paper industry with a long history. Nokia had historical traces all the way back to 1865, but was really created in 1967 when Suomen Kaapelitehdas (Finnish Cable Works, founded in 1917 and active in the telecommunications cable and electronics businesses) was merged with Suomen Gummi-tehdas (Finnish Rubber Works) and Nokia, a 100-year-old wood grinding mill. Other parts of the economy, such as the food retail sector, had a strong presence of small companies tied together in co-operatives.

Developments in the 1980s Economic growth in the 1980s was driven by rising government expenditure that led to increasing inflationary pressure. Growing government budgets were financed by public sector deficits and an increasing tax share of GDP. In October 1982 the Bank of Finland devalued the Finnish Markka, first by 3.8% and then by 5.7%.

Throughout the 1980s, a series of policy changes were made in reaction to a growing perception that Finland's economy was losing ground internationally. In science and technology, R&D expenditure as a share of GDP was increased continuously beginning in the early 1980s. Public R&D spending was increased at an annual rate of about 10%, soon making Finland one of the leading OECD countries in public R&D spending relative to GDP.

In 1983 the National Technology Agency (Tekes) was founded, which became the main implementer of technology policy. In March 1987, another research related body, the Science and Technology Policy Council, was founded. Headed by the Prime Minister and including the Ministers of Finance, Trade and Industry, Education, and four other Ministers together with representatives from the main research organizations, the Council was to direct overall research policy and develop strategies in three-year cycles.

In financial market regulation, existing policies came under increasing pressure in the 1980s for making Finland uncompetitive. In the second half of the 1980s the financial markets were liberalized, as they were in Norway and Sweden, making lending much easier for banks. Access to international capital markets was also made easier.

Emergence of the Finnish telecommunications cluster

Unlike in most other European countries, the Finnish telephone network was never monopolized by the state. The deliberately fragmented market structure reflected security concerns dating back to the late nineteenth century when Finland was a Russian Grand Duchy. At the time, the Finnish Senate had granted many licenses for telephone operations in order to complicate any effort by the Tsar to seize the national telephone system.

After independence, a national public telecommunications operator (PTT) Telecom Finland was established to operate the network left behind by Russia. The PTT was not only an operator but also the regulatory body for the industry. There were several attempts over the decades to nationalize poorly performing private operators in the name of harmonizing infrastructure, but these had met with political resistance and never materialized. The threat of nationalizing weak companies, however, stimulated private operators to upgrade their technology. In 1921, the private telephone operators founded the 'Association of Telephone Companies' for administrative cooperation and joint actions vis-à-vis the PTT. The Association became a powerful competitor to the PTT, dominating local telephone operations in major cities while the PTT had a monopoly over long distance and international calls. In the 1930s, there were no less than 815 private local telephone companies in Finland. Finnish operators, who were quite advanced technologically, engaged actively in R&D cooperation with equipment manufacturers.

The seeds of the Finnish radiophone and mobile phone industries were planted in the 1920s in three companies: Salora, established in 1928, was a regional manufacturer of TV and radio sets. It began the development of radiophones in 1964 after the Finnish Army issued an invitation for tenders; the first in a series of orders by the government which required companies to meet demanding requirements in the development of radio technology. Valtion Sähköpaja (lit. State Electric Works), established in 1925, as the radio laboratory of the Ministry of Defense, was founded to strengthen national development and production of radio technology. Valtion Sähköpaja was merged after the War with the R&D unit of the PTT, renamed Televa. Finally, Suomen Kaapelitehdas (lit. Finnish Cable Works), founded in 1917, was a producer of telecommunications cables, and merged into Nokia in 1967. By the 1970s, Televa and Nokia viewed the Finnish market as too small and its resources too scarce for parallel development of digital exchanges, and combined their R&D and marketing efforts in digital transfer technology in a joint venture, Telefenno. Telefenno introduced the first digital exchange in 1982, only shortly after Ericsson, Alcatel, ITT and Siemens. For years, the product became Nokia's most successful export.

The first two decades of the mobile era In 1969, the 'Nordic Telecom Conference', a body for formal and informal technical cooperation between the Nordic PTTs (in Denmark, Finland, Norway and Sweden), initiated a project on an automatic (analog) Nordic Mobile Telephone (NMT) network. The NMT system, launched in 1981, was unique in several respects. Most importantly, it developed roaming technology (later used in other systems around the world) that made it possible for the system to know where a telephone was located, making it possible to travel across national borders using the same phone. Furthermore, NMT was an open standard. The introduction of the NMT made the Nordic region the world's largest single mobile market at the time.

Expanding at a rapid rate, the market began to attract private operators and manufacturers. In Finland, private license applications were rejected by the PTT in its role as regulator. The Finnish PTT argued that competition would preclude economies of scale and that mobile communications was a natural monopoly. As a countermove, the Association of Telephone Companies formed a joint venture in 1988, Radiolinja, to operate a private network.

The introduction of the NMT marked the start of a fast-expanding new industry. The design of the NMT standard brought the Nordic telecommunications administrators and providers into close cooperation. While active in the development of mobile phones, the Finnish industry had in the past not been able to provide network infrastructure. In 1981, however, pressure from the Finnish PTT led the domestic industry to develop a base station (see Appendix for an overview of the technologies involved). By 1985, the NMT standard had a leading position in a number of foreign markets, and an average annual growth rate of 50%. Several Nordic manufacturers of mobile phones and network infrastructure soon entered the market. In other countries, with closed standards, there was only one operator that also supplied the phones.

By the late 1980s there were some 15 competitors active in the Nordic mobile phone markets. The only other country that had significant competition was the UK, which had a similar number of competitors, while each of the other European markets had about five. In terms of user penetration, the Nordic region was the first to take off. The Nordic region had 523,000 subscribers in June of 1988, The U.K. had 366,000, Germany 70,000, France 69,000, Austria 34,000 and Switzerland 14,000.

With the NMT under way, Nokia and Salora created a 50-50 owned joint venture in 1979 named Mobira (later Nokia-Mobira) to market and develop radio technology, especially new NMT phones. Before 1980 Nokia had sold approximately half of its production in the domestic market. The rest was exported mostly to neighboring countries. During the 1980s, Mobira allied itself with distributors and mobile operators around the world, and the company learned about building a global consumer brand. Nokia began to strengthen its international operations by also acquiring several electronics companies including Luxor (a Swedish manufacturer of TV sets and personal computers) and Standard Elektrik Lorenz's consumer electronics businesses (a German manufacturer of TV sets and other electronics). Nokia also acquired the PC and office electronics business of Ericsson,

Ericsson Information Systems. The acquired units operated mostly in the electronics industry and manufactured products such as TV sets, monitors and videos sold directly to consumers. Through these acquisitions Nokia became the largest consumer electronics company in the Nordic region during the 1980s. Nokia's mobile phone unit, Mobira, expanded through global alliances. Together with Tandy Corporation, for example, Nokia established joint ventures in Korea and the United States. Mobile phones were sold under different brand names, including the private label brands of dealers (e.g. Radio Shack in the U.S.) and service operators.

During this period, the Finnish telecommunication equipment industry was further consolidated in Nokia, still a large conglomerate. Through a series of mergers finalized in 1987, Salora, Telefenno, and Televa became parts of Nokia. Salora and units of Suomen Kaapelitehdas ultimately became Nokia Mobile Phones in 1989, and Telefenno and Televa became Nokia Telecommunications (the exchange business) in 1992.

After rapid growth through acquisitions and alliances, however, Nokia ran into a financial crisis. With CEO Kari Kairamo's untimely death in 1988 a new CEO was brought in to try to establish some focus in the company as well as to regain cost control. Company employment decreased by around 15,000 between 1989 and 1992 (see **Exhibit 2**).

Finnish economic policy in the 1990s

The 1990s began with the most severe crisis the Finnish economy had ever experienced. In 1991, real GDP fell by 6.2%. In 1992, it lost another 3.3%. Exports dropped by 13% in dollar terms in 1991. Unemployment rose from 3.5% in 1990 to 17.9% in 1993.

The Berlin wall had come down in 1989 and the Soviet Union was dissolving. Almost overnight, exports to what had been the most important market for Finnish exports dried up. German reunification and the economic integration of Eastern Germany led to an increase in real interest rates throughout Europe. Finland was also experiencing a deteriorating terms-of-trade due to falling world pulp and paper prices, its main export industry. The problems were compounded by domestic economic conditions: In the late 1980s, the Finnish economy had experienced a huge increase in credits from the liberalized banking sector. Property prices increased sharply and inflation rose. The savings rate fell to 12.1% in 1992, less than half of the 24.9% ten years earlier. As a result of the external problems and internal overheating, the Finnish exchange rate came under pressure. In November 1991 the Marka was devaluated by 12%, and in September 1992, Finland was forced to float its currency and fundamentally revisit its economic policy.

Tight macroeconomic policies were quickly adopted. The earlier creeping increase in the tax burden was halted, and tax rates stabilized. With wage growth and profits weak during the crisis, tax revenues on these two items as a share of GDP fell from 19.3% in 1990 to 18.1% in 1995. Government expenditures were cut by nearly 10% of GDP, targeting budget surpluses by the end of the 1990s compared to a deficit of 7.3% of GDP in 1993. Monetary policy was changed to adopt an inflation target of 2% beginning 1995. Interest rates were the main policy instrument, initially reaching levels above 13% on 10-year government bonds in 1992, implying an interest rate differential of up to 500 basis points relative to Germany.

Finland's economy began to rebound in 1993 with real GDP growth reaching 4% and staying between 3.8 and 6.3% throughout the rest of the 1990s. Inflation fell continuously from its peak of almost 7% in 1990 to under 2% from 1993 onwards. Interest rates came down continuously to reach about 6% at the end of 1997, eliminating the differential with Germany. Finland was able to re-establish a stable parity to European Union member currencies in 1996.

During the 1990s, the changes in the science and technology policies initiated in the preceding decade were accelerated. While some parts of the budget were severely cut in the 1992 crisis, the government decided to make additional resources available for research and development (see **Table 1**). Already in 1990, the Science and Technology Policy Council conducted a major review of Finland's economic position that had resulted in two reform initiatives to strengthen the country's national innovative capacity. The Center of Expertise Program, focused on 'strengthening regional competitiveness by increasing innovation, renewing the regional production structure, and creating new jobs in selected expertise areas'. The Cluster Program focused on developing the innovative capacity of industrial clusters by supporting cluster-specific R&D efforts. In parallel, the government set up 15 incubators in proximity to regional clusters throughout Finland to make venture capital available for start-up companies.

Table 1 Finnish research and development expenditure, 1989–1999 (€ millions)

	1989	1991	1993	1995	1997	1998	1999
Enterprises	€924.8	€975.1	€1,048.5	€1,373.4	€1,916.7	€2,252.8	€2,643.9
Public sector[a]	286.1	357.5	379.7	374.4	408.6	443.8	470.1
University sector[b]	290.2	378.0	367.5	424.6	579.5	657.9	764.8
Total	1,501.2	1,710.6	1,795.8	2,172.4	2,904.9	3,354.5	3,878.8
as % of GDP	1.8	2.0	2.2	2.3	2.7	2.9	3.2[c]
Enterprises	61.6%	57.0%	58.4%	63.2%	66.0%	67.2%	68.2%
Public sector[a]	19.1	20.9	21.1	17.2	14.1	13.2	12.1
University sector[b]	19.3	22.1	20.5	19.6	20.0	19.6	19.7
Total	100	100	100	100	100	100	100

Source: *Statistics Finland*, Science and technology statistics.
[a] Including private nonprofit sector.
[b] Including central university hospitals since 1997 and polytechnics since 1999.
[c] Preliminary data

The cluster approach was introduced in Finland through a study coordinated by the Research Institute of the Finnish Economy (ETLA) in the early 1990s. The approach set the design of policy guidelines outlined in 1993 in the White Paper 'A National Industrial Strategy' by the Ministry of Trade and Industry. The central message for policy makers was that all government actions had implications for national competitiveness. Therefore, economic and industrial policies needed to be considered from an extended perspective, beyond sectoral ministries' administrative boundaries. The cluster model stimulated new forums for interaction and coordination between ministries, public and private research units, and companies. The study served to convince policymakers of the relevance of the evolving policy direction first began in the 1980s, clarifying the role of the government as the creator of favorable framework conditions, and emphasizing interorganizational cooperation as well as accumulation and transfer of know-how. Policies concerning technology, education and competition became center stage of the new Finnish industrial policy.

The increasing focus on R&D and technology-intensive activities increased the demand for skilled employees. The government reacted by expanding the capacity of higher education. Between 1993-1998, the total intake of students in universities nearly doubled, and in polytechnics it nearly tripled. Despite growing enrollment, however, Finland ranked 14th—well below the OECD average—in expenditures per student at the tertiary level. In early 1998, the government adopted a program to expand education in the information and communication field between 1998–2001.

The liberalization of the Finnish capital markets that had begun already in the 1980s continued. In 1991, for example, households were allowed to borrow in foreign currency. More rivalry in the domestic banking market and easier access to foreign capital reshaped the traditionally tight relations between companies and their banks. In 1993, restrictions on foreign ownership of Finnish firms were removed. Venture capitalists emerged during the 1990s, stimulated in part by government-sponsored incubators. Successful business plans at the turn of the century attracted increasing amounts of venture capital, which had emerged as the most common source of capital for start-ups. Investors had become more specialized due to the increased number of funds and investment companies. The availability of venture capital had reshaped the role of public funding, traditionally the prime source of capital for risky enterprises. New kinds of investment syndicates were established where the public sector invested alongside venture capitalists.

In 1994, the policy-making powers of the regions were significantly strengthened through the Regional Development Act. Regions were encouraged to develop their own economic development activities and integrate the 'Center's of Excellence' concept developed as part of the new technology policy.

The attitude towards competition shifted in favor of more intense rivalry. However, mark-ups in many Finnish industries still remained above the levels of the United States and other European countries. The centralized wage setting mechanisms between unions and employer organizations remained in place.

Internationally, Finland was redirecting attention from the East to the West: In 1993, Finland joined the European Economic Area (EEA); a decision that eliminated many trade and investment barriers to other Nordic and European countries. Germany, Sweden, and the United Kingdom became Finland's most important export markets. The United States doubled its share of Finnish exports, while the Russian share fell to 4.5%.

In 1995, Finland became a member of the European Union, entering together with its neighbor Sweden. EU membership brought further integration into the European Common Market, and the harmonization of many laws and regulations with the other EU countries. With the opening towards the west, the Finnish economy attracted significant amounts of inward FDI. Large mergers between Swedish and Finnish firms in banking (Nordea), engineering (ABB), electronics (Nokia) and pulp and paper (Stora-Enso, UPM-Kymmene) created larger and more focused Finnish firms with global reach. In 1998, Swedish firms accounted for 50% of FDI in Finland, and 34% of Finnish FDI took place in Sweden. In 1985, the stock of Finnish inward and outward foreign direct investment had been 1.3% and 1.8% of GDP respectively. In 1998, these ratios had increased to 18.3% and 33.8%.

The transformation of Finnish industry could also

be seen in the composition of the economy: In 1999, electronics and telecommunications equipment had become the leading sector, accounting for 21% of value added, followed by pulp and paper (15%), chemicals (10%), and machinery and equipment (9.5%). Within these and other fields the corporate landscape had changed significantly. The pulp and paper cluster, for example, was considered to be a leader in global markets with a broad array of companies including specialized machine manufacturers and service companies.

The three largest sectors also increasingly dominated exports. In 1999, pulp and paper and electronics products each accounted for about 30% of exports. Engineered metal products accounted for another 20%.

In the second half of the 1990s, Finland's average GDP growth rose to about 5%, with Nokia's growth contributing close to 1%. Unemployment rates came down but stayed above the 10%-level throughout the 1990s. In 1999, youth unemployment was above 20%, higher than in other European countries and more than twice as high as ten years earlier.

Finnish telecommunications policy in the 1990s

The Finnish telecommunications sector was subject to standard competition and consumer protection legislation. The telecommunications authorities pursued a policy of minimum interference, acting mainly in cases of insufficient competition, an approach different from most other OECD countries. Some mandatory EU requirements had been enforced in Finland rather reluctantly, as they were considered to go against the liberal functioning of markets.

In 1987, a new Telecommunications Services Act had separated the regulatory and operator functions of the PTT, transferring regulatory authority from the PTT to an independent body under the Ministry of Transport and Communications. The Act also established the right of private companies to offer mobile communication network services. This legislation ended a long dispute over the PTTs monopoly rights that dated back already to the 1960s.[1]

---

[1] The operative Imperial Telephone Decree of 1886 did not provide an unambiguous interpretation of the statutory rights to provide novel network services, such as data transfer, telefax and teletext.

In 1991, privately-owned Radiolinja was the first operator in the world to launch a commercial GSM network. Liberalization meant fundamental organizational changes for the PTT, which was turned into a public company. The PTT began to improve service and worked hard to launch its GSM service soon after Radiolinja, becoming one of the first PTTs in Europe to do so. The government started reducing its ownership in the PTT and indicated further privatization. In 1998, the name of the company was changed to Sonera to reflect a new strategic focus on fixed, mobile and media services.

At the end of the 1990s, the government was mandated by parliament to withdraw from the telecommunications business. These intentions were later frustrated by Sonera's large expenditures on UMTS licenses in Europe which created large borrowings. In 2001, the Government decided to save the company by infusing new equity. This move came despite the government's decision to limit intervention in the sector as much as possible. Finland had, for example, decided not to engage in direct, high-speed network capacity provision, despite the political goal of providing leading infrastructure. This decision, different from neighboring Sweden and more in line with the United Kingdom and other continental European countries, was made to insure technology neutrality and the free functioning of the market. In line with the same liberal policy principles, Finland granted third-generation mobile network licenses without restricting the choice of standards.

The international mobile telecommunications sector

The mobile telecommunications sector grew out of the combination of radiophone technology with wired telephone systems. The basic technology of so-called cellular systems had been developed already in the 1950s in the United States. With the exception of small city systems in some parts of the world, however, cellular or mobile telephony did not develop as a market until the early 1980s.

In 2001, over 500 million mobile phones were sold worldwide. The industry was divided into two parts: mobile communication infrastructure and mobile handsets (often called cellular phones in the

United States. See the **Appendix**). Each part had different competitive characteristics, though the big three, Motorola, Ericsson (including Sony Ericsson) and Nokia were all active in both infrastructure and handsets in 2001.

The use of mobile phones was highest in the Nordic countries, with penetration rates of over 70% in 2000. Italy and Austria also had penetration rates above 70%, whereas most other European countries were around 60%. Japan had a penetration rate of about 50%, the United States 40%, and South East Asia around 10%.

Evolving standards

In 1986, there were mobile networks in 32 countries, most of which were incompatible accross national borders. In 2001, this list had grown to over 150 countries and an emerging global standard had begun to be installed across the most advanced nations. This third generation system, referred to as UMTS, integrated voice and high-speed data communication (see **Table 2**).

First generation systems in the 1980s were analog and incompatible. In Europe alone, there were six systems: NMT, Comvik, TACS, Radiocom 2000, C-450, and RTMS. The leading system was the Nordic NMT system, the only one offering international compatibility (first throughout the Nordic region, and in 1988, in Switzerland and the Benelux region). Comvik was used in Sweden in parallel to the PTT-controlled NMT system. The TACS system from the United States was brought to Ireland and the U.K. in 1985. The Radiocom 2000 system was developed by Matra and used only in France. The C-450 system was developed by Siemens for the German market, and adopted by Portugal. The Italian RTMS system was introduced in Italy in 1985. In the United States, several competing systems and standards evolved, covering limited areas of the nation that were also adopted in Latin America.

Second generation systems involved a shift to digital technology, and were introduced earlier in Europe than in the United States. Digital technology provided major benefits in terms of operating costs, system capacity and enhanced service offerings to customers. The Nordic Conference in 1982 played an active role in initiating the pan-European digital mobile network, or GSM system (an alternative standard proposed by German and French interests was later withdrawn). GSM was launched in 1990 and covered all of Europe, later spreading to Asia and the United States. A GSM group had been

Table 2 Mobile telecommunication standards

	First Generation	**Second Generation**	**Third Generation**
Application	◆ National/local systems ◆ Portable phones ◆ Car phones	◆ Regional systems ◆ Pocket phones ◆ Digital voice services ◆ Digital text: SMS (short message service) ◆ First-generation WAP	◆ Global system ◆ Integrated high-quality audio and data ◆ Music and video ◆ Narrowband and broadband ◆ Multimedia services
Type of System	◆ Analog cellular technology ◆ Macro-cellular systems	◆ Digital cellular technology ◆ Micro-cellular and pico-cellular ◆ Enhanced cordless technology	◆ Digital broadband ◆ Information compression ◆ Higher frequency spectrum ◆ IP packet switching
Standards	◆ AMPS, ETACS, NMT 450, NMT 900, TACS, Radiocom 2000, C-450, RTMS, Comvik	◆ GSM, CDMA, TDMA, PDC, GPRS	◆ WCDMA, CDMA 2000, TDMA 136

formed to secure Europe against Japanese competition and involved cooperation through alliances. For example, Nokia-Mobira developed systems and handsets together with AEG and Alcatel, and had an alliance for processor chip development together with AT&T. Motorola was also active in GSM technology, with a focus on Europe.

In the United States, two digital standards emerged, TDMA and CDMA. In the late 1990s, a number of GSM systems were established offering the ability to use a single phone in Europe and the United States. Qualcomm's Code Division Multiple Access (CDMA) followed a restrictive licensing strategy. Nokia decided not to license the technology and developed its own CDMA phone. In March of 1999, Qualcomm sold its manufacturing operations to Ericsson after a long patent fight. TDMA was championed by AT&T Wireless, Bell South, and Southwestern Bell Mobile. In 2000, GSM had 69% of digital subscribers worldwide, CDMA 13%, TDMA 10% and the Japanese system PDC 8%.

There was fierce competition over third-generation standards. GPRS, sometimes referred to as the 2-1/2 generation system, had been developed in Europe to maintain momentum. The emerging leader in 3G systems was the European WCDMA. Together with Qualcomm's new CDMA 2000 and the leading Japanese companies, WCDMA formed a 'global family' allowing phones to be used all over the world. U.S. proponents of the TDMA system also introduced a third generation system under the name of TDMA 136. The transition to the third generation system was slow and in 2001/2002 investment plans were delayed in most countries. Japan and Korea were the first movers.

Mobile telecommunication systems had initially been separate from the Internet. A first standard allowing access to certain Internet services was the Wireless Application Protocol (WAP), introduced on high-end phones in the late 1990s. With increased bandwidth in third-generation systems, mobile Internet was emerging.

The mobile communications value system

Mobile service was provided by network operators (Figure 1). Once a monopoly in many countries, mobile service providers faced fierce competition in 2001. Three or more mobile operators typically competed in each local market. Verizon Wireless was the largest mobile operator in the United States in 2001 with some 30 million subscribers. Operators had internationalized, and a few global firms or 'families' of firms had emerged.

Operators had begun to segment their services to cater to the differing usage needs of business and residential customers. Handset manufacturers had also begun developing handsets focused on segments.

The growth of fixed-line systems was slowing in advanced countries, and the paging market had recently begun to slow as well. Leading paging manufacturers such as Motorola and Glenayre in the United States were adding more functionality to paging with two-way paging and voice paging. Satellite phones were a long-term threat to mobile phones, but remained expensive in 2001.

Mobile telephone equipment could be divided into infrastructure and handsets; each accounting for about one half of the total manufacturing market. Infrastructure, consisting of base stations and switching equipment, was produced by major telecommunications manufacturers such as Ericsson, Motorola, and Nokia. Handsets, or mobile phones, were manufactured by many new companies, especially as standards became more established.

As the mobile communications industry emerged in the 1980s, two companies became leaders: Motorola from the United States and Nokia-Mobira from Finland (see **Table 3**). Suppliers of first generation analog infrastructure (such as Ericsson, Siemens, Philips, Alcatel, NEC) also developed proprietary phones for their own systems, and some also manufactured phones for open systems such as NMT. Rapid industry growth attracted new handset competitors, many with a background in consumer electronics (such as Samsung, Panasonic, Mitsubishi, Sony). Ericsson and Samsung gained substantial market share in the 1990s, while NEC, Mitsubishi and Toshiba were the losers. In 2002 positions had shifted considerably with Sony-Ericsson (the two companies merged their handset businesses in 2000) far behind Nokia, Motorola, Samsung and Siemens.

Mobile handsets were sold through service operators as well as through independent dealers.

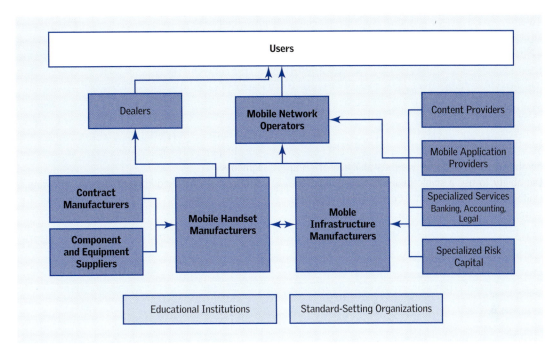

Figure 1 The mobile phone value system
Source: Case writer

Some operators sold phones directly to consumers (sometimes branding the phone themselves or jointly with the OEM), while others concentrated exclusively on subsidized sales of phones through independent dealers, with which they typically had exclusive relationships.

The components for mobile phones included the casing, LCD, circuits, battery, and antenna. Phone manufacturers made some parts themselves but contracted many components from outside suppliers. Some phone manufacturers such as Motorola, Nokia and Samsung had integrated backwards into semiconductors in an attempt to reduce costs and help shorten new product development cycles. In addition, software constituted an increasingly important part of the value of a phone.

Competition

All mobile phone manufacturers were facing intense competition in 2001. Growth rates in major consumer markets were slowing, and incumbents together with new entrants from the consumer electronics industry had capacities that outstripped market demand. Phone companies, were also under financial pressure and less willing to subsidize phones in order to stimulate demand. The three leading competitors in 2001, were Nokia, Motorola, and SonyEricsson.

Motorola Based in the United States, Motorola had long been a leader in two-way radios, paging, mobile phone handsets and mobile infrastructure. Founded by Paul V. Galvin, Motorola successfully commercialized car radios under the brand name 'Motorola' in the 1930s. In the 1960s, the company became a leader in military, space and commercial communications, as well as semiconductors and consumer electronics. It also began expanding into international markets.

After divesting its consumer electronics business, Motorola had, by the end of the 1980s, became the leading worldwide supplier of mobile phones and mobile infrastructure. In the 1990s Motorola invested several hundred million dollars in a new satellite phone system, the Iridium, which did not grow as expected.

Table 3 World market shares of leading mobile equipment competitors

Company	Home Base	Mobile Phones		Infrastructure
		2000	1988	1999
Nokia	Finland	31%	14%	10%
Motorola	United States	15	13	13
Ericsson	Sweden	10	3	30
Samsung	Korea	6	–	–
Siemens	Germany	6	2	6
Panasonic	Japan	5	9	–
Alcatel	France	5	6	3
Philips	Netherlands	3	3	–
Sagem	France	3	–	–
NEC	Japan	3	12	7
Mitsubishi	Japan	2	8	–
Qualcomm	United States	2	–	–
Toshiba	Japan	2	8	–
LG	Korea	1	–	–
Lucent	United States	–	–	11
Nortel	Canada	–	–	9
Fujitsu	Japan	–	–	2
OKI	Japan	–	6	–
Others		6	16	9

Source: 'Nokia-Mobira OY,' Harvard Business School case No. 589-112; Gardner Dataquest.
Note: – = not active or less than 1% share.

Motorola's small and light mobile phones had garnered a strong following. In 1989, the MicroTAC phone was the smallest and lightest phone in the market. In 1996 the 3.1-ounce StarTAC was introduced. The company controlled almost 25% of the world market in the 1990s. However, Motorola was slow to shift from analog to digital phones, and lost its leadership position in the late 1990s. In 2001, Motorola held the number two spot in both mobile networks (13%) and phones (15%). The company was vertically integrated into semiconductors and other components.

Ericsson Founded as a telegraph repair shop in 1876 by Lars Magnus Ericsson, Ericsson copied the newly invented Bell telephone which had not been patented by Bell in Sweden. When Bell entered the Swedish market in 1880, a spirited rivalry began. Ericsson introduced the first half-automatic switch in 1883. Because the Swedish PTT began to manufacture its own telephone equipment, Ericsson turned to international markets in the late 19th century. Ericsson had manufacturing operations in Russia and sales subsidiaries in China and Mexico as early as the 1890s. By 2001, Ericsson served over 130 markets worldwide. Ericsson had entered the radio industry in 1919.

In 1977, when NMT specifications were issued, Ericsson developed a mobile phone and exchange infrastructure. The mobile handset business was seen as peripheral and Ericsson considered selling the division several times. Throughout the 1980s and 1990s, Ericsson became a world leader in network technologies, especially through its digital switches, for both mobile and fixed-line telecommunication systems. Ericsson was known for its strong focus on technology, and invested 16% of revenues in R&D.

In 2000 and 2001, Ericsson sold off or closed a large number of units, concentrating on mobile telecom infrastructure where it was considered the world leader. In handsets, market share fell from 15% in 1998 to less than 10% a few years later. In 2000, Ericsson and Sony decided to join forces, establishing a 50/50-owned company, SonyEricsson, headquartered in London. As 3rd generation mobile systems were implemented beginning in the Japanese market, Ericsson had taken a lead with over 40% of the worldwide infrastructure market.

Exhibit 3 presents comparative data sales, profitability, and employment for the major manufacturers throughout the 1990s.

The Finnish telecommunications cluster in 2001

Finns had been early adopters of mobile phones. As Nokia became an international success story, Finns came to see the mobile phone as a 'national symbol.' Finland was among the world leaders in mobile penetration. In 1998 mobile subscribers outnumbered wired subscribers, and 20% of households had cancelled fixed line service and relied solely on mobile communications.

Finland had also been early to adopt the Internet in the late 1980s, led by students. The world's first graphic-based Internet browser was developed in an IT class at the Helsinki University of Technology in 1992, a year before Mosaic and Netscape. The students were not interested in commercializing the software, but other Finnish students, Tatu Ylönen (SSH encryption program) and Linus Torvalds (Linux operating system) went on to become legends in their own time. Finland ranked number one in the rate of Internet host penetration by 1999. A rapid increase in ISDN subscriptions, due to growing Internet penetration, was driving renewed demand for fixed line services in Finland.

From a modest base in the 1960s and 1970s, the Finnish telecommunications cluster began to emerge in earnest in the 1990s. By 2000, the cluster employed some 83,000 people (just under 4% of national employment) in over 4,000 firms, representing 6.9% of GDP (see **Table 4**). The total value of shipments was EUR 21.4 billion, with manufacturing of equipment and electronic components representing 70% of revenues. The cluster had grown at an average annual rate of 20% (manufacturing 32% and services 12%). See **Table 4**.

Operators In 2001, there were over 100 telecommunications operators in Finland, though most of them utilized leased network capacity. Sonera (formerly Telecom Finland) and the Finnet Group (the renamed Association of Telephone Companies) held 95% of revenue. Sonera had restructured during the 1990s and upgraded employee skill levels. In mobile services, Sonera's main competitor was Radiolinja, owned by the largest private operator Elisa Communications. Swedish Telia had not succeeded in capturing any significant share of the Finnish market since its entry in 1997. The fourth mobile operator, DNA Finland, was launched in early 2001 by a group of private investors. Finland granted licenses for 3rd generation systems (called UMTS) to all four GSM operators, the first country in the world to do so.

Content providers There were over 300 Finnish companies engaged in the provision of digital content, including media, services (e.g., banks and travel agencies) and Internet portals. An expanding number of services were targeted at professional groups (e.g., in health care and education). Nokia offered tools and support for entertainment service providers in an open virtual forum. The National Technology Agency, Tekes, had assumed the role of a facilitator in the emerging digital media industry, and facilitated interaction between firms, venture capitalists, universities, and research institutes.

Equipment manufacturers Nokia was the dominant equipment manufacturer in Finland, producing both handsets and infrastructure. There were also other manufacturers such as Benefon, a company founded by ex-Nokia managers. Much of Nokia's manufacturing was also outsourced to contract manufacturers such as Elcoteq.

Suppliers A large number of specialized suppliers

Table 4 Key economic indicators of the telecommunications cluster (2000)

	Telecom Manufacturing		Telecom Services				Cluster Total	
			Telecom		Related Software and IT Services			
	EUR Million	Share of Production	EUR Million	Share of Production	EUR Million	Share of Production	EUR Million	Share of Production
Revenues	14,805		3,678		2,947		21,431	
Exports	12,125	82%	118	3%	1,009	34%	13,252	62%
Imports	4,185	28%	151	4%	605	21%	4,941	23%
No. of firms	414		216		3,463		4,093	
No. of employees	38,385		19,294		25,284		82,963	

Source: Adapted from L. Paija (ed), 'Finnish ICT Cluster in the Digital Economy,' Helsinki: ETLA – the Research Institute of the Finnish Economy).
Note: Smaller amounts of non-telecom IT software and services are included in the figures.

and contract manufacturers had emerged in Finland, in part driven by the growth of Nokia. Finnish suppliers tended to produce highly customized inputs (e.g. ASIC, rf filters, customized circuit boards, hybrid circuits), while standard components were imported. Other Finnish companies specialized in process technologies such as surface mounting, robots, and precision moulding equipment for telecom use. Increased outsourcing was coupled with extensive cooperation and long-term commitments between manufacturers and suppliers. Increased technological complexity and shortening product life cycles had pushed firms to closer interaction and risk sharing. Finnish suppliers such as Perlos Ltd, Eimo Ltd and Elcoteq Networks Ltd followed Nokia by establishing or acquiring manufacturing units in such countries as China and the United States.

Equity capital A venture capital market had emerged as a new and important source of funding in the 1990s. In 1999 some EUR 285 million of venture capital was invested in new Finnish companies. A Finnish Venture Capital Association had been formed, which included 36 members in 2001. Some 30% of all venture capital was directed towards telecommunications.

In part due to Nokia, investors and venture capitalists from around the world sought out other leading-edge technology companies in Finland. As a consequence, a number of small Finnish high-tech companies had obtained financing from abroad. The majority of the capital raised in recent private placements in companies such as Solid, Digia, Riot, AVS and LPG came from international venture capitalists. Most of the money went to first or second round investments, rather than seed stage financing. Since the early 1990s, a growing number of foreign portfolio investors had added Nokia to their portfolios. In 1993, Nokia's foreign ownership was 46%, and by July 2001 the share had reached 90%. Nokia's share of the total market capitalization of the Helsinki Stock Exchange (HEX) peaked at 71% in November 2000. Although Nokia was listed in a number of markets, Helsinki had retained its position as the most important place to trade Nokia shares.

Education and research There were 12 colleges and universities in Finland providing education and conducting research in information technology and telecommunications. Finland was recognized as a location for highly skilled IT professionals.

Investment in IT and telecommunications-related R&D had risen substantially, mostly driven by a huge

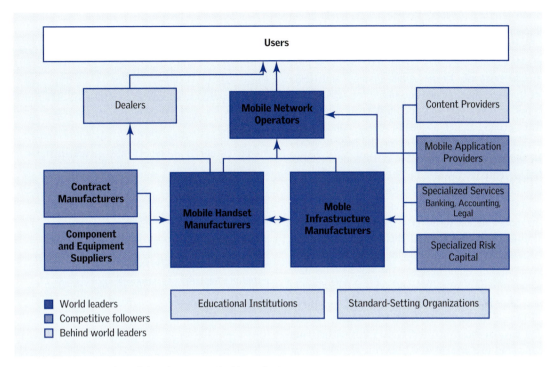

Figure 2 The Finnish mobile telecommunications cluster
Source: Case writer

increase in private sector R&D. University and other public-sector R&D also increased substantially in absolute terms, but not as rapidly as investments by companies. Increased R&D led to an average annual growth rate in patenting of 42%, in these fields between 1992 and 1998. Almost 30% of the United States patents granted to Finnish inventors were in IT and communications. During the 1990s, a number of international companies such as ICL, IBM, Siemens, Hewlett Packard and Ericsson had established R&D activities in Finland. Nokia conducted close to 60% of its research in Finland, and accounted for approximately 45% of all private R&D expenditure in the country.

Nokia in 2001

Nokia's sales were EUR 30.4 billion in 2000, with an operating profit of EUR 5.8 billion, an above average margin. The company employed 60,289 people, 24,000 of whom were located in Finland. The company had production locations in 10 countries, R&D in 15 countries, and sales to over 130 countries.

Nokia had weathered a crisis in the late 1980s as the company tried to cope with growth and diversity. A new CEO cut employment, but Nokia registered large losses in 1992. Jorma Olilla, 41, became CEO in 1992. New capital was raised through a private placement in the United States in 1993, and Nokia was listed on the New York Stock Exchange the following year. In 1994, Olilla got board approved to divest all of Nokia's businesses outside of telecommunications.

Olilla and his team also began to build a new culture. The four fundamental values of Nokia, the 'Nokia Way', were introduced in 1992: customer satisfaction, respect for the individual, achievement, and continuous learning. Nokia's strong culture, shared especially among the Finnish management team, substituted for detailed systems when the company entered new geographies. Nokia was seen as mirroring the Finnish national character: pragmatic, honest, quiet, and serious. The business press often referred to Nokia as 'non-political' and as an informal organization built on trust.

In 2001, Nokia was organized into three business groups: Nokia Networks (GSM and 3rd generation mobile systems), Nokia Mobile Phones, and Nokia Ventures. Mobile phones accounted for 72% of revenues in 2000, and was the most profitable of the three groups. It sold phones for every standard and in just about every market in the world. Nokia Networks accounted for 25% of revenue in 2000. Nokia Ventures, founded in 1998 to search for new business opportunities, accounted for 3%.

In the early 1990s, Nokia controlled about 12% of the global market for handsets, with a goal of 25%. The new sleek Nokia 2100 phone was designed by Los Angeles freelance designer Frank Nuovo (who later became head designer for Nokia). The new phone offered a larger screen and a scrolling menu that later became the industry standard. The Nokia 2100 was Nokia's first consumer-targeted model and was launched in 1994, selling 20 million units compared to a goal of 400,000. Nokia would go on to define a mobile phone as a fashion item and consumer good, instead of a technology product. Nokia's strategy was to serve distinct customer segments with differing needs using technology compatible to whatever standard was utilized in a particular regional market.

In the 1990s Nokia became the world leader in digital phones with a market share of 31% in 2000. The company offered the widest line of phones, covering every segment of the market, and had the broadest geographical coverage. In 1998 Nokia announced that 'mobile Internet' was to be the future guiding star of the company. Foreign sales accounted for 98% of revenue in 2000, up from 70% in 1990. In 2001, Nokia had a total of 19 manufacturing facilities in ten countries. Nokia Networks had five plants in Finland, five plants in China and one in Malaysia. Nokia Mobile Phones had production units in eight countries. See **Table 5**.

Nokia had R&D units located in 14 different countries, although just over half of total R&D activities were located in Finland. R&D facilities were typically located close to leading universities and research centers. At the end of the 1990s, Nokia spent close to 9% of its revenues on R&D, up from 6% in the first half of the 1990s.

Table 5 Nokia's operations in different countries (2000)

R&D Units	Production Facilities	Listings on Stock Exchanges
Finland	Finland	Finland
Germany	Germany	Germany
United States	United States	United States
Hungary	Hungary	Sweden
China	China	U.K.
Malaysia	Malaysia	France
South Korea	South Korea	
Australia	Brazil	
United Kingdom	Mexico	
Japan		
Italy		
Canada		
Sweden		
Denmark		

In the 1980s, Nokia had used subcontractors mainly as buffers to stabilize its manufacturing capacity. In the 1990s Nokia turned to outsourcing through long-term cooperation agreements. In the latter part of the 1990s, cooperation was gradually expanded from accessories to other components. Nokia also reorganized its supply chain to include contract manufacturers. Furthermore, Nokia began to contract for some software development and R&D. Some of Nokia's partners and subcontractors began international operations, including exports and production abroad not only to Nokia's foreign units but also to other customers. The outsourcing activities of Nokia had created some public concerns, that manufacturing operations would shift to low-cost countries in Eastern Europe and Asia.

One of the main challenges facing Nokia in 2001 was the evolution of standards. New standards in 3rd generation systems were being developed in mobile Internet services as well as software and hardware for phones and infrastructure. Personal digital assistants (PDA), electronic organizers, palmtops, and small-screen handsets were proliferating. A large number of firms and standards were competing, many of which sought enhanced mobility. For example, Microsoft had developed Stinger software and Palm had its own system. Nokia had licensed parts of its phone software and components to other handset manufacturers to encourage the adoption of its standard globally. In November 2001, Nokia announced it would license the source code for its mobile Internet browser and advanced text messaging technology to Samsung in Korea.

Together with Ericsson, Motorola and Phone.com (a small U.S. company), Nokia had established the WAP (Wireless Application Protocol) Forum. By 2000, there were over 200 members. Nokia introduced the first WAP phone in 1999, though the early products encountered some technical problems. In Japan, the i-mode system led by NTT had attracted large demand with millions of users.

Together with Sony, Ericsson (who invented the technology in 1994), Microsoft, IBM, Intel and others, Nokia had also developed Bluetooth, a standard used for short-range (under 30 feet) wireless connectivity. The main competing standard was called WiFi. Bluetooth chips used far less power than WiFi devices and were much cheaper, though WiFi offered a much higher bandwidth.

Research efforts were geared at developing 'smart' mobile phones with multimedia messaging, connections to the Internet, and the possibility of downloading information from Web sites. Here Nokia was pushing the Symbian operating system used by more than 70% of the mobile phone market. Motorola, Sony Ericsson, Psion, (a U.K. based manufacturer of PDAs), and Japan's Matsushita were Nokia's partners in this effort.

Finland in 2001

While Finland had maintained its ranking as a leading competitive nation in 2001, the nation was facing challenges. Overall growth rates were declining, and major export markets appeared weak. The telecommunications cluster especially was experiencing a severe downturn, and Nokia had seen its revenue and profits fall. Given the large role of Nokia and the cluster in Finland's economy, concerns about the level of exposure to one company and one cluster were becoming louder.

Finland was also facing shortages of skilled engineers and scientists. As demand for skilled labor was expected to increase, some universities had started offering programs tailored for foreign students to attract people to Finland. At the same time as IT jobs went begging, however, there was increasing unemployment, especially among the young and the low skilled. The differences in prosperity was creating strains on the traditionally egalitarian Finnish society.

Exhibit 1 Government ownership stakes in the top 25 Finnish companies

Sales Rank	Company	Industry	Government Share (%)
1	Nokia	Electronics	–
2	Stora Enso*	Forestry	15.1
3	Fortum	Energy	70.7
4	UPM-Kymmene	Forestry	–
5	*Metsäliitto*	Forestry	–
6	Kesko	Wholesale trade	–
7	Sampo	Finance	40.2
8	Pohjola	Finance	–
9	Nordea*	Finance	–
10	Metso	Mining / Metals	11.6
11	Varma-Sampo	Finance	–
12	Outokumpu	Mining / Metals	40.0
13	Ilmarinen	Finance	–
14	Tamro	Pharmaceuticals trade	–
15	Huhtamäki	Food	–
16	SOK	Retail	–
17	Rautarruukki	Mining / Metals	40.1
18	Wärtsilä	Machinery / Shipyards	–
19	Kone	Machinery / Shipyards	–
20	Partek	Mining / Metals	30.2
21	Kemira	Chemicals/ Plastics	56.2
22	Elcoteq Network	Electronics	–
23	Merita Henkivakuutus	Finance	–
24	Ahlström	Forestry	–
25	Sonera	Telecommunication	52.8

Source: Talouselämä, Finland's Top500 Companies, 2000.
Note: * indicates companies with broad Nordic Ownership. – = 0% or not applicable.

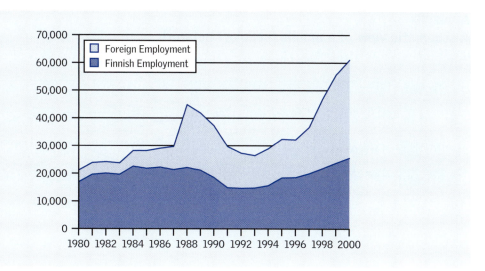

Exhibit 2 Nokia employment, 1980–2001
Source: L. Paija (ed), 'Finnish ICT Cluster in the Digital Economy,' Helsinki: ETLA – the Research Institute of the Finnish Economy and Taloustieto Oy, 2001.

Exhibit 3 Financial overview, major mobile telecommunication manufacturers

	1992	1993	1994	1995	1996	1997	1998	1999	2000
Nokia									
Sales ($ mil)	3,451	4,079	6,368	8,400	8,446	9,702	15,553	19,954	28,608
Net Income ($ mil)	(78)	132	632	509	745	1,154	2,043	2,601	3,709
Employees	26,700	25,800	28,600	31,948	31,723	36,647	44,543	51,777	60,000
Ericsson									
Sales ($ mil)	6,644	7,622	11,342	14,902	18,291	21,219	22,760	25,267	29,026
Net Income ($ mil)	68	340	531	813	1,033	1,511	1,609	1,423	2,230
Employees	66,232	69,597	76,144	84,513	93,949	100,774	103,667	103,290	105,129
Motorola									
Sales ($ mil)	13,303	16,963	22,245	27,037	27,973	29,794	29,398	30,931	37,580
Net Income ($ mil)	453	1,022	1,560	1,781	1,154	1,180	(962)	817	1,318
Employees	107,000	120,000	132,000	142,000	139,000	150,000	133,000	121,000	147,000

Source: Adapted from Hoover's, Inc.
Note: Motorola figures include a number of business units outside the mobile telecommunications sector.

Appendix
A schematic view of a mobile (cellular) network

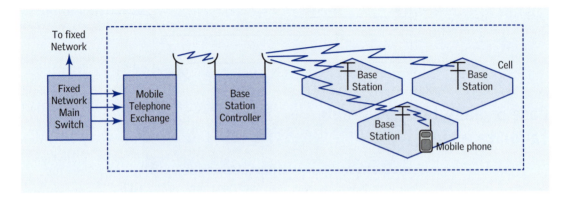

The base station controller coordinates calls among the base stations; it controls and routes calls back to the main switch for routing to other base station controllers or the fixed line system depending on the call. The base station controller is also connected to the base station via fixed line or microwave. The base station covers a certain geographic area, which is called a cell. Base stations are strategically located so as to overlap and connect geographically to surrounding base stations. The combination of these base stations or cells is the overall coverage area of the cellular network. The base station connects to handsets, i.e. mobile phones, via radio signals. These radio signals have traditionally been transmitted using analog coding technology (e.g., AMPS, ETACS, NMT) but are now using digital technology (e.g. GSM, GPRS, TDMA, CDMA and WCDMA) for cost and capacity reasons.

The cellular network broadly consists of base stations (cells), a base station controller, and a mobile telephone exchange (MTX). The cellular concept had been developed by Bell laboratories in the United States already in the 1950s. The MTX is the central coordinator (similar to the CPU in a computer) in the cellular network and gateway to the fixed wire-line system. As the central coordinator, the main switch coordinates/routes calls within the cellular network and externally to the fixed line system. The cellular network customer database and call information reside in the main switch. The MTX connects to the base station controller either via fixed line or microwave. Traditional manufacturers of telephone exchanges for fixed networks, such as Ericsson, had developed the MTX technology based on their expertise in building large-scale switching systems.

Case 5 easyJet: the web's favorite airline

The safest way to become a millionaire is to start as a billionaire and invest in the airline industry.

Richard Branson,
Founder, the Virgin Group

'If you create the right expectations and you meet or exceed those expectations, then you will have happy customers,' proclaimed Stelios Haji-Ioannou, the 32 year-old founder and CEO of easyJet airlines. Since its launch in November 1995, easyJet had become one of Europe's leading low-cost airlines by adopting an efficiency-driven operational model, creating brand awareness, and maintaining high levels of customer satisfaction.

Stelios, who preferred to be addressed by his first name only, considered himself a serial entrepreneur. Although he gained international fame as a pioneer

Research Associate Brian Rogers prepared this case under the supervision of Professor Nirmalya Kumar as a basis for class discussion rather than to illustrate either effective or ineffective handling of a business situation.

This case was the **Overall Winner** of the **2002 European Case Awards**, granted by ECCH in association with Business Week.

This case also won the **2001 European Case Award**, in the category of **Policy & General Management**, granted by ECCH in association with Business Week.

IMD-3-0873 (EM 873)
V. 11.12.2002

in the airline industry, he first achieved business success at the age of 25 when he created Stelmar, a specialized tanker company. Anxious to replicate his past successes, Stelios aggressively pursued any business opportunity that he believed he could operate profitably.

Despite its early success, easyJet airlines still faced internal challenges that were typical of many start-up companies. Growing competition from other small, low-cost carriers, as well as threats from Europe's major carriers, required much of the company's attention and resources. Undeterred, Stelios relished the challenge and moved ahead in his mission 'to offer low-cost airline service to the masses.'

Stelios believed that in order to be successful, it was important to be first to market and to saturate the geographic market. 'You don't need to conquer the world in order to be profitable,' he argued. His strategy for market entry had been successful in the airline industry, but many wondered if he could transfer his low-cost business model to Internet cafés, rental cars, and Internet banking, three ventures he considered in 1999.

Company background

Stelios first became interested in the idea of a European low-cost airline in May 1994, after being asked to invest in a Virgin Atlantic Airlines franchisee. Although he refused, soon thereafter, he flew on Southwest Airlines, a successful low-cost carrier in the US. That experience became the catalyst in his decision to create easyJet. Stelios asked his father, Lukas Haji-Ioannou, a Greek shipping tycoon, to invest in his startup airline. In November 1995, after receiving £5 million from his father, Stelios began operating easyJet with two leased aircraft and a staff primarily comprised of teenagers who served as reservation agents. Although London's Heathrow and Gatwick were major international airports with higher passenger traffic, Stelios chose Luton because it offered lower labor costs and close proximity to downtown London, and charged lower airport fees.

The first easyJet flight, from London to Glasgow, was advertised for a one-way fare of £29. The flight was completely full, in large part because Stelios had launched an extensive public relations and advertising campaign with the slogan, 'Fly to Scotland for the price of a pair of jeans!' Increasing demand soon led to flight service to Edinburgh and Aberdeen. Over the next two years, Stelios raised an additional £50 million in debt and equity to finance the purchase of four additional aircraft and to speed expansion. By early 1998, easyJet owned a fleet of six Boeing 737-300s and flew 12 routes in five countries. However, by November 1999 easyJet owned and/or leased 18 Boeing 737-300s, and flew 27 routes in Europe.

Stelios modeled easyJet after Southwest Airlines. He researched Southwest intensively and even met with the airline's CEO, Herb Kelleher, before launching easyJet. Stelios deeply admired the concept behind Southwest Airlines: one type of aircraft, point-to-point short-haul travel, no in-flight meals, rapid turnaround time and very high aircraft utilization. However, Stelios added his own twist to the Southwest concept: he completely avoided travel agents, issued no tickets, encouraged direct sales over the Internet, and flew brand new Boeing 737s using the maximum seat capacity of 149 seats. Moreover, he decided not to offer free drinks or peanuts; everything would be for sale. Stelios championed the idea of no-frills travel; the only free item on board an easyJet flight was easyRider, the airline's in-flight magazine. He argued, 'When someone is on a bus, he doesn't expect any free lunch. I couldn't see why we cannot educate our customers to expect no frills on board.' (*Refer to Exhibit 1 to view items available from the easyKiosk.*)

The company's headquarters, referred to as 'easyLand,' was located at London's Luton airport. Just like the airline, easyLand was no-frills. Employees were instructed to dress casually, and Stelios sat in the same open-plan office as everyone else. He had no personal secretary, maintained a paperless office, and expected everybody else to do the same.

In 1996/97 easyJet suffered pre-tax losses of £3.3 million.[1] However, in 1998 the company announced annual pre-tax profits of £2.3 million, the first time the airline had posted a profit in its brief history. (*Refer to Exhibit 2 to review easyJet's financial performance.*)

---

[1] £1.0 = US$1.60.

Deregulation of the European Airline Industry

Until the early 1990s the European airline industry had been highly regulated, in large part because individual countries wanted to protect their own national carriers, commonly referred to as 'flag carriers.' However, in December 1992 the European Union passed legislation that deregulated the airline industry. Similar to the deregulation of the US airline industry in the 1980s, the new directive meant that any European carrier could fly to any destination and demand landing slots.

The proliferation of airlines offering highly competitive fares after December 1992 revolutionized European air travel, especially from the United Kingdom. New airlines were created, and travelers could fly from most airports in the UK to almost anywhere in the world for very low prices. This prompted one commentator to reply, 'You can now fly from one end of Europe to the other for the cost of two hardback books.' Richard Wright of the Civil Aviation Authority, which regulated British aviation, postulated that many new carriers set up operations from the UK, rather than other European countries, because the British, along with the Germans, traveled most often.

Deregulation in Europe, however, spawned fewer new competitors than in the US. In 1999, only 3% to 5% of passengers in Europe flew on a low-cost carrier, compared to 24% in the US. On some routes in Europe, high speed rail service competed directly with airlines. Furthermore, industry experts believed that the cost of running an airline in Europe was, on average, 40% higher than in the US.

Understandably, few low-cost carriers enjoyed the same success as easyJet. Of the 80 carriers that had begun operations after 1992, 60 had already gone bankrupt by 1996. Still, analysts predicted that the European low-cost market could grow by as much as 300% by 2004.

Competing on cost

Because easyJet offered low fares, it sought to minimize costs where possible. For example, easyJet saved £14 per passenger by not offering meal service, and estimated that by flying into London's Luton Airport instead of Gatwick, it saved £10 per passenger. The airline also shaved costs by not offering business class seating, thus allowing for more overall seating capacity. (*Refer to Exhibit 3 to view a comparison of the costs of easyJet and other carriers.*)

Moreover, easyJet encouraged Internet sales. In March 1999, Internet sales accounted for 15% of revenues; however, by October 1999, Internet sales had soared to 60% of revenues. Stelios offered discounted fares to customers who purchased over the Internet because such sales reduced the need to hire additional reservation agents. He avoided computer reservation systems and travel agents because he believed that they added 25% to total operating costs.

Illustration: Saying No To Travel Agents

In 1998, Stelios enraged travel agents in Greece by selling cheap daily flights to Athens and flaunting his commission-free service by advertising to 'forget your travel agent.' Travel agents there took him to court. He won and then immediately thumbed his nose at his foes by plastering 'say no to travel agents' in bright orange letters across the first plane to fly from London to Athens, earning him huge amounts of press.

The airline also turned its airplanes around faster, flying planes 11.5 hours per day, instead of 6 hours, the industry average. Because easyJet flew its planes more hours, Stelios claimed that he could fly just 2 planes, and do the work of 3. Although easyJet had achieved profitability in 1999, margins were quite small; the airline earned £1.50 profit per passenger.

Even though easyJet carefully monitored costs, Stelios emphasized that safety was never compromised. The airline only flew brand new Boeing 737s, and only hired experienced pilots who were paid market rates. Stelios commented:

If you advertise a very cheap price, people expect an old airplane. But when they come on board and see a brand new plane, they are impressed. Likewise, many customers expect an unhappy staff because they believe they are not paid well, but they come on board and see the staff is smiling!

Table 1 Cost of an easyJet flight from London to Geneva

Cost Item	£	%
Airport charges	600	15%
Aircraft ownership	560	14%
Air traffic control	480	12%
Crew	400	10%
Marketing/sales	400	10%
Fuel	400	10%
Maintenance	400	10%
Overhead	400	10%
Ground handling	360	9%
Total Costs	£4,000	100%

Assumptions: The table approximates easyJet's costs for a one-way trip. All costs are fixed.
Source: easyJet

Competing on service

One of the distinguishing characteristics of easyJet was its approach to customer satisfaction. Stelios flew on at least four flights per week, and enjoyed interacting with customers. He had even been known to work the phones selling tickets. Stelios was wary of market research, preferring to cull information directly from passengers. He also read and replied to many of the emails he received from customers. He considered himself a man of the people and worked hard to cultivate this image. (*Refer to Exhibit 4 to view an example of his communication with customers.*)

> To provide our customers with safe, low-cost, good value, point-to-point air services. To offer a consistent and reliable product at fares appealing to leisure and business markets from our bases to a range of domestic and European destinations. To achieve this we will develop our people and establish lasting partnerships with our suppliers.

Figure 1 easyJet mission statement
Source: easyJet

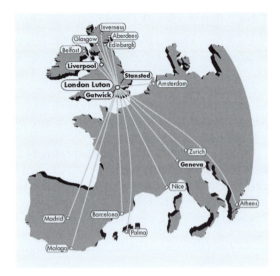

Figure 2 Destinations served from London's Luton Airport
Source: easyJet, November 1999

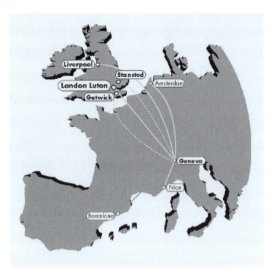

Figure 3 Destinations served from Geneva
Source: easyJet, November 1999

All of easyJet's fares were one-way fares and had the same restrictions. The cost to change a flight was £10 plus the difference between the two fares. Only 4% of customers failed to show up for their flights, and easyJet offered no reimbursement for missed flights.

To book a flight, customers either purchased their tickets over the Internet or they called a local number and were connected to one of easyJet's reservation agents in easyLand. Because easyJet was a 100% direct-sell operation, the marketing department knew the relative effectiveness of different media and could react quickly. Oftentimes, the company placed different phone numbers on different types of advertisements to measure consumer response precisely.

Customers were required to pay by credit card, after which they received a six-character booking reference number. This reference number was the only information passengers needed to board the plane. Reservation agents were paid on a commission basis, at a rate of £0.80 per seat sold, and could sell 60 to 90 seats during an average eight-hour shift.

The airline did not offer any pre-assigned seating, but instead utilized a priority boarding procedure. Passengers were given a number based on the time they checked in, and those passengers who arrived late for check-in had to sit in whatever seats remained.

Generally speaking, easyJet defined its target customers as 'people who pay for travel from their own pockets.' The target group consisted of travelers visiting relatives, leisure travelers making brief trips, as well as entrepreneurs and managers working for small firms. While easyJet typically ignored the large market of business travelers, on some routes, such as London-Glasgow, London-Edinburgh, and London-Amsterdam, business travelers represented 50% of the passengers. Stelios argued that larger airlines ripped off traveling business customers who usually did not want to stay over a Saturday night or who wanted complete flexibility to change their travel plans.

Using yield management, easyJet tried to fill as many seats as possible. Seats were sold in what could be considered a lottery system; the more people demanded a particular flight, the higher the fare. Put differently, if the load factor (percentage of seats sold) was higher than normal, prices automatically increased. This system worked well for easyJet because it helped avoid selling out popular flights months in advance.

Yield management also served another purpose: it drew potential customers who were in search of

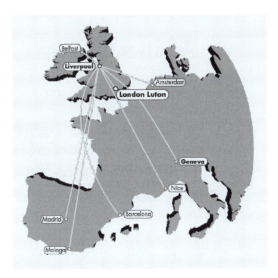

Figure 4 Destinations served from Liverpool
Source: easyJet, November 1999

cheap fares. Once they found there were no more cheap seats, they usually bought a ticket anyway, since the next highest fare was still cheaper than easyJet's competitors. Stelios defended his policy vigorously: 'We decided that people who are willing to give us their money early should get a better price, and those who want the flexibility of booking late should pay a bit more.' (*Refer to Exhibit 5 to view a report on availability of fares.*)

Punctuality at easyJet was important. Because customer satisfaction was linked so closely to punctuality, responding adequately to the needs of customers was very important to Stelios. If a flight arrived more than four hours late, Stelios instructed his staff to write a letter of apology with his signature and to issue a full refund. Because the airline had many repeat customers, Stelios was confident that customer satisfaction was high. (*Refer to Exhibit 6 to view additional data on punctuality.*)

Outsourcing

Initially, Stelios had outsourced many of the airline's operations because it lowered costs and increased efficiency. Typically, the airline provided the planes, pilots, cabin crew, marketing and sales people. Subcontractors handled all other responsibilities, from check-in to the on-site customer information desk.

By early 1998, however, easyJet had acquired its own operating certificate and reached a scale where it would have been possible to bring certain operations in-house. Nevertheless, Stelios still maintained that it made more sense to continue working with subcontractors. The airline's ability to remain ticketless, meet its goal of a 20-minute turnaround at the gate, and maintain its safety depended on subcontractors.

To improve its relationships with these outside vendors, easyJet often led workshops, role-reversal exercises, and simulations to explain its objectives and expectations. The company evaluated subcontractors not only on quantitative criteria, such as percentage of on-time flights, but also on qualitative criteria, such as understanding of the easyJet concept.

Creating brand awareness

Because Stelios felt that brand awareness was critical to the success of the airline, approximately 10% of easyJet's revenues were spent on newspaper, magazine, and radio advertising. Because of its marketing approach, easyJet's top management believed that easyJet was able to differentiate itself from its competitors. Management was also of the opinion that its efforts had been rewarded through a significant growth in sales and through the company's high level of brand awareness. A 1998 industry poll indicated that the easyJet brand had a recognition rate of 88% in London; in Geneva, brand awareness was 82%.

Stelios also generated publicity for easyJet through highly publicized, and often full-scale attacks on his competitors. According to Philippe Vignon, marketing director, 'Whenever there is an opportunity to make some news, we do it!' (*Refer to Exhibits 7 and 8 to view examples of easyJet's attacking ads.*)

Illustration: The Barcelona Controversy

In early 1999, easyJet advertised for months that the airline was planning to offer service to Barcelona [from Geneva], and had even sold 7,000 seats. However, this new service was contingent upon approval from the Swiss authorities. Swissair, which had a monopoly over the Barcelona-Geneva route, fought against easyJet's entry into the market. The Swiss government ruled in favor of Swissair, stating that easyJet could not fly scheduled flights between the two cities. On the inaugural flight to Barcelona, Stelios appeared and personally issued refunds to passengers, in essence, giving them a free trip to Barcelona. He even emblazoned the words, 'Say no to Swissair monopoly' in bright orange letters across the fuselage of the plane. During the flight, he asked for a donation from passengers in order to 'protect consumers against the Swissair monopoly.' Surprisingly, 50% to 60% of the money he refunded was donated back to easyJet. Undeterred, easyJet found a loophole. The company set up a new company, called easyJet Tours, which offered chartered service to Barcelona as part of a package that included the flight, a bus ticket, and the right to stay in a tent on a campsite near the city. (Staying in the tent was not a requirement.) Stelios believed such acts created affinity. In addition to building brand loyalty, the extra media attention helped easyJet gain widespread support in Switzerland for its willingness to stand its ground against Swissair.

Source: easyJet

Corporate culture

Stelios wanted to build a strong, inclusive employee-culture at easyJet, which led to the creation of the easyJet Culture Committee. The committee, an elected group drawn from company staff, was responsible for establishing company policy on the working environment, communications between management and staff, and social events such as staff parties for the airline's 1,000 employees. Every Friday at Luton, easyJet held a company-sponsored barbecue that the staff used to get to know one another better.

Stelios believed in complete transparency, and all documents had to be scanned and placed on the computer system, so that anyone in the company could access them. This included mail, internal memos, press cuttings, business plans, and sales data (the only confidential information was payroll-related).

Stelios stressed that culture was not something leaders can create overnight. As he put it, 'You build your legend slowly, bit by bit, battle by battle. You talk about it, and then you get together and have fun. I believe that work should be fun.'

Illustration: The Fight with Go

In 1996, Bob Ayling, British Airway's chief, approached Stelios in what appeared to be an offer to buy easyJet. Instead, after a three month courtship, British Airways abandoned the deal, and one year later, launched Go, its own budget airline. Still angry over the incident, Stelios got his revenge by buying several rows of seats on Go's first flight. He commanded his staff to don orange boiler jackets, and they all boarded the flight like a group of merry pranksters, offering free flights on easyJet to Go's passengers. Barbara Cassani, chief executive of Go airlines, was on the inaugural flight to welcome new passengers. When she saw what was occurring, she lapsed into stunned silence. The publicity stunt paid off for easyJet. Go Airlines announced losses of £22 million in 1999. However, Stelios was wounded yet again when British Airways hired away easyJet's lawyer at an estimated annual salary of £500,000.

Source: easyJet

Stelios strongly believed that being the underdog in such a highly competitive industry strengthened his team and brought them closer together. He recalled:

I noticed how much more motivated the staff was when British Airways launched the Go airline and when the whole country was talking about us and we were on television every night. All of these things created a sense of pride for the company. The same thing happened in Switzerland. People at TEA, a Swiss charter airline, were no longer motivated, so we bought the company and turned it around. As soon as we had the run-in with Swissair, morale really picked up. We were the underdogs. Our employees would go home and their neighbors had heard about the company they work for, which gave them the courage to stay and fight.

Because of the airline's high-profile battles, Stelios had become famous and people began to recognize him when he was out in public. When asked about his increasing popularity, he replied:

> It is nice to be considered as sort of a Robin Hood, and have people stop you in the street and say, 'Thank you for flying to London. Now I can go and see my family.' My father was a very successful shipper, but no one ever stopped him in the street and said, 'Thank you for transporting oil to my house.' It is very satisfying to be recognized and to be appreciated.

Competition

Ryanair

Ryanair, based in Ireland, was established in 1985. Initially, Ryanair was a full-service, traditional airline with two classes of seating, but in the early 1990s, the airline changed its focus to become a no-frills carrier. Unlike easyJet, Ryanair used travel agents, issued tickets, and participated in the global distribution system. Utilizing a fleet of 20 Boeing 737s and servicing 26 destinations, the airline had more than 100 scheduled flights per day in late 1999, and planned to expand both its route base and the size of its fleet. (*Refer to Exhibits 9 and 10 for additional information on easyJet's competitors.*)

In 1999, Ryanair experienced its ninth straight year of strong growth. For the six month period ending June 30, 1999, Ryanair had sales of IR£66.2 million[2], and the operating profit margin was 28%.

Go

Go was established by British Airways in May 1998 as a no-frills airline to compete in the low-cost segment of the European market. Financed with £25 million from British Airways, Go was founded in large part to defend British Airway's market share, since easyJet was stealing its passengers. In 1999 the company suffered financial losses, although Go's CEO, Barbara Cassani, expected to achieve profitability by 2001. For the period ending March 31, 1999, Go had sales of £31.6 million, and operating losses of £22 million. Before Go announced that the airline was losing money, Stelios set up a contest offering free easyJet flights to whoever came closest to guessing the amount of Go's losses.

Go's flights were based out of London's Stansted Airport instead of London's Heathrow Airport, where British Airways was headquartered. Stelios considered Go a copycat of easyJet, and believed that Go was heavily influenced by parent company British Airways in the way it structured its fares. Stelios also suspected that British Airways unfairly subsidized Go; therefore, he filed a lawsuit alleging that British Airways violated Article 86 of the Treaty of Rome, which says that dominant players in a market should not operate at below the cost of production.

Virgin Express

Virgin Express Holdings plc, headquartered in Belgium, was set up in 1996 when the Virgin Group acquired a controlling stake in EuroBelgian Airlines. Virgin Express Holdings plc was principally engaged as a low-fare carrier, and provided short to medium-haul jet service to markets principally within continental Europe from the company's base in Brussels. For the fiscal year ending December 31, 1998, Virgin Express had sales of BEF 10.5 billion.[3]

Virgin Express differentiated itself from other low-cost carriers in that it had formed an alliance with Sabena Airlines, the flag carrier in Belgium. This relationship provided Virgin Express with a steady stream of contractual revenue, since Sabena bought seats on Virgin Express in order to offer better connections to destinations throughout Europe.

Buzz

In September 1999 KLM announced that it would enter the low-cost segment of the market with Buzz airlines. From its base at London's Stansted airport, Buzz planned to offer service to Berlin, Dusseldorf, Frankfurt, Milan, Vienna, Paris, and Lyon. KLM already had one brand in place at London Stansted, KLM UK. To avoid confusion, management stated that KLM flights would go to Amsterdam, while Buzz would fly to all other destinations.

---

[2] IR£1.00 = US$1.30.

[3] BEF 40 = US$1.00.

Challenges

Stelios faced several challenges at easyJet. In November 1999, he struggled with the decision of whether to take his privately held company public. On one hand, he believed he could better motivate his staff by offering them shares in the company. On the other hand, however, his team of advisors feared his management style was too entrepreneurial. Regarding the decision to refund passengers who had already paid for the Geneva-Barcelona flight during the battle with Swissair, he remarked, 'Do you think the finance director of a public company would say, "Refund every customer on the Geneva flight" like I did? My finance director was pulling his hair out!' Although plans were underway to float the company on the London Stock Exchange and NASDAQ in early 2000, Stelios frequently asked himself and others around him if the market would trust him to run the company the way he felt was best.

Second, the airline had a history of using subcontractors, but found that at times, the outsourcing of vital functions posed certain problems. For example, at some airports that were not frequently serviced, easyJet hired external ground handlers. Because the handlers were not easyJet employees, they did not attend to customers' needs in a manner that satisfied Stelios. He commented:

Making sure that these subcontractors meet the quality standards we have set is very difficult. The weakest link in the chain is in Mallorca. There, we have people who maybe work on an easyJet flight once a day or once a week, and therefore don't know the company very well. I've been telling my staff, 'If I hear another ground handler refer to easyJet in the third person, I will sack him!' There is nothing worse for a customer to go to a check-in desk and say, 'When is the flight?' and the person responds, 'easyJet is an hour late.' When the customer asks why, the person responds, 'Ask easyJet!'

Third, Stelios believed that easyJet needed to become more corporate in its processes. In his opinion, it took certain skills to start a company from scratch, and people who were good at starting companies were not necessarily good at running

big companies. In late 1999, the company was recruiting 3 or 4 senior managers.

A fourth challenge at easyJet was the relative youth and inexperience of some employees. Although it was not unusual to find a 24 year-old handling a monthly budget of £500,000, the airline nonetheless had high rates of absenteeism among phone operators.

Recognizing that easyJet was in a phase where it needed to stabilize itself internally, Stelios decided not to enter any new markets in the short-term. He felt that he needed to consolidate and do more in the countries where they had already set up operations. He asked, 'What's wrong with flying 10 times a day between London and Geneva?' He added, 'One of the biggest mistakes that airlines make is spreading themselves too thin.'

When asked how many low-cost carriers could survive in Europe, Stelios replied:

The market is bigger than most people think, although availability of slots at airports is a problem. London is getting a bit crowded, but then again, London is a big place and just about any city out of London can work as a destination. Start looking around Europe, and there aren't many other low-cost carriers. [...] The big prize in Europe is Paris. There is no low-cost flying in and out of Paris whatsoever. Any city with 3 or 4 million people should be capable of sustaining a low cost airline.

From easyJet to easyEverything

Pleased with his success in the airline industry, Stelios was ready to try his hand at other businesses in 1999. Among his pet projects was the creation of a cybercafé business called easyEverything café. The idea behind easyEverything was 'to offer the Internet to the masses' and 'to be the cheapest way to access the web.' Charging £1 per hour of Web access, Stelios stated that surfing the Internet at easyEverything was less than the cost of a phone call in London. He hoped that customers would come to the café not only to surf the Internet, but also to send emails and do their online shopping. Stelios joked, 'If flying people to Scotland for £29 is crazy, this is crazier!'

The first easyEverything café debuted in London on June 21, 1999 near Victoria Station and was open non-stop 24 hours per day. It was quickly considered one of the hot spots in London, and there was often a queue to get inside, even at 3 AM. Customers could purchase coffee and snacks or rent the services of a tutor, who showed them how to use the Internet to access online bargains.

In June 1999, Stelios signed four more leases for bigger locations in London. The key to success for the café was thought to be size; the first café contained 400 terminals. Another perceived advantage was the use of state-of-the-art hardware, including flat screens and fiber-optic communication lines, which offered much faster connection and downloading than most home systems.

Not content to stop with cybercafés, Stelios also considered entering the rental car business and starting up an Internet-based bank. He wondered if he could successfully apply the concept behind easyJet to these new businesses. Given that Stelios was known to be rather risk-averse, the decision would not be an easy one.[4]

4   The case was written using interviews and materials provided by the company. Among the materials provided were a case study from the February 1999 issue of the *European Management Journal* written by Don Sull, and an article on easyJet from the November 1999 issue of *Bilan* magazine written by Giuseppe Melillo, which we would like to gratefully acknowledge.

easyKiosk

There's no such thing as a free lunch... so on easyJet we don't give one – we've taken a big bite out of flight costs instead.

£2.80
A fresh Granary Bloomer filled with Four Cheeses and a salad garnish

Pringles **90p** each

Danish Pastries £**1.60** each

£3.20
All Day Breakfast – a Soft White Bloomer filled with egg and bacon in mayonnaise

£3.80
Fresh Focaccia Wedge, one side filled with Char-Grilled Chicken, Tomato and Lollo Rosso, and the other with Soft Cheese and Roasted Vegetables. Served with a moist Flapjack

KitKat **50p** each

Hot Drinks
Tea, Coffee, Cappuccino, Hot Chocolate . . . All £**1.00** each

Drinks from the bar

Lagers
Stella Artois £1.50
Budweiser £1.50

Wines
Red Wine £2.50
White Wine £2.50

Champagne
Champagne £8.00

Spirits
Polignac Brandy . . £2.00
Gordons Gin £2.00
Whyte & Mackay Whisky£2.00
Smirnoff Red Vodka£2.00
Bacardi Rum £2.00

Soft Drinks & Mixers
Pepsi 330ml £1.00
Pepsi 150ml 50p
Diet Pepsi 50p
Lemonade 50p
Tonic Water 50p
Ginger Ale 50p
Tomato Juice 50p
Orange Juice 50p
Tango 50p
Sparkling Water 150ml50p
Still Water 330ml . . . 80p
Apple Juice 200ml . . 70p

Other Products
easyJet Model Aircraft. . . . £8.00

Our cabin crew would be delighted to assist you with your purchases. In return please have the correct change ready, if possible. Thank you.

The only alcohol permitted to be consumed on board is that which has been purchased from the cabin crew.

Prices and information correct at time of going to press. However, we reserve the right to alter or amend them without notice. Any communication regarding the contents must be directed to Alpha Flight Services. All products subject to availability. Sandwich filling may vary depending on originating airport. Your cabin crew will be happy to advise you on what's available today.

ALPHA
FLIGHT SERVICES

Provost Way, Luton Airport, Luton, Bedfordshire LU2 9LY. +44 (0)1582 737411

Exhibit 1 Food selections from the easyKiosk
Source: easyJet

Exhibit 2 Financial performance, 1997-1998

easyJet Airline Company Limited PROFIT AND LOSS ACCOUNT	1997 £	1998 £
Turnover	46,034,549	77,000,035
Cost of Sales	(38,963,150)	(61,525,257)
Gross Profit	7,071,399	15,474,778
Distribution and marketing	(6,324,068)	(7,748,225)
Administrative expenses	(4,491,338)	(6,260,124)
Operating profit/(loss)	(3,744,007)	1,466,429
Other interest receivable and similar income	607,392	978,268
Interest payable and similar charges	(135,250)	(125,759)
Profit/(loss) on ordinary activities before taxation	(3,271,865)	2,318,938
Tax on profit on ordinary activities	–	–
Retained profit/(loss) for the year	(3,271,865)	2,318,938
Retained loss brought forward	(5,872,621)	(9,144,486)
Retained loss carried forward	(9,144,486)	(6,825,548)

easyJet Airline Company Limited BALANCE SHEET	1997 £	1998 £
Fixed assets		
Tangible assets	1,529,161	2,601,184
Current assets		
Restricted deposits	343,476	1,416,457
Debtors	3,888,546	10,887,761
Cash at bank and in hand	16,877,623	12,506,665
Creditors	(17,783,292)	(20,237,615)
Net current assets	3,326,353	4,573,268
Net assets	4,855,514	7,174,452
Capital and reserves		
Called up share capital	14,000,000	14,000,000
Profit and loss account	(9,144,486)	(6,825,548)
Equity shareholders' funds	4,855,514	7,174,452

Source: Directors' report and financial statements, September 30, 1998

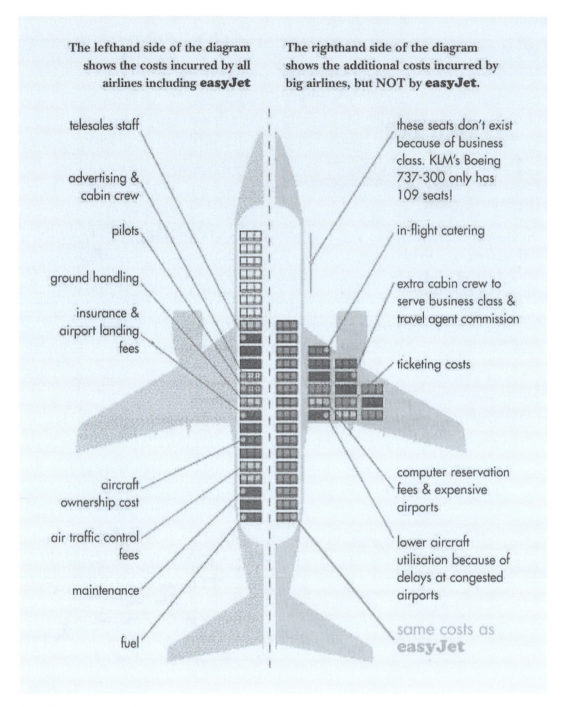

The lefthand side of the diagram shows the costs incurred by all airlines including easyJet

The righthand side of the diagram shows the additional costs incurred by big airlines, but NOT by easyJet.

telesales staff

advertising & cabin crew

pilots

ground handling

insurance & airport landing fees

aircraft ownership cost

air traffic control fees

maintenance

fuel

these seats don't exist because of business class. KLM's Boeing 737-300 only has 109 seats!

in-flight catering

extra cabin crew to serve business class & travel agent commission

ticketing costs

computer reservation fees & expensive airports

lower aircraft utilisation because of delays at congested airports

same costs as easyJet

Exhibit 3 Cost comparison
Source: easyRider magazine, July 1999

We have arrived! (Well, sort of.) The ultimate magazine for fat cat business travelers did a poll of its readers, and we were voted the best low-cost airline. What pleases me more than anything is that we beat the low-cost clone by British Airways (BA). It's not bad if you think that they lost £22m in the first year alone trying to break into our market.

So we must be doing something right. With our fleet of 18 Boeing 737-300s, one of the youngest in the world, and a far better punctuality record than BA and other so-called flag carriers, we are flying fuller than ever before. We now have 27 routes, and not only will we fly more frequently on our existing routes, but we are also planning new ones later in the year 2000, when the next 15 brand new 737-700s start arriving.

On other fronts, my Internet shops are doing very well and I will expand easyEverything in all the cities that easyJet flies as soon as I can. At the time of publishing this message on the web site, we have signed for five in London with a total of 2300 seats (yes – the biggest has 630 seats!), and have already signed for sites in Edinburgh and Amsterdam.

My easyRentacar.com project is on track for being up and running by April 2000, and you should be able to rent an 'orange car' over the Internet for £9/day.

As you can see, the common theme for all my ventures is the heavy use of the Internet. Take my word for it, all the best deals on the airline will be available on the Net from now on. So, if you don't get online you might lose out. Remember you can always use an easyEverything Internet shop to book your flight or car, coming to a place near you soon!

On another subject, we continue our battle against Swissair. As you may remember, in July we were blocked from operating a scheduled service between Geneva and Barcelona, due to political pressure from Swissair who wanted to preserve their monopoly on this route. So, to get round this, I set up easyJet Tours, a charter operation which offers passengers return flights, transfers, and accommodation (even though this is only a tent!). This service has proved very popular (I mean the flights, not the tents), and we will continue to fly this route throughout the winter. In the meantime, we will carry on lobbying the Swiss government to make changes to the law. I am encouraged by the fact that a large number of Swiss MPs have signed a motion supporting this cause, even before it is debated in Parliament.

Thank you for visiting our web site.

Stelios

Exhibit 4 Message from Stelios
Source: easyJet, November 1999

Four weeks before travel date:

I had to wait 10 minutes before speaking to Richard, a sales assistant. I asked for the cheapest fare to Barcelona, leaving Saturday, September 26 and staying two nights. Richard said that a ticket for the 8:10 PM flight would cost £49 one way (an earlier flight would be much more expensive). The return would cost £99 for the 4:45 PM flight, or £69 for the 6:50 AM flight. So the cheapest fare was £118 including tax. Richard warned me that the 4:45 PM flight was filling up fast and prices would only go up.

Three weeks before travel date:

Prices were the same, but there were then only six seats for the return leg. I felt pressured to book, so I did. There was no charge for using my credit card and no hard sell to take easyJet insurance. I was given a reference number and told I won't be issued a ticket. Confirmation of my flight was faxed through about an hour later; the paperwork arrived in the post a week later, with a discount voucher for train travel.

Two weeks before travel date:

The prices had risen by £10 for the outward flight; the 4:45 PM flight was sold out.

One week before travel date:

My outward flight was £64; there were only two seats left. Interestingly, seven seats were available again on the return flight at £129.

One day before travel date:

The outward flight cost £69, and the return flight cost £139.

Exhibit 5 A Sunday Times reporter investigates availability of easyJet's low fares
Source: 'Fare Play.' *Sunday Times*, October 18, 1998

Exhibit 6 Airline punctuality comparisons for the period ending August 1999: arrivals and departures

		Percentage of Flights Late				
		Early to 15 minutes	16 to 30 minutes	31 to 60 minutes	1 to 3 hours	3 to 6 hours
easyJet	London–Glasgow	90%	8%	2%	0%	0%
	London–Zurich	52%	33%	11%	4%	0%
	London–Mallorca	79%	13%	6%	2%	0%
go	London–Malaga	64%	18%	9%	6%	3%
	London–Mallorca	53%	8%	25%	14%	0%
RYANAIR	London–Dublin	63%	20%	10%	7%	0%
Virgin Express	London–Malaga	70%	0%	10%	20%	0%
	London–Mallorca	78%	11%	11%	0%	0%
swissair	London–Zurich	43%	31%	18%	8%	0%
BRITISH AIRWAYS	London–Glasgow	88%	6%	3%	3%	0%
	London–Zurich	69%	23%	6%	2%	0%

Source: UK Civil Aviation Authority

It's time BA came out of the closet!

On 25 May 1999, British Airways announced their 1998/99 results, but they still refuse to disclose how much of the £25 million they put in their low-cost airline has been lost over that period. Last year **easyJet** convinced a High Court Judge that any cross subsidy between BA and its subsidiary could be illegal. The case is still pending, and BA is doing everything it can to avoid disclosure of the facts.

We are so convinced that BA's low-cost airline has made a substantial loss in their first year that we are having a competition over the Internet to guess the total amount lost in its first year of trading.

The 50 entrants nearest the correct figure will win themselves a pair of **easyJet** flights anywhere on the **easyJet** network! If there are more than 50 correct answers a tie-breaker will apply. The competition will close as soon as the results are released. In due course they will have to file them with Companies House. So if you want the chance to win a prize sooner, why not e-mail Bob Ayling at BA and persuade him to release the results.

COMPETITION
50 pairs of **easyJet** flights up for grabs!

Entries will ONLY be accepted over the Internet at

www.**easyJet**.com
the web's favourite airline

Exhibit 7   Ad attacking British Airways
Source: easyJet

Stelios' pet hates

Air Miles = Air Bribes

Air Miles is a bribery scheme invented by British Airways and designed to induce business travellers to waste their companies' money by travelling business class and then collecting the reward for their personal benefit. (Usually lavish holidays in the Caribbean frequently in the company of their secretaries)!

Those Chief Executives with the best interest of the company and its shareholders at heart must ban the collection of air miles by their staff while travelling on business. It's not going to be a popular decision, which goes to prove the degree of corruption!

In addition, the taxman has done British Airways a huge favour by miraculously not including air miles as a taxable perk, in the same way that company cars are taxed.

Write to your MP about the great Government rip-off!

The last Tory Chancellor increased airport tax (officially called Air Passenger Duty or APD) from £5 to £10. Zurich, outside the EU, has an even higher tax at £20. Contrary to popular belief this money does not contribute to the improvement of airports, but ends up in the pocket of the taxman. This tax is totally unfair to **easyJet** customers as on some occasions the tax has been more than our one-way air fare (Yes, we have sold seats for £8.50). Please write to your MP expressing your dissatisfaction and suggesting that APD should be a percentage of the fare, just like VAT.

www.**easyJet**.com

Exhibit 8 Stelios' pet hates
Source: easyJet

Exhibit 9 Airlines routes of competing low cost carriers

	easyJet	go	RYANAIR THE LOW FARES AIRLINE	Virgin Express
Belgium			Brussels	Brussels*
Czech Republic		Prague		
Denmark		Copenhagen	Århus	Copenhagen
France	Nice	Lyon	Biarritz, Carcassonne, Dinnard, Lyon, Paris, St. Etienne, Toulouse	Nice
Germany		Munich	Frankfurt	
Greece	Athens			
Ireland	Belfast		Cork, Derry, Dublin*, Kerry, Knock	Shannon
Italy		Bologna, Milan, Rome, Venice	Ancona, Genoa, Pisa, Rimini, Turin, Venice	Milan, Rome
The Netherlands	Amsterdam			Rotterdam
Norway			Oslo	
Portugal		Faro, Lisbon		
Scotland	Aberdeen, Edinburgh, Glasgow, Inverness	Edinburgh	Glasgow*	
Spain	Barcelona, Madrid, Malaga, Mallorca	Alicante, Barcelona, Bilbao, Madrid, Malaga, Mallorca		Barcelona, Madrid, Malaga, Mallorca
Sweden			Kristianstad, Malmö, Stockholm	
Switzerland	Geneva*, Zurich	Zurich		
United Kingdom	Liverpool*, London*	London*	Birmingham, Bournemouth, Bristol, Cardiff, Leeds Bradford, Liverpool, London*, Manchester, Teesside	London

* Represents a hub

Sources: <http://www.easyJet.com>; <http://www.Go-Fly.com>; <http://www.Ryanair.com>; <http://www.Virgin-Express.com>.

Exhibit 10 Comparative financial & operational statistics for selected airlines

	easyJet[1]	Go[2]	Ryanair[3]	Virgin Express[4]	Southwest[5]	British Airways[6]	Swissair[7]
	US$ million	US$ million	US$ million	US$ million	US$ million	US$ million	US$ million
Revenue	123	51	303	262	4,164	14,264	7,290
Operating expenses	121	83	233	261	3,480	13,557	6,897
Operating profit/(loss)	2	(32)	70	1	684	806	452
Net profit/(loss)	4	(22)	59	(3)	433	330	233
Market Capitalization	n/a	n/a	1,794	95	8,197	6,504	2,439
Pre-tax Profit Margin	3.0	(63)	25.6	0.5	16.9	2.5	4.9
Return on Assets	32.3	(57)	18.8	(2.8)	9.7	1.6	2.6
Return on Equity	16.6	(177)	31.6	(6.6)	19.7	6.1	13.0
Debt/Equity	1.4	n/a	59.3	140.3	96.7	282.2	385.2
Sales to Assets	10.7	91.1	96.9	292.0	92.9	69.5	82.5
Price-Earnings Ratio	n/a	n/a	21.7	170.8	20.4	21.4	10.0
Capacity (000) – ASKM[a]	2,801,000	2,052,000	3,000,000[b]	2,657,814	76,069,624	161,291,000	40,560,000
Load Factor	75%	53%	71%	75%	66%	71%	72%
Passengers per year	1,714,761	2,000,000	4,900,000	2,600,000	52,586,400	45,049,000	12,199,000
Number of Aircraft	8	13	20	20	280	278	129
Employees	394	500	1094	639	25,844	63,779	43,696

[1] For the period ending 30.09.98.
[4,5,7] For the period ending 31.12.98.
[2,3,6] For the period ending 31.03.99.
[a] ASKM = Available Seat Kilometers; [b] This figure is an estimate.
Source: Company Annual Reports, Reuters Business Briefing

Case 6 **Hewlett-Packard: Creating a virtual supply chain (A)**

I want Hewlett-Packard to be able to produce and deliver a tape drive in five days, from supplied parts to customers.

Research Associate Petri Lehtivaara prepared this case under the supervision of Professors Carlos Cordon, Ralf W. Seifert and Thomas E. Vollmann as a basis for class discussion rather than to illustrate either effective or ineffective handling of a business situation.

This case series won the Supply Chain Management Award in the 2003 European Case Writing Competition organized by the European Foundation for Management Development (efmd).

IMD-6-0251
V. 17.12.2003

The words that Derek Gray, supply chain manager in the tape drive unit of Hewlett-Packard, had uttered just hours earlier to a couple of external visitors echoed in his head.

It was early July 2001. Gray sat down in his cubicle in HP's open-plan office in Bristol, United Kingdom. He was preparing for the next day's management meeting at which he had to present his recommendations for moving toward virtual manufacturing.

Gray had been managing a project – started some years ago – to create a virtual supply chain. He had gathered vast experience on the way and wanted to use this knowledge to recommend a good solution. Gray had three alternative routes to choose from:

◆ Path of least resistance: Outsource the final assembly, testing and configuration to one of the suppliers of a major part (Philips).

◆ Create the ultimate supply chain: Develop a lowest total cost supply chain; invest in further redesign and resourcing to maximize long-term efficiency.

◆ Consolidation of the industry: Join forces with a competitor and outsource the final assembly, testing and configuration to it.

HP needed to take manufacturing to the next stage – standing still was not an option.

Hewlett-Packard Company

Hewlett-Packard Company (HP) was a global provider of computing and imaging solutions and services for business and home. In 2000 its sales

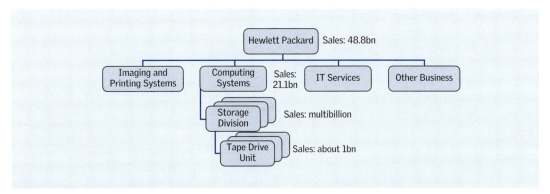

Figure 1 Tape Drive Business Unit
Note: 2000 figures, in $

were US$48.8 billion and it employed 89,000 people. HP's three main segments were imaging and printing systems (41%), computing systems (42%) and IT services (14%); other business accounted for 3%.

CEO Carly Fiorina had reorganized HP to become more customer oriented. The reorganization created a back-end, including product generation units, and a front-end devoted to sales and marketing, delivery channels and the client relationship. In addition, the focus changed from a functional one to a matrix.

Tape drives in HP

The tape drive business unit employed 700 people, 550 of them based in Bristol. The headquarters of the unit was in the United States. (*Refer to* **Figure** *1 for the organizational position of tape drives in HP.*)

Products

HP's tape drive business unit had three main areas: digital data storage (DDS), Ultrium and Storage solutions. In 2000 sales were just under $1 billion, with DDS generating most of this. Ultrium was the product of the future; it was based on an open standard – called linear tape open (LTO) – developed together with IBM and Seagate.

Tape drive business

The tape drive business was part of the storage market. The storage market in general was expanding due to customers' business transformation. Customers were (1) taking advantage of opportunities on the Internet, (2) increasing their demands and need for information and (3) evolving IT to meet these unpredictable demands. Storage was potentially a large market – estimated at $46 billion in 2003.

Tapes were an economical way to store large volumes of digital data. Although the market had reached maturity and the time for major growth had passed, tapes still had their advantages compared with disks. As Gray explained:

> The tapes are regularly 7 to 10 times better than disks in cost/gigabyte stored. They will remain around for at least the next seven years.

The type of tape drives most often used had also started to change, and demand was increasingly for higher capacity, more complex equipment.

The performance and quality of the product were qualifying criteria in the business. The key success factors were time-to-market and cost of the product. The cost was especially important in sales to original equipment manufacturers (OEMs).

The life cycle of a product was typically four years. This meant that getting product to market as quickly as possible was critical for the company, to ensure highest possible sales volumes and margins. In the future merely having a good product would not be good enough; it would have to be part of a system.

The business in transition

Tape technology was in a transitional phase. New technology – LTO and super digital linear tape (SDLT) – had been introduced to upgrade from the traditional technologies of DDS and digital linear tape (DLT). Quantum was the major producer of DLT and was the overall market leader in the tape drive business, particularly the high-end segment. HP had kept its lead in the medium segment. DDS technology-based products were still a profitable product line. (*Refer to* **Figure 2** *for characteristics of tape drive products.*)

One emerging trend in the industry was the link between sales of tape drives and media (tape). The media business was a large and growing one. Gray noted:

> There is less money in the tape drive business. The money is increasingly in media. The business is increasingly like selling razor blades. This is the strategy that many of our key competitors are using with their high-end tape drives.

HP's supply chain in the tape drive business

The supply chain consisted of four phases before final delivery to the customer. (*Refer to* **Figure 3** *for supply chain of DDS product family.*) HP sourced the main components from third parties because they had special technology and expertise that HP did not have in-house.

Characteristics	Traditional Technology		New Technology
	Medium segment	High-end segment	
Competing products	DDS, AIT	DLT, AIT, Mammoth, 34XX	Super digital linear tape (SDLT), linear tape open (LTO)
Volume (per annum)	1.75 million	400,000	Low
Price comparison	$1,000 (reference price*)	3× to 5×	7× to 10×
Main producers (and market share)	HP (50%–55%), Sony (30%), Seagate	Quantum (80%)	Quantum, IBM, HP, Seagate

Figure 2 Characteristics of tape drive products
* A disguised price that does not reflect actuals.

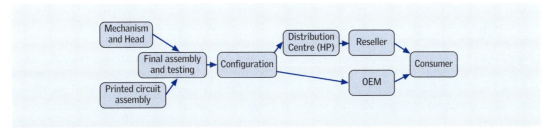

Figure 3 Supply chain for DDS products

Two channels to market

The tape drives were sold to the end consumer either through OEMs or resellers. In volume terms the OEM channel was larger; in sales terms the reseller channel was larger. The reseller channel was pretty profitable for HP, whereas the OEM channel was less so. Danny Berry, OEM supply chain manager, explained:

OEMs are very demanding. On the other hand, if we deliver it is a good reference. In addition we have a lot of contact with the engineers.

HP delivered the product to its resellers through three regional warehouses – Asia-Pacific, Europe and the US – which had varying degrees of performance. Gray expressed his views on the deliveries:

[In the reseller channel] we had significant problems with on-time delivery. I am not sure if we

need distribution centers in our business. I think we should be able to deliver product directly from production to the reseller.

The OEM channel received the products directly from the factory. This worked well and HP had even won awards from Sun Microsystems for being a good supplier.

Outsourcing of DDS products

In 1997 HP decided to start developing the LTO standard together with IBM and Seagate. This meant that the requirement for space and investment in the factory increased, but the manufacturing manager indicated there was no more space or investment for manufacturing. Outsourcing of manufacturing was the only option, even if many people had initially been against it.

Players in the Outsourced Supply Chain with Different Models of DDS					
Model	Start	Mechanism and Head	PCA	FAST	Configuration
DDS1	1990	Sony	CM A	HP Bristol	HP Bristol
DDS2	1997	Mitsumi	CM A	CM A (Scotland)	CM A (Ireland)
DDS3	1998	Mitsumi	CM B	CM A (Scotland)	CM A (Ireland)
DDS4	1999	Mitsumi	CM A	Mitsumi	CM C (Ireland)

Figure 4 Evolution of the partners in the supply chain
Note: CM = Contract manufacturer

Between 1997 and 2000 HP outsourced all its models in the DDS product family, one by one. The organization did not have an overall strategy. The solutions were tailored to each individual situation. *(Refer to Figure 4 for evolution of the partners in the supply chain.)* HP always started the manufacturing in its own facilities in Bristol and transferred production to the contract manufacturer after the ramp-up had been done.

OEM customers had an ambivalent reaction to outsourcing. On the one hand, they did not want to go through a new approval process of a new supplier for the product. On the other hand, their attitude to outsourcing was: 'Just make sure that this is invisible to us in terms of quality, delivery performance and cost.'

Outsourcing assembly and configuration

HP decided to outsource the final assembly and configuration of DDS2. It chose a contract manufacturer in Scotland to keep the risk of outsourcing low: the contract manufacturer was close to HP, the engineering people liked it and the price was competitive, although not the lowest.

Relatively soon after the deal, it became evident that the contract manufacturer could produce drives at a significantly lower cost than HP, largely because of overhead. Both companies put a lot of effort into managing the relationship. HP had three or four people constantly in Scotland and the companies had regular team meetings. The core team consisted of people from materials, finance, engineering and logistics areas in the two companies. There was also a communications matrix by which HP people talked to their counterparts at the manufacturer. Both companies seemed happy with the situation.

HP also outsourced production of the DDS3 model to the same contract manufacturer. The decision was based on capacity and cost. In this case, HP was concerned about the resourcing of the project. Davey Maclachlan, procurement manager, explained:

We wanted the contract manufacturer to have a new product introduction team [for DDS3]. It had one team that needed to manage both DDS2 and DDS3. I think the margins were so small that they had to cut resources. We also noted that they were fire fighting. It felt like their departments were not talking to each other. They fixed one problem and the next came up as a consequence. The vendor management, inbound logistics and throughput suffered.

Divisional finance involvement

In 1998 HP's divisional finance function became involved. It had been investigating opportunities for taking advantage of regional benefits. The tape drive unit assessed whether this would work for them and decided on a location in Ireland. This meant that configuration should move there. Legal issues complicated the matter as HP had to have the management of the operation in Ireland, so communication from Bristol went to the factory via the Irish office.

The regional benefits were so significant that the organization was willing to complicate matters operationally. Calculations showed that the financial advantages would be equal to double the normal returns from supply chain savings and efficiencies.

Worsening relations with the contract manufacturer

The relationship with the contract manufacturer deteriorated. Maclachlan explained:

> I went to visit the CM with a colleague in a positive mood. We thought that we would propose some additional business to them. When we met the team we were surprised by their response. Their motivation had clearly diminished and all they could see were problems. We assumed that something had happened to cause their change of heart, potentially in their assessment of the real costs of doing the work. We also felt it necessary to alert them to our needs to consider lower cost geographies (within the same company) and this was not well received.

New outsourcing partner

For the DDS4 model, HP opted to work mainly with Mitsumi and another contract manufacturer. For the new contract manufacturer, which had to configure only one product, this arrangement was not ideal. Also the supply chain had become complex. Gray explained:

> We now had three major deals with different generations of DDS products. The relationships

with the earlier contract manufacturers were becoming quite difficult due to the limited future. We had hoped to grow the business with the new CM but were having operational problems. The Mitsumi relationship was working very well, however the overhead to manage all of these various relationships was going through the roof. At this stage we also started to have quite heated debates between the functions (accountants, supply chain and engineering) about the relative benefits of each outsourcing decision.

Launch of the new technology: Ultrium

Work on developing Ultrium started in 1997. HP partnered with IBM and Seagate to develop the standard, which was in competition with the Quantum one. Production of Ultrium began in late 2000. The supply chain looked similar to that for DDS products, with three main components: mechanism, PCA and head (refer to **Figure 5**).

After six months' production of Ultrium, Gray decided to collect data to better understand the ramp-up period. He was amazed to see the level of inventory in the supply chain since production began. (Refer to **Exhibit 1** for information on the supply chain.)

The lead time across the supply chain was theoretically 90 days. Gray's ambition was to be able to deliver a tape drive to the customer in five days. He commented:

> It does not take more than a day to manufacture one, and four days are enough for logistics.

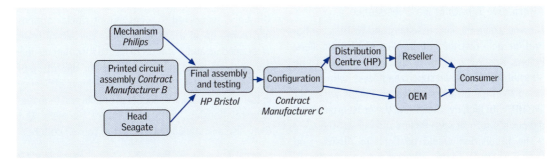

Figure 5 Supply chain for Ultrium

Future alternatives

Gray had come to the conclusion that HP needed to move toward virtual manufacturing and not produce any part of Ultrium. He identified four key issues that should determine the choice of the future alternative:

1 Strategic alignment
2 Total cost of ownership
3 Partner choice
4 Cost of production

The first two were the most important criteria. Strategic alignment included both supply chain and overall strategy of the storage division and meant that HP's investment would be low with quick returns.

Many other companies in the industry had also moved toward outsourcing or virtual manufacturing. Outsourcing had seen the development of a new industry around contract manufacturers, the largest of which had global operations with high-level manufacturing and supply chain management skills. During 1999 and 2000 the deals had become larger, reaching multibillion levels in 2001.

HP had not been convinced of its contract manufacturers' capabilities in tape engineering. HP's experience was that its fixed cost was not reducing as much as expected, as it had to do the engineering itself. In the future HP wanted to move away from its original practice of ramping up the production in-house for six months and moving the production out after that. Now it wanted to change its manufacturing approach radically and get its partner involved from day one. To this end, it had outlined three main alternatives.

Alternative 1: path of least resistance

HP would give the final assembly and testing, configuration and distribution to one of its suppliers, Philips. According to Gray this was an easy-to-do alternative. Philips had superb engineers, who understood the tape business. However, Philips was a bit like HP, with high overhead, and the outsourcing deal did not seem to fit with Philips' overall strategy.

The production would be done in Austria and Hungary with five or six HP people always on site. In this case Gray needed to persuade the accountants of the intangible benefits, since the apparent savings were lower. The key issue was: What would it take for Philips to take on this business and what would be left for HP?

Alternative 2: the ultimate supply chain

This would involve designing the supply chain in the right way, from scratch. HP had talked with Mitsumi, which would ultimately have capabilities to manufacture both the head and mechanism and would also take care of final assembly and testing, configuration and – potentially – distribution. Mitsumi would emerge as a major tape drive manufacturer.

Gray assumed the investment would be high, but that the return would also be high. Ultimately this alternative would provide low cost and flexibility. At the moment Mitsumi did not have enough buying power and capabilities to produce the mechanism. HP would need to assist it with technology development for Ultrium. In the past, HP had had positive experiences working with Mitsumi. However, this time HP would need to assist Mitsumi with technology development and was unsure about the implications of moving in this direction.

Alternative 3: consolidation

The third alternative included collaborating with a competitor. This approach would assume consolidation was necessary in the industry and would concentrate on supply chain efficiency rather than competition. This would be especially true as both companies would be competing against Quantum's standard. The main question would be: Should you help a competitor to survive? The relationship would be complex and troublesome.

Decision looming

Gray also wondered to what extent similar options had come up in other industries. The alternatives were lined up and it was up to him to recommend one. The decision could be a crucial one for the future of the tape drive unit. Gray wanted to achieve efficiency in the supply chain, low cost of products and manageable relationships with HP's future partners. But Gray also acknowledged the fact of the HP culture:

HP is big on consensus. Any one person can kill the proposal.

Exhibit 1 Cumulative volume of parts in the supply chain and sales of ultrium

Month (end)	Supplier to PCA	Head	PCA	Mechanism	FAST	Config.	Sales
Aug 2000	33	9	18	20	4	4	0
Sep 2000	62	26	32	46	13	13	1
Oct 2000	129	34	43	46	21	17	1
Nov 2000	150	70	71	74	42	35	9
Dec 2000	204	100	127	120	73	51	14
Jan 2001	270	136	204	155	96	66	21
Feb 2001	367	185	266	208	130	101	38
Mar 2001	636	237	320	264	174	116	62
Apr 2001	733	294	418	332	220	161	78
May 2001	1,021	343	448	367	265	192	100

Note: The volume information is proportional, with sales in May 2001 being 100 and other volumes proportional to that.
Source: Company information

INTERNATIONAL

Hewlett-Packard: Creating a virtual supply chain (B)

Another 12 months had passed. Derek Gray took a deep breath and sat back and reflected on the developments that had taken place in this time.

We took a long time to decide, but now we are ready to move forward. A lot of people were involved in the decision and we also lived through some internal organizational changes. The pending merger with Compaq further complicated the process on our side, but frankly there were also a number of surprises on the part of our potential partners.

Gray was relaxed as the roller-coaster experience of reaching the outsourcing decision was behind him and he could look forward to his new challenge of ramping up production at the supplier. It was July 2002. Gray had just moved to Vienna, Austria. This was not the original intention, but Gray explained:

In autumn 2001 we decided on a variation of the Mitsumi option. We believed that it was worth

Research Associate Petri Lehtivaara prepared this case under the supervision of Professors Carlos Cordon and Ralf W. Seifert as a basis for class discussion rather than to illustrate either effective or ineffective handling of a business situation.

This case series won the Supply Chain Management Award in the **2003 European Case Writing Competition** organized by the European Foundation for Management Development (efmd).

IMD-6-0252
V. 17.12.2003

winning the battle for the tape drive business and thus wanted to create the ultimate supply chain, removing as many nodes as possible to improve efficiency. The idea with the Mitsumi option was to move our mechanism production, including equipment, technology and tools, from Philips to Mitsumi.

We discussed our decision with the Philips executive and reached agreement on the matter. Somewhat unexpectedly, however, his team resisted the transfer and [through organizational play] effectively made it impossible for us to proceed.

More time passed and Gray needed to take a fresh look at the Philips option. Philips came back with the alternative suggestion of using Flextronics as a contract manufacturer. Flextronics had an assembly plant in Hungary, few hours away from Vienna, where the Philips division was based. Gray noted:

We got quite excited about this option, as it would provide the lower manufacturing cost but with the engineering expertise of Philips. It felt like Christmas to us, it could be a win-win-win situation. The Philips and Flextronics executives were long-time friends and this helped to establish the relationship. We felt that in the circumstances, this would be a deal worth going for. By then we had finally said no to the Mitsumi option, and our negotiations with Seagate had slowly gone cold. Shortly afterwards, we learned about a management change at Philips. The new executive also subscribed to Philips strategy, but interpreted it slightly differently: It was no longer desirable for Philips to divest the mechanism manufacturing business to Flextronics as was previously proposed. At that point we had gone through all the options and in view of the significant loss of time decided simply to go ahead with Flextronics anyway. The Flextronics option provided ample opportunity for supply chain integration and was geographically close to Philips. It also provided low cost manufacturing capability in its Hungarian facility.

Gray's learning points from the outsourcing decisions

While reflecting on the ups and downs with the outsourcing, Gray was able to identify four dimensions of learning for himself.

- *'People buy from people'* Individuals make a difference and can alter decisions. A change of individuals will have a huge impact on potential deals.

- *'You get the vendor you deserve'* Vendor management and vendor development is extremely important. A partner who is constantly driven on cost is likely to cut resources to the point of poor performance. The vendor's performance often reflects the poorly developed vendor management practices of the customer, and indeed the other customers that the vendor works with.

- *'We need more accountants and lawyers than engineers'* Regional benefits are extremely significant and can distort people's thinking. The supply chain should still be the primary driver of decisions but there is a great deal of opportunity to be taken through these regional benefits.

- *'Like herding cats'* Large companies have difficulty organizing themselves. Bureaucracy and unclear accountability render decision making difficult. This applies to many multinationals and can be frustrating when two multinational companies try to work together.

Gray described the central learning:

> *Any team halfway capable but focused could make any of the options work, as long as they want to make things happen and have shared values with the supplier. One should not underestimate the value of the right team and the right skills in making almost any option work.*

New challenges

Gray and two other people from HP's Bristol plant moved to Vienna to oversee the transition of manufacturing operations to Flextronics. Gray's challenge was to quickly transfer the manufacturing knowledge to the contract manufacturers. This time he wanted to follow a different approach and work toward a true partnership. With this in mind, Gray had to decide on two issues.

- What would be the best approach for knowledge transfer from the HP team to Flextronics?

- How should he define success for himself?

INSEAD

Case 7　Canon: Competing on capabilities

In 1961, following the runaway success of the company's model 914 office copier, Joseph C. Wilson, President of Xerox Corporation, was reported to have said, 'I keep asking myself, when am I going to wake up? Things just aren't this good in life'. Indeed, the following decade turned out to be better than anything Wilson could have dreamed. Between 1960 and 1970, Xerox increased its sales 40 percent per year from $40 million to $1.7 billion and raised its after-tax profits from $2.6 million to $187.7 million. In 1970, with 93 percent market share world-wide and a brand name that was synonymous with copying, Xerox appeared as invincible in its industry as any company ever could.

When Canon, 'the camera company from Japan', jumped into the business in the late 1960s, most observers were sceptical. Less than a tenth the size of Xerox, Canon had no direct sales or service organization to reach the corporate market for copiers, nor did it have a process technology to by-pass the 500 patents that guarded Xerox's Plain Paper Copier (PPC) process. Reacting to the spate of recent entries in the business including Canon, Arthur D. Little predicted in 1969 that no company would be able to challenge Xerox's monopoly in PPCs in the 1970s because its patents presented an insurmountable barrier.

Yet, over the next two decades, Canon rewrote the rule book on how copiers were supposed to be produced and sold as it built up $5 billion in revenues in the business, emerging as the second largest global player in terms of sales and surpassing Xerox in the

This case was prepared by Mary Ackenhusen, Research Associate, under the supervision of Sumantra Ghoshal, Associate Professor at INSEAD. It is intended to be used as a basis for class discussion rather than to illustrate either effective or ineffective handling of an administrative situation.

05/92-2253

number of units sold. According to the Canon Handbook, the company's formula for success as displayed initially in the copier business is 'synergistic management of the total technological capabilities of the company, combining the full measure of Canon's know how in fine optics, precision mechanics, electronics and fine chemicals'. Canon continues to grow and diversify using this strategy. Its vision, as described in 1991 by Ryuzaburo Kaku, President of the company, is 'to become a premier global company of the size of IBM combined with Matsushita'.

Industry background

The photocopying machine has often been compared with the typewriter as one of the few triggers that have fundamentally changed the ways of office work. But, while a mechanical Memograph machine for copying had been introduced by the A.B. Dick company of Chicago as far back as 1887, it was only in the second half of this century that the copier market exploded with Xerox's commercialisation of the 'electrophotography' process invented by Chester Carlson.

Xerox

Carlson's invention used an electrostatic process to transfer images from one sheet of paper to another. Licensed to Xerox in 1948, this invention led to two different photocopying technologies. The Coated Paper Copying (CPC) technology transferred the reflection of an image from the original directly to specialized zinc-oxide coated paper, while the Plain Paper Copying (PPC) technology transferred the image indirectly to ordinary paper through a rotating drum coated with charged particles. While either dry or liquid toner could be used to develop the image, the dry toner was generally preferable in both technologies. A large number of companies entered the CPC market in the 1950s and 1960s based on technology licensed from Xerox or RCA (to whom Xerox had earlier licensed this technology). However, PPC remained a Xerox monopoly since the company had refused to license any technology remotely connected to the PPC process and had protected the technology with over 500 patents.

Because of the need for specialized coated paper, the cost per copy was higher for CPC. Also, this process could produce only one copy at a time, and the copies tended to fade when exposed to heat or light. PPC, on the other hand, produced copies at a lower operating cost that were also indistinguishable from the original. The PPC machines were much more expensive, however, and were much larger in size. Therefore, they required a central location in the user's office. The smaller and less expensive CPC machines, in contrast, could be placed on individual desks. Over time, the cost and quality advantages of PPC, together with its ability to make multiple copies at high speed, made it the dominant technology and, with it, Xerox's model of centralized copying, the industry norm.

This business concept of centralized copying required a set of capabilities that Xerox developed and which, in turn, served as its major strengths and as key barriers to entry to the business. Given the advantages of volume and speed, all large companies found centralized copying highly attractive and they became the key customers for photocopying machines. In order to support this corporate customer base, Xerox's product designs and upgrades emphasized economies of higher volume copying. To market the product effectively to these customers, Xerox also built up an extensive direct sales and service organization of over 12,000 sales representatives and 15,000 service people. Forty percent of the sales reps' time was spent 'hand holding' to prevent even minor dissatisfaction. Service reps, dressed in suits and carrying their tools in briefcases, performed preventative maintenance and prided themselves on reducing the average time between breakdown and repair to a few hours.

Further, with the high cost of each machine and the fast rate of model introductions, Xerox developed a strategy of leasing rather than selling machines to customers. Various options were available, but typically the customers paid a monthly charge on the number of copies made. The charge covered not only machine costs but also those of the paper and toner that Xerox supplied and the service visits. This lease strategy, together with the carefully cultivated service image, served as key safeguards from competition, as they tied the

customers into Xerox and significantly raised their switching costs.

Unlike some other American corporations, Xerox had an international orientation right from the beginning. Even before it had a successful commercial copier, Xerox built up an international presence through joint ventures which allowed the company to minimize its capital investment abroad. In 1956, it ventured with the Rank Organization Ltd. in the U.K. to form Rank Xerox. In 1962, Rank Xerox became a 50 percent partner with Fuji Photo to form Fuji Xerox which sold copiers in Japan. Through these joint ventures, Xerox built up sales and service capabilities in these key markets similar to those it had in the United States. There were some 5,000 sales people in Europe, 3,000 in Japan and over 7,000 and 3,000 service reps, respectively. Xerox also built limited design capabilities in both the joint ventures for local market customization, which developed into significant research establishments in their own rights in later years.

Simultaneously, Xerox maintained high levels of investment in both technology and manufacturing to support its growing market. It continued to spend over $100 million a year in R&D, exceeding the total revenues from the copier business that any of its competitors were earning in the early 70s, and also invested heavily in large-size plants not only in the U.S., but also in the U.K. and Japan.

Competition in the 1970s

Xerox's PPC patents began to expire in the 1970s, heralding a storm of new entrants. In 1970, IBM offered the first PPC copier not sold by Xerox, which resulted in Xerox suing IBM for patent infringement and violation of trade secrets. Canon marketed a PPC copier the same year through the development of an independent PPC technology which they licensed selectively to others. By 1973, competition had expanded to include players from the office equipment industry (IBM, SCM, Litton, Pitney Bowes), the electronics industry (Toshiba, Sharp), the reprographics industry (Ricoh, Mita, Copyer, 3M, AB Dick, Addressograph/Multigraph), the photographic equipment industry (Canon, Kodak, Minolta, Konishiroku) and the suppliers of copy paper (Nashua, Dennison, Saxon).

By the 1980s many of these new entrants,

including IBM, had lost large amounts of money and exited the business. A few of the newcomers managed to achieve a high level of success, however, and copiers became a major business for them. Specifically, copiers were generating 40 percent of Canon's revenues by 1990.

Canon

Canon was founded in 1933 with the ambition to produce a sophisticated 35mm camera to rival that of Germany's world-class Leica model. In only two years' time, it had emerged as Japan's leading producer of high-class cameras. During the war, Canon utilized its optics expertise to produce an X-ray machine which was adopted by the Japanese military. After the war, Canon was able to successfully market its high-end camera, and by the mid-1950s it was the largest camera manufacturer in Japan. Building off its optics technology, Canon then expanded its product line to include a mid-range camera, an 8mm video camera, television lenses and micrographic equipment. It also began developing markets for its products outside of Japan, mainly in the U.S. and Canada.

Diversification was always very important to Canon in order to further its growth, and a new products R&D section was established in 1962 to explore the fields of copy machines, auto-focusing cameras, strobe-integrated cameras, home VCRs and electronic calculators. A separate, special operating unit was also established to introduce new non-camera products resulting from the diversification effort.

The first product to be targeted was the electronic calculator. This product was challenging because it required Canon engineers to develop new expertise in microelectronics in order to incorporate thousands of transistors and diodes in a compact, desk model machine. Tekeshi Mitarai, President of Canon at that time, was against developing the product because it was seen to be too difficult and risky. Nevertheless, a dedicated group of engineers believed in the challenge and developed the calculator in secrecy. Over a year later, top management gave their support to the project. In 1964, the result of the development effort was introduced as the Canola 130, the world's first 10-key numeric pad calculator. With this

product line, Canon dominated the Japanese electronic calculator market in the 1960s.

Not every diversification effort was a success, however. In 1956, Canon began development of the synchroreader, a device for writing and reading with a sheet of paper coated with magnetic material. When introduced in 1959, the product received high praise for its technology. But, because the design was not patented, another firm introduced a similar product at half the price. There was no market for the high priced and incredibly heavy Canon product. Ultimately, the firm was forced to disassemble the finished inventories and sell off the usable parts in the 'once-used' components market.

Move into copiers

Canon began research into copier technology in 1959, and, in 1962, it formed a research group dedicated to developing a plain paper copier (PPC) technology. The only known PPC process was protected by hundreds of Xerox patents, but Canon felt that only this technology promised sufficient quality, speed, economy and ease of maintenance to successfully capture a large portion of the market. Therefore, corporate management challenged the researchers to develop a new PPC process which would not violate the Xerox patents.

In the meantime, the company entered the copier business by licensing the 'inferior' CPC technology in 1965 from RCA. Canon decided not to put the name of the company on this product and marketed it under the brand name Confax 1000 in Japan only. Three years later, Canon licensed a liquid toner technology from an Australian company and combined this with the RCA technology to introduce the CanAll Series. To sell the copier in Japan, Canon formed a separate company, International Image Industry. The copier was sold as an OEM to Scott Paper in the U.S. who sold it under its own brand name.

Canon's research aiming at developing a PPC technical alternative to xerography paid off with the announcement of the 'New Process' (NP) in 1968. This successful research effort not only produced an alternative process but also taught Canon the importance of patent law: how not to violate patents and how to protect new technology. The NP process was soon protected by close to 500 patents.

The first machine with the NP technology, the NP1100, was introduced in Japan in 1970. It was the first copier sold by Canon to carry the Canon brand name. It produced 10 copies per minute and utilized dry toner. As was the standard in the Japanese market, the copier line was sold outright to customers from the beginning. After two years of experience in the domestic market, Canon entered the overseas market, except North America, with this machine.

The second generation of the NP system was introduced in Japan in 1972 as the NPL7. It was a marked improvement because it eliminated a complex fusing technology, simplified developing and cleaning, and made toner supply easier through a new system developed to use liquid toner. Compared with the Xerox equivalent, it was more economical, more compact, more reliable and still had the same or better quality of copies.

With the NP system, Canon began a sideline which was to become quite profitable: licensing. The first generation NP system was licensed to AM, and Canon also provided it with machines on an OEM basis. The second generation was again licensed to AM as well as to Saxon, Ricoh, and Copyer. Canon accumulated an estimated $32 million in license fees between 1975 and 1982.

Canon continued its product introductions with a stream of state-of-the-art technological innovations throughout the seventies. In 1973 it added colour to the NP system; in 1975, it added laser beam printing technology. Its first entry into high volume copiers took place in 1978 with a model which was targeted at the Xerox 9200. The NP200 was introduced in 1979 and went on to win a gold medal at the Leipzig Fair for being the most economical and productive copier available. By 1982, copiers had surpassed cameras as the company's largest revenue generator (see **Exhibits 1 and 2** for Canon's financials and sales by product line).

The personal copier

In the late 1970s, top management began searching for a new market for the PPC copier. They had recently experienced a huge success with the introduction of the AE-1 camera in 1976 and wanted a similar success in copiers. The AE-1 was a very compact single-lens reflex camera, the first camera that used a microprocessor to control electronically functions of exposure, film rewind and strobe. The product had been developed through a focused, cross-functional project team effort which had resulted in a substantial reduction in the number of components, as well as in automated assembly and the use of unitized parts. Because of these improvements, the AE-1 enjoyed a 20 percent cost advantage over competitive models in the same class.

After studying the distribution of offices in Japan by size (see **Exhibit 3**), Canon decided to focus on a latent segment that Xerox had ignored. This was the segment comprised of small offices (segment E) who could benefit from the functionality offered by photocopiers but did not require the high speed machines available in the market. Canon management believed that a low volume 'value for money' machine could generate a large demand in this segment. From this analysis emerged the business concept of a 'personal side desk' machine which could not only create a new market in small offices, but potentially also induce decentralization of the copy function in large offices. Over time, the machine might even create demand for a personal copier for home use. This would be a copier that up to now no one had thought possible. Canon felt that, to be successful in this market, the product had to cost half the price of a conventional copier (target price $1,000), be maintenance free, and provide ten times more reliability.

Top management took their 'dream' to the engineers, who, after careful consideration, took on the challenge. The machine would build off their previous expertise in microelectronics but would go much further in terms of material, functional component, design and production engineering technologies. The team's slogan was 'Let's make the AE-1 of copiers!', expressing the necessity of know-how transfer between the camera and copier divisions as well as their desire for a similar type of success. The effort was led by the director of the Reprographic Production Development Center. His cross-functional team of 200 was the second largest ever assembled at Canon (the largest had been that of the AE-1 camera).

During the development effort, a major issue arose concerning the paper size that the new copier would accept. Canon Sales (the sales organization for Japan) wanted the machine to use a larger-than-letter-size paper which accounted for 60 percent of the Japanese market. This size was not necessary for sales outside of Japan and would add 20–30 percent to the machine's cost as well as make the copier more difficult to service. After much debate world-wide, the decision was made to forego the ability to utilize the larger paper size in the interest of better serving the global market.

Three years later the concept was a reality. The new PC (personal copier) employed a new-cartridge based technology which allowed the user to replace the photoreceptive drum, charging device, toner assembly and cleaner with a cartridge every 2,000 copies, thus eliminating the need to maintain the copier regularly. This enabled Canon engineers to meet the cost and reliability targets. The revolutionary product was the smallest, lightest copier ever sold, and created a large market which had previously not existed. Large offices adjusted their copying strategies to include decentralized copying, and many small offices and even homes could now afford a personal copier. Again, Canon's patent knowledge was utilized to protect this research, and the cartridge technology was not licensed to other manufacturers. Canon has maintained its leadership in personal copiers into the 1990s.

Building capabilities

Canon is admired for its technical innovations, marketing expertise, and low-cost quality manufacturing. These are the result of a long-term strategy to become a premier company. Canon has frequently acquired outside expertise so that it could better focus internal investments on skills of strategic importance. This approach of extensive outsourcing and focused internal development has required consistent direction from top management and the patience to allow the company to become well grounded in one skill area before tasking the organization with the next objective.

Technology

Canon's many innovative products, which enabled the company to grow quickly in the seventies and eighties are in large part the result of a carefully orchestrated use of technology and the capacity for managing rapid technological change. Attesting to its prolific output of original research is the fact that Canon has been among the leaders in number of patents issued world-wide throughout the eighties. These successes have been achieved in an organization that has firmly pursued a strategy of decentralized R&D. Most of Canon's R&D personnel are employed by the product divisions where 80–90 percent of the company's patentable inventions originate. Each product division has its own development center which is tasked with short- to medium-term product design and improvement of production systems. Most product development is performed by cross-functional teams. The work of the development groups is coordinated by an R&D headquarters group.

The Corporate Technical Planning and Operation centre is responsible for long-term strategic R&D planning. Canon also has a main research centre which supports state-of-the-art research in optics, electronics, new materials and information technology. There are three other corporate research centres which apply this state-of-the-art research to product development.

Canon acknowledges that it has neither the resources nor the time to develop all necessary technologies and has therefore often traded or bought specific technologies from a variety of external partners. Furthermore, it has used joint ventures and technology transfers as a strategic tool for mitigating foreign trade tensions in Europe and the United States. For example, Canon had two purposes in mind when it made an equity participation in CPF Deutsch, an office equipment marketing firm in Germany. Primarily, it believed that this move would help develop the German market for its copiers; but it did not go unnoticed among top management that CPF owned Tetras, a copier maker who at that time was pressing dumping charges against Japanese copier makers. Canon also used Burroughs as an OEM for office automation equipment in order to acquire Burroughs software and know-how and participated in joint development agreements with Eastman Kodak and Texas Instruments. **Exhibit 4** provides a list of the company's major joint ventures. Canon also recognizes that its continued market success depends on its ability to exploit new research into marketable products quickly. It has worked hard to reduce the new product introduction cycle through a cross-functional programme called TS 1/2 whose purpose is to cut development time by 50 percent on a continuous basis. The main thrust of this programme is the classification of development projects by total time required and the critical human resources needed so that these two parameters can be optimized for each product depending on its importance for Canon's corporate strategy. This allows product teams to be formed around several classifications of product development priorities of which 'best sellers' will receive the most emphasis. These are the products aimed at new markets or segments with large potential demands. Other classifications include products necessary to catch up with competitive offerings, product refinements intended to enhance customer satisfaction, and long-run marathon products which will take considerable time to develop. In all development classifications, Canon emphasizes three factors to reduce time to market: the fostering of engineering ability, efficient technical support systems, and careful reviews of product development at all stages.

Canon is also working to divert its traditional product focus into more of a market focus. To this end, Canon R&D personnel participate in international product strategy meetings, carry out consumer research, join in marketing activities, and attend meetings in the field at both domestic and foreign sales subsidiaries.

Marketing

Canon's effective marketing is the result of step-by-step, calculated introduction strategies. Normally, the product is first introduced and perfected in the home market before being sold internationally. Canon has learned how to capture learning from the Japanese market quickly so that the time span between introduction in Japan and abroad is as short as a few months. Furthermore, the company will not simultaneously launch a new product through a new distribution channel – its strategy is to minimize risk by introducing a new product through known channels first. New channels will only be created, if necessary, after the product has proven to be successful.

The launch of the NP copier exemplifies this strategy. Canon initially sold these copiers in Japan by direct sales through its Business Machines Sales organization, which had been set up in 1968 to sell the calculator product line. This sales organization was merged with the camera sales organization in 1971 to form Canon Sales. By 1972, after three years of experience in producing the NP product line, the company entered into a new distribution channel, that of dealers, to supplement direct selling.

The NP copier line was not marketed in the U.S. until 1974, after production and distribution were running smoothly in Japan. The U.S. distribution system was similar to that used in Japan, with seven sales subsidiaries for direct selling and a network of independent dealers.

By the late 1970s, Canon had built up a strong dealer network in the U.S. which supported both sales and service of the copiers. The dealer channel was responsible for rapid growth in copier sales, and, by the early 1980s, Canon copiers were sold almost exclusively through this channel. Canon enthusiastically supported the dealers with attractive sales incentive programmes, management training and social outings. Dealers were certified to sell copiers only after completing a course in service training. The company felt that a close relationship with its dealers was a vital asset that allowed it to understand and react to customers' needs and problems in a timely manner. At the same time, Canon also maintained a direct selling mechanism through wholly owned sales subsidiaries in Japan, the U.S. and Europe in order to target large customers and government accounts.

The introduction of its low-end personal copier in 1983 was similarly planned to minimize risk. Initially, Canon's NP dealers in Japan were not interested in the product due to its low maintenance needs and inability to utilize large paper sizes. Thus, PCs were distributed through the firm's office supply stores who were already selling its personal calculators. After seeing the success of the PC, the NP dealers began to carry the copier.

In the U.S., the PC was initially sold only through existing dealers and direct sales channels due to limited availability of the product. Later, it was sold through competitors' dealers and office supply stores, and, eventually, the distribution channels were extended to include mass merchandisers. Canon already had considerable experience in mass merchandising from its camera business.

Advertising has always been an integral part of Canon's marketing strategy. President Kaku believes that Canon must have a corporate brand name which is outstanding to succeed in its diversification effort. 'Customers must prefer products because they bear the name Canon', he says. As described by the company's finance director, 'If a brand name is unknown, and there is no advertising, you have to sell it cheap. It's not our policy to buy share with a low price. We establish our brand with advertising at a reasonably high price'.

Therefore, when the NP-200 was introduced in 1980, 10 percent of the selling price was spent on advertising; for the launch of the personal copier, advertising expenditure was estimated to be 20 percent of the selling price. Canon has also sponsored various sporting events including World Cup football, the Williams motor racing team, and the ice dancers Torvill and Dean. The company expects its current expansion into the home automation market to be greatly enhanced by the brand image it has built in office equipment (see **Exhibit 1** for Canon's advertising expenditures through 1990).

Manufacturing

Canon's goal in manufacturing is to produce the best quality at the lowest cost with the best delivery. To drive down costs, a key philosophy of the production system is to organize the manufacture of each product so that the minimum amount of time, energy and resources are required. Canon therefore places strong emphasis on tight inventory management through a stable production planning process, careful material planning, close supplier relationships, and adherence to the **kanban** system of inventory movement. Additionally, a formal waste elimination programme saved Canon 177 billion yen between 1976 and 1985. Overall, Canon accomplished a 30 percent increase in productivity per year from 1976 to 1982 and over 10 percent thereafter through automation and innovative process improvements.

The workforce is held in high regard at Canon. A philosophy of 'stop and fix it' empowers any worker to stop the production line if he or she is not able to perform a task properly or observes a quality problem. Workers are responsible for their own machine maintenance governed by rules which stress prevention. Targets for quality and production and other critical data are presented to the workers with on-line feedback. Most workers also participate in voluntary 'small group activity' for problem solving. The result of these systems is a workforce that feels individually responsible for the success of the products it manufactures.

Canon sponsors a highly regarded suggestion programme for its workers in order to directly involve those most familiar with the work processes in improving the business. The programme was originally initiated in 1952 with only limited success, but in the early 1980s, participation soared with more than seventy suggestions per employee per year. All suggestions are reviewed by a hierarchy of committees with monetary prizes awarded monthly and yearly depending on the importance of the suggestion. The quality and effectiveness of the process are demonstrated by a 90 percent implementation rate of the suggestions offered and corporate savings of $202 million in 1985 (against a total expenditure of $2 million in running the programme, over 90 percent of it in prize money).

Canon chooses to backward integrate only on parts with unique technologies. For other components, the company prefers to develop long-term relationships with its suppliers and it retains two sources for most parts. In 1990, over 80 percent of Canon's copiers were assembled from purchased parts, with only the drums and toner being manufactured in-house. The company also maintains its own in-house capability for doing pilot production of all parts so as to understand better the technology and the vendors' costs.

Another key to Canon's high quality and low cost is the attention given to parts commonality between models. Between some adjacent copier models, the commonality is as high as 60 percent.

Copier manufacture was primarily located in Toride, Japan, in the early years but then spread to Germany, California and Virginia in the U.S., France, Italy and Korea. In order to mitigate trade and investment friction, Canon is working to increase the local content of parts as it expands globally. In Europe it exceeds the EC standard by 5 percent. It is also adding R&D capability to some of its overseas operations. Mr. Kaku emphasizes the importance of friendly trading partners:

> Frictions cannot be erased by merely transferring our manufacturing facilities overseas. The earnings after tax must be reinvested in the country; we must transfer our technology to the country. This is the only way our overseas expansion will be welcomed.

Leveraging expertise

Canon places critical importance on continued growth through diversification into new product fields. Mr. Kaku observed,

> Whenever Canon introduced a new product, profits surged forward. Whenever innovation lagged, on the other hand, so did the earnings ... In order to survive in the coming era of extreme competition, Canon must possess at least a dozen proprietary state-of-the-art technologies that will enable it to develop unique products.

While an avid supporter of diversification, Mr. Kaku was cautious.

> In order to ensure the enduring survival of Canon, we have to continue diversifying in order to adapt to environmental changes. However, we must be wise in choosing ways toward diversification. In other words, we must minimize the risks. Entering a new business which requires either a technology unrelated to Canon's current expertise or a different marketing channel than Canon currently uses incurs a 50 percent risk. If Canon attempts to enter a new business which requires both a new technology and a new marketing channel which are unfamiliar to Canon, the risk entailed in such ventures would be 100 percent. There are two prerequisites that have to be satisfied before launching such new ventures. First, our operation must be debt-free; second, we will have to secure the personnel capable of competently undertaking such ventures. I feel we shall have to wait until the twenty-first century before we are ready.

Combining capabilities

Through its R&D strategy, Canon has worked to build up specialized expertise in several areas and then link them to offer innovative, state-of-the-art products. Through the fifties and sixties, Canon focused on products related to its main business and expertise, cameras. This prompted the introduction of the 8 mm movie camera and the Canon range of mid-market cameras. There was minimal risk because the optics technology was the same and the marketing outlet, camera shops, remained the same.

Entrance into the calculator market pushed Canon into developing expertise in the field of microelectronics, which it later innovatively combined with its optics capability to introduce one of its most successful products, the personal copier. From copiers, Canon utilized the replaceable cartridge system to introduce a successful desktop laser printer.

In the early seventies, Canon entered the business of marketing micro-chip semiconductor production equipment. In 1980, the company entered into the development and manufacture of unique proprietary ICs in order to strengthen further its expertise in electronics technology. This development effort was expanded in the late eighties to focus on opto-electronic ICs. According to Mr. Kaku:

> We are now seriously committed to R&D in ICs because our vision for the future foresees the arrival of the opto-electronic era. When the time arrives for the opto-electronic IC to replace the current ultra-LSI, we intend to go into making large-scale computers. Presently we cannot compete with the IBMs and NECs using the ultra-LSIs. When the era of the opto-electronic IC arrives, the technology of designing the computer will be radically transformed; that will be our chance for making entry into the field of the large-scale computer.

Creative destruction

In 1975 Canon produced the first laser printer. Over the next fifteen years, laser printers evolved as a highly successful product line under the Canon brand name. The company also provides the 'engine' as an OEM to Hewlett Packard and other laser printer manufacturers which when added to its own branded sales supports a total of 84 percent of world-wide demand.

The biggest threat to the laser printer industry is substitution by the newly developed bubble jet printer. With a new technology which squirts out thin streams of ink under heat, a high-quality silent printer can be produced at half the price of the laser printer. The technology was invented accidentally in the Canon research labs. It keys on a print head which has up to 400 fine nozzles per inch, each with its own heater to warm the ink until it shoots out tiny ink droplets. This invention utilizes Canon's competencies in fine chemicals for producing the ink and its expertise in semiconductors, materials, and electronics for manufacturing the print heads. Canon is moving full steam forward to develop the bubble jet technology, even though it might destroy a business that the company dominates. The new product is even more closely tied to the company's core capabilities, and management believes that successful development of this business will help broaden further its expertise in semiconductors.

Challenge of the 1990s

Canon sees the office automation business as its key growth opportunity for the nineties. It already has a well-established brand name in home and office automation products through its offerings of copiers, facsimiles, electronic typewriters, laser printers, word processing equipment and personal computers. The next challenge for the company is to link these discrete products into a multifunctional system which will perform the tasks of a copier, facsimile, printer, and scanner and interface with a computer so that all the functions can be performed from one keyboard. In 1988, with this target, Canon introduced a personal computer which incorporated a PC, a fax, a telephone and a word processor. Canon has also introduced a colour laser copier which hooks up to a computer to serve as a colour printer. A series of additional integrated OA offerings are scheduled for introduction in 1992, and the company expects these products to serve as its growth engine in the first half of the 1990s.

Managing the process

Undergirding this impressive history of continuously building new corporate capabilities and of exploiting those capabilities to create a fountain of innovative new products lies a rather unique management process. Canon has institutionalized corporate entrepreneurship through its highly autonomous and market focused business unit structure. A set of powerful functional committees provide the bridge between the entrepreneurial business units and the company's core capabilities in technology, manufacturing and marketing. Finally, an extraordinarily high level of corporate ambition drives this innovation engine, which is fuelled by the creativity of its people and by top management's continuous striving for ever higher levels of performance.

Driving entrepreneurship: the business units

Mr. Kaku had promoted the concept of the entrepreneurial business unit from his earliest days with Canon, but it was not until the company had suffered significant losses in 1975 that his voice was heard. His plan was implemented shortly before he became president of the company.

Mr. Kaku believed that Canon's diversification strategy could only succeed if the business units were empowered to act on their own, free of central controls. Therefore, two independent operating units were formed in 1978, one for cameras and one for office equipment, to be managed as business units. Optical Instruments, the third business unit, had always been separate. Since that time, an additional three business units have been spun off. The original three business units were then given clear profitability targets, as well as highly ambitious growth objectives, and were allowed the freedom to devise their own ways to achieve these goals. One immediate result of this decentralization was the recognition that Canon's past practice of mixing production of different products in the same manufacturing facility would no longer work. Manufacturing was reorganized so that no plant produced more than one type of product.

Mr. Kaku describes the head of each unit as a surrogate of the CEO empowered to make quick decisions. This allows him, as president of Canon, to devote himself exclusively to his main task of creating and implementing the long-term corporate strategy. In explaining the benefits of the system, he said:

Previously, the president was in exclusive charge of all decision making; his subordinates had to form a queue to await their turn in presenting their problems to him. This kind of system hinders the development of the young managers' potential for decision-making.

Furthermore, take the case of the desktop calculator. Whereas, I can devote only about two hours each day on problems concerning the calculator, the CEO of Casio Calculator could devote 24 hours to the calculator ... In the fiercely competitive market, we lost out because our then CEO was slow in coping with the problem.

In contrast to the Western philosophy of stand-alone SBUs encompassing all functions including engineering, sales, marketing and production, Canon has chosen to separate its product divisions from its sales and marketing arm. This separation allows for a clear focus on the challenges that Canon faces in selling products on a global scale. Through a five-year plan initiated in 1977, Seiichi Takigawa, the president of Canon Sales (the sales organization for Japan), stressed the need to 'make sales a science'. After proving the profitability of this approach, Canon Sales took on the responsibility for worldwide marketing, sales and service. In 1981, Canon Sales was listed on the Tokyo stock exchange, reaffirming its independence.

Canon also allows its overseas subsidiaries free rein, though it holds the majority of stock. The philosophy is to create the maximum operational leeway for each subsidiary to act on its own initiative. Kaku describes the philosophy through an analogy:

Canon's system of managing subsidiaries is similar to the policy of the Tokugawa government, which established secure hegemony over the warlords, who were granted autonomy in their territory. I am 'shogun' [head of the Tokugawa regime] and the subsidiaries' presidents are the 'daimyo' [warlords]. The difference between Canon and the Tokugawa government is that the latter was a zero-sum society; its policy was repressive. On the other hand, Canon's objective is to enhance the prosperity of all subsidiaries through efficient mutual collaboration.

Canon has also promoted the growth of intrapreneurial ventures within the company by spinning these ventures off as wholly owned subsidiaries. The first venture to be spun off was Canon Components, which produces electronic components and devices, in 1984.

Building integration: functional committees

As Canon continues to grow and diversify, it becomes increasingly difficult but also ever more important to link its product divisions in order to realize the benefits possible only in a large multi-product corporation. The basis of Canon's integration is a three dimensional management approach in which the first dimension is the independent business unit, the second a network of functional committees, and the third the regional companies focused on geographic markets (see Exhibit 5).

Kaku feels there are four basic requirements for the success of a diversified business: 1) a level of competence in research and development; 2) quality, low-cost manufacturing technology; 3) superior marketing strength; and 4) an outstanding corporate identity, culture and brand name. Therefore, he has established separate functional committees to address the first three requirements of development, production and marketing, while the fourth task has been kept as a direct responsibility of corporate management. The three functional committees, in turn, have been made responsible for company-wide administration of three key management systems:

- The Canon Development System (CDS) whose objectives are to foster the research and creation of new products and technologies by studying and continuously improving the development process;

- The Canon Production System (CPS) whose goal is to achieve optimum quality by minimizing waste in all areas of manufacturing;

- The Canon Marketing System (CMS), later renamed the Canon International Marketing System (CIMS), which is tasked to expand and strengthen Canon's independent domestic and overseas sales networks by building a high quality service and sales force.

Separate offices have been created at headquarters for each of these critical committees, and over time their role has broadened to encompass general improvement of the processes used to support their functions. The chairpersons of the committees are members of Canon's management committee, which gives them the ability to ensure consistency and communicate process improvements throughout the multiproduct, multinational corporation.

Using information technology to integrate its world-wide operations, Canon began development of the Global Information System for Harmonious Growth Administration (GINGA) in 1987. The system will consist of a high-speed digital communications network to interconnect all parts of Canon into a global database and allow for the timely flow of information among managers in any location of the company's world-wide organization. GINGA is planned to include separate but integrated systems for computer integrated manufacturing, global marketing and distribution, R&D and product design, financial reporting, and personnel database tracking, as well as some advances in intelligent office automation. As described by Mr. Kaku, the main objective of this system is to supplement Canon's efficient vertical communications structure with a lateral one that will facilitate direct information exchange among managers across businesses, countries, and functions on all operational matters concerning the company. The system is being developed at a total cost of 20 billion yen and it is targeted for completion in 1992.

Managing renewal: challenges and change

Mr. Kaku was very forthright about some of the management weaknesses of Canon prior to 1975:

In short, our skill in management – the software of our enterprise – was weak. Management policy must be guided by a soundly created software on management; if the software is weak, the firm will lack clearly defined ideals and objectives. In the beginning we had a clearly defined objective, to overtake West Germany's Leica. Since then our management policy has been changing like the colours of a chameleon.

In the past our management would order employees to reach the peak of Mount Fuji,

and then before the vanguard of climbers had barely started climbing, they would be ordered to climb Mount Tsukuba far to the north. Then the order would again be suddenly changed to climb Mount Yatsugatake to the west. After experiencing these kind of shifts in policy, the smarter employees would opt to take things easy by taking naps on the bank of the river Tamagawa. As a result, vitality would be sapped from our work force – a situation that should have been forestalled by all means.

Mr. Kaku's first action as President of Canon was to start the firm on the path to global leadership through establishing the first 'premier company plan', a six-year plan designed to make Canon a top company in Japan. The plan outlined a policy for diversification and required consistently recurring profits exceeding 10 percent on sales.

The aim of any Japanese corporation is ensuring its perpetual survival. Unlike the venture businesses and U.S. corporations, our greatest objective is not to maximize short-term profits. Our vital objective is to continually earn profits on a stable basis for ensuring survival. To implement this goal, we must diversify.

By the time the original six-year plan expired in 1981, Canon had become a highly respected company in Japan. The plan was then renewed through 1986 and then again into the 1990s. The challenge was to become a premier global company, defined as having recurring profits exceeding 15 percent of sales. R&D spending was gradually increased from 6 percent of sales in 1980 to 9 percent in 1985 as a prerequisite for global excellence. As described by Mr. Kaku:

By implementing our first plan for becoming a premier company we have succeeded in attaining the allegorical top of Mount Fuji. Our next objective is the Everest. With a firm determination, we could have climbed Fuji wearing sandals. However, sandals are highly inappropriate for climbing Everest; it may cause our death.

According to Mr. Kaku, such ambitions also require a company to build up the ability to absorb temporary reversals without panic; ambition without stability makes the corporate ship lose its way. To illustrate, he described the situation at Canon during the time the yen depreciated from 236 to the dollar in 1985 to 168 to the dollar in 1986. With 74 percent of Canon's Japanese production going to export markets, this sudden change caused earnings to fall to 4.6 billion yen, one tenth of the previous year. Some board members at Canon sought drastic action such as a major restructuring of the company and cutting the R&D budget. Mr. Kaku had successfully argued the opposite:

> *What I did was calm them down. If a person gets lost in climbing a high mountain, he must avoid excessive use of his energy; otherwise his predicament will deepen ... Our ongoing strategy for becoming the premier company remains the best, even under this crisis; there is no need to panic. Even if we have to forego dividends for two or three times, we shall surely overcome this crisis.*

While celebrating the company's past successes, Mr. Kaku also constantly reminds his colleagues that no organizational form or process holds the eternal truth. The need to change with a changing world is inevitable. For example, despite being the creator of the product division-marketing company split, he was considering rejoining these two in the nineties:

> *In the future, our major efforts in marketing must be concentrated on clearly defining and differentiating the markets of the respective products and creating appropriate marketing systems for them. In order to make this feasible, we may have to recombine our sales subsidiaries with the parent company and restructure their functions to fully meet the market's needs.*

While constantly aware of the need to change, Kaku also recognizes the difficulties managers face in changing the very approaches and strategies that have led to past successes:

> *In order for a company to survive forever, the company must have the courage to be able to deny at one point what it has been doing in the past; the biological concept of 'ecdysis' – casting off the skin to emerge to new form. But it is difficult for human beings to deny and destruct what they have been building up. But if they cannot do that, it is certain that the firm can not survive forever. Speaking about myself, it is difficult to deny what I've done in the past. So when such time comes that I have to deny the past, I inevitably would have to step down.*

Exhibit 1 Canon, Inc. – Ten-year financial summary (millions of yen expect par share amounts)

	1990	1989	1988	1987	1986	1985	1984	1983	1982	1981
Net sales:										
Domestic ¥	508,747	413,854	348,462	290,382	274,174	272,966	240,656	198,577	168,178	144,898
Overseas	1,219,201	937,063	757,548	686,329	615,043	682,814	589,732	458,748	412,322	326,364
Total	1,727,948	1,350,917	1,106,010	976,711	889,217	955,780	830,388	657,325	580,500	471,262
Percentage to previous year	127.9%	122.1	113.2	109.8	93.0	115.1	126.3	113.2	123.2	112.5
Net income	61,408	38,293	37,100	13,244	10,728	37,056	35,029	28,420	22,358	16,216
Percentage to sales	3.6%	2.8	3.4	1.4	1.2	3.9	4.2	4.3	3.9	3.4
Advertising expense	72,234	54,394	41,509	38,280	37,362	50,080	51,318	41,902	37,532	23,555
Research and development	86,008	75,566	65,522	57,085	55,330	49,461	38,256	28,526	23,554	14,491
Depreciation	78,351	64,861	57,627	57,153	55,391	47,440	39,995	30,744	27,865	22,732
Capital expenditure	137,298	107,290	83,069	63,497	81,273	91,763	75,894	53,411	46,208	54,532
Long-term debt	262,886	277,556	206,083	222,784	166,722	134,366	99,490	60,636	53,210	39,301
Stockholders' equity	617,566	550,841	416,465	371,198	336,456	333,148	304,310	264,629	235,026	168,735
Total assets	1,827,945	1,636,380	1,299,843	1,133,881	1,009,504	1,001,044	916,651	731,642	606,101	505,169
Per share data:										
Net income:										
Common and common equivalent share	78.29	50.16	51.27	19.65	16.67	53.38	53.63	46.31	41.17	34.04
Assuming full dilution	78.12	49.31	51.26	19.64	16.67	53.25	53.37	45.02	38.89	33.35
Cash dividends declared	12.50	11.93	11.36	9.09	11.36	11.36	9.88	9.43	8.23	7.84
Stock price:										
High	1,940	2,040	1,536	1,282	1,109	1,364	1,336	1,294	934	1,248
Low	1,220	1,236	823	620	791	800	830	755	417	513
Average number of common and common equivalent shares in thousands	788,765	780,546	747,059	747,053	746,108	727,257	675,153	645,473	564,349	515,593
Number of employees	54,381	44,401	40,740	37,521	35,498	34,129	30,302	27,266	25,607	24,300
Average exchange rate ($1 =)	143	129	127	143	167	235	239	238	248	222

Source: Canon 1990 Annual Report.

Exhibit 2 Canon – Sales by product (millions of yen)

Year	Cameras	Copiers	Other Business Machines	Optical & Other Products	Total
1981	201,635	175,389	52,798	40,222	470,044
1982	224,619	242,161	67,815	45,905	580,500
1983	219,443	291,805	97,412	48,665	657,325
1984	226,645	349,986	180,661	73,096	830,388
1985	197,284	410,840	271,190	76,466	955,780
1986	159,106	368,558	290,630	70,923	889,217
1987	177,729	393,581	342,895	62,506	976,711
1988	159,151	436,924	434,634	75,301	1,106,010
1989	177,597	533,115	547,170	93,035	1,350,917
1990	250,494	686,077	676,095	115,282	1,727,948

Source: Canon Annual Report, 1981–1990

Exhibit 3 Office size distribution, Japan 1979

Copier Market Segment	Number of Office Workers	Number of Offices	Working Population
A	300+	200,000	9,300,000
B	100–299	30,000	4,800,000
C	30–99	170,000	8,300,000
D	5–29	1,820,000	15,400,000
E	1–4	4,110,000	8,700,000

Source: Breakthrough: The Development of the Canon Personal Copier, Teruo Yamanouchi, *Long Range Planning*, Vol. 22, October 1989, p. 4.

Exhibit 4 Canon's major international joint ventures

Category	Partner	Description
Office Equipment	Eastman Kodak (U.S.)	Distributes Kodak medical equipment in Japan; exports copiers to Kodak
	CPF Germany	Equity participation in CPF which markets Canon copiers
	Olivetti (Italy) Lotte (Korea)	Joint venture for manufacture of copier
Computers	Hewlett-Packard (U.S.)	Receives OEM mini-computer from HP; supplies laser printer to HP
	Apple Computer (U.S.)	Distributes Apple computers in Japan; supplies laser printer to Apple
	Next, Inc. (U.S.)	Equity participation; Canon has marketing rights for Asia
Semiconductors	National Semiconductor (U.S.)	Joint development of MPU & software for Canon office equipment
	Intel (U.S.)	Joint development of LSI for Canon copier, manufactured by Intel
Telecommunications	Siemens (Germany)	Development of ISDN interface for Canon facsimile; Siemens supplies Canon with digital PBX
	DHL (U.S.)	Equity participation; Canon supplies terminals to DHL
Camera	Kinsei Seimitsu (Korea)	Canon licenses technology on 35 mm Camera
Other	ECD (U.S.)	Equity participation because Canon values its research on amorphous materials

Source: Canon Asia, Nomura Management School.

Exhibit 5 Canon Organization Chart

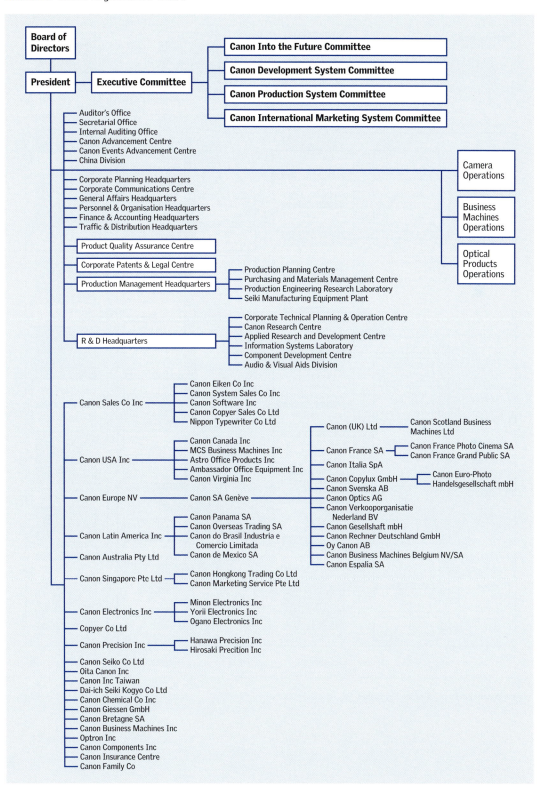

Exhibit 5 continued

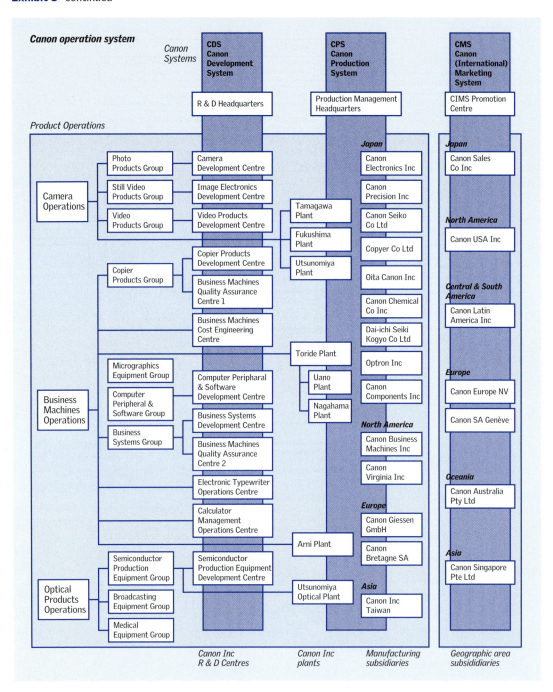

Source: Canon Handbook, published by Canon, Inc.

Case 8 LVMH: Managing the multi-brand conglomerate

LVMH Moët Hennessy Louis Vuitton, based in France, is one of the world's leading luxury goods companies. It operates in wines, spirits, fashion goods, leather goods, perfumes, cosmetics, watches, jewellery and retailing. The company employs approximately 56,000 employees. Its global distribution network grew from 828 stores in 1998 to 1,592 stores in 2004. The majority of sales are derived from the fashion and leather goods division, with Europe (including France) being the biggest regional contributor. The company is the largest and most widely spread luxury goods company, with a strong brand portfolio and distribution skills. LVMH's 'star brands' is a key foundation of the group's strategy. It has built over time one of the strongest brand portfolios in the sector, counting 60 top brands among its five divisions and other operations. At the core of the fashion and leather business is the Louis Vuitton brand itself. This 'star of star brands' is estimated to generate over 80% of earnings in the segment.

....

The case was written by Ashok Som, Assistant Professor of Strategy and Management at ESSEC Business School. It is intended to be used as a basis for class discussion rather than to illustrate either effective or ineffective handling of a business situation. The author gratefully acknowledges Lilly Liu, Deepak Yachamaneni, ESSEC MBA Exchange students, and Boris Gbahoué, ESSEC MBA student, for their research help. The case was compiled from published sources and generalised experience.

Distributed by The European Case Clearing House, England and USA.

North America: phone: 11 781 239 5884, fax: 11 781 239 5885, e-mail: ECCHBabson@aol.com.

Rest of the World: phone: 144 (0)1234 750903, fax: 144 (0)1234 751125, e-mail: ECCH@cranfield.ac.uk.

The case discusses the following critical challenges for LVMH:

♦ sustaining its organic growth strategy

♦ competition strategy

♦ managing multi-brand strategy with star brands

♦ managing a decentralized conglomerate

♦ the leadership and charisma of Bernard Arnault in creating, maintaining and managing a global conglomerate

♦ people issues in the luxury industry.

Introduction

The mission of the LVMH group is to represent the most refined qualities of Western 'Art de Vivre' around the world. LVMH must continue to be synonymous with both elegance and creativity. Our products, and the cultural values they embody, blend tradition and innovation, and kindle dream and fantasy. (www.lvmh.com)

On 4 March 2004, 54-year-old Bernard Arnault stood under his Picasso painting at the LVMH headquarters in Paris and pondered the future of his fashion empire. He had just announced a 30% rise in net income for 2003, with improved profits for all sectors of the business except watches and jewellery. Margins for the flagship leather goods brand Louis Vuitton topped 45%, due to the increased publicity spending featuring the actress Jennifer Lopez in its latest global ad campaign.

As the chief shareholder in LVMH Moët Hennessy Louis Vuitton, and his ownership stakes in the high-profile labels of Christian Dior, Givenchy, Louis Vuitton, Christian Lacroix, Kenzo, Céline, Emilio Pucci, Fendi, Loewe, Donna Karan, and a substantial investment in Marc Jacobs, much of the future of world fashion is in his hands. His properties also include Tag Heuer watches, Moët and Chandon champagne, and a chain of duty-free shops that dot many international airports. The fashion conglomerate's leadership in the luxury sector has been sustained by new product launches, store openings and an increased investment in communications. The group has continued its new launches and initiatives in 2004, including the new leather goods Damier Geant line, the Théda bags, an entire new jewellery line at Louis Vuitton, a new perfume for women at Dior, a new fragrance for men at Guerlain, an array of watch and jewellery creations, and the new Ellipse Cognac from Hennessy.

LVMH has continued to develop its worldwide distribution network. The Louis Vuitton brand, which celebrated its 150th anniversary, opened its largest store in the world in New York. Advancements in markets with significant potential for luxury products, such as Asia, have also bolstered the group's performance. Future focus will be likely on new growth markets and regions such as China, a market with considerable potential for cognac, fashion and perfumes; Russia with promise notably for Sephora, which has already shown promise in several Central and Eastern European countries; India, where Louis Vuitton opened its first store in 2003.

However, the €12 billion fashion and liquor conglomerate controlled by Bernard Arnault is not without worries. Wall Street continues to question whether the company's multi-brand strategy can be sustained. He has to consider the increasing importance of succession as he is approaching the legal retirement age; he would soon need to plan about his successor, someone to replace him at the helm of his group.

Company background

History

Established in 1987, LVMH was created by the fusion of two fashion houses: Louis Vuitton, a leather goods specialist founded in 1834, and Moët-Hennessy, a wine and spirits group created in 1971. The luxury group grew through key acquisitions and the development of new products. Under the leadership of Bernard Arnault, the 1990s saw a period of great expansion with the purchase of large stakes in the company's subsidiaries. In recent years, the luxury group has begun to shed some of its portfolio, with the strategy of focusing on its 'star' brands, defined by Arnault as 'timeless, modern, fast-growing and highly profitable' brands (see Exhibit 1 for a list of the recent acquisitions and divestitures). Observers comment that 'This collection of global brands was the stepping stone for realizing lucrative synergies in the fashion business, which would add to the bottom line.'

With over 56,000 employees and approximately €12 billion in revenues during the fiscal year 2003, the LVMH group operates in five primary sectors: wines and spirits; fashion and leather goods; perfumes and cosmetics; watches and jewellery; and selective retailing. LVMH today controls more than 60 luxury brands across its product lines. The acquisition strategy at LVMH always focused on brands that had strong brand power, resulting in the company reaching leadership positions in almost every segment it served. Each division functions as a strategic business unit (SBU) with its own general manager and a top management team. These divisions also manage overseas sales of their respective lines.

Wines and spirits

The wines and spirits division contributed 18% of sales and 36% of the operating profit in 2003. LVMH, through Hennessy, holds 40% of the cognac market and between 20% and 25% of the overall champagne market. In the premium champagne segment, LVMH has a dominant share of 50% built around exclusive brands such as Moët Chandon and Veuve Clicquot. It has also ventured outside the traditional wine belts in France and Italy to acquire high-end wine producers in California and Australia. Given the rising prominence of both California and Australia in the wine business, these moves allowed the company to market a truly global selection of wines and champagnes. However, considering the total liquor market, LVMH does not figure in the top 10 due to the absence of its drinks in the 'popular segments' such as beers, whisky and vodka. However, this is in line with LVMH's strategy to focus only on high-margin activities. Analysts have suggested spinning off the wines and spirits businesses as a separate unit as they consider it to be non-core to LVMH's fashion image. For example, the sale of Pommery, a profitable champagne brand, in 2001 was a strategic move by LVMH. The brand was bought for the vast lands it owned in the Champagne region; as high-quality land is limited in this region, LVMH wanted more land to produce more grapes for its Moët and Veuve brands of champagne. When Pommery was purchased, its land was also acquired, but when it was sold, the land was retained and only the brand was sold.

Fashion and leather goods

The fashion and leather goods division contributed 35% of sales and 60% of the operating profit in 2003 and had an operating margin of 32%. Much of the sales of this division are concentrated in the Asia-Pacific region, particularly Japan, which accounts for 33% of the sales. Sales in this segment are directly attributable to the Louis Vuitton brand. This label has grown by leaps and bounds under the leadership of its legendary designer, Mr Marc Jacobs. Demand for Louis Vuitton products has often exceeded supply, requiring customers to go on a waiting list that often took several months to clear. The Louis Vuitton label, combined with the strength of the LVMH group, has provided opportunities for expanding into new brands and products. Using this as a launching pad, the company engaged in significant brand expansion efforts to reach a wider audience. These efforts were well supported by fashion buyers.

The company has been able to leverage synergies across its fashion brands. For example, its Kenzo production facility has been transformed into a logistics platform for men's ready-to-wear products serving other brands such as Givenchy and Christian Lacroix. Given the historically lower profit margins in the ready-to-wear market, synergies resulting in cost savings have boosted profitability. As Muriel Zingraff, Harrods' fashion and beauty director, observed:

> What I will say is that we may have more patience with smaller brands if they are owned by a parent company such as LVMH or the Gucci Group.

Perfumes and cosmetics

The perfumes and cosmetics (P&C) division contributed 18% of sales and 8% of the operating profit in 2003. This division has an enviable collection of brands such as Christian Dior, Guerlain, Kenzo, and Givenchy. The company has recently acquired popular US brands such as Bliss, Hard Candy, Urban Decay and Fresh that were geared towards a younger clientele. These acquisitions are an integral part of the drive to internationalize LVMH's perfumes and cosmetics offerings. Europe is the largest market for perfumes, perhaps due to the heritage of the brands that the company offered. The P&C division has been able to leverage R&D synergies across brands; while its R&D expenditure is in line with the industry norms, LVMH has been able to generate twice the average growth rate in the industry. It is believed that these R&D skills would help boost sales of the acquired companies. As part of a larger drive to consolidate margin in this division, the company has been integrating R&D, production, distribution, sourcing and other back-office operations across brands. These moves have been beneficial. For example, integrating the purchasing function across brands has resulted in cost savings in raw materials of 20%. Analysts believe that this division is well positioned to reap the spillover benefits arising from the co-branding strategy under which many of the brands are linked directly to ready-to-wear apparel brands, a unique avenue of differentiation at LVMH.

Watches and jewellery

The latest portfolio addition at LVMH, watches and jewellery, contributed 4% of sales and 2% of the operating profit in 2003. In the watches section, the company owned prestigious brands that included Tag Heuer, Ebel and Zenith, and in the jewellery section, Fred Joallier and Chaumet. The purchase of the Zenith brand was crucial to LVMH's strategy to expand its watches operations. Most watches have an identical manufacturing process and brands reflect minor differences in quality. According to industry sources, there are only three manufacturers in the world from whom all the luxury watchmakers source their products. It is noteworthy that Zenith is the only manufacturer in the world of a certain component used in every watch. LVMH wanted a platform to sell more watches by utilizing its design experience and the production know-how of Zenith. Watches can be one of the most lucrative segments at LVMH with margins as high as 80%.

Unlike its constellation of brands in other divisions, many think that the company does not have quite the same star power in watches and jewellery. Competitors such as Richemont, Hermès and Bulgari seem to have more recognizable brands and more upscale products in this category. However, tangible synergies appear to be a definite possibility because the division could centralize the manufacturing and utilize Tag Heuer's expertise in retail distribution across all brands. The jewellery business is also extremely competitive due to the presence of leading brands such as Cartier and Van Cleef & Arpels. Despite the Place Vendôme heritage of both Chaumet and Fred Joallier, neither of them is currently profitable.

Selective retailing

The selective retailing division contributed 25% of the sales and 5% of the operating profit in 2003. The vertical integration strategy of LVMH came to fruition when the selective retailing arm was established. This division manages LVMH investments in Sephora, DFS Galleria, and Miami Cruiseline Services. While this division contributed 26% of company sales in 2002, it had not made a profit in the previous three years. DFS Galleria, with 150 duty-free and general merchandise stores, is the world's largest travel retailer. Acquired in 1996, this business was a victim of poor timing, since the Asian financial crisis hit soon thereafter. LVMH has since instituted several good management practices, including the execution of a strategy that would reduce DFS's reliance on Asian airports, selective closing of underperforming stores and the creation of DFS Galleria stores in large metropolitan areas. Despite these changes, Japanese travellers are still its most important and loyal customers and any economic development that hurt Japanese travel will invariably find its way to DFS's bottom line.

Miami Cruiseline Services (MCS) was acquired in January 2000. It offers retail services on board cruise ships and includes 76% of the world's major cruise lines (over 100 ships) as its customers. Conceived as an extension of the DFS concept, Miami Cruiseline focuses primarily (90%) on North American passengers, thus counterbalancing the over-reliance on Japanese tourists. It also manages duty-free operations at the Miami International Airport, the gateway to Latin America, opening possibilities of strengthening LVMH's brands in a region of the world where they are still underrepresented.

In addition to these distribution-based assets, LVMH has recently acquired La Samaritaine, the prestigious Paris department store. The company has also entered the retailing end of the made-to-order tailoring business with the acquisition of Thomas Pink, the legendary Mayfair tailoring house

that has a worldwide reputation for excellence in shirts. Thomas Pink has retail outlets in the United States as well. LVMH has also taken a minority stake in the 200-year-old UK fashion retailer Asprey & Garrard, which has global aspirations of its own.

Functioning of the group

LVMH's five product groups are decentralized into production and distribution subsidiaries. Some of the major brands have their own national subsidiaries. Overlaying this, there is a regional structure, with corporate headquarters in Paris, New York, Tokyo and Amsterdam. The wine and spirits operations of Moët Hennessy have their own headquarters, with main offices in France and regional headquarters in Singapore.

Depending on the geographic region, LVMH has different organizational set-ups. In France, the hub of LVMH has individual headquarters for every brand, with an LVMH headquarters handling some centralized activities. In contrast, in New York, the central LVMH office houses the LVMH and Givenchy brands, while Dior and Fendi have their own US-offices. Tokyo centralizes the human resources function, and each brand operates independently on all aspects of business.

The Group's decentralized organizational structure helps the company to foster efficiency, productivity and creativity. LVMH strives to create a highly motivating and dynamic atmosphere for its employees, emphasizing individual initiative and offers real responsibilities – often early on in one's career. LVMH gives each brand almost complete freedom to pursue its creative vision. However, it does realize synergies through almost 20% discount in advertising by negotiating in bulk for all its brands.

The challenge of this structure is that it requires highly entrepreneurial executive teams in each company within the Group. This entrepreneurial spirit requires a healthy dose of common sense from managers, as well as hard work, pragmatism, efficiency and the ability to motivate people in the pursuit of ambitious goals.

Bernard Arnault: 'The Pope of Fashion'

Dubbed the 'Pope of Fashion', Bernard Arnault has spent the past 15 years building LVMH from a small clothing manufacturer to a conglomerate comprising approximately 50 of the world's most powerful brands. Trained as an engineer at the Ecole Polytechnique in France, Arnault joined his family's construction business where he worked for 13 years, before becoming the president of the company in 1978. In 1984, he left his family business to reorganize a French state-owned holding company, Boussac, which owned Christian Dior. In the late 1980s, Bernard Arnault took control of LVMH. With growing success in his business, Bernard Arnault acquired Givenchy (1988) and Kenzo (1993). Today, through a complex web of partnerships, Bernard Arnault owns at least 33% of the company's stock. Bernard Arnault is deeply involved in the creative process, far more than his peers. He believes that in the creative and highly seasonal fashion business, the ability to match effective CEOs with temperamental designers can make the difference between a star and a failure. He believes that *to have the right DNA in a team is very rare. It's almost like a miracle.'* Deemed the *Billionaire Matchmaker*, in the past 15 years he has formed close creative bonds with designer John Galliano, whose collections for Christian Dior have been hailed by fashion critics. His selection of Hedi Slimane has done wonders for Dior Homme, and his pairing of Marc Jacobs with Luis Vuitton has been a critical and financial success. His vision of the luxury and fashion industry, as he states, is:

> This link to creativity, it's not far from art, and I like it very much. You must like to be with designers and creators. You have to like an image. That's also a key to success. And at the same time, you must be able to organize a business worldwide.

Industry background

> Luxury is not the contrary to poverty, but a contrary to vulgarity. (Gianni Versace)
>   We are in the business of selling dreams. The strength of a brand depends on how many dreams it inspires. (Chanel)

The luxury products industry has been estimated to be worth $58 billion, excluding automobiles and travel. The breakdown by sector is shown in **Exhibit 2**.

Major players in the global luxury goods market include: LVMH Moët Hennessey Louis Vuitton, Richemont, Christian Dior, Gucci, Tiffany, Hermes, Swatch and Bulgari. Traditionally, the luxury sector has been highly fragmented, characterized by a large number of family-owned and medium-sized enterprises. In the past two decades, it has been increasingly dominated by multi-brand luxury conglomerates. Although smaller companies still thrive in this environment by serving niche markets, larger luxury goods companies have acquired or overtaken many of their smaller competitors. (See **Exhibit 3** for luxury market growth, by sector.)

Survival of the multi-brand strategy?

LVMH and France's biggest retail-to-luxury group Pinault-Printemps-Redoute (PPR), which controls Gucci, led the consolidation spree in the luxury industry in the late 1990s. More luxury conglomerates have emerged through acquisitions: many separate brands have united under a holding company structure intended to spread best practice and impose commercial and financial discipline. The goal is to allow firms to grow strongly without overexploiting a particular brand and killing exclusivity. However, Michael Zaoui, Morgan Stanley's head of mergers and acquisitions in Europe, has doubts on the viability of the multi-brand model, citing the slump in luxury M&A activity since 1999. *'It's a hotly debated issue ... but is the multi-brand model holding up?'* asks Zaoui, whose investment bank has been involved in every Gucci acquisition since 1999 as well as the initial public offerings of Bulgari SpA and Burberry PLC.

According to Zaoui, M&A in luxury goods slumped to $800 million in 2002 from $10 billion in 1999, and the rate of return on capital employed in the sector has dropped to 20% in 2001 from 32% in 1997. As companies seek to stretch their brands to target new customers, some 1,400 new luxury goods stores have been opened since 1999 – equivalent to strategic investments of $4.5 billion. Large advertising budgets are required to attract people to these new stores. According to Zaoui, the 10 leading luxury companies spent $1.1 billion on advertising in 2001, equivalent to 8% of sales, compared with 6%

of revenue in 1995. '*This expansion trend increases the inflexibility of the cost base … it can reduce margins if the growth's not there.*'

'Luxury for the masses'

There has been a systemic change in the luxury products market. In the past decade Gucci sunglasses, Prada handbags, and Louis Vuitton suitcases have become must-have items for many thousands of middle-class buyers. According to the Boston Consulting Group's newly released book, *Trading Up: The Transforming Power of New Luxury*, the trend in the market is towards mass elitism. While traditional luxury brands such as Louis Vuitton, Rolls-Royce and Hermes remain items for the elite, luxury has been democratized for all. According to BCG, 'new luxury' could range from a Starbucks frappuccino to a Porsche and can be extended across categories such as personal care, homewares and appliances, oral care, toys, restaurants and wines.

Consumers are in a 'state of heightened emotionalism' and often address feelings of being overworked, isolated, lonely, worried and unhappy by shopping for premium-priced products. 'New' luxury is the idea that middle-class consumers trade up to premium products because of emotional needs, to give them a sense of indulgence and personal fulfilment. They spend a disproportionate amount of their income on such goods, and trade down in other categories that are perceived to be less important. For example, a consumer may visit a Dior boutique to spend several hundred dollars on a Gucci handbag, and then go to a Wal-Mart or Carrefour to buy cotton socks.

This new middle-class market for luxury products creates a wide range of challenges for luxury conglomerates such as Gucci and Louis Vuitton, as they have to understand and cater to a different target consumer.

Market trends

In 2003, the luxury retail market segment was adversely affected by SARS (Severe Acute Respiratory Syndrome) in Asia, the US-led war against Iraq, the strengthening of the euro and a weak 'feel good factor' worldwide. SARS in Asia – which represents 30% of the sales in the luxury retail market segment – led to a general decline in travel and spending. Consumers in the United States also spent less in 2003 due to the war in Iraq and a weak economy. According to a study by Cotton Inc., published by *Women's Wear Daily*, consumers put 39% of their disposable income into savings and 14% to pay down debt in 2003. The strengthening of the euro has also led to a drop in tourism, which translated into lower sales in the luxury retail segment since a significant portion of luxury retail sales is generated by Japanese tourists. A strong euro also means equal sales in foreign currencies now appear as less euro revenues. All of these events contributed to the weak 'feel good factor' in 2003.

The luxury sector is cyclical and partially correlated to economic conditions. The luxury retail market segment appears to be rebounding in 2004 after two years of lacklustre performance. Mr Arnault predicted that the coming years will be '*very good for luxury because the world economy is doing well. The US is booming, interest rates are very low and there is a lot of optimism, Japan recovering, and China and the Far East are growing fast.*' Consumers dug into their pockets during the 2003/2004 holiday season to purchase more of the finer things in life. This turnaround in the luxury retail market segment ends the slump that plagued the market since the 11 September 2001 terrorist attacks.

So, signs of a turnaround in the luxury retail market are surfacing as consumer confidence improves and spending increases. In addition, performance in the luxury retail market segment is expected to improve throughout 2004. According to Mike Niemira, chief economist for the New York-based International Council of Shopping Centers, '*2004 will be a year of transition. Luxury items are strong and I think they are going to continue to be strong.*' Consumer spending in the United States is being propelled by the rebounding stock markets, President Bush's $350 billion tax-cut plan, and improving employment rates. Consumer spending in Asia is also recovering after the SARS epidemic.

In the long term, growth opportunities for the luxury retail market remain positive. The luxury retail market is currently driven by Japan, Europe and the United States. However, this market will include other parts of Asia such as China and

Eastern Europe in the future as these regions become richer.

Competition

Traditionally, the luxury goods sector has been very fragmented and was dominated by small and medium-sized companies that have over the years developed expertise in a particular product. But since the late 1990s – the boom years – the sector has been governed by multi-product and multi-brand conglomerates. Growth by acquisitions has been an important strategy for all the major players in this industry. Conglomerates have been trying to pre-empt each other in acquiring brands that have managed to survive successfully. This race has changed the dynamics of the industry from being 'creativity focused' to more 'financially focused'. The years since 2000 have seriously dampened spirits as sales stagnated and the conglomerates are paying a heavy price for their acquisition spree.

As the luxury goods industry looks to move beyond the three turbulent years, the independent and family-controlled companies that yielded the spotlight to sprawling conglomerates during the boom years are claiming a measure of vindication. The heads of several of the world's leading fashion houses said that their strategy of resisting corporate advances had worked. It gave them better control over production direction at a time when consumers are showing signs of weariness with the glitz and hype of some of fashion's biggest names. *'Never be exploited; don't give up control of design,'* says Giorgio Armani, head of the company he owns.

While keeping it in the family may make sense from a brand-development standpoint, it does have limitations. During the past three years, a weak global economy has tested the financial resources of a number of family-owned luxury goods houses. There is also the question of what happens to companies that become associated with the name, charisma and creativity of a larger-than-life founder. While Armani himself has steadfastly resisted the idea of offering shares to the public, he refused to rule out the option of bringing in a big strategic investor, expressing willingness to partner with LVMH or PPR.

Selling to a bigger holding company does not always mean that a formerly privately controlled designer has to compromise on identity. When Phillips-Van Heusen bought Calvin Klein to help the biggest US shirt-maker compete against department stores, industry insiders were sceptical that Klein would be able to retain complete design control over his empire. Finances at one of the world's most recognizable brands were dismal. The designer had reportedly been losing up to $25 million a year on its couture collection and millions more on retail operations. Rather than clamping down on Klein's creativity, Phillips spun the label into two new mid-range sportswear lines and pledged to cut costs while keeping Klein's 100 designers. Klein continues to play an important role in the image-making of the company. This is an example that shows how designers can funnel their creative energies and coexist with large conglomerates that offer substantial financial support – as both parties have adopted a middle path in the quest for control.

GUCCI–PPR: what after Tom Ford?

Originally a reseller of luggage that was imported from Germany, Gucci took advantage of the economic expansion following the First World War. Since then, the company has displayed an innovative streak, improvising leather alternatives. After the Second World War, Gucci began its global expansion strategy with a store in New York in 1953. The company suffered setbacks in the 1970s and 1980s after scandals and murder plots. There was intense fighting within the Gucci family that resulted in poor strategy and dilution of valuable brand equity. In the late 1980s, Investcorp bought 50% of the company. The revival of Gucci commenced with the appointment of Mr Domenico De Sole as the CEO. The new CEO hired Tom Ford, a highly acclaimed designer who revamped Gucci's product designs. The company took firmer control of the brand, its products, and the distribution. Investcorp sold its holdings through an IPO in 1996, making a fivefold return on its original investment. This was followed by a bitter battle for control of Gucci by LVMH and PPR. Finally, after poison pill measures taken by the Gucci management, which did not deter LVMH, PPR raised its offer and took control of the group. The move was welcomed by the Gucci management comprising Domenico De Sole and Tom Ford, who preferred PPR to LVMH for fear of losing their 'creative license' if LVMH took over Gucci.

Gucci started a multi-brand model later than LVMH. It acquired Yves Saint Laurent's fragrance and ready-to-wear apparel lines and added the renowned shoemaker Sergio Rossi to its umbrella of brands. The multi-brand strategy was expected to deliver important synergies. Unfortunately, the benefits were never realized and YSL pulled down the group's earnings year after year. In the meantime, Gucci continued its aggressive ascent choreographed by De Sole and Ford. The brand is strong in North America today and its strategy of portraying Gucci as a youthful and sensuous brand has appealed immensely to the Americans.

After the PPR group acquired a majority control of Gucci, it started 'infringing' on the independence enjoyed by the creative duo of De Sole and Ford. It is ironic that the very same group that was supposedly chosen to protect the creative freedom was curtailing it. Tensions with the chairman of PPR group, Pinault, led to both De Sole and Ford refusing to renew their three-year contracts after 2004.

According to analysts, 'The decade of revival of Gucci from almost a dead brand to one of the most promising ones today made Mr Tom Ford a bigger name than Gucci and PPR would have immense trouble replacing him.' Adding to PPR's woes, in September 2003 a US court began investigating Pinault for fraud in an unrelated acquisition in the 1990s. These drawbacks have indeed put a question mark on whether Gucci and PPR can continue their growth in the future after Tom Ford exits.

A nagging concern for the PPR group is whether Tom Ford is going to be lapped up by the rival LVMH group. Bernard Arnault has been openly critical of Pinault and De Sole but has refrained from saying anything against Tom Ford since the Gucci episode in 2000. He has recently been quoted as crediting Ford as 'one of the best designers of his time'. These may reflect Arnault's intention to hire Mr Ford after his exit from Gucci. It could significantly affect the dynamics at LVMH if it can lure Tom Ford to its fold. Sources familiar with the situation feel that Tom Ford is more likely to join a smaller company or launch his own label than join LVMH. The reason for his quitting is the constraint over his freedom and,

given the temperament of Mr Arnault, Mr Ford's association with LVMH might not result.

This has created a buzz in the industry as to where Tom Ford is headed and also whom would PPR recruit to replace him. It seems particularly interesting as the new job profile for the position of head of Gucci is to be a person 'out of the Luxury Industry'. It remains to be seen if this proves to be a good option and whether a key figure in this industry can make, break or manage a conglomerate.

Managing a multi-brand conglomerate

Creativity and innovation are synonymous to success in the fashion business. As two analysts recently observed, 'Luxury brands must foster an appreciation and tolerance for creativity that is unconstrained by commercial or production constraints'. In almost all its acquisitions, LVMH had maintained the creative talent as an independent pool without attempting to generate synergies across product lines or brands. Lately though, the sourcing is slowly being centralized to gain synergies and cost savings with a centralized purchasing mechanism.

Bernard Arnault believes that 'If you think and act like a typical manager around creative people – with rules, policies, data on customer preferences, and so forth – you will quickly kill their talent.' The company has been decentralized by design and has a very small cadre of managers.

However, industry insiders cite that all is not well with a financial man like Bernard Arnault at the helm. His management style is described as providing 'constrained freedom'. For example, a manager for Céline could recruit someone himself, independent of the central LVMH human resources department, but he has to send a copy of the CV of the person he hired so that head office is kept aware of the new development. Though Arnault's managers are given autonomy, they know they are being watched and who has the final word in case of any conflict.

Another concern is the ruthless pursuit towards the bottom line. LVMH believes in 'running businesses profitably'. Managers are supported as long as they make money over the stipulated minimum: 'You have the freedom as long as you exceed *your targets. Once you do not … there is no freedom any more.'* The emphasis is on profit and if any division or company does not deliver, it will promptly be sold off. This approach contrasts with the traditional and creative view of 'Haute Couture', which accepts losses on some collections but waits for the market to accept its designs over a period of time.

Managing 'star brands'

The core pillar of LVMH's current business strategy is 'star brands,' coupled with innovation and quality. More specifically, Bernard Arnault describes the group's stellar financial performance in 2003 as '*a consequence of the priority placed on internal growth and profitability, the development of brands around the dual goals of innovation and quality, and the conquest of new markets.'* (See **Exhibit 5** for key financials.) According to Bernard Arnault, a star brand is one that is:

> *timeless, modern, fast-growing, and highly profitable … There are fewer than ten star brands in the luxury world, because it is very hard to balance all four characteristics at once – after all, fast growth is often at odds with high profitability – but that is what makes them stars. If you have a star brand, then basically you can be sure you have mastered a paradox.*

According to him, star brands are born only when a company manages to make products that '*speak to the ages*' but the feel is intensely modern. Such products are designed to sell fast, raking in profits for the fashion empire. This is a paradox and he confides that '*mastering the paradox of star brands is very difficult and rare.'*

Bernard Arnault has never specified exactly what those ten 'star brands' were but, using his criteria, the following luxury labels could be considered as star brands: Christian Dior, Louis Vuitton, Hermes, Cartier, Giorgio Armani, Gucci, Chanel and Prada. Of these, LVMH controls just two – Dior and Vuitton, of which he says:

> *if you take Vuitton, which has existed for more than 150 years, I think, today, it is also modern. Dior has been there for 50 years, but also I think it is the most hip fashion brand today.*

Innovation

Bernard Arnault believes that innovation '*is the ultimate driver, of growth and profitability. Our whole business is based on giving our artists and designers complete freedom to invent without limits.'* He has acknowledged past mistakes, including the rapid expansion of the Sephora beauty and fragrance supermarkets, for which he said LVMH had paid too much. After expanding too quickly in the United States, the company had to close stores and reposition the unit. In a business based on giving artists and designers the freedom to create without limits, LVMH allows each brand to run itself, headed by a creative director. Only 250 out of the over 56,000 employees are based in the Paris headquarters; the essence of the business is to identify the right creative people to stimulate new and cutting edge ideas, and trusting their instincts.

Quality

In the luxury products business, quality is essential in production as well as in product development. This is also an essential element in LVMH's success strategy. For example, to exercise the utmost control over the quality of its Louis Vuitton 'star brand,' the company owns manufacturing facilities employing over 4,000 in France, Spain and in the United States, among other countries. While LVMH produces its Louis Vuitton brand in-house, the firm outsources part of the production of its other fashion labels, such as Céline and Fendi. '*For all of our brands we manufacture part of the overall production within our facilities to be sure that there is a consistency between what is done by external subcontractors and what we do,'* explained Jean-Paul Vivier, executive vice president of the LVMH Fashion Group.

Managing people

Human resources and management talent are critical for the luxury conglomerate. When Arnault first began his consolidation, the group was full of problems, and only a few of the companies were profitable. HR Director Concetta Lanciaux confided that his primary concern was to '*have the best managers*'. Lanciaux's challenge was particularly difficult because there was a scarcity of executives in luxury goods at the time. Most firms were small, family-owned companies, without graduates or succession planning. LVMH had to recruit and develop talent from different fields. Regarding the mobilization of LVMH's resources, Bernard Arnault said:

> In a global context the progress of LVMH in 2003 will be based above all on the excellence of the fundamentals and its capacity to mobilize its internal resources. We can rely on our traditional strengths – namely the talent of our managers and employees and their determination to make the difference, the appeal of our major brands, the certain values – more than ever in a difficult period; the creativity and excellence of our products and the power of our distribution networks.
>
> We are continuing to deploy the organic growth strategy ... while still carrying out the sale of non-strategic assets, we will maintain strict management focus, enabling us to reinvest the cost savings achieved in the driving forces of our growth.

LVMH has encouraged and passed on the know-how, skills, the spirit of excellence, and the ethic that conveys, through its creations and products, an exceptional art of living, which is appreciated worldwide. The awakening and education of young people to these values has always constituted an essential part of the Group's goal. LVMH has carried out various original initiatives for young people in France and abroad. It is through these initiatives that primary school children, high school students, art students, young artists and designers, as well as those closer to the Group's new work opportunities such as college and higher education students, can benefit. In 1991, for example, LVMH partnered with Paris-based business school ESSEC to launch the luxury brand marketing LVMH ESSEC chair, funded with FF10 million. Further partnerships have since been launched in Asia as well.

The company had to hire people with experience in other industries, such as consumer goods, and select people with 'good taste'. Lanciaux cited engineering and business schools as specific sources of talent. LVMH also instituted strong company-wide induction and training programmes as well as on-the-job training to introduce the world of luxury to its capable, bright novices. Lanciaux explained:

> With some 40 brands potentially competing against each other in the Group, recruitment and everyday business becomes complex. In the case of our Group, what builds value and profits is the ability to act in an autonomous way and create new products. The business is built on the number of innovative products that come out every year – 20% to 30% of the turnover is based on new products. Therefore, our companies' senior executives have to have a large dose of autonomy and creative capacity. People use these as aspirational products, so we need people who manage and dream – and make others dream.

Despite the group's aggressive growth through acquisition, LVMH has tried to treat such moves sensitively, with a vision of integration. Lanciaux commented:

> First of all, it was about respecting, identifying and then preserving all of the assets of the company – not changing everything at once. One of the mistakes that companies in this situation make is that they want to change everything and bring in their own culture. When we buy these brands, we buy them to develop them. To develop the brand, the first thing you need to know is what makes that brand. Very often it's a number of people who are behind it, often invisible ... You have to find them, make them visible. This means that we have been able to preserve the integrity of these brands. Our style is not to go in there and replace everybody – never.

Jean-Paul Vivier, executive vice president of the LVMH Fashion Group, agrees that the Group seeks to foster creativity not just among its design teams, but also with professionals throughout the business. He compares the process to mixing the perfect cocktail – LVMH tries to build a work environment that promotes creativity and at the same time adheres to strict business disciplines.

Integration, training and top management seminars designed to support business strategies played an essential role in the professional development of the LVMH Group. Since 2001, it steadily increased the number of training days for all personnel categories within the Group and in centres located in Paris, New York, Hong Kong and Tokyo. The total number of training days in 2001 was 103,585 worldwide. Each of the companies is developing a specific training programme that reflects its own vision of excellence and its strategic objectives. At Louis Vuitton, which operates in 44 countries, vendors from all over the world participate in 'brand immersion' seminars organized in Asnières, the company's birthplace and communications centre. They tour the workshops built in 1859 and the Louis Vuitton travel museum. These sites are filled with the spirit of the company, which has remained constant even as it adapts to changing fashions and trends – a spirit embodied in the skills of the craftsmen, the details, and a unique talent for anticipating, analysing and meeting the requirements of the contemporary world. In 1999, Hennessy developed a teaching game called 'Strateco' that takes place over two days. It is designed to make all non-managerial employees more aware of economic influences affecting the companies and their operating realities. Another programme, 'Decompartmentalizing people and their jobs', presents the mission, organization and business of each department in the company's portfolio and brings together participants from the various departments. Finally, the intercompany seminars offered to all the Group's managers focus on topics of mutual interest and are primarily designed to develop or perfect management, communication and leadership skills.

American designer Michael Kors joined LVMH and successfully revived Céline, a dusty brand. However, it didn't seem that anyone at LVMH noticed. During Kors's six-and-a-half-year tenure at Céline, the position of chief executive officer turned five times, from Nan Legeai, to Bernard Divisia, Yves Carcelle, Thierry Andretta and, finally, to Jean-Marc Loubier. At the same time, Bernard Arnault attended only two of Kors's fashion shows for Céline. In total, Kors estimated that he spent a total of three hours in Bernard Arnault's company, including the two shows and two 'hellos' when he ran into Arnault at the Dior store in Paris. Kors said:

Was I mistreated? No. Was I neglected? Yes. I never felt as though there was a strategy at LVMH as far as pitting the designers against each other or the brands against each other.

It's just that I never felt anyone was watching the smaller companies at all, but everybody was spending their time on the two first-born children – Louis Vuitton and Christian Dior. In a way, if you're a nice kid, no one pays attention to you. If you are a bad kid, you get spoiled.

Interesting is the case of Marc Jacobs. In 1997, Marc Jacobs was struggling to keep his namesake brand afloat. Bernard Arnault approached him with an irresistible offer to lend his creative flair to the venerable but stodgy Louis Vuitton label, in return for LVMH underwriting his beleaguered design firm. Jacobs's designs have helped boost sales and buzz around the $3.8 billion Louis Vuitton brand, which accounts for 60% of LVMH's operating profit. His multicoloured Murakami handbag alone drove over $300 million in sales. The 41-year-old designer was also able to develop his own Marc Jacobs label, which soared to about $75 million in sales in 2003, helped by a $50 million investment from LVMH.

However, tensions have arisen between the designer and the company. Mr Jacobs believes his ambitions to develop his own brand are being hindered by LVMH. He complains that the French conglomerate hasn't invested enough in the Marc Jacobs business and has locked him out of critical decisions about the operations at his own line. For example, in May 2003, LVMH, while closing its US fragrance division, sold the Marc Jacobs perfume to Coty Inc. without informing or consulting the designer. None of the proceeds went to Jacobs, instead heading directly to LVMH.

Due to its heavy dependence on creative and modern designs, the departure of key creative personnel would be devastating to Vuitton. Early this year, there was speculation that Jacobs might leave unless LVMH gave more backing to his clothing line. As seen in the example of Tom Ford and Domenico De Sole's departures from luxury rival Gucci, losing its young star designer may spell trouble for the Louis Vuitton brand.

In May 2004 a spokesman in Paris confirmed that Moët Hennessy Louis Vuitton SA has resolved a year-long dispute with the New York designer Marc Jacobs, artistic director of Louis Vuitton, and his business partner Robert Duffy, 49-year-old President of Marc Jacobs, by signing them to new

10-year employment contracts and committing to invest in the partners' Marc Jacobs International fashion house. Under the new agreement, Marc Jacobs and Robert Duffy received salary raises and – for the first time – stock options. According to Robert Duffy, *'Now, Marc and I can achieve our dream of turning Marc Jacobs into a global power-house'*.

Conclusion

Although the Louis Vuitton brand is enormously profitable, none of the other labels rival its level of commercial success. With its current dependence on star designers such as John Galliano and Marc Jacobs, the Group's success is highly correlated to the whim of the creative. Given the current internal politics and recent departure of Michael Kors, will consumers remain loyal to the brand or the designer? The bigger questions are, can LVMH oversee so many luxury brands, make them all profitable and maintain the highest standards of creativity? After Bernard Arnault, how can one manage this 'loose' conglomerate that he has created in the last decade?

Case Questions

1   What does globalization mean in the luxury industry? What is the international strategy of LVMH? How does it differ from its competitors?

2   What are the factors influencing companies to seek growth by acquisitions in this industry? How are they managing and integrating these acquisitions? Is this growth sustainable?

3   Does LVMH's structure support its multi-brand strategy and functioning of the Group?

4   Comment on the nature of the competition in the luxury industry and the multi-brand strategy?

5   How is LVMH managing its creative talents? Does it differ from its competitors? If yes, how? If not, why not?

6   Comment on the leadership of Bernard Arnault and his management style. How is LVMH 'cultivating' leaders for tomorrow?

Exhibit 1 LVMH conglomerate at a glance

Wine & Spirits	Watches & Jewellery	Fashion & Leather	Selective Retailing	Perfumes & Cosmetics
Moët & Chandon*	TAG Heuer*	Louis Vuitton*	DFS*	Parfums Christian Dior*
Dom Pérignon	Ebel*	Loewe*	Miami Cruiseline Services*	Guerlain*
Veuve Clicquot*	Zenith*	Céline*	Sephora*	Parfums Givenchy*
Krug	Christian Dior Watches*	Berluti*	Le Bon Marché*	Kenzo Parfums*
Mercier	Fred*	Kenzo*	La Samaritaine*	Laflachère*
Ruinart	Chaumet*	Givenchy*		Bliss*
Château d'Yquem*	OMAS*	Christian Lacroix*		BeneFit Cosmetics*
Chandon Estates*		Marc Jacobs*		Fresh*
Hennessy*		Fendi*		Make Up For Ever*
Cloudy Bay		StefanoBi		Acqua di Parma*
Cape Mentelle		Emilio Pucci*		Perfumes Loewe*
Newton		Thomas Pink*		
MountAdam		Donna Karan*		

* indicates company status.

Acquisitions

1987   Fashion house Céline

1988   Fashion house Givenchy

1991   Champagne brand Pommery

1993   Fashion house Kenzo

1994   Perfume company Kenzo, cosmetics company Guerlain

1995   Jeweller Fred

1996   Leather goods specialist Loewe

1997   DFS, the luxury goods distribution network

1998   Sephora, the fragrance and cosmetics retail chain

1999   Champagne producer Krug and the watch manufacturer TAG Heuer, a 34% minority stake in the Italian luxury goods maker Gucci

2000   LVMH purchased the US start-up Urban Decay, and Donna Karan apparel line

2001   La Samaritaine department store, Acqua di Parma perfumes, a stake in Fendi

2002   Millennium & Company, prestige wines and alcohol

New business creations

1987   Christian Lacroix

2001   Newton and MountAdam vineyards

        Marketing De Beers diamond jewellery in a 50–50 joint venture

Divestitures

2001   Sale of stake in Gucci to Pinault Printemps Redoute

2002   Pommery champagne brand, Hard Candy and Urban Decay

2003   Canard-Duchene to the Alain Thienot Group

        Final stake of 27.5% in Phillips, de Pury & Luxembourg, an auction house

        Minority stake in Michael Kors, including cosmetics and fragrance licences

        Marc Jacobs and Kenneth Cole fragrance divisions

        Bliss spa line & Ebel watches

Exhibit 2 Breakdown of luxury goods industry

Sector	Percentage share
Tableware	4
Ready-to-wear apparel	26
Leather goods and accessories	17
Wines and spirits	15
Fragrances	12
Cosmetics	12
Watches	9
Jewellery	5

Source: Merrill Lynch Research.

Exhibit 3 Luxury market growth, by sector

Sectors of the luxury products industry	Annual sales growth 1998–2002 (%)
Home fashions	10
Ready-to-wear	10
Accessories	10
Leather goods	10
Watches and jewellery	8
Perfume and cosmetics	6
Crystal and silverware	5
Shoes	4

Source: Eurostat.

Exhibit 4 Representative primary competitors, by business unit

Product Sector	LVMH Businesses	Primary Competitors
Fashion and Leather Goods	Louis Vuitton, Loewe, Céline Berluti, Kenzo, Christian Lacroix, Givenchy, Marc Jacobs, Fendi, StefanoBi, Emilio Pucci, Thomas Pink, Donna Karan	Prada, Versace, Armani, Saint-Laurent, Chanel, Ralph Lauren, MaxMara, Burberry, Ferragamo, Hugo Boss, Gucci, Hermès, Bulgari, Lancel, etc.
Jewellery and Watches	TAG Heuer, Zenith, Dior Watches, FRED, Chaumet, OMAS*	Oméga, Breitling, Vendôme-Cartier, Cartier, Van Cleef & Arpels, Rolex, Ebel*, Baume et Mercier
Perfume and Cosmetics	Parfums Christian Dior, Guerlain, Parfums Givenchy, Kenzo Parfums, Laflachère, BeneFit Cosmetics, Fresh, Make Up For Ever, Acqua di Parma, Perfumes Loewe*	Many brands, including Lancôme, Lanvin et Armani, all brands under L'Oréal, Chanel, Yves Saint-Laurent, Gautier, Calvin Klein, Ralph Lauren, Estée Lauder, Shiseido, Hard Candy*, Bliss*, specialty perfumeries, etc.
Wines and Spirits	Moët & Chandon, Dom Pérignon, Veuve Clicquot, Krug, Mercier, Ruinart, Château d'Yquem, Chandon Estates, Hennessy, Cloudy Bay, Cape Mentelle, Newton, MountAdam	Pommery*, Marne et Champagne, Laurent Perrier, Seagram, Johnny Walker, Smirnoff, Rémy Cointreau, Rémy Martin, Courvoisier, etc.
Distribution	DFS, Le Bon Marché, La Samaritaine, Séphora, sephora.com, Miami Cruiseline Services	Many stores and retailing franchises

* Indicates former LVMH businesses.

Exhibit 5 Consolidated group performance (€million)

	2002	2001	2000	1999	1998	5-Year Growth
Total Current Assets	7,168	8,260	8,280	6,887	5,414	32.40%
Total Current Liabilities	6,890	8,017	9,829	8,615	6,328	8.88%
Total Assets	20,658	22,540	21,124	19,671	16,008	29.05%
Total Liabilities	12,864	15,122	14,947	13,194	9,408	36.73%
Total Common Equity	6,022	5,618	4,696	5,400	5,7365	4.99%
Income Statement	**2002**	**2001**	**2000**	**1999**	**1998**	**5-Year Growth**
Sales	12,693	12,229	11,581	8,547	6,936	83.00%
Cost Of Goods Sold	3,806	3,466	3,821	2,698	2,197	73.25%
Net Income	556	10	705	636	429	29.65%

Source: Thomson Analytics Financial Database.

Exhibit 6a Net sales by business group

Group	2001 (€m)	2001 % total sales	2002 (€m)	2002 % total sales	2003 (€m)	2003 % total sales
Wines & Spirits	2,232	18%	2,266	18%	2,116	18%
Fashion & Leather Goods	3,612	30%	4,207	33%	4,149	35%
Perfumes & Cosmetics	2,231	18%	2,336	18%	2,181	18%
Watches & Jewellery	548	4%	552	4%	503	4%
Selective Retailing	3,493	29%	3,337	26%	3,039	25%
Other businesses and eliminations	113	1%	5	0%	25	0%
Total	12,229		12,693		11,963	

Source: LVMH 2003 Annual Report.

Exhibit 6b Income from operations by business group

Group	2001			2002			2003		
	€m	% total sales	op. margin	€m	% total sales	op. margin	€m	% total sales	op. margin
Wines & Spirits	676	43%	30%	750	37%	33%	796	36%	38%
Fashion & Leather Goods	1,274	82%	35%	1,280	64%	30%	1,311	60%	32%
Perfumes & Cosmetics	149	10%	7%	161	8%	7%	178	8%	8%
Watches & Jewellery	27	2%	5%	13	21%	N/S	48	22%	N/S
Selective Retailing	213	214%	N/S	20	1%	1%	106	5%	3%
Other businesses and eliminations	353	223%	N/S	190	29%	N/S	161	27%	N/S
Total	1,560			2,008			2,182		

Source: LVMH 2003 Annual Report.

Exhibit 7 Net sales by geographic region

2002	
Other markets	6%
United States	27%
France	17%
Rest of Europe	20%
Japan	15%
Rest of Asia	15%
2003	
Other markets	7%
United States	26%
France	17%
Rest of Europe	21%
Japan	16%
Rest of Asia	13%

Source: LVMH 2003 Annual Report.

Exhibit 8 LVMH global reach (number of stores in 2003)

North America	344
Latin America	16
France	277
Europe	401
Africa & Middle East	6
Asia	287
Japan	232
Pacific Region	29

Source: LVMH 2003 Annual Report.

Exhibit 9 Benchmarking Louis Vuitton vs. other luxury brands

Brand	2003 sales ($bn)	Percentage change*	Operating margin (%)
Louis Vuitton	3.80	16.0	45.0
Prada	1.95	0.0	13.0
Gucci**	1.85	21.0	27.0
Hermes	1.57	7.7	25.4
Coach	1.20	134.0	29.9

* At constant rate of exchange
** Gucci division of Gucci Group
Source: Company reports, *Business Week*.

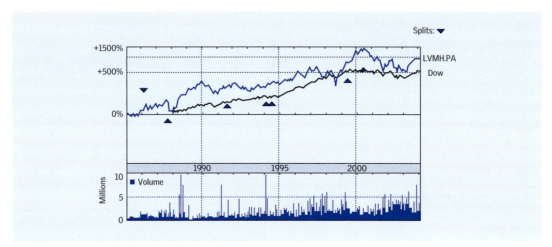

Exhibit 10 LVMH stock performance, 1985 to March 2004
Source: http://uk.finance.yahoo.com. Copyright 2003 Yahoo! Inc.

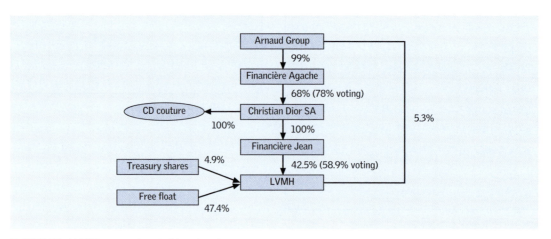

Exhibit 11 LVMH group shareholder structure
Source: Company data, UBS Warburg.

Exhibit 12 The 15 leadership factors
Identified by 450 LVMH Group senior executives during LVMH house sessions (October 2001)

Creativity

Comes up with a lot of new and unique ideas; easily makes connections among previously unrelated notions; tends to be seen as original and value-added in brainstorming sessions.

Strategic Agility

Sees ahead clearly; can anticipate future consequences and trends accurately; has broad knowledge and perspective; is future oriented; can articulately paint credible picture and visions of possibilities and likelihood; can create competitive and breakthrough strategies and plans.

Innovation Management

Is good at bringing the creative ideas of others to market; has good judgement about creative process of others; can facilitate effective brainstorming; can project how potential ideas may play out in the market place.

Managing Vision and Purpose

Communicates a compelling and inspired vision or sense of core purpose; talks beyond today; talks about possibilities; is optimistic; creates mileposts and symbols to rally support behind the vision; makes the vision sharable by everyone; can inspire and motivate entire units or organizations.

Customer Focus

Is dedicated to meeting the expectations and requirements of internal and external customers; gets first-hand customer information and uses it for improvements in products and services; acts with customers in mind; establishes and maintains effective relationships with customers and gains their trust and respect.

Priority Setting

Spends his/her time and the time of others on what's important; quickly zeros in on the critical few and puts the trivial many aside; can quickly sense what will help or hinder accomplishing a goal; eliminates roadblocks; creates focus.

Building Effective Teams

Blends people into teams when needed; creates strong morale and spirit in his/her team; shares wins and successes; fosters open dialogue; lets people finish and be responsible for their work; defines success in terms of the whole team; creates a feeling of belonging in the team.

Action Oriented

Enjoys working hard; is action oriented and full of energy for the things he/she sees as challenging; not fearful of acting with a minimum of planning; seizes more opportunities than others.

Drive for Results

Can be counted on to exceed goals successfully; is constantly and consistently one of the top performers; very bottom-line oriented; steadfastly pushes self and others for results.

Hiring and Staffing

Has a nose for talent; hires the best people available from inside or outside; is not afraid of selecting strong people; assembles talented staffs.

Motivating Others

Creates a climate in which people want to do their best; can motivate many kinds of direct reports and team or project members; can assess each person's hot button and use it to get the best out of him/her; pushes tasks and decisions down; empowers others; invites input from each person and shares ownership and visibility; makes each individual feel his/her work is important; is someone people like working for and with.

Business Acumen

Knows how businesses work; knowledgeable in current and possible future policies, practices, trends, and information affecting his/her business and organization; knows the competition; is aware of how strategies and tactics work in the market place.

Integrity and Trust

Is widely trusted: is seen as a direct, truthful individual; can present the unvarnished truth in an appropriate and helpful manner; keeps confidences; admits mistakes; doesn't misrepresent him/herself for personal gain.

Learning on the Fly

Learns quickly when facing new problems; a relentless and versatile learner; open to change; analyses both successes and failures for clues to improvement; experiments and will try anything to find solutions; enjoys the challenge of unfamiliar tasks; quickly grasps the essence and the underlying structure of anything.

Delegation

Clearly and comfortably delegates both routine and important tasks and decisions; broadly shares both responsibility and accountability; tends to trust people to perform; lets direct reports finish their own work.

INSEAD

Case 9 HSBC: Migrating for value

In September 2000, Raymond Or Ching Fai, General Manager of the Hong Kong and Shanghai Banking Corporation Ltd (HSBC), a subsidiary of HSBC Holdings plc, returned to Hong Kong from a one-week executive workshop at the group's London headquarters. The workshop had been designed to review the progress of each subsidiary in implementing the corporate strategy, 'Managing for Value' (MfV), introduced in 1998. Within HSBC, initial progress had been slow, yet employee grievances and internal conflicts had already emerged. While he agreed with his colleagues in London that it made the best 'commercial sense' for HSBC, Or was not looking forward to his latest task: migrating functions from the company's Network Services Centre (NSC) in Hong Kong to its global processing centre on the Chinese mainland.

HSBC Holdings plc

The HSBC name is derived from the Hongkong and Shanghai Banking Corporation, founded in 1865 in Hong Kong, to provide larger scale and more sophisticated banking facilities to local businesses. Almost immediately after its establishment, the new bank opened an office in Shanghai and began to build a network of offices with an emphasis on China and the rest of the Asia-Pacific region. The group's international acquisition programme did not begin until much later, in 1959, by which time a near monopolistic position in Hong Kong provided a secure foundation from which to finance global expansion.

In 1980, HSBC opened a representative office in Beijing, followed by representative offices in Guangzhou, Shenzen and Xiamen. In 1984, it became the first foreign bank since 1949 to be granted a banking licence, enabling the Shenzen office to be upgraded to a branch. In 1997, HSBC was one of the first banks to be granted permission to conduct renminbi[1] (RMB) business at its Shanghai Pudong Branch. By 1999 it had a network of 19 offices in mainland China, with an expanded renminbi business.

HSBC had also achieved a broad geographical balance of businesses outside Asia. By 2000, it represented one of the largest banking and financial services organizations in the world providing a complete range of personal banking, commercial banking and related financial services through some 5,000 offices in 80 countries and territories worldwide.

Managing for value

In 1998, HSBC responded to global developments in the banking industry by introducing a major group-wide change initiative, *Managing for Value: HSBC into the 21st Century* (MfV). On the banking giant's web site, the introduction to its corporate values emphasised the priorities of this programme:

> As a commercial organisation, our governing objective is to provide a satisfactory return on our shareholders' capital.

The MfV strategy aimed to double shareholder value in the five-year period 1999–2003 and again every five years thereafter. A series of initiatives were introduced across the HSBC group in a bid to align the organisation with this primary objective. These included:

This case was written by Sarah Meegan, Research Fellow, and Steven White, Professor of Asian Business and Comparative Management at INSEAD. It is intended to be used as a basis for class discussion rather than to illustrate either effective or ineffective handling of an administrative situation.

[1] The renminbi (translated literally as 'people's currency') is the official currency of the People's Republic of China. It is sometimes confused with the *yuan*, which is the currency's base unit.

- Transforming traditional branches to financial service centres.

- Strengthening the salesforce by recruiting dedicated Financial Services Executives (FSE) and re-deploying back-office staff to frontline operations.

- Streamlining the business processes and procedures.

- Migrating back-office operations, currently centralized in the Network Services Center (NSC) in Hong Kong, to the Guangzhou Data Center (GZC) in mainland China.

It was this final initiative which would prove most disruptive to Or's operation in Hong Kong, requiring careful planning and management, and raising myriad issues and concerns across the company.

Back-end jobs to low-cost centres

A guiding principle of the MfV programme was to pursue economies of scale across the various countries and territories covered by the HSBC group. As Keith Whitson, Group Chief Executive, had proclaimed:

A key initiative is the introduction of global processing. We now have two centers, the first of which was established in Guangzhou, China in 1996, and the second in Hyderabad, India in October 2000. These centers currently employ more than 1,000 people to handle routine workflow from both the UK and the Hong Kong Special Administrative Region (SAR). We plan to double our global processing capacity in 2001.[2]

Previously associated with the manufacturing sector, similar shifts in service industries worldwide had demonstrated an acceleration in the trend of basing low-end jobs in low-cost countries. The acceleration could be attributed, in part, to improvements in infrastructure such as internet connections and falling telecom costs in the host countries. It had also resulted from a corporate desire to concentrate resources on brand-name and customer relations,

leaving the back-office work to contractors. US companies, including General Electric and American Express, had been shifting back-end jobs to lower-cost centres since the mid-1980s, transferring credit card service centres to countries such as India. Other beneficiaries included Malaysia, the Philippines and Australia, as multinationals transferred data entry functions, accounts and call centre work worth millions of dollars.

Network Services Center (NSC) in Hong Kong

The Network Services Center (NSC) in Hong Kong represented HSBC's back-end operations hub, processing all transactions and customer requests on behalf of the branch network. By 2000, the NSC employed more than 1,000 staff divided between five key departments: Account Services (ASV), Payment Services (PSV), Credit Services Personal Banking (CSP), Collections and Recoveries-Secured (CRU-S), and Collections and Recoveries-Unsecured (CRU-U) (**Exhibit 1**).

Traditional processing and control

Since the NSC had been established, clear segregation of duties and responsibilities had operated across the various departments and between different levels of staff. To iron out a number of grey areas that had arisen over the years, complete sets of operating procedures had been produced and distributed to all employees. For the operations staff in particular, work patterns were extremely routine.

In order to manage the risk exposure and minimize potential errors, the NSC had adopted a 'dual control' approach to most processes: each data-entry input by an operator was subsequently checked by a verifier. In addition to this, a comprehensive set of checks and control measures were enforced, including a maintenance register for transaction processing, multi-level credit approval, and referral to branches/customers for information clarification. Some NSC staff was specifically assigned to perform stringent audit checks on tasks conducted by their colleagues.

Having worked in such a controlled environment for many years, most of the bank's operations staff were focused solely on their own tasks.

---

[2] The Implementation of HSBC's Strategy: a Review by the Group Chief Executive, HSBC Holdings plc, 2000 annual review.

Despite various improvements in the bank's internal systems and a corresponding reduction in risk, over the years the old procedures and practices continued to hold.

NSC review

As part of the bank's major change programme, Or instigated a review of the NSC operation which was carried out between November 2000 and January 2001. The objectives of the study were fourfold:

◆ To reduce the cost structure of the NSC.
◆ To identify suitable functions for cross-border processing.
◆ To identify revenue opportunities in the NSC.
◆ To optimize customer service levels through re-engineering activities.

Several hundred recommendations on the stream-lining of operational processes, simplification of control procedures, and development of new sources of revenue generation were proposed in the first round of the initiative. One of the most significant suggestions was the migration of functions from the NSC to the Guangzhou Processing Center (GZC), 180km north of Hong Kong, in line with the Chief Executive's directive on global processing. HSBC anticipated creating or facilitating a range of savings from this exercise, including reduction of head-count in the NSC division, reduction in the use of paper, release of premises for business unit expansion, introduction of fee-based services, enhanced process quality, and improved customer service levels.

Function migration to Guangzhou

The processing center at Guangzhou, established in 1996, was designed to house routine clerical tasks which required low-level skills and virtually no decision-making. It was ideally suited to tasks that could be automated and either partially or wholly replaced by computer systems, such as data entry. More complex jobs, which were time-critical, required specialized knowledge or skills, or involved important interactions with other departments such as credit approval or legal matters, would remain at the NSC. As a first step in the migration initiative, the bank conducted a series of re-engineering

projects in order to identify process stages already eligible for migration to GZC, and streamline others that could also be transferred. Opportunities for function migration to GZC were greatly increased through the extensive application of computer systems by HSBC.

One of the primary sources of cost reduction achieved through the move to GZC was the pay roll. The average salary of operations staff in GZC was as low as one-fifth of that in the NSC. In addition, a range of fringe benefits enjoyed by staff in Hong Kong, such as low-interest mortgage loans and pension funds, were not offered to their mainland counterparts.

Job losses at NSC

In March 2001, HSBC announced the migration of up to 300 posts (2% of its 14,000 strong workforce) to Guangzhou. Given the variation in duties and responsibilities, relocation of head-count was unevenly distributed across the five departments at NSC: 28% of ASV, 44% of PSV, 26% of CSP, 7% of CRU-S, and 36% of CRU-U would be moved to GZC.

While the NSC would become much smaller, the GZC data center was expanding at an increasing rate. The bank planned to achieve the head-count reduction in the NSC through staff re-deployment, natural attrition, and redundancies. Staff selected for re-deployment would be provided with an intensive one-month training programme to convert them to direct sales positions such as financial services executives. For the new GZC staff, the bank felt that minimal job training was required given the more simple nature of their duties. The bank also considered that each target function could be switched from the NSC to GZC overnight with no requirement for a period of parallel operations or trials.

Employee empowerment

During the NSC Review it had also been concluded that the operating environment was too heavily controlled: excessive checking, unnecessary referrals to branches and customers, and complex and redundant approvals. In order to avoid duplicate efforts, increase the productivity of the center, and better utilize its staff for value-added activities, the decision was taken to relax most of these measures and grant employees greater authority and autonomy in making decisions. For transaction posting and data capture tasks, where error rates had proven negligible, the traditional 100% duplicate checking was replaced by 10% random checking. The widespread use of registers in the NSC was also targeted for elimination.

To compensate for the simplification of the approval structure and decision levels, NSC staff were encouraged to take up additional roles and responsibilities. The existing transaction and credit approval limits, e.g. for invoice signing, loan application, loan restructuring and bad debt write-off, were revised upward for all staff categories and staff at lower grades were authorised to approve transactions below a pre-defined threshold. Employees were also encouraged to take certain decisions without referral to their superiors or further approval from senior management. The clerical staff, for example, could verify customers' signatures by themselves, staff officers (SOs) and section heads (SHs) could post payments to accounts without constant referral to the department manager, and the CRU manager approve a loan reconstruction without counter-approval from a senior manager. At the operations level, the clerical staff and SOs were empowered to amend simple data submission errors at their discretion without referring to the branches or customers. Staff in lower grades were also empowered to sign official documents or letters on behalf of their superiors.

Embarking on the function migration

In mid-March 2001, HSBC management briefed the 1,200 employees in Hong Kong who would be directly affected by the job relocation to GZC. On the same day, copies of a nine-page letter signed by the General Manager explaining the relocation were circulated to all 14,000 employees. In the letter,[3] Or explained:

Whilst we must increase the number of customer interface and sales roles if we are to meet our customers' future needs, back-office

processing and support services can more easily be transferred to low-cost offshore locations such as Guangzhou ... The resultant strategy will mean a change in the skills profile and the nature and mix of jobs between Hong Kong and Guangzhou.

The transformation of traditional transaction-based banking into a sales-oriented financial services organization was also confirmed in the letter:

We are now embarking on a major redeployment exercise for those immediately affected ... Equally, we will actually be growing the numbers of employees engaged in positions such as Mandatory Provident Fund[4] processing, customer service and product sales, so the total number employed by the bank in Hong Kong will remain around 14,000 or even increase somewhat over the next three years ... At the maximum, we expect no more than one to two per cent of our total workforce to leave the bank in 2001 as a result of this exercise, and we will be doing all we can to keep this number as low as possible.

However, there was no explicit reference to the exact number of jobs affected or to recent speculation that the bank planned to close many of its branches in Hong Kong. Or's letter remained vague on these points:

Historically, we have been very successful in redeploying those whose jobs have migrated to Guangzhou and elsewhere, and we will make every effort to do so again, through retraining and working with other Group companies in Hong Kong. However, we cannot guarantee that we will be successful in finding redeployment opportunities for everyone.

With the public announcement of the first job move to Guangzhou in March 2001, rumours abounded in the Hong Kong market that HSBC planned to cut as

---

[3] HSBC move may set trend: Group predicts more jobs will switch to 'cheap' mainland as it announces hundreds of transfers, *South China Morning Post*, 14 March 2001.

[4] MFP, the Mandatory Provident Fund was a fully funded, privately managed compulsory retirement scheme implemented by the Hong Kong Government in December 2000. Both the employer and the employee were required to contribute 5% of the employee's monthly cash income.

many as 1,200 jobs. Or responded by dismissing speculation on massive job cuts:

> The reports are all speculative ... this is an ongoing process. The bank would be committed to retraining and to allow the staff to adapt to a new environment.

He urged the bank staff, moreover, 'to adopt a positive attitude and try to upgrade themselves'.[5]

Morale, however, was extremely low and staff were left hoping for an early decision on their fate. Some were quite concerned, especially those who had negative-value assets because of the collapse in the secondary housing market.

Employee reactions

An officer in the hotline section of the bank's card center explained that even if he was fortunate enough to be re-deployed to a new frontline sales position, he had little confidence in performing as well as the existing salesforce because he lacked the practical experience and was not personally suited to that type of role. A white-collar staff member in his late forties he preferred the routine provided in his current post, but concluded that he would accept the bank's decision since it was commercially-driven.

Another employee, who had worked in NSC for over 10 years, was worried that she might not fulfil the sales job requirements. However, she needed to retain the low-interest mortgage that came with the job to reduce the burden of her negative-value apartment:

> The bank has neglected our interests. I work very hard to meet the bank's stringent requirements and plan to stay here until I retire. HSBC has recorded huge profits from Hong Kong virtually every year and we have always had trust in our senior management. The bank should have a moral obligation to provide employment opportunities to us first before offering them to people outside Hong Kong.[6]

Unlike London and New York, where those released could move to other parts of their respective countries, most employees would find starting a new career in the mainland an unattractive option not least because of its contrasting culture and inferior health-care system. On the other hand, some Hong Kong residents not employed by the bank were considering moving across the border where the price of an apartment was a fraction of the equivalent property in Hong Kong.

A background briefing paper entitled 'Migration of Jobs to Guangzhou—Questions and Answers' distributed to employees with the letter from Raymond Or, had confirmed that labour costs were a significant factor (**Exhibit 2**):

> The pay packages of Guangzhou employees are structured in accordance with local market conditions. As you will be aware, living costs and salaries in mainland China are, in general, substantially lower than in Hong Kong.[7]

Reactions from Guangzhou

Contrary to their counterparts in Hong Kong, staff in the GZC processing center welcomed the bank's policy of relocating jobs across the border.[8] In a recent recruitment exercise conducted in Guangzhou, HSBC had hired Derek Cheung, a 28-year-old credit processing officer who had worked previously for the China Construction Bank. When asked why he was interested in working for HSBC, Cheung explained:

> It is a golden opportunity to work in a company with such a global brand name like HSBC. I will definitely be admired by every one if I succeed. Apart from this, the salary offered is higher, almost double that of similar posts in other banks. There are also opportunities for me to shift to other job positions and learn different operations in a bank.

Jobs in the banking industry were considered above average if not prestigious. Most employees—usually

---

[5] HSBC confirms moving HK backroom ops to China, *The Business Times Singapore*, 14 March 2001.
[6] Interview with HSBC employee.

[7] HSBC move may set trend: Group predicts more jobs will switch to 'cheap' mainland as it announces hundreds of transfers, *South China Morning Post*, 14 March 2001.
[8] Mainlanders eager for HSBC jobs: Guangzhou staff willing to work for quarter of salaries paid in morale-hit SAR, *South China Morning Post*, 15 March 2001.

university educated—enjoyed housing allowances and received higher wages than the average worker. Vera Wong had already worked in the GZC processing center as a data entry clerk for one year since graduating from Guangzhou University with a Bachelor's Degree in Business Administration. When asked why she chose to stay at HSBC when she had such good qualifications, Miss Wong replied:

> I think it is good to learn and work from the basics. The working experience here will definitely make my resume look better.

Market reaction

In addition to problems within the bank, HSBC faced increasing opposition from the Hong Kong market, and not just from concerned customers. With 220 branches serving 75% of Hong Kong's adult population, the bank found itself at the centre of a controversy over its objectives. Letters and comments from angry residents flooded in to local newspapers:

> I take it that only bottom-line considerations are being taken into account by management to ensure that the bank remains viable amid the increasingly competitive global financial-services market ... Any entity that carries the Hong Kong name but intends to subjugate the job security and welfare of its local staff in order to achieve the practical bottom line should obviously not be allowed to make representations of the SAR in any manner.[9]
>
> Mainlanders used to look up to Hong Kong for everything from the skyscrapers to its vibrant economy. But the sense of envy has eroded since the handover. Guangzhou is getting close to being on a par with it, so Hong Kong should sense the risk it faces in the future.[10]
>
> It may make commercial sense for HSBC to start to transfer its operations to the mainland, but it shows a lamentable disloyalty to the place

that has made the bank one of the richest and most profitable in the world. For generations it has held a privileged position here in Hong Kong, being virtually the central bank of the territory and wielding huge influence over government policy—and never in a way which has been to its own advantage ... It might be thought that all this would promote an allegiance to Hong Kong which goes a little beyond the easy dollars to be made by employing cheap staff in Guangzhou.[11]

The local community was concerned that, as a huge and influential organisation, HSBC was liable to set a trend. HSBC itself had predicted that its relocation to Guangzhou would signal off a trend that other companies would follow. In his nine-page letter to employees, Or explained that:

> While the bank is taking a lead, we believe that more and more Hong Kong companies will undertake similar migration exercises for processing roles.[12]

The company's latest announcement had come on the back of Standard Chartered Bank's attempt to cut staff by 20% by centralising back-office processing and customer support in India and Malaysia. These moves had also sparked alarm among local unions who warned that Hong Kong could see more hollowing out of low-end service sector jobs, as had happened in the 1980s. In a recent protest, several activists from the Confederation of Trade Unions had blindfolded one of the landmark lion sculptures outside HSBC headquarters in Central, symbolising what they perceived as the bank's failure to see the suffering of the people of Hong Kong.

David Hall, HSBC's Head of Public Affairs, was quick to assert that:

> If we are going to make changes, we have to do it in a sensitive way. Will we upset some people? We may. We hope not. We do see the importance of not upsetting the people of Hong Kong

---

[9] Guangzhou & Shanghai Bank a more apt name, Letters to the Editor, *South China Morning Post*, 1 April 2001.

[10] Mainlanders eager for HSBC jobs: Guangzhou staff willing to work for quarter of salaries paid in morale-hit SAR, *South China Morning Post*, 15 March 2001.

[11] Bank's move could start wounding exodus, Letters to the Editor, *South China Morning Post*, 1 April 2001.

[12] HSBC move may set trend: Group predicts more jobs will switch to 'cheap' mainland as it announces hundreds of transfers, *South China Morning Post*, 14 March 2001.

but we live and operate in a commercial and changing environment.[13]

Hall maintained that the group cared deeply about business ethics and supported two international codes of conduct for multinational companies – the United Nations Global Impact and the Global Sullivan Principles.[14]

Hong Kong vs. Mainland China

In addition to the eroding advantages from differences in costs, Hong Kong's position as the gateway to China was also under threat. By mid 2001, the mainland port of Shenzen had boosted the number of containers sixfold since 1996, and with 300,000 Taiwanese working on the mainland and direct shipping and air links across the straits imminent, the comparative erosion was expected to continue. Cities such as Beijing, Shanghai and Shenzen were closing the infrastructure gap as billions of dollars were ploughed into port roads and telecommunications. Moreover, the quality of life in many of China's centres in terms of golf courses, shops, western goods, and high quality housing, meant that Hong Kong was no longer the only—or even preferred—choice for expatriates.

Accordingly, it was not just manufacturing jobs that were moving to the mainland but also service jobs, such as consulting. It was also becoming apparent that large Chinese companies, having established their credibility by listing on the Hong Kong or New York Exchanges, were turning to the higher-rated Shanghai market, giving the underwriting fees to Chinese firms in many cases.

Guangzhou and other Chinese cities near Hong Kong were attractive to employers—even though labour costs were among the highest on the mainland—because the local population spoke Cantonese, the same Chinese dialect used in Hong Kong. The proximity to Hong Kong also meant that documents for processing could be transported by road in a few hours.

---

[13] For Love or Money? *South China Morning Post*, 31 March 2001.

[14] The two codes lay down principles in such areas as protecting human rights, avoiding discrimination, and eliminating forced and child labour.

Cooperation between NSC and GZC

Within a short period of the first tasks being migrated to Guangzhou, it became apparent to Or that the new operations were not running as smoothly as anticipated.

One example of the emerging problems was the processing of customer instructions, such as correspondence address updates, which were received from customers at bank branches and traditionally passed to the NSC. Before the function migration to GZC, the NSC staff were responsible for checking whether the address had been completed or any required fields had been left blank before any information was put into the computer system. After the migration, however, the NSC was only required to consolidate the requests from all branches before forwarding them to GZC for data entry. Within a matter of weeks both branches and the NSC started receiving complaints from customers who had not been sent the standard letters and bills from the bank, or whose account information was incorrect. After checking the customer instructions against the records in the computer systems, it was found that the data was either not entered into the system in the exact format (e.g. wrong order in flat, floor and block) or was simply incorrect (e.g. confusing a 'P' with a 'D' or an 'F' with an 'E').

The NSC staff complained that their GZC colleagues did not understand the format being used and were trying to decipher customers' handwriting themselves rather than checking with NSC first. They also felt that the GZC staff had poor English and a limited knowledge of personal reference fields such as address format and district names, in Hong Kong. They further claimed that the GZC staff were not duly concerned about reading the data carefully as they were not in direct contact with customers and so did not have to answer complaints. Conversely, the GZC staff believed that the NSC was to blame for not checking the data before sending the forms to Guangzhou for data entry and insisted that it was the responsibility of the NSC or the branches to verify data accuracy before forwarding the files to GZC for processing.

A second round

In October 2001, HSBC announced that it would open a second data processing centre in mainland China (Shanghai) in the first quarter of 2002. The group had already moved its China headquarters from Hong Kong to Pudong in Shanghai in 2000.

Pending approval, a wholly-owned subsidiary, HSBC Data Processing (Shanghai), would be established, occupying six floors in Ciro's Plaza in Nanjing Xi Lu, in the Huangpu district of Puxi. The centre was expected to employ 250 people initially, with plans to increase this to 550 by the end of the year, and 1,000 over the next few years. HSBC's Chairman, David Eldon, stressed that although the opening of the new centre represented a transfer of jobs from Hong Kong to the mainland, it did not necessarily mean that staff in Hong Kong would be made redundant.[15] The Shanghai Centre would be engaged in data entry and account maintenance for HSBC operations in the Asia-Pacific in addition to the parent holding company's operations in Canada and Europe. It would be the third such centre serving Asia, alongside the Guangzhou office and a further centre in India. A second centre was also planned for India. Eldon claimed that HSBC would try to avoid involuntary staff cuts but could not guarantee that it would be successful in this endeavour.

Responding to the announcement of a second back-office service centre in China, Or predicted 'obvious' job losses in Hong Kong but countered this with other plans:

> Let's hope we are going to create new jobs by getting into other business areas ... I mean this year we went into Mandatory Provident Fund and that helped to create quite a number of jobs to absorb the surplus staff being released due to the migration of jobs to Guangzhou.[16]

In October 2001, HSBC announced that it would be freezing salaries for the bank's 14,000 staff. It was clear that it was still struggling to implement more cost effective work structures and procedures.

---

[15] HSBC arm to freeze staff pay, *Financial Times*, 20 October 2001

[16] HSBC in second mainland centre, *South China Morning Post*, 25 October 2001.

How could the bank learn from its earlier experiences in Guangzhou to facilitate a smoother function migration to Shanghai? What alternative approaches could Or/HSBC have employed in the first round of function migration?

At the same time, HSBC was seeking to significantly expand its business operations in the world's fastest growing market by acquiring stakes in mainland banks. In early 2002, it paid RMB 518 million for an 8% stake in the Bank of Shanghai (BoS). By April 2002, it was in talks with two further mainland banks—Beijing City Commercial Bank (BCCB) and Citic Industrial Bank, owned by mainland giant China International Trust & Investment Corporation (Citic). BCCB and BoS were both local banks, while Citic Industrial Bank was a national concern with 239 branches in 26 leading mainland cities. On 3 April 2002, HSBC became the second Hong Kong bank to obtain a licence to conduct foreign exchange business with mainlanders.

While China represented huge opportunities for new growth and cost-savings, implementing strategies had already proven difficult. HSBC had faced difficult challenges coordinating operations internally as well as harsh criticism from its own employees and customers in Hong Kong. How could the bank achieve a smoother transition and stem the backlash that future changes were likely to elicit?

Functions of NSC

The Account Services (ASV) Department provides account services support to customers. It is responsible for processing automatic payments, performing transactions and maintenance for international deposits, handling pre-processing and post-processing of maintenance requests and supporting all other types of account services such as court order, audit confirmation, Inland Revenue Department enquiries and document microfilming and retrieval.

The Payment Services (PSV) Department handles payments related to transactions and performs all kinds of pre-payment and post-payment processing. These include all types of outward and inward telegraphic transfer, clean cheques, and demand draft.

The Credit Services Personal Banking (CSP) Department conducts the processing of Home Mortgage Loans, Packaged Loans and Personal Financial Services General Banking Facilities.

The handling of Unauthorized Overdrafts and Effects Not Cleared items are also centralized in this department from the branch network.

The Collection & Recoveries Unit—Secured Credit (CRU-S) Department is mainly responsible for the collection and recovery of Home Mortgage Loans, Wayfoon Finance Hire Purchase and General Banking Facilities, arrangement of repossession of distressed properties and legal actions, handling of insurance claims as well as processing of voucher transactions and account maintenance.

The Collections & Recoveries Unit—Unsecured Packaged Product (CRU-U) Department is mainly responsible for the collection and recovery of delinquent or overdue payments on credit cards, and packaged products such as Personal Installment Loan, Personal Overdraft, and SuperEase accounts.

Exhibit 1 Structure of Network Service Centre in Hong Kong

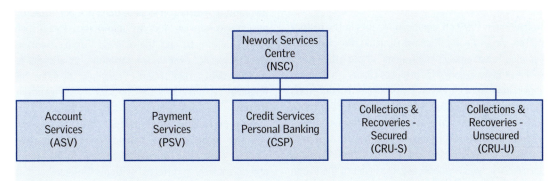

Exhibit 2 A price comparison between Hong Kong and Mainland China

	Hong Kong	Mainland China
Prime Office Space (rent)	US $6.30/sq.ft	US $1.90/sq.ft
Two-bedroom Apartment	$3,500/month	$1,000
Personal Assistant	$3,500/month	$500
International School	$14,500–$16,000/yr.	$17,000–$20,000/yr.
Business Lunch for Two	$51	$24
Taxi to Airport from Downtown	$48	$24
Commercial Broadband	up to $390/month	$180
Office Blessing (by Geomancer)	50 cents/sq.ft	6 cents/sq.ft

Source: A City Under Siege, Business Week International Edition, 23 July 2001.

INSEAD

Case 10 The house that Branson built: Virgin's entry into the new millennium

The music stops

Reflecting in 1999 on significant events in the history of the Virgin Group, Richard Branson, its chairman, remained extremely ambivalent about the most momentous decision of his business career – a decision that had been made seven years earlier. It concerned his acceptance of a £510 million cash offer from Thorn EMI, a UK conglomerate with extensive music interests, for his record label Virgin Music. A private company with tangible assets of less than £4 million, Virgin Music was, symbolically, the heart of the Virgin Group, having its roots in the late 1960s, when Branson and his first collaborators founded a record mail-order business in London. Its sale, therefore, meant a great deal more to Branson than simply another business transaction. He would part company with many people he had known since childhood and hand over a business that had been built painstakingly on cash flow using a combination of guile, flair, and luck.

In March 1992, Branson was a reluctant seller, but he was also a realist. He recognized that the cards were heavily stacked against him. The world economy – the airline industry in particular – was in the doldrums in the aftermath of the Gulf War. Virgin Atlantic, the airline he had founded in the mid '80s, had been badly affected by the turmoil in the Middle East. Moreover, it was being targeted in a competitive war by British Airways, which (it would later transpire) was using dubious tactics to gain advantage. Further complicating matters, the media were speculating on Virgin's financial health (prompted, if Branson's allegations are accurate, by misleading stories fed to journalists by British Airways); and behind the scenes, Virgin's bankers were pressing ever more strongly for a sale to reduce debt, reinforcing Branson's disdain for financial organizations that he saw as fair-weather friends.

More personally, Simon Draper, Branson's cousin and the creative force behind Virgin Music, had made it clear that he wanted to cash in his equity and do something different with his life. A vehement opponent of Virgin's move into the airline business from the outset, he envisaged his life's work collapsing with the airline, which was surviving only on the cash flow and guarantees provided by Virgin Music. And Virgin Music provided strong support indeed: only months before, the music label had signed the Rolling Stones, a sign of the position it had attained in the worldwide music business.

Branson realized that the sale of Virgin Music would transform Virgin's financial situation. After settling with the Japanese company Fujisankei, a 25 percent shareholder, and with Simon Draper and Ken Berry (a key collaborator and minority shareholder who had started at Virgin as an accounts clerk and who now runs Thorn EMI's music business), Branson would be left with over £350 million in cash – more than enough to 'fulfill [my] wildest dreams.'[1]

---

[1] Richard Branson, *Losing my Virginity* (London: Virgin Publishing 1998), p. 413.

Growing a business: a strategy for fun

'Putting the world to rights'

Richard Branson's business career started when, at the age of seventeen, he founded *Student* magazine – the 'Voice of Youth' – while still at boarding school. Based on co-operative principles, the magazine employed fellow students as workers and a nearby public pay phone as an office. *Student* was a product of the 1960s, the decade when the post-war 'baby boomers' came of age. Across Western Europe and North America, young people enjoyed educational, employment, and lifestyle opportunities unknown to their parents, all made possible by rapid economic growth. The decade became known for its promotion of a youth culture in which authority was challenged, fashions changed rapidly, and rock stars were the global gurus of a new age.

The initial success of the magazine (Branson optimistically claimed a circulation of 100,000) was not sustained. Seeking new activities to boost his flagging business, he decided to try to tap the potential he saw in the sale of records, still overpriced despite the abolition of retail price maintenance, a UK government policy designed to support certain industries by allowing manufacturers and suppliers to 'recommend' prices to retailers.

Lacking the capital to start a retail outlet, Branson and his associates simply placed an advertisement in the last issue of Student to test the market, listing only records likely to appeal to young people. Prices discounted those offered in stores by as much as 15 percent, and orders (accompanied by cash) came flooding in. Casting around for a name for his new business, he finally accepted a suggestion made jokingly by one of his coterie, who claimed that what they needed was a name that proclaimed their commercial innocence but also had a certain shock value, in keeping with the anti-establishment mood of the times. What better, therefore, than 'Virgin'? The name appealed to Branson and was adopted despite objections from the registration authorities, who deemed it to be in poor taste.

Branson quickly realized that buying and selling records in bulk required proper controls and systems. He turned to a childhood friend, Nik Powell, to help him manage his new business, offering in return a 40 percent stake in the company.

Methodical where Branson was erratic, cautious where Branson would overextend himself, Nik Powell became the ideal counterbalance in the record mail-order company.

In 1971 a national postal strike threatened to push the mail-order company into bankruptcy. Immediately Branson rented retail space, transferred his stock of records, and launched Virgin Retail. True to the emerging Virgin style, the shop's decor was a mix of the outrageous and the shabby, attracting customers more bent on enjoying an experience than spending money. Later that year, Virgin received its first overseas order. Realizing that records intended for export could be purchased by Virgin tax-free, Branson gave in to the temptation to make a quick cash profit by selling 'exported' records through his London store – until the tax authorities pounced.

Shocked and humiliated, Branson spent an uncomfortable night in prison. He was released only after a tearful appeal to his parents to put up £30,000 bail, using their home as security. Eventually, formal charges were dropped in return for an out-of-court financial settlement. Later, Branson would laughingly dismiss his night in a cell, but the pain and embarrassment he caused his parents made him resolve to 'avoid sleepless nights and pay taxes.' Even so, Branson remains an unwilling tax-payer and holds his Virgin shareholding in secret off-shore family trusts, preferring 'to reinvest profits in the business.'

While these setbacks were taking place, Branson had a piece of good fortune. Simon Draper persuaded him to consider backing Mike Oldfield, a nervous, troubled, and talented young musician who arrived at Virgin clutching a handful of recording tapes. Having already been rejected by the major recording studios, the young man was looking for friends and supporters. At Virgin he found them, and his first recording, Tubular Bells, was to launch him and Virgin into the big time.

Tubular Bells and the Sex Pistols

Released in 1973, Tubular Bells was an immediate hit, eventually selling over five million copies worldwide. The massive inflow of funds transformed the company. For Branson, this was the ideal opportunity to launch the Virgin record label and join the ranks of the small independent record producers that were active in the UK market at that time. Within two years, however, financial pressure forced Virgin to reassess its position to avoid becoming a one-hit record label. Its original creative policy, which focused on non-mainstream artists, was not working. Branson needed something fast to re-establish the Virgin name with the record-buying public. He achieved his aim in 1977 with a notorious punk rock band: the Sex Pistols. Debauched and drug-crazed, foul-mouthed and obscene, the Sex Pistols were the subject of intense media coverage and speculation until one of its members, already facing a murder charge, died of a drug overdose and the band disintegrated. But their short existence was a considerable fillip for Virgin.

By the end of the '70s, Virgin comprised a record label, recording studios, music retail outlets, music and book publishing, night-clubs, and cinemas. Virgin had prospered in a buoyant UK market. But as the decade closed, recession and high inflation, com-bined with changing consumer tastes, severely affected the music business worldwide. Sales con-tracted and few record companies earned profits. Virgin registered losses of £400,000 in 1980 and £900,000 in 1981. Although well-established, the record company was still a small player living hand-to-mouth in a business dominated by large multinationals.

With financial pressure mounting, Branson was forced to act. Looking to Nik Powell for solutions, he was offered belt-tightening measures that inevitably included laying off personnel, a task Branson has always found daunting and has avoided whenever possible, usually by delegation. The anxiety and ill-feeling that the various measures caused led to talk of union representation.

To some extent Branson himself had inflamed dis-content in his company. His personal business philosophy was simple: Why worry about the past? It is over and done. Look to the future to solve diffi-culties through new opportunities, expansion, and growth. Even as the company was firing staff, closing its US office, and cutting its roster of bands, Branson used scarce financial resources to purchase two night-clubs – Heaven, London's largest venue for homosexuals, and the struggling Roof Garden. He also launched a new London entertainment guide,

Event, founded to challenge the strike-bound market leader, Time Out. The launch was unsuccessful; within a year Event closed at a cost to Virgin of £750,000.

Branson's expansion-oriented actions created tension between him and his senior management, particularly Nik Powell. As Powell's working relationship with Branson soured, he realized that his ambitions were likely to remain unfulfilled while he was number two. Matters came to head over cre-ative policy. Despite limited funds, Simon Draper wanted to invest in new bands and to continue financing existing artists whom he believed would eventually be profitable. Nik Powell, advocating a more cautious, corporate-type approach, pressed for the pruning of loss-making bands. Obligated to make the choice that would settle matters, Branson, with some reluctance and sadness, backed Draper's artistic judgement over the more conventional approach offered by Powell.

His instinct proved right: within a short span of time, Virgin had some of the most profitable bands of the '80s – Phil Collins, Human League, Simple Minds, and the hugely successful Culture Club, led by the transvestite Boy George. Virgin successfully maneuvered itself out of the recession, nearly dou-bling its turnover from £48 million in 1982 to £94 million in 1983, with profits soaring to over £11 million. But Nik Powell was not around to share the success. Dissatisfied with his position, he had left the company in 1981, selling his shareholding in return for £1 million, Virgin's cinema interests, and a video recording studio. Branson was once again the 100 percent owner of Virgin, with two trusted lieu-tenants: Simon Draper and Ken Berry. (Both later acquired holdings in the record company after lengthy negotiations.) Branson, depending on Draper for creative decisions and on Berry for contracts and management, kept himself out of the day-to-day administration of the company to concentrate on new ventures.

In France, Germany, and Italy, Virgin companies were established to add local artists to the company roster and to represent UK bands. In the US, the Virgin label was re-established. The huge success of Virgin artists attracted increasing numbers of estab-lished and emerging bands to the Virgin stable, creating a portfolio of talent that challenged the industry leaders. In circumstances such as these, conventional business practice would dictate that success should be consolidated and expansion restricted to complementary activities. Such, however, was not to be Branson's way. He wanted to expand his company in a completely new direction. To the astonishment of music industry observers, the horror of Simon Draper, and the ridicule of the music press, Richard Branson was off on a new path: he was going to found an airline.

'Never let the facts get in the way of a good idea'

In early 1984, Branson received a call from Randolph Fields, the 31-year-old California-born lawyer who had founded British Atlantic, a transatlantic airline not yet off the ground that hoped to target business travelers. Fields, one of an increasing number of people arriving at Branson's door with ideas that needed backing, was seeking additional financing to get his airline airborne. Branson was all too aware of the dangers in entering the airline business: his company had no experience in that arena, the business was capital intensive, and revenue was highly seasonal. Furthermore, he recalled the recent experience of a UK cut-price airline, Laker Airlines, which had been pushed into bankruptcy by high debts, currency fluctuations, and ferocious competition from established national airlines. The industry Goliaths had slaughtered the upstart David in a battle whose echoes were still straining UK/US trade diplomacy in the mid '80s.

Yet, despite all these reservations and obstacles, Branson was persuaded by Fields's proposal. Within a week – 'We can decide something in the morning and have it running in the afternoon' is Branson's proud boast – he had formed a partnership with Fields, renaming the airline Virgin Atlantic. It was later dubbed by jokers the airline that Boy George built, a reference to the supposed source of cash injected by Branson into his new project. The launch in June 1984 saw him playing to the cameras dressed as a World War I pilot in leather jacket and goggles, the first in a long line of publicity stunts that were to become Branson's trademark.

One of a number of ex-Laker managers recruited by Branson was David Tait, now President of Virgin Atlantic North America, based in Norwalk, Connecticut. Recalling the launch of the airline he said:

> *I thought that Virgin was the most stupid name ever for an airline, and I told him that his plan [for business class only] was not a good idea and explained why. But with Richard, you never let the facts get in the way of a good idea! ... Despite what people think, it was never a budget proposition either – more a mix of economy and business class, which in those days only Air Florida had tried with success. Since we went into Newark and not JFK, we could also offer lower fares with less chance of reprisal. But our real secret was to offer value-for-money. Charge the same or slightly less for a much better product: first-class travel at business-class rates.*

The creation of his airline took Branson into unfamiliar territory. His business needed skills not previously required in the unregulated, open-market environment of the record industry. The airline business, by contrast, was – and remains – highly political: the awarding of jealously guarded international landing rights to (mostly) nationalized airlines involved protracted inter-governmental negotiations, requiring Branson to lobby the Thatcher government. Informally advised by Freddy Laker, Branson also had an eye to the future; he anticipated predatory pricing from the major airlines that would jeopardize his cost advantage – the Laker scenario all over again.

Randolph Fields, who had brought the airline idea to Branson, did not stay long with Virgin. His management style, Branson concluded, did not fit either the Virgin ethos or the detailed operation of an airline, although Branson recognized Fields's contribution in putting together the initial proposal. Behind the scenes, relations between the two became so acrimonious that Branson felt forced to oust Fields in 1985, buying his shareholding for £1 million. Fields later said that he had fallen in love with Branson on the day they met, but that Branson had fallen in love only with Fields's idea.

'From the rock market to the stock market'

In late 1986 a series of press and TV advertisements appeared in the UK under the slogan 'From the Rock Market to the Stock Market.' The advertisements invited the public to buy shares in the Virgin Group. Richard Branson, for so long a champion of private company status and the independence of entrepreneurs, had succumbed to the blandishments of City investment bankers to sell part of his company during the '80s bull market. He saw the move as an opportunity to raise capital quickly to reduce the company's dependence on short-term bank borrowing – and what Branson saw as demanding and short-sighted bankers – and to further expand without losing control of his company. (When the public company was eventually floated, Branson and his senior collaborators retained control of 63 percent of the voting stock.)

Much of the detail work of the flotation had been handled by Don Cruickshank, appointed Group Managing Director in 1984. A Scottish accountant with an MBA from Manchester Business School, Cruickshank had worked for the consulting firm McKinsey and had been in general management in the media industry. At ease in City circles, he was the kind of executive with whom bankers felt comfortable, an important factor in Branson's decision to recruit him via head-hunters.

Despite the demand for shares, the stock market flotation was not the success that Branson or the investors had expected. Although recording better-than-expected profits, Virgin's share price performed badly post-flotation and later fell precipitously when the London exchange crashed in October 1987. Moreover, relations between Virgin management and City analysts were at best uneasy. Branson was unsuited to cultivating the type of relationship that the chairman of a public company must have with institutional investors. While appreciating the discipline that being a public company had imposed on his company, he nevertheless felt that the City undervalued Virgin and failed to understand the entrepreneurial nature of his business, especially the music division. The analysts in turn were uncomfortable with the vagaries of a business where, it seemed to them, most of the assets – rock musicians and their creative output – were valued against the ephemeral nature of public taste. (More recently there has been evidence to show that established artists can create a steady revenue stream against which investment decisions can be calculated. The sale in 1997 of David Bowie's work via a securitized bond placement is a case in point.)

The analysts' doubts and concerns were reinforced by the unpredictable nature of the Chairman and the demands on his time from his publicity stunts, airline business, and charitable activities. Unwilling to tolerate the constraints placed upon him but determined to help the many small investors who had seen the value of their investment diminish, Branson finally resolved to quit the stock market. In July 1988 he announced his decision to raise privately £200 million to be used to buy out the publicly held shares at the original asking price, in effect compensating the original shareholders, both private and corporate, who at that point faced a considerable paper loss. Richard Branson thus honored a moral debt he felt he owed and was once more master of his own destiny.

'Too old to rock, too young to fly'

The unsuccessful flotation had forced Branson to review Virgin's activities and modus operandi. With a major debt to repay and still in need of a substantial capital injection to finance his ambitions for the company, Branson recognized that he needed external investors. However, his approach in the light of his stock market experience was to be more circumspect.

In the years following privatization, Branson, while still an opportunistic entrepreneur, nevertheless followed a path of growth through joint ventures with established companies. This approach permitted his company to expand, in terms of both product and geography. The most significant deal was the sale in 1989 of 25 percent of Virgin Records to Fujisankei, Japan's largest media company, for £115 million. That same year, another Japanese company – Seibu Saison, the hotel chain – paid £10 million for 10 percent of Virgin Travel, which had recently acquired landing rights in Tokyo through Virgin Atlantic.

In the UK, Virgin's retail interests were consolidated around the Megastore concept in a joint venture with a major retailer. In prestige locations in major cities, Megastores began to sell home-entertainment products – music, videos, and books – on a large scale. They replaced the string of small secondary retail outlets for which Virgin had become known. The success of the Megastore concept was exported to major cities throughout the world, frequently through joint ventures.

Virgin Atlantic had also advanced dramatically from the original operation envisaged by Randolph Fields. Although still a relatively small player, it now competed with the major carriers on the main routes out of London, winning awards for innovation and service as well as plaudits from vital business travelers. Virgin Atlantic had become a serious threat to the major airlines – none more so than British Airways (BA), the UK's national carrier, led by the ebullient and forthright Lord King.

However, the airline had suffered financially as a result of the recession and the Gulf War, perhaps more than Branson was prepared to admit publicly. He was reconciled to finding a major capital investment to ensure the airline's long-term survival, an ambition close to his heart. Internally, such capital could realistically come only from the sale of the record business – the jewel in the Virgin crown and the largest remaining independent record company in the world.

After long discussions with his immediate team, and wrenching soul-searching, Branson, advised by the investment bank Goldman Sachs, entered into negotiations with Bertelsmann of Germany and Thorn EMI, calculating that the time was ripe to conclude a sale on his terms. Thorn's offer of cash or shares (Branson took the cash) to a value of £510 million won the day, allowing Branson to clear his debts and to plan the expansion of his airline in the way he sought. Commercial to the last, Branson and Berry managed to win £9 million on currency speculation by delaying payment to Fujisankei to the last contractual moment.

Virgin Music was combined with EMI records, creating a music business with 18 percent of the world market. City comments that Thorn had overpaid for Virgin were quickly discounted. A rationalization of Virgin staff and bands improved Thorn's profits by more than £80 million in 1993–94. At the time of the sale, some Virgin Music employees felt that they had been let down by Branson. They had assumed they would share in the profits from the sale of the company, although no promises had been made. Many of the long-serving staff attended an emotional farewell party where a tearful Branson and Draper assured them that Ken Berry would be staying with Virgin and that its future independence within the Thorn EMI group was guaranteed. After the sale, Branson said, 'Too many entrepreneurs have gone down because they were not prepared to cash in their chips at the right time.'

The battle between British Airways and Virgin Atlantic, personalized around its two leaders (Lord King dismissing Richard Branson as 'too old to rock and too young to fly'), became increasingly acrimonious. Matters came to a head when a television program alleged that BA had used dirty tricks against Virgin Atlantic, breaking into its computer system to target its customers, spreading misinformation about Virgin's financial state, and diverting its customers at US airports to BA flights. Branson immediately sued BA for damages, claiming £11 million. Lord King's rebuttal was libelous and Branson won substantial damages, humiliating the BA chairman and accelerating his retirement after an otherwise distinguished business career. As a gesture to the airline staff, Branson divided the damages among them.

Coming of age?

The sale of the record company in 1992 saw the departure of many long-serving staff. This, combined with the evolutionary changes in retail, the growth of the airline, and the creation of new companies, moved Virgin away from its roots and previous management structure. From 1992 to 1997, the company was overseen by a triumvirate: Richard Branson, Trevor Abbott (the Group's Finance Director, brought in by Cruickshank), and Robert Devereux (Branson's brother-in-law, who headed the media and entertainment interests). These latter are no longer with Virgin. Robert Devereux, now a wealthy man, has achieved his aim of 'semi-retiring at forty' and spends his time climbing mountains; Trevor Abbott took his own life, motivated, it is believed, by serious personal problems and his diminishing role at Virgin. Their functions are now fulfilled by Simon Burke and Steven Murphy, respectively.

Research on the Virgin brand name in the early 1990s demonstrated the impact over time of quirky advertising and publicity stunts. The brand was recognized by 96 percent of UK consumers, and Richard Branson was correctly identified by 95 percent as the company's founder. The Virgin name was associated by respondents with words such as fun, innovation, success, and trust and identified with a range of businesses, confirming what Branson and others had believed: in principle, there were no product or service boundaries limiting a brand name, provided it was associated with a quality offering.

Encouraged by the research, Virgin began entering new sectors outside of its core activities of travel and retail. Virgin businesses as diverse as radio broadcasting, book publishing, and computer games found a home in the same stable as hotels, railways, personal computers, cola drinks, cinemas, and financial services. To manage this complex empire, Virgin increasingly employed the type of structure and people more usually associated with conventional companies. Branson continued to work at the center, supported by a small business-development group, a press office, and key senior advisors in the areas of strategy and finance. Although the firm is now housed in more elegant surroundings, the early Virgin style of informality and openness remains. There is not the feel of a traditional corporate head office: neckties are rarely worn, denim jeans are common, and everybody is on first-name terms.

Building on that evolutionary process started in the mid '80s, Virgin today is more likely to employ people (particularly at the management level) with direct experience of a relevant business activity, either through a career at Virgin or through training with a competitor. The policy of promotion-from-within that Branson practiced in the early days remains in force, especially in the larger companies, but has become more organized and less driven by short-term exigencies and Branson's whims. In acknowledgement of the fact that promotion cannot always provide the best candidate, the use of head-hunters is now an established practice for senior posts. Human resource tools such as assessment centers, personality profiling, and employee development are commonly used. Moreover, many managers have formal business training and qualifications, along with experience with multinationals or management consultancies, a profile that would have been unknown at Virgin in its early days. Despite this, there is still a belief, held by most of the senior management, that there are 'Virgin people' – those who, through their personality, style, or outlook on life, are better suited than others for the organization. (See **Exhibit 4**: Virgin People.)

Having a center did not mean a centralized operation, a notion that Branson resisted – at least until recently. Each operating unit was expected to stand alone, having little interaction with either the head office or other units. Unit managers networked informally (usually at parties and similar events) but were not obliged to follow prescriptive corporate policies; these were 'understood' rather than codified. For example, there was no common human resource policy. Managers knew that employees must be treated 'fairly,' since 'that is what Richard would want,' and they complied in their own way, whether in the UK or overseas. Similarly, there was no group information-technology strategist or central purchasing function, because Branson believed that those roles would constitute interference and discourage managerial creativity. In the same way there was no systematic seeking out of synergy, either at the center or by unit managers. Whenever synergy emerged, it was because the unit managers saw mutual advantage, not because a corporate policy dictated it.

This strategy was Virgin's modus operandi until 1999, when a chance remark from one of his senior executives made Branson rethink his approach. The executive mentioned to Branson that the managing director of a rival organization had commented that if Virgin companies ever decided to collaborate, they would be unstoppable. To test whether this was true, Branson immediately – and for the first time – brought together all his managing directors (some thirty in all) for a retreat at his hotel in Mallorca. The agenda was open, but two themes dominated – e-commerce and a proposed unifying document, the Virgin Charter.

During the discussion at the Mallorca meeting, the participants realized that, more by happenstance than planning, Virgin had found itself in businesses 'that are ideally suited to e-commerce and in which growth is expected to occur – travel, financial services, publishing, music, entertainment.' To exploit this potential, the participants decided to use tomorrow's technology to give all Virgin customers a small mobile device from which they could purchase any Virgin product – from a rail or cinema ticket to a CD or a savings product – and streamline online services with a single Virgin web address: Virgin.com. Virgin Net, another venture, is an Internet service provider created as a joint venture between Virgin and the UK subsidiary of NTL, a US computer technology company. Virgin is responsible for creative content and marketing; NTL provides the backup systems and software. Virgin Net targets the UK consumer market and wants to compete on 'value-for-money, speed, excellent customer service, and compelling content,' according to David Clarke, Managing Director. Much of its content is sourced from specialist suppliers (for example, the Independent newspaper for news). This idea took off in 1999; Virgin Net became a free service, and Virgin.com continued its expansion in e-commerce with a wide range of connections from Megastores online to train booking facilities (total internet revenues 1999 – £150 million).

During the meeting in Mallorca, the group also endorsed Branson's proposed Virgin Charter. Running to some sixty pages, the charter is an agreement between Virgin Management Ltd (in effect, the holding company) and all the subsidiaries. It defines the role of the center vis-à-vis the subsidiaries. The principal benefit the Virgin Charter is expected to bring is to create clearer information and communication flows between the Virgin shareholders, Virgin Management Ltd, and the Virgin companies. It covers topics such as taxation, legal affairs, intellectual property, and real estate, but it also outlines closer links in areas previously left to individual units: IT, people, purchasing. Thus the charter sets out ways for Virgin companies to tackle common activities with a common approach. (**Exhibit 5** shows Richard Branson's introduction to the charter.)

Branson has compared his current operation to a venture capital firm based on the Virgin brand. At the center, ideas (whether sourced internally or externally) are debated and analyzed, deals are struck, and new ventures are created. Potentially good ideas are disseminated outwards – quite often by Branson, who will 'call up [a manager] in his half-apologetic way and ask you to think about

a suggestion.' When deals or joint ventures are finalized, the implementation is delegated out, usually with considerable autonomy. A small example of the process is Virgin Brides. In 1995 Ailsa Petchley joined Virgin Atlantic as a member of its cabin crew. On one of her early flights she met Branson and got talking about weddings and the poor, often disjointed service offered to prospective brides. When she mentioned that she had a business idea offering a comprehensive service, she was given a few months to put together a plan. The net result was the creation of Virgin Brides, with Ailsa in the role of marketing manager, working in collaboration with a bridal-wear specialist from the US. The company is established but has a way to go to be profitable.

Along with the development of Virgin.com, Branson's last bold move at the close of the century was his deal with Singapore Airlines. During 1999 Branson had intimated that he might float part of the airline to raise capital for expansion. As the year was closing, however, he announced a surprise deal with Singapore Airlines that, in terms of fleet and revenues, is about three times the size of Virgin Atlantic. If the deal goes through, in 2000 Singapore will acquire a 49% stake in Virgin Atlantic at a cost of £600 million. The two airlines will work in partnership to maximise cost cutting synergies (eg maintenance, ground facilities, code sharing) but retain their respective identities and develop their own products. Industry observers saw the logic of the deal since in many ways the two airlines are complementary – their routes do not overlap and they both enjoy excellent reputations for service and innovation. There were, however, doubts expressed at the price that Singapore was paying, valuing Virgin Atlantic at more than £1.2 billion, a high figure in many observers' view.

The Virgin Group in 2000 comprised twenty-four individual companies or groups of companies (see Exhibits 2 and 3 for commentary and summary). Nearly all are private and owned entirely by the Virgin Group or by Richard Branson's family trusts. Branson sits on the board of most of the companies and usually, but by no means always, attends board meetings. He relies on others to bring serious problems to his attention: he has little time for reading long operational reports, market research, financial statements, and the like.

Richard Branson: a portrait

Jailbird or millionaire?

Richard Branson was born in July 1950, the first child and the only son of Ted Branson and his wife, Eve, née Huntley-Flint. He was later joined by two sisters, Lindi and Vanessa. The family has remained close, all enjoying what Richard was later to describe as a 'happy and secure' childhood.

Both Ted and Eve came from comfortable Establishment backgrounds. Ted was the son and grandson of eminent lawyers, a fact impressed on young Richard when he visited Tussaud's waxworks museum in London with his father and saw models of murderers sentenced to hang by Sir George Branson, his grandfather. Following family tradition, Ted left his Quaker-run school to study law at Cambridge University. After military service in World War II, he eventually qualified as a lawyer, but (perhaps because of his Quaker education or his naturally kindly disposition) his career in advocacy, where adversarial skills are vital, was slow to get started.

Eve Huntley-Flint came from a family of clerics, farmers, and stockbrokers whose womenfolk were expected to have horizons beyond the home. While still a young girl, she trained as a dancer and appeared in London theatres, both in dance reviews and as an actress, a somewhat risqué career for someone of her background. By the time she met Ted Branson, she had become an air stewardess, travelling to South America when air travel still contained a significant element of adventure and danger. Determined, self-assured and ambitious, at twenty-seven Eve was an attractive, outgoing young woman when she married Ted Branson, the reserved and fair-minded young lawyer.

Eve had decided views on child-rearing. While she was never a martinet, she pushed her children to be self-reliant and responsible, to take control of their own destinies rather than relying on others. One summer afternoon as she and four-year-old Richard were on their way home after visiting his grandparents, Eve told Richard to get out of the car and try to find his own way back. The farmhouse where they were staying was not far, but Richard got lost, ending up at the neighbor's farm to be collected by his alarmed parents. Eve Branson now admits that she may have been overly enthusiastic about encouraging Richard's independence, but she has never regretted it. Clearly, Eve admired strength of character. Furthermore, she was convinced that shyness in children was simply bad manners and a self-indulgence to be discouraged. She believed that her children's ability to overcome challenges would encourage the kind of spirit she wanted to see in them. Accordingly, she used her own considerable energy to organize activities, games, and projects for her children that were not only fun but also served a useful purpose. Holidays, weekends, and other free time were used productively. In line with that goal, the Branson household had no television, since it was 'time-wasting.' If money was short (as it was in the early days, when Ted's father cut off his allowance to protest his precipitate marriage), a solution could always be found in small money-making schemes that Eve thought up. Bemoaning one's lot was never acceptable to Eve, and she lived up to her own standards.

Ted Branson was never a strict and remote father figure. Rather, he acted as a calm and considerate backdrop to Eve's daily management of the children. Sympathetic and supportive by preference, a half-hearted disciplinarian if really necessary, Ted was less directly ambitious for his children than Eve, who expected, for example, that 'Richard [would] one day be Prime Minister.'

Richard grew up to be the archetypal naughty boy, frequently in minor scrapes, scolded for innumerable misdemeanors, and hyperactive in all he did. His parents found him both endearing and fatiguing. According to his father, Branson began his first business venture when he was eleven or twelve years old. He planted a thousand seedlings and then went back to school convinced that he would make a killing selling Christmas trees. Rabbits soon ate the trees, however. About a year later he tried another venture. This time the scheme involved budgerigars, a highly fecund type of small parrot. Another failure.

Richard's parents were particularly concerned about his progress at school, where – thanks to a strong physique and a competitive spirit – his main accomplishments were on the sports field. His schoolboy heroes were sportsmen, particularly cricketers, and adventurers such as Scott of the Antarctic, the famous British explorer and a distant relation by marriage. A serious leg injury, however, forestalled a promising career in athletics, while a period of forced intensive study finally gained his admittance to Stowe School, an exclusive English boys' private school with a liberal reputation. His indifference to schoolwork (not helped by long-undetected poor eyesight and dyslexia) continued, and he achieved only average results, ruling out a legal or other professional career. By contrast, Student magazine excited Branson with its possibilities and offered a timely and convenient exit from the educational treadmill. So, with his parents' reluctant blessing – his father's support was particularly influential – he quit school.

Branson left few friends behind him. While he was not unpopular, his energetic and single-minded pursuit of that which pleased him left little room for others. His indifference to the contemporary social mores and allegiances common in a school like Stowe left him somewhat isolated. His few friends were those he managed to inveigle into his varied and numerous projects. Commenting on the end of his schooldays, Branson said, 'Having left school without going to university, I decided to make money.... I never considered failure.' His headmaster had definite views about his future: 'Richard, you will either go to prison or become a millionaire.'

Working with family and friends

For a long time, Branson's office and home shared quarters in a canal houseboat. One bedroom served as the office of his two secretaries, while Branson operated from a dining table in the small sitting room. On occasion the bathroom served as the boardroom, with Branson conducting meetings from his bath. Eventually, when his two children 'started to answer the phones,' Branson was forced to move to a larger home, but he kept the houseboat as a private office. Nowadays, he runs his business empire from a large, elegant townhouse situated in London's diplomatic quarter. His home is in a similar building nearby.

His (second) wife, a down-to-earth Glaswegian from a working-class background, has no interest or role in his business life. She remains out of the limelight in the interests of their two children, providing an intimate family life to which Branson can retreat. Her stance is something of an anomaly at Virgin.

Contrary to conventional wisdom, Branson has always been a great believer in working with family and friends, convinced that the advantages outweigh the risks. Over time, his cousins, aunts, school and childhood friends, parents, and former girlfriends have all been drawn into his various business activities. His first wife found the situation difficult to accept, but even she is now in a joint venture with Branson, developing hotels in Spain.

The charges of nepotism that such arrangements usually engender were muted at Virgin, because of Branson's promotion-from-within policy. He has given many of his staff opportunities that their gender, lack of experience, or training would have precluded in more conventional companies. Of course, Virgin has been unconventional in other ways, too. Somehow, Branson has created the impression that people work at Virgin for fun rather than simply as a means of earning a living. ('More than any other element, fun is the secret of Virgin's success,'[2] he believes.) Notoriously indifferent to material possessions and unconcerned about everyday financial matters, the young Branson saw no problem in paying modest salaries provided people enjoyed themselves and felt part of an idiosyncratic enterprise that had a heart. If people were down, a party would revive spirits and, incidentally, give Branson the chance to play a practical joke on newcomers, an embarrassing rite of passage at Virgin that is partially maintained to this day. For example, when Branson hands out 'wings' to newly appointed cabin crew, he douses them in champagne. Similarly, the traditional annual company party that Branson used to throw at the recording studios (and now holds at his country home) has grown from a small Sunday event for 200 or so in the '70s to a marathon jamboree to which all Virgin staff and their family and friends can come.

A business philosophy

Much of Virgin's operating style was established not so much by design as by the exigencies of the time when Virgin was getting started. Nonetheless, it has proved to be a successful model that Branson believes he can replicate. His practice is to immerse

---

[2] Ibid. p. 431.

himself in a new venture until he understands the ins and outs of the business, then hand it over to a good managing director and financial controller, the two of whom are usually given a stake and then expected to make the company take off. (Branson can usually be relied on to engage in a publicity stunt of some kind that will give the company some initial awareness, jumpstarting the process. In the case of Virgin Bride, for example, he shaved off his beard and was photographed in a bridal gown).

Branson knows that expansion through the creation of additional discrete legal entities not only protects the Virgin Group but also gives people a sense of involvement with and loyalty to the smaller unit to which they belong, particularly if he trusts the managers of subsidiaries with full authority and offers them minority share options. He is proud of the fact that Virgin has produced a considerable number of millionaires. He has said that he does not want his best people to leave the company to start a venture outside; he prefers to make millionaires within.

His use of joint ventures, an extension of this model, has been reinforced by his dealings with the Japanese. Branson has been impressed by the Japanese approach to business, admiring their commitment to the long term and the way they take time to build a business through organic growth rather than acquisitions. He sees similarities between the Japanese *keiretsu* system (small companies interlocking in a collaborative network) and the structure he has created at Virgin, with numerous small companies around the world operated quasi-independently by the right people. Both systems embody the maxims 'Small is beautiful' and 'People matter.'

Branson explained these and other business maxims that he believes are necessary for success in a speech in London in 1993.[3] 'Staff first, then customers and shareholders' – this should be the chairman's priority if an organization wants better performance, according to Branson. Happy staff who are proud of their company make for happy customers who return. Job satisfaction is hampered when management is remote from all levels of staff,

relying, for example, on trade unions for communication. Branson cites his decision to keep 200 airline staff on the payroll, rather than lay them off during a recession, as a practical manifestation of this staff-first philosophy. Businesses should be 'shaped around the people,' Branson believes, citing his experience of subdividing the record company as it grew. Each new record label was given to up-and-coming managers, creating in-house entrepreneurs who were 'far more motivated to build a business' with which they, and the staff, identified. A natural extension of this is the notion of growing a business organically: 'Build, don't buy.' In accordance with that maxim, Branson has never made a major acquisition (as that term is usually understood).

His rivalry with British Airways illustrates his views on competition: 'Be best not biggest; compete on quality as well as price.' And his habit, since the early days, of recording good ideas in notebooks (dozens of these books have accumulated over time) supports his notion that the innovative business must 'capture every fleeting idea.' In a restless, creative business with an emphasis on experiment and development, 'ideas are lifeblood.' 'Drive for change' is another guiding principle in the Branson business philosophy. Branson is impatient with what he sees as the risk-aversive nature of British industry and commerce, and indeed society at large. 'It is great for tourism ... and airlines ... but has no place in industry.... We [at Virgin] experiment endlessly with new methods, new companies, and new marketing, especially when we can get others to pay for it!'

Formally expounding a business philosophy, however, is not a regular Branson activity. Indeed, in his autobiography he commented, 'Academics analyze ... we just hit the phones and get on with the business.'[4]

'Hero of the World'

In 1990, Richard Branson found himself in northern Japan preparing for take-off in an attempt to make the first-ever trans-Pacific crossing in a hot-air balloon, an event timed to coincide with Virgin Atlantic's inaugural flight to Tokyo. His Japanese hosts had invited a huge crowd to witness the event,

---

[3] Institute of Directors, London, 1993.

[4] Branson, *Losing my Virginity*, p. 12.

and banners had been hung declaring him to be the 'Hero of the World.'

The attempt was just one in a series of exploits undertaken by Branson. They began in 1985 when he attempted to cross the Atlantic in a high-powered speedboat to win the coveted Blue Riband, the prize awarded to the vessel and crew with the fastest time. The vessel sank off Ireland, but a similar attempt the following year was successful. In 1987, he and Per Lindstrand, an experienced balloonist, attempted the fastest trans-Atlantic balloon crossing, an aim achieved – but only after both barely escaped with their lives when the balloon made a forced landing in the Irish Sea. His latest endeavor, a round-the-world balloon flight, has now been abandoned following a rival's successful attempt.

Branson is happy to admit that these exploits were started as an inexpensive way of publicizing his trans-Atlantic airline, but with time they seemed to gain a momentum of their own. Asked how the chairman of a major corporation can justify the risks and expense, he replied, 'People who have to ask the question don't understand.'

Whatever his motives, Branson has come to be seen as a modern buccaneer with an appealing, devil-may-care attitude to physical danger as well as business risks. At the same time, he supports charitable, radical, and humanitarian causes. For example, he still funds a sex counseling clinic that he helped found in his Student days when his girlfriend became pregnant and they had nowhere to turn for advice. He also launched a new brand of condoms, Mates, as a response to the government's laissez-faire attitude towards AIDS and condom use. This is the kind of project that appeals to Branson: there is a benefit for society, money is raised for charity, and he has fun doing it. More controversially, he boycotted a magazine that refused to carry advertisements supporting the legalization of marijuana, although he personally dislikes illegal drugs following an ill-fated experiment with LSD. 'Richard could not stand to be out of control,' according to his girlfriend at the time.

Branson's exploits and causes are diverse, ranging from a health-care foundation supporting AIDS research to financial support for a new political publication. He bought and published a banned video on security matters, used his aircraft to rescue people trapped by the Gulf War, and led an initiative to help unemployed teenagers (although the initiative soon wound down). He submitted a bid to run the new National Lottery in the UK on a charitable rather than profit-making basis. He lost, later claiming that the winning consortium's representative had tried to bribe him to withdraw from the bidding. The representative sued but lost in court, paying heavy damages to Branson and standing down from his position.

Branson's esteem in UK public opinion at all levels is regularly demonstrated. In the 1980s he was the darling of the former Prime Minister, Margaret Thatcher; in the late 1990s he enjoyed good relations with Tony Blair's Labour government. He has been nominated for awards for enterprise, voted the most popular businessman, and named in polls by Londoners as the preferred choice for the new post of mayor, even though he has never put his name forward. In recognition of his services to entrepreneurship, the Blair government nominated Branson for a knighthood in the new millennium honours list. The soon-to-be Sir Richard Branson expressed his delight at the award, noting that 'neither I nor Virgin have ever made a political donation', underlining his long-held apolitical stance.

In general, Branson is the point of reference whenever comparisons are made between the traditional business leader and emerging entrepreneurs of the '80s and '90s. He is, however, a man of contrasts. The public persona is that of a warm, friendly, idealistic family man. Yet he is also a highly competitive workaholic and an extremely tough negotiator who thrives on bargaining.

The 'real' Richard Branson

Richard Branson has become an international celebrity, the subject of numerous profiles in gossip magazines, the business press, and television programs. Generally, this coverage has been sympathetic – especially in the UK, where he has achieved folk-hero status. Writers focus on his eccentric lifestyle, derring-do exploits, and new business ventures, comparing him favorably to more staid and conventional business leaders. Even the London tabloids, not known for their generosity to celebrities – indeed, often seeking out sensational stories about their private lives – seem willing to give Branson a relatively soft ride. They generally adopt a tone of friendly mockery about his exploits (although the failure to meet expectations in his rail company is starting to encourage negative press). He is frequently cited as a role model by young people wanting a successful business career that does not compromise personal ethics.

His detractors see Branson in different terms: a me-too operator, simply copying other people's ideas; an arch manipulator, fooling staff and consumers with warm words to mask his own grasping ambition; a fool with a death wish, driven by demons from his childhood to undertake ever-more risky exploits – whether commercial or physical – until eventually everything collapses about him.

Whichever point of view is right, in material terms Branson is undoubtedly successful. He became one of the UK's richest people before he turned forty, and recently he ranked as the eleventh-wealthiest person in the UK, with an estimated net worth of £900 million. Asked to explain the strategy that got him to this point, he talks of minimizing risks: 'Protect the downside, always be ready to walk away,' he says. 'But I have never thought of myself as a businessman. In my first venture I saw myself as an editor, only becoming a businessman to make sure my magazine survived.'

Over the years he has made strategic statements that, with hindsight, have not related closely to subsequent events. Most frequently, however, he eschews strategy in favor of fun: he says he simply wants to enjoy himself. But can a strategy for fun really explain the creation of a music company by a founder who, paradoxically, has little interest in or knowledge of music? Equally, it is difficult to explain how a shy man, ill at ease when speaking publicly or in private conversation with strangers, can become a supreme self-publicist. Or how an establishment-born figure with intrinsically conventional views can become the champion of radical and libertarian causes. Or how the man who is almost obsessive about fair play can negotiate ferociously for the last penny in a deal.

A London Sunday Times report on the British Airways affair quoted Lord King as saying, 'If Richard Branson had worn a pair of steel-rimmed glasses, a double-breasted suit and shaved off his beard, I would have taken him seriously. As it was I couldn't.... I underestimated him.' Perhaps Lord King is not alone in being misled by the hippie entrepreneur image that surrounds Branson. But if that image is not the real Richard Branson, then what is?

Virgin in the new millennium

In the year 2000, when Richard Branson celebrates his fiftieth birthday, he will have been leading Virgin for thirty-two years. (See **Exhibit 1** for key dates.) How many more years will he be at the helm? Can a company founded on youth, fun, and anti-establishment sentiments be run by someone with retirement on the horizon? Indeed, will Richard Branson ever *want* to retire? If not, what implications would his continuation have for Virgin and its management? If he does plan to withdraw, either partly or wholly, what impact would his retirement have, given that his persona is so closely associated in the eyes of the public and investors with Virgin and its ethos? Is there anyone else who could act as the public face of Virgin, who could step into Branson's shoes? He has children, but they are still in their teens; the elder, his daughter, has ambitions to become a doctor.

Typically, entrepreneurs do not pass on their heritage successfully. What needs to be done to ensure that Virgin endures? What potential dangers are there, and what preventative steps should be taken? Will it take a commercial or other calamity to force Branson to take a back seat, or will someone (family? friend? business associate?) be able to 'control' his instinctive tendency for expansion, growth, and risk taking, directing his energies towards an orderly transition?

Or is the only real danger the sudden loss of Branson himself? Branson argues that he is not the sole source of the company's success, that each major Virgin company could stand alone, led by an experienced management team. The Virgin brand, he says, is an independent entity that has an existence beyond its association with him. Moreover, the organization has the momentum and strength that would see it through a crisis. Is this assertion correct? If Branson goes, would the company lose the impetus for innovation and the 'can-do' culture that has for so long been its hallmark? Who would maintain the elaborate structure of financial deals, joint ventures, and interlinked companies? Would the abrupt departure of Richard Branson create a crisis of confidence so severe as to endanger the very survival of Virgin?

As time passes, questions about the future of Virgin (often brought to the fore by Branson's dangerous exploits) will increasingly be in the minds of shareholders, bankers, senior managers, potential partners, and myriad other interested parties. Has Virgin come of age to face a robust future, or is it on the cusp, about to enter terminal decline?

Exhibit 1 Key dates

1968	First issue of Student magazine published.
1970/71	Virgin mail-order operation started; first Virgin record shop opened in Oxford Street.
1972/73	First Virgin recording studio opened at The Manor near Oxford; Tubular Bells released; Virgin record label launched; music publishing operation established in the UK.
1977	The Sex Pistols signed by Virgin.
1978/80	First Virgin night-club (The Venue) opened; Human League signed to Virgin; Virgin Records presence in overseas markets expanded.
1981/82	Phil Collins, Boy George, and Culture Club signed to Virgin.
1983/84	Virgin Vision formed: film and video distribution, TV, broadcasting; Virgin Games launched; Virgin Atlantic Airways and Virgin Cargo launched; first luxury hotel launched (in Mallorca); the Music Channel, a 24-hour satellite-delivered music station, launched by Virgin Vision, which also produced the award-winning film 1984, starring Richard Burton and John Hurt.
1985/86	Business Enterprise Award for company of the year won by Virgin; Virgin Holidays formed; £25 million raised via convertible stock; Virgin Group floated on London stock exchange.
1987	Virgin Records America launched; Japanese subsidiary established; Rushes Video, London, acquired; 525, Virgin Communications LA-based post-production facility, launched; Virgin served as founding member of British Satellite Broadcasting Plc; majority holding in Music Channel sold; UK distribution rights for Sega computer games acquired; Virgin balloon company launched; first results from Virgin Group Plc made available – turnover: £279 million; pbt: £28 million.
1988	Olympic Recording Studios opened in London; Virgin Classics established to specialize in high-quality classical music repertoire; first Virgin Megastores opened in Australia, Glasgow, and Paris; smaller UK retail outlets sold to W. H. Smith for £23 million; Virgin Broadcasting formed to further develop Virgin's interests in radio and TV; three major business-class awards won by Virgin Atlantic, designated Britain's second-most-popular long-haul carrier; management buyout announced by Branson following the 1987 October stock market crash.
1989	Doubled pre-tax profits at £10 million announced by Virgin Atlantic, which also established its own engineering operations; 10 percent of Virgin Travel sold to Seibu Saison, Japan; 25 percent of Virgin Music sold to Fujisankei, Japan; long-term European distribution for Sega Video Games signed by Virgin Mastertronics as Sega became the number-one brand for video games in Europe; Virgin Vision sold to Management Company Entertainment Group (MCEG) of Los Angeles for $83 million.

➤

1990   Virgin Music Group launched second US record company based in New York; Megastores opened in Marseilles, Bordeaux, and Belfast; West One Television, a UK post-production company, created by Virgin Communications; joint venture signed with Marui retail group to operate Megastores in Japan.

1991   Ruling by the Civil Aviation Authority (CAA) won by Virgin Atlantic, allowing it to operate extra services to Tokyo by transfer of rights from BA; right won by Virgin Atlantic to operate services out of Heathrow (London) in addition to Gatwick (London), along with UK government approval to fly to South Africa; Virgin Mastertronic, Virgin Communications' European computer games distributor, sold to Sega of Japan for £40 million (though Virgin Communications retained the publishing division and began a rapid expansion of Virgin Games); Virgin Book Publishing formed in joint venture with W. H. Smith and Allison & Busby.

1992   Virgin Music Group sold to Thorn EMI Plc; first video-game software in Europe released by Virgin Games; Westwood Studios Inc., a Las Vegas–based developer of computer software, acquired; Virgin Games SA established in Paris; purchase of DC-3 announced to establish new US carrier Vintage Airtours, to operate a daily service of nostalgic trips from Orlando to the Florida Keys; UK's first national radio rock station launched in joint venture with TV-am Plc; post-production interests consolidated by Virgin TV, which also planned international expansion; Megastores opened in Spain, Netherlands, Australia, USA; joint venture formed by Virgin Retail with Blockbuster of Florida to expand Megastores in Europe, Australia, and North America; Euro-Magnetic, a specialist supplier of PC consumables, acquired by Virgin.

1993   Libel settlement of £610,000 against Lord King and BA won by Virgin Atlantic, which was voted Executive Travel's Airline of the Year for the third year running; Virgin Games K.K established in Tokyo by Virgin Games, which sold minority interests to Hasbro Inc and Blockbuster; the PC market entered by Virgin Euromagnetics, which launched its first range of personal computers; first management contract obtained by Virgin Hotels; daily flight to Hong Kong and San Francisco launched by Virgin Atlantic; joint venture announced with Wheelock Pacific to form Virgin Megastores Hong Kong, aimed at Chinese-speaking Asia market; Our Price chain in UK acquired by Virgin Retail; Saehan Virgin Megastores Korea established in joint venture with Saehan Media.

1994   Virgin Games renamed Virgin Interactive Entertainment (VIE) and Blockbuster raise stake to 75 percent; creative design and brand-development consultancy formed in partnership with Rodney Fitch and Co; Virgin City Jet service launched in January between Dublin and London City Airport; joint venture formed by Virgin Hotels with Shirayama Shokusan to develop London's County Hall; management contracts for four UK hotels awarded to Virgin Hotels; 100 percent ownership of three hotels previously held in joint venture taken by Virgin Hotels, which also acquired 50 percent ownership of the luxury restaurant Le Manoir aux Quat' Saisons; Virgin Hotels Marketing launched to promote owner-managed small hotels operating in Virgin style; Virgin Television Mexico formed; Virgin Trading formed to market FMCG under the Virgin brand name, with first venture in partnership with W. Grant and Sons to market Virgin Vodka; Virgin Radio awarded FM license in London; Virgin Cola Company formed by Virgin Retail and COTT of Canada.

1995	Agreement reached by Virgin Atlantic and Malaysian Airways to operate a twice-daily flight to Kuala Lumpur; agreement between Virgin Atlantic and Delta Airways approved by the US Department of Transportation; Virgin Direct Financial Services launched in a joint venture with Norwich Union Insurance; joint venture formed to acquire MGM Cinemas; Norwich Union bought out by Australian Mutual Provident (AMP); Virgin Atlantic voted airline of the year by Executive Travel magazine; Virgin Cola launched to compete with Coca-Cola and Pepsi; British Airways sued again by Branson, who this time claimed damages in the US.
1996	Flights started by Virgin Atlantic to Orlando and Washington DC; Euro Belgian Airlines acquired by Virgin Travel, which renamed it Virgin Express; Virgin Bride, Europe's largest bridal-wear shop, opened; Virgin Net formed to enter the Internet market; V2 Music launched, signing its first two bands; £3 billion contract to build Channel Tunnel Link and operate Eurostar services to Paris and Brussels awarded to London and Continental Railways, in which Virgin is a minority shareholder; Virgin Rail awarded franchise to operate rail passenger service covering 130 stations in England, Scotland, and Wales; Virgin Atlantic voted best business class and best transatlantic carrier by Executive Travel magazine for the sixth year running.
1997	Virgin Rail awarded InterCity West Coast franchise; three hotels in Wales acquired by Virgin Hotels; 50 percent share in London Broncos rugby team acquired by Branson; Virgin Express quoted on the Brussels and NASDAQ exchanges; Virgin Cinemas and Virgin Megastores World-wide (excluding the UK) merged to form Virgin Entertainment Group; four stores in UK opened by Virgin Vie, a joint venture in cosmetics and beauty care; first banking product – Virgin One Account – launched by Virgin Direct (Financial Services) in joint venture with Royal Bank of Scotland; Virgin Radio sold for £85 million; COTT's share of Virgin Cola bought out by Virgin Trading.
1998	Richard Branson wins G-Tech court case, involving G-Tech the lottery equipment supplier and Guy Snowden its former chairman; 'Diana', the tribute album for Diana, Princess of Wales, released by V2 Records on behalf of the record industry raises over £40m for charity; Virgin Sun, Virgin Holidays' first foray into short-haul holidays is launched; Virgin Express starts flights from Stansted to Continental Europe; Rail Regulator, John Swift, approves Virgin Trains' and Railtrack's massive upgrade of the UK's West Coast Main Line; Stagecoach buys 49% of Virgin Rail Group and Virgin increases its stake from 41% to 51%; Virgin Entertainment Group buys WHSmith's 75% holding in Virgin Our Price retail chain in Great Britain and Ireland.
1999	Virgin Rail Group completes the financing of new high speed tilting trains for both its franchises – West Coast and Cross Country. A total of over £4 billion of private sector investment secured with the introduction of the new trains still on track for 2001-2002. The first new 'Pendolino' destined for the West Coast Mainline rolls off the production line in December 1999; Virgin Atlantic announces further expansion plans on the back of continuing growth and increased profitability. 1999 will see the launch of new routes to Chicago, Shanghai and other destinations. Virgin Sun's first charter flights commence in May 1999. Virgin Atlantic's fleet of wide body jets grows to 28. In December, Singapore Airlines and Virgin announce that the former will buy a 49% stake in Virgin Atlantic for £600m cash. In the same month, Virgin Atlantic also announces a deal with Air India which

➤

will give the airline access to the sub-continent for the first time, with flights due to start in July 2000; Virgin Group announces its intention to enter the telecommunications business; Virgin Net goes free and Virgin continues its expansion in e-commerce with a wide range of connections from Megastores online to train booking facilities (total internet revenues 1999—£150 million); Virgin Mobile, Virgin's first consumer telecommunications venture, announces creation of 500 jobs in Trowbridge, West Wiltshire. The company will establish a management, customer service and call centre from which to market mobile telephony products (joint venture with Deutsche Telekom's One2One unit); Virgin Megastores continue their expansion world-wide with store openings in Miami, Glasgow, Piccadilly Circus, Bluewater, Strasburg, Okayama in Japan, bringing the total of Megastores total up to 381 stores world-wide. As a result of its more focussed retail strategy, Virgin Entertainment Group accepts an offer of £215m from UGC of France to buy Virgin Cinemas, the deal completes in November 1999; Virgin Active launches the first of its expected chain health and lifestyle centres, in Preston, Leeds and Stockley Park; Virgin Express starts a new service from Stansted to Berlin. Virgin also confirms the intention to set up a new independent low cost airline in Australia; Virgin opens its first game park in South Africa. The company also confirms that it has sold some of its smaller UK hotels to a private investor as part of its plan to refocus on exclusive properties around the world.

2000   Virgin Spectrum Limited is formed to participate in SpectrumCo, a new company formed by a number of shareholders to bid for a 3rd Generation Mobile Telephony license in the UK in March 2000. Other partners in the bid include Tesco, EMI, Sonera, Nextel, Marconi and a number of large private equity funds; Virgin Rail Group confirms its intention to bid for the East Coast Mainline; Virgin confirms its intention to launch Virgin.com/cars, a new e-commerce business, selling a wide range of cars direct to the consumer online.

Exhibit 2 Virgin group of companies in 1999: commentary on Major Operations

It is generally acknowledged, both within and outside Virgin, that **Virgin Travel**, especially Virgin Atlantic, is the company closest to Branson's heart. It is the only company in which employees have Branson's direct telephone number and are encouraged to call or write to him with ideas or feedback on customer satisfaction. Branson regularly travels on his planes, helping to serve meals, talking to passengers and cabin crew, and generally listening for suggestions for improvements.

With twenty-nine aircraft and routes from London to about a dozen major cities outside Europe, **Virgin Atlantic** remains a niche player in an industry dominated by global carriers and state airlines. Since its founding, the airline has relied on service, value-for-money, and innovation, dished up with panache and flair, to differentiate itself in the market. On the first flights, cabin crew in business class were dressed as butlers, serving bought in food from Maxims. Later, in-flight magicians, masseuses, and musicians were used; a limousine service to the airport for upper-class passengers was instituted; and multi-channel music and video systems that can be customized to a passenger's individual needs were installed. More recently, luxurious Virgin Atlantic clubhouses have appeared at London's two airports as well as in Hong Kong, Washington, and San Francisco. Not all of these ideas originated at Virgin, but Branson will happily copy good practice if he sees an advantage. Judging by the numerous awards and citations the airline has won, his approach seems to work.

During 1999 Branson had intimated that he might float part of the airline to raise capital for expansion. As the year was closing, however, he announced a surprise deal with Singapore Airlines that, in terms of fleet and revenues, is about three times the size of Virgin Atlantic. If the deal goes through, in 2000 Singapore will acquire a 49% stake in Virgin Atlantic at a cost of £600 million. The two airlines will work in partnership to maximise cost cutting synergies (eg maintenance, ground facilities, code sharing) but retain their respective identities and develop their own products. Industry observers saw the logic of the deal since in many ways the two airlines are complementary – their routes do not overlap and they both enjoy excellent reputations for service and innovation. There were, however, doubts expressed at the price that Singapore was paying, valuing Virgin Atlantic at more than £1.2 billion, a high figure in many observers' view.

Also included in the deal are the other divisions of Virgin Atlantic—Virgin Holidays, Virgin Sun and Virgin Aviation Services, the group's cargo division. Managing Director Ron Simms describes **Virgin Holidays** as 'the world's largest long-haul tour operator in terms of numbers carried.' The holiday company grew on the back of the airline and has recently moved into the short-haul business. The main destination is Florida, where Virgin is the Disney hotels' biggest customer.

Virgin Entertainment owns **Virgin Cinemas**, a cinema chain formed from the purchase of MGM cinemas. Virgin sold the ninety small sites it acquired, retaining the remainder for conversion to 'Megaplexes.' After substantial refurbishment, Megaplexes offer cafe/bars, shops, and spacious seating; those that offer 'Premier Screen' also have personalized service – coats are taken, drinks are served at the seat, extra legroom is provided. Virgin plans to develop the chain through purpose-built Megaplexes.

Virgin Entertainment is also the Virgin partner in joint ventures that run overseas Megastores. The Megastore concept is exported and refined to adapt to the local culture, but it retains its core values: fun, good design, value-for-money, and choice.

Virgin Retail's core activity is the chain of fifty-plus Megastores in the UK, in partnership with W. H. Smith, a retail chain. It also owns Caroline International, an importer/exporter of music and video media, and has an interest in Sound & Media, a specialist music supplier.

Based in Brussels, **Virgin Express Holdings Plc** is a scheduled airline company serving the main European cities, offering single-class airfares substantially below the norm. It offers its customers a no-frills, simple-to-understand service in which even ticketing has been reduced to a booking confirmation number.

Virgin Direct and **Virgin Direct Personal Finance** were founded to bring Virgin into the personal financial services market, where Branson saw an industry 'ripe for reform': poor service, high charges, disreputable practices, dissatisfied customers. In addition, the market was forecast to grow as people took more responsibility for their own financial security in old age.

Relying for competitive advantage on the Virgin brand's association with trust and value-for-money, **Virgin Direct** was initially a joint venture with Norwich Union Assurance, a large insurance group that supplied the technology and back-office support while Virgin supplied the marketing. Norwich Union withdrew shortly after the launch in favor of Australian Mutual Provident.

Virgin Direct differentiates itself in several ways. First, it does not use a commission-led sales force or agents, relying instead on advertising and telesales, contrary to accepted industry practice. Second, it offers simple saving products, based on tracking financial indices, that the average person can understand. Simplicity of product and lack of commission mean lower costs, which are passed on as lower administration charges. The transparency of its charges are a key selling point in its advertising. In 1999, after four years in operation, Virgin Direct has over 200,000 customers with more than £1 billion under management. Its main products are PEPS (a tax-efficient personal equity plan under a 'tax wrapper'), personal pensions, and life insurance.

Virgin Direct Personal Finance links Virgin Direct with Royal Bank of Scotland to offer the *One* account, a combined, highly flexible mortgage and bank account with a single rate for all lending purposes: car loan, house purchase, overdraft, credit card, etc.

The most recent major investment by Virgin, **Virgin Rail** consists of twenty-year franchises to operate two networks: CrossCountry, a series of routes that traverse the UK, and West Coast, the main route from London to Glasgow and intermediate stations. The franchises were awarded by competitive tendering as part of the long-term denationalization program of the Conservative government. Virgin inherited rolling stock, ticketing offices, and staff, all previously under British Rail ownership and management. The tracks, signaling, and stations are owned and operated by Railtrack.

British Rail was not seen as a customer-friendly and efficient organization. Furthermore, years of under-investment had had an impact on the infrastructure. The result was high prices, unhappy customers, and demotivated (sometimes antagonistic) staff. Industry observers, City analysts, and media commentators all had reservations about the prospects for franchisees given the major turnaround required. In Virgin's case, they forecast considerable damage to the brand. Branson recognized that there was a risk but believed that his project to undertake major investment in modern trains and convert the staff to a customer-service culture would pay off in the long term, particularly with passenger numbers forecast to rise. In the short term, however, Virgin Rail has suffered from poor public relations, with horror stories surfacing frequently about delayed trains, poor food, and dirty trains. Virgin Rail management explains that improvements cannot come overnight.

Virgin Rail was initially a joint venture between Virgin and venture capitalists. In 1998, Branson made plans to float Virgin Rail, intending to offer part of the equity to the public to allow the initial investors to withdraw. There were doubts in the City about whether this would be a success. At the last moment, Brian Souter, chairman of Stagecoach, a private bus company operating mainly in the UK but also overseas, offered to take a 49 percent holding. A Scottish entrepreneur from a modest background, Souter is a born-again Christian with a reputation for running a tight and hard-nosed operation. His company has been accused of predatory actions against competitors, for example. His business was founded in the early '80s and prospered when the Thatcher government privatized many bus companies. With the reputation for being somewhat eccentric (i.e., in the Branson mold), Souter sees synergy between his bus networks and trains.

Obliged by contract to stay out of the music business for three years after the sale of Virgin Music, **V2 Music** is Branson's return to the industry that got him started. It was founded as a global business with a presence in many countries. Still a small, loss-making operator, V2 Music has yet to sign any major artists, but it is investing in creative personnel to seek out new talent.

Virgin Net is an Internet service provider created as a joint venture between Virgin and the UK subsidiary of NTL, a US computer technology company. Virgin is responsible for creative content and marketing; NTL provides the backup systems and software. Virgin Net targets the UK consumer market and wants to compete on 'value-for-money, speed, excellent customer service, and compelling content,' according to David Clarke, Managing Director. Much of its content is sourced from specialist suppliers (for example, the Independent newspaper for news).

Exhibit 3 Virgin group of companies in 1999: summary

Virgin Company	% Virgin interests	Other major shareholders	Turnover 97/98 £m*	Employees	Trading location(s)	Launch date
Virgin Travel Group	100%			4,750	Worldwide	
– Virgin Atlantic Airways	100%		678			1984
– Virgin Holidays	100%		177			1985
– Virgin Aviation Services	90%	Held by management	15			1985
Virgin Entertainment Group	70%	Texas Pacific Group, Colony				
– Cinemas	100%	Capital	100	800	UK	1995
– US Megastores	100%	(formerly MGM Cinemas)	80	400	USA	1992
– Japan Megastores	50%		68	100	Japan	1990
– European Megastores	100%	Marui Co	150	300	Continental Europe	1988
Virgin Retail Group	100%					
– Virgin Retail (Our Price, UK Megastores)	25%	W H Smith	500	4,500	UK	1971
– Caroline International	100%		20	62	UK	1972
– Sound & Media	50%	Held by management (Virgin interest since 1994)	8	68	UK	1994
Virgin Trading Group	100%					
– Virgin Cola, Virgin Vodka	100%		21	45	UK	1994
– Virgin Limobikes	100%		0.3	5	UK	1996
V Entertainment Group	100%					
– Virgin Digital Studios (525, Rushes, W1TV)	100%		27	340	UK, USA	1986
– Virgin Publishing	60%	Robert Devereux	10	42	Worldwide	1991
– John Brown Enterprises	20%	John Brown	12	68	UK	1984
– Rapido TV	50%	Rapido TV Investments	4	12	Mexico	1991
Ginger Media Group	20%	Chris Evans, Apax partners				
– Virgin Radio	100%		18	64	UK	1993
Virgin Express Holdings Plc	50.1%	Guarantee Nominees Ltd, management	150	800	Continental Europe	1996
Virgin Hotels Group	100%					
– Virgin Clubs, La Residencia, Woodhouse Securities, Cribyn	100%		21	587	UK, Spain	1988
– Le Manoir Aux Quat' Saisons	50%	Held by management	7	120	UK	1994
Virgin Direct Ltd	50%	Australian Mutual Provident				
– Virgin Direct Personal Services	100%	(AMP)	608**	450	UK	1995
Virgin Direct Personal Finance	25%	AMP, Royal Bank of Scotland		150	UK	1998
Victory Corporation Plc	49%	Clerical Medical, Foreign & Colonial, GRE				
– Virgin Vie	100%	Morgan Grenfell, Commercial	2.5	150	UK	1997
– Virgin Clothing	100%	Union, McCarthy Corporation		57	UK	1998
Virgin Rail Group	51%	Stagecoach Group	423	3,450	UK	1997
– West Coast Trains	100%					
– CrossCountry Trains	100%					
V2 Music	66%	McCarthy Corporation	10	200	UK	1996
Virgin Net	51%	NTL	10	60	UK	1996
Vanson Developments (property)	100%		30	14	UK	1983
Virgin Bride	100%		0.9	25	UK	1996
Neckar (island resort)	100%		2.5	33	Virgin Islands, WI	1984
Heaven	100%		3	43	London	1982
Virgin Vouchers	100%		0.1	2	UK	1996
London Broncos	50.1%	BAT Trustees (Jersey), King Investments	2	50	London	1997
Virgin Helicopters	100%		0.8	12	UK	1997
The Lightship Group	50%	Lightship America	9	215	UK, USA	1990
Virgin Airships & Balloons	75%	Nerorate	8	47	UK	1987
Storm Model Management	50%	held by management	6	22	Worldwide	1985

* Financial year-ends not concurrent   **Gross Sales   Plc indicates publicly quoted company

Exhibit 4 Virgin people

Is there a 'Virgin person'? From Richard Branson to the most humble employee, those who work for Virgin seem to believe that only a certain type of person will fit into the sprawling Virgin empire, despite its diverse range of businesses. What follows are selected extracts from interviews with Virgin staff, who talked about what it takes to work at Virgin:

Stephen Murphy, Group Financial Director based in Geneva: *We like to hire smart people, people who have had all the schooling and education but who are pissed off with management consultancies, investment banks, and the like. We had one woman who was thrown out of a well-known consultancy because she had a nose earring. We took her on. We don't have those kinds of prejudices.*

Dan Higgott, International Brand Development Manager, Megastores (formerly Manager of the flagship Megastore on London's Oxford Street): *After five years with Virgin, I still find it difficult to describe a Virgin person. You need common sense and need not to be overly concerned with status and formality, but these could apply to any successful business. There are no preconceptions about people at Virgin, and I'm a good example. My training was in fashion, and I fell into retail management by accident. In Virgin Retail we have quite a formal process for developing people, so I've been given opportunities to progress. At twenty-nine I was running a £35 million business. I believe those opportunities genuinely apply to any of the 230 people who worked for me at the Oxford Street store.*

Kenneth Ibbett, Chairman, Virgin Media Group: *I joined Virgin so that I could come to work on a bicycle and not wear a tie – and took a 25 percent pay cut! We don't necessarily pay the best rates, and we're quite open about that. One problem at Virgin is that senior people with creativity and flair move on when they cash in their options. We miss people like that – Robert Devereux is a good example. When recruiting, you have to be open-minded and recognize that you're not looking* for clones. *I've just recruited someone who has nothing in common with me, but she's just right to run our TV business. As to the attributes we look for, it's probably easier to list the negatives to avoid: complacency, fear of failure, lack of integrity, and stupidity are probably the important ones.*

Lene Byrne, Flight Supervisor, Virgin Atlantic: *I came from Denmark to college in England and had wanted to fly for a couple of years. That was nine years ago. We've grown a lot since then and are more systemized, less easygoing, but we also have more chance to be transferred or promoted. I like the way we have fun at Virgin; it's more like a family where I know everyone, and that wouldn't be the same at BA, for example. To be employed at Virgin Atlantic you have to have the Virgin Flair – that's the big one – which means thinking young, having a sense of humor, being easygoing but professional at the same time. The longer you're here, the more you get to know Richard. Personally he's a very nice man, very genuine; but when it comes to business, he doesn't do anything without a reason – he's good at it!*

Will Whitehorn, Director of Corporate Affairs, Virgin Group: *Virgin has grown a lot recently and brought in a lot of new people. [To avoid difficulties in a start-up,] a new team will be made up of Virgin people plus new people. The new telecommunications business is a good example of that. We've brought in technical expertise and linked it to our marketing skills. The kind of people we look for are those who want to be the boss sometime and can work in the culture here at Virgin that gives you the confidence to do that. We want people with a clear idea of why they want to be with us, who don't beat around the bush when it comes to expressing a vision they may have. The organization doesn't like 'yes' people or political people; we want people who are happy to enter a discourse and debate things.*

Tim McIntosh, Manager, Union Square Megastore, New York: *In New York the staff do have the feeling that they work for Richard*

►

Branson and an English company because they've seen him and talked to him when he comes by for [promotional] events. For many of them this is their first job, but they know the history because of the book [Branson's autobiography] and the Virgin record label. We look at resumes [of potential recruits] and on paper they look good but not when you meet them. We're looking for personality – someone you'll notice, friendly and upbeat, people who look like they're going to try. It takes time to find the right people. Once they're here, they have to do a pretty bad thing to get fired –

stealing, racial slurs, drinking, fighting, and that kind of thing. At a senior level, one bad business decision won't get a hatchet thrown at you, but you don't make that decision again.

Whatever the profile of the Virgin Person, the company should not have difficulty in persuading young people to join, at least in the UK. According to a 1999 survey,[5] UK graduates ranked Virgin Group second only to the BBC as the best place to work, ahead of its rival British Airways (ranked sixth) and the accounting and consulting firms.

Exhibit 5 Richard Branson's introduction to the Virgin charter

Virgin is a unique brand, and behind that brand sits an equally unique corporate structure. Over the years Virgin has evolved into something between a branded venture capital organization and a Japanese-style keiretsu (family of businesses).

The consequences of this evolving structure have been twofold. Firstly, each business has become focused and been able to develop in a more autonomous and entrepreneurial environment than their equivalent subsidiaries in large conglomerates. Secondly, the Virgin brand has built up a world-wide reputation out of all proportion to the actual size and market share of any individual Virgin company. Much in the way that other brands have become household names without being associated to any one product, so Virgin is becoming a household name, bound only by the attributes that people want to associate it with – namely, value for money, quality, innovation, challenge and fun.

In a hectic and dynamic business environment, however, autonomy can have its downside – and communication links are usually the first to suffer. This can lead to flaws in the decision-making process and, ultimately, to companies acting on their own and without the common good of the Virgin shareholders in mind. As more responsibility is devolved to a range of individually significant businesses in their own right, links become stretched and frustrated and information stops flowing.

We need to prevent this from happening while respecting and maintaining the spirit of Virgin. Hence the Virgin Charter.

It is intended that the Virgin Charter will evolve into a management system that will allow all Virgin companies to be the best they can possibly be, without the need for obstructive hierarchies which can so easily impede rapid decision-making by those who know their own business.

In the longer term we hope that the Virgin Charter will become a mechanism through which both the individual companies, Virgin Management Ltd. and the Virgin brand can quickly take advantage of the truly exciting opportunities that lie ahead, both in our core businesses and the new frontiers of global electronic commerce. As we move into the twenty-first century there is a real opportunity to turn Virgin into one of the leading global brands, by looking at strategic opportunities for the existing businesses and by forming new ones.

Finally, please don't forget that Virgin's success, both now and in the future, rests with each of us. We are a people brand and a people business in the purest sense of the word.

My greatest hope is that the Virgin Charter will continue to create a culture of praise rather than blame, and family rather than alienation. If that alone can be achieved then all our efforts will have been worthwhile.

---

[5] Universum, Stockholm 1999, graduate survey.

INSEAD

Case 11 Rank Xerox, A, B, C

Rank Xerox (A): Global transfer of best practices

It was early 1995 and Carlos Camarero, the get-things-done, results-oriented leader of Rank Xerox's Team C initiative, was troubled. Over six months into the implementation of Wave II he was perplexed by its negligible impact on Rank Xerox's approach to selling products. The absence of financial benefits from Wave II was particularly worrying compared with the resounding success of Team C's Wave I initiative which had generated US$100 million net benefit in 1994.

The early 1990s had been a time of tremendous change at the European Rank Xerox and its parent company, Xerox Corporation, based in Stamford, Connecticut, US. Faced with changing competitive and technological dynamics in the world copier market, Xerox Corporation CEO Paul Allaire had repositioned the firm as *The Document Company*

This case received the 2003 European Foundation for Management Development Case of the Year Award in the category 'Knowledge Management and Learning in Organisations'

This original version of the case was written by Gary M. Deutsch, Wharton MBA 1997 and Joanna Fueyo, Research Assistant, under the supervision of Gabriel Szulanski, Associate Professor of Strategy at INSEAD. Michael Casaburi, Wharton MBA 1998 and Doctoral Student at Wharton, wrote this revised version. The case is intended to be used as a basis for class discussion rather than to illustrate either effective or ineffective handling of an administrative situation.

06/2004-5138

and transformed its centralized organizational structure into one based on product-centric business divisions. Rank Xerox, however, did not similarly redesign its organizational structure at that time.

In September 1992, Managing Director Bernard Fournier announced the *Rank Xerox 2000* initiative to remedy the company's recent performance ills and restructure its organization using the more customer-responsive business division model of the master corporation. At the core of the 2000 initiative was the concept of best practice transfer – the identification and transfer of best practices across Rank Xerox's individual countries of operation – in response to the realization that valuable information was not being successfully shared between countries.

Fournier had formed a series of expert teams to meet his objectives – Teams A, B and C – and gave them each a specific set of goals and objectives. Team A had been successful in transforming the organizational structure into an information-sharing and customer-focused matrix. Team B had succeeded in slashing costs and eliminating bureaucracy at Rank Xerox's corporate headquarters in Marlow, England. Wave I of Team C's initiative had achieved remarkable revenue improvements by identifying, documenting and transferring best practices associated with discrete sales processes and the marketing of specific products. Next came Wave II, a broader attempt to define overarching sales best practices which was targeted at the core processes of the predominantly sales-focused company. Although Wave II was led by Camarero – as was its predecessor – its results had not been as successful as those of Wave I.

As he prepared to meet with Fournier to discuss Wave II's status, Carlos pondered the intricacies of best practice transfer and analyzed the similarities and differences between Waves I and II.

Rank Xerox

Originally an English motion picture firm, Rank first became involved with Xerox through a joint venture in 1955. Later, Rank became Rank Xerox, the European subsidiary of Xerox Corporation. Rank Xerox was organized into 15 independent national operating companies (OpCos) centered on its European headquarters in Marlow, England. The heads of the largest OpCos reported directly to Fournier. Smaller OpCos were organized into regional clusters whose heads reported to regional general managers who reported to Fournier.

Over the years, Rank Xerox had learned to cope with the difficulties of being a multinational corporation operating across the various countries and cultures of Europe. Some countries were natural rivals (Portugal and Spain, Britain and France, Belgium and Holland) and Rank Xerox managers had come to recognize that certain ideas and initiatives would be better received in some places than others. For instance, calls for technological advancement met with approval more quickly in Holland than in Italy. Likewise, customer demands and needs varied by country.

In 1992 Fournier was concerned about Rank Xerox's recent financial performance, particularly variance across the OpCos. For many years it had been less profitable than Xerox US and its return on assets (ROA) was well below the 20% profit seen in the US. Fournier believed Rank Xerox had the potential to make up the US$200 million cost gap between itself and Xerox US and to improve ROA by 5% or 6% by 1996, but first he felt he needed to align Rank Xerox's organizational structure with that of Xerox US.

Moving toward a solution

Fundamental to Fournier's desired changes was the identification of the strengths of each element of the organisation – features that he wanted to maintain and perhaps use in best practice transfer. Initial examination of the OpCos showed that performance lacked uniformity since Holland, Belgium, Austria, Switzerland, Denmark and Portugal – with ROAs greater than 20% – outperformed other OpCos and Rank Xerox as a whole.

Pressure from Stamford was increasing on Rank Xerox to devise an organizational structure more congruent with its own, and show a dramatic improvement in profits: Stamford set goals of a 40% increase in 1994 and a 38% increase in 1995. In response, Fournier announced the Rank Xerox 2000 initiative in September 1992 with three main objectives. The first was to make the new organization

cost effective, flexible, synergistic and pro-active. This meant closing the US$200 million cost gap between Rank Xerox and Xerox US, simplifying processes and increasing productivity, sharing resources and skills at all levels, and getting closer to the customer and thus better able to serve customer needs. The second objective was to position Rank Xerox to move closer to the idea of *The Document Company,* and the third was to restructure the company in line with the organization of the Xerox business divisions.

Team B

Team B was created for the organizational restructuring and streamlining of activities at European headquarters – a focus designed to partially fulfill objectives one and three above. It involved identifying and eliminating activities and layers that did not add direct value to the company or its customers. Team B quickly achieved results and four months into the project had already saved the company US$50 million, mostly by downsizing the corporate workforce.

Team A

Much broader in scope than Team B, Team A was mandated to redesign the Rank Xerox organization. Fournier specifically instructed Team A to propose a structure for the OpCos more congruent with the corporate business divisions model. Team A concluded that a matrix design was best for Rank Xerox. The new organization was centered on the formation of small regional profit centers known as Customer Business Units (CBUs). For the most part, each European country was its own CBU. A CBU had its own sales support, financial analysis, and human resource/quality functions and its general manager held profit/loss responsibility.

CBUs were grouped into territorial 'Entities' that provided governance across the CBUs. France, the UK and Germany were large enough to constitute their own Entities; the other countries were grouped into the Nordic, Central, or Southern Entity. Their role did not involve day-to-day operations (which were now the domain of the CBU); their purpose was to provide resource support to CBUs and help determine national-level policy. To interact adequately with and follow the design of the business division model of Xerox Corporation, Rank Xerox's new structure also included product-line focused Business Division Units (BDUs).

The bottom line impact of Team A's work was dramatic: it was estimated that the reorganization of Rank Xerox led to a US$240 million reduction in the 1993 cost base. However, that was not enough to put Rank Xerox on course to meet the profit improvement goals set by Xerox Corporation for 1994 and 1995 (i.e., projected cost savings would generate 11% profit growth in 1994 and 1995, well below the respective 40% and 38% goals set by Stamford).

Team C

The results for diverse products and services varied dramatically across countries and it was obvious that some CBUs outperformed others. After the success of Teams A and B and their resulting cost savings, Fournier focused on revenues. He created Team C to identify, validate, and document best practices and to mandate their implementation with the overall goal of revenue creation.

Fournier appointed a Spaniard, Carlos Camarero, to lead Team C. In 1993 he had been at Rank Xerox for 22 years, having served as Managing Director in Italy and Portugal as well as in Rank Xerox's Asia-Pacific operations. He had also spent time as Director of Operations in Spain and Region A, which, under the old structure, included all countries in Europe except France, Germany and the UK. Just months before his appointment, Carlos had been transferred from Italy to corporate headquarters in Marlow to assume the position of Corporate Business Division Director. He maintained his responsibilities in that position while committing approximately one-third of his time to the management of Team C. Known for his direct style and get-things-done attitude, he was selected for his operational experience in various OpCos as well as his ability to motivate people and drive projects to fruition. Fournier believed Carlos was vital to the success of Team C since he could negotiate productive agreement between multiple parties.

Since Team C's revenue initiatives would be transferred across the diverse cultures and nationalities of Rank Xerox, Carlos was quick to recognize that its work would have to be simple and easily implementable. He did not want Team C to get lost in the outer realms of 'strategic thinking'. To ensure the accessibility of its work to all the CBUs, Carlos enlisted 'doers' – 25 senior managers (product managers, marketing directors, operations directors and general managers) from CBUs who had ultimate responsibility for confirming that Team C's ideas and plans were realistic and implementable. Both Carlos and Fournier agreed that doers must be the top people in their respective CBUs. To allay possible fears that doers might hurt their careers by spending time away from their CBUs and 'best practicing' themselves out of a job, top management guaranteed their futures in the firm.

It was critical that Team C rapidly identify the origin of revenue growth opportunity best practices and not waste time on the inconsequential. Carlos continually emphasized that they must be broken down into their core drivers, stressing the identification of each best practice by a small number of underlying 'Key Success Factors.' In addition to contributing knowledge and experience, the doers would be instrumental in the prompt implementation of Team C's work. Fournier and Carlos anticipated that the acceptance of Team C initiatives by the top CBU people would inspire their rapid adoption by their CBU peers and subordinates.

Team C's Wave I initiative

Team C's initial project, Wave I, served to identify, document and transfer best practices involved in bringing specific products to market. Beginning in 1994, Team C devoted six months to draw up a list of best practices to be later implemented across different CBUs. Their objective was to find discrete policies within each CBU that could be taught and transferred to others, with the originating CBU serving as model for their specific practice. The original implementation goal was modest – to implement 50% of best practice transfer opportunities in 75% of the CBUs.

Defining the opportunities

Team C laid out the following actions to be taken to successfully identify best practices:

◆ Deep analysis of internal reporting database.
◆ Appointment of 'knowledge' person (Best Practice Champion).

◆ Promotion of the idea of best practice sharing.

◆ Creation of the right team to include skills and expertise.

◆ Recognition that identification effort is not enough.

◆ Building best practice transfer into annual business planning.

◆ 100% commitment and support from top managers.

◆ They also recognized the following potential difficulties in identifying best practices:

◆ Gaining complete understanding when best practice is complex, cross functional and sequential.

◆ Establishing sufficient common measurements.

◆ Thorough documentation of best practices.

◆ Justification of the opportunity.

◆ Identification of critical success factors at an early stage.

Since Team C's overall goal was to increase revenue, they began by scanning CBUs for potential easy-to-implement revenue growth opportunities. Opportunities currently being fully implemented by at least one of the CBUs were identified. Carlos described the identification process:

> We searched for best performance. Some we found through the database. The others were not so easy. We wrote to every key person (intermediate level) asking them for the best idea from their country. Out of approximately 40 ideas it was very easy to identify the best 10. We then went to each country to observe and understand, and the entire process took six months.

Once the revenue growth opportunities had been identified, Team C benchmarked those CBUs already optimizing such opportunities – essentially making them role models for the company-wide implementation of their specific opportunity. Team C personnel next worked with salespeople and managers at the benchmark CBUs to define the extent of the revenue opportunity as well as to determine a logical scope of implementation. Lastly, a consortium of Team C and CBU personnel laid out a set of Key Success Factors to be implemented simultaneously which served as an action plan for other CBUs.

Carlos believed that although multiple Key Success Factors for each revenue growth opportunity were listed, each opportunity hinged on the identification of one or two core best practices. He illustrated his point with the following story:

> In the North of Spain I stumbled across the finest fish restaurant I have ever found. I had to know what the chef was doing to prepare his fish so excellently. Through my persistence, I convinced him to give me his recipe. However, when I tried to duplicate his masterpiece at home I had no luck. The chef later told me with a sly grin that the key to the recipe was not the ingredients per se, rather the precise order in which they are mixed together. For Team C, we knew that we not only had to find the key ingredients of success, but also understand the key drivers which enabled the ingredients to optimally work together.

From their work, Team C developed the following list of nine revenue growth opportunities/best practices that were to be implemented across the CBUs:

◆ MajestiK: An initiative to increase market share in the European colour copier market.

◆ Customer Retention: A plan to encourage current customers to repurchase equipment from Rank Xerox by providing special incentives to salespeople for customer retention as well as technological database aids for tracking customer equipment stocks, usage requirements and contract expiration dates.

◆ DocuTech: An initiative to sell offset printers to commercial and educational users by focusing on overall document solutions rather than on traditional product or price selling.

◆ New Business Major Accounts: A plan to establish salespeople whose sole responsibility is generating new business.

◆ DocuPrint: A plan to accelerate sales of the newly launched line of high-speed network printers, particularly to the banking and insurance industries, by emphasizing the product's image printing capabilities and systems integration features.

◆ CSO Competitive MIF Identification: An initiative for rapid updating of the Rank Xerox company-wide sales database to track competitive information and provide salespeople with reliable leads.

◆ Analyst Time Billing: A plan to sell the value-adding, problem-solving consulting services of Rank Xerox technical analysts.

◆ XBS: A plan to educate salespeople on how to sell facilities management services effectively through the creation of simple packages and pricing options (i.e., Rank Xerox providing the customer with a packaged service consisting of both equipment and manpower).

◆ Secondhand CEP: An initiative to regain control of the secondhand market for centralized mainframe printers (typically found in data centers) by repurchasing secondhand machines, refurbishing and reselling them to targeted accounts for which price sensitivity is high.

Implementing the opportunities

The first step in the implementation process was convincing Entity and CBU managers that Team C's findings were significant. Carlos and his team had the benefit of Fournier's support but also of hard data which were critical in convincing them of the importance of Wave I. Carlos explained:

We prepared 180 slides full of statistics to convince top management. Even before seeing them the big bosses said, 'Forget it. Everybody here is an expert in marketing and sales. It will never work.' I said, 'Forget it? No! You are going to see the slides. If after that you tell me to forget it, I will forget it. But you are not going to tell me to forget it before you see this.' After only 35 slides we got the go-ahead.

Once Wave I was underway, one of the first challenges facing Team C was logistical coordination and planning. With Team C members scattered throughout Europe holding meeting after meeting and writing up new documentation, it was critical that valuable information did not get lost in the process. Team C enlisted the aid of two secretaries who were immediately immersed in the blood and guts of the project – compiling text, managing schedules and coordinating meetings. The secretaries also became instrumental in the massive

editing project that ensued once the data and ideas for the Wave I implementation books had been gathered.

Team C had essentially created a new corporate language for Rank Xerox. Carlos knew it was critical that the revenue growth opportunities, carefully selected for their simple underlying Key Success Factors, be described in a way that was equally simple and straightforward. Developing such a language proved to be a challenging task requiring several iterations. Several 'laymen' and 'non-experts' in the CBUs were enlisted to read the evolving drafts of the Wave I books. They rejected the first draft due to its complexity and corporate jargon.

Once an easily comprehensible set of Team C books had been completed and distributed, the implementation effort began to gain momentum from the benchmark CBUs. They were more than happy to talk up the best practice for which they had been highlighted. Team C figured that their input, combined with the abundance of data, would help to alleviate many of the problems that typically result when business people in different European countries are asked to agree on a standard. Effectively, Carlos and his team could turn to managers in a given CBU and say, 'You may not think that the French (or Swiss or English or Portuguese, etc.) can do this better than you, but they do, and here are the numbers to prove it.'

Fournier was happy with the way Wave I was proceeding. However, he was still concerned about how the CBU managers would react to change. In an attempt to minimize possible CBU stress, Fournier gave instructions that Entities avoid implementing all nine revenue opportunities at once. Rather, he suggested they pick their four favorites and concentrate on them before proceeding with the other five – a feasible approach as the opportunities were mutually exclusive.

Carlos and Team C believed that as the impact of Wave I would be felt throughout Rank Xerox over a multiple-month roll out, the key to successful implementation would be close monitoring of the process. During implementation, Team C's core group of 10 people dedicated 30% to 40% of their time to traveling to the CBUs for two-day visits to explain the best practices. Carlos was a proponent of a 'champion' system whereby each Entity would dedicate one senior-level person outside Team C to monitor implementation. This would involve monthly progress meetings between the champion, a Team C steering committee, and managers and key people within the CBU. At the meeting, the CBU manager would present a monthly results report detailing the CBU's performance against a set of goals and benchmarks. A major positive side effect of these meetings was that Team C was able to develop a set of 'best practices' for the implementation of the Wave I best practices which could be quickly transmitted across all the other countries.

Success

Wave I proved to be relatively easy to implement despite the fact that some revenue growth opportunities were more challenging than others and that e Entity Champions only gave 50% of their time to the team. Fournier felt that Team C's approach was effective since it entailed each country receiving all information so that the reinvention of the wheel could be minimized. This led to the generation of superb documentation which was followed by the launch of Wave I, the results of which were immediately apparent: it yielded revenue improvements of US$100 million in the first year (1994). All the more impressive was the cost of Team C which was estimated to be about US$1 million.

Fournier was so impressed by Team C's performance that he rewarded team members with significant spot bonuses, dividing participants into three categories of involvement with the project, with the largest bonuses going to the biggest contributors. The two secretaries who dedicated themselves to planning Team C logistics and editing the Wave I books were rewarded at the highest level.

Team C's Wave II initiative

With the success of Wave I, Team C set its sights on a more challenging objective: defining overarching best practices for the company's core sales processes, specifically salesforce productivity and sales process management. Carlos and Team C felt that their efforts could be escalated to a more sophisticated level in Wave II.

Wave II was based upon the concept of best practice transfer and focused predominantly on salesforce productivity. At its core was the notion that a set of best practices – identified by the team from a number of countries – could be combined into a series of modules covering key activities in the Salesforce Management Activities Model. The best practice modules did not exist as a finite, discrete entity. Rather, elements of each existed in several units. Although Wave II would be more difficult to implement than Wave I, Team C felt the bottom line rewards of Wave II could triple those of its predecessor. The highly competitive environment in Europe and the lofty profit growth goals set by Xerox Corporation in Stamford added urgency to their new mission.

Team C knew that replicating the success of Wave I would not be easy. In concrete terms, implementing a comprehensive salesforce management process meant telling salespeople how to do almost every aspect of their job and, in many cases, dramatic changes in a salesperson's assumptions and behavior. For example, it was traditionally believed that the more time a salesperson spent on the road, the more contacts could be made and the more sales closed. By that logic, salespeople should spend as little time as possible in the office and as much time as possible out making contacts. However, the analysis of best practices by Team C showed that salespeople in the best-performing offices spent more time in the office preparing intelligently for their field trips and optimizing the choice of prospects and the timing of visits. Since Rank Xerox was historically a sales-focused company with 5,000 'experts' devoted to the sales process, considerable effort would be needed to change their behavior. Also, in Wave II Team C would be losing one of its strongest proponents from Wave I – the benchmark CBUs.

Generating a new set of opportunities

In practical terms, Wave II differed most from Wave I in that it was a theoretical laboratory model that was a composite of little pieces of information from best practices identified across many countries. Team C sought to develop a model that would optimize salesforce management and all salesforce activities. Specifically, it aimed to identify optimal sales behaviors that were spread randomly (and sometimes deceptively) throughout the CBUs and devise a model that, in essence, would define new action plans for each aspect of the Rank Xerox sales process: territory planning, field salesforce activity management, market engagement programs, lead generation, product training, sales pay and incentive plans. A unique software module would be developed for each of these aspects linked to a market database containing schedules, performance figures, leads, contacts, and other information from all the CBUs. Salespeople would each have a portable computer to access the database at any time. Additionally, managers would be able to track salesperson activity at all times.

Tim Spooner, who was in charge of formulating the Wave II model, describes the generation of the idea as follows:

> We started with data. We sought out the CBUs which were performing best in areas like revenue growth and coverage-to-buy ratios. We then visited those countries and simply sat around for a while, talking with salespeople and watching what they were doing. It was key for us to dig below the sometimes rather slick surface to determine what was really going on. A lot of best practices are hidden, and many of the countries weren't exactly aware of what they are doing right and wrong. The danger we faced was that we would hone in on only the best-performing countries and assume that everything they did was the best thing. It was important that we look at all countries. Actually, the worst-performing countries played an important role in our analysis: we used them to confirm that certain practices were certainly not best. Over time, we did find that most of the 'building blocks' we ended up incorporating into our final model could be found in the best-performing countries, although they were never fully in place.

Implementation

Once Team C had generated its Wave II model and again produced a set of implementation books, it was time to return to the CBUs to put the model into action. But Team C faced several barriers

to implementation: a lack of urgency on the part of the CBUs and additional complications. The CBUs' response was very different second time around and there was no urgency for change. Team C knew that getting mass buy-in to a revolutionary plan would be difficult when so many people had the attitude 'We had an excellent 1994 ... outperforming Xerox US, so why make changes? There is no crisis.'

In effect, Team C's ability to convince CBU personnel of the need for further change via Wave II was confounded by the resounding success of Wave I. Additionally, because Wave II was based on a laboratory model, Team C did not have voluminous data to support their cause. In fact, they had no directly applicable data. Neither did they have the help of the benchmark CBUs. For Carlos and Team C, the key to successful implementation for Wave II was somewhere between a rock and a hard place. They also knew that it represented fundamental change for the Rank Xerox environment – a shift from 100% salesforce empowerment to strong process management – and that all players in the implementation would need to be on the same page from day one.

Team C felt that the complexity of implementation highlighted the need for strong leadership and not only from both the Team C doers and top managers: Wave II would require full-time Entity Champions. Unfortunately, just as implementation was gearing up, Team C learned that Fournier and top managers were unwilling to appoint full-time Wave II Entity Champions.

Adding to the complexity of implementation was the timeline aspect of Wave II. Adoption of the various modules had to follow a tight schedule and the software modules had to be installed sequentially. This meant it was much more challenging to implement than Wave I, which had no such constraints since each of its nine revenue opportunities could be implemented separately in any order.

Another complicating factor was the computer hardware and software required for Wave II. First, it injected a group of outside players (computer consultants and technicians) into the process. Second, because it relied more heavily on technology than its predecessor and required greater technological skills from participants, it underscored differences in technical aptitude across the CBUs. Further, a keystone to the Wave II model was the market database software which depended on all databases being at a standard level of quality. Although each CBU had maintained its own database for many years, data quality varied tremendously across countries. Carlos and his team worried about these technology barriers and feared that the less computer adept Southern Europeans would have more difficulty meeting Wave II's strict software/database management demands than the computer savvy Central and Northern Europeans.

The fact that the Wave II initiatives were more process-oriented than the simpler Wave I initiatives highlighted one of the major differences among Rank Xerox CBUs. Although Rank Xerox had a long history as a multinational company successfully operating across the diverse cultures of Europe, Carlos was concerned that while the English, for example, would find comfort in the rigid structure of Wave II's implementation, the Italians and Spanish would hate it. Rank Xerox had long fostered an open and democratic culture in which everyone was encouraged to generate ideas, and he feared a mass rejection since a company-wide program for reinventing everyone's job could evoke some very negative emotions.

Waiting for results

Six months into the implementation of Wave II, no more than 10% of salespeople were using the new software. Team C had run into an empowerment conflict with the CBUs since no one wanted to surrender control of the sales process. Revenue improvements associated with Wave II were negligible in comparison with those of its predecessor. Team C was left wondering what had gone wrong and how it could be successfully re-implemented in the future. Sitting in the lobby of Fournier's office, Carlos compared Waves I and II and contemplated the reasons for the latter's unsuccessful implementation.

Exhibit 1 Team C results

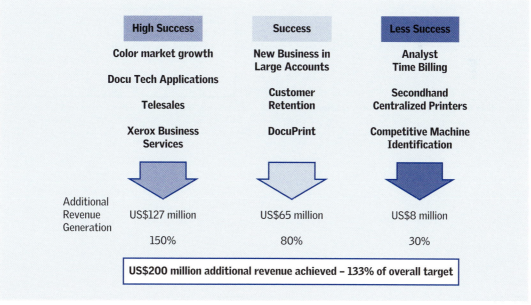

High Success	Success	Less Success
Color market growth	New Business in Large Accounts	Analyst Time Billing
Docu Tech Applications	Customer Retention	Secondhand Centralized Printers
Telesales	DocuPrint	Competitive Machine Identification
Xerox Business Services		

Additional Revenue Generation

US$127 million	US$65 million	US$8 million
150%	80%	30%

US$200 million additional revenue achieved – 133% of overall target

Source: Rank Xerox.

Exhibit 2 Assessments of Team C, Wave I implementation

	UK Jan 95	GERMANY Sept 95	SWITZ Dec 95	AUSTRIA Jun 95	SPAIN Nov 95	NORDIC Sept 95
MajestiK	3	4	4	4	4	4
Customer Retention	3	4	4	4	4	3
Docutech	4	3	4	4	4	4
DocuPrint	3	3	4	4	3	4
New Business Major Accounts	5	-	3	4	5	2
Compet MIF	3	4	2	4	3	3
Analyst Time Billing	3	4	5	3	4	3
Second Hand CEP	4	5	5	1	4	5
XBS	5	5	3	5	4	3

Validation of Implementation status (1–5 rating)
1 = Not implemented
2 = Planned implementation in next 3 months
3 = Implemented / major improvements required
4 = Implemented / minor improvements required
5 = Best practice implemented

Source: Rank Xerox Policy Committee 24–26 January 1996.

Exhibit 3 Database-driven marketing and sales processes

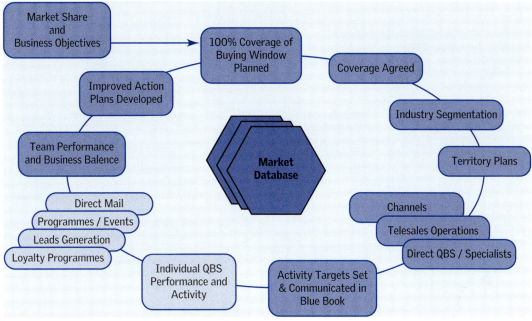

Source: Rank Xerox Policy Committee 24–26 January 1996.

Exhibit 4 Best practice transfer overview

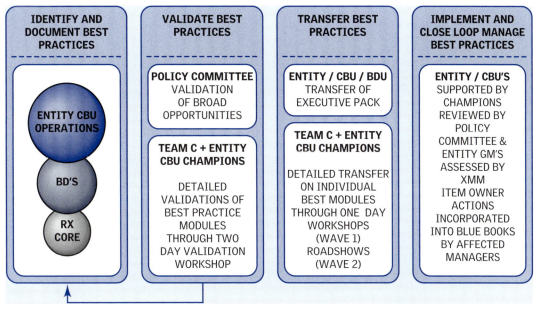

Source: Rank Xerox.

Exhibit 5 Best practice transfer key success factors (sample)

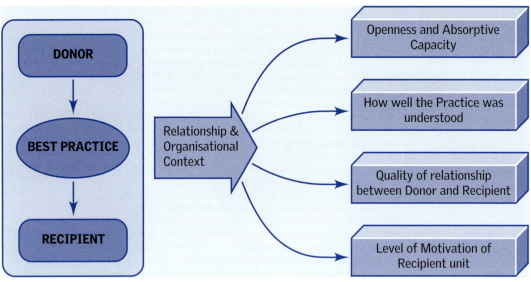

Source: Rank Xerox

INSEAD

Rank Xerox (B): Is 'telemarketing' the answer?

This case received the 2003 European Foundation for Management Development Case of the Year Award in the category 'Knowledge Management and Learning in Organisations'

It was mid-1995 and Carlos Camarero, leader of Rank Xerox's Team C, was not pleased. Having led Wave I to achieve remarkable revenue improvements (over US$100 million in incremental revenue in 1994) by identifying, documenting and disseminating best practices associated with discrete sales processes and the marketing of specific products, his subsequent project, Wave II, was faltering.

Carlos and Team C had set a more challenging objective for Wave II: defining overarching best practices for the company's core sales processes, specifically salesforce productivity and sales process management. But it was producing only lackluster results – for example, sales coverage (the key metric) had remained static.

Carlos asked Bernard Fournier, Rank Xerox's Managing Director, if they could change the approach to implementing Wave II and try again, but the request was rejected: 'Forget it. I'm not going to put my name on something that is never

....

This case was written by Michael Casaburi, Wharton MBA 1998 and Doctoral Student at Wharton under the supervision of Gabriel Szulanski, Associate Professor of Strategy at INSEAD. The case is intended to be used as a basis for class discussion rather than to illustrate either effective or ineffective handling of an administrative situation.

06/2004-5138

going to fly.' Instead, Fournier said that he would like him to investigate something else.

In the early 1990s, in the search for revenue generating opportunities, Fournier had visited various Rank Xerox offices. What struck him was that in Colombia and Dubai (United Arab Emirates) salespeople contacted and interacted with customers primarily by telephone rather than through face-to-face contact. (Dubai called this process 'telemarketing', although the processes involved were very different from those commonly associated with the term.) Contrary to the approach used in Europe, telephone selling was used extensively in these locations because salespeople preferred to be indoors – in Colombia to avoid the risk of being shot while driving, and in Dubai to avoid the heat (typical temperatures exceeded 44°C). During his visits to Colombia and Dubai, local managers made presentations that showed substantially better sales productivity than Fournier had seen in Europe.

Fournier asked Carlos to visit Colombia and Dubai to see first-hand how telemarketing worked and determine whether it was of potential interest for adoption at other Rank Xerox offices. Carlos thought such a trip would be a 'waste of time' – telemarketing intuitively did not make sense, customers needed face-to-face contact before they purchased a copier. Neither Rank Xerox nor its competitors used the telephone in such a way in Europe. Even if Colombia and Dubai had great success with telephone sales, they might simply be special cases because of their small size and unique circumstances.

But given the apparent impending failure of Wave II, Fournier's rejection of his request to re-implement Wave II, and the state of sales operations, Carlos thought he had little to lose by visiting Colombia and Dubai and had his flights booked.

Rank Xerox's sales operations were not performing well. It had less than 30% coverage of buying window decisions; 40% of its customers at risk were not contacted in the six months before the loss of the business to a competitor; and sales costs, which were already high, were rising.

Surprise in Colombia

When Carlos arrived in Colombia, the performance of the operations there appeared, on the face of it, to be astounding: sales were reported by local management to be growing at 40% annually with a 70% profit margin. But he soon learned that all was not as it appeared, as he explained:

The general manager [in Colombia] made a beautiful presentation, but I couldn't believe it. I developed a huge curiosity to know what it [the truth] was. I couldn't sleep that night. ... In the morning I said to myself, 'If I ask about the details they are not going to tell me.' So what I did was go back and say, 'I would like to talk to someone about commissions and remuneration of the salesforce ...' They looked at me very strangely. Here comes this big guy from Europe to talk to the secretary ... What happened was that I got into the office of that young lady and she started to explain to me what was really going on: the [dollar value of the] revenue and profit [being reported] were correct but they came from different sources [e.g., selling paper to customers] and not from selling Xerox copiers!

What Carlos could see, however, was that Colombia had an excellent operation selling small equipment and other items over the telephone. Salespeople closed deals over the telephone without face-to-face contact with customers. Even with his concern that the products being sold were not what he (or probably anyone else at Xerox outside of Colombia) expected, the telephone operation was intriguing:

I came back [from Colombia] and said, 'Somehow this looks bloody good.' At the time I was not able to understand the [potential] power of that process. But instinctively you could see that this could be something special.

Carlos's next stop was Dubai.

'Little' Dubai

Compared with the major European countries where Rank Xerox did most of its business, Dubai is very small. A city of approximately 700,000 people, it is the second largest city (after the capital Abu Dhabi) in a country of about two million people with a GDP of US$132 billion (1993). The country's geography is extensive and there are a limited number of

geographic concentrations of businesses. Rank Xerox's Dubai location had close to US$5 million in revenue in 1994, compared to approximately US$5 billion for the company overall.

Carlos watched the salesforce in action and interviewed people at all levels of the organization (from clerks to the general manager). He found that Dubai had been using telemarketing since April 1993. Unlike Colombia, he uncovered no surprises as to what was being sold.

Telemarketing originated from the desire of the salesforce to escape the harsh climate. At one point, sales managers in Dubai decided to minimize the frequency of salespeople using the telephone to solicit and transact business because they wanted them to meet customers face-to-face (which they thought was a more effective sales approach). The sales managers set a goal that each salesperson make six face-to-face sales calls per day (given the area's geographic expanse this entailed a lot of traveling). The salesforce protested and as a 'capitulation solution' management agreed to let them stay in the office if they made 40 telephone calls daily with no requirement to make a daily face-to-face sales call.

'Telemarketing' was in some ways a misnomer: while salespeople conducted most of their activities over the telephone (e.g., interviewing potential customers), they still visited customers periodically in-person as required (e.g., to provide demonstrations or to close the transaction). Carlos explained:

Eventually, there is a big deal [opportunity] available [to bid on] ... [W]hen it is the right time, they go [to the customer or potential customer] for a face-to-face meeting and not before then.

The key objectives of telemarketing were to maximize coverage (i.e., the percentage of buying decisions that Rank Xerox bid on), improve sales productivity and controls, conduct accurate sales analysis, and improve the prospect and customer database.

Increasing coverage was critical because the more buying decisions that Rank Xerox was aware of, the more opportunities it had to bid, and thus the greater the number of contracts it would win. Knowing the timing of the contract bid window in advance was therefore valuable. Using the telephone to call prospects (and existing Rank Xerox customers) to identify such timing was more efficient than setting up face-to-face meetings.

The concept that salespeople would be more productive, however, relied on more than increased coverage. Salespeople also needed better and more information about prospects and existing customers (through an improved database) and to have the hardware and software to fully leverage that data.

A critical part of telemarketing was the central database that was compiled from existing databases and by the salesforce through telephone calls. Using the telephone helped increase the quality of the database much faster than face-to-face visits, as Carlos observed:

> The secret of their success was their [database] ... because it is so easy and takes five minutes to make a telephone call. Physically you can do six [in person] visits a day, five are to customers. On the telephone you can make 40 calls a day to non-customers.

Sample information in the database included:

- Company name, location, telephone number, number of employees, etc.
- Identification of decision-making unit (DMU) (i.e., the part of a company that makes the decision as to which copier to purchase).
- Market segmentation data.
- Impression volume (e.g., of Rank Xerox and competitors).
- Contact history (e.g. when salesperson called a prospect and what transpired).
- Selling cycle tracking (e.g., date of demonstration, proposal, close, order, and implementation).

The salesforce had clear performance objectives. Sales managers could provide direction and control on a daily (sometimes hourly) basis and had to approve visits by salespeople to prospects or customers. Software measured performance on many of these objectives (e.g., number of calls, call duration, new contacts versus follow-up contacts, prospects, proposals, and orders) and provided managers with tailor-made reports regarding sales statistics, activity levels, and individual/group productivity.

While the technical staff in Dubai was still refining the telemarketing system, Dubai had performed very well on its objectives. For example, from August 1993 to February 1994, the number of companies (decision-making units) in the database had increased over 400% to about 12,000 and Dubai was making several thousand telemarketing phone calls per month.

Moreover, its sales productivity far outpaced that of other countries. In Europe, the average number of contacts-per-day and revenue-per-salesperson were six contacts and US$300,000, whereas in Dubai it was 40 contacts and US$1.2 million respectively (after adjusting revenues for the small size of the Dubai market).

On the return flight, Carlos was elated about the possibilities that telemarketing offered. But would it work outside of Dubai? He knew he had to get the opinion of Ricardo Morias, an expert in relational database management who was well respected within Rank Xerox for his ability to bridge the technical and practical domains. Ricardo had worked with Carlos on a variety of projects (often without additional pay on top of a significant amount of other work) and he trusted Ricardo's judgment regarding practical business issues as much as on technical issues, as he recalled:

> [Telemarketing would need to be] translated to our culture, our language, our physical and graphic life, and the only person that could do that was him ... I knew that if he [Ricardo] bought [into] the concept, he had the technical capabilities to put that in a package [that would be extremely valuable].
>
> When I came back from Dubai, I said to Ricardo, 'I've found something shocking.' He asked me, 'What have you found?' and I don't remember what I said but Ricardo said, 'You must be joking!' because, at the time, everyone reacted like that. So, I said, 'Go to Dubai and take a look. Take a plane and go there.'... So he went to Dubai, and I thought, 'Oh geez, let's see if Ricardo likes it or doesn't like it, because if he doesn't like it, we'll start again.

Ricardo was thinking in similar terms:

> Carlos came to me and told me about Dubai. At that time I was working on a project [for Rank

*Xerox's International Region] looking into poten-
tial software systems we could us ... It matched
perfectly for me to go to Dubai as I wanted to
see what they had and what could be done
with it.*

Dubai revisited

Ricardo's mission was to understand telemarketing
and assess its value for use in other parts of Rank
Xerox. He was concerned that it would not be possible to sell large copiers over the telephone and
wanted to see how Dubai handled such orders.

During the visit, Ricardo was impressed:

*... I was impressed even though their operation
was on a small scale. I saw myself how they sold
through the telephone ... [The] supervisors
showed me information that they had available
by pointing to a [computer] screen and saying
'Look what this guy [salesperson] is doing now
... in the morning he made five contacts ... he is
not doing much now, I am going to have to see
him later.' I was shocked. ... We had spent
US$140 million in the [United] States on soft-
ware development by X [an outside consultant]
and we did not have a clue how to collect information automatically.*

Ricardo found that the telemarketing operations
covered clients of all sizes, from major accounts to
other commercial customers, and included selling
large and smaller copiers.

Telemarketing was a primitive technical system
that Ricardo thought was appropriate for Dubai's
environment. For example, the database had limited
fields for a prospect company's address because
there were no street names in many parts of Dubai.

But he instantly realized that without the
'TeleMagic' software that was the glue holding it
together, there 'would be no telemarketing'. Key
elements regarding database management,
reporting and record keeping were embedded in
TeleMagic, which was the most recent public version
available and was based on the Disk Operating
System (DOS).

To help salespeople fully leverage the power of the
database, TeleMagic put the following productivity
tools at their fingertips:

- Automatic telephone number dialing and tele-
  phone call logging (including call length).
- Electronic diary (controlling appointments and
  meeting scheduling).
- Automatic reminders (e.g., to tell a salesperson
  to call a particular prospect on a given day).
- Mail merge and email.
- Sales quotation and proposal generation models.
- Territory planning.

Each salesperson had a computer and a modem that
was set up in the office and connected to a network.
Salespeople were fully dependent on the workstation, software, database, and telephone/facsimile –
there was no need for 'pen and paper' or secretarial
support.

Ricardo saw a lot of potential in applying telemarketing elsewhere. But he rejected the idea of using
Dubai's version of TeleMagic because as a DOS
program it was outdated. It would need to be available in a Microsoft Windows environment for him to
even attempt to upgrade the software for different
and larger environments (e.g., European operations).

As part of his investigation for Rank Xerox's
International Region, Ricardo had spoken with staff
at the company that sold TeleMagic about potentially purchasing the software. He later found out
that if he were to proceed with upgrading telemarketing, they would provide him with a Windows
version of TeleMagic and all the other things he
needed to customize the software (e.g., Windows
Professional version, hooks, etc.) along with full
information and technical support to assist his
efforts. As he explained:

*Dubai was using something [TeleMagic] that I
knew there was a new version of ... they had
never heard [about]. If I could not get the
Windows version, I would not consider creating
a new package for telemarketing.*

Ricardo came back from Dubai ready to get the ball
rolling on improving telemarketing for use system-
wide in Rank Xerox, as Carlos explained:

*Ricardo came back saying, 'Excellent!' Already in
the plane he was creating out of that [Dubai's]
package a package that was one-hundred*

times better, which was what I knew he was going to do. And, he came like a lion, saying '... I can do it one hundred times better!'

Outside of Dubai

Sales operations in Europe differed from those within Dubai in many ways.

First, no competitor in Europe was using telephone sales to sell copiers. Moreover, while Dubai sold copiers of many sizes via telemarketing, it was unclear whether customers elsewhere would buy copiers, particularly large ones, with such heavy dependence on the telephone by the vendor.

Second, Rank Xerox had a 'marketing buccaneer' culture. The salesforce was used to making decisions independently (e.g., who to approach and how to sell to them) with little management control. The existing approach was to focus on generating revenue by spending as much time on the road (seeing people face-to-face) and as little time in the office as possible. Because salesforce bonuses were based on performance (i.e., revenue generated) and not activity (e.g., prospects contacted), salespeople put greater priority on obtaining signed orders than

on making contact with non-customers to generate leads.

Third, salespeople outside of Dubai had not used computers in the selling process in any substantial way – they were used to pen and paper and secretarial support.

Clearly, considerable effort would be needed to change their behavior, as Carlos noted:

Cultural traditions and history [at Rank Xerox] are as tough as granite ... To change the behavior of salespeople is impossible.

Next move

As he sat in his office, Carlos was still trying to recover from Wave II's waning performance. He was buoyed, however, by the thought of what he had seen in Dubai and how excited Ricardo was about upgrading and implementing telemarketing.

It was now time to decide: should he tell Fournier that he had found a revolutionary tool that would transform Rank Xerox's sales operations, or should he put the whole idea aside and not share the secrets of Dubai?

Exhibit 1 Dubai revenues (1992 to 1994)

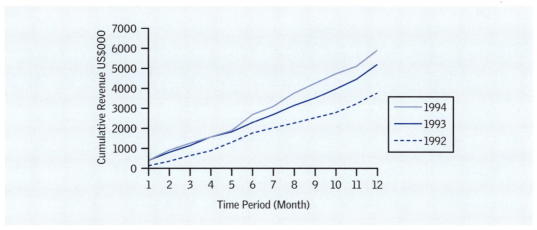

Source: Rank Xerox Order Tracker (Sales).

Exhibit 2 Dubai telemarketing activity (1993 to late 1995)

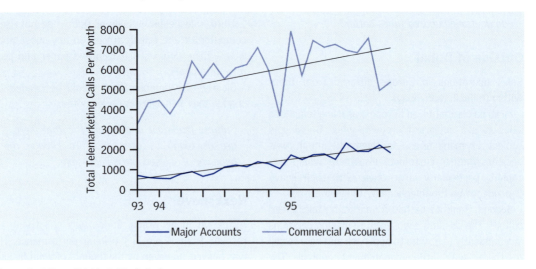

Source: Rank Xerox TeleMagic (Marketing).

INSEAD

Rank Xerox (C): The success of telesales

This case received the 2003 European Foundation for Management Development Case of the Year Award in the category 'Knowledge Management and Learning in Organisations'

It was 1997 and Carlos Camarero was a happy man. His last initiative leading Team C, Telesales, was a resounding success. Within the first six weeks of launch, over 2,000 TeleMagic licenses were sold within Rank Xerox. Within a year, Telesales had been fully implemented in 19 countries (all 15 major Rank Xerox European countries as well as Turkey, Hungary, the Czech Republic, and Morocco) and average sales coverage had increased by 11% over 1995 levels with some units increasing by as much as 30%. The Chairman's Statement in Rank Xerox's 1996 Annual Report noted that Telesales helped improve coverage (i.e., percentage of copier buying decisions that Rank Xerox bid on) and increase market share. Its success was lasting. Over the next two years, direct sales productivity (annual per person revenue) had risen from US$385,000 to US$481,000.

'Telesales' was Carlos's retitled version of 'Telemarketing'. He saw Telemarketing in action first-hand when he visited Rank Xerox's Dubai, United Arab Emirates location. Telemarketing involved increased use of the telephone by salespeople to capture information from prospects and customers to increase coverage and improve salesforce productivity. Carlos described and marketed it as 'Telesales' because it sounded more impressive (which was important when trying to get people at all levels of the organization buy in to the approach). After he had visited Dubai, Carlos obtained approval from senior management to pilot, and ultimately broadly implement Telesales. Telesales was piloted outside of Dubai in 1995 and was launched broadly among Rank Xerox's European offices in 1996.

The Telesales concept was originally a small piece of the Wave I initiative. Hardly anyone, even Carlos, the Team C leader, had noticed at that time or several years later that Telesales was technically part of Wave I. Telesales was presented in 1995 as another module to Wave II, which was struggling at that time. There was such an enormous acceptance of Telesales that Wave II was ultimately declared dead and Team C focused on Telesales.

Carlos, however, was surprised at Telesales' success. He recalled that at a senior committee meeting to gain approval to pilot Telesales, people were asking 'Where is Dubai?' Some executives even scoffed at the idea of attempting to spread a practice from such a small country. When Carlos told Bernard Fournier, Rank Xerox's Managing Director, of the Telesales plan he was impressed but wondered who was going to pay for it. When Carlos told him that Ricardo Morias, a relational database expert within Rank Xerox, was going to do this as a voluntary service (without extra pay) during the night (while working on other responsibilities during the day), Fournier laughed but gave the approval to proceed. Under such circumstances, Carlos wondered how Telesales had become so successful.

Telesales development and pilots

Carlos's objective to implement Telesales in European countries was to restore the momentum lost in Wave II. Following Team C methodology (as used in Wave I and Wave II), Carlos and his team extracted the key elements of the Dubai practice. They then put together a 40 page booklet similar to those used in Wave I detailing the extraordinary

This case was written by Michael Casaburi, Wharton MBA 1998 and Doctoral Student at Wharton under the supervision of Gabriel Szulanski, Associate Professor of Strategy at INSEAD. The case is intended to be used as a basis for class discussion rather than to illustrate either effective or ineffective handling of an administrative situation.

06/2004-5138

performance of Dubai, describing the key factors of the Telesales practice, and explaining how to implement it.

The management in Dubai had embedded the key elements having to do with database management, reporting, and record keeping in a piece of DOS software entitled 'TeleMagic'. Ricardo purchased an upgrade to TeleMagic which operated in a Microsoft Windows environment and then changed the coding in the software so that the language identifying the various fields matched the daily language of Rank Xerox exactly (the company selling TeleMagic gave Rank Xerox the rights to modify the software). Ricardo developed computer screens that were easy to read and easy to use. Ricardo also increased the reporting capabilities of the software and connected it to headquarters' central computers. As Carlos summarized:

> We decided to buy the best package in the market [TeleMagic] and modify and link it to our database. Ricardo Morias did that … He did a beautiful job. It took him two months. He [worked with] a company in Portugal and for US$50,000, we developed the most amazing piece of sales software … it basically fills the database and helps salespeople try to get 100% coverage of buying windows by using industry segmentation and territory planning, organizing activity targets, and monitoring of activities (not performance) …

Telesales was initially implemented in late 1995 in Europe in a series of pilots beginning in Lisbon and later in Birmingham, Lyon, Brussels, and Madrid. To persuade the managers of these units to undertake the initiative, Carlos not only shared with them data proving the superior performance of Dubai but he also flew them to Dubai personally to observe the operations. This approach was effective. As Carlos described:

> It was an opportunistic exercise where theory turned into practice. It allowed potential recipients to see, eat, chew and touch the practice. It was seeing with their eyes that 2+2=4, not just being told.

The Telesales practice is considerably larger and more complex than those transferred in Wave I and implementation was not as smooth as originally anticipated. It took a number of months for the pilots to begin to reproduce the superior results found at Dubai along with a number of iterations back to Dubai to answer questions that were originally unforeseen.

For example, after implementation had been under way in Lisbon for a couple of months they discovered that they didn't know how to operate Telesales for salespeople responsible for Key Accounts, accounts with major corporations. Calling such corporations on the phone to sell copiers did not at first sound like an intelligent idea. However, Carlos went back to Dubai to observe what they did. In Dubai, those responsible for Key Accounts used the telephone as much or more than those responsible for smaller firms because the units of large corporations often buy separately and are headed by people who are too busy for numerous personal visits.

Telesales roll-out

Once the pilot units were operational they were designated as benchmarks for the rest of the corporation. As he had in persuading the pilots, Carlos brought dozens and dozens of managers to the pilot in Lisbon to personally observe the operations in an explicit attempt to increase the motivation to adopt the new practice. The managers who visited Dubai were impressed by the potential opportunity they saw in implementing Telesales in their countries. As Carlos explained:

> It was a cosmic exercise, of almost insulting simplicity. We found out that [in Europe] our salespeople were averaging ten customer visits a day, but only one of them was effective. This way (i.e., using Telesales) they could rapidly complete the effective transaction and had plenty of time left to average 2.5 effective transactions per day, thus doubling their productivity.

In rolling out Telesales, Team C offered a complete package. It was like many franchise operations, according to Ricardo, in that all the necessary elements were pulled together and were easy to follow. Team C integrated the equipment, space, facilities, and network requirements and provided training and support. As Ricardo recalled, 'We even told them how to organize the workspace with the new computers in the office'. Carlos and his team did not publicize the control aspects of the software, which allowed sales managers to closely monitor salepersons' behavior (even by the minute).

Salespeople saw the benefits of using Telesales. As Ricardo explained:

> Sales people did not like having to write up their activities (e.g., who they called and when) and the software was viewed as great because the computer was now doing this for them ... The solution is simple. You contact 24 customers instead of 6 customers. People thought, 'I'll buy it' ... it was a magic box.

Salespeople also accepted the introduction of computers (and the attendant requirement to populate the database with data) because the Internet age was emerging and it was seen as being 'high tech'. As Carlos noted:

> The computer was fashionable as it was the time of the Internet explosion ... we did not have to explain to them that they would fill in [populate] the database ... we said 'This is state of the art technology and we are helping you' ... it was sexy and fashionable and we did not need to convince them with data [that they should use Telesales].

Looking back

As Carlos reflected on his work with Team C, he tried to piece together what lessons could be learned. Why was Telesales successful? Would Telesales have worked independent of the initial attempt to implement Wave II? Was Telesales Wave II reborn? What were the factors that made Wave I and Telesales successful but Wave II unsuccessful? What could others learn from his experience?

Exhibit 1 Telesales performance

	1995	1996 (Jan – Oct)	1997 (Jan – Oct)	% Difference
Level of Implementation	Pilots in Nine Countries	Jan: 49/59 subunits July: 58/59 subunits	Fully implemented in all countries and all but one of 59 subunits	
Revenue attributable directly to Telesales		US$42 million (US$60 million in all of 1996)	US$47 million	11.9%
Revenue per Teleseller		US$180,000	US$220,140	22.3%
Orders per Teleseller		33	43	29.2%
Boxes per Operator		3.2	4.1	28.5%

Source: Rank Xerox documents.

Exhibit 2 Wave I, Wave II, and telesales metrics

	Pre Wave I (1993)	Post Wave I /Pre Wave II (1994)	Post Wave II /Pre Telesales (1995)	Post Telesales (1996)	Telesales Lagged (1997)
Mean Sales Coverage	Not available	29.14	29.14	32.36	33.11
Mean Direct Sales Revenue/sales person ($US 000)	368	400	385	Not Available	481
Mean Ratio of gross profit to selling expenses	Not available	1.06	1.19	Not Available	2.02

Note: 1995 sales coverage data is available only by geographic region (Northern, Southern, and Central) except for the three largest countries (Germany, France, and the U.K) for a total sample size of seven.
Source: Rank Xerox documents.

Ivey

Richard Ivey School of Business

The University of Western Ontario

Case 12 **Cola wars in China: The future is here**

On July 7, 2002, Zong Qinghou, the general manager of the Wahaha Group (Wahaha), China's largest soft drink producer, was reviewing market data on Wahaha's Future Cola brand in his office in Hangzhou, Zhejiang Province. Wahaha Future Cola had been launched four years earlier to compete with products from Coca Cola and PepsiCo, the dominant players in the category. At the launch, Zong and his management team had been

Nancy Dai prepared this case under the supervision of Professor Niraj Dawar solely to provide material for class discussion. The authors do not intend to illustrate either effective or ineffective handling of a managerial situation. The authors may have disguised certain names and other identifying information to protect confidentiality.

Version: (A) 2004-07-13

tremendously energized by the opportunity to compete with some of the world's best companies. Four years later, despite the failure of several other domestic colas, Wahaha Future Cola and other Future Series carbonated drinks had achieved an impressive 18 per cent of the carbonated drinks market in the first half of 2002. However, as Future Cola's share grew, Zong was preoccupied with how his multinational competitors would respond, how Wahaha should prepare for these responses, and how it should continue to increase its market share. Competition for share in the high-stakes market of the world's most populated country was intensifying.

Wahaha group

Company profile

With 2001 sales revenue of RMB6.23 billion, and profits of RMB914 million,[1] the Wahaha Hangzhou Group Co. Ltd. consisted of more than 40 wholly-owned subsidiaries and majority holding companies in 23 provinces, autonomous regions and cities. With total assets of RMB6 billion and 14,000 employees, the group operated more than 68 advanced auto-mated production lines at various locations. Unlike many other Chinese companies of its size, the group had a solid cash position and no long-term bank debt. Wahaha's 2002 target was to achieve sales revenues of RMB8 billion, and a profit of RMB1.3 billion. In the longer term, the Wahaha Group aimed to become a truly national, and even international, player. Specifically, it was working on establishing subsidiaries in most provinces, maintaining its leading position in water, milk drinks and mixed congee, and on increasing its market share in carbonated beverages, tea and juice drinks.

In 2002, Wahaha competed in six major product categories: milk drinks, packaged water, carbonated drinks, tea and juice drinks, canned food and health-care products. For several years, its milk drink, packaged water and canned mixed congee had been leaders in their respective categories. For the first half of 2002, the total soft drink output for Wahaha was 1.83 million tons (1.66 billion litres), while its

[1] *An exchange rate of US$1 = RMB8.27 applied in 2002.*

closest competitors — Coca Cola and PepsiCo — sold 1.61 million tons (1.461 billion litres) and 0.76 million tons (0.689 billion litres), respectively. This was the first time that a domestic company's soft drink output had exceeded that of Coca Cola in China. It was also an unusual situation for Coca Cola that a local competitor had seemingly come out of nowhere to upstage the global giant. In a nation of 1.3 billion people, per capita consumption of Wahaha beverages in China was more than 10 bottles a year.

Wahaha's development

Wahaha was founded in 1987, when it began selling bottled soda water, ice cream and stationery to the children in Hangzhou, Zhejiang Province. Founder Zong Qinghou and two employees discovered in 1988 that although there were 38 companies nationwide producing nutritional drinks, none was specifically targeted toward children. The one-child policy had created a whole generation of 'little emperors' who, due to their parents' and grandparents' indulgences, were fastidious with food, and presented a potentially huge opportunity. By some estimates there were 200 million such children in China. The company developed a nutritious drink called the Wahaha Natrient Beverage for Children and aggressively pursued the children's market. (The brand Wahaha means 'to make children happy.') The product was supported with the slogan 'Drinking Wahaha boosts appetite.' The product was an instant success, propelling corporate revenues to RMB400 million and profits to RMB70 million by 1990.

Management quickly realized that it was not easy to sustain growth with a single product that had low entry barriers and low technical content. Competitors followed close on the heels of Wahaha. Between 1992 and 1994, 3,000 companies entered the market for children's beverages. Zong decided to expand the product range, entering the fruit-flavored milk drinks market. At the time, a couple of companies had already launched fruit-flavored milk drinks, and the product had won market acceptance. Zong felt this was the best time to enter. In what was to become a pattern in several product categories, Wahaha was a fast follower that quickly ramped up production and achieved high retail coverage with its nationwide production facilities, well-known brand,

and well-established distribution network. Its wide range of products made it competitive relative to other domestic producers who tended to have a narrow product line. By the end of 1991, Wahaha launched its fruit-flavored milk drink, followed quickly by Wahaha Milk enriched with vitamins A and D, and calcium. Its catchy advertising jingles rolled off the tongues of tots in many provinces. In 1996, amidst concerns over polluted tap water in several provinces, the company launched Wahaha purified water, which rapidly achieved leading market share, contributing to corporate sales revenues of over RMB1 billion in that year.

Wahaha's brand extensions had aroused much debate among industry observers who held that Wahaha was mainly a children's brand and extending it to categories such as mixed congee and purified water would either not work, or would dilute the brand. Zong, while admitting the advantages of launching different brands for different product categories, held that it would spread the limited financial resources of most Chinese enterprises too thin. Wahaha's logic had been to continue to extend the brand into food and beverage categories in which there was no dominant player. For consumers, the connotation of the Wahaha brand broadened and came to represent health, wholesomeness, happiness, quality and reliability, and not just a brand for children's nutritious drinks. Results from the market rewarded and justified Wahaha's approach. After a series of brand extensions, Wahaha's sales revenue exceeded RMB2 billion in 1997, and the revenue of Wahaha purified water and mixed congee exceeded RMB500 million and 100 million respectively. This was a rare achievement, even in China's rapidly growing food and beverage industry. In 1998, spurred by its success in other beverage categories, Wahaha decided to tackle the prize: the carbonated drinks market. Industry observers were skeptical and predicted that it would last no more than a few months on the market.

Corporate growth was powered not just by the launch of new products, but also through acquisitions, such as loss-making companies that were several times larger, but poorly managed. Acquisitions supported geographic expansion and allowed Wahaha to produce locally in various provincial markets, as well as to increase its market share and brand awareness in other provinces. By 2002, over a third of Wahaha's output was produced outside its home province.

Wahaha's joint ventures with Danone

In 1996, despite Wahaha's excellent performance, management realized that it needed to scale its operations quickly and obtain world-class production technology if it was to survive competition from both local and multinational competitors. After careful consideration, it chose to partner with the giant French food company, Groupe Danone. The two companies established several production-oriented joint ventures. While Danone eventually held a 51 per cent share of the joint ventures, Wahaha retained control of management and marketing. In 2002, among Wahaha Group's 42 companies and RMB3.5 billion registered capital, Danone's investment was 32 per cent. With the injection of capital from Danone, Wahaha launched Wahaha Future Cola and introduced advanced production lines for bottling water, milk and tea. Prior to the joint venture, the annual increase in revenues and profits was about RMB100 million and RMB10 million respectively. Since 1996, both revenue and profit had grown even more rapidly (see Exhibit 1).

Zong Qinghou's management style

Founder and general manager Zong Qinghou was a charismatic leader who liked to 'put his eggs in the baskets he knew best.' Like most of his generation of the Cultural Revolution, he spent 15 years in the countryside after finishing junior school. This experience taught him a lot about rural China. When he came back to his hometown, Hangzhou, he worked in a factory, first as a worker and then in sales. During this period, he traveled extensively throughout China, deepening his knowledge of markets and consumers in various regions. He was 42 when he began his career as sales manager of the two person sales team at the factory. His job included delivering goods to retailers on his cycle.

When asked what made Wahaha so successful, Zong responded that the company understood the Chinese market well:

Market research reports in China are not reliable. You pay the market research firms large amounts of money and you don't know where the money was spent. However, our own marketing people are our market research staff since we are always collecting information about the market, and we make decisions based on their understanding of the market.

Now in his late 50s, Zong worked long hours and still traveled more than 200 days every year 'to keep a finger on the pulse of the market.' He hosted most of the marketing meetings at Wahaha and participated in every product launch and marketing planning activity.

Wahaha's marketing

Marketing, research and development (R&D) and logistics management were centralized at headquarters, while the subsidiaries were engaged in production. Wahaha's marketing was clearly home-grown.

Wahaha's advertising

A typical new product launch followed a pattern established early on in Wahaha's history. In an early launch of Wahaha Natrient Beverage, Zong signed advertising deals worth several hundred thousand RMB with local television stations, exceeding even the company's cash reserves at the time. In its advertisement, Wahaha highlighted data from reports about children's malnutrition and endorsements from experts about Wahaha Natrient Beverage's nutritional benefits for children. On the strength of the advertising, Wahaha would convince the local government-controlled distribution companies to carry the product. If distributors hesitated, Wahaha's marketing staff would call every retailer and smaller distributor in the local yellow pages to inquire if they carried Wahaha Natrient Beverage. This created a buzz that usually resulted in the product being listed with the distribution companies.

In 2001, Wahaha was among the top 10 advertisers in China's US$11.2 billion advertising market, and the only beverage company in the group.[2] Wahaha's total advertising expenditures amounted

---

[2] 'China Market racks up largest ad spending in Asia-Pacific,' www1.chinadaily.com.cn/bw/2002–03–05/60571.html, March 12, 2002.

to more than RMB500 million, with media buys accounting for 80 per cent. Comparatively, Coca Cola's 2001 media expense in China (including cinema, TV, radio, print, and outdoor) was US$19 million. Wahaha's television advertising was mainly intended to build brand awareness and recognition, while print advertising elaborated on product benefits and promotions. Wahaha spent 75 per cent of its marketing budget on television advertising, and half of that was on CCTV Channel 1 (the national news channel). The remainder was spent on print media (five per cent), promotion (10 per cent) and outdoor advertising (10 per cent). Wahaha's advertising targeted the mass market, and not just the wealthier urban consumers. The prices of its products were usually lower than those of comparable products from its multinational competitors.

In addition to Wahaha's advertising, its sponsorship activities had helped build positive associations for its brand. Wahaha established Wahaha elementary school, Wahaha Children's Palace (a recreation center for children), Wahaha Children's Art Troupe and Wahaha Summer Camps to underscore its involvement in child development. In 2001, Wahaha held a campaign to celebrate Children's Day and Beijing's application to host the 2008 Summer Olympic Games.

Wahaha was also the first among Chinese companies to use celebrity product endorsement for its products. In 1996, Jinggangshan, a pop singer, was signed to endorse Wahaha purified water. Celebrity endorsement was also used for Wahaha Future Cola and Wahaha Tea series.

Wahaha's distribution

Key success factors for Wahaha were the unique relationships developed with distributors over the previous 10 years. In a vast country where logistics are notoriously difficult, Wahaha's network was able to quickly deliver its products, reaching even remote corners of China within days. Unlike many multinational and domestic companies which preferred to establish their own distribution networks, Wahaha focused on partnering with local distributors, and its initial promotional efforts on entry into a region included distributors rather than end-consumers alone.

Partnerships with local distributors were not without problems. In particular, accounts receivable and bad debts were a perennial headache and the main reason why multinationals shunned this mode of distribution. In 1994, Wahaha concluded that the problem of accounts receivable was serious enough to jeopardize its growth and success. The company tackled the issue head-on by developing a radical new policy that ensured compliance and on-time payment by introducing incentives for channel members to play for long-term gain: distributors were required to pay an annual security deposit in advance and operate according to Wahaha's payment policy. In return, Wahaha would pay a higher-than-bank interest rate on the security deposit and offered discounts for early payment. At the end of the year, bonuses were awarded to distributors making prompt payments. The policy was replicated down the chain as distributors, in turn, developed secondary wholesalers, some of whom enjoyed preferential policies by paying security deposits to the distributors. It took Wahaha two years to implement the policy. In the process, a number of distributors that had low credibility dropped out of the system. Those that remained were more committed than ever to Wahaha.

Wahaha established offices in more than 30 provinces with sales staff co-ordinating operations with the distributors. Distributors were in charge of carrying inventory, providing funds and delivering to the retailers, and Wahaha's local offices supported them in retail coverage, inventory management, advertising and promotion. Wahaha established coordination teams to monitor prices in different areas to protect the interests of local distributors. Wahaha's staff collected information from the market and provided feedback to headquarters, which enabled the company to adjust its sales strategy and develop new products. Today, Wahaha's 2,000 sales staff work closely with more than 1,000 influential distributors that have the credibility and infrastructure to sell large volumes. Loyalty and stability of the distributors are key, and bad debts have decreased substantially. In 2002, Wahaha began implementing an information system that would enable distributors and Wahaha to exchange information in real time.

The world soft-drink industry

The term 'soft drinks' refers to beverages that do not contain alcohol, and includes packaged water, carbonated drinks, juices and juice drinks, ready-to-drink tea, as well as sports and energy drinks.

In 2000, global soft drink consumption reached 320.2 billion litres. That total was split into 170 billion litres (53 per cent) of carbonated drinks, 77 billion litres (24 per cent) of packaged water, and the 'other' category which included juices, ready-to-drink tea, sports and energy drinks, and miscellaneous drinks accounting for 73.2 billion litres (23 per cent). Worldwide, the growth of carbonated drinks had been slowing in recent years from an average annual rate of four per cent between 1994 and 2000 to a predicted rate of only two per cent in 2003 (see **Exhibit 2**). These numbers masked fast growth in countries such as China and India, which compensated for declines in the more mature markets of North America and Europe. Packaged water was growing worldwide, in some markets due to consumer trends toward a healthier lifestyle, and in others due to the poor quality of tap water. The 'other' category had great growth potential due to increased demand for more healthy, nutritious and tasty drinks. The size of this category had rapidly grown from 52.7 billion litres in 1994 to 73.2 billion litres in 2000. By 2003 volumes were forecast to reach 85.6 billion litres. Within this category, 'ready-to-drink tea' had had the fastest growth since 1994, with an annual increase of over 11 per cent and industry observers believed it still had plenty of untapped potential.

The players in China

The leading soft drink producers in the world included Coca Cola, PepsiCo, Nestlé and Danone, and all four were also present in China. Globally, the first two were dominant in the carbonated category with more than 70 per cent combined market share, while the latter two were strong in the ready-to-drink tea and water categories.

Coca Cola Coca Cola was the world's largest soft-drink company, and the fifth-largest food and beverage company. Its 2001 revenues were US$20.092 billion, with a net income of US$3.969 billion. The firm sold about 300 drink brands, including coffees, juices, sports drinks and teas in 200 nations. Its major brands included Coca Cola Classic, Diet Coke, Sprite, Fanta (carbonated drinks), Minute Maid (juice), POWERade (sports drink) and Dasani (water). It distributed Danone's Evian water in North America and Danone's spring water brands in the United States. Beverage Partner Worldwide, its joint venture with Nestlé, S.A., marketed ready-to-drink coffee and tea. More than 60 per cent of its sales revenues came from outside the United States. Coca Cola's stated aim was to become an all-around beverage company. In 2001, water was the second largest contributor to its growth after carbonated drinks. Coca Cola had recently instituted a 'think local, act local, but leverage global' mandate to empower local decision-makers, in recognition of the need to both respond to local preferences and react to local competitors. In response, its local subsidiaries had launched a wide variety of drinks aimed at local needs.

Coca Cola first opened bottling plants in Shanghai and Tianjin in 1927, which were shut after the communist revolution in 1949. In 1979, when Coca Cola re-entered China, following the re-establishment of relations between China and the United States, it became the first American consumer product to return to China. In 2000, it moved its marketing headquarters for China from Hong Kong to Shanghai. By 2002, Coca Cola had a total of 28 bottling plants in China, with a total investment of US$1.1 billion. In most of these joint ventures, Coca Cola didn't have majority shareholding. Its soft-drink output in China was 16 per cent of the national total in 2001 and its carbonated drink output was about 35 per cent of total carbonated drink output. China was the sixth largest market for the company worldwide. In addition to its global carbonated drink brands such as Coca Cola, Diet Coke, Fanta and Sprite, the company also developed local brands such as Heaven and Earth (non-carbonated fruit juice, tea, water), Jinmeile (tea), Smart (fruit-flavored carbonated drink), Lanfeng (honey green tea) and Qoo (juice drink). In 2001, it launched its water brand 'Sensation' (at the remarkably low wholesale price point of RMB0.50, while the market leader Wahaha water was selling at RMB0.90). In its advertising, the company included Chinese cultural icons such as windmills and dragons. Local film and sports stars were engaged as endorsers, including diver Fu Mingxia, the three-time Olympic gold medalist. It also sponsored the Coca Cola Cup National Youth Soccer Tournament and the China national soccer teams at all levels. Coca Cola also extended its sponsorship contracts with the International Olympic Committee up to 2008, which included US$1 billion in funding for the Beijing Games. In 2001, the total revenue for Coca Cola China was about US$189 million and revenue from carbonated drinks was about US$186 million. However, the annual per capita consumption of Coca Cola products in China was a meager eight servings (about 0.2268 litre per serving). Consumption was still a far cry from the average 415 servings consumed in the United States, 163 in Japan, 98 in Europe and 68 in South Korea.

PepsiCo After the merger with Quaker in 2001, PepsiCo became the fourth-largest food and beverage company in the world. Its 2001 total sales revenue of US$26.935 billion included beverage revenue and profit of US$10.44 billion and US$1.678 billion respectively. Forty-two per cent of its sales were outside the United States. Its powerful soft drink brands included Pepsi-Cola, Diet Pepsi, Mountain Dew, 7Up, Miranda, Gatorade (sports drink), Tropicana (juice), Lipton teas and Aquafina (water).

In 1981, PepsiCo signed a deal with the Chinese government to establish a joint-venture bottling plant in Shenzhen. By 2002, the company had invested a total of US$500 million in China on 14 bottling plants and employed close to 10,000 people. Unlike Coca Cola, PepsiCo sought a majority share in the joint ventures. Its flagship carbonated drink brands in China were Pepsi-Cola, Pepsi Light, Pepsi Twist, 7Up, Miranda and Mountain Dew. It also owned local brands such as Asia, Arctic and Tianfu. Its non-carbonated drink brands in China included Gatorade and Dole (fruit juice). Its non-beverage brands included Lay's potato chips, Doritos and Cheetos. Its soft-drink output in China was about eight per cent of the national total in 2001. According to A.C. Nielsen's market data in Asia, Pepsi-Cola was the most popular soft drink brand for young consumers, a reflection of its positioning for that demographic market. In its advertising in China, PepsiCo used popular entertainers such as Faye Wang, Guo Fuchen and Chen Huiling as endorsers. Despite its marketing efforts and popularity among China's youth, PepsiCo China had not been profitable during its 20 years in China: high marketing costs and conflicts with joint venture partners were holding the company back.[3]

Nestlé S.A. With revenues of CHF84.698 billion[4] (approximately US$56 billion) and profit of CHF6.681 billion (approx. US$4 billion) in 2001, Nestlé was the world's largest food and beverage company. Its major products included coffee, water, dairy products, breakfast cereals, culinary products, ice cream, frozen food, chocolate and confectionary, and pet care. Its major water brands included Nestlé Pure Life, Nestlé Aquarel, Perrier and Vittel. Other beverage brands included Nestea, Nesquik, Nescau, Milo, Carnation, Libby's and Caro. In 2001, Nestlé was the world leader in bottled water with a market share of 16.3 per cent. Nestlé owned four of the top six water brands in the world.

Nestlé came to China in 1979. By 2002 it had established 14 fully owned enterprises, 19 joint ventures and one R&D center for a total investment of US$72 million. Its 2001 sales in China amounted to US$570 million. Due to the growth of packaged water and its profitability, Nestlé China aimed to be the market leader in this category. It established plants for producing packaged water in Tianjin and Shanghai and was expanding its own sales network to co-operate with distributors.

Groupe Danone The French company ranked sixth in the global food and beverage industry. In 2001, it had revenues of €14.470 billion (approximately US$14 billion), with net income of €132 million (approximately US$127.7 million). It operated in three core businesses: fresh dairy products, beverages and cereal biscuits and snacks. Its major brands included Danone and Dannon for fresh dairy products, Evian, Volvic and Aqua for mineral water, and LU for biscuits. Its leading position worldwide was based on a portfolio of major international brands

---

[3] Yan Shi, 'Pepsi's Business Model Encountering Trust Crisis in China', Economic Observation, April 24, 2002.

[4] 1 U.S. dollar (US$) 5 1.35 Swiss Francs (CHF).

and a solid presence in local markets (about 70 per cent of global sales came from brands that were local market leaders in which Danone had shares). As part of a recent push toward globalization, the company had made about 40 acquisitions in Asia, Latin America, Central Europe, Africa and the Middle East.

Danone's major products in China included biscuits, water, yogurt and milk. Most of these products were sold under the Danone brand. In 1987, the company had begun operations in China by establishing the Guangzhou Danone Yogurt Company. This was followed in 1992 by the Shanghai Danone Biscuit Company. Since then, it had acquired a number of companies: in 1996 it purchased 63.2 per cent of Haomen Beer, 54.2 per cent of Wuhan Donghu Beer and its stake in the five joint ventures with Wahaha. In 1998 it owned 54.2 per cent of Shenzhen Danone Yili Beverages Co. Ltd., and in 2000 it purchased 92 per cent of Robust Group, one of the top 10 Chinese soft-drink producers. In December 2000, it had acquired a five per cent stake in Shanghai Bright Dairy, one of the top milk producers in China. It also purchased 50 per cent of Meilin-Zhengguanghe Water Company and 10 per cent of Zhengguanghe Online Shopping Company.

China's soft-drink industry

With the entry of multinationals into the Chinese market in the 1980s, marketing, advanced production technology and cutting-edge management expertise were injected into China's soft-drink industry, spurring its development. Over the past 20 years, the industry had grown at an annual rate of over 21 per cent, and annual output had increased from 0.288 million tons (261 million litres) in 1980 to 16.69 million tons (15.141 billion litres) in 2001 (see Exhibit 3). Per capita consumption increased from 0.3 litre per annum in 1982 to eight litres per annum in 2001, 27 times that of 1982. Total revenues exceeded RMB40 billion in 2000. In urban areas, soft drinks were no longer seen as an occasional luxury to be consumed only in restaurants and hotels, but a regularly consumed product. Drink package formats diversified to meet new consumption patterns, and now included cans, polyethylene terephtalate (PET) and paper packs.

China's soft-drink industry had sped through three major development stages in a short time: the rise of carbonated drinks in the 1980s, packaged water in the 1990s and tea in the 2000s. In 2001, packaged water accounted for 40.6 per cent of total sales, carbonated drinks for 27 per cent and the 'other' category for 32.4 per cent. The fastest growing product was bottled tea because of its low-calorie, low-fat and low-sugar content, and convenience. It had a share of about 12 per cent and an annual growth of 85 per cent. It was predicted that juice and milk drinks would become the catalyst for growth in the next phase of development. Despite rapid growth, China's national per capita consumption was still only 20 per cent of the world average and 33 per cent of the United States average. Growth potential for all categories remained high. It was predicted that over the next 10 to 15 years, industry output would grow at an annual rate of about 10 per cent, reaching 22.65 million tons (20.548 billion litres) in 2005, and 37 million tons (33.566 billion litres) by 2015. With China's entry into World Trade Organization (WTO) in 2001, China's soft-drink industry was expected to develop even more rapidly and competition was already intensifying as restrictions on foreign investment were lifted.

A number of large companies and brands were present on the national stage, yet the industry remained fragmented in comparison to developed markets. In 2001, the combined output of the top 10 domestic soft-drink producers in China (see Exhibit 4) accounted for 40 per cent of the national total.[5] With Coca Cola China and PepsiCo China, the total output of the top players represented 63 per cent of national output. In the 2000s, several of the top 10 companies were undergoing major changes: Jianlibao, a large domestic player, was in crisis; Danone invested in Wahaha, Robust and Meilin-Zhengguanghe; Xuri Group, the largest tea producer, failed in its competition with two iced-tea brands from Taiwan (named Mr. Kon and President), which now held 75 per cent share, with combined revenues of RMB3.5 billion. Nestlé, despite its leading position in the global tea market, did not do as well in China. Robust, in which Danone had a majority share, had its own problems. Five of its top executives resigned

---

[5] *Data from China Soft Drink Industry Association.*

due to the company's failure to meet growth targets and because of differences of opinion on the future strategy of the company with Danone. Danone China's CEO took over the management role.

Consumers

According to research conducted in 2001, the target customers for soft drinks were people in the 11 to 40 age group. Income and education level were positively related to soft drink purchase. When purchasing soft drinks, taste was a key criterion. In addition, young consumers were concerned with brand, lifestyle and fashion. Older consumers cared more about health and nutrition. Women and children preferred sweeter drinks, men and young consumers preferred a crisp taste, while older consumers preferred a light taste. Most consumers purchased soft drinks in supermarkets for reasons of price, choice, and the quality assurance the retailer provided. Drinks were also sold through convenience stores, ice cream shops and roadside stalls, especially those near residential areas and schools.

Marketing in the soft drink industry had changed in recent years. Prior to 1997, the emphasis had been on brand-building, and companies had spent heavily on advertising. However, with brand proliferation and several companies adopting similar positioning, distribution had become a key battleground for gaining competitive advantage.

Cola in China

Thanks to Coca Cola and PepsiCo, cola was the most popular soft drink worldwide, with consumption amounting to 70 billion litres, and accounting for 20 per cent of all soft-drink sales. Cola sales were still on the rise, though its role in the overall soft-drinks mix was diminishing.

In the early 1980s, before Coca Cola and PepsiCo entered China, more than 10 domestic cola manufacturers produced cola, but with little marketing, revenues remained small. With the arrival of the two multinational giants, the local producers found it hard to compete, and gradually withdrew from the market or established joint bottling ventures with the two giants.

Coca Cola and PepsiCo's sales volumes rose in line with overall sales of cola until they dominated China's carbonated drink market. The two

companies had replicated their global rivalry in China and were initially determined to seize market share from domestic cola producers, even at the cost of profitability. The headquarters of both companies in China co-ordinated the marketing efforts of the bottling plants. Both used heavy advertising and sponsoring to support their cola brands. By 2000, Coca Cola had an average of 85 per cent distribution penetration in cities, while PepsiCo stood at about 65 per cent but was growing faster (3.7 per cent growth rate versus Coca Coca's 1.3 per cent).[6] Coca Cola expanded its sales nationwide: it first targeted the 150 cities with a population greater than one million by establishing sales channels there. Next, it continued to roll out into cities with populations greater than 0.5 million, and so on. In comparison, PepsiCo focused on key markets and in cities such as Shanghai, Chongqing, Chengdu, Wuhan and Shenzhen, where it had a higher share than its rival.

In 1998 some domestic soft-drink producers, attracted by the rapidly growing market, launched their own cola brands. Among them were Wahaha Future Cola from Wahaha, and Fenhuang Cola from Guangzhou Fenhuang Food Company. Both advertised heavily on CCTV. Wahaha launched its Wahaha Future Cola brand during the soccer World Cup and utilized its well-established distribution channels. Fenhuang Cola signed up the famous martial arts actor Jackie Chan to endorse its brand. Both brands emphasized a 'China's own cola' positioning, and were targeting smaller cities and the rural market where the two big foreign cola producers were comparatively weak. This revitalization of domestic cola brought other competitors into the fray, including Alishan Zhonghua Cola and Yanjing Cola in 2000, as well as Jianlibao's Huating Cola in 2001.

Wahaha Future Cola

By 1998, Wahaha had firmly established its production and distribution system, and its dominant position in non-carbonated drinks was secure. Wahaha could not, for long, neglect the carbonates market which represented almost half of the volume

---

6 'An Analysis of the Competition Between Coca Cola and PepsiCo in China,' China Business, October 16, 2001. Market penetration refers to the percentage of consumers of a certain cola brand among total cola consumers.

of the soft-drink industry. Entering the market would provide a much better utilization of its distribution network, and leverage its marketing skills. But it would also mean direct competition with Coca Cola and PepsiCo. In 1997, the total cola output in China was 1.36 million tons (1.234 billion litres) and Coca Cola and PepsiCo held a combined market share of 80 per cent. In 1998, Coca Cola's total beverage output in China was two million tons and PepsiCo 0.8 million tons. Wahaha, despite its number one position among domestic producers, had a total output of 0.93 million tons. Coca Cola and PepsiCo's success against the domestic cola producers in the early stages and their strong brand name and sales network in big cities formed a high entry barrier for new competitors.

Zong firmly believed local companies were capable of competing with the multinational players. He pointed to the computer industry, where domestic companies such as Legend were dominating the local market, and even building global brands. He pointed out that in the food and beverage industry where the technical requirements were relatively low and an understanding of domestic preferences was a distinct advantage, domestic companies had an edge. He concluded that the failure of domestic colas in the early stages was due to their lack of marketing and brand management skills, and that Wahaha had proven that it had these skills. As well, he believed some domestic producers did not want to compete with the multinationals because they lacked the confidence to compete against the giants. Confidence was not lacking at Wahaha.

Zong decided to target the rural market first because he knew and understood this market, and because it was not the focus of Coca Cola and PepsiCo. He reasoned that cola had the potential to be a mass-market product, and the rural areas were where the mass market resided. The 1.1 billion people in the rural market were impossible to ignore. Over the years, China's rural population had become wealthier. In 2000, rural residents' average income was 36 per cent of that of an urban resident (see **Exhibit 5**), but due to their large numbers, they accounted for two-thirds of national spending. A rural resident's spending on food and beverage totaled RMB820.52 a year, 42 per cent that of an urban resident. Meanwhile, the development of mass

communication had made the rural population more accessible, and exposed it to the outside world. Zong believed these trends represented an unparalleled and untapped opportunity.

To develop the product, Wahaha co-operated with R&D institutes and leading domestic flavor producers. To ensure that its cola would be of a high quality, Wahaha sought the advice of global beverage experts and conducted thousands of taste tests worldwide. Its taste was designed to be close to international colas, but a little bit sweeter and stronger to cater to the Chinese consumers' taste. In domestic blind taste tests, consumers preferred Wahaha Future Cola to other colas.

The name Wahaha Future Cola was put forward by Wahaha's employees. The Chinese characters of the brand meant 'unusual,' a reference to the unusual move of launching against entrenched and strong competitive rivals.

Wahaha did not intend to start a price war in the cola category, but it prepared to win such a war if one broke out. At launch, Wahaha offered three pack sizes, the same as Coca Cola and PepsiCo: 355 ml, 500 ml and 1.25 litres. A standard unit case (12 bottles of 500 ml) of Wahaha Future Cola was priced at RMB19 (wholesale), RMB7 lower than Coca Cola and Pepsi-Cola. This translated into a price difference of approximately RMB0.50 per bottle at retail. One reason for the lower price, Wahaha executives explained, was that Future Cola was aimed at the rural market which was more price-sensitive than the urban markets where the international competitors focused. Assessing potential competitive responses, Zong said:

It is possible that Coca Cola might reduce its price. But if it lowers the price per bottle of cola by RMB0.10, it will probably lose profit of about RMB0.5 billion; if it cuts price by RM0.50 it stands to lose RMB2.5 billion. If it is willing to do so, we are willing to follow.

Wahaha reasoned that its revenues from other products could support Future Cola through a price war. As it happened, Wahaha maintained the price difference with Coca Cola and PepsiCo over the years despite the launch of new pack sizes (see **Exhibit 6**).

Wahaha supported the launch with an RMB33.9-million TV campaign, including RMB12.44 million spent on CCTV during the soccer World Cup. Simultaneously, Wahaha greatly increased its brand-building efforts. In 1998, total TV advertising of Wahaha reached RMB368.7 million, of which RMB65.18 million was devoted to Future Cola. CCTV's coverage (national, including rural areas) and credibility (as a domestic national voice) among consumers made it an excellent channel to convey Wahaha Future Cola's brand image. According to a national survey, 61 per cent of rural consumers said TV was their most important source of information and 33.8 per cent said CCTV Channel 1 was the most frequently viewed channel. Favorite programs for rural residents included films, TV series and CCTV news. Prime advertising time was 7 p.m. to 10 p.m. It helped that Wahaha had been advertising on CCTV for 10 years and already had high brand awareness among rural consumers.

Wahaha relied on its nationwide distribution network to get the product to rural consumers. While Coca Cola and PepsiCo had the advantage in large cities where chain stores and supermarkets accounted for half the grocery trade, Wahaha played on its strength in the countryside where the trade was fragmented, and reachable primarily through multi-layered wholesale markets. Distributors who had been working with Wahaha for years and who had benefited from Wahaha's remarkable growth supported the launch of the cola.

The initial success of the cola surprised even Wahaha. The company could not meet demand using its own bottling facilities and even resorted to outsourcing bottling to other bottlers. When Coca Cola bottlers were approached, the answer was a firm 'no.' At the same time, many of Coca Cola's distributors noticed that if they sold Wahaha Future Cola, Coca Cola would stop supplying them and refuse end-of-year bonuses.[7]

On average, advertising expenses of Wahaha Future Cola comprised about 20 to 30 per cent of the company's total advertising expenditure, adjusted for seasonal and promotional focus. Besides advertising on CCTV and other local TV channels, Wahaha used outdoor advertising and point-of-sale

advertising. In particular, to tackle the rural market, it used 'wall advertising' — painting walls with advertising slogans — a cost-effective way to promote brand awareness. At busy roads and fairs, Wahaha set up large brand and slogan banners. It also sponsored traveling troupes that performed in rural markets and at fairs. In villages where there was no cinema, Wahaha sponsored traveling film shows. These activities catered to the needs of rural customers and quickly increased Wahaha Future Cola's awareness in the rural market.

In 2000, Yu Chen Qing, a pop singer from Taiwan, was signed on to endorse Wahaha Future Cola, while Coco Li Wen, another pop singer from Taiwan, endorsed the Future Lemon carbonated drink. In 2000 and 2001, Wahaha was the exclusive sponsor for CCTV's spring festival party, a program that attracted a mass audience, building national brand awareness.

In 2001, Wahaha Future Cola launched a new advertising slogan 'Future Cola, the choice for happy occasions.' To support this association, Wahaha provided free cola to wedding parties in some key markets. A co-promotion with liquor producers further reinforced the association.

Before the spring festival in 2002, Zong noticed that Coca Cola changed its original paper case packaging to plastic wrap to save costs. Zong saw this as an opportunity to promote Wahaha Future Cola's paper packaging, which was easier to carry and looked better than plastic wrap. Sales staff promoted the paper case as a gift item for the festival, inserting posters of the image of the god of fortune in each case.

Wahaha Future Cola's focus on rural markets meant that 60 per cent to 70 per cent of total sales came from rural areas. In 2002, Wahaha launched carbonated drinks with fresh apple juice and orange juice. With the wider product range, it increased its sales efforts in supermarkets and big stores, and in larger cities.

During the same period, Coca Cola and PepsiCo began to notice and respond to the domestic upstart, while continuing to compete with each other. In a few markets they offered their cola products at a lower price than Wahaha Future Cola. Meanwhile, they further localized their marketing. For example, Coca Cola adjusted its advertising strategy and

---

[7] *Wu Xiaobo and Hu Honwei,* Extraordinary Marketing Strategy, *Zhejiang People's Publishing House, 2002, pp. 230–231.*

increased its advertising on CCTV. It also signed on pop singers from Taiwan and Hong Kong, Zhang Huimei and Xie Tingfeng, to endorse its brand. In 2001, to celebrate Beijing's victory in its bid to host the 2008 Olympics Games, Coca Cola announced a new thematic pack design just 22 minutes after the news announcement. The following day the new design (in gold, integrating various architectural and sports themes in Beijing) was launched in key markets. In 2001 during the Spring Festival, Coca Cola packs carried a picture of a traditional Chinese clay doll 'A Fu' (a symbol of luck).

Coca Cola and PepsiCo also began to actively develop the non-carbonated drink market while continuing to promote their carbonate products. Pepsi promoted non-carbonate drinks such as Dole (100 per cent fruit juice) and Gatorade. Coca Cola launched 'Sensation' water in 2001 without any advertising support, and with a wholesale price that was 40 per cent lower than Wahaha purified water in some regions. In 2002, it launched new 600 ml, 1.5 litre and 2.25 litre packages for its cola without increases in price over the 500 ml, 1.25 litre and two litre respectively. Coca Cola also announced its intention to increase the number of bottling plants to 34 from 28 within five years, growing especially in the mainly rural western region.

Both Coca Cola and PepsiCo were also working on their distribution policy, according to a report in *China Business*.[8] Coca Cola and PepsiCo had never been directly involved in the sales of their products. Instead, their bottlers managed sales in their assigned territory, relying on distributors to cover areas their own systems could not serve. The two companies' practice was to set stringent sales targets for bottlers, and in turn bottlers would set targets for distributors. Bonuses were contingent on reaching these goals. Distributors paid upfront for goods and couldn't return unsold merchandise. However, different wholesale prices in different regions and the incentive of the bonus resulted in distributors selling across provinces to achieve their sales targets, even though both companies had strict policies against cross-territory sales. Recognizing

the problems of the current system, the two companies had recently redefined the roles of bottlers and distributors: distributors were in charge of carrying inventory and delivering to the retailer and their profit would come from the volume handled, but they no longer had any discretion over selling prices; bottlers were responsible for order taking, promotion and product display at the retail end, and retained ownership of the product until the retailer bought it. In comparison, Wahaha's sales company bought the products from its wholly-owned bottling subsidiaries and then co-ordinated sales and marketing on a national scale. Its sales company directly dealt with the distributors (see **Exhibit 7**). Coca Cola and PepsiCo both made money from the sales of concentrate, thus limiting the potential profitability (and price flexibility) of third-party bottlers. Wahaha made money from the sales of the final product, as the production of concentrate and the final product was handled by its own subsidiaries. This gave Wahaha greater pricing flexibility in the field.

In 2002, PepsiCo encountered some problems with a local joint-venture partner. PepsiCo was applying to a commercial arbitration court in Stockholm to cancel its contracts with the joint-venture partner in Chengdu, Sichuan Province — a key Pepsi-Cola market. PepsiCo contended that it had been prevented from exercising its rights under the joint-venture contract, and alleged that there were major financial irregularities within the local company, while the latter accused PepsiCo China of bugging its phones. This was unprecedented in PepsiCo's 20 years in China. While PepsiCo was distracted by these internal problems, Coca Cola was launching a campaign to seize market share in Sichuan and Chongqing — other key markets for PepsiCo.

In the meantime, Wahaha steadily increased sales and market share of Future Cola. Between 1998 and 2001, Wahaha Future series' sales volume increased from 73,800 tons (66.95 million litres) to 0.64 million tons (580 million litres), a share of 14 per cent of the carbonated drink market (see **Exhibit 8**). In comparison, 2001 carbonated-drink sales for Coca Cola and PepsiCo were 1.9 million tons (1.724 billion litres) and 1.07 million tons (971 million litres) respectively. In June 2002, Future series market share reached 18 per cent, with sales revenues of RMB930 million.

---

[8] Ma Qiang, 'Comments on Banning the Association of PepsiCo's Bottlers,' China Business, August 1, 2002.

In some provinces such as Hunan, Xinjiang, Jiangxi and the three provinces in northern China, Future's market share was higher than that of Coca Cola and Pepsi-Cola. In some provinces, Wahaha Future Cola was the only cola brand carried by retailers. In 2001, the Future brand was extended to tea drinks.

Coca Cola now admitted that it faced competition from domestic companies. According to a *Wall Street Journal* article, Coca Cola had been aggressively ramping up its sales efforts and 'by opening more bottling plants and using recyclable bottles, it has brought the price down to one yuan for a single serving in remote towns.'

During the past three years, Coke and its bottlers have been trying to map every supermarket, restaurant, barbershop or market stall where a can of soda might be consumed throughout much of China. Their army of more than 10,000 sales representatives makes regular visits, often on bicycle or foot, to each outlet to ensure there is enough in stock and to record how much was sold. All the information goes into a central database, updated daily, that gives Coke some of the most accurate consumer profiles available in China. Those data help Coke get closer to its customers, whether they are in large hypermarkets, spartan noodle shops or schools. ... And in a strategy proven in markets such as Africa and India, Coke lets local distributors gradually own their own assets, whether these be tricycles used for deliveries or small refrigeration units.[9]

Wahaha, in the meantime, was planning on expanding its sales and marketing staff from 2,000 to 8,000 in 2002.

As Zong Qinghou reviewed the progress of Wahaha Future Cola, he knew that his strategy had allowed Wahaha to quickly become a player in the soft-drink business in China. As Coca Cola and PepsiCo realized the threat from Chinese domestic cola producers and the vast market potential in the countryside, they would certainly take action to protect their position in the carbonated-drink market and tackle the rural market. Zong wondered what steps he should take next with Wahaha Future Cola and the carbonated-drink market. Meanwhile, changes in the soft-drink industry also posed challenges for all participants. The rapid growth of new drink categories offered both opportunities and risks. As the general manager of China's number one soft-drink producer, he also needed to consider competition in the rapidly growing non-carbonated drink market and the future growth of Wahaha.

Exhibit 1 Wahaha group sales revenue and profit 1996 to 2001 (in RMB million)

	1996	1997	1998	1999	2000	2001
Sales revenue	1,110	2,110	2,870	4,510	5,440	6,230
Profit	155	334	501	875	906	914
Profit margin	14%	16%	17%	19%	17%	15%

Source: Company files.

[9] *Gabriel Kahn, 'Coke Works Harder at Being The Real Thing in Hinterland', Wall Street Journal, November 26, 2002.*

Exhibit 2 World soft drink average annual growth rate 1994 to 2003

category	1994–2000	2001–2003
Carbonated drinks	4%	2%
Packaged water	8%	6%
Other*	5.70%	5.30%
Juice and nectars	4.10%	4.20%
Non-carbonated drinks	4.90%	6.30%
Iced tea	11.70%	5.80%
Sports and energy drinks	6.40%	5.90%

'Other' category includes juice and nectars, still drinks, iced tea, sports and energy drinks.

Global soft drink category development (billions of litres)

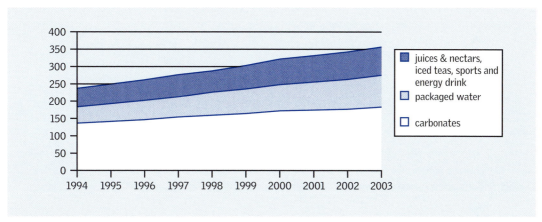

Source: Canadean Ltd.

Exhibit 3 China's soft drink output

Year	Soft Drinks output (in millions of tons)	Carbonated Drinks output (in millions of tons)	Carbonated Drinks as a percentage of total Soft Drinks
1994	6.29	3.14	50%
1995	9.82	5.21	53%
1996	8.84	4.29	49%
1997	10.69	4.92	46%
1998	12.00	5.40	45%
1999	11.86	4.27	36%
2000	14.91	4.62	31%
2001	16.69	4.57	27%

Source: The beverage industry.

Exhibit 4 Top ten domestic soft drink producers in China

Company	Major Soft Drink	Major Brand
Robust (Guangdong) Food & Beverage Co., Ltd.	non-carbonated drink	Robust
Guangdong Jianlibao Beverage Co., Ltd.	sport drink	Jianlibao
Shanghai Maling Aquarius (Group) Corporation	canned food, packaged water	Zhengguanghe
Beijing Huiyuan Juice Group Corporation	juice	Huiyuan
Hebei Xurishen Co. Ltd.	tea	Xurishen
Hebei Lolo Co. Ltd.	almond drink	Lolo
Hangzhou Wahaha Group Corporation	packaged water, carbonated drinks, tea, dairy drink	Wahaha, Future
Hainan Coconut Palm Group Corporation	coconut milk	Coconut Palm
Shenzhen Danone Yili Beverage Co., Ltd.	mineral water	Yili
Cestbon Food & Beverage (shenzhen) Co., Ltd	distilled water	Cestbon

Source: China Soft Drink Industry Association.

Exhibit 5 Comparison of urban residents' and rural residents' disposable income in China

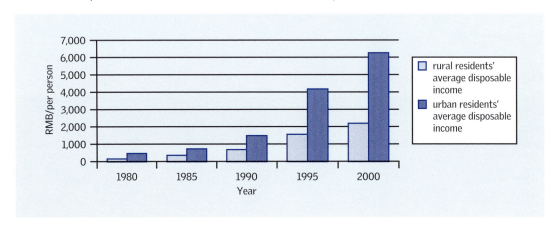

Exhibit 6 Retail price comparison of various pack sizes in 2002 (in RMB)

Size	Coca Cola	Pepsi Cola	Wahaha Future Cola
355 ml	1.8–2.2	1.8–2.2	1.7–2.0
500 ml	2.2–2.5	2.2–2.5	1.9–2.2
600 ml	2.2–2.5	2.2–2.5	none
1.25 l	4.4–4.9	4.4–4.9	3.8
1.5 l	4.4–4.9	4.4–4.9	none
2 l	6.5	6.5	6.0–6.5
2.25 l	6.5	6.5	none

Note: Both Coca Cola and Pepsi Cola offered 600 ml, 1.5 l and 2.25 l at the same price as 500 ml, 1.25 l and 2 l as promotion prices.
Source: Company files.

Exhibit 7 Comparison of product flow and revenue flow

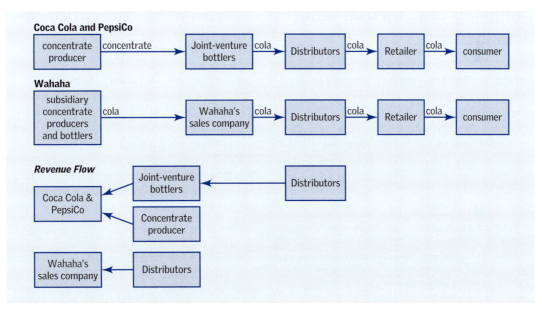

Exhibit 8 Comparison of Coca Cola, PepsiCo. and Wahaha's carbonate sales

	1998		1999		2000		2001	
	Total (in tons)	Market Share	Total	Market Share	Total	Market Share	Total	Market Share
Coca Cola	1,940.0	36%	2,040.0	48%	2,180.0	47%	1,920.0	42%
PepsiCo's	760.0	14%	910.0	21%	1,090.0	24%	1,066.7	23%
Wahaha	73.8	1%	399.0	9%	480.0	10%	640.0	14%
China's total carbonated drink sales	5,400.0	100%	4,273.8	100%	4,620.0	100%	4,571.4	100%

IVEY

Richard Ivey School of Business

The University of Western Ontario

Case 13 The Leo Burnett Company Ltd.: virtual team management

On July 2, 2001, Janet Carmichael, global account director for The Leo Burnett Company Ltd. (LB), United Kingdom, sat in her office wondering how to structure her global advertising team. The team was responsible for the introduction of a skin care product of one of LB's most important clients, Ontann Beauty Care (OBC). The product had

launched in the Canadian and Taiwanese test markets earlier that year. Taiwanese sales and awareness levels for the product had been high but were low for the Canadian market. Typically, at this stage in the launch process, Carmichael would decentralize the communications management in each market, but the poor performance in the Canadian market left her with a difficult decision: should she maintain centralized control over the Canadian side of her team? In three days, she would leave for meetings at LB's Toronto, Canada, office, where the team would expect her decision.

The Leo Burnett Company Ltd. background

LB, which was founded in Chicago in 1935, was one of North America's premier advertising agencies. It had created numerous well-recognized North American brand icons, including The Marlboro Man, Kellogg's Tony the Tiger, and the Pillsbury Dough Boy.

By 1999, LB had expanded around the globe to include 93 offices in 83 markets. The company employed approximately 9,000 people, and worldwide revenues were approximately US$9 billion. In 2000, LB merged with two other global agencies to form b|com[3] (the actual company name), one of the largest advertising holding companies in the world, but each LB office retained the Leo Burnett company name.

LB services and products

As a full-service agency, LB offered the complete range of marketing and communications services and products (see Exhibits 1 and 2). The company's marketing philosophy was to build 'brand belief.' The idea driving this philosophy was that true loyalty went beyond mere buying behavior. LB defined 'believers' as customers who demonstrated both a believing attitude and loyal purchase behavior. The company strove to convert buyers into believers by building lasting customer affinity for the brand.

One of the most important measures of an agency's success was the quality of the creative product that was developed to connect brands to their end consumers. Each local office strove to produce outstanding creative advertising to break through the clutter of marketing messages that the general public was subjected to daily and truly reach the consumer in a memorable way. Award shows were held nationally and internationally to recognize this effort, one of the most prestigious being the annual festival in Cannes, France. With each award, individual employees (usually the art director and copy writer who had worked together to develop the ad) were recognized, as was the local agency office where they worked. These creative accolades were instrumental in helping an office win new client business. Even within the global LB network, awards were given to the local offices that produced the most outstanding creative work.

LB internal team structures

A multidisciplinary team serviced each brand. Each team had representatives from all core areas of the agency as well as members from the specialized services as appropriate for the brand. In most cases, team members had two sets of reporting lines.

First and formally, they directly reported to the supervisor of their home department (for example, account management). It was this formal supervisor who was responsible for conducting performance evaluations and assigning and managing an employee's workload.

Informally, the team members reported to a project team leader, the senior account services person, who usually was an account director or a vice-president of client services director. It was this team leader's responsibility to manage the project in question, ensure that the client was satisfied with project progress, and build and manage the overall relationship between the client and the agency. Employees on the project team would be responsible to this person for meeting project deadlines and managing their individual client relationships. This team leader would often provide input to a team member's performance evaluation, along with other agency colleagues (see **Exhibit 3**).

At any given time, an agency employee typically worked on two or three different brand teams, virtually all of them face-to-face teams servicing local clients.

LB typical office environment

Most LB employees were young (in their 20s and 30s) and worked about 60 hours per week. Client needs and project deadlines dictated work priorities, and the volume of work often required late nights at the office. Agency office environments were often open-concept and social. Employees spent many hours each day up and about, discussing projects with colleagues and responding to client requests. The pace was fast and the general spirit was one of camaraderie; it was common for LB employees to socialize together after a late night at the office.

LB Toronto

LB's Toronto office was founded in 1952 to service the Canadian arms of the Chicago-based clients. It was LB's first expansion beyond Chicago. In 2001, it employed a staff of approximately 200 people and billings were approximately $200 million.

LB United Kingdom

LB acquired its London, United Kingdom, office in the mid-1970s as part of an expansion into Europe. By 2001, the office had grown to over 350 employees and billings were approximately $400 million. London was also the regional LB headquarters for all European, Middle Eastern and African offices.

LB's relationship with Ontann Beauty Care

Ontann Beauty Care (OBC)

OBC was a leading global manufacturer of health and beauty care products. In the late 1990s, OBC made a strategic decision to centralize the global marketing of its brands and products, designating a global team to define the global strategy for a given brand and develop the core communication materials as templates for local markets to follow. Local offices were given the responsibility for adapting the global materials and developing local 'below the line' (BTL) materials which would synergize with the global vision and creative templates. Below the line materials included direct marketing, in-store materials, digital marketing, public relations and promotions (that is, everything except strict advertising). In practice, on established brands with well-defined communication templates and strong local knowledge, some local markets (at least key regional markets) were awarded more opportunity to develop their own communication material.

The global team, however, retained veto power to ensure all communications were building a consistent personality and look for the brand.

Each OBC global office had as many teams as it had brands. An OBC brand team usually consisted of the global category director, the brand manager and an assistant brand manager, plus a representative from each of the various departments: marketing technology, consumer, trade/distribution, PR, sales, product development, and production.

Relationship between LB and OBC

OBC, which, like LB, was founded in Chicago, was one of LB's original clients. In 2001, as one of the top three LB clients worldwide, OBC did business with most LB offices. OBC, however, awarded its business to advertising agencies brand-by-brand. As a result, other advertising agencies also had business with OBC. Competition among advertising agencies for OBC business was strong, in particular when they had to work together on joint brand promotions.

OBC had been a client of LB's Toronto office since 1958 and of LB's London office since its acquisition in the mid-1970s. Both the Toronto and London offices initially developed advertising and communications materials for various OBC facial care brands and eventually also worked on OBC's skin care brands.

To better service OBC, LB also centralized its decision marking for this client's brands and appointed expanded and strengthened global teams with the power to make global decisions. For its other clients, LB's global teams were significantly smaller, tending to consist simply of one very senior LB manager who shared learning from across the globe with a given client's senior management.

A new OBC brand: Forever Young

In the fall of 1998, the OBC London office announced a new skin care line called 'Forever Young'. Product formulas were based on a newly patented process that addressed the needs of aging skin. For OBC, this brand presented an opportunity to address a new market segment: the rapidly growing population of people over the age of 50. The product line was more extensive than other OBC skin care brands. It also represented the company's first foray into premium priced skin care products. Product cost, on average, was double that of most other OBC brands, falling between drug store products and designer products. OBC intended Forever Young to be its next big global launch and awarded the Forever Young advertising and brand communications business to LB.

Global advertising and communications team for Forever Young

Team formation

For LB, a successful launch of this new product would significantly increase revenues and the likelihood of acquiring additional global OBC brands. An unsuccessful launch would risk the relationship with OBC that LB had built over so many years. LB management in Chicago decided that LB London would be the global team headquarters. This decision reflected the experience that the London office had in leading global business teams and the proximity to the OBC global team for Forever Young. It was also likely that the United Kingdom would be the test market for the new product.

In LB's London office, Janet Carmichael was assigned as brand team leader for the Forever Young product line effective January 1, 1999. Carmichael was the global account director for OBC. The 41-year-old Carmichael, a Canadian, had begun her career at LB Toronto as an account executive in 1985, after completing an MBA degree at the University of Toronto. In 1987, Carmichael moved to Europe, where she continued her career with LB. She became an account supervisor in Italy, an account director in Belgium, and finally a regional and global account director in Germany before taking on a global account director role on OBC brands in the United Kingdom in 1996. She was very familiar with OBC's business and had built excellent relationships with the OBC skin care client group.

LB's initial Forever Young brand team had six members who all were employees of the London office: Carmichael as the team leader, an account director, an account executive (she formally supervised these two employees), the agency's creative director, and two 'creatives' (an art director and a copy writer). Carmichael outlined a project timetable (see **Exhibit 4**). The LB team worked with the OBC team on consumer research, market exploration, brand creative concepts (creative), packaging samples and global copy testing throughout North America and Europe. Carmichael viewed marketing a new product to a new consumer segment in a crowded category as challenging; however, after several months of testing, LB's Forever Young brand team developed a unique creative concept that was well received by OBC.

In the fall of 1999, OBC decided that the United Kingdom would be the lead market for another skin care product. Because North America was a priority for the Forever Young brand and Canada was 'clean' (that is, OBC was not testing other products in Canada at that time), Canada became the new primary test market for Forever Young. In addition, Canadians' personal skin care habits and the distribution process for skin care products were more reflective of overall Western practices (i.e., the Western world) than were those in other potential test markets. Taiwan became the secondary test market for Asian consumers. These choices were consistent with OBC's interest in global brand validation.

In keeping with OBC's team structures, LB maintained the global brand team in London and, in January of 2000, formed satellite teams in Toronto, Canada, and Taipei, Taiwan, to manage material execution in their local markets. It was up to the LB Toronto and Taipei offices to determine their members in the Forever Young satellite teams. In Taipei, Cathy Lee, an account director who was particularly interested in the assignment, took the lead on local agency activities. In Toronto, Geoff Davids, an account supervisor from the direct marketing group, was assigned to lead the Toronto team. The global brand team and the two satellite teams now formed the LB side of the global advertising and communications team for Forever Young (see **Exhibit 5**).

Kick-off meeting

In February 2000, a face-to-face kick-off meeting took place in Toronto with the intent to bring all senior members of LB's and OBC's London, Toronto, and Taipei teams onto the same page regarding the new brand and the status of the launch process. One or two senior representatives from OBC London, Toronto, and Taipei participated in the meeting. From LB, the complete London team participated, along with Geoff Davids and a senior agency representative from the Toronto office, and Cathy Lee and a senior agency representative from the Taipei office. Carmichael and her U.K. team members shared their initial brand creative concepts, which had already garnered admiration throughout the LB network, and their knowledge about the product and target audience.

It was decided that Davids and Lee would serve as the main links to LB's London-based global brand team. Specifically, Davids and Lee reported to Annabel Forin, Carmichael's account director in the United Kingdom. Forin then reported to Carmichael and OBC's London team. Besides Forin, Carmichael's primary contacts would be Annabelle Manning, the global creative director at LB United Kingdom and Sarah Jones, OBC's global vice-president of skin care in London. All work produced by LB's satellite teams would require approval from LB's London team.

The creative assignments

The creative assignments for the Canadian and Taiwanese teams were slightly different from each other. Normally, the global team would produce a creative template for a brand (meaning the design of the advertising and communications materials), which would then be passed to the satellite teams to be adapted for the local market.

In the Taiwanese market, this would be the case. The Taiwanese LB team would be responsible for adapting the advertising materials, which would include re-filming the television ad to star an Asian actress, as well as retaking photos for the print ads, again, to demonstrate product benefits on Asian skin. The brand message (meaning the text in print ads and the vocal message in television ads) would be adapted to appeal to the Taiwanese audience.

In Toronto, however, the assignment broke from this traditional format. The LB team in London would produce English television and print advertising, which would be used in the Canadian market. The LB team in Toronto would design and produce the direct marketing and Web site materials because the London office did not have strong in-house capabilities in these areas. While the Toronto office would have control of the design of these communication pieces, the U.K. office would require that certain elements be incorporated into the design (for example, specific photos and colors), in order for the pieces to be visually consistent with the print advertising.

Events leading up to the launch

LB's Taipei office

After returning to Taipei from the kick-off meeting, Lee formed her local team, which consisted of an account executive (Tanya Yang) and a creative team (one art director and one copy writer). In co-operation with OBC's Taipei team, Lee and her team focused first on recreating the television ad. The ad followed the original creative idea developed in the United Kingdom but used a popular Taiwanese actress in the lead. The character differentiation was necessary to demonstrate the product's benefit to Asian skin because the original ad featured a blond, Caucasian actress as the lead. The team moved on to adapt the brand's print advertising and direct marketing pieces and developed a public relations campaign to meet local market needs. These communication elements were visually and strategically consistent with the television ad as they incorporated photos of the same Taiwanese actress.

Throughout this process, the Taipei team regularly updated LB's and OBC's London teams about its progress. Although all work required U.K. approval, the Taiwanese team worked with a significant amount of autonomy because of the cultural differences present in its market. Carmichael and Manning occasionally travelled to Taiwan to meet with the team and approve its creative work, which they generally received well. In addition, the Taipei team communicated with the London offices through videoconference calls and e-mail. The LB Taipei and Toronto teams had contact with each other only during the global team videoconference meetings, held every two months.

LB's Toronto office

After the kick-off meeting, Davids, with the approval of LB's Toronto management, assigned representatives from the direct marketing group and the interactive marketing group to the brand team. This included account management (Tara Powell, account executive for direct; and Liz Nelson, account supervisor; and Alexis Jacobs, project manager for interactive) and creative staff (Shirley Watson, creative director; and one copy writer from each of the direct and interactive groups).

In co-operation with OBC's Toronto team, the LB Toronto team was responsible for developing a full communication plan for its local market. Along with running the television and print ads developed in the United Kingdom, the team would focus on producing the brand's below the line materials (i.e., direct mail, Web site). These communication elements served as the education pieces that supplemented the TV ad. Davids conducted an internal team debrief, outlining the information he had received at the kick-off meeting. From this, the team developed a communications plan that, in Carmichael's opinion, was 'on-brief' (i.e., consistent with the original brand strategic direction) and included some very innovative thinking.

Next, the team began determining a creative look and feel for the direct mail pieces. The look and feel could be different from the television creative but had to be consistent across all of the paper-based (print ads, direct mail pieces and in-store materials) and online communication elements. The creatives in LB's Toronto team developed the direct marketing materials, and simultaneously the creatives in LB's U.K. team developed the print advertising. The two sides' creative work evolved in different directions, but each side hoped that the other would adapt their look and feel. Eventually, however, LB's Toronto team told its London counterpart to 'figure it out,' and they would follow London's lead. Communication between the two sides mostly flowed through Davids and Forin to Carmichael. Carmichael, however, had received a copy of the following e-mail from Watson to Davids:

Geoff, as you know, it's always a challenge to work with someone else's art direction. I don't think the model that London chose is right for this market, and the photography we have to work with doesn't have as contemporary a feel as I would like.

This would be easier if I could connect directly with Annabelle [Manning] but she's on the road so much of the time it's hard to catch her. We weren't asked for our opinion initially and, given the timing constraints at this point, we don't have much choice but to use what they've sent us, but could you please convey to Annabel [Forin] that in the future, if possible, we'd like to have the chance to input on the photography before it's taken? It will help us develop good direct mail creative.

For now, though, I think we'll be able to do something with what they've sent us. Thanks.

There had been other challenges for LB's Toronto team. Davids described an incident that had occurred when his direct marketing team tried to present its creative concept to the team in the United Kingdom during a videoconference meeting:

Our direct mail concept was a three-panel, folded piece. We sent two flat files to the United Kingdom via e-mail, which were to be cut out, pasted back-to-back [to form the front and back of the piece] and then folded into thirds. It took us so long to explain how to do that — somehow we just weren't getting through! Our colleagues in London cut and folded and pasted in different places, and what should have been a simple pre-liminary procedure took up 45 minutes of our one-hour videoconference meeting! By the time we actually got around to discussing the layout of the piece, everyone on the call was frustrated. That's never a good frame of mind to be in when reviewing and critiquing a new layout. It's too bad our clients were on that call as well.

A greater challenge came in September 2000, when the team was behind schedule in the development of the Web site after encountering difficulties with OBC's technology standards. The budgeting for the Web site development came out of the global budget, not the local budget. This meant that the members of LB's Toronto team who were responsible for the Web site development ('interactive marketing') received directions from OBC's London team. The budgeting for direct marketing, however, came out of the local budget, and the members of LB's Toronto team, who were responsible for the development of the direct marketing materials, dealt with OBC's Toronto team. The instructions from

these two OBC teams were often inconsistent. Compounding matters, the two OBC client teams repeatedly requested changes of the Web and direct marketing materials, which made these materials even more different from each other and forced the LB Toronto team into extremely tight timeframes.

Carmichael learned about this sort of difficulty mostly through the direct supervisors of the team members. She frequently received calls from LB Toronto's Interactive Marketing Group and Direct Marketing Group senior managers. Carmichael repeatedly had to explain the basic project compo-nents to these senior managers and wished that the members of LB's Toronto team would just follow the team communications protocol and forward their concerns to Davids, who would then take up matters as necessary with the U.K. team.

Canadian pre-launch test

Despite these challenges, LB's Toronto team produced the materials in time for the Canadian pre-launch test in October of 2000. The pre-launch test was a launch of the complete communications program (TV ad, newspaper inserts, distribution of trial packs, direct mail, and a Web site launch) in a market whose media could be completely isolated. A small town in the interior of British Columbia, Canada's most westerly province, met these conditions. In terms of product trial and product sales as a percentage of market share, the test indexed 120 against its objectives, which had a base index of 100. Subsequently, OBC and LB decided to move immediately into research to test the advertising in the U.S. market. The global OBC and LB teams worked with their Canadian counter-parts to conduct this research, the results of which were very poor. As a result, OBC London required that LB's London and Toronto teams revised the adver-tising materials even before the Canadian launch.

Canadian national launch

The days before the launch were panic-filled, as LB's London and Toronto teams scrambled to revise the advertising. In February 2001, the campaign was launched in Canada with the following elements:

- One 30-second TV ad;
- One direct mail piece;

- The English Web site;

- Product samples available from the Web from direct mail piece, and from an in-store coupon;

- Specially designed in-store displays;

- Trial-sized package bundles (one week's worth);

- A public relations campaign; and

- Five print ads in national magazines.

Research following the national launch showed that the brand did not perform well among Canadian consumers. It indexed 50 against a base index of 100. Because of the success of the Canadian pre-launch test, OBC and LB were surprised. The Forever Young global advertising and communications team attributed the discrepancy between the pre-launch test and national launch, in part, to the fact that the pre-launch test conditions were not replicable on a national scale. The audience penetration in the small B.C. town, the pre-test site, was significantly greater than it was in the national launch. OBC decided that the results of the Canadian launch were below 'action standards,' meaning that OBC would not even consider a rollout into the U.S. market at the current time.

The tension levels on both LB's side and OBC's side of the Forever Young global advertising and communications team were high. LB's future business on the brand was in jeopardy. The OBC side was under tremendous pressure internally to improve brand trial and market share metrics and already planned to decentralize the local teams for the global product rollout. Despite numerous revisions to the advertising, it never tested well enough to convince OBC that a U.S. or European launch would be successful.

A different story in Asia

In Taiwan, the product launch was successful. Test results showed that the brand was indexing 120 per cent against brand objectives. Research also showed that Taiwanese consumers, in contrast to Canadian consumers, did not perceive some of the advertising elements as 'violent.' Moreover, in Taiwan, overall research scores in terms of 'likeability' and 'whether or not the advertising would inspire you to try the product' were higher, leading to higher sales.

By June of 2001, the Taiwanese team was ready to take on more local-market responsibility and move into the post-launch phase of the advertising campaign. This phase would involve creating new ads to build on the initial success and grow sales in the market.

Recovery plan for Canada

By June of 2001, LB needed to take drastic measures to develop a new Forever Young campaign in order to improve the brand's performance in the Canadian marketplace. Whereas, before the launch, there had been a clear division of responsibilities (with the United Kingdom developing the television and print advertising and Canada developing direct marketing, in-store and Web site communications), now the global LB team in London decided that it would be necessary to have all hands on deck. New creative teams from the mass advertising department in the Toronto office, as well as supplementary creative teams from the London office, were briefed to develop new campaign ideas. Each team had only three weeks to develop their new ideas, less than half of the eight weeks they would normally have, and the teams had to work independent of each other. The London and Toronto creative teams had to present their concepts to the entire global OBC and LB team at the same time. Subsequently, the results of market research would determine the winning creative concept. Squabbling between the offices began over which team would present first, which office received what compensation for the development, and whether or not overall remuneration packages were fair. Moreover, the communication between the account services members of LB's London and Toronto teams, which was the primary communication channel between the two agencies, became less frequent, less candid and more formal. The presentations took place on June 25, 2001, in Toronto. Watson, the creative director in Toronto commented:

This process has been exciting, but we're near the ends of our collective ropes now. We have a new mass advertising creative team [who specialized in TV ads] on the business in Toronto, and they're being expected to produce world-class creative results for a brand they've only

*heard about for the past few days. They don't —
and couldn't possibly — have the same passion
for the brand that the direct marketing creative
team members have after working on it for so
long. I'm having a hard time motivating them to
work under these tight timelines.*

*We're even more isolated now in Toronto. Our
connection to the creative teams and the global
creative director in London was distant at best,
and now it's non-existent. And our relationship
with the local OBC client feels very remote, too.
Still, we're moving forward with our work. We're
trying to learn from the Taiwanese experience
and are considering what success we would
have with a nationally recognized actress star-
ring in our television ads.*

Evolution of the Forever Young global advertising and communications team

Personnel changes

Between January and June of 2001, numerous personnel changes in the Forever Young global
advertising and communications team occurred (see
Exhibit 5). In LB's London office, Forin, the U.K.
account director, had been replaced following her
departure for maternity leave. In OBC's London
office, Sarah Jones, the global vice-president for
skin care, took early retirement without putting a
succession plan in place. In LB's Toronto office,
Davids, the Toronto brand team leader, had left the
agency. Tara Powell, who had reported to Davids,
took on his responsibilities, but she had not met
most of the global team members. Liz Nelson, the
account supervisor for interactive, left LB's Toronto
office to return to school. Alexis Jacobs, who had
managed the Web site development, took over her
responsibilities. Powell and Jacobs did not have
close relationships with their international counterparts. At OBC Toronto, Sally Burns, the local brand
manager, who had been LB's main contact in the
local market and had been with the brand since
inception, left OBC. LB's and OBC's Taiwanese
teams remained stable over time. Cathy Lee worked
with a team that was nearly identical to her initial
team.

Communications

Early on (between February and May 2000),
Carmichael had orchestrated frequent face-to-face
meetings to ensure clarity of communication and
sufficient information sharing. In the following
months, the team relied on videoconferences and
phone calls, with visits back and forth between
London and Toronto on occasion. Since early 2001,
the team had relied increasingly on e-mails and telephone calls to communicate. In June 2001,
Carmichael noted that the communication had
become more formal, and she had lost the feeling of
being part of a global team. She wondered if giving
the LB's Toronto team more autonomy to develop
the brand in their market would help the brand
progress. Working together as a smaller team might
improve the Toronto group's team dynamic as well.
Carmichael was concerned that the current discord
between LB's London and Toronto offices would
negatively affect the relationship to OBC.

Budget problems

The extra creative teams assigned to the redevelop-
ment of the brand's television advertising and the
unexpected changes to the Forever Young communication materials had meant that LB's costs to staff
the project had been higher than originally estimated
and higher than the revenues that had been negotiated with OBC. Since OBC did not want to pay
more for its advertising than had been originally
budgeted, LB faced tremendous internal pressure to
finish the project as soon as possible. This situation
created conflict between LB and OBC in the United
Kingdom, who was responsible for negotiating LB's
overall fees. Because all fees were paid to the global
brand office (in this case, LB's London office) and
then transferred to the local satellite teams, this
situation also created conflict between LB's London
and Toronto teams, who had both expended
additional staff time to revise the advertising
materials and wanted 'fair' compensation.

What next?

In three days, Carmichael had to leave for Toronto
to sit in research sessions to test the recently presented new creative concepts. In the meetings that
followed, she would present to the team her

recommendation for how to move forward with the brand. Carmichael reviewed the brand events and team interaction of the past two years (see Exhibit 4) to determine the best global team structure for salvaging the Forever Young brand and maintaining the relationship between OBC and LB.

Carmichael felt torn in her loyalties. On the one hand, she was Canadian and knew LB's Toronto office well — she knew that LB's Toronto brand team worked hard, and she wished them every success. On the other hand, she had now worked in LB's London office for several years, and she had always liked the creative that the U.K. team had initially produced. If she maintained the current form of centralized control of the team, either creative concept might be chosen; however, if she decentralized team control, the Toronto team would almost certainly choose their own creative concept for the television ads. Since the creative direction chosen now would become the brand's advertising in most North American and European markets, it needed to be top calibre. Carmichael thought this posed a risk if the creative development was left to the new Toronto-based mass advertising creative team. It would be a shame to lose the U.K. team's original creative concept.

In making her decision on whether to decentralize the team, Carmichael considered the following:

1   Where was the knowledge necessary to create a competitive advantage for the brand in Canada? Would it be in the Canadian marketplace because they understood the market, or would it be in London because they had more in-depth knowledge of the brand?

2   Where was the client responsibility, and where should it be? Now that the London-based global vice-president of skin care was retiring, the client was considering creating a virtual global team to manage the brand, headquartered in the United States but composed of members of the original United Kingdom OBC team, in preparation for a U.S. launch. If the client team had its headquarters in North America, should LB also structure its team this way?

3   If Carmichael decentralized the brand and gave the Toronto team greater autonomy, who would lead the brand in Toronto now that Davids had left the agency? How would the necessary knowledge be imparted to the new leader?

4   If they remained centralized, would the team make it through before it self-destructed? How much would this risk the client relationship? To what extent would it strain the already tight budget?

Carmichael had to make a decision that was best for the brand, LB and OBC.

Exhibit 1 LB Agency Services

Traditional core agency services included:

Account Management

Account management worked in close partnership with planning, creative, media, production and the client to craft tightly focused advertising strategies, based on a deep understanding of the client's products, goals and competition, as well as insights into contemporary consumer behavior.

Creative Services

In most LB offices, creative was the largest department. Creatives focused its visual art and copywriting talents on turning strategic insights into advertising ideas. This department was a key part of each client's brand team and often interacted with both clients and clients' customers.

Planning

Planners conducted research to gain insights about the consumer and the marketplace. They also provided valuable input to the strategic and creative agency processes in the form of the implications raised by that research, specifically combining that learning with information about a given product, the social context in which it fit and the psychology of the people who used it.

Media

Starcom was the media division for LB's parent holding company. Its role was to identify the most influential and efficient media vehicles to deliver brand communications to the appropriate audience.

Production

Production staff brought creative ideas to life with the highest quality execution in television, cinema, radio, print, outdoor, direct, point of sale, interactive or any other medium.

In addition to these core services, most offices also offered expertise in more specialized services, including:

- B2B Technology Marketing
- Direct and Database Marketing
- Health-care Marketing
- Interactive Marketing
- Multicultural Marketing
- Public Relations
- Sales Promotion and Event Marketing

Exhibit 2 LB agency products

Traditional Advertising Products

Television Broadcast Advertising — Usually 30-second (:30s) or 60-second (:60s) TV ads that ran during local or national television programming. This also included sponsoring specific programs, which usually consisted of a five-second announcement before or after the show, i.e., 'This program is brought to you by …' accompanied by the visual of the sponsoring company's logo.

Radio Broadcast Advertising — Usually 15-, 20-, or 30-second (:15s, :20s, :30s) radio ads that were placed throughout local or national radio programming. Radio ads could include sponsoring specific programs, which usually consisted of a five-second announcement before or after the show, i.e. 'This program brought to you by …'

Print Advertising — Included black and white and color print ads in local, national or trade newspapers, journals and magazines. Magazine ads could be single-page ads or double-page spreads (two pages facing each other).

Non-Traditional or 'Below the Line' Advertising Products

Direct Marketing — Normally a series of mail-out items (letters, post cards, product samples, etc.) sent to a specifically targeted population(s) called 'cells', e.g., companies might send promotional mail-outs to current customers, former customers who have not shopped with the company for a period or time, and new prospective customers — each of these groups would be considered a cell.

Digital or Interactive Marketing — Any marketing efforts that were delivered to the consumer online or by wireless networks (e.g., hand-held wireless devices). This could include Web site design and production, banner advertising and promotions on other Web sites, e-mail marketing, and internal corporate marketing tools such as customer relationship marketing or database building tools.

Collateral — Any piece of print material that was not strictly advertising, for instance brochures, annual reports, posters, flyers and in-store materials.

Promotions — Any marketing effort that included a time-limited offer or incentive to either purchase a product or offer personal data. Promotions could involve advertising, direct marketing, interactive marketing, product packaging and/or outdoor marketing.

Exhibit 3 LB agency formal and informal reporting lines

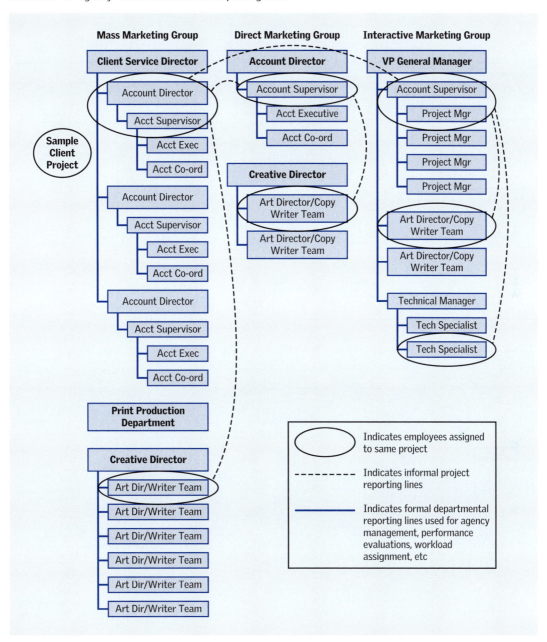

Exhibit 4 Brand development chronology

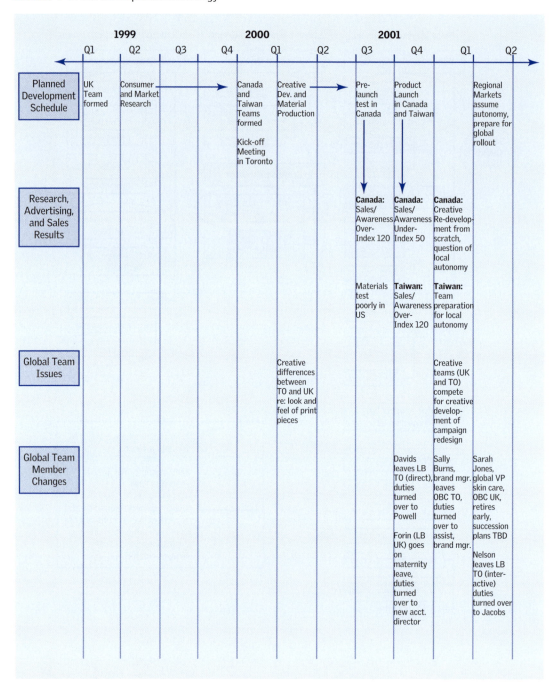

	1999				2000			2001			
	Q1	Q2	Q3	Q4	Q1	Q2	Q3	Q4	Q1	Q2	
Planned Development Schedule	UK Team formed	Consumer and Market Research		Canada and Taiwan Teams formed Kick-off Meeting in Toronto	Creative Dev. and Material Production		Pre-launch test in Canada	Product Launch in Canada and Taiwan		Regional Markets assume autonomy, prepare for global rollout	
Research, Advertising, and Sales Results							Canada: Sales/Awareness Over-Index 120 Materials test poorly in US	Canada: Sales/Awareness Under-Index 50 Taiwan: Sales/Awareness Over-Index 120	Canada: Creative Re-development from scratch, question of local autonomy Taiwan: Team preparation for local autonomy		
Global Team Issues					Creative differences between TO and UK re: look and feel of print pieces				Creative teams (UK and TO) compete for creative development of campaign redesign		
Global Team Member Changes							Davids leaves LB TO (direct) duties turned over to Powell Forin (LB UK) goes on maternity leave, duties turned over to new acct. director	Sally Burns, brand mgr. leaves OBC TO, duties turned over to assist. brand mgr.	Sarah Jones, global VP skin care, OBC UK, retires early, succession plans TBD Nelson leaves LB TO (interactive) duties turned over to Jacobs		

Exhibit 5 The Global Forever Young team

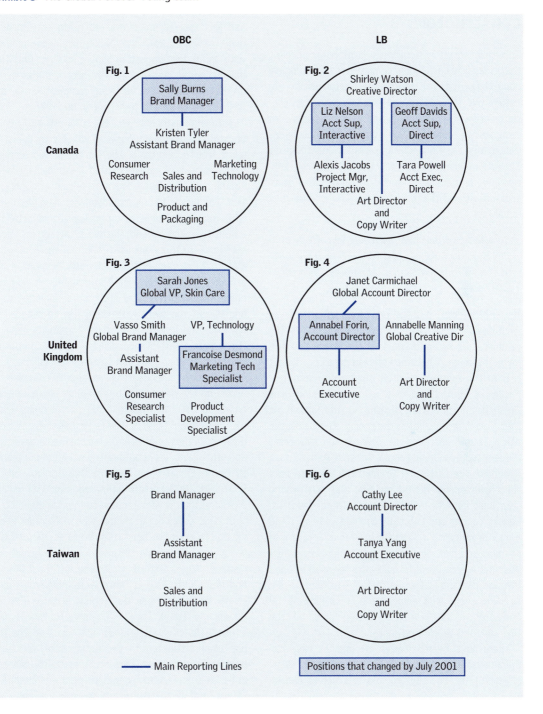

Case 14 The Formula 1 constructors

This case describes four periods of dominance by particular firms in a highly competitive technological context. Formula 1 (F1) motorsport is the pinnacle of automotive technology and involves highly specialized constructors designing and building single-seat racecars to compete for annual championships which bring huge financial and reputational rewards. These four eras explore the stories of three contrasting companies in terms of how they both created and lost the basis for sustained competitive advantage.

Between two and four on a Sunday afternoon this is a sport. All the rest of the time it's commerce. (Frank Williams, Managing Director, Williams F1)

In 1945 the Fédération Internationale de l'Automobile (FIA) established Formula A as the premier level of motorsport. In the years that followed Formula A became referred to as Formula 1 (F1) and a drivers' world championship was introduced in 1950. The first world champion was Giuseppe Farina of Italy, driving an Alfa Romeo. At that time Alfa dominated the racing along with the other Italian marques of Ferrari and Maserati. Drivers such as Juan Fangio, Alberto Ascari, Jack Brabham, Jim Clark and Graham Hill were to take the championship during the 50s and 60s driving cars built by Alfa Romeo, Ferrari, Mercedes-Benz, Lancia, Cooper and Lotus. By the mid sixties F1 had moved from being a basis for car manufacturers to promote and test their products to a highly specialist business where purpose built cars were developed through leading edge technology to win a TV sporting event that enjoyed the third highest TV audience in the world, surpassed only by the Olympics and World Cup soccer.

There have been between 10 and 14 race car manufacturers or constructors competing in F1 at any one time. The constructors themselves can be grouped into a number of different categories. In 2003 the top three teams were Ferrari, Williams and McLaren, all medium-sized businesses turning over between $250 and $350 million per annum, with estimates suggesting that it took around $50 million capital investment in research facilities to set up the minimum basis for being competitive. For the first three years of their entry into F1 in 2002 Toyota were estimated to have committed $1 billion on capital and running costs of which only one-fifth came from sponsorship. The top teams would typically have their own testing and development equipment, including wind-tunnels and other facilities. The larger teams employed between 450 and 800 people in their F1 operations, a quarter of whom travelled around the world attending races every two to three weeks throughout the F1 season (March to November). Labour costs accounted for around 25% of the budget. All the teams would have highly qualified technical staff which included race engineers (who work with the driver to set up the car), designers, aerodynamicists, composite experts (to work with specialized carbon-composite materials) and information systems specialists.

In addition to sponsorship, revenue is provided by prize money generated by winning championship points; in 2003 this was allocated on a sliding scale for the first eight places. The prize money is a way of dividing up the royalties earned from media coverage and other revenues negotiated on behalf of the teams by Bernie Ecclestone's Formula One Administration (FOA). In 2003 Ferrari estimated that $30 million (9.7%) of their revenues came from prize money.

In 2003 seven out of the ten F1 constructors were located in what has been referred to as 'motorsport valley', an area of the UK described by a broad arc centred around Oxford, stretching into East Anglia and down into Surrey. There were, however, other teams located outside this region, such as Ferrari (Maranello, Italy), Toyota (Cologne, Germany) and Sauber (Hinwil, Switzerland). The focus on the UK has been attributed to the network of specialist engineering talent which is fundamental to success in F1, as summarized by the principal of RenaultF1, Flavio Briatore: '*If you like proscuitto you come to Italy. If you like champagne, you come to France. For Formula 1 you come to England. I don't like the English weather, but the best engineering is here.*'

By Mark Jenkins

© 2004, M. Jenkins, Nottingham University Business School.

The Formula 1 constructors provide a unique context to consider the competitive advantage of different multi-million-pound organizations over time. The pace of change and the basis of advantage is constantly changing, shown by the fact that since the start of the world championships, only two constructors have won the championship consecutively more than four times (McLaren 1988–91; Ferrari 1999–2003) and only Ferrari (1975–1977) and Williams (1992–1994) have won for three consecutive years. The remainder of the case considers each of these periods of competitive dominance in chronological order.

Ferrari 1975–1979

The period 1975–77 saw a renaissance for the Ferrari team. Their previous F1 World Championship had been won in 1964, one of the few reminders of the glorious 50s and early 60s when the bright red cars of Ferrari dominated motor racing. In the mid 70s they won 15 of the 45 races during 1975, 1976 and 1977.

Ferrari are the oldest of all the Grand Prix teams still racing. Their heritage gives them a special place in the hearts of all motor racing enthusiasts. Founded by Enzo Ferrari, an ex-driver and manager of the Alfa Romeo racing team in 1950, they and other Italian marques of Maserati and Alfa dominated the sport during the 1950s. By the end of 2003 Ferraris had taken part in more than 550 Grand Prix and, despite the variable nature of the team's performance, drivers continue to view a contract with Ferrari as something very special. Perhaps this is why world champions such as Alain Prost, Nigel Mansell and Michael Schumacher have been attracted to the team at times when their cars have been far from the fastest or most reliable.

In an era when the majority of constructors are British specialists who buy in components such as engines and gearboxes, Ferrari had always done everything themselves. Engine, gearbox, suspension, chassis were all made at their Maranello factory, which enjoys the most up-to-date facilities in terms of designing, developing and building all the necessary components of a race-car. While other constructors such as McLaren and Williams would paint their cars whatever colour was required by their flagship sponsor, Ferraris had always been blood red, the national colour of Italy, a throwback from the time when F1 cars were colour coded by country of origin. There was also very little evidence of sponsorship on the Ferrari cars; it has always been the Ferrari emblem – a black prancing horse on a yellow shield – which has the most prominent position. The Italian public see Ferrari as a national icon, as observed by Niki Lauda:

> *The Italians love you when you win and hate you when you lose and whatever you do, win, lose or simply break wind everyone in Italy wants to know about it!*

The influence of Enzo Ferrari, or Il Commendatore as he was frequently known, was pervasive and the myths and stories surrounding him still permeate the team. It was legendary that Ferrari himself hardly ever attended a race and rarely left the Maranello factory where his beloved cars were made. He relied on the media and his advisors for information, which often created a highly political atmosphere in the team. Ferrari's first love was motor racing, this was despite having created a very successful range of road-going cars which he saw primarily as the source of funding for his racing. The merger between Fiat and Ferrari in 1969, when Fiat acquired a 50% stake in the company, provided Ferrari with a huge cash injection. While Fiat would manage the production of the road cars, Enzo, who was then 71, would retain control of the racing operation to concentrate on his first love, motor racing at the highest level: Formula 1.

The resources which Ferrari had at their disposal were the envy of every other team. They had always built their own engines and have a large technical team dedicated to the task of engine design and development. In 1971 they opened their own test track at Fiorano, a few hundred yards from the Maranello factory. At the time it was the most advanced and sophisticated test circuit in the world, enabling the cars to be constantly tested and developed between the track and the factory. This effectively gave Ferrari their own Grand Prix circuit. All their competitors were obliged to hire a circuit such as Silverstone in the UK and transport their cars and equipment for a two- or three-day test. Ferrari himself attended most of the tests and would make sure he was kept informed as to exactly what was being tested and why. Enzo himself had always declared his love for the distinctive sound and power of a Ferrari engine, as indicated by former Ferrari driver Nigel Mansel: '*Enzo Ferrari believed that the engine was the most important part of the race car. Colin [Chapman – head of British constructor Lotus] believed it was the chassis.*'

The early seventies were difficult for Ferrari. The new ownership and influence from Fiat meant increased resources, but also increased pressure for results. At this time F1 was dominated by the Ford DFV engine. Built by Cosworth Engineering near Northampton and funded by the Ford Motor Company, the DFV was purpose built for F1. It was light, powerful and relatively inexpensive. In 1968 the engines were available for £7500 each and were fully capable of winning a Grand Prix. This enabled the British constructors, which specialized in chassis design, to become increasingly competitive. In 1971 and 1973 every Grand Prix was won by a car using a DFV engine.

In 1971 the Ferrari racecars were very fast, but unreliable. It got worse in 1972 and 1973, with cars only finishing every other race and rarely in the points. Enzo himself had been suffering poor health and the team seemed unable to turn around despite having the huge resources of Fiat at its disposal. However, through 1974 things began to change. A few years earlier Ferrari engineers had commissioned a small firm in the UK, TC prototypes to build three chassis for the 1974 car using a monocoque structure, derived from aircraft design and favoured by the English constructors. Mauro Forghieri had also been recalled to Ferrari in 1973 as technical director. Forghieri had been responsible for some of the more successful Ferraris of the 1960s but had fallen from grace and spent the later part of the 1960s working on 'special projects'.

In addition to the arrival of Forghieri, a new team boss was also appointed to try to turn Ferrari fortunes around. At 25 years old and a qualified lawyer with connections to the Agnelli family who owned Fiat, Luca di Montezemolo was an unlikely right-hand man for Il Commendatore. However, he was given a relatively free hand by Ferrari and brought much needed management discipline to the team. While there had always been a huge supply of talent at Ferrari, particularly in the design and development of engines, gearboxes and suspension systems, it had not always reached its collective potential. Enzo's autocratic style of 'divide and rule' had created much confusion and rivalry within the team. Montezemolo defined strict areas of responsibility in order to reduce the amount of interference and internal politics. This created a situation where the various technical teams (chassis and suspension; engine; gearbox) concentrated on, and were fully accountable for, their own area. Montezemolo was also instrumental in the recruitment of driver Niki Lauda. Lauda was of Austrian aristocratic descent, but was totally committed to his racing. He had been very successful in Formula Two but was having a torrid time with the ailing BRM team in F1. In 1973 Enzo Ferrari told Lauda he wanted him to drive for Ferrari, an offer which very few drivers have ever refused.

In 1974 Lauda and the design team had embarked upon an exhaustive testing and development programme at the Fiorano test track. The new car, the 312B, was very fast. However, there were still reliability problems and although Lauda was leading the championship at the British Grand Prix, the lead was lost through technical problems which resulted in Emerson Fittipaldi in a McLaren taking the eventual honours.

In 1975 the fruits of Forghieri's creative ideas and the intensive testing at Fiorano were exemplified in the new 312T, which featured a wide low body with a powerful 'flat-12' 12-cylinder engine and a revolutionary transverse (sideways mounted) gearbox which improved the balance of the car, making it handle extremely well. While the new car was not ready until the season had already started, Lauda, with the support of team-mate Regazzoni, was easily able to secure both the drivers' and constructors' world championships. The Ferraris dominated the 1975 season. With their elegant handling and the power advantage of the engine, they were in a class of their own. Because the majority of the competition all had the same engine gearbox combination (Ford DFV and Hewland gearbox), they were unable to respond to a chassis/gearbox/engine combination which was unique to Ferrari.

The following year, 1976, continued in much the same vein, with Lauda and Regazzoni winning the early races. The intensive testing did not let up and new ideas and innovations, such as a revised rear suspension system, were constantly being tried out. On the management front, Montezemolo had been promoted to head up Fiat's entire motorsport operation, which included the Lancia rally programme as well as Ferrari. Daniele Audetto was moved from managing the rally team to Sporting Director at Ferrari. However, things were not to go as smoothly as in 1975. At the German Grand Prix Lauda lost control of the car in the wet and crashed in flames. He was rescued by four other drivers, but not before suffering severe burns and inhaling toxic fumes. His life was in the balance for some weeks while the Grand Prix series continued with James Hunt (McLaren) reducing Lauda's lead in the championship. Miraculously Lauda recovered from his injuries, and although still badly scarred, he returned to race for Ferrari. He and Hunt went into the last Grand Prix of 1976 (Japan) with Lauda leading by three points. There was heavy rain and Lauda pulled out of the race leaving the drivers' championship to Hunt, although Ferrari still collected the constructors' championship. While, on paper, it was a good year, by rights Ferrari should have dominated 1976 as they had 1975. Audetto, who had been unable to live up to the role created by Montezemolo, returned to the world of rallying. Ferrari went into 1977 in a state of disarray.

In 1977 Ferrari were still the team to beat, although the testing and development lost through Lauda's six-week convalescence had undermined the crushing dominance which the team had earlier demonstrated. The competition were beginning to find ways of catching up. The Brabham team moved away from the Ford DFV and used an Alfa Romeo 'flat-12', similar to the Ferrari engine. Tyrrell launched the revolutionary P34 six-wheeled car which seemed to be the only car able to stay with the Ferrari in 1976. Ferrari themselves were not standing still and launched the 312T2 which was a significant development of the original 312T. Ferrari won the 1977 drivers' and constructors' championship, but this was the end of the partnership with Niki Lauda; the relationship had never been the same since the Nurburgring accident. Lauda left to join Brabham. While Lauda was not perhaps the fastest racer on the track, he was always able to develop a

car and build relationships with the design team which enabled Ferrari to translate the driver's senses into reliable technical solutions.

The unprecedented run of Ferrari success continued in 1978 with the 312T3 car driven by two highly talented drivers: Argentinean Carlos Reutemann was joined by the flamboyant Gilles Villeneuve and, while they were not able to win the constructors' championship, they achieved a very strong second place. In 1979 Reutemann was replaced by South African Jody Scheckter, whose consistency contrasted with Villeneuve's erratic speed. Scheckter won the drivers' championship, with Ferrari taking the constructors' championship. Their greatest moment was when Scheckter and Villeneuve finished first and second in the Italian Grand Prix at Monza.

However, 1979 was the last time that Ferrari were to win a drivers' world championship for 21 years. 1980 was something of a disaster for Ferrari. Scheckter and Villeneuve were totally uncompetitive in the 312T5 car which, while a significant development from the 312T4, was outclassed by the competition. New innovations in aerodynamics brought the 'ground effect' revolution, pioneered by Lotus and quickly adopted by Williams and Brabham. Here the underside of the car featured two 'venturi', or channels, either side of the driver. These were aerodynamically designed to create a low-pressure area under the car which sucked the car to the track, allowing faster cornering. Sliding strips of material or 'skirts' were used to create a seal for the air flowing under the car. While the Ferrari's engine was one of the most powerful, it was a flat-12 meaning that the cylinders were horizontal to the ground, creating a low and wide barrier which gave no opportunity to create the ground effect achieved with the slimmer V8 DFV engines. In 1978 Alfa Romeo had launched a V12 engine to replace their flat-12 for this very reason. No such initiative had been taken at Ferrari which was concentrating on a longer-term project to develop a V6 turbo-charged engine. *Autosport* correspondent Nigel Roebuck commented on this change of fortune: 'Maranello's flat-12, still a magnificent racing engine, is incompatible with modern chassis. Villeneuve and Scheckter were competing in yesterday's cars.' The lowest point came in the Canadian Grand Prix when the reigning world champion, Jody Scheckter, failed to qualify his Ferrari for the race. Once again the full wrath of the Italian press descended on the team.

McLaren Honda 1988–1991

The period from 1988 to 1991 was unusual in the hyper-competitive world of F1, where the pace of change is rarely matched in any other competitive environment. This period was notable because of the dominance of one constructor. In one year the McLaren team won 15 of the 16 races. Such dominance had not been seen before and is unlikely to occur again.

Founded by New Zealander and F1 driver Bruce McLaren in 1966, the McLaren team had their first victory in the Belgian Grand Prix of 1968. Tragically McLaren himself was killed two years later while testing. Lawyer and family friend Teddy Mayer took over as team principal. The team continued to develop and in 1974 secured a long-term sponsorship from Philip Morris to promote the Marlboro brand of cigarettes. This was a partnership that was to last until 1996, probably the most enduring relationship between a constructor and a 'flagship' sponsor. However, in the late seventies McLaren found itself left behind by some of the new aerodynamic advances. In September 1980 Ron Dennis became joint team principal with Mayer, a position which he took over solely in 1982, when Mayer was 'encouraged' by Philip Morris to take a less active role in the management of McLaren. In the previous year McLaren moved from their modest site in Colnbrook to a modern facility at Woking in Surrey, South of London.

Dennis had been a mechanic for the highly successful Cooper team in 1966, but left to set up his own Formula 2 (a smaller, less expensive formula) team in 1971. By the end of the 70s he had built up a reputation for professionalism and immaculate presentation. His Project Four company brought in designer John Barnard, who had some radical ideas about using carbon fibre, rather than metal, as the basis for a race car chassis. These ideas were to provide the basis for the radical MP4 car. Both Dennis and Barnard were perfectionists, with Dennis's obsession with immaculate presentation and attention to detail complemented by Barnard's

uncompromising quest for technical excellence. As John Barnard observed in an interview, the entire nature of the organization shifted: '*We changed from being mechanic-led to a team which was totally controlled by the drawing office. Ron used to tell everyone time and time again, "I don't care if we're the last two cars on the grid, we'll be the smartest and the best presented" and that attitude built into the company once it was launched.*'

In 1986 John Barnard left to join the struggling Ferrari team. Barnard was considered by many to be the reason for McLaren's developing dominance. The partnership between Dennis and Barnard had been stormy, but a huge amount had been achieved through the energy of these two individuals. Dennis provided the managerial and commercial acumen and Barnard the highly innovative design skills. To replace Barnard, Brabham designer Gordon Murray was brought into the team, perhaps best known for developing the innovative 'fan car' for Brabham in 1978. Murray, like Barnard, was at the leading edge of F1 car design.

A further factor in McLaren's success had been their relationship with engine suppliers. In the mid eighties turbo-charging became the key technology and in 1983 they used a Porsche turbo engine which was funded by the electronics' company TAG, a sponsor which had previously been with the Williams team. However, the emerging force in engine development was Honda, which had re-entered F1 in 1983 in partnership with Williams. Importantly, the engines were supported by a significant commitment from Honda in both people and resources. Honda used the relationship as an opportunity to develop some of their most talented engineers and to transfer F1 design and development capabilities to their production car programme. In the mid eighties the Williams/Honda partnership was very successful, but following Frank Williams' road accident in 1986, Honda began to have doubts about the future of the Williams team and agreed to supply both McLaren and Lotus for the 1987 season.

Halfway through 1987 McLaren announced that they had recruited two of the top drivers in F1 to their team for the 1988 season: Alain Prost and Ayrton Senna. This was unusual as most teams tended to have a clear hierarchy with a lead driver being supported by a 'number two', who was either regarded as less skilful and/or less experienced than the lead driver. However, McLaren appeared to feel that they would be able to deal with the potential problems which such a structure could cause, as reported in *Motorsport*:

Ayrton Senna is being moved from Lotus to McLaren to join Prost in one of the most professional and well balanced teams of all time. Prost and Senna have been announced as joint number one drivers, and McLaren International has shown in the past that it is well capable of handling two top drivers, which few other teams have managed.

Ayrton Senna, the young Brazilian, had made a name for himself as being extremely talented and totally committed, but very difficult to manage. In his previous team, Lotus, he is alleged to have blocked the recruitment of second driver Derek Warwick as he regarded him too great a threat and persuaded the team to bring in the less experienced and younger Johnny Dumfries. Prost and Senna were real contrasts: Senna was fast, determined and ruthless. Prost was fast too, but a great tactician and adept at team politics, making sure that the whole team was behind him. It was rumoured that a key reason for Honda moving to McLaren was that they now had Alain Prost. However, it was ultimately Senna who was able to win the psychological battle and change the balance of power within the team.

In 1988 the Honda-powered MP4 car was without question the fastest and most reliable car on the circuit. This meant that effectively the only real competition for Prost and Senna was each other. This competition between two highly committed and talented drivers resulted in one of the most enduring and bitter feuds the sport has ever known. In 1988 Senna swerved at Prost as they raced wheel to wheel at 190 mph. Prost told him, '*If you want the world championship badly enough to die for it, you are welcome*'. In 1990 the acrimony with Senna culminated in Prost moving to Ferrari. Senna now had the team to himself. But the battle between them continued, reaching a dramatic climax at the Japanese Grand Prix when Senna forced Prost's Ferrari off the road, and as a consequence became world champion.

Ron Dennis and his professional management style was synonymous with the success of McLaren, indicating that the era of the 'one-man band' Formula One constructor was past. Eddie Jordan, principal of the Jordan team made the following statement when planning to enter F1 in 1990:

I know it sounds far fetched, but I want to emulate Ron Dennis. He's won that many Grand Prix, he's won that many championships, he's been on pole that many times and he's got the best drivers. Everyone hates him; but they only hate him because he's the best. I believe I'm as good as he is: I believe I'm in the same league, but only time will tell.

Dennis's negotiating and marketing abilities were legendary throughout Formula One. McLaren also created their own marketing consultancy operation where the smaller teams engaged them to find sponsors. In 1991 *Management Week* had Ron Dennis on the front cover with the question, 'Is Ron Dennis Britain's best manager?' Dennis likens the management of McLaren to that of a game of chess: '*... you've got to get all the elements right, the overall package, the budget, the designer, the engine, the drivers, the organization.*' John Barnard once likened working with Dennis as: '*being in a room with a hand grenade rolling about without its pin, about to go off and make a horrible mess.*' Dennis is renowned for being hyper-competitive and allegedly once chastised a driver who was delighted with finishing second with the comment, '*Remember, you're only the first of the losers*'. Dennis's ambitions went beyond F1 and in 1988 he began a project to build a road-going car, the McLaren F1. In many ways this mirrored the development of Ferrari, which had made the progression from producing dedicated race cars to also develop road-going cars. The McLaren F1 was launched in 1994 and, with a price tag of £634,000 and a top speed of 231 mph, became the most expensive and fastest road-going car in the world.

The McLaren Honda combination had dominated F1 from 1988 through to 1991, and it was difficult to see what more could be achieved. In September 1992, following widespread speculation, Honda confirmed that that they were pulling out of F1 racing. Honda's reasons were simple: they had been hugely successful and achieved all of their objectives; it was now time to stand back from F1 and find some new challenges. While Dennis had been told about Honda's thinking in late 1991, it appeared that he hadn't taken it seriously enough and the team had no realistic alternatives. This meant they lost valuable winter development time as they tried to find a new engine supplier. In 1993 they competed with customer Ford engines available to any team that had the cash to buy them. Senna's skills still gave McLaren five victories, despite having a less than competitive car. However, at the end of 1993 Senna left the McLaren team to move to Williams, which he saw as having the superior car and engine combination. Former world champion and adviser to Ferrari, Niki Lauda saw this as the terminal blow: '*Senna was a leader. He told them exactly what was wrong with the car. Hakkinen* (Senna's replacement) *is not in a position to do that, so the reaction time is much longer. Senna motivated the designers.*' John Hogan, VP of European marketing for Philip Morris and holder of the McLaren purse strings, saw the problem as design leadership and was advocating that Barnard be brought back to McLaren.

The mid nineties was a particularly difficult period for McLaren. Having tried Peugeot engines in 1994, they moved to Mercedes in 1995. However, 1995 was perhaps best remembered for the debacle at the start when neither Nigel Mansell nor Mika Hakinnen could fit into the new £50 million MP4/10 and then Mansell's alleged £4.5 million contract to race for the year fell apart when neither he nor the car came up to expectations. On a more positive note, 1995 was significant in that it heralded a new partnership between McLaren and Mercedes. Mercedes had been considering a major commitment to F1 and in 1995 they concluded a deal which involved their taking equity stakes in McLaren (40%) and also in specialist engine builder Ilmor Engineering, based near Northampton (25%, increased in 2002 to 55%) which was to build the Mercedes engines used in F1. This relationship was wider than just F1 and would lead to the design and manufacture of the new Mercedes SLR sports car using F1 technology and materials.

Williams Renault 1992–1994

If the McLaren MP4 was the dominant car in the late eighties, the Williams F1 FW15 and 16 powered by a Renault V10 was the car to beat in the early 1990s. During the period 1992–94 Williams cars won 27 out of 48 races, they secured the F1 constructors' title for all three years and the world championship for drivers was won in a Williams in 1992 (Nigel Mansell) and 1993 (Alain Prost).

Like most of the founders of the Formula One constructors, Frank Williams began as a driver, perhaps not of the same standing as Bruce McLaren or Jack Brabham, but nonetheless someone who lived, breathed and loved motor racing. His desire to remain in the sport led him to develop a business buying and selling racing cars and spare parts and in 1968 Frank Williams (Racing Cars) Ltd was formed. A series of triumphs, tragedies and near bankruptcies led up to the establishment of Williams Grand Prix Engineering in 1977 when Frank Williams teamed up with technical director Patrick Head. His approach and style owed a lot to the difficult years in the seventies when he survived on his wits and very little else. At one time he was making calls to sponsors from a public telephone box near the workshop as the phones were disconnected because he hadn't been able to pay the bill. His style could be described as autocratic, entrepreneurial and certainly frugal, despite the multi-million-pound funding he managed to extract from the likes of Canon, R.J. Reynolds and Rothmans. Williams saw his role as providing the resources to build the best car; therefore, anything that didn't directly make the car go faster was a waste of money as far as Frank was concerned. His long-standing relationship with Head was pivotal to the team and brought together a blend of entrepreneurial energy and technical excellence needed to succeed in F1.

The first car from this new alliance was the FW06, designed by Patrick Head and with support from Saudi Airlines. The team enjoyed their first real success in 1980/81 by winning the constructors' championship and with Alan Jones winning the drivers' title in 1980. Jones was a forthright Australian who knew what he wanted and was not afraid to voice his opinions; he also simply got on with the job of driving with little fuss or expectations of special treatment. His approach to working with the team was very influential and coloured Frank Williams' view of drivers: '*I took a very masculine attitude towards drivers and assumed that they should behave – or should be treated – like Alan.'*

A further success occurred in 1986/87 with Nelson Piquet winning the drivers' title in 1987 and Williams the constructors' title in both years. This was despite the road accident in 1986, which left Frank Williams tetraplegic and confined to a wheelchair. However, 1988 was Williams' worst season, with Honda having switched to supplying McLaren, they were forced to suddenly switch to 'off the shelf' Judd V10 engines which were available to anyone who wanted one. Williams didn't win a single race, while McLaren won 15 out of the 16 Grand Prix of 1988 and a disillusioned Nigel Mansell left and went to Ferrari. Frank Williams had to search frantically for a new engine deal which he found in 1990 with Renault. At the end of 1985 Renault had withdrawn from Formula One as a constructor, having failed to win a world championship over the previous eight seasons. However, they continued their engine development activities with the aim of building a new F1 engine to meet the new non-turbo standards due to be introduced in 1989. Frank Williams was able to form an agreement for Renault to supply him with the new V10 engine. This relationship became a far reaching and durable one, with Renault putting human and financial resources into the project with Williams. They also sought to develop the relationship further and extended their activities with Renault by running their team of saloon cars for the British Touring Car Championship, and also provided engineering input and the Williams name for a special edition of the Renault Clio.

In 1990 a lack of driver talent meant that the team were only able to win two races. In 1991 Nigel Mansell was persuaded to return from retirement by Frank Williams and narrowly missed taking the 1991 title, but in 1992 the team dominated the circuits, effectively winning the championship by the middle of the season. Nigel Mansell went into the record books by winning the first five consecutive races of the season. However, deterioration in the relationship between Williams and Mansell led to the driver's retirement from F1 at the end of the year.

The Williams approach to design and development of a car was always the highest priority. Patrick Head had always been one of the more conspicuous of the technical directors in Formula One, a role which is often put into the shade by the team principal and driver. In a sport where personnel change teams frequently, the stable relationship between Williams and Head provided enviable continuity compared with the rest of the field. While Head's designs had often been functional rather than innovative, he had always been able to take a good idea and develop it further. These have included ground effect (originally developed by Lotus), carbon-composite monocoque (McLaren), semi-automatic gearbox (Ferrari), and active suspension (Lotus). The car development process was always a top priority at Williams and Head was supported by many junior designers who then went on to be highly influential in Formula One, such as Neil Oatley and Adrian Newey (both with McLaren), Frank Dernie (Ligier, Lotus and Arrows), Geoff Willis (BAR) and Ross Brawn (Benetton and then Ferrari).

This focus on developing the car and engine combination sometimes meant that the driver took second place in the Williams philosophy, despite the fact that a good driver, who could tell the technicians what needed to be done to the car to improve its performance, was essential to the development process. There had been a number of high-profile disputes between drivers and Williams which had, in part, been attributable to Frank Williams' 'masculine' approach to dealing with drivers. Controversy broke out when the relationship between Williams and two top British drivers broke down. In 1992 Nigel Mansell left when he felt his 'number one' driver position was threatened by the recruitment of Alain Prost for 1993 (although Prost himself left the following year for the same reason regarding the hiring of Ayrton Senna). A similar situation arose when the 1996 world champion, Damon Hill was not retained for the 1997 season and was replaced with Heinz-Harald Frentzen. In an interview with the *Sunday Times* Patrick Head set out the reasons for the decision not to hold on to Hill: '*We are an engineering company and that is what we focus on. Ferrari are probably the only team where you can say the driver is of paramount importance and that is because* [Michael] *Schumacher is three-quarters of a second a lap quicker than anyone else.'*

This emphasis on the driver being only part of the equation was not lost on Paul Stewart, who was concentrating on developing the Stewart Grand Prix entry to F1 in 1996:

If you haven't got the money none of it is poss-ible, so money is one key to success – but what makes a difference is how the money is used. It's not down to any one thing like a driver or an engine, but the interaction that matters. If you look at the Williams team, they rely on a solid framework, their organization, their engine, their car design is all amalgamated into something that gives a platform for everyone to work on. They don't believe putting millions into a driver is going to make all the difference.

Williams' emphatic dominance in the 1992 season was due to a number of factors: the development of the powerful and reliable Renault engine was per-fectly complemented by the FW15 chassis which incorporated Patrick Head's development of some of the innovations of the early nineties, namely semi-automatic gearboxes, drive-by-wire technology and their own active suspension system. As summarized by a senior manager at Williams F1: '*I think we actu-ally were better able to exploit the technology that was available and led that technology revolution. We were better able to exploit it to the full, before the others caught up … it wasn't just one thing but a combination of many things, each one giving you another 200/300th of a second, if you add them up you a get a couple of seconds of advantage.*'

However, other teams were also able to use these innovations and in 1993 the Benetton team made a great deal of progress with both the gearbox and suspension innovations largely attributed to the development skills of their new driver, Michael Schumacher. Williams' technical lead coupled with the tactical race skills of Alain Prost, supported by promoted test driver Damon Hill (due to Mansell's sudden exit) secured the 1993 world championship and constructors' championship for Williams F1.

1994 was a disastrous year, but not for reasons of performance as Williams won the constructors' championship for the third successive year (this was always their declared primary objective, with the drivers' championship very much a secondary aim). Frank Williams had, for some time, regarded Brazilian Ayrton Senna as the best driver around and now, with the obvious performance advantage of the FW15 chassis and the Renault V10 engine, Senna was keen to move to Williams. The problem

was that a bitter and prolonged feud between Senna and Prost, originating from their time together at McLaren, meant that if Senna arrived, Prost would leave. This was exactly what happened. Prost decided to retire (though he returned to run his own team) and Ayrton Senna was partnered by Damon Hill for the 1994 season. However, tragedy struck in the San Marino Grand Prix at Imola on 1 May 1994 when Senna was killed in an accident, an event which not only devastated the Williams team but the sport as a whole.

For the remainder of the season Hill found himself as lead driver supported by the new test driver David Coulthard and a couple of 'comebacks' from Nigel Mansell. While Williams lost the drivers' title to the rising star of German driver Michael Schumacher, despite these huge setbacks Williams retained the constructors' title for 1994.

In 1995 the Benetton team was eclipsing the Williams domination. Benetton had developed a car using many of the technological innovations used by Williams (with the help of ex-Williams designer Ross Brawn). In addition, Renault's ambitions to match Honda's previous domination of the sport as an engine supplier from 1986–1991 led them to supply Benetton with their engines as well as Williams, a decision which incensed Head and Williams. 1995 was the year of Benetton and Michael Schumacher, breaking the three-year domination of the Williams team. However, in 1996 Schumacher moved to the then uncompetitive Ferrari team for £27 million, putting him in 3rd place in the Forbes chart of sports top earners. This left the way clear for Williams to dominate the season, with Benetton failing to fill the gap left by Schumacher.

Ferrari: 1999–2003

The 1980s were a difficult period for Ferrari; more and more investment was poured into the Italian facilities but with no effect on performance. A key problem was that new developments in aerody-namics and the use of composite materials had emerged from the UK's motorsport valley. Ferrari had traditionally focused on the engine as their key competitive advantage. This made perfect sense as, unlike most of the competition who outsourced their engines, Ferrari designed and manufactured their own engines. However, it appeared that these new technologies were substituting superior engine power with enhanced grip due to aerodynamic downforce and improved chassis rigidity.

In 1984, in an effort to introduce a greater understanding of aerodynamics in Ferrari, British designer Harvey Postlethwaite became the first non-Italian Technical Director of Ferrari. In 1986 British designer John Barnard was recruited to the top technical role. However, Barnard was not prepared to move to Italy as he felt that his technical team and network of contacts in the UK would be essential to the success of his position. Surprisingly Enzo Ferrari allowed him to establish a design and manufacturing facility near Guildford in Surrey that became known as the Ferrari 'GTO' or Guildford Technical Office. It seemed that rather than being a unique and distinctively Italian F1 team, Ferrari were now prepared to imitate the British constructors who Enzo had once, rather contemptuously, referred to as the 'Garagistes'. The concept of the GTO was that it was concerned with longer-term research and development and would concentrate on the design of the following year's car, whereas in Maranello, under Postlethwaite, they would focus on building and racing the current car. However, the fact that Barnard was defining the technical direction of Ferrari meant that he became increasingly involved in activities at both sites.

Enzo Ferrari's death in 1988 created a vacuum which was filled by executives from the Fiat organization for a number of years. It was written into the contract that on Enzo's death Fiat's original stake would be increased to 90%; this greater investment led to attempts to run Ferrari as a formal subsidiary of the Fiat group. Barnard became frustrated with the interference and politics of the situation and left to join Benetton in 1989. However, at the end of 1991 Fiat brought Luca di Montezemolo back to Ferrari, this time as CEO with a mandate to do whatever was needed to take Ferrari back to the top. Montezemolo had been team manager with Ferrari during the successful period in the mid seventies. After leaving Ferrari he had taken on a range of high-profile management roles including running Italy's hosting of the soccer World Cup in 1990. One of Montezemolo's first actions was to re-appoint John Barnard as technical director and

re-establish GTO. He was quoted in *The Times* as follows: '*In Italy we are cut away from the Silicon Valley of Formula One that has sprung up in England.*' With an Englishman heading up design he followed this up with the appointment of a Frenchman, Jean Todt, to handle the overall management of the team. Both appointments were clear signals to all involved in Ferrari that things were going to change. Todt had no experience in F1 but had been in motorsport management for many years and had recently led a successful rally and sportscar programme at Peugeot.

However, the physical separation between design and development in Guildford and the racing operation in Maranello led to increased problems and eventually Barnard and Ferrari parted company in 1996. This opened the way for Ferrari to recruit a number of the key individuals in the Benetton technical team to join driver Michael Schumacher who had moved from Benetton to start the 1996 season with the Maranello team. Todt and Montezemolo also chose not to make a direct replacement for the role of technical supremo who would both lead the design of the car and the management of the technical activity. They split the role between a chief designer, Rory Byrne, who had overall responsibility for designing the car, and Ross Brawn, who managed the entire technical operation, roles which both had undertaken in working with Schumacher at Benetton. However, the contractual arrangement with John Barnard had been one where the GTO designers were paid through his private company. When he left they all went with him and Byrne and Brawn faced the task of building up from scratch a new design department – around 50 people, based in Italy.

Along with their recruitment of Michael Schumacher in 1996, Ferrari entered into a commercial partnership with tobacco giant Phillip Morris to use their Marlboro brand on the Ferrari cars. In a novel arrangement Phillip Morris, rather than Ferrari, paid Schumacher's salary, and also made a significant contribution to Ferrari's annual operating budget. However, there was one price to pay which troubled many long-term Ferrari officiandos: the blood-red Ferrari of old was now replaced by a vivid red which more closely matched Marlboro 'rocket red' and also, importantly was more effective on television. There was much speculation about the wisdom of these changes, but Montezemolo was clear that these had to be made to move forward:

For me the company's human resources are critical, the atmosphere is extremely important. I want people, first of all, who love Ferrari and are totally willing to work as a team. You need people able to work together and look forward at the same time. OK, the company has a long history, which holds the lessons for the future, but I don't want people to look at it and stop. The past is the past, important as a point of reference but that's it.

Ferrari also entered into a long-term partnership with Shell to provide both financial and technical support to the team. In these kinds of arrangements Ferrari led a trend away from selling space on cars to long-term commercial arrangements, with coordinated marketing strategies for commercial partners to maximize the benefits of their investments.

This rejuvenated team provided the basis for Michael Schumacher's dominance of F1 in the early part of the 21st century. In 1997 they raced the Barnard-developed Ferrari and finished second in the constructors' championship. Their competitiveness continued to improve and in 1999 they won their first constructors' championship for 12 years – although with an injured Schumacher missing six Grand Prix, the driver's championship went to Mika Hakkinen in a McLaren-Mercedes. However, in 2000 Ferrari secured both championships and it was at this point that they felt they had truly returned to the glory of the mid seventies, it having been 21 years since their last drivers' world championship. In 2002 Schumacher and Ferrari were so dominant that a series of regulation changes were introduced to try to make the racing more competitive. These changes were also prompted by Ferrari's tradition of having a lead driver, which meant that often the second driver was asked to move over in order for the lead driver to maximize his world championship points. This happened at the 2002 Austrian Grand Prix when Ferrari driver Rubens Barrichello moved over just before the finish line to allow Michael Schumacher to win. This produced an angry reaction from fans worldwide and made both the governing body – the FIA – and Ferrari reflect on the wisdom of such a blatant use of team orders.

While Schumacher's talent as a driver and a motivator of the team (he learnt Japanese to converse with an engine technician recruited from Honda) was clearly critical, another key aspect in Ferrari's advantage for 2002 had been their relationship with Bridgestone tyres. Tyres were regarded as a 'black art' in F1, with differing compounds of rubber and different tyre wall construction suiting different cars and different drivers; whereas with changes in aerodynamics teams could make improvements in 100ths of a second, with the right tyre the improvements could result in an advantage in terms of whole seconds rather than tenths or hundredths. In 2000 Bridgestone had been the sole supplier to all F1 teams and therefore tyres were not a source of competitive advantage. However, in 2001 Michelin entered F1 and Ferrari's main rivals – Williams, McLaren and Renault – all switched to Michelin. At the time the regulations stipulated that each manufacturer could create only two specific tyre compounds. For Bridgestone, which now only supplied Ferrari and a number of less competitive teams, the choice was clear: they had to design and develop their compounds specifically for Michael Schumacher and Ferrari. Everyone else would have to make do with this specification. For Michelin the problem was more complex, with many top teams and drivers vying for a compound that specifically suited their car and driving style. Inevitably the Michelin solution was a compromise across many drivers and teams. However, in 2003 the regulations were relaxed and they were able to develop specific compounds for each team/driver. Despite stronger competition from Williams, McLaren and Renault, in 2003 Ferrari were able to secure a record-breaking fifth consecutive constructors title and Michael Schumacher a sixth world championship, breaking Juan Fangio's record which had stood since 1957.

For Montezemolo, all of this was the culmination of a process which had started from the moment of his appointment in 1991:

At the beginning of the '90s, we reorganized the team and invested a lot in new technology. Now we're getting the benefit of what we did three, four years ago; in Formula 1, you can't change everything in 12 months. We had a strong mechanical knowledge, and it was important to keep that, but we had to find out about things we didn't know such as aerodynamics, electronics and, perhaps most importantly, team work. It's because of all that change that we have a very strong team today.

Appendix A: summary of world champions

Year	Driver	Car/Engine	Constructor's Cup
1950	Giuseppe Farina	Alfa Romeo	
1951	Juan Manuel Fangio	Alfa Romeo	
1952	Alberto Ascari	Ferrari	
1953	Alberto Ascari	Ferrari	
1954	Juan Manuel Fangio	Maserati	
1955	Juan Manuel Fangio	Mercedes-Benz	
1956	Juan Manuel Fangio	Lancia-Ferrari	
1957	Juan Manuel Fangio	Maserati	
1958	Mike Hawthorn	Ferrari	Vanwall
1959	Jack Brabham	Cooper/Climax	Cooper/Climax
1960	Jack Brabham	Cooper/Climax	Cooper/Climax
1961	Phil Hill	Ferrari	Ferrari
1962	Graham Hill	BRM	BRM
1963	Jim Clark	Lotus/Climax	Lotus/Climax
1964	John Surtees	Ferrari	Ferrari
1965	Jim Clark	Lotus/Climax	Lotus/Climax
1966	Jack Brabham	Brabham/Repco	Brabham/Repco
1967	Denny Hulme	Brabham/Repco	Brabham/Repco
1968	Graham Hill	Lotus/Ford	Lotus/Ford
1969	Jackie Stewart	Matra/Ford	Matra/Ford
1970	Jochen Rindt	Lotus/Ford	Lotus/Ford
1971	Jackie Stewart	Tyrrell/Ford	Tyrrell/Ford
1972	Emerson Fittipaldi	Lotus/Ford	Lotus/Ford
1973	Jackie Stewart	Tyrrell/Ford	Lotus/Ford
1974	Emerson Fittipaldi	McLaren/Ford	McLaren/Ford
1975	Niki Lauda	Ferrari	Ferrari
1976	James Hunt	McLaren/Ford	Ferrari
1977	Niki Lauda	Ferrari	Ferrari
1978	Mario Andretti	Lotus/Ford	Lotus/Ford
1979	Jody Scheckter	Ferrari	Ferrari
1980	Alan Jones	Williams/Ford	Williams/Ford
1981	Nelson Piquet	Brabham/Ford	Williams/Ford
1982	Keke Rosberg	Williams/Ford	Ferrari
1983	Nelson Piquet	Brabham/BMW	Ferrari
1984	Niki Lauda	McLaren/Porsche	McLaren/Porsche
1985	Alain Prost	McLaren/Porsche	McLaren/Porsche
1986	Alain Prost	McLaren/Porsche	Williams/Honda
1987	Nelson Piquet	Williams/Honda	Williams/Honda
1988	Ayrton Senna	McLaren/Honda	McLaren/Honda
1989	Alain Prost	McLaren/Honda	McLaren/Honda
1990	Ayrton Senna	McLaren/Honda	McLaren/Honda
1991	Ayrton Senna	McLaren/Honda	McLaren/Honda
1992	Nigel Mansell	Williams/Renault	Williams/Renault
1993	Alain Prost	Williams/Renault	Williams/Renault

1994	Michael Schumacher	Benetton/Ford	Williams/Renault
1995	Michael Schumacher	Benetton/Renault	Benetton/Renault
1996	Damon Hill	Williams/Renault	Williams/Renault
1997	Jacques Villeneuve	Williams/Renault	Williams/Renault
1998	Mika Hakkinen	McLaren/Mercedes	McLaren/Mercedes
1999	Mika Hakkinen	McLaren/Mercedes	Ferrari
2000	Michael Schumacher	Ferrari	Ferrari
2001	Michael Schumacher	Ferrari	Ferrari
2002	Michael Schumacher	Ferrari	Ferrari
2003	Michael Schumacher	Ferrari	Ferrari

Note: Constructors' championship is based on the cumulative points gained by a team during the season. Currently each team is limited to entering two cars and drivers per race.

Case 15 Transforming the prancing horse: Ferrari 1950–2003

This case describes the transformation of the Ferrari Formula 1 team from 1950 through to the end of 2003. It focuses in particular on the way in which Ferrari reinvented itself during the 1990s into a winning force which has dominated Formula 1 in the early part of the 21st century.

Breaking all the records

In 2003 Ferrari won their fifth successive Formula 1 (F1) constructors' world championship title, the first time this had ever happened since the award began in 1958. Furthermore, driver Michael Schumacher won his fourth successive drivers' world championship, the first time a driver had ever achieved such a concentrated dominance. His previous world championships for the Benetton team in 1994 and 1995 also meant that he had now surpassed Juan Manuel Fangio's record of five world championships with a total of six, making him the most successful world champion since F1 began in 1950. However, this success had not come without controversy: at the Austrian Grand Prix of 2002 Ferrari were accused of unsporting behaviour when their second driver, Rubens Barrichello, having dominated the race, moved over to allow Michael Schumacher to win, thereby maximizing Schumacher's world championship points. While there was a furore in the press, the Ferrari management remained stoical about their approach. After all, this success had been a long time coming, their 1999 constructors' title had been their first for sixteen years, during which the honours had been dominated by the British-based Williams, McLaren and Benetton teams. Moreover Ferrari's focus had always been to secure the drivers' championship and Schumacher's title in 2000 had been Ferrari's first since Jody Scheckter in 1979, a gap of 21 years. The roots of Ferrari's 2000 victory can be traced back to the appointment

By Mark Jenkins

© 2004, M. Jenkins, Nottingham University Business School.

of a new chairman, Luca di Montezemolo, in 1991 and the fact that it took Ferrari almost ten years to reinvent itself into a world championship winner meant that those involved in this journey felt justified in savouring the fruits of victory for as long as possible.

The prancing horse

Born in 1898, Enzo Ferrari achieved his boyhood ambition of becoming a racing driver. Legend has it that on his first victory at the 1923 Circuito del Savio he was presented the prize by Countess Paolina Baracca, the mother of a First World War fighter pilot who had used the image of a prancing horse on the side of his plane. The countess offered Ferrari the horse emblem so that he could use it for his racing cars, an offer he gratefully accepted. However, Ferrari's career as a driver was soon behind him and in November 1929 he created Scuderia Ferrari (SF) based in Modena, between Parma and Bologna in northern Italy. SF focused on the preparation and competition of racecars for enthusiasts, thereby creating one of the first specialist motorsport companies. They exclusively raced Alfa Romeo cars and in 1932 Alfa Romeo outsourced all its motorsport activity to be run by SF; 1932 was also the year that Ferrari used the prancing horse logo, a black horse on a yellow background – the historic colour of Modena – to symbolize Scuderia Ferrari. The partnership with Alfa Romeo proved to be very successful, winning 144 out of 225 races in the period up to 1937. However, during the late thirties the German Mercedes and Auto-Unions began to dominate racing and, following the Second World War, Alfa Romeo split with SF and Enzo Ferrari went on to build his first car.

The Ferrari 125 made its debut in May 1947, having been designed and developed over the previous two years. Most of the design and development had focused on the creation of the Ferrari supercharged 12-cylinder engine, the first in a long line of Ferrari *dodici cilindri* engines. The Ferrari 125 entered the new F1 championship when it began in 1950, but it was not until 1951 that a Ferrari won a Grand Prix and in 1952 driver Alberto Ascari won the drivers' world championship. The early fifties were of unparalleled success for Ferrari and the other Italian teams of Alfa Romeo and Maserati, which were all based in northern Italy. Italy was now the world leader in motorsport engineering with designs that focused on supercharged 4.5 litre engines positioned in front of the driver, their blood red cars a reflection of the earlier days of Grand Prix racing when cars were colour coded by country of origin, with British racing green for the Vanwalls and BRMs, and the silver Mercedes and Auto-Unions from Germany.

The 1950s were also a tragic time for Ferrari; overall safety standards were poor and many drivers died in Ferrari cars. As a consequence Ferrari often had to endure a great deal of criticism from the press; Enzo Ferrari had lost his son Dino in 1956, and for many this loss hardened his attitude to life and to the loss of drivers. The role of the driver was simply to do a job – bring victory to the red cars of Ferrari and if they did not there was always another to take their place. He was also very frugal about drivers' wages, as former world champion Phil Hill remarked: *'The Old Man's line was very much that you drove for Ferrari for the honour of it. And he wasn't kidding.'* Similarly, it was also claimed that Enzo liked to manage the situation so no particular driver was able to gain the credit for success, as former driver Stirling Moss records: *'I never drove for him, but I've no doubts that in my day he would allow different drivers to win by giving them better cars sometimes, thereby giving the impression that the driver didn't count for anything – that it was the car which had won.'*

Ferrai himself had a rather enigmatic approach to running the company. After the death of his son Dino he very rarely left the Modena area, and hardly ever attended races, preferring to spend his time either in the factory or at the Ferrari test facilities. He relied on the Italian media – which had always shown a keen interest in Ferrari – and his closest advisors for information; this often created a highly political atmosphere in the team.

However, Italian supremacy in F1 was soon to end. The British constructor Cooper produced small 2.0 litre cars with the engine positioned behind the driver (mid-engine layout), designed to maximize mechanical grip, as opposed to relying on sheer engine power as preferred by the Italians. Cooper dominated the world championships of 1959 and 1960 using the 'bought in' Coventry Climax engine, which had been originally designed to power water pumps for fire engines. They were followed by Lotus which, like Cooper, produced lightweight agile cars with high levels of mechanical grip.

Ferrari initially resisted this trend and referred to the British constructors as *'assemblatori'* or *'garagistes'*. He defended the engine layout of the Ferrari with the analogy that the 'horse' had always pulled, not pushed, the cart. Although not an engineer himself, the designers who Ferrari employed (Alberto Massimino, Gioachino Colombo, Carlo Chiti and Mauro Forghieri) had learnt their trade as engine designers and so the design of a new car would always start with the engine. Ferrari often referred to *'the song of the twelve,'* underlining the distinctive high-pitched note of the Ferrari engine. However, by 1960 the dominance of the British cars was undeniable and Ferrari built a lighter mid-engine layout car using a highly effective V6 engine. The Dino 156 (1.5 litre, V6) or 'shark nose' dominated 1961 and gave Ferrari a further world title. However, the advances made in chassis construction by other teams had meant that it was increasingly uncompetitive and in 1964 the Ferrari 158 was launched with a similar monocoque-type chassis to the Lotus 25 of 1962. In 1964 Ferrari tried out the 'flat-12' engine developed by Mauro Forghieri, it was this 12-cylinder unit that was seen to be the future for Ferrari.

Ferrari renaissance: the mid seventies

In 1969 SF merged with Italian automotive manufacturer Fiat. This was, in all but name, a benign acquisition, with Fiat acquiring 50% of Ferrari equity. This provided a huge injection of cash to support research and development activities, symbolized by the construction of a purpose-built circuit at Fiorano, close to the SF factory at Maranello, in 1972. The technical team used this facility to engage in a period of intensive development focusing on the 'flat-12' engine.

The new ownership and influence from Fiat meant increased resources, but also increased pressure for results. In the early seventies F1 was dominated by the Ford DFV engine. Built by Cosworth Engineering near Northampton and funded by the Ford

Motor Company, the DFV was purpose-built for F1: it was light, powerful and relatively inexpensive. In 1968 the engines were available for £7500 each and were fully capable of winning a Grand Prix. This enabled the British constructors, which specialized in chassis design, to become increasingly competitive. In 1971 and 1973 every Grand Prix was won by a car using a DFV engine. The DFV engine made the cars both very light and very powerful; at a time when tyre technology was relatively primitive, this left the designers searching for other ways to increase grip. The answer came from aerodynamics with aircraft-type 'wings' being used to create downforce, or aerodynamic grip, allowing the cars to both enter and exit corners at vastly increased speeds.

During this time Enzo, now in his seventies, had been suffering from ill health. He appointed a team manager to help run the day-to-day activities of the F1 team. Luca di Montezemolo was a 25-year-old lawyer who was connected to Fiat's Agnelli dynasty. In addition Mauro Forghieri had been recalled to Ferrari in 1973 as technical director. In 1975 the fruits of Forghieri's creative ideas and the intensive testing at Fiorano were exemplified in the new 312T, which featured a wide low body with a powerful flat-12 cylinder unit and a revolutionary transverse (sideways mounted) gearbox which improved the balance of the car, making it handle extremely well. While the new car was not ready until the season had already started, driver Niki Lauda, with the support of team-mate Clay Regazzoni, was easily able to secure both the drivers' and constructors' world championships. The Ferraris dominated the 1975 season. With their elegant handling and the power advantage of the engine, they were in a class of their own. This unprecedented run of Ferrari success continued through to 1978 and in 1979 when they won both the drivers' and constructors' championships. Their greatest moment came in 1979 when Ferrari's finished first and second at the Italian Grand Prix at Monza, sending the fanatical Italian fans or *tifosi,* and the Italian press into a complete frenzy.

Ferrari: the end of an era, 1980–1990

However, in 1980 the 312T5 car was outclassed by the competition. New innovations in aerodynamics

brought the 'ground effect' revolution, pioneered by Lotus and quickly adopted by Williams and Brabham. Here the underside of the car featured two 'venturi', or channels, either side of the driver. These were aerodynamically designed to create a low-pressure area under the car which sucked it to the track, allowing faster cornering. Sliding strips of material or 'skirts' were used to create a seal for the air flowing under the car. While the Ferrari's engine was one of the most powerful, it was a flat 12, meaning that the cylinders were horizontal to the ground creating a low and wide barrier which gave little opportunity to create the ground effect achieved with the slimmer V8 DFV engines. In 1978 Alfa Romeo had launched a V12 engine to replace its flat-12 for this very reason. No such initiative had been taken at Ferrari, which was concentrating on a longer-term project to develop a V6 turbocharged engine. *Autosport* correspondent Nigel Roebuck commented on this change of fortune: '*Maranello's flat-12, still a magnificent racing engine, is incompatible with modern chassis. Villeneuve and Scheckter were competing in yesterdays cars.*' The lowest point came in the Canadian Grand Prix when the reigning world champion, Jody Scheckter, failed to qualify his Ferrari for the race. This was a disaster equivalent to Italy failing to qualify for the soccer World Cup. Once again the full wrath of the Italian press descended on the team.

In the mid-eighties more and more investment was poured into the Italian facilities but to no effect on performance. A key problem was that new developments in aerodynamics and the use of composite materials had emerged from the UK. This was concentrated in an area to the south and west of London known as motorsport valley, an area which developed from a network of small engineering firms developed from the automotive and aerospace industries.

In 1986 British designer John Barnard was recruited to the top technical role – he was the second senior non-Italian engineer to take up a position with Ferrari, following the recruitment of Dr Harvey Postlethwaite two years earlier. However, unlike Postlethwaite, Barnard was not prepared to move to Italy as he felt that his technical team and network of contacts in the UK would be essential to the success of his position. Surprisingly Enzo accepted his terms and allowed him to establish a design and manufacturing facility near Guildford in Surrey; it subsequently became known as the Ferrari 'GTO' or Guildford Technical Office. The fact that Barnard was defining the technical direction of Ferrari meant that he became increasingly involved in activities at both Guildford and Maranello. However, the geographical separation between the car and engine departments led to development of various 'factions' within Ferrari, making Barnard's job increasingly difficult. In 1987 there was uproar from the workforce when he ordered a ban on the consumption of wine at the midday canteen in Maranello, many seeing this as an insult to their professionalism.

Enzo Ferrari's death in 1988 created a vacuum which was filled by a series of executives from the Fiat organization for a number of years. It was written into the contract that on Enzo's death Fiat's original stake would be increased to 90%, this greater investment led to attempts to run Ferrari as a formal subsidiary of the Fiat group. Barnard became frustrated with the interference and politics of the situation and left to join the Benetton F1 team in 1989. Ferrari had recruited world champion Alain Prost to drive for them in 1990 but, while the car was both competitive and elegant (an example of this Ferrari 641 now resides in New York's Museum of Modern Art), the organization was falling apart and in 1991 Prost was fired by the Ferrari management for criticizing the car and therefore the sacred name of Ferrari. Former driver Patrick Tambay commented on the situation as follows: 'No one's in charge any more. When the Old Man was alive the buck stopped with him. Maybe he took some curious decisions – but at least he took them. I'm not saying that Ferrari will never win again, but the fabric of what the name meant has gone. There are so many layers of management, so many bosses reporting to bosses, until ultimately it gets to Gianni Agnelli (Chairman of Fiat).'

Transforming the prancing horse: 1990–2003

At the end of 1991, Fiat's chairman Gianni Agnelli appointed Luca di Montezemolo as CEO of Ferrari. His mandate was simple, to do whatever was needed to take them back to the top. After his role as team manager for Ferrari during the successful period in the mid seventies, Montezemolo had taken on a range of high-profile management roles including running Italy's hosting of the soccer World Cup in 1990. Di Montezemolo accepted the role on the basis that Ferrari, and in particular, the racing operation, was independent of Fiat: 'I have not been in the Fiat management stream for ten years. Maranello is another world and has to be treated as such.' In an article in *Autosport* he described the situation as follows:

After I arrived last December (1991) I spent five months working to understand the situation. To understand the manpower, to understand the potential of the car. Once I had absorbed all this I decided to approach the whole situation in a completely different manner. Ferrari had become an inflexible monolith of a company which was no good for racing. As a result I decided to divide it into three small departments: future developments and special projects in the UK under John Barnard; the engine department in Maranello under Paolo Massai and finally the Scuderia Ferrari under Harvey Postlethwaite which is the place where we build the cars and manage the team.

I also wanted to build up a a strong relationship between our UK facility and Italy in order to take full advantage of the F1 'silicon valley' in England for chassis development and specialist sub-contractors while still harnessing the huge potential of Maranello.

When asked why he was repeating the 'GTO' initiative which Enzo Ferrari had set up with Barnard and which had ultimately ended with Barnard leaving, Montezemolo had a very clear response:

I think that the GTO concept of Enzo Ferrari was a super idea. Unfortunately, at the time Ferrari was very old and the situation was managed in a bad way. But the fundamental idea was very good. For me the approach is slightly different. First of all, I am in charge of the company with full powers, so I can take a decision without anyone else taking a parallel initiative. I take my responsibilities and I want the people in the company to follow my ideas. If they follow, I am very happy. If they don't then there are many other doors, many possibilities available to them outside Ferrari.

My objective is to create a smaller racing department which contains less bureaucracy; of course, there will be a lot of discussion between the engine and chassis departments. In Maranello we have a huge organization geared to building cars, but I want to take advantage of the UK facilities, and for a world-wide company like Ferrari it is certainly not a scandal to have an affiliate in the UK. If you want to make pasta, then you have to be in Parma, I want to make a sophisticated F1 project so I want to be involved in England. Then it is up to me to put everything together.

In August 1992 John Barnard signed a five-year contract with Ferrari to design and develop its new cars. In an effort to avoid a 'them and us' situation between the UK and Italy a number of technical people were swapped over between the UK and Italy.

At the launch of the 1992 car, Montezemolo broke with tradition and introduced a new numbering system based on the year a car would be racing. Prior to this point the numbering of many Ferrari cars had been based on the characteristics of the engine – the 312 of 1971 representing 3.0 litre 12 cylinders, the 126C4 of 1984 representing a 120° 'V' angle with 6 cylinders, and C standing for 'Compression' or turbo-charging:

At Ferrari we have always devoted and will continue to devote, great attention to racing, racing is part of the history, the culture and the traditions of this company. We live in a country which, especially in recent times, people have yelled and complained a bit too much. We hope that the only noise around here will be our engine as it sets new lap records at Fiorano. We are looking for a revival here, and with an eye to the future we have tried to put together a group which combines young engineers, many of them with the highest qualifications, and people whose enthusiasm and abilities will make a notable contribution. We have a lot of work to do, we have a lot of ground to make up on the opposition. We have code-named the new car F92A to demonstrate that we are turning a new page in our history.

When asked about drivers in 1992 he also gave some indication of his thinking: *'The main priority is the new organization. We are lucky because it is a big challenge to offer a driver the chance to help re-establish Ferrari to a competitive level. I want a driver who is motivated and prepared to work with us. Motivation is everything in a driver, as Niki Lauda reminds us!'*

In addition to the structural changes, Montezemolo had also brought in some familiar faces from Ferrari's successful period in the mid seventies, driver Niki Lauda acted as a consultant to the team and Sante Ghedini took on the role of team manager. With an Englishman heading up design he followed this up with the appointment of a Frenchman, Jean Todt, to handle the overall management of the team. Todt had no experience in F1, but had been in motorsport management for many years and had recently led a successful rally and sportscar programme at Peugeot. Driver Gerhard Bergher commented on Todt's team building skills: *'I was able to bring some links in the chain to Ferrari, but it took Todt to join them together. Ferrari is now working as a team for the first time. He has made a huge difference.'* Chief Mechanic Nigel Stepney joined Ferrari in 1993, but his first impressions were not positive. *'When I joined Ferrari at the beginning of 1993, it was like being thrown into the lion's den. I was in a non-position, regarded as John Barnard's spy and not allowed to take any responsibility.'* However, he recalled the arrival of Jean Todt as a turning point in the team: *'It was like Julius Caesar every day. People getting sacked and leaving every five minutes. You never knew who was boss – not until Jean Todt arrived, took control of the situation and instilled organization, stability and loyalty into the team.'*

However, the physical separation between design and development in Guildford and the racing operation in Maranello led to increased problems and eventually Barnard and Ferrari parted company for the second time at the end of 1996. At the start of the year Ferrari had recruited F1 World Champion

Michael Schumacher, formerly with the Benetton team. The departure of Barnard now opened the way for Ferrari to recruit a number of the key individuals from the Benetton technical team which had helped Schumacher to his world titles in 1994 and 1995. The arrival of Schumacher also provided new impetus for the team, as Nigel Stepney recounted: 'Once Schumacher arrived, everyone started putting us under incredible pressure. We weren't quite ready as we still needed key people, but at some point you just have to go for it and get the best driver around. He was the icing on the cake and it sent out signals that we were serious again.'

Todt and Montezemolo also chose not to make a direct replacement for the role of technical supremo who would both lead the design of the car and the management of the technical activity. They split the role between a chief designer, Rory Byrne, who had overall responsibility for designing the car, and Ross Brawn, who managed the entire technical operation; these were roles which both had undertaken in working with Schumacher at Benetton. However, the contractual arrangement with John Barnard had been one where the GTO designers were paid through his private company. When he left they all went with him and Byrne and Brawn faced the task of building up from scratch a new design department – around 50 people, based in Italy. The engine department continued to develop Ferrari's engines but, in line with new technologies and developments, these were now lighter V10s to compete with the Renault and Mercedes engines, rather than the beloved, but now dated, Ferrari *dodici cilindri*.

Along with its recruitment of Michael Schumacher in 1996, Ferrari entered into a commercial partnership with tobacco giant Phillip Morris to use their Marlboro brand on the Ferrari cars. In a novel arrangement Phillip Morris, rather than Ferrari, paid Schumacher's salary, and also made a significant contribution to Ferrari's annual operating budget. However, there was one price to pay which troubled many long-term Ferrari officiandos: the blood-red Ferrari of old was now replaced by a vivid red which more closely matched Marlboro 'rocket red' and also, importantly was more effective on television. There was much speculation about the wisdom of these changes, but Montezemolo was clear that these had to be made to move forward:

For me the company's human resources are critical, the atmosphere is extremely important. I want people, first of all, who love Ferrari and are totally willing to work as a team. You need people able to work together and look forward at the same time. OK, the company has a long history, which holds the lessons for the future, but I don't want people to look at it and stop. The past is the past, important as a point of reference but that's it.

In addition to Marlboro, Ferrari also entered into a long-term partnership with Shell to provide both financial and technical support to the team. In these kinds of arrangements Ferrari led a trend away from selling space on cars to long-term commercial arrangements, with coordinated marketing strategies for commercial partners to maximize the benefits of their investments.

There were also concerns about the way the team now revolved around Schumacher, rather than, as in the past, when the drivers were secondary to the cars of Ferrari. Jean Alesi, a former Ferrari driver observed that 'Schumacher does whatever he wants, and they do whatever he says.. This was in marked contrast to Enzo Ferrari who had famously rejected a number of top-class drivers because they wanted too much money, such as Jackie Stewart in 1970 and Ayrton Senna in 1986 whose wage demands Enzo described as 'imaginativo!'

This rejuvenated team provided the basis for Michael Schumacher's dominance of F1. In 1997 it raced the Barnard-developed Ferrari and finished second in the constructors' championship. Although as this was Ferrari's 50th anniversary and there was high anticipation that this was to be their year – but, as Nigel Stepney recounts: '1997 was a great disappointment for the team as we so nearly won the championship, we felt we had the right way of working; we just had to keep at it and not panic.' Their competitiveness continued to improve and in 1999 they won the constructors' championship – although the drivers' championship went to Mika Hakkinen in a McLaren-Mercedes, Stepney again recalls: 'It was a very stressful year, we lost Michael Schumacher after he broke his leg at Silverstone. Then we made mistakes such as the pit-stop at the Nurburgring. But although we paid the price in *one respect, we gained from the experiences. We realized that as a team, we had to pace ourselves, to switch off and recharge our batteries sometime.'*

There was clear momentum in the company now to secure the world championships and what followed was a complete domination by Ferrari in the period 2000–2003. For Montezemolo this was the culmination of a process which had started from the moment of his appointment in 1991: *'At the beginning of the '90s, we reorganized the team and*

invested a lot in new technology. Now we're getting the benefit of what we did three, four years ago; in Formula 1, you can't change everything in 12 months. We had a strong mechanical knowledge, and it was important to keep that, but we had to find out about things we didn't know such as aerodynamics, electronics and, perhaps most importantly, team work. It's because of all that change that we have a very strong team today.'

Appendix A: summary of world champions			
Year	Driver	Car/Engine	Constructor's Cup
1950	Giuseppe Farina	Alfa Romeo	
1951	Juan Manuel Fangio	Alfa Romeo	
1952	Alberto Ascari	Ferrari	
1953	Alberto Ascari	Ferrari	
1954	Juan Manuel Fangio	Maserati	
1955	Juan Manuel Fangio	Mercedes-Benz	
1956	Juan Manuel Fangio	Lancia-Ferrari	
1957	Juan Manuel Fangio	Maserati	
1958	Mike Hawthorn	Ferrari	Vanwall
1959	Jack Brabham	Cooper/Climax	Cooper/Climax
1960	Jack Brabham	Cooper/Climax	Cooper/Climax
1961	Phil Hill	Ferrari	Ferrari
1962	Graham Hill	BRM	BRM
1963	Jim Clark	Lotus/Climax	Lotus/Climax
1964	John Surtees	Ferrari	Ferrari
1965	Jim Clark	Lotus/Climax	Lotus/Climax
1966	Jack Brabham	Brabham/Repco	Brabham/Repco
1967	Denny Hulme	Brabham/Repco	Brabham/Repco
1968	Graham Hill	Lotus/Ford	Lotus/Ford
1969	Jackie Stewart	Matra/Ford	Matra/Ford
1970	Jochen Rindt	Lotus/Ford	Lotus/Ford
1971	Jackie Stewart	Tyrrell/Ford	Tyrrell/Ford
1972	Emerson Fittipaldi	Lotus/Ford	Lotus/Ford
1973	Jackie Stewart	Tyrrell/Ford	Lotus/Ford
1974	Emerson Fittipaldi	McLaren/Ford	McLaren/Ford
1975	Niki Lauda	Ferrari	Ferrari
1976	James Hunt	McLaren/Ford	Ferrari
1977	Niki Lauda	Ferrari	Ferrari
1978	Mario Andretti	Lotus/Ford	Lotus/Ford
1979	Jody Scheckter	Ferrari	Ferrari
1980	Alan Jones	Williams/Ford	Williams/Ford
1981	Nelson Piquet	Brabham/Ford	Williams/Ford
1982	Keke Rosberg	Williams/Ford	Ferrari
1983	Nelson Piquet	Brabham/BMW	Ferrari
1984	Niki Lauda	McLaren/Porsche	McLaren/Porsche
1985	Alain Prost	McLaren/Porsche	McLaren/Porsche

1986	Alain Prost	McLaren/Porsche	Williams/Honda
1987	Nelson Piquet	Williams/Honda	Williams/Honda
1988	Ayrton Senna	McLaren/Honda	McLaren/Honda
1989	Alain Prost	McLaren/Honda	McLaren/Honda
1990	Ayrton Senna	McLaren/Honda	McLaren/Honda
1991	Ayrton Senna	McLaren/Honda	McLaren/Honda
1992	Nigel Mansell	Williams/Renault	Williams/Renault
1993	Alain Prost	Williams/Renault	Williams/Renault
1994	Michael Schumacher	Benetton/Ford	Williams/Renault
1995	Michael Schumacher	Benetton/Renault	Benetton/Renault
1996	Damon Hill	Williams/Renault	Williams/Renault
1997	Jacques Villeneuve	Williams/Renault	Williams/Renault
1998	Mika Hakkinen	McLaren/Mercedes	McLaren/Mercedes
1999	Mika Hakkinen	McLaren/Mercedes	Ferrari
2000	Michael Schumacher	Ferrari	Ferrari
2001	Michael Schumacher	Ferrari	Ferrari
2002	Michael Schumacher	Ferrari	Ferrari
2003	Michael Schumacher	Ferrari	Ferrari

Note: Constructors' championship is based on the cumulative points gained by a team during the season. Currently each team is limited to entering two cars and drivers per race.

This case study is drawn from material contained in Performance at the Limit: Business Lessons from Formula 1 Motor Racing (2005) Jenkins, M. Pasternak, K. and West, R., Cambridge University Press, Cambridge, UK.

CHAMBRE DE COMMERCE ET D' INDUSTRIE DE PARIS
CENTRE DE PERFECTIONNEMENT AUX AFFAIRES

Case 16 IKEA culture as competitive advantage

I IKEA the worldwide standard setter

After firmly attaining leadership within Sweden, where it holds more than 20% of the overall market, IKEA has succeeded over the last twenty five years to do what no furniture distributor has ever attempted: to become a global player in an industry considered by nature to be local.

Today IKEA delivers low priced quality furniture to key markets throughout the world. It is the only distributor in its field to have successfully established itself in all parts of Europe, including Southern and Eastern Europe, and more notably in North America, including the USA. It has stores today in the Middle East, Singapore and Hong Kong and is preparing to enter the Chinese market sometime in the early part of the next century. Recently Ingvar Kamprad has secured his position in Europe with the acquisition of British based Habitat, IKEA'S chief rival in the UK and France.

To provide some idea of its worldwide presence, IKEA receives annually over 120 million visitors in its 125 stores, and distributes 35 million catalogues. Its sales revenues increased steadily over the last 10 years by an average of 12% annually, in spite of the flattening out of its business in Western Europe which still represents nearly 80% of its annual volume. (See **Exhibit 1.**)

Founder Ingvar Kamprad's stubborn insistence that people will buy more furniture if the price is low enough, the furniture of decent quality and no delays in delivery has gradually revolutionized the conservative national furniture markets in Europe and beyond. Kamprad intuitively anticipated the rise of consumerism in the 1950's and 60's, and virtually invented the practices of cash and carry, self-service, and volume buying in Europe.

IKEA was to invent many other concepts and new ways of dealing with logistics, sourcing, and retailing, many of these innovations have become industry standards: knock-down furniture that can be stored and shipped in flat boxes; involving customers in the value adding process by handling the transportation and doing easy home-assembly themselves; and turning shopping into a family event by creating attractive open store environments that contain IKEA trademarks like the children's areas with brightly colored plastic balls, and the buffet style restaurants where you can eat Swedish meatballs.

IKEA has affected the way furniture is sold and distributed in every country where it is doing business, inspiring imitation and drawing respect, sometimes begrudgingly, from traditional furniture dealers.

One aspect of IKEA'S success has been the development of unique product design capabilities, based on an almost religious dedication to the simple, yet graceful design of contemporary Swedish furniture. In so doing it has introduced millions of households around the world to the Swedish style that it more than others have come to typify. (See **Exhibit 2.**)

IKEA'S strength today comes from their mastery of three key aspects of the value chain: **unique design capabilities, unique sourcing, and tightly controlled logistics**. This means that they are able to produce products that are distinctive enough to provide market recognition, secure sourcing for long runs at profitable levels, and reduce inventory costs through regional warehouses which work very closely with stores. In this way they have been able to buck industry trends and steadily increase their share of slow growing, sometimes shrinking markets.

IKEA has become a household reference as much in Warsaw, as in Los Angeles, attracting customers who just want to come to a store, look around and have some fun. Something universally irresistible about IKEA makes it very difficult for people to come away from one of its stores without making a purchase and instills unprecedented loyalty among its customers and employees.

IKEA's successful development, particular organizational capabilities, and the bold and inspired leadership of its entrepreneur-founder have all been largely written up and commented on. Its organization, communication, marketing, product range, and store layouts all tell the same story – the story of the 'IKEA-Way'. A way strongly rooted in the personality of found Ingvar Kamprad and the Swedish (regional) culture that he grew up in.

II THE 'IKEA-way': doing things differently

What is it that makes IKEA so different? Is it just 'low priced quality goods at affordable prices'? Or is there a deeper explanation? When asked these questions, IKEA managers and personnel become mystical and somewhat vague. 'It is really a winning combination of price and a merry feeling, a feeling of delight' a Dutch marketing manager answers. This feeling and a conscious awareness that, in addition to the competitive advantage there is something strong and intangible at IKEA that drives and motivates its success, is shared by IKEAns throughout the organization. Could it be that the IKEA-Way's combination of vision, charismatic leadership, sound business principles is subtly reinforced by the influence of Swedish culture? Could it be that Swedish, or Scandinavian culture contains elements that facilitates international expansion?

Can a company's national culture in this case be a competitive advantage? Throughout our investigation of IKEA we have kept these questions in the back of our minds, and we invite you to consider them as we explore the IKEA-Way more closely.

How it all started

IKEA's name is derived from the initials of the company's founder, architect, and driving force

Ingvar Kamprad, those of the farm where he was raised, Elmtaryd, and those of his native village Agunnaryd, located in Smaland a poor farming region in the south-east of Sweden. Coming from a modest background, Kamprad began as a trader in everything from matches to Christmas cards, he almost accidentally got into the furniture business after buying out a failed furniture plant in the early 1950's. He demonstrated from the very beginning a combination of strong salesmanship, practical business acumen, thrift, an identity with ordinary people, and an unconventional perseverance in the face of adversity. Always modest he was none the less a true entrepreneur, and more significantly a nonconformist who was not the least bit restrained by the conventions and traditions of the Swedish furniture trade of his day.

His habit of staying close to his customers and his reluctance to own manufacturing furniture plants gave him freedom to focus and innovate on all the facets of distribution. With nearly furniture producers he co-designed furniture to meet very specific requirements for quality products that average customers could afford, and then printed them up in catalogues, which he had discovered as an economical and effective way of marketing to a growing customer base in his early days as a trader.

In 1953 he opened his first showroom at the furniture plant he had bought earlier in Almhult which has become the heart of his furniture empire. The only transportation link to the factory was by road at a time when more and more working class Swedes were purchasing their first automobiles, so what was originally a problem would become a solution.

Kamprad was obsessed with low prices, and the only way to offer them was to keep costs as low as possible: this conviction became a driving force of his business development. He would constantly seek new ways to lower prices. For example he bought fabrics for his furniture directly from textile mills, placing large orders and then supplying the material himself to his network of small furniture manufacturers. In this way at the same time he was able to cut costs a bit more, and ensure that his customers would have a wider selection of upholstery to choose from in the catalogue. Unwittingly he had introduced the notion of vertical integration, which provided

IKEA even then with a strong competitive advantage compared to traditional distributors who only displayed and sold furniture.

Such practices enabled him to have close contact with his suppliers, and eventually to learn intimately the parameters of furniture production. His relationship between him and his suppliers were so good that to obtain their commitment he needed only to draw rough sketches of the furniture he wanted and discuss with them how to adapt production to their capabilities. In so doing, he established over the years another cornerstone of his business philosophy: marrying the customers' need for low prices with the suppliers' need for profit through efficiency and long production runs. This was a strong departure from the kind of relationship that distributors traditionally maintained with their suppliers, buying furniture as it was ordered piece by piece at high prices with long waiting periods for delivery.

Balancing customers' requirements and producers' needs, which enabled him to sell furniture at prices 30 to 50% below traditional distributors, is now the foundation of the IKEA-Way. This notion is so basic and even imperative that a store manager in Germany told me, when walking through the accessories department where some Chinese gadgets were displayed, that this balancing of optimal product design with the supplier with the needs of the customer is the 'Yin and Yang' of the IKEA strategy. It was already present in the way Ingvar Kamprad developed his business through the fifties when his innovative ways provoked stubborn counter attacks from his more established Swedish competitors.

A legendary showdown took place at the Sankt Erik's Fair in Stockholm where, for the first time, IKEA introduced its products. Feeling threatened by Kamprad's unexpected success and many new customers, the Swedish furniture cartel tried to block IKEA's entry at the fair. They failed, but soon thereafter managed a successful boycott of IKEA by Swedish furniture manufacturers accusing Kamprad of unfair practices. Undaunted by this seemingly insurmountable obstacle, Kamprad looked for and found new suppliers in Poland at the height of the Cold War.

Although Polish manufacturers were willing to sell at prices well below their counterparts in Sweden, the cost of transportation offset this advantage. This new obstacle was at the origin of yet another IKEA invention, as Kamprad discovered that by 'knocking down' furniture into disassembled parts it could be packed and shipped in flat cardboard reducing by more than 80% the cost of transporation. To further save on costs, the furniture could be sold directly to customers in these same flat boxes. To help customers participate in the distribution cycle IKEA offered to rent roof racks and invented the simple assembly tool which had become another of its trademarks.

To reach the largest possible market and benefit fully from volume sales, in 1964 IKEA opened Europe's first large 'warehouse scale' store in Stockholm. Unexpectedly large crowds of people attended the grand opening causing yet another problem. Seemingly endless queues formed at the check-out stands as employees scurried to the storage areas to fetch the purchased furniture. Instead of hiring more employees, Kamprad simply opened the storage area to customers and invited them to fetch the furniture themselves. Such practices were unheard of then, but understanding that this would lead to lower prices, customers willingly complied. In just a few years IKEA had invented the concept of 'prosumers' whereby customers actively participate in the distribution cycle.

Suddenly the whole system was in place: customers were able to purchase attractive quality furniture at low prices; furniture suppliers benefited from long production runs, and IKEA, through volume sales, was able to make a considerable profit from small margins.

IKEA's business strategy did not evolve from 'strategic planning' which is still scorned today in the company as 'too sophisticated'. It evolved from creative responses to difficult problems, turning them into solutions pragmatically and often with considerable risk. Not going by the book, or adopting conventional solutions. Learning by doing appears to be a distinguishing trait of Ingvar Kamprad's and IKEA's intuitive way of doing business.

The IKEA mission

As IKEA grew Ingvar Kamprad found ways to explain his unique way of doing business always using simple language and metaphors. He has consistently maintained that IKEA's mission is **to offer 'a wide range of home furnishing items of good design and function, at prices so low that the majority of people can afford to buy them'**. This statement is at the heart of the IKEA's philosophy and has shaped all of the phases of its business, particularly product range. The concept is protected through numerous guidelines and special legal entities. Changes in the criteria for product range can only be made by joint decisions of INGKA Holding BV and Inter IKEA Systems BV both of which are outside the sphere of management.

The essential guidelines appear in a 1976 publication 'Testament of a Furniture Dealer' in which Kamprad emphasizes the company's ambition to cover furnishing and decorative needs of the total home area with a distinctive style that reflect 'our thoughts and be as simple and straightforward as ourselves'. The guidelines also express such modern ideals as furniture that is durable and easy to live with, reflects a natural and free life style, and appeals to youthfulness with color and joy. Most of IKEA's products are designed by Swedes in Almhult who consciously reproduce the designs that reflect these values which are very consistent with Swedish culture. At the same time there is something universally appealing in that specific design in markets throughout the world.

Business principles

IKEA has developed unique competencies and ability to deliver products which are distinctly Swedish, attractively presented in warm value adding environments, and at consistently lower prices than competition.

What has made IKEA so different from other distributors is the balanced focus it has maintained on product range, sourcing, vertical integration, mass marketing, cost leadership, and a distinctive image. As such they are not market driven, and tend to react rather slowly to new consumer trends, studying them to see how they can fit into their operating systems and what value IKEA can add within their proven framework, before adopting them into their range. The issue of range is vital for them as, when they introduce new products they must insure that the volumes they produce are leveraged from within sourcing-logistics-store layouts.

The Yin/Yang metaphor mentioned earlier illustrates the imperative balance of strategic sourcing and marketing mix.

The balance and complementariness of:

Strategic Sourcing   and   the Marketing Mix

In the area of **strategic sourcing**, IKEA has established a long-standing competitive advantage. The durable partnerships that it has developed with furniture producers and other suppliers is based on the producers capacity to provide long runs of parts, and their willingness to comply with IKEA's quality standards and IKEA's guaranteed purchase of all parts produced. IKEA considers their producers as key stakeholders and provide them with technical assistance to increase their productivity sometimes underwriting investments of new technology. Together they actively contribute to both cost reduction and quality enhancement, that optimise the marketing mix.

Through such partnerships IKEA has virtually integrated production into its value-added chain without the heavy investments of actually owning and running its own furniture plants.

Management style and practices

IKEA management style is described by non-Swedish members as informal, open, and caring. Hierarchy is not emphasized and in a typical store there are only three levels of responsibility between the store manager and co-workers (which is what employees are called). A pragmatic approach to problem solving and consensus-based decision-making are also strongly embedded in IKEA management practice.

Co-workers at all levels are encouraged to take initiatives, and making mistakes is considered a necessary part of 'learning by doing'. Managers are expected not only to share information with co-workers but also their knowledge and skills. IKEA wants their co-workers to feel important, they can express their ideas, and should feel responsible for improving the way things are done.

An entrepreneurial zeal for getting the job done in the most direct way and a distaste for bureaucratic procedure are basic managerial attitudes that have long been promoted within IKEA. Managers are expected to be close to their co-workers with few if any status barriers, and not to take themselves seriously. This egalitarian approach to management has also made it easy for motivated employees to work their way up the organization with little formal training. It is significant that Swedish managers' titles do not appear on their business cards, and that company cars are the same economy models for all of those who need them for work or business regardless of their position.

Rather than establish extensive training programs and detailed rules on procedures to propagate its unique culture, IKEA prefers a softer approach through discussion and explanation. The IKEA-Way has been spelled out through wide distribution of Kamprad's 'Testament', which has been translated into a dozen languages. Kamprad himself explains that IKEA has 'a strong and living culture' based on doing things differently. 'It has grown step by step', and together with its business principles is the 'cornerstone of our operations. ... Which helps us retain the spirit and vitality of the early years ... and create a feeling of belonging in a large international organization. Our corporate culture binds us together.' To ensure that the IKEA-Way is understood, the organization relies heavily on managers to act as 'missionaries' carrying all that it embodies through their example and willingness to explain to new and older employees why things are done the way they are. This, as much as anything else, provides the reason for the extensive presence of Swedish managers in IKEA's international units, as their knowledge stems from their direct exposure to Ingvar Kamprad and IKEA's subtle way of doing business and managing people. For those managers who do not have that exposure, week-long IKEA-Way seminars are organized periodically in Almhult, the IKEA equivalent of Mecca and the heart of its culture.

III IKEA's strategy of international expansion: flexibility within established parameters

Patterns of international expansion

IKEA's international expansion has taken place progressively over the last twenty-five years with an eye towards markets in countries with growth potential. Expansion outside of Scandinavia was driven by Ingvar Kamprad's intuitive quest for new opportunities, and his previous successful search for suppliers outside of Sweden more than by any formal development strategy. Some insights are provided by one of IKEA's Swedish executives, an early companion of Ingvar Kamprad. 'When we opened our first store outside Scandinavia in Switzerland, people asked why there? It was a difficult market. Ingvar said that if we could succeed there, we should succeed anywhere. He had intuitions, he spoke to people on the streets to learn what they were looking for.' Such an empirical experiential approach goes against the orthodox rules of international retailing which are preaching extensive market studies before entering a new market, catering to local tastes, and gaining expertise through acquisitions and joint ventures.

When IKEA expanded into Germany, competition was strong and German distributors didn't take them seriously. 'They called us those crazy Swedes, but we didn't mind, we even used this label in our advertising. It took them five years to really react, but by then we had eight stores and were setting the standards.'

Charting its own course, IKEA has developed internationally, finding cheap land for stores, availability of sourcing, proximity to central warehouses, or lowering marketing costs. When in the late 70's they decided to go into Belgium because it was cost effective to service the country from their central warehouse in Germany they ran into problems with building permits and so decided to develop in France instead. The preference has been for leveraging market costs by concentrating several stores in the same area. This explains why they opened four stores in the Philadelphia/Washington DC/New Jersey area sometimes in locations that were rather isolated. They also preferred concentrating four stores in the Paris area even if this could dilute store sales and creates potential competition between stores.

Typically development has been done on a store by store basis. IKEA opens a beachhead in a given country with a group of trusted and experienced Swedish 'Missionaries'. Together they form a right-knit group who can solve problems and make decisions quickly. They supervise the building, lead operational teams who open the store, and run the store until local management has learned how the system works. After a short while store management is turned over to local managers, while most of the key national positions remain in the hands of Swedes until the operation and market has reached maturity.

Adapting to national markets

Adapting to new markets in Western Europe throughout the 70's and early 80's was fairly simple. Catalogue offerings were virtually the same. However concessions had to be made, particularly in bedroom furnishings since bedding could be substantially different from country to country.

'When we entered a new country we did things our way. The idea was to be IKEA everywhere, after all, our furniture is a cultural statement. But as the years went by we learned to be more flexible, particularly when demand in Sweden declined and we became more dependent on our non-Scandinavian markets.'

Adapting to the US market was a real learning experience for IKEA, since many standards were different. Few product managers from IKEA of Sweden had traveled to North America since the price of air travel was prohibitive to IKEA's cost-conscience policies. They expected their European range to sell just as easily in the US, which did not turn out to be the case. As a former US country manager explains: 'IKEA ran into problems in the US so we had to ask ourselves what can we offer to Americans. Should we become an American company, or merely adapt our merchandising to American customers? We finally decided on a solution: Merchandising to the American customer by speaking English with a Swedish accent. Capitalizing on our strengths as an outsider.'

Development of the range is now closely monitored by IKEA of Sweden (IOS) and the Board of Directors of INGKA Holding. The issue of range is vital for them as, when they introduce new products they must ensure that the volumes they produce are balanced from within (sourcing-logistics-store layouts). It took IKEA of Sweden several years to introduce 'futons' in Europe, and American store managers had to work hard to convince them that a 'Home Entertainment' line was feasible in North America.

As a former French country manager described, obtaining concessions from product managers to take into account specific national preferences was a consensual process that required many negotiation skills. 'Some room is allowed for national considerations in our catalogue range. But since changes mean that it will be more expensive for the country manager, only a limited number is requested. Still 90% of our range is the same all over, only 5 to 10% is country specific. The product manager has the final word, but he usually listens to the country manager. There is a healthy tension between the two and this enables us to adapt but not to over-adapt and weaken our cost effectiveness.'

Although IKEA's stated mission is to provide home furnishing for the 'greatest number' and its business is conducted on a volume basis, outside of Scandinavia it is in reality a niche player, appealing to the educated population with mid to upper level incomes. This segment is looking for non-traditional lines of furniture, and finds the Swedish style of IKEA suitable to its modern taste.

'In spite of our image as the "common man's store" the majority of our customers have a university degree' admits a French store manager. This may appear paradoxical considering IKEA's avowed mission statement, but the paradox has proven successful as it keeps IKEA at the same time close to its roots and still makes it highly distinctive in foreign market places. It also plays neatly into its strengths of sourcing, volume, long runs, and cost-efficient distribution.

Human resource management

Management of international operations has largely followed the IKEA-Way and its strong Swedish flavor. The belief in IKEA is that their way of managing people has universal appeal. 'People like to participate in making decisions. They like to feel respected, and that they can take responsibility', one Swedish expatriate states.

For recruitment, IKEA looks for people who have good communication skills, open minds, positive work attitudes and have good potential without necessarily having diplomas. It attracts people with its pleasant working environment, job security, and the **care that shows** towards the individual. IKEA employees regardless of nationality are more than likely to have strong preferences for cooperative informal relations, being independent and have a tolerant approach to others. 'We look for people who know how to listen, and who are able to transmit their knowledge to others. They should not feel they are better than others and be curious about what is going on around them.'

Being an IKEA manager overseas isn't just running the stores and distribution systems smoothly. They must be able to explain to employees and managers why things are done that way, and win people's hearts and minds to the 'IKEA-Way'. They are expected to be ambassadors and must educate their non-Swedish co-workers through patience, common understanding, and example. It is not always easy to transmit IKEA's egalitarian management style. While it goes down easily in the Netherlands, it is less easy for Germany or for France. But for different reasons. In the United States long term employees generally feel more comfortable with Scandinavian managers than with Americans, younger American managers don't seem to know how to show **'equalness'**.

The challenge IKEA may be facing is that, with its extended international network, it is becoming more difficult to find enough Swedish IKEA managers who are willing to work overseas for long periods. IKEA had to hire Swedes from outside the company. In the past the company has not systematically searched out and developed its international 'high potentials' early enough, although it does send its most loyal and successful foreign managers to week-long seminars in Sweden and encourages its co-workers to learn something about the culture.

It is still very difficult for non-Scandinavians to work their way up the corporate ladder. To do so they need to learn all of IKEA's key trades: retailing, logistics, product design, and purchasing. Non Swedes can work their way up in retailing through

the national organizations and sometimes in the logistical organizations which are run regionally, but very few have gone into product management because this function is part of IKEA of Sweden in Almhult, where IKEA's product managers and furniture school are located. It is a very remote area and only Swedish is spoken. So, speaking the language as well and knowing the culture becomes a prerequisite that very few managers from the foreign branch have been able to fill.

There are no formal career paths for advancement as a long term Swedish expatriate executive admits. 'To get ahead in IKEA you first have to know the range intimately, then you have to know and use the informal internal network, and then you have to understand the subtleties of the IKEA-Way, its cultural roots. It is really difficult for an outsider to know his way around. In reality it is a difficult company to understand. Humbleness is not a sign of weakness. It comes from Ingvar. People are expected to learn from their experience, and this takes time and patience, you can't be in a hurry to move up the ladder.'

Dealing with the Europeans – Germany

Germany is the largest national organization of the IKEA group accounting for ±30% of the total group sales with more than 20 stores, including the nearly opened stores in former East Germany.

Although IKEA has been established in Germany for more than two decades, (its first store was opened in Munich in 1974), Swedish management is still perceived by German IKEA members as peculiar. As described by Thomas Larson, the store manager of Cologne: 'Some older co-workers still have problems addressing me by my first name or use the German "Du" (the informal equivalent for you, "tu" in French).' 'Dutzen', using the informal you, is often felt as undermining the respect and prestige of the boss. As Heike Oestreich, the personnel manager said: 'There are two different "Du's", the IKEA Du and the Du which is used between friends.'

The Germans are very disciplined and precise. They do exactly what the boss asks them to do and what is agreed is put down in writing. A problem is that the Swedish notion and cornerstone of our work policy 'to take your own responsibility' is not perceived in the same way by the Germans. There is a tendency to adhere very closely to precisely defined rules and instructions. When IKEA translated the corporate brochure 'the IKEA-Way' into German, a need was felt to sharpen and make more explicit the original Swedish text, which presented key IKEA concepts in sometimes vague terms in order to give freedom to people to adapt them and take personal responsibility for carrying them out. Once Anders Moberg, I. Kamprad's successor, suggested in a letter that certain merchandising displays could be used in a variety of places. In Germany department managers interpreted this as an order, and systematically set up the displays in every part of their stores.

In general German employees feel that the Swedes are more result oriented and treat every problem as a challenge that should be met. However they believe that Swedish management does not sufficiently assess risks before taking action. According to Heike Oestreich, Human Resource Manager in Cologne: 'The Swedes', to reduce bureaucracy, 'would like to dump all our office desks in the back yard'. The lack of formality is also dismaying to Germans. To implement a decision 'notes on the back of a cigarette package are often sufficient' for the Swedes. In contrast, Germans are more comfortable adhering to formal procedures; 'We need procedures and forms. Germans love administration because it provides them with security.'

Dealing with the Europeans – France

Development in France, which has fewer than half the number of stores in Germany, was always considered problematic because of multiple administrative regulations on the retail trade and a hostile attitude towards discounters that prevailed in the late 70's and early 80's. By carefully avoiding too much public attention and with only a limited number of store openings it managed to secure a safe place for itself on the market and develop an 8% share of market.

The main challenge for IKEA management in France is the French tendency to judge informality as a sign of weakness, or indecision. People here are accustomed to formal rules and strong hierarchy. In the words of a former Swedish country manager when IKEA first started in France: 'Some French managers felt that with Swedish informality they could do whatever they wanted. When we told them that they should inform their subordinates they did not take us seriously.' Some aspects of the informality can be irritating to the French at such as the lack of formal job descriptions and written procedures. Whereas Swedish managers will justify this by saying that they don't like to limit responsibility, and that they get more out of people with an informal approach, the French tend to be suspicious of informality for the same reasons.

In the view of IKEA's French Human Resource manager: 'Working here isn't for everyone. It is very difficult for someone over 35, because this place is different from all of the others in France. When you join IKEA, you enter another world: we do not behave like a normal French company. Status is not recognized which can cause an identity problem: everyone is put on the same level – no one stands out, and you can get lost in the crowd. It is hard to explain what IKEA is, everyone will give a different answer, one shouldn't freeze the system, it is flexible, it should stay that way.'

Two of the main reasons given for IKEA's appeal to French candidates are:

♦ The esthetics of our stores – they look nice and are pleasant to work in.

♦ Also the intelligent way in which we work – it makes sense!

However, to make things clearer to employees, a formal communication platform has been developed in France to spell out in facts and figures which compare IKEA's benefits to those of competitors. Also more formal training programs are being developed because in France 'learning by doing' is not perceived as credible way of developing competency. You typically would not trust your boss to develop your skills in France, and more faith is placed in 'off-site programs'. In France tolerance has its limits and when IKEA hired 'too many' people of non-French origins, they received complaints from their customers, so now they make a point of keeping 'non-French' workers to a minimum.

Four years ago relations with unions were hostile. There was a nasty strike and widespread discontent. French labor unions did not trust or understand IKEA's Swedish management style with its tendency to seek consensus. More recently IKEA's management has taken a more affirmative attitude, and relations have improved notably. They may continue to improve now that IKEA France is run by a Frenchman, Jean Louis Baillot whose wife is Swedish and who has worked in Almhult.

Doing things differently in the United States

Expanding into the US market in the 80's was certainly the boldest developmental decision that IKEA had made up to that time. From an historical perspective the venture seemed unlikely to succeed. First the culturally specific requirements for home furnishing in the United States are considerably different than the European markets, particularly concerning the size and functions of furniture. Secondly the American market had come to be known as the 'graveyard' of European retailers with a long list of unfortunate ventures by such successful firms as Casino, Carrefour, and Marks & Spencer. But somehow IKEA seemed confident that going about it in their own way would prove an exception to the laws of failure that seemed to doom European entrants to the US market.

Initially development in the US was quite consistent with IKEA's pattern in Europe: Identifying prime markets with volume potential; purchasing cheap land in the periphery of big cities; relying on mass advertising and a unique message emphasizing its Swedishness; focusing on range and price through the catalogue, establishing a beachhead from which to launch and develop its organization. Also its approach was empirical and pragmatic, and it did not set out to take the US by storm, but merely to test its tried and true formula and learn through experience how they could succeed. In fact from the mid seventies to the early 80's IKEA opened a series of franchised stores in Canada, developing during this time its logistic capabilities and demonstrating that its European range could sell in America's back yard, before it finally entered the US market in 1985.

Its first stage of development in the US began on the East Coast with the opening of Plymouth Meeting in Philadelphia's northwest suburbs, followed by a cluster of four other stores. 'Development was initially based on the potato field approach. Find someplace where there is cheap land, build and the people will follow.' This approach ignored the rule of American retailing based on fine tuned segmentation and targeting. Their choice of locations, driven by cost-consciousness, led them to establish their stores in shopping centers that had no upscale 'anchors stores' to draw the high income customers that IKEA appeals to. This should have been a relative disadvantage, since competitors like Home Depot locate their stores in centers with 'anchors' like Nordstrom's and Macy's. But by maintaining the profile of a 'different kind of store', very Swedish, with a wide range of products, it apparently has overcome this obstacle. Here the catalogue has served them well, as people can plan their purchases before they come and thus optimize their time investment.

Up until the early 90's IKEA enjoyed a honeymoon of sorts. The American public was attracted by the novelty of Scandinavian style, and IKEA's unique merchandising, which resembles a European village market place. Its advertising was a success. People drove six to eight hours to come to the stores and they initially came in large numbers. Riding on a high dollar, IKEA had appeared to have gotten off to a fast start as they had in Germany and other European markets. The honeymoon ended abruptly in the late eighties when the dollar went down, revealing multiple weaknesses.

First and foremost even if Americans were initially attracted by IKEA's advertising and novelty, their range of furniture was unsuited to American standards and sold poorly. One often told anecdote illustrates just how far from those standards they really were. Customers would purchase flower vases thinking they were American size drinking glasses. Americans furnish their master bedrooms with king-size beds, whereas IKEA's largest beds were 5 inches narrower. Also Americans are harder on sitting room furniture, and IKEA's soft and armchair offerings proved too lightly dimensioned. Additionally IKEA did not offer furniture suitable to the 'Home Entertainment Centers' that blossomed through the 80's and into the 90's in American households with proliferation of widescreen television, VCR, and hi-fi equipment. With declining sales revenue and shrinking profits, by 1989 the 'graveyard effect' seemed to have caught up with IKEA.

A courageous decision was then made by Anders Moberg and a new management team was brought in to head the US organization. Faced with the alternatives of: holding on and waiting for better times, withdrawing humbly, or fighting back, the latter course was chosen. In 1990 the American retail management group, under the leadership of Göran Carstedt, recently hired from Volvo, convinced the product managers at IKEA of Sweden that the IKEA European range has to be adapted and American based sourcing stepped up while reassuring them that IKEA would not lose its soul. In the words of Carstedt: 'The IKEA strategy in North America will still be blue and yellow, but we will put more stars and stripes and more maple leaves in it.'

It was not easy but they succeeded in changing the design of many household products. To make the point one US manager brought a plastic American-sized turkey with him to Almhult and before a surprised group of product managers placed it on one of the best selling dining tables in the European range. Given the size of the bird there was only room for two table settings instead of the normal six. He had made his point.

However there was a condition attached to adapting the range, and that condition was volume. Lines of furniture specifically designed for the American market would have to be produced in long enough lines to meet IKEA's commitment to suppliers and be priced at the lowest levels possible.

A combination of luck and bold counter attacking led to an unexpected expansion on the West Coast that was to ease pressure on its pricing and provide needed growth to its retail business. An imitator 'Stor' inspired by IKEA's success had illicitly acquired knowledge of IKEA's floor plan and merchandising schemes and successfully opened four stores primarily around Los Angeles, far from IKEA's base on the East Coast. Responding as much to the threat to their image as to the opportunity to capitalize on Stor's advertising of Swedish style furniture, IKEA decided to counter attack. It opened a store in Los Angeles and eventually, through its price and sourcing advantage, drove Stor to the brink of bankruptcy. It then bought out its imitator at a bargain price and established a solid base in a prime market on the West Coast. If IKEA's low profile stance stressed its humble origins and culture, it definitely did not mean that the company was a weakling. IKEA showed that it could be tough and decisive in that

toughest of tough markets. The current US country manager Jan Kjellman is comparing the US market to his previous European experience used the following words: 'The biggest difference is competition. Competitors are everywhere, and they are strong. The market is crowded, but still there always seem to be new competitors. Even with a million and a half customers, we are small. It is a total struggle for us, and it is tough to survive.' Could IKEA adapt to such competition and still remain faithful to the 'IKEA-Way'?

Swedish managers are impressed with the professionalism of American salesmanship. 'Over here retailing is a profession. Sales persons are subjected to a lot of pressure for short term results because large retailers are publicly owned and shareholders measure quarterly results. So they are very time-efficient and masters of the hard sell,' relates Kjellman. IKEA has always maintained a soft approach believing that people know what they want, so that sales personnel are there to help them find it. Moreover the strategy is that most of the selling is done by the catalogue so that people arrive with specific purchases in mind. Impulse buying takes place for smaller items like candleholders, or accessories that are sought for as bargains. On this point IKEA has stood firm, and sales personnel from competitors such as Macy's or Bloomingdale have to unlearn the hard sell approach.

Americans are always looking for convenience, which means more space, more information, anything that reduces effort and saves time. To respond to these demands IKEA had to redesign its store layouts providing more directions and short cuts for people who don't want to just wander through the store. 'Customers were screaming: let us out, before we remodelled our layout' reports a store manager, 'They couldn't find their way out of our maze of displays, there were no windows or signs they felt lost and panicky.' While making these adjustments in store layout, which have been criticized by IKEA International headquarters, IKEA has maintained its policy of minimal service. Customers who want home delivery or someone to assemble their furniture must pay the full add-on cost. In fact IKEA stores carefully outsource these services to local providers and they never promote such services in their advertising, they rather encourage their customers to do it the IKEA-Way, which means renting a roof rack and assembling it yourself.

Adapting IKEA's floor plans and furniture to American dimensions paid off, and sales has increased 25 to 30% compared to the late 80's. By 1994 IKEA had turned around the situation in the USA. Through its acquisition of Stor and by adapting its range to US requirements sales have increased steadily by about 10% annually providing them with the volume base necessary to sustain long production lines and keep prices low. Whereas only 15% of the furniture in American stores was produced locally, the figure is now at about 50%.

In the view of several IKEA senior US managers, the key to this successful turn around was the granting of more autonomy to the American country management than their European counterparts had enjoyed. 'You can't steer America from Europe', admitted Anders Moberg in 1994. 'When we went in we hadn't planned a clear strategy of how to supply the American market at a low cost'. Learning how to succeed in the United States through its own painful expense took more than five years. Although its US operation has shown a profit over the last three years it still has not received its initial investment. With flat growth in Europe, heavy investment in longer term expansion into Eastern Europe and China putting pressure on IKEA's capital reserves, focus in the US is now on developing sales and profit from its existing stores before expanding into new regions. Following its bold actions in the early 90's, IKEA has entered into a more conservative phase of consolidation, perhaps it has also learned that the price of being different means that you also have to be more careful about where you invest.

Unresolved issues: management and human resource development

From an American perspective Swedish managers don't show emotion in the work place, 'praise is given for looking calm in all situations. They do not feel comfortable in conflictual situations. Also they tend not to set themselves apart, and self-promotion is frowned upon. They don't like drum beating, or cheer leading in a culture where both are common ways of motivating workers.'

'The biggest conflicts stem from the Americans who need to know who's in charge. People expect their managers to tell them what to do here.' However, at IKEA the manager's role is more subtle and they tend to have a long-term approach to management. 'It takes longer but we want to train people to know how to do things the IKEA-Way.' Since there are few written procedures, the golden rule for managers is helping people understand why things are done in a particular way. This can be taken for indecision by American employees new to IKEA who are more used to rules and procedures spelled out clearly and managers who take responsibility for quick decision making.

American employees perceive IKEA as being more employee oriented than average American employers. IKEA attracts and selects people who value security, job enrichment, and benefits, which are more generous than American typical employers (like five weeks of paid holiday) more than career advancement. However, with full employment in the US it is becoming more difficult to find candidates, particularly for management positions, who have the necessary job qualifications and whose values match IKEA's.

Although IKEA has recently initiated an American style performance review procedure, which requires documenting employee's individual performance strengths and weaknesses, Swedish managers feel uncomfortable with the formality of the system and the need to provide negative feedback. Since they hold the more senior positions their ambivalence has resulted in little real discrimination in pay increases which are directly linked to the reviews. Although turnover at IKEA is lower than the industry average, and co-workers generally appreciate IKEA's caring environment, there is some latent discontent with the way pay increases are distributed even among long term employees who feel that their individual achievements are not always rewarded.

In the opinion of one American manager 'A lot of people have left IKEA because they can't move up fast enough here. Some left the store to go to the Service Center (IKEA's national headquarters) then left because it was too hard for them to adjust, there was not clear frame of reference – policies, procedures. We have lost some key American managers because they didn't have a clear idea of their role or future in the organization.'

Acknowledging that there are not enough American managers in senior positions, IKEA is trying to attract management trainees through presentations at Business Schools. However its low keyed image and lack of structured career pathing is not easy to sell to 'high potentials' more attuned to the packages offered by retailers such as Home Depot which forcefully promote rapid promotion and individualized pay incentives. There is a general consensus that IKEA needs to develop young American managers who can play a bigger role in the organization than at present. However there is no agreement yet on how critical the need is, nor on how to solve the problem.

Two differing views that could be overheard in a fictitious debate between two long term Ikeans illustrate the unresolved issues facing IKEA USA at the end of 1996:

The view of a young American manager: *There is a glass ceiling here. I am at a level at which my growth will stop because I'm not Swedish. IKEA should be made less complicated for Americans, easier for us to adapt to, and develop in. Our management needs to be much more professional in managing human resources. We need to bring new people into the organization and reward individual accountability for results. This would lead to a better balance between the IKEA-Way and American management. Becoming a successful manager at IKEA requires a lot of time and effort to understand how everything fits together. Yet not everyone can go to Sweden or learn Swedish and today too many talented Americans choose to go to the competition. Competition is catching up on us in terms of benefits, and with full employment we should be much more competitive than we are on the American job market.*

The Swedish view: *Being the underdog, not doing things the traditional way over here is vital to IKEA's success in the United States. We must keep a unique image and work better at getting our message across to employees and customers so that they understand why we are successful. Pride in being a part of IKEA must be built locally and since our system is unique this takes time. The real danger is assimilation. We are becoming too American. Giving people bonuses and pay incentives doesn't make them*

more intelligent; people are motivated by learning and improving in an organization that provides them room to grow. Rewards should be more on a give and take basis, when the company makes more it can give more, but we must remain flexible. Although we must seek balance between adapting and sticking to our proven ways we must protect our unique concepts and way of doing. This means that we will always need a strong Swedish presence in the US, they are our 'on site missionaries' who can develop loyalty to and understanding of our uniqueness.

IV Clouds on the horizon

By the mid 90's, in spite of its undisputed international success and expansion over the past 25 years, signs appeared that the pattern of growth and steady profit were slowing down. Costs were rising, complaints on quality were more frequent, and unaccustomed delays appeared in product delivery. External factors had changed from the early times in Europe. Economic growth slowed as baby boomers moved into middle age with new tastes and demands, and fewer new homes being sold. Competition had also learned from IKEA's pioneering distribution and were offering better furniture at lower prices, seeking low cost furniture suppliers in eastern Europe which put pressure on IKEA's unique sourcing.

IKEA had become a rather large international organization and in an effort to adapt to the requirements of its many domestic markets its product range had grown from 10.000 to 14.000 items thus weakening returns from long product runs and overburdening logistic supply lines. Increasingly greater attention had to be given to bringing costs down, often through productivity gains which put unprecedented pressure on retail staffs to improve sales to staff ratios. During the years of rapid growth many recruits were bought in from outside the company, who were not steeped in IKEA culture. The company's extended network made it difficult to provide employees and mid-level managers with a clear perception of how their local business impacted on the corporation as a whole. Local initiatives were taken without regard to their impact on the whole system.

Was this the price of diversity or was IKEA in many ways suffering from too much decentralization.

In 1993 to cope with this situation, Anders Moberg and IKEA'S senior management launched a company wide operation 'Nytt Läge' (New Situation) with task forces and project teams to suggest ways of improving communication and eliminating snags in distribution. Many suggestions were implemented, including creation of new regional divisions in Europe for closer coordination of country operations, and the hiring of more professionals at headquarters to provide guidelines and more efficient corporate control systems. Although the 'Nytt Läge' program met with a lot of enthusiasm and did achieve improvement in some areas, it soon became clear to Ingvar Kamprad that a more radical change in the organization was needed.

In early 1996 a major organizational change was introduced to 'shorten the value chain' between customers and suppliers. Regional organizations were eliminated to bring stores in more direct contact with IKEA of Sweden. New emphasis was given to the importance of a living corporate culture based on the IKEA values of simplicity and self-discipline, rather than relying on formal policies and procedures. At the same time IKEA'S expansion plans in Europe and the United States were delayed. The fear at corporate headquarters was that the IKEA had drifted too far from the basic principles that were behind its legendary success.

Back to the roots

In May Ingvar Kamprad gathered IKEA'S 250 worldwide store managers and senior managers at an important meeting in Poland to explain IKEA'S need to re-focus and re-direct its efforts. He actually used the word 'rejuvenate'.

'Our product range and purchasing people often have an unequal battle with retailers and their far too many interests. Many of our suppliers got stuck in the middle. Our IKEA idea as one of the world's few production oriented companies is under threat.

Perhaps we were blinded by the boom years of the 80's, which increased geographical spread of our operations to new markets, both on retail and the trading side. Internal communication also became difficult, our administration expanded and our overheads became increasingly heavy. Our costs rose, and our customers and suppliers felt lost, many of them got in touch with me directly.

Decision-making took longer and longer, and endless discussions took place. It became more difficult to see the company as a whole. Far too much of our product development had too little to do with the tastes and wallets of the majority of people. Our product range expanded in every direction and could not be handled in a reasonable way on our sales floors. Our price advantage compared to competitors began to shrink. Even IKEA'S soul, our fine corporate culture was in danger. Have we forgotten to explain to our new workers about the IKEA-Way? Have our desks removed us too far from reality? Have we lost our way?'

The managers who attended that meeting felt galvanized by their founder's strong message, and their confidence and belief in the IKEA-Way had been doubtlessly reinforced. In an increasingly complex world environment, simplicity indeed appeared to be a true virtue that had guided the company in the past. Several wondered as they left how Kamprad's intuitive ability to see through the complexity of a worldwide organization and re-ignite the dynamics of IKEA'S success could be transmitted throughout the organization? Others wondered if they would have as much autonomy as they had previously enjoyed in adapting to very different markets? Some wondered if the company could regain its developmental thrust through the late 90's.

Case 17 BSkyB: Embracing the digital revolution

Introduction

At the end of 1998 BSkyB faced multiple challenges to its immensely profitable position as the dominant player in UK pay-TV. The imminent launch of digital television meant the end of channel scarcity and created opportunities for new entrants to grab a share of the growing pay-TV market. ONdigital, backed by the UK's two main commercial terrestrial broadcasters and offering consumers digital television via their existing TV aerials, was gearing up for a mass-market launch in November. Another challenge came from the three largest cable companies. Cable and Wireless, Telewest, and NTL were all planning to offer low-cost 'triple-play' packages that included digital television, telephony, and internet access from early 1999. With so many competitors moving into digital television it seemed only a matter of time before BSkyB's margins and market-share were eroded and its dominant position in pay-TV came to an end.

By the end of 2002, however, the picture was very different. BSkyB had doubled its annual revenues to £2.8 billion, almost doubled its subscriber base to 6.6 million, and increased its market-share to 70% of the pay-TV market. By contrast most of its competitors were either down or out. ONdigital, renamed ITV Digital in 2001, had shut down in May 2002 with losses of £1.25 billion (although Freeview – a free-to-access service backed by the BBC – rose from the ashes six months later). The two remaining cable companies, NTL and Telewest, were more focused on restructuring their combined £15 billion debt and simply surviving than on leading the digital revolution.

This case study was researched and written by Ian Maude under the supervision of John McGee, Warwick Business School. Special thanks to Claire Enders and Toby Syfret for their help with proof-reading. Also thanks to Jon Beaumont, Tom Betts, David Chance, David Elstein, Chris Goodall, Mathew Horsman, Marija Radaković, David Raybould, Paul Simmonds, Joe Smithies, Ray Snoddy, David Thatcher, and several others that cannot be named for their assistance.

How did BSkyB manage to see off the competition and extend its domination of pay-TV into the digital era? Why did its competitors fail so spectacularly? What were BSkyB's strategic advantages and how did they change over time? By 2002 BSkyB had fully converted its customer franchise to digital but was the decision to launch Sky Digital in 1998 the right one? What other options did BSkyB have? Finally what threats, challenges, and opportunities lie ahead for the satellite television company?

The analogue era

UK pay-TV up to 1998

By 1998 pay-TV had grown significantly in the UK since its launch in the 1980s. At the end of the year 6.3 million UK households – 25% of TV households – received cable or satellite television.[1] The majority subscribed to Sky's satellite service although an increasing number was signing up to cable services such as those run by Cable & Wireless and Telewest.

Until the mid-1980s the UK had only four terrestrial free-to-air television channels: BBC1 and BBC2, advertising-free channels owned by the public service BBC and funded by a compulsory television licence, ITV, a commercial channel formed by a number of independent regional franchises, and Channel 4, a public service commercial channel. In 1986 the television regulator invited bids to broadcast television channels into UK homes via a government-controlled satellite. At the time Rupert Murdoch's Sky was a small satellite television company broadcasting a single advertising-supported channel across Europe. Sky bid for the new UK satellite licence but lost out to British Satellite Broadcasting (BSB), a consortium including Granada and Anglia, two of the ITV regional franchises, and Richard Branson's Virgin Group. BSB's plan was to launch a high-quality subscription-based service in late 1989. Unwilling to give up, Murdoch decided to launch a competing, advertising-supported free-to-access service before BSB went

---

[1] *UK: TV Market Overview*, Screen Digest, London, November 2003.

on air. Sky bought content rights, leased transponder capacity on the Luxembourg-based Astra satellite, and set up alliances with consumer electronics companies to develop set-top boxes and satellite dishes. Cash was tight and much of the necessary equipment had to be leased rather than bought. Hollywood studios refused to license their movies to Sky until Murdoch restricted access to paying customers. Movies were 'must-have' content so Murdoch was forced to switch from his original advertising-based business model to a subscription-based model. To control access to Sky's channels he invested in encryption technology and subscriber management systems.[2]

The revamped Sky went on air on 5 February 1989 with four channels: Sky News, the UK's first 24-hour news channel, Sky TV, an entertainment channel, Sky Movies, and Eurosport. Retailers were initially reluctant to stock the set-top boxes required to access the new service so Murdoch hired hundreds of salesmen to sell Sky door-to-door. News Corporation, Sky's parent company, promoted the service heavily in its UK media assets which included *The Sun* and *The Times* newspapers. When BSB finally launched in April 1990 Sky had around 750,000 subscribers. Sky's earlier launch and aggressive marketing enabled it to attract far more subscribers but the competition between the rival services drove up costs and increased uncertainty amongst consumers, resulting in both companies haemorrhaging cash. By the end of 1990 the competitors were forced to merge to stave off bankruptcy. Rumour had it Murdoch himself approached the Prime Minister, Margaret Thatcher, who nodded the deal through. Although touted as a merger, Murdoch's News Corporation had a controlling share and Murdoch wasted no time in exercising it. Almost all BSB's staff were sacked. Brutal cost-cutting by Sam Chisholm, the pugnacious Australian television boss picked by Murdoch to run the merged company, helped British Sky Broadcasting (BSkyB)

to achieve its first operating profit in 1992.[3] But massive debt meant the company was still losing money.

The new Premier League presented an opportunity and Chisholm grabbed it. The Premier League (also known as the Premiership) was formed in 1992 by the top 22 football clubs in the UK Football League breaking away to have more control over their own destiny and specifically over television rights. Sport in the UK is dominated by the top football clubs and Chisholm saw the potential of the new league to drive subscriptions. BSkyB bid £191.5 million for exclusive broadcast rights to live Premier League football for five years from 1992/93. With the addition of the BBC's bid for exclusive recorded highlights, the combined BSkyB/BBC offer was £214 million – significantly more than was bid by ITV for live rights and recorded highlights. It was alleged Chisholm resubmitted his bid after being told the value of ITV's offer but for a company with a turnover of £93 million and which lost £759 million in 1991 it was still a very big bet. It paid off immediately. After it was announced Sky had exclusive live Premier League football Chisholm said subscriptions rolled in as if it was 'Christmas every day'.[4] Within two years Sky doubled in size to more than 2.5 million satellite (also known as direct-to-home or DTH) subscribers. In 1994 BSkyB achieved its first pre-tax profit of £93 million on revenues of £550 million. Murdoch immediately capitalised on Sky's success and floated 17.5% of BSkyB's stock on the London and New York Stock Exchanges, valuing the company at £4.4 billion.

Over the next few years BSkyB took advantage of additional satellite capacity to add more channels. It negotiated exclusive carriage deals with popular US cable channels and moved into new areas such as pay-per-view (PPV). In 1996 660,000 subscribers each paid up to £15 to watch Mike Tyson's heavyweight boxing match with Frank Bruno. That same year BSkyB negotiated a new contract with the Premier League, paying £670 million for exclusive live rights for another four years. Its negotiating position was aided by a clause in the 1992 contract

2 Murdoch realised secure encryption was key to charging for content over networks. In 1988 he invested $3.6 million in News Datacom Research Ltd which had licensed Israeli academic Adi Shamir's encryption algorithms, the basis for the VideoCrypt conditional access system later used by Sky.

3 The pay-TV service continued to operate under the Sky brand name.

4 'Everything to play for at BSkyB', John Cassy, *The Guardian*, Manchester, 23 April 2003, p.19.

that allowed it to match any other bid. BSkyB also tied up rights for the Football League, the three professional football divisions below the Premier League, for five years for £125 million. By now Sky offered 33 basic and seven premium channels. In 1997 BSkyB had 3.5 million DTH subscribers and generated profits of £374 million on turnover of £1.25 billion. The broadcaster was the dominant player in UK pay-TV but subscriptions had stagnated. BSkyB had become highly profitable on the back of exclusive live Premiership football but it looked as if the football dividend had been used up. Sky also had a downmarket image in part due to the large satellite dishes required to receive the weak Astra signal. Analysts began to question BSkyB's prospects and by the end of 1997 its market value had fallen 30% from a peak of £12.7 billion.

Cable television launched in the UK in 1984 with licences based on geographic areas. Unlike the US, networks had to be installed underground and the high cost meant there was little money for original programming. By 1990 there were 26 cable operators but only 270,000 subscribers. In 1991, to kick-start the market, the Government granted cable companies the right to provide telephony. Offering cheap telephone calls gave them a competitive edge over Sky but it was this that drove much of their growth. This was compounded by a lack of compelling, attractively-priced programming. US cable companies built their franchises on the back of premium content but in the UK BSkyB had exclusive rights to 90% of first-run Hollywood movies and, from 1992, live Premiership football. UK cable operators felt obliged to go to BSkyB for content. It didn't refuse access but it did require them to take a range of channels and set strict rules about packaging through the use of Minimum Carriage Requirements (MCRs) and buy-through conditions.[5] These forced cable operators to sell Sky channels on the same basis of tiering and buy-through as did Sky.

This meant including Sky's basic channels in their basic tiers and its premium channels in a premium tier with subscribers having to buy through a basic tier to subscribe to premium channels. Sky's wholesale prices were based on 59% of its retail prices with discounts and penalties according to several factors that included the Pay-to-Basic Ratio (PBR), the ratio of premium Sky channel subscribers (weighted for the number of premium Sky channels to which they subscribed) to basic subscribers. Some cable companies argued such policies made pay-TV more expensive by making it more premium-oriented and preventing price competition and meant it was impossible to resell Sky channels profitably. In late 1995 BSkyB's position in the wholesale pay-TV market became the subject of an Office of Fair Trading (OFT) investigation. In its defence BSkyB argued it did not dominate the supply of premium or other content, pricing policies such as tiering and buy-through were commonplace in pay-TV markets, and an efficient company would eventually make a profit reselling its channels. After a year-long inquiry the OFT announced there was no evidence BSkyB was abusing its position although it asked the company to make certain voluntary undertakings, to which it agreed.[6] These included publishing its wholesale pricing and discount policy and agreeing to submit any future changes to the OFT for approval. Other undertakings included reducing the upper limit on MCRs from 100% to 80% of a cable operator's base and publicly reaffirming other broadcasters had non-discriminatory access to its conditional access system (which had become the de facto UK standard). The OFT also referred the Premier League and its broadcast agreements with BSkyB and the BBC to the Restrictive Practices Court on the basis the League was acting as a cartel by brokering exclusive deals which reduced consumer choice and increased the cost of watching games on television.

The huge costs of installing underground networks and resulting losses led to rapid consolidation in the cable industry and by 1998 there were only five major operators. But despite its problems cable had

---

[5] Minimum Carriage Requirements required channels to be made available to a certain proportion of a cable operator's subscriber base. An MCR of 100% meant a channel had to be included in an operator's most widely available tier. Buy-through conditions applied to premium channels. They required pay-TV subscribers to buy through a basic tier before they could subscribe to a premium channel.

[6] *The Director General's Review of BSkyB's position in the Wholesale TV Market*, OFT, London, December 1996.

started to grow rapidly. By 1997 there were 2.3 million cable television subscribers compared to Sky's 3.5 million and in 1998 cable subscriptions increased by 20% compared with virtually no growth in satellite.[7] Some analysts predicted it would not be long before cable overtook satellite as the dominant pay-TV platform in the UK, as it was elsewhere in Europe and in the US.

The game's afoot

Government Acts

Digital technology converts sound and pictures into a digital format – a series of 1s and 0s – which is compressed before transmission. Six or more digital television channels can be supported by the same 'bandwidth' (broadcast spectrum or frequency) required for a single analogue channel. This allows broadcasters to deliver more channels as well as other services and makes transmission costs per channel far cheaper. Transmitting digital signals also reduces data loss enabling higher quality sound and pictures to be delivered.

In 1996 Parliament passed the Broadcasting Act which set out the legislative framework for the development of digital terrestrial television (DTT) in the UK.[8] This came into force in October 1996 when the Independent Television Commission (ITC), the commercial television regulator, invited bids for four digital terrestrial multiplexes (equivalent to analogue channel licences). Two additional multiplexes were reserved, one for the BBC and one for ITV/Channel 4. Channel 5, a terrestrial channel launched in 1997, and S4C, a Welsh-language channel, were guaranteed carriage on a non-specified multiplex. Value was added to the multiplexes by the fact the Government planned to switch off analogue television by 2006–2010 so the spectrum could be sold off for other purposes.

In June 1997 three multiplexes were awarded to British Digital Broadcasting (BDB), a three-way venture owned by Carlton and Granada, the two largest regional ITV broadcasters, and BSkyB.

Under pressure from EU competition authorities, however, the ITC forced BSkyB to pull out of the consortium because of concern its position as both programme buyer and seller could allow it to control prices. In May 1998 the fourth multiplex was awarded to SDN Ltd, owned by NTL, S4C, and United News & Media, the latter being a major shareholder in Channel 5.

The arrival of DTT meant digital television could now be broadcast via three different platforms:

- DTT: signals are received via a conventional aerial but require a digital adaptor (set-top box) or integrated digital television (including a digital adaptor) to decode them back into analogue form.

- Cable: digitally encoded signals are piped into the home via cable and decoded via a set-top box.

- Satellite: received via a satellite dish the digital signals are decoded via a digital adaptor or integrated digital television.

Since cable and satellite broadcasters controlled their own networks they could transmit as many channels as they wanted, limited only by the capacity of the technology they used, and switch to digital whenever they wished.

Digital ambition

The key groups planning to launch digital television services in the UK were the BBC, ITV/Channel 4, BDB, BSkyB, and the cable companies.

The licence fee funded BBC planned to make its two existing channels plus three new channels available on all three digital platforms. It also planned to launch four more channels as part of a commercial venture with Flextech, the programme supplier. The first digital channel, BBC News 24, was scheduled to launch in November 1997, to be followed by BBC Choice and BBC Parliament in 1998. To help to fund its digital expansion the BBC sold its transmitter network to Crown Transmission Services Ltd for £244 million.

ITV and Channel 4 set up a joint venture, Digital 3&4 Ltd, to manage their multiplex and planned to launch existing and new channels on all digital platforms by the end of 1998. New channels included ITV2, a free-to-access entertainment and sports channel, and FilmFour, a subscription-based movie channel. Free-to-access channels would be available

[7] *UK: TV Market Overview*, Screen Digest, London, November 2003.

[8] *Broadcasting Act 1996*, HMSO, London, July 1996.

to anyone with an integrated digital television or set-top box but subscription channels would only be accessible via pay-TV services.

BDB, holder of three digital multiplexes, planned to launch in late 1998. After BSkyB's forced withdrawal Granada and Carlton became sole owners with Carlton's Chairman, Michael Green, becoming Chairman of BDB. Green recruited Stephen Grabiner, Managing Director at Express Newspapers, to be BDB's CEO. With the 12-year DTT licences won and the analogue switch-off scheduled for 2006–2010, confidence at BDB was high. Grabiner and his team spent 1998 putting together the new service. They set up a transmission agreement, awarded the contract for the encryption system to Canal+ subsidiary SECA, appointed BT to handle subscriber management, and placed orders for set-top boxes with six consumer electronics companies. In July BDB changed its name to ONdigital and announced it would launch with 15 channels. These included 12 basic channels from Granada, Carlton, and BBC/Flextech, and three premium channels from Sky. Free-to-air channels would also be available. The big selling point was consumers wishing to access these channels had only to plug the ONdigital set-top box into their existing aerial and television – they didn't need a new aerial, cable, or satellite dish. The DTT broadcaster was targeting what Green called 'Middle England' or the three quarters of the UK population that didn't subscribe to multi-channel television and it had ambitious targets, aiming to double the size of the UK pay-TV market by signing up around six million subscribers.[9] Grabiner told analysts ONdigital would achieve breakeven with two million subscribers and make annual profits of £165 million once it reached three million.[10] In late September the company confirmed it would launch its service on 15 November with set-top boxes costing £199 and a range of subscription packages starting from £7.99 a month. With a marketing budget of £90 million, plus promotion on the ITV network, it would be one of the largest ever launches of a consumer product in the UK.

At BSkyB Chisholm was not sold on digital television, believing it would reduce profitability. However Murdoch saw 'digital' as the future and thought it was essential to switch before the competition, so Chisholm pushed on. Despite his reservations Chisholm was determined not to let anything loosen BSkyB's highly lucrative grip on UK pay-TV. As well as planning a satellite-based service, dubbed Sky Digital, he entered into a joint venture with Carlton to bid for the DTT licences. Chisholm believed the best approach was to be platform agnostic, telling analysts 'Sky is in everything ... it's a horizontally integrated business, that's why it's in digital terrestrial, cable, satellite, smoke signals, whatever the platforms are, we're a programme deliverer'.[11] He also set up British Interactive Broadcasting (BIB), a consortium of BSkyB, BT, HSBC, and Matsushita, which would offer a range of interactive services such as home banking and shopping via a set-top box. Initially the partners were to invest £265 million in BIB, which was projected to breakeven after five years. Sky Digital and other services would be accessed via set-top boxes developed by BIB. These would feature an Electronic Programme Guide (EPG), an on-screen display controlled by a dedicated remote control which would enable viewers to search and select channels and services. Return-path information for interactive services would be via a telephone connection. Conditional access technology would be supplied by NDS (formerly News Datacom Research Ltd), a News Corporation subsidiary, and subscriber management would be handled by BSkyB's state-of-the-art customer service centre.

Murdoch and Chisholm had considered launching Sky Digital as early as May 1996 but delayed several times. Ostensibly this was for technical reasons but Chisholm's concern about the impact on profitability and the lack of pressure from the competition were also factors. The delays did have one upside in that Sky's digital set-top box and EPG technology was, in the words of one executive, 'road-tested to death'.[12] On 17 June 1997 it was announced Chisholm was to step down as BSkyB's CEO because of ill-health.

---

[9] *Sky High: The Inside Story of BSkyB*, Mathew Horsman, Orion, London, 1998, p.247.

[10] 'UK's BDB stays on track for Q4 digital TV launch', *Reuters Newswire*, London, 8 May 1998.

[11] Horsman, op. cit., p.198.

[12] Case study interview, June 2004.

A few days later news leaked out BSkyB would have to pull out of BDB and David Chance, Chisholm's highly regarded deputy, would leave later in the year. That same week the *Financial Times* ran a story that the Premier League was considering setting up its own pay-TV venture.[13] In the space of a few days the shares fell 24%, reducing the company's value by £2.6 billion. Before he left, one of Chisholm's last significant acts was to negotiate a settlement with Granada and Carlton in which they agreed to pay £75 million for BSkyB's stake in BDB. As part of the deal BSkyB contracted to supply certain of its premium channels to BDB for five years, although the DTT broadcaster had to consent to a high Pay-to-Basic Ratio.

Two weeks before Chisholm's departure was announced Murdoch appointed Mark Booth, COO at JSkyB – News Corporation's Japanese pay-TV operation, as his successor. There were plenty of issues for the new CEO to deal with. From February 1998 BSkyB was in dispute with Carlton and Granada, claiming it was owed £60 million for the programming it was due to supply to BDB. Granada had agreed to pay but Carlton's Green held out on the basis BSkyB hadn't delivered the promised content. It had emerged BSkyB's deals for Premiership football and Hollywood movies didn't include digital terrestrial rights and Green refused to pay the full amount after slow progress made him believe BSkyB hadn't tried hard enough to resolve the issue. In April BDB's decision to use SECA's MediaGuard conditional access system rather than VideoCrypt from NDS led Booth to issue a writ against BDB, arguing this breached a commitment to make its set-top boxes interoperable. BSkyB also had to deal with an ITC investigation into its policy of requiring cable companies to purchase two Sky movie channels if they wished to carry the Disney Channel (the company dropped the requirement prior to the outcome of the inquiry).[14] All this time BSkyB's share price was falling.

Despite these issues BSkyB's digital plans moved ahead. The company negotiated exclusive or preferential carriage deals with key channel providers such as Disney, Turner Broadcasting, and Viacom, and set up PPV deals with the major film studios. It also leased transponder capacity on digital satellites from SES-Astra and ordered set-top boxes from Pace and other manufacturers. In May, after BSkyB and BT had made concessions, the EU commission gave BIB, now renamed Open, the go ahead.[15] The following month the row with ONdigital over its conditional access system was settled after Booth accepted viewers only needed a plug-in adaptor to switch to Sky Digital. In July BSkyB signed agreements with the BBC, Flextech, Discovery, and Channel 4 to add their channels to its digital service. Not everything went BSkyB's way. Following an investigation into channel bundling and in an attempt to make access to pay-TV cheaper, the ITC announced MCRs were to be prohibited. Even so BSkyB saw it could turn the situation to its advantage by creating a low-cost entry level package for Sky Digital with only a few channels included (in effect ditching channels it didn't own from the basic package) while leaving prices for top tier packages unchanged.

Available to a limited number of analogue subscribers from June, Sky Digital's official launch was scheduled for 1 October. Initially it would offer 140 channels. Many of these were extensions of channels on Sky's analogue service, multiplexed PPV movie channels showing the same movies at short intervals (known as Near Video On Demand or NVOD), and audio-only music channels. Booth's business strategy remained the same as Chisholm's but a new marketing strategy focused on attracting premium subscribers to Sky Digital by emphasising its extensive movie and sports content whilst continuing to market the basic analogue service to value-conscious consumers. A smaller, redesigned satellite dish aided Sky Digital's more upscale positioning.

The three leading cable companies – Cable & Wireless, Telewest, and NTL – planned to launch

---

[13] 'Top football clubs consider pay-TV launch: Premier League told it could fare better without BSkyB', Patrick Harverson, *Financial Times*, London, 24 June 1997, p.1.

[14] BSkyB had exclusive UK distribution rights for the Disney Channel.

[15] The concessions included guaranteeing third parties access to the set-top box and removing the requirement for users to sign up for BSkyB's pay-TV service. BT also had to agree to divest its UK cable television interests.

cable-based digital television services from late 1998/early 1999.

At the end of 1997 the UK's largest cable operator, Cable & Wireless Communications (CWC), a subsidiary of telecoms giant Cable & Wireless plc, had 5.9 million passed homes and nearly 600,000 cable television subscribers. In early 1998 CWC committed £100 million to developing its digital television service, started consumer trials, and made plans to roll the service out to all the homes covered by its network the following year. In October 1998 the company ordered 100,000 digital set-top boxes in anticipation of launching the service in spring 1999.

Telewest Communications plc was set up in 1992 as a joint venture between US West, one of the Baby Bell telcos, and TCI, the US cable operator. By 1998 it had a cable network covering 20% of the UK and 600,000 television subscribers. At £281 per annum Telewest had the highest average revenue per user (ARPU) of all cable television companies although it also had the highest churn, losing 34% of its customers a year. In March it bid £666 million for General Cable and announced it would buy Comcast's cable franchises in Birmingham and London, to be financed by share issues and debt. After these acquisitions Telewest had more than 720,000 cable television subscribers and debts of £2.3 billion. At the end of the year the company announced plans to launch a digital service by the end of 1999.

National Transcommunications Ltd (NTL) began life as the UK's transmission network for commercial television. In 1996 it was bought by CableTel, a fibre optic network company which owned cable licences for several UK cities. In 1997 NASDAQ-listed CableTel renamed itself NTL and set about buying more cable licences. That same year it led an unsuccessful bid for the DTT multiplexes. In April 1998 CEO Barclay Knapp announced plans to launch a 'triple-play' of digital services later in the year saying, 'We just want to pump everything we can down the wires'.[16] Telephony and internet access would be available from September with digital television to follow. As was the case with all

cable companies, NTL's services could only be accessed in areas covered by its network. After acquiring Diamond Cable and the majority of Comcast's UK cable operations, NTL reached 5.2 million homes and had 690,000 cable television subscribers. Knapp and his team spent the year raising money, planning acquisitions, and managing the company's debt. They even bought a stake in Newcastle United football club.[17] By the end of 1998 debt had risen to $5 billion but delays in agreeing technical specifications meant there was still no firm launch date for NTL's digital services.

Digital TV arrives

DSAT and DTT launch

Sky Digital went on air on 1 October 1998. It offered a range of pricing options starting from £6.99 per month for a six channel package up to all 140 channels including all Sky Sports and Sky Movies channels for £29.99 a month.[18] To access Sky Digital viewers had to purchase a new set-top box, the Sky Digibox, and satellite dish for £200 (£160 for existing subscribers) and pay an installation fee of £30 (£25).[19] BSkyB promoted the new service aggressively with TV spots on Sky's analogue service and the terrestrial television channels. *The Times* and *The Sun* ran daily promotions. At the end of the month Booth announced Sky Digital had 100,000 subscribers.

ONdigital went live six weeks after Sky Digital. Although available in less than 70% of households and despite problems with delivery of set-top boxes, hopes were high with Grabiner proclaiming, 'Digital television made simple, through an aerial, is here' (BSkyB's Booth responded by saying ONdigital was

---

16 'Hot wires', *The Economist*, London, 20 June 1998, p.98.

17 This aped an earlier bid by BSkyB for Manchester United football club. NTL planned to make a full bid for Newcastle United but drew back after the OFT disallowed BSkyB's bid for Manchester United in April 1999.

18 The entry level package for Sky's analogue service cost £11.99 a month – all 40 analogue channels cost £29.99 a month.

19 Subscribers who didn't renew their subscriptions could still access free-to-air digital satellite channels via their set-top box.

more 'plug and pray' than 'plug and play').[20] ONdigital's set-top boxes cost £200 and there was a £20 connection fee. The basic subscription package cost £7.99 a month. This included six out of a possible 15 subscription channels, plus the free-to-air channels from the BBC, ITV, Channel 4, and Channel 5. Five premium channels were also available – the most expensive being Sky Sports 1, featuring live Premiership football, which cost an extra £11 per month. All 31 channels were available for £29.99 a month.

Analysts were quick to predict rapid growth in consumer take-up of digital television. Almost all saw digital television as a non-zero-sum game since there were more than enough households not yet subscribing to multi-channel television to support Sky Digital, ONdigital, and, eventually, the cable companies. Henderson Crosthwaite forecast by 2005 Sky Digital would have 3.8 million subscribers with 2.7 million on ONdigital and 4.7 million for digital cable.[21]

At BSkyB Booth was determined to ensure Sky Digital offered the widest possible choice and was incensed when ITV made its channels available via cable but not on satellite. He complained to the OFT and the ITC, claiming ITV's decision was anti-competitive. He complained again to the ITC when Carlton and Granada refused to carry commercials for Premiership football on Sky Digital. At the end of 1998 Sky Digital had 225,000 subscribers, mostly existing customers switching to digital. ONdigital's decision not to release year-end figures was somewhat undermined by a statement in mid-January by Philips, the only supplier to have distributed set-top boxes for the new service, which said, 'By the end of January, we hope to have sold 100,000 ONdigital boxes'.[22]

The battle between BSkyB and ONdigital was also fought out over content rights, mostly for sporting events. In February 1999 ITV and ONdigital successfully bid £265 million for exclusive broadcast rights to UEFA Champions League football for four years.[23] Matches would be shown exclusively on ITV and ITV2 which were not available on Sky Digital. In retaliation BSkyB switched events, such as Ryder Cup golf, from Sky Sports 1, which was available on ONdigital, to Sky Sports 2, which was not. Grabiner complained to the ITC that BSkyB was abusing its position by refusing to supply Sky Sports 2 to ONdigital. BSkyB countered by arguing doing so might put it in breach of the Broadcasting Act's limits on the supply of services by one supplier. In March the ITC found against Carlton and Granada over their refusal to carry ads promoting Premiership football on Sky Digital but decided ITV should not be forced to supply ITV or ITV2 for satellite distribution (the OFT later came to the same conclusion). Even without the ITV channels Sky Digital grew faster than ONdigital and by the end of March had 350,000 subscribers compared to 110,000 on the DTT service.

Cable consolidation and free set-top boxes

In January 1999 Microsoft agreed to buy 5.25% of NTL's convertible preferred stock for $500 million. In return NTL undertook to use Microsoft servers and software in its digital services. Whilst undoubtedly a high profile strategic partnership, the deal meant further delays before NTL could confirm the technical specifications for its digital cable service. At Telewest (where Microsoft also took a non-controlling stake) the management team spent the first part of the year organising credit facilities for acquisitions. To a degree the cable companies' focus on deal-making was understandable. Analogue cable subscriptions continued to grow and the stock markets were charging ahead, particularly in the US where the Dow Jones and NASDAQ Composite both rose 20% in the first half of the year. Media stocks were being valued on a per subscriber basis and investors were rewarding scale and ambition. Further consolidation seemed inevitable. In fact the first move was made by CWC which, having decided

[20] 'First shots in Digital TV war', *BBC News web site*, 15 November 1998, <URL:http://news.bbc.co.uk/1/hi/business/the_company_file/214809.stm>, Accessed 1 June 2004.

[21] 'First shots in Digital TV war', op. cit.

[22] 'The First 100k ... we hope!', *Digital TV Group web site*, 16 January 1998, <URL: http://www.dtg.org.uk/news/archive/sum_9801.htm>, Accessed 4 June 2004.

[23] UEFA Champions League football is an annual cup competition between the top 32 European football clubs.

to focus on business and data services, started talks about selling its cable division to Telewest. The cable operators finally made their first digital moves in May when CWC started trials of its digital cable service, offering a package of 14 television channels and a telephone line for £10 a month. The following month NTL announced it would launch its digital service in September. Knapp confidently predicted NTL would have 250,000 digital subscribers by mid-2000 with customers attracted by the company's low cost packages.

Although Sky Digital was growing, Sky's overall DTH subscriber numbers had been static at 3.5 million since 1997. With cable about to enter the race it was clear something dramatic was needed to boost growth. Free trials were not feasible but Martin Stewart, BSkyB's CFO, suggested giving away the set-top box to new digital subscribers in return for a 12 month commitment.[24] It was estimated the subsidy would cost £187 million in 1999. Booth approved the strategy but, as with all key decisions, the critical approval was that of Murdoch. To help finance the promotion the company made a provision of £450 million in its accounts. Booth also raised Sky Digital's retail prices by £2 a month, increased the installation fee to £40, and cancelled dividend payments until further notice. The offer started on 5 May and encouraged mass-market retailers like Dixons, Comet, and Argos, to offer Sky on a national basis for the first time – although their commission per sale went down BSkyB was able to persuade the retailers higher volumes would more than compensate. Again the bet paid off. BSkyB had to hire an extra 2,000 installation engineers and 600 call centre staff to cope with demand.

Grabiner knew ONdigital had to match Sky's free set-top box offer. It did so two weeks later, even offering free connection as an additional inducement, but the £220 per subscriber subsidy wasn't factored into the business plan, forcing Carlton and Granada to allow it to draw down

more cash.[25] However, the move did encourage analysts to increase their forecasts for the DTT service. Merrill Lynch raised its forecast to 480,000 subscribers by the end of 1999 and 1.66 million by 2002.[26]

Back in April Booth had announced he was leaving BSkyB in June to head up e-partners – a venture capital fund set up by News Corporation. Murdoch quickly appointed Tony Ball, President of News Corporation's Fox Sports network in the US, as the new CEO. Soon after, ONdigital also lost its CEO when Grabiner resigned after a series of disagreements with Green. During the summer ONdigital lost a number of other key staff and Carlton and Granada were forced to restructure the management team. Grabiner was replaced by Stuart Prebble, previously Director of Channels at Granada and regarded as having strong management and programming skills.

By the end of June Telewest still hadn't agreed terms with Cable & Wireless. NTL's Knapp decided to contact CWC with an offer and within a few weeks the deal was agreed. NTL would buy CWC's cable business for £8.2 billion. NTL was backed by France Telecom which agreed to pay $5.5 billion for 25% of the merged company. When the deal closed NTL would be the UK's biggest cable operator with a network covering half the country and 2.8 million residential customers. According to Knapp, NTL/CWC would have the scale to compete with BT in telephony and with BSkyB in pay-TV. But with management focused on completing the buyout, which was referred to the competition authorities after BSkyB objected, the launch of NTL's digital service was delayed once more.

Declaring 'I don't just want Sky in every home – I want it watched in every home', BSkyB's Ball set his team the goal of changing Sky from a sports-led broadcaster to an all-round entertainment service.[27]

---

[24] Chisholm and Chance had used the same razor-and-blades strategy in the analogue era. Free trials were not considered viable or desirable, mainly due to the cost of dish installation. Under the terms of the free set-top box offer subscribers had to connect the set-top box to their telephone line.

[25] Unlike Sky, ONdigital required the free set-top box to be returned when the subscription came to an end or was cancelled.

[26] 'Cheap integrated sets and free boxes push button for high-street blast-off', Hugo Davenport, *New Media Markets*, 27 May 1999, p.1.

[27] 'Tony Ball: Murdoch's solid enforcer', Ian Youngs, *BBC News web site*, 23 September 2003, <URL: http://news.bbc.co.uk/1/hi/entertainment/tv_and_radio/313020 6.stm>, Accessed 29 May 2004.

More family-oriented channels were signed up but it was the free set-top box offer that drove take-up. By July Sky Digital had 1.2 million subscribers although BSkyB's results revealed the high cost – the previous year's profit had become a loss of £388 million. Ball publicly announced targets of 5 million DTH subscribers and ARPU of £300 per annum (including £50 from interactive) by the end of 2000 and suggested Sky's analogue service could be switched off by the end of 2001. The company also moved into interactive services. In July it added internet access and discounted telephone calls to Sky Digital's offering. The following month saw the launch of Sky Sports Extra – an on-screen interactive icon which provided the ability to change camera angles and call up replays during football matches. Also in August, Open, the interactive banking and shopping service backed by BIB, finally launched. There was good news on another front when the Restrictive Practices Court rejected the OFT's case against the Premier League's practice of collective bargaining of broadcast rights.[28] The markets welcomed the company's subscriber land-grab and interactive strategy and by the end of September BSkyB was valued at over £20 billion.

At ONdigital Prebble and his team faced a number of challenges:

♦ Lower than expected signal strength for DTT transmissions meant less than 70% of the UK population could receive ONdigital rather than 90% as per the business plan.

♦ Although its marketing focused heavily on the plug and play nature of ONdigital some viewers experienced poor reception and picture quality unless they upgraded their TV aerials.

♦ Significant numbers of customers were cancelling their subscriptions with many switching to other providers of multi-channel television.

♦ ONdigital's encryption technology had been hacked making piracy commonplace.[29]

In spite of its problems ONdigital had 411,000 subscribers by September, ahead of expectations and on track to its target of two million by May 2002. Whilst Sky Digital had more subscribers many of these were existing customers switching to digital whereas, as Prebble regularly pointed out, 90% of ONdigital's subscribers were new to multi-channel television. Many commentators felt ONdigital's simple offering and ease of installation would attract customers that had so far resisted the lure of pay-TV. The company was certainly making progress, adding channels such as MTV, Nickelodeon and, after a long battle with BSkyB, Sky Sports 2 to its line-up. New marketing programmes had been launched such as 'pre-paid' set-top boxes which included a year's subscription to ONdigital for £119. These could be bought in stores, taken home, and plugged in for instant digital television – a significant advantage over Sky where customers had to wait up to seven weeks for the dish to be installed. Low-cost integrated digital televisions (idTV) with built-in ONdigital decoders were also coming onto the market. Analysts believed idTVs would soon represent a big slice of the 4 million televisions sold in the UK every year and become the main driver of ONdigital's growth. In the meantime the free set-top box offer was severely affecting the company's cash flow. Merrill Lynch estimated the subsidy accounted for over 90% of revenues in 1999.[30] Nevertheless the company received a boost when the Government restated its goal of switching off analogue television by 2010.

Increasing consumer choice

Digital cable finally arrived in October 1999 when Telewest launched Active Digital. This offered 150 television and radio channels, including 50 PPV

---

28 *1996 No.1 (E&W) in the Restrictive Practices Court (in England and Wales)*, The Court Service, London, 28 July 1999. Although the Court agreed the agreements were restrictive it found they were in the public interest as they helped to fund ground improvements and the money was shared equitably by the clubs.

29 By 2002 ONdigital estimated there were over 100,000 hacked smart cards in circulation. In March 2002 Canal+, makers of the MediaGuard conditional access system used by ONdigital and other pay-TV broadcasters, filed a lawsuit against NDS alleging it had leaked the encryption code. No link was proven and the case was settled out of court.

30 'ONdigital terrestrial TV forecasts', *New Media Markets*, op. cit., p.3.

movie channels, and low-cost telephony with the promise of broadband internet access to come. The basic package, including 18 television channels and a telephone line, was priced at £13 per month. Additional channels, costing between £2 and £12 a month, could be picked from an 'à la carte' menu which allowed subscribers to select and pay for only those they wanted. Subscribers had to pay a connection fee of £30 but the set-top box came free.[31] To attract new customers Telewest even offered a free one-month trial. The company planned to rollout the new service to the 4.2 million homes covered by its network by the middle of 2000. Telewest also moved into interactive services. In December it announced a flat-rate internet access service, SurfUnlimited, for £10 a month – the first company in the UK to do so. It also announced plans to offer home banking, home shopping, email, and internet access via its high speed cable network from early 2000.

Most analysts assumed it would not be long before the acquisitive Knapp made a play for Telewest. Instead Telewest sprang its own surprise when it announced the takeover of Flextech, the programme supplier which owned or had a stake in 13 television channels.[32] Telewest's shareholders would own 80% of the merged company, worth £10.5 billion, with 20% owned by Flextech's shareholders. Adam Singer, CEO of the smaller Flextech, would be CEO. Singer's strategy was to build mass and increase ARPU by using the company's low-cost bundled packages to attract customers and then persuading them to trade up to higher margin services such as high speed internet access. Singer pushed the idea that Telewest/Flextech's branded content, high speed network, and focus on new interactive services would create the UK's first 'Broadbandcaster'.[33] Investor reaction was positive and by the end of the year the share price had risen over 40% in two months, valuing the pre-merger Telewest at over £10 billion.

In May 2000 NTL at last launched its digital cable service. NTL Digital Plus featured the much-vaunted 'triple-play' of digital television, telephony, and internet access, although the latter would only be available from July. Channel packs and premium channels could be bolted onto the basic package which cost £13 per month and included a telephone line, 14 television channels, and access to multi-plexed PPV movies. Whilst the set-top box came free subscribers had to pay a £40 connection fee.[34] Like Telewest, NTL planned a phased rollout. NTL also put heavy emphasis on interactivity, promising full web-browsing via both TV and PC. Knapp believed NTL's interactive services would distinguish it from its competitors and set a target of 500,000 digital subscribers by the end of 2000. Later that month the last regulatory obstacle to NTL's buyout of CWC's cable business was cleared when France Telecom received approval for its investment in NTL/CWC.

The view from 30,000 feet

By June Continental Research estimated there were 4.65 million digital television subscribers in the UK, equivalent to 19% of TV households.[35] In many areas, consumers could now choose between three different services: Sky Digital, ONdigital, and either Telewest or NTL. Heavyweight marketing campaigns from the key players throughout the year increased consumer demand. In a survey by Gallup, 44% of adults said they intended to get digital television within three years with greater choice of viewing and better quality sound and pictures the main attractions.[36]

The UK was the first country to launch digital terrestrial television but digital cable- and satellite-based services had launched in the US, France, Germany, and elsewhere from 1994 onwards.

---

[31] In fact the set-top box was rented and had to be returned if the subscriber cancelled their subscription.

[32] The deal was partly driven by fears that OFTEL, the telecoms regulator, would open up cable networks to competition.

[33] *1st Quarter Results 2000*, Telewest, London, 18 May 2000, p.2.

[34] As with Telewest the set-top box was rented and had to be returned if the subscription was cancelled.

[35] *Digital Satellite and Cable Monitor No. 135*, Continental Research, June 2000.

[36] 'Digital TV Hitting Home', *Pace Micro Technology web site*, 30 November 2000, <URL: http://www.pace.co.uk/news room/index.asp>, Accessed 10 June 2004

By 2000 a number of governments had set firm dates for analogue switch-off. National regulatory regimes as well as language and cultural differences had conspired against the creation of global or even regional television companies but the development of digital technology and the resulting convergence of television, telecommunications and the internet were creating new opportunities.

Murdoch was keen to establish satellite operations in Europe and the US but, with much of the world's television industry still highly regulated, genuine opportunities were hard to find. At the end of 1999 he decided to take a minority share in Premiere World, a fledgling German digital satellite pay-TV service, via a 24% stake in KirchPayTV Gmbh, with a view to securing a position in Europe's largest television market. The £962 million investment was made through BSkyB, funded by cash and shares.[37] NTL's Knapp also had ambitions beyond the UK, spending over $5 billion on his corporate credit card to acquire or take stakes in a number of cable companies across Europe.

Football matters

In the latter half of 1999 and early part of 2000 the stock markets were rising fast, largely driven by increasing internet frenzy. BSkyB's Ball invested in a number of dotcom ventures including spending £287 million to acquire Sports Internet Group, a sports web site and online betting service. The satellite broadcaster also continued to buy sports rights, adding more cricket and rugby union to its roster. However the biggest prize was top flight football. BSkyB had maximised its return from the Premiership over the previous eight years but the television rights were up for negotiation once more and this time Sky's competitors had a better understanding of their potential value. In May 2000 the League invited sealed bids for four broadcast packages each lasting three years. Rumours of a massive bid from NTL led to a 40% drop in BSkyB's share price, wiping £13.8 billion off its market value in less than three weeks.[38] On 9 June Richard Scudamore,

Managing Director of the Premier League, announced there would be a second round with only three packages on offer. Any one bidder could win only one package and winning bids had to be 10% higher than the next offer or a new round would be held. The deadline for bids was 2pm on Wednesday 14 June.

The three Premier League broadcast packages were:

- The Main Deal: the most valuable package, comprising 66 live games each season.
- The Pay-Per-View Deal: consisting of 40 PPV games per season in which all 20 teams had to be featured at least once.
- The Terrestrial Deal: open only to free-to-air terrestrial broadcasters: the BBC; ITV companies; Channel 4; and Channel 5; this only included recorded highlights.

BSkyB's bid team was led by Tony Ball supported by the company's in-house strategic planning team. The only package they were really interested in was the Main Deal. Stories that Bill Gates was bankrolling NTL and Barclay Knapp would bid £1.7 billion were all over the press and BSkyB's share price bounced up and down as the markets considered the implications. Ball and his team agonised over how much to offer. Finally they decided NTL wouldn't bid more than £1 billion for the live rights. Ball added 10% and another £10 million for good measure. BSkyB's bid was £1.11 billion.[39] If NTL bid less than £1.01 billion BSkyB would win. If NTL bid more than £1.01 billion but less than £1.22 billion BSkyB would have another chance. But if Knapp bid more than £1.22 billion NTL would walk away with the prize and BSkyB would lose its 'battering ram'.[40]

If Ball was at all uncertain, analysts seemed to have a clear sense of how much he should bid. Mathew Horsman, Research Director at Investec, told the BBC, 'If they [BSkyB] pay less than £1.2 billon and win it, we will be buying the shares. If they pay substantially more, we will be back sharpening

---

[37] Murdoch also invested in several other pay-TV companies around the world via News Corporation.

[38] BSkyB's share price had peaked at £22.64 on 7 March 2000, valuing the company at more than £43 billion.

[39] *Virtual Murdoch: Reality Wars on the Information Superhighway*, N Chenoweth, Vintage, London, 2000, p.335.

[40] Murdoch's famous description of how sports could be used to drive pay-TV subscriptions.

our pencils, but if they lose them altogether we will watch the shares dive.'[41]

An hour after the deadline on 14 June, Scudamore telephoned BSkyB to tell them they had won the live broadcast package outright. NTL won the PPV deal for £328 million and ITV outbid the BBC for the recorded highlights with a bid of £183 million. In total the auction generated over £1.6 billion. The general view of most analysts was BSkyB had won the live rights with a high but justifiable bid but NTL had overbid for the PPV package.[42]

Prebble was determined to find a 'killer-app' to drive ONdigital subscriptions. An opportunity came in the form of the Football League, consisting of the 72 clubs below the Premier League, whose broadcast rights were up for sale at the same time. Although the Premiership grabbed the headlines, more fans attended Football League matches every week. ONdigital quickly won exclusive rights with a bid of £315 million for a three year deal starting in 2001/02. The deal gave ONdigital the right to show 88 live matches plus a number of PPV matches every season. The contract was signed by the Football League and ONdigital on 15 June. With exclusive live UEFA Champions League and Football League matches as well as Premiership football via Sky Sports, ONdigital could now legitimately claim it offered more comprehensive coverage of the national sport than any other broadcaster. Soon afterwards ONdigital also announced its interactive service – ONnet, offering internet access and email via TV for £5 a month, would launch in September.

Sky high

Regardless of the competition Sky Digital maintained its rapid, if costly, growth. In July 2000 Ball announced it had more than 3.6 million subscribers and set a new target of seven million by the end of 2003. With digital churn a mere 3.5%, customer satisfaction was rising, as was ARPU, up to £287 per annum. Sky Digital's growth pushed revenues in 1999/2000 up to £1.85 billion but the set-top box subsidy continued to hit the bottom line with pre-tax losses exceeding £260 million. Investor reaction to the results was downbeat with analysts expressing concern about the costs of going digital, although the fading love affair with technology, media, and telecoms stocks was also a factor. In July BSkyB was forced to buy out HSBC and Matsushita from Open, its underperforming interactive shopping service, for £525 million in an all-share deal – that same month Murdoch told all his senior managers there was to be no more spending on internet businesses. By September Sky Digital had over 4.5 million subscribers, well on track to the year-end target of five million DTH subscribers, but BSkyB's share price had halved from its peak of six months earlier.

BSkyB's competitors faced their own problems. In August Carlton and Granada had announced plans to float ONdigital in the autumn with a capitalisation of between £1.5 and £2 billion, partly to raise funds to support the DTT broadcaster through to 2003 when it was expected to move into profit. However, the initial public offering (IPO) was postponed after several analysts downgraded their valuations to under £1 billion. As many predicted, NTL couldn't make the numbers add up for its PPV deal with the Premier League. Knapp had planned to offer free games to attract new subscribers and to bundle games with other programming but the Premier League objected. The row still wasn't resolved by the start of the 2000/01 football season and in October NTL pulled out of the deal.[43] At Telewest problems with the supply of set-top boxes, sourced exclusively from Pace, and service reliability forced it to relaunch Active Digital and reduce its targets for digital subscribers.

In November BSkyB raised its retail prices for Sky Digital – the second set of increases since launch – triggering rises of up £4 a month in Sky's

---

[41] 'TV giants gamble on sport', *BBC News web site*, 14 June 2000, <URL: http://news.bbc.co.uk/1/hi/business/791321.stm>, Accessed 10 June 2004.

[42] The logic for believing NTL had overbid was as follows. Each game would cost NTL £2.7 million. If NTL charged £5 per match, after factoring in costs of say £1, it needed to attract over 680,000 viewers per game – more than the UK record for a PPV event. Since many matches would be between less popular teams and NTL had only 1.26 million cable TV subscribers such a target seemed unattainable.

---

[43] Eventually the Premier League made the PPV rights available on a non-exclusive basis. This raised £181 million.

wholesale prices. Prebble complained BSkyB was behaving as a monopoly leading the OFT to announce it was reopening its investigation into Sky's wholesale pricing. ONdigital's priority however was to hit its target of one million subscribers by the end of the year. With Granada and Carlton planning an IPO for the DTT broadcaster and profits unlikely in the near future the subscriber target was critical. As the year-end approached there were reports of subscribers threatening to cancel being offered packages worth £37 a month for as little as £1 a month. Whatever the tactics ONdigital hit its target. By the end of the year the Digital TV Group estimated the number of digital television homes had risen to nearly 7 million, including satellite, DTT and cable services.[44] A fourth platform was also opening up. After regulations preventing the delivery of broadcast television via telephone lines were lifted, BT confirmed it was considering launching a digital television service in 2001 using high-speed ADSL (Asymmetric Digital Subscriber Line) technology.

Decreasing investor patience

After the longest bull market in history the Dow Jones, NASDAQ Composite, and FTSE-100 had all fallen in 2000. By 2001 slowing economic growth in the US and Europe was having a significant impact on global equity markets. Business confidence and capital investment were declining for the first time in nearly a decade. For businesses still in the investment phase and with little experience of managing in a bear market the situation was problematic to say the least.

By spring 2001 the stock market bubble had burst and Telewest and NTL faced mounting pressure from shareholders. NTL's shares had fallen to less than a quarter of their peak value of $110. Despite losses of more than $3 billion in 2000 and debts in excess of $15 billion Knapp was as confident as ever,

predicting NTL would achieve breakeven by 2004 and cable would soon overtake BSkyB to become the dominant DTV platform in the UK. Not everyone agreed – with interest payments of more than $1 billion a year some questioned how NTL could survive. At the end of March, although churn was still 25%, Telewest's digital television service had reached 500,000 subscribers. But by now its share price had fallen from a high of 569 pence to around 115 pence. In spite of this Singer was able to restructure £2.25 billion of Telewest/Flextech's debt and free up £300 million for expansion.

The deteriorating economy and dotcom crash also had a negative impact on the advertising market. As advertising was their sole source of revenue this was especially hard on Granada and Carlton whose shares fell throughout the latter half of 2000 and early 2001. At ONdigital Prebble told journalists the company's target of achieving two million subscribers and breakeven by 2002 'is not a hope, it is entirely realisable' but net subscriber growth in the first quarter of 2001 was rumoured to be less than 40,000.[45] This was partly due to high churn caused by pre-paid customers returning set-top boxes at the end of the 12-month subscription. Sales of ONdigital-enabled idTVs had also been very disappointing. Granada and Carlton decided a new approach was needed for their main businesses and ONdigital. In April Charles Allen, Granada's Chairman, and Carlton's Green announced plans to reorganise their assets under the ITV banner and to rebrand ONdigital as ITV Digital. Prebble was appointed CEO with responsibility for ITV's terrestrial network, ITV Digital, and ITV.com. ITC rules had restricted the level of promotion ITV could offer ONdigital but the new structure would allow it to promote ITV Digital more heavily. At a press conference to publicise the new structure Prebble announced new goals for the DTT broadcaster. ITV Digital's targets for the end of 2002 included:

♦ Reaching 1.6 million subscribers.

♦ Increasing ARPU from £225 to £300 (including VAT).

---

[44] 'Another digital milestone!' *Digital TV Group web site*, 20 December 2000, <URL: http://www.dtg.org.uk/news/archive/sum_0012.htm>, Accessed 17 June 2004. As well as nearly five million Sky Digital and one million ONdigital subscribers, this included 500,000 NTL and 300,000 Telewest digital cable subscribers. In addition it was estimated 100,000 digital television sets, allowing access to free-to-air channels, had been sold.

[45] 'Ondigital fights for growth', *BBC News web site*, 17 January 2001, <URL: http://news.bbc.co.uk/1/hi/business/1121929.stm> Accessed 18 June 2004.

- Reducing churn from 25% to 18%.
- Cutting acquisition costs from £200 to £120 per subscriber.
- Achieving a gross margin of 44% on programming.[46]

Prebble planned to use sport to grow ITV Digital the same way Sam Chisholm had done at Sky in the early 1990s. As part of this strategy the different ITV units were to pool their sports rights to create a new subscription-based channel, ITV Sport, which would launch on ITV Digital the following August. For £6.99 subscribers would be able to watch live UEFA Champions League and Football League matches as well as various other sports. A new marketing campaign would promote ITV Digital and the new ITV Sport channel. Prebble planned to boost ARPU through a mixture of price rises and increasing the Pay-to-Basic Ratio by selling more premium channels such as ITV Sport.[47] Falling set-top box prices would cut acquisition costs and programming costs would be reduced by renegotiating contracts with suppliers – a clear reference to BSkyB. If all the targets were achieved ITV Digital would breakeven by 2003/04. Reaction to the strategy was mixed with some analysts seeing it as long overdue and others seeing it as the last throw of the dice.

Since advertising represented a small proportion of its revenues BSkyB was less vulnerable to falling advertising spend than Carlton and Granada. The free set-top box offer continued to drive growth and by June 2001 Sky Digital had more than 5.5 million digital subscribers, allowing Ball to bring forward the analogue switch-off to September. More digital than analogue subscribers took the top tier package,

helping to push ARPU up to £313 per annum (including £11 in interactive ARPU). BSkyB continued to innovate by launching Sky+, a Sky-branded Personal Video Recorder (PVR) enabling programmes to be recorded onto a hard drive. It wasn't all good news. Losses had doubled over the previous year to £515 million and net debt had risen to £1.55 billion. BSkyB had been forced to buy out BT from Open and many of the company's investments had gone sour. Despite owning the rights to Bundesliga football (the German Premier League) and other high profile sports, Premiere World had struggled in the traditionally free-to-air German television market. By 2001 KirchPayTV was staggering under the weight of debt taken on to buy broadcast rights at what turned out to be the top of the market. Ball's new media investments fared no better. BSkyB had invested over £800 million in interactive services but the only interactive bet that paid off (and even this was debatable) was TV betting which generated £78 million in 2000/01 out of total interactive revenues of £93 million, the rest coming from Open. In July the EU Commission announced it would investigate an agreement between BSkyB and Disney which prevented the latter from offering its channels to ITV Digital. In spite of the challenges Ball and Stewart forged ahead, promising to increase ARPU to £400 per annum by 2005 and to deliver positive cash flow by the end of the year and profits by 2002–2004.

Cash is king

By the end of 2001 falling stock markets and declining ad spend meant cash was king. Telewest continued to grow its digital television service, up to 644,000 subscribers by October, but debt was now £4.7 billion. In November, with its share price down to 25 pence and under pressure from bondholders, Singer announced plans to convert Telewest's debts into equity. At NTL, in spite of reaching 1.25 million digital subscribers, Knapp announced the company would have to shed 8,000 staff and increase prices to meet its cash flow targets. He also put many of NTL's assets up for sale, although most were worth a fraction of their purchase price – leading to write-downs of $11.5 billion. With TV advertising revenues down an estimated 25% year-on-year in the last quarter, cash flow was also becoming a problem for

---

[46] *ITV Digital – Between a Rock and a Hard Place*?, Claire Enders, Enders Analysis, Dundee, July 2001, p.2.

[47] The high PBR that had been agreed with BSkyB back in 1997 as part of the deal for Sky programming meant that, in the words of a senior manager at one of ITV Digital's shareholders, "When we sell one pay channel to a subscriber, we lose money. When we sell two, we break even. When we sell three, we make between 0 and 5%. When we sell four, we make between 5 and 10%". Quote from *The Gross Margin from Retailing Premium Pay-TV Channels*, Chris Goodall, Enders Analysis, Dundee, July 2001, p.5.

Granada and Carlton. They had pumped £800 million into ITV Digital and analysts were now openly calling for them to pull the plug. While admitting to considering their options they continued to support their DTT offspring. In part this was because of signs of improvement at ITV Digital but it was also in the belief the Government would soon set a firm date for analogue shutdown. However in November they succumbed to pressure from advertisers and signed a deal with BSkyB for carriage of ITV1 (previously ITV) and ITV2 on Sky Digital.[48] Despite losing one of ITV Digital's key selling points versus Sky, with subscriptions up to 1.2 million Prebble was still upbeat. But the underlying situation was worsening. ITV Sport was not attracting significant numbers of subscribers to ITV Digital, forcing the DTT broadcaster to seek additional distribution for the new channel. A carriage fee was agreed with NTL but Telewest and BSkyB refused to take ITV Sport on the terms offered.[49] The Football League deal bombed. Some matches had such poor viewing figures Prebble was compelled to try to renegotiate the cost but the League refused. As the year ended BSkyB's competitors were at last able to claim a victory. In December the OFT announced it proposed to find the satellite broadcaster guilty of infringing UK competition law by unfairly squeezing the margins of its premium channel distributors and using its wholesale pricing policies to prevent rival premium channel providers from entering the market.[50] Possible sanctions included a fine of 10% of turnover for up to three years. Unusually BSkyB's shares rose on the news, reflecting the markets' confidence it would beat the rap.

At the end of the year the fierce competition between the different service providers had driven penetration of digital television up to 37% of all TV households.[51] However a poll in November found switching to digital was still not on the radar for 30% of the population.[52]

Winners and losers

ITV and the cable companies

Poor sales in the last quarter of 2001 and early 2002 and continuing losses of £1 million a day led Granada and Carlton to announce ITV Digital needed a 'fundamental restructuring ... as a matter of urgency'.[53] In February they called in Deloitte & Touche. The accountants laid off 500 staff and attempted to cut ITV Digital's costs although not everyone was sympathetic. One source quoted Adam Singer, Telewest's CEO, as saying 'If ITV Digital come to us and say we have to lower our prices or they die, then as a competing platform owner the death bit sounds good to me. Bring it on.'[54] Attention focused on the deal with the Football League. Deloitte & Touche tried to persuade the League to accept less than the £178.5 million it was still owed but the League rejected all offers, believing it could force Carlton and Granada to honour the original agreement. After failing to restructure the business or find a buyer Deloitte & Touche finally shut ITV Digital down on 1 May 2002 with the loss of 1,300 jobs and debts of £1.25 billion. The pioneering digital

---

[48] As well as increasing their audience reach the agreement increased the rebate Granada and Carlton received from the Government against the levy they paid for their analogue licences. Analysts estimated adding BSkyB's subscribers to ITV's digital audience would generate an annual windfall of £50 million for the network owners. ITV also received undisclosed carriage fees from BSkyB for ITV2, which became part of Sky's pay-TV packages. Against this the network had to pay BSkyB's conditional access charges of £17 million.

[49] NTL was rumoured to have agreed to pay a guaranteed carriage fee of around £40 million per annum. The offers rejected by BSkyB and Telewest were reputed to be £80 million and £20 million per annum respectively. There were also discussions with BSkyB based on the idea of marketing ITV Sport directly to satellite TV viewers using Sky's conditional access system but ITV didn't pursue the idea.

[50] *OFT proposes to find BSkyB in breach of law PN 51/01*, OFT, London, 17 December 2001.

[51] *2001 Report: Commercial Television in the UK: an overview*, ITC, London, April 2002.

[52] 'Digital Switch Fails to Spark Public Imagination', *Pace Micro Technology web site*, 16 November 2001, op. cit.

[53] 'ITV Digital in crisis, owners say', *BBC News web site*, 27 February 2002, <URL: http://news.bbc.co.uk/1/hi/business/1843673.stm>, Accessed 17 June 2004.

[54] 'ITV Digital's flickering future', Nick Higham, *BBC News web site*, 5 March 2002, <URL: http://news.bbc.co.uk/1/hi/entertainment/tv_and_radio/1853678.stm>, Accessed 15 June 2004.

terrestrial pay-TV service had been unable to compete with BSkyB. In total Carlton and Granada had pumped £1.2 billion into the venture.

In the glory days the cable companies had pushed their 'convergence' model but by 2002 they were just trying to stay alive. In the last months of 2001 NTL sold assets to cut debt and made thousands of staff redundant to cut costs. It even shut down its marketing department as it couldn't afford to take on new customers. It was all too late and the shares continued to fall until being suspended at the end of March 2002, trading at 20 cents. NTL finally sought the refuge of Chapter 11 bankruptcy protection in May, emerging the following January after bond-holders forgave $10.9 billion of debt in return for control of the company. Telewest fared little better. In February 2002 it announced it had lost £1.9 billion in 2001 – mostly a write-down against Flextech. Having lost the confidence of his fellow directors, Singer resigned in July to be replaced by Charles Burdick, the Finance Director. Telewest narrowly avoided administration with a financial restructuring which gave bondholders 98.5% of the company. The cable companies had stopped building out their networks in 2000. By the end of 2002 they faced scaling back their ambitions even further and the number of cable television subscribers was in decline.

The BBC

Although the Government rejected a BBC plea for a digital levy in 2000, above-inflation rises in the licence fee and internal cost cutting enabled it to expand its digital television services to eight channels by 2002. When bids were invited for the defunct ITV Digital's DTT multiplexes the BBC approached BSkyB and Crown Castle (formerly Crown Transmission Services) with the idea of launching a low cost free-to-air service. After winning the licence, subject to the condition BSkyB wasn't involved in running the new service, the BBC-led consortium moved quickly. Freeview launched in October 2002 with 30 channels, including free-to-air channels from the BBC, ITV, Channel 4, Five (previously Channel 5), and BSkyB. Consumers wishing to access the new service only required a set-top box costing £99 or an integrated digital television, no subscription was needed. Ex-ITV Digital subscribers

could also access it via their set-top boxes. Freeview got off to a flying start and by the end of 2002 over 330,000 people had bought set-top boxes for the new service. The BBC had taken control of a key digital distribution channel and made a significant and politically astute contribution towards the Government's goal of switching off analogue television by 2010.

BSkyB

In the year to June 2002 BSkyB made an operating profit of £115 million on turnover of £2.76 billion. The former became a loss of £1.28 billion after goodwill and exceptional charges (principally a write-down of the investment in KirchPayTV) but Ball and Stewart delivered on their promise of generating positive cash flow (albeit only £18 million). They also continued to improve the Sky Digital offering, increasing the number of channels to 380. The demise of ITV Digital helped Sky grow to 6.6 million DTH subscribers by the end of 2002. With net growth of over 200,000 per quarter and ARPU of £350 per annum the company was well on track to its targets of 7 million subscribers and ARPU of £400 with the prospect of significant free cash flow. Throughout 2002 the OFT's provisional decision to find BSkyB in breach of the 1998 Competition Act had hung over the company but in December, following further submissions by the satellite broadcaster, the regulator announced there was insufficient evidence it had abused its position.[55] With the threat of action by the UK competition authorities removed BSkyB was able to face the future with confidence. Despite the enormous risks and challenges it had managed the transition to digital and reinforced its position as the dominant UK pay-TV platform. Furthermore, through its partnership with the BBC and Crown Castle, it had secured distribution for several of its channels on the new free-to-air DTT service.

At the end of 2002 BSkyB's position seemed unassailable, although the emergence of Freeview and increasing interest of EU regulators presented potential future threats. How would BSkyB deal

---

[55] *Decision of the Director General of Fair Trading No CA98/20/2002*, OFT, London, 17 December 2002.

with these and other challenges? Could it ever again produce the 30% margins it achieved in 1997? With over 40% of the UK population already signed up for digital television and another 30% seemingly uninterested, where would long-term growth come from?

Exhibit 1 Glossary

ADSL (Asymmetric Digital Subscriber Line)	Digital technology allowing high speed data transfer over copper wire.
Analogue	Traditional method of transmitting information in continuous wave form.
ARPU (Average Revenue Per User)	The average revenue generated by a user in a specific period, usually per month or per annum.
Buy-through	The practice of forcing pay-TV subscribers to buy through basic channel packages before they are allowed to subscribe to premium channels.
Churn	The ratio of subscribers cancelling their subscriptions to total subscribers within a specific period, usually per annum.
Conditional access system	A system for encrypting content to control access. Users require a decoder in the form of a set-top box or integrated digital television.
Digital	Digital technology converts information into binary digits which can be compressed, allowing more efficient transmission with less data loss.
DTV (Digital television)	Television signals are converted into digital format, transmitted and decoded back into sound and pictures.
DTT (Digital Terrestrial Television)	Digital television received via an aerial.
DTH (Direct-to-Home)	Satellite signals received via a dish receiver. Also known as satellite TV.
EPG (Electronic Programming Guide)	An application enabling users to search and select channels and services via an on-screen display, usually controlled by a dedicated remote control.
FTA (Free-to-air or free-to-access)	Free channels or services.
idTV (integrated digital television)	A television with an integrated digital decoder.
MCRs (Minimum Carriage Requirements)	Agreements requiring channels to be carried to a pre-set percentage, usually 80%, of a platform's subscribers. Banned, with some exceptions, by the UK's commercial television regulator in 1998.
Mux (Multiplex)	A stream of digital data able to carry several channels or services.
Passed homes	The number of homes covered by a cable network.
Pay-TV	Encrypted television services only accessible by paying subscribers.
PBR (Pay-to-Basic Ratio)	Ratio of premium channel subscribers (weighted for the number of premium channels to which they subscribe) to total subscribers.
PPV (Pay-Per-View)	Service allowing specific programmes such as movies or sports events to be ordered in return for a one-off payment.
PVR (Personal Video Recorder)	An enhanced set-top box which enables television programmes to be recorded onto an internal hard-drive.
Subscriber acquisition cost	The average cost of acquiring a new customer or subscriber.
STB (Set-top box)	Device enabling television signals to be decoded and accessed.
Tiering	The practice of creating separate basic and premium pay-TV channel packages (see buy-through).
VOD (Video On Demand)	Service allowing customers to order and see a specific programme at a time of their choosing.

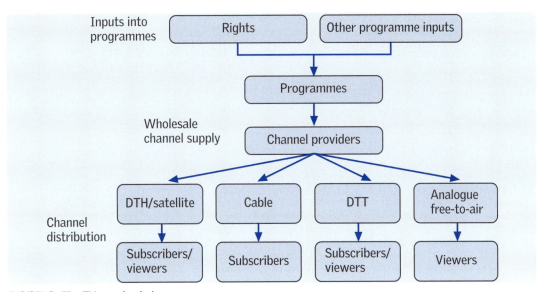

Exhibit 2 The TV supply chain
Source: *Decision of the Director General of Fair Trading No CA98/20/2002*, OFT, London, 17 December 2002, p.6.

Exhibit 3 The history of multichannel TV in the UK

1989	Sky Television launches UK satellite TV with a four channel service.
1990	British Satellite Broadcasting (BSB) launches. Sky and BSB merge to form British Sky Broadcasting (BSkyB).
1992	BSkyB buys exclusive rights to live FA Premier League football coverage.
1993	Sky launches multichannel pay TV package.
1997	Independent Television Commission licenses digital terrestrial TV multiplexes to Digital 3&4 and British Digital Broadcasting. The BBC is also allocated one multiplex.
1998	BSkyB launches UK's first digital TV service and attracts 100,000 customers in its first month. Digital terrestrial TV broadcasts start. British Digital Broadcasting launches its pay TV service under the ONdigital brand name.
1999	Sky and ONdigital begin to offer free set-top boxes. NTL and Telewest launch digital cable TV services. Sky introduces interactive services. Secretary of State announces ambition to complete digital switchover and defines switchover targets.
2000	NTL acquires the consumer operations of Cable and Wireless Communications (CWC) to become largest cable operator. Telewest merges with Flextech.
2001	BSkyB reaches five million digital subscribers and switches off its analogue service. ONdigital relaunched as ITV Digital. NTL and Telewest launch broadband Internet services. Government launches Digital TV Action Plan.
2002	ITV Digital closes down. Freeview launched. New BBC digital TV and radio services begin broadcasting. NTL applies for Chapter 11 protection in the US; it later secures recapitalisation. Half of all UK viewers have multichannel TV.

Source: *Driving digital switchover: a report to the Secretary of State*, OFCOM, London, April 2004, p.29.

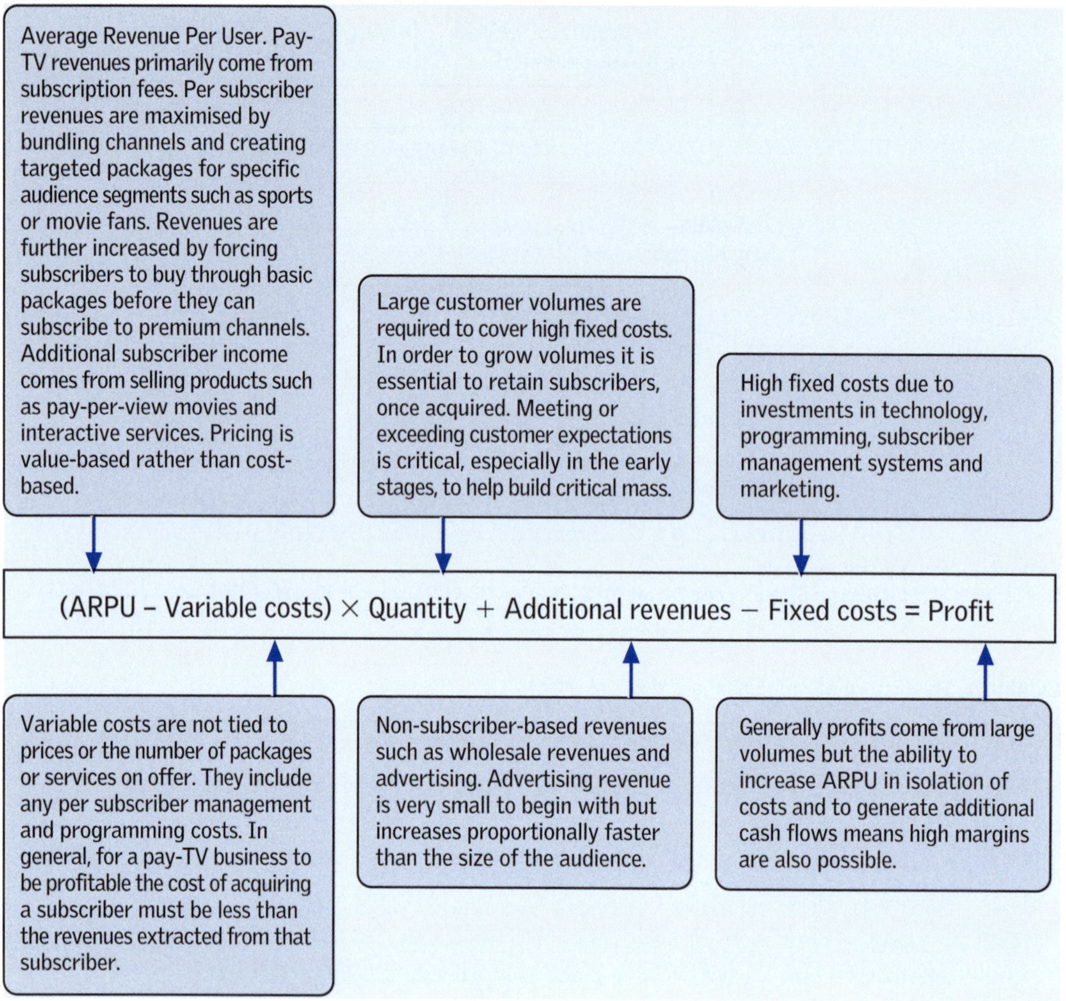

Average Revenue Per User. Pay-TV revenues primarily come from subscription fees. Per subscriber revenues are maximised by bundling channels and creating targeted packages for specific audience segments such as sports or movie fans. Revenues are further increased by forcing subscribers to buy through basic packages before they can subscribe to premium channels. Additional subscriber income comes from selling products such as pay-per-view movies and interactive services. Pricing is value-based rather than cost-based.

Large customer volumes are required to cover high fixed costs. In order to grow volumes it is essential to retain subscribers, once acquired. Meeting or exceeding customer expectations is critical, especially in the early stages, to help build critical mass.

High fixed costs due to investments in technology, programming, subscriber management systems and marketing.

$$(\text{ARPU} - \text{Variable costs}) \times \text{Quantity} + \text{Additional revenues} - \text{Fixed costs} = \text{Profit}$$

Variable costs are not tied to prices or the number of packages or services on offer. They include any per subscriber management and programming costs. In general, for a pay-TV business to be profitable the cost of acquiring a subscriber must be less than the revenues extracted from that subscriber.

Non-subscriber-based revenues such as wholesale revenues and advertising. Advertising revenue is very small to begin with but increases proportionally faster than the size of the audience.

Generally profits come from large volumes but the ability to increase ARPU in isolation of costs and to generate additional cash flows means high margins are also possible.

Exhibit 4 Pay-TV business model

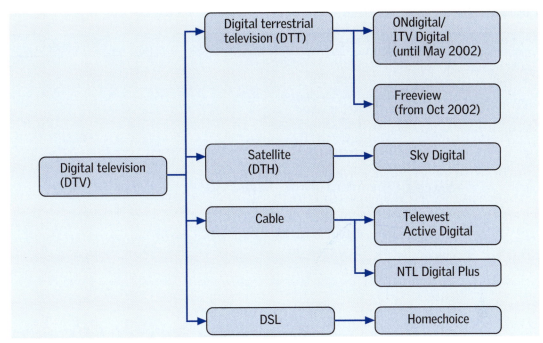

Exhibit 5 Digital television platforms and key service providers

Source: Adapted from *Digital television for all: A report on usability and accessible design*, DTI, London, September 2003, p.9. Freeview can be accessed by anyone with an idTV or digital set-top box and doesn't require a subscription. Other companies providing free-to-air digital channels accessible via an idTV or digital set-top box include the BBC, Digital 3&4 Ltd, and SDN Ltd. Other digital cable service providers include Kingston Interactive Television and Isle of Wight Cable. By the end of 2002 DSL-based digital television services delivered via a telephone connection, such as Homechoice, had a user base of a few thousand homes.

Exhibit 6 Digital terrestrial multiplexes

Multiplex	Operator	Free to air	Subscription	Coverage
1	BBC	BBC1 BBC2 BBC Choice BBC News 24 BBC Knowledge BBC Text BBC Parliament (audio only)		91%
2	Digital 3 & 4	ITV ITV2 Channel 4 Teletext digital	Film Four*	91%
A	SDN	Channel 5 S4C		90%
B	Ondigital		Carlton Cinema Cartoon Network Sky One British Eurosport Sky Sports 1* and 3 Sky Premier*	88%
C	Ondigital		Granada Plus Shop!** UK Gold MTV ON Sport** Sky MovieMax*	77%
D	Ondigital		UK Style UK Horizons (BBC) UK Play Discovery Kids AM Carlton Food Network Granada Breeze Discovery Wings PM Adult Channel Granada Men & Motors	69%

* Premium channel ** Free bonus channels
Note that this listing is subject to change quite dynamically.
Source: *Development of Digital TV in Europe: 2000 report: United Kingdom*, iDate, Montpellier, Decemeber 2000, p.9–10.

Exhibit 7 Sky Digital channel line-up

Sky One	Sky Sports Extra	Discovery Animal Planet	VH1
UK Gold	MUTV	Cartoon Network	VH1 Classic
UK Gold 2	Skysports.comTV	Nickelodeon	The Box
Living	British Eurosport	CNBC	UK Play
Granada Plus	Sky Premier	Discovery	44 Music Choice channels
Challenge TV	Sky Premier 2	Discovery Travel & Adv.	QVC
Bravo	Sky Premier 3	Discovery Civilisation	BBC1
Paramount Comedy Channel	Sky Premier 4	Discovery Sci-Trek	BBC2
Sci-Fi	Sky Premier Widescreen	Adventure One	Channel 4
Discovery Home & Leisure	Sky MovieMax	The History Channel	Channel 5
Granada Breeze	Sky MovieMax 2	UK Horizons	BBC Choice
Granada Men & Motors	Sky MovieMax 3	[.tv]	S4C
Sky Travel	Sky MovieMax 4	Nick Jr.	BBC News 24
UK Style	Sky MovieMax 5	Trouble	BBC Parliament
UK Drama	Sky Cinema	Fox Kids	CNN International
TARA Television	Sky Cinema 2	Disney Channel	BBC Knowledge
Hallmark Entertainment	FilmFour	MTV	Money Channel
Sky Sports 1	Sky Box Office	MTV Extra	22 digital radio channels
Sky Sports 2	Sky News	MTV Base	
Sky Sports 3	Bloomberg	MTV2	

Source: *2000 Annual Report*, BSkyB, Isleworth, June 2000, p.38–39.

Exhibit 8 ONdigital channel line-up

BBC1	Carlton Cinema	Granada Men & Motors	Sky Sports 1
BBC2	Carlton Food Network	Granada Plus	Sky Sports 2
ITV	Carlton Kids	ITV2	Sky Sports 3
Channel 4	Carlton Select	MTV	UK Gold
Channel 5	Carlton World	Nickelodeon	UK Horizons
BBC Choice	Cartoon Network	S4C	UK Play
BBC Knowledge	Eurosport	Sky MovieMax	
BBC News 24	FilmFour	Sky One	
BBC Parliament	Granada Breeze	Sky Premier	

Source: *D2K: Just Zeros and Ones? A Report into Viewing Behaviour in Digital Homes*, Television Research Partnership, Taunton, December 1999, p.12.

Exhibit 9 Telewest Active Digital channel line-up

Sky One	Challenge TV	Channel One Liverpool	Zee TV
UK Gold	Granada Men & Motors	Turner Classic Movies	B4U
Granada Plus	UK Style	FilmFour	QVC
Paramount Comedy	Travel Channel	Front Row Guide	Shop!
Sci-Fi Channel	Discovery Home & Leis.	Television X	TV Travel Shop
Bravo	Discovery Travel & Adv.	Playboy	Travel Deals Direct
Scene One	Granada Breeze	Sky Sports 1	Screenshop
E4	Carlton Food Network	Sky Sports 2	BBC1
UK Drama	MTV	British Eurosport	BBC2
Play UK	MTV2	Racing Channel	BBC News 24
Tara	MTV Base	Sky News	BBC Choice
Carlton Cinema	MTV Extra	CNN	BBC Parliament
Discovery	VH1	Bloomberg	BBC Knowledge
Discovery Animal Planet	VH1 Classic	Cartoon Network	ITV
Discovery Civilisations	Performance Channel	Nickelodeon	ITV2
Sci-Trek	Sky Premier	Nick Jr.	ITN News 24
UK Horizons	Sky MovieMax	Disney Channel	regional ITV
National Geographic	Sky Cinema	Trouble	Channel 4
The History Channel	CNBC	Asianet	Channel 5
Living	The Money Channel	Sony Entertainment TV	S2

Source: Zap (Telewest Digital magazine), January 2001

Exhibit 10 NTL Digital Plus channel line-up

BBC1	Sky News	UK Play	Sky Sports 2
BBC	The Box	BET Jazz International	Sky Sports 3
ITV	UK Drama	MTV	Sky Premier
Channel 4	Tara TV	VH1	Sky Moviemax
Channel 5	Challenge TV	Cartoon Network	Sky Cinema
BBC News 24	Carlton Cinema	Rapture	Disney Channel
BBC Choice	Granada Plus	Trouble	Playboy TV
BBC Knowledge	Carlton Food Network	Nickelodeon	Adult Channel
BBC Parliament	UK Gold	Discovery	Television X
CBBC Digital	Performance Channel	UK Horizons	The Fantasy Channel
BBC Cbeebies	Discovery Home & Leis.	Discovery Civilisation	FilmFour
TV Travelshop	Granada Breeze	Discovery Travel & Adv.	Racing Channel
Bloomberg	UK Style	Discovery Sci-Trek	Sony Entertainment TV
MTV2	Sci-Fi	Discovery Animal Planet	Christian Channel
British Eurosport	TCM	History Channel	Zee TV
QVC	Granada Men & Motors	CNN	Front Row PPV movies
ITN News	Bravo	National Geographic	PPV Events
E4	Living	Travel Channel	8 Music Choice channels
Sky One	Paramount Comedy Ch.	Sky Sports 1	

Source: Adapted from NTL Home Digital Pricing NI, *Irish Cable & Digital Guide* web site, c. 2002, <URL:
http://myhome.iolfree.ie/~icdg/tuning_ntl_nidigital.htm>, Accessed 22 August 2004. Excludes channels only available in Northern
Ireland.

Exhibit 11 Cost of digital television

All figs £	Connection Fee	Basic Package	Basic with Movies	Basic with Sport	Basic with Both	Full Range
NTL	40	120	324	360	396	468
ONdigital	Free	84	264	264	324	396
Sky Digital	40	84	324	324	384	384
Telewest	20	108	288	288	348	504

Source: 'Annual Cost of Digital Television', *Which?* magazine, December 2000.

Exhibit 12 Sky Digital retail prices

All figs £	1998	1999	2000	2001	2002
Entry level package	7	7	7	10	10
Entry level plus Movies	25	27	27	28	30
Entry level plus Sports	25	27	27	30	30
All channels	30	32	32	34	37

Source: Enders Analysis. All prices per month.

Exhibit 13 Estimated BSkyB wholesale pricing

All figs £	Wholesale price from BSkyB	Approximate market retail price (ex-VAT)
1 Premium channel	10.50–11.00	10.00–13.00
2 Premium channels	13.50–14.10	13.50–17.00
3 Premium channels	15.20–15.90	16.50–17.50
4 Premium channels	16.45–17.25	18.00–20.00

Source: *The Gross Margin from Retailing Premium Pay-TV Channels*, Chris Goodall, Enders Analysis, Dundee, July 2001, p.5. All prices per subscriber per month. UK VAT is 17.5%.

Exhibit 14 UK digital TV households

All figs 000s	1998	1999	2000	2001	2002
Sky Digital	225	2,075	4,669	5,716	6,562
ONdigital/ITV Digital	c.100	552	1,012	1,263	–
NTL/CWC	–	c.100	531	1,253	1,229
Telewest	–	23	339	724	857
Free-to-air/Freeview	–	–	c.100	c.275	c.1,550
Total	c.325	c.2,750	c.6,651	c.9,231	c.10,198

Sources: Company reports, ITC. All figures to end December. Free-to-air/Freeview figure for 2002 includes integrated digital televisions, legacy ITV Digital set-top boxes and 25% of Sky Digital's former subscribers as well as Freeview set-top boxes.

Exhibit 15 Integrated digital TV sales forecasts

All figs 000s	1999	2000	2001	2002	2003	2004	2005
ABN Amro	21	114	185	338	613	1,060	1,710
BREMA	27	93	195	375	375	1,500	3,000

Source: *Future Reflections: Data and Context*, ITC, London, November 2001, p.4. According to the report 'BREMA's forecast of 195,000 idTV sales in 2001 is already looking doubtful; in reality, sales could be as low as 130,000 this year and 200,000 in 2002'.

Exhibit 16 UK: TV market overview

		1997	1998	1999	2000	2001	2002
UK population	000s	59,090	59,357	59,623	59,863	60,120	60,148
UK households	000s	25,089	25,429	25,597	25,820	26,048	26,197
TV households	000s	24,239	24,489	24,639	24,972	25,267	25,411
Cable penetration	%	9.79	11.54	13.17	14.26	14.32	13.21
DTH penetration (pay)	%	14.78	14.12	16.1	20.23	22.62	25.82
DTH penetration (free)	%	2.98	4.54	3.51	0.99	3.46	2.2
DTH penetration (total)	%	17.76	18.66	19.61	21.21	26.08	28.02
DTT penetration (pay)	%	–	0.11	2.24	4.05	5	–
DTT penetration (free)	%	–	–	–	–	–	5.23
DTT penetration (total)	%	–	0.11	2.24	4.05	5	5.23
Analogue terrestrial penetration	%	–	–	–	–	–	–
Analogue pay TV penetration	%	24.57	24.74	20.54	12.31	6.49	4.97
Digital pay TV penetration	%	–	1.03	10.97	26.23	35.45	34.06
Pay TV penetration	%	24.57	25.77	31.51	38.54	41.94	39.03
Digital TV penetration (pay & free)	%	–	1.03	10.97	26.23	35.45	39.29

Source: 'UK: TV Market Overview', *Screen Digest*, London, November 2003.

Exhibit 17 UK digital TV forecasts

All figs millions	2002	2003	2004	2005	2006
Digital satellite TV households	6.30	6.75	7.10	7.25	7.40
Digital cable TV households	2.09	2.25	2.40	2.55	2.65
Digital terrestrial TV households	0.70	0.95	1.15	1.30	1.50
Digital TV dual platform households	0.22	0.25	0.27	0.29	0.30
All digital TV households	8.87	9.70	10.38	10.81	11.25
Analogue cable TV households	1.30	1.10	0.90	0.80	0.70
Free-to-air satellite	0.30	0.35	0.40	0.45	0.50
Multi-channel TV households	10.47	11.15	11.68	12.06	12.45

Source: *UK Digital TV Forecasts: 2002–2006*, Enders Analysis, Dundee, November 2002, p.6.

Exhibit 18 BSkyB results

	2002 £m	2001 £m	2000 £m	1999 £m	1998 £m	1997 £m
DTH subscriber revenues	1,929	1,537	1,189	979	968	861
Cable and DTT subscriber revenues	279	299	303	253	228	191
Advertising revenues	251	271	242	217	195	150
Interactive revenues	186	93	5	–	–	–
Other revenues	131	106	108	96	43	48
Turnover	2,776	2,306	1,847	1,545	1,434	1,249
Programming	−1,439	−1,134	−946	−787	−688	−569
Transmission and related functions	−147	−129	−105	−91	−70	−47
Marketing	−417	−378	−381	−216	−168	−102
Subscriber management	−291	−243	−200	−154	−92	−92
Administration	−203	−187	−130	−112	−76	−65
Gaming	−88	−75	–	–	–	–
Operating expenses, net	−2,585	−2,146	−1,762	−1,360	−1,094	−875
Goodwill amortisation and exceptional items	−137	−67	−105	−456	–	–
Operating profit	54	93	−20	−271	341	374
Share of operating results of joint ventures	−76	−256	−122	−58	−17	−10
Joint ventures' goodwill amortisation	−1,070	−101	−14	–	–	–
Profit on sales of fixed assets	2	−70	−15	–	–	–
Amounts written off fixed assets investments	−60	−39	–	–	–	–
Release of provision for loss on disposals	10	−10	–	–	–	–
Net interest payable	−137	−132	−92	−60	−53	−50
Profit on ordinary activities before tax	−1,277	−515	−263	−389	271	314
Tax on profit on ordinary activities	−107	−24	65	103	−22	−26
Profit on ordinary activities after tax	−1,384	−539	−198	−286	249	288
Capital expenditure	101	133	58	76	82	42
Fixed assets	1,129	2,411	1,886	343	219	148
Working capital	−17	15	32	2	90	150
Provisions, tax and dividend	115	182	−127	−305	−92	−92
Net debt	−1,528	−1,547	−1,145	−665	−518	−628
Net assets	−301	1,061	646	−625	−301	−422
Direct-to-home (DTH) subscribers (000s)	6,101	5,453	4,513	3,460	3,547	3,532
Sky Digital subscribers (000s)	6,101	5,308	3,583	753	–	–
Cable subscribers (000s)	4,091	3,486	3,735	3,778	3,352	2,327
DTT subscribers (000s)	0	1,105	740	204	–	–
Total subscribers (000s)	10,192	10,044	8,988	7,442	6,899	5,859
DTH subscriber acquisition cost (£)	234	250	n/a	n/a	n/a	n/a
DTH annual churn (%)	10.5	10	10.5	13.4	15.1	12.2
DTH ARPU (£ per annum)	347	313	287	281	272	252
DTH pay-to-basic ratio (%)	267	272	284	291	302	253

Sources: Company reports (UK GAAP), company presentations, Merrill Lynch. Annual results to end June. ARPU includes revenues from television and interactive services and is net of VAT.

Exhibit 19 NTL results

	2002 $m	2001 $m	2000 $m	1999 $m	1998 $m
Consumer revenues	2,074	2,515	1,820	834	355
Business revenues	880	841	720	453	249
Broadcast and other revenues	311	344	319	297	140
Total revenues	3,265	3,699	2,841	1,584	747
Operating expenses	−1,503	−1,809	−1,388	−799	−372
Selling, general and admin.	−770	−1,182	−1,109	−575	−300
EBITDA	993	708	344	211	75
Asset impairment	−445	−11,124	–	–	–
Other charges and expenses	−408	−409	−140	−62	−38
Depreciation and Amortisation	−1,542	−3,181	−2,123	−791	−266
Operating profit	−1,402	14,006	−1,919	−643	−229
Net interest	−750	−1,390	−1,035	−631	−283
Profits from investments	−98	−399	−121	506	4
Recapitalisation	−152	–	–	–	–
Profit before tax	−2,402	15,795	−3,075	−768	−507
Income tax	26	−63	111	35	3
Profit from early extinguishment of debt	–	–	–	−3	−31
Net profit	−2,376	15,858	−2,964	−736	−535
Preferred stock dividends	–	−326	−194	−74	−19
Net profit to common shareholders	2.376	−16,184	−3,158	−809	−553
Working capital	−554	18.151	−849	2,261	601
Fixed assets, net	7,894	12,573	12,693	5,598	3,854
Total assets	11,248	16,834	28,384	12,212	6.194
Long term debt	6,540	102	15,044	8,798	5,044
Redeemable preferred stock	–	2,774	2,083	142	124
Shareholders' equity	2,928	−6,542	8,367	2,137	355
Homes passed (000s)	8,404	8,404	8,800	4,291	n/a
Telephony subscribers (000s)	2,412	2,589	2,537	n/a	n/a
Cable TV subscribers (000s)	2,055	2,262	2,301	n/a	n/a
Digital Plus subscribers (000s)	1,229	1,253	531	c.100	–
Internet subscribers (000s)	987	845	859	625	200
Total subscribers (000s)	2,686	2,840	2,842	1,846	1,172
Annual churn (%)	15.9	21.3	20.4	12.7	n/a
ARPU (£ per annum)	492	488	428	420	n/a
Pay-to-basic ratio (%)	n/a	n/a	n/a	91	n/a

Source: Company reports (UK GAAP). Annual results to end December. Assets and liabilities for 2002 are pro-forma. Digital Plus subscribers includes all NTL/CWC digital TV subscribers. ARPU is annualised Q4 ARPU, includes revenues from telephony, cable TV and internet services, and is net of VAT.

Exhibit 20 Telewest results

	2002 £m	2001 £m	2000 £m	1999 £m	1998 £m
Residential cable TV	336	329	279	258	202
Residential telephony	495	488	445	343	233
Internet and other	79	40	16	17	21
Business telephony & services	267	274	271	174	84
Content division (inc UKTV backout)	42	66	82	–	–
Total	1,283	1,260	1,093	793	539
Programming costs	−128	−142	−132	132	−103
Telephony costs	−218	−238	−235	158	−82
Content division costs	−70	−83	−46	–	–
Selling, general and admin. costs	−499	−491	−445	281	−208
Total costs of revenue	−915	−954	−846	571	−393
EBITDA	368	306	247	222	146
Depreciation and amortisation	−609	−626	−541	−403	−238
Operating profit	−241	−320	−294	−181	−92
Total interest payable and similar charges	−274	−477	−407	−349	−234
Profit before income taxes	−506	−797	−701	−530	−314
Income tax	−1	−5	−5	–	–
Extraordinary items	−1,712	−1,134	–	–	–
Net profit	−2,219	−1,936	−706	−530	−312
Fixed assets	3,911	5,789	6,891	4,086	3,405
Current assets	640	340	235	236	353
Net current assets	−3,770	−330	−270	−270	23
Creditors: amounts due after > 1 year	−1,932	−5,031	−3,580	−3,061	−2,570
Net assets	−1,790	427	2,355	754	858
Equity shareholders' funds	−1,790	427	2,355	754	858
Homes passed (000s)	4,896	4,914	4,922	4,918	4,183
Cable TV subscribers (000s)	1,293	1,342	1,250	1,192	999
Active Digital subscribers (000s)	857	724	339	23	–
Residential telephony subscribers (000s)	1,614	1,616	1,538	1,476	1,261
Internet subscribers (000s)	540	388	287	70	–
Total subscribers (000s)	1,759	1,766	1,691	1,649	1,370
Cable TV annual churn (%)	21.5	18.7	26.0	26.7	29.7
Cable TV ARPU (£ per annum)	250	249	234	253	270
Pay-to-basic ratio (%)	80	72	n/a	n/a	n/a

Source: Company reports (UK GAAP). Annual results to end December. ARPU is net of VAT. Pay-to-basic ratio is for Q4.

Exhibit 21 ONdigital operating results

	2001 £m	2000 £m	1999 £m	1998 £m
Revenues	176	107	n/a	n/a
Cost of sales	−104	−69	n/a	n/a
Gross profit	72	37	n/a	n/a
Subscriber management	−71	−54	n/a	n/a
Fixed costs	−69	−61	n/a	n/a
Customer acquisition costs	−134	−106	n/a	n/a
Direct costs	−47	−58	n/a	n/a
ITVSelect/ITVActive/Sport	−92	−47	n/a	n/a
Rebranding	−10	–	–	–
Profit before interest and tax	−351	−289	−153	−31
Fixed assets	104	104	n/a	n/a
Current assets	206	228	n/a	n/a
Gross liabilities	−1,034	−560	n/a	n/a
Subscribers (000s)	1,263	896	411	–
Subscriber acquisition cost (£)	200	n/a	n/a	n/a
Annual churn (%)	25	n/a	n/a	n/a
ARPU (£ per annum)	225	n/a	n/a	n/a

Sources: Carlton, Enders Analysis. Annual results to end September. Figures for 2000 and 2001 include ITV Digital and ITV Sport channel. SAC, ARPU and churn for 2001 taken from *ITV Digital – Between a Rock and a Hard Place?*, Claire Enders, Enders Analysis, Dundee, July 2001, p.2. ARPU includes VAT at 17.5%.

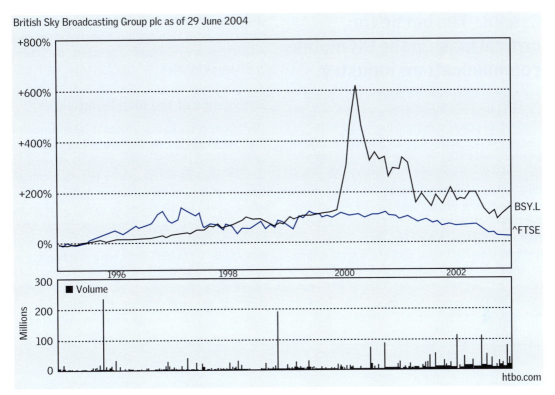

British Sky Broadcasting Group plc as of 29 June 2004

Exhibit 22 BSkyB share price performance

Source: *Yahoo! UK & Ireland Finance web site*, 28 June 2004, URL:http://uk.finance.yahoo.com/q?s=bsy.l&d=c>, Accessed 29 June 2004.

Case 18 The battle for critical mass in the UK mobile communications industry

The mobile communications industry is a fascinating case of interacting forces each working to retain a threshold of power over the future of the networks. The mobile telecommunications industry is a highly interconnected industry. It is interconnected with the competitors and with its customers on a long-term basis. Industry players in the mobile communications market moderate their strategic behaviour and opt for strategies that imply a form of complex adaptive behaviour. The common goal becomes the collective survival of the firms in order to eliminate the probability that one firm will prevail and the rest will fail. A set of isomorphic (copy-cat) strategies emerges at the level of technical standards, network platforms and the consumer platform. As a result market shares of competing firms become almost equal and network externalities are reconfigured to act for the benefit of the whole industry.

Emergence of the mobile networks

The UK subscriber base increased to 50 million users from 1985 to 2004. Most of the industry's growth occurred from 1999 to 2000 when 30 million subscribers joined the four networks. This represents an increase of 66% of the subscriber base in just two years, out of a total industry life span of 17 years, as seen in Figure 1. The industry's history has been through a period of duopoly and a period of increased competition. Up to 1993 there were only two operators, Cellnet[i] and Vodafone. The competitors were banned from selling directly to the public. A supply chain with an independent level of dealers and service providers sold mobile equipment and subscription

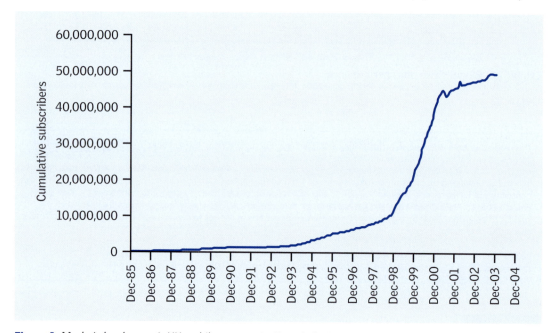

Figure 1 Market development: UK mobile communications industry

By Tanya Sammut-Bonnici

The material in this case is taken from original research conducted by the author at Warwick Business School under the supervision of John McGee.

© Tanya Sammut-Bonnici, 2004

[i] Cellnet later became 02 in November 2001.
[ii] One2One became T-Mobile in April 2002.

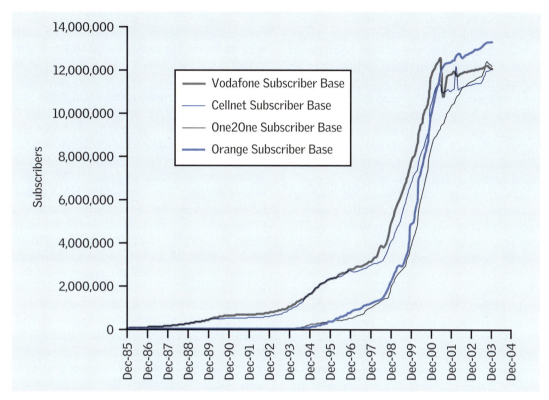

Figure 2 Industry network performance

airtime to consumers. One2One[ii] and Orange entered the market in 1993 and 1994 respectively.

The UK Government granted licences to Vodafone and Cellnet for the operation of mobile communications networks in 1983. Vodafone was initially owned by Racal Electronics and was later floated on the stock exchange as a separate company. Cellnet was 60% owned by British Telecom, and 40% by Securicor. The two companies launched their networks concurrently in 1985. Further licences were granted to One2One and Orange in 1993 and 1994 respectively. One2One, was originally owned by Mercury Personal Communications. Orange was created by the Microtel consortium led by British Aerospace, which was subsequently purchased by Hutchison Telecommunications. The industry started with analogue networks in 1985 and moved on to digital network in the 1990s. Vodafone and Cellnet switched on digital networks in 1992 and 1994. One2One and Orange entered the market with digital networks from their launch date.

Industry leadership

Figure 2 summarises the network size of the four MNOs from 1985 to date. Three out of the four MNOs held the position of the largest networks at different periods. Only One2One failed to attain the largest subscriber base at any point in its history. Cellnet, Vodafone, and Orange became industry leaders in 1985, 1986 and 2001 respectively.

Cellnet was the industry leader up to the third quarter of 1985. The company never regained the lead position but came close to having the same market share as Vodafone in 1996 and in 2001. The Cellnet story defeats the idea of 'first mover advantage', and the concept of a seed value[iii] from the innovations diffusion literature.

Cellnet started to relinquish market share to

[iii] The seed value, which is the initial size of a network, is thought to provide enough impetus for a network to grow at an increasing rate, outstripping competitors.

Racal-Vodafone[iv] in mid 1986. At that point, it had 32,000 subscribers, representing 54% of the UK mobile market. In just nine months, Cellnet made three price changes in fixed and variable rates. Its pricing structure was cheaper in the London areas, but more expensive in what were called the provincial areas. Growth in connections and traffic in the provincial areas was increasing in significance. Cellnet suffered because of real and perceived price differentials, and its miscalculation of growth potential of non-London territories.

In an effort to protect margins, Cellnet attempted to increase its connection and standing charges in April 1986. It withdrew them only four days after they had been introduced. The move followed the decision by the rival operator, Racal-Vodafone, to hold its prices steady and to increase the usage charge. Racal-Vodafone's increase was confined to the London area. Cellnet increased all its call charges at the beginning of this month. Racal, which had 27,000 customers at the time, said that its move was not designed to put pressure on Cellnet. Its mix of charges was intended to meet its target of another 35,000 customers over the next year, and that it decided to hold down connection and standing charges. These types of charges were viewed as the 'most emotive issues' for customers. Vodafone intended to act according to the psychological response of the consumer.

The fact that Cellnet cancelled its plans to increase prices meant that it would not meet its planned target to reach break-even point by 1987. The company, which was 60% owned by British Telecom, thought that the proposed increases would be reasonable, and that they would have been acceptable to the market. The results showed otherwise, and new customers drifted slowly towards Racal-Vodafone. In spite of the freeze in prices, Cellnet continued to lose market share. It claimed that the average customer would pay 6% less than under Racal, but it believed that customers perceived the Vodafone offering to be better. As a result, Cellnet was losing out in provincial areas where Racal's charges were cheaper. At that point in the industry's timeline, Vodafone was getting about 60% of its traffic from outside London, while Cellnet got 40–50%.

By January 1987, the pressure from customers increased and Cellnet was forced to introduce a new price structure. The move marked an attempt by Cellnet to win back market share from Racal, which had gained 53% of the UK's 114,000 subscribers. Cellnet announced a decrease in price of its basic cell phone by £450 to £899. However, the company lost its opportunity to gain a price differential in the eyes of its customers because Racal-Vodac followed suit the next day. Cellnet had started another price war. When sales were slow in August 1986, Cellnet brought the price of its cheapest unit below £1,000 for the first time. This move was the subject of a complaint to Oftel, but it did not lead to an investigation since Cellnet put its prices up again after six weeks. In May 1987, Cellnet instigated another price war against Vodafone with the announcement that new subscribers to its network would only pay half the subscription price for the first six months.

The competition battles were played through pricing strategies as well as advertising strategies. In May 1987, Cellnet unveiled a £5 million promotional drive, including a £1 million TV campaign through its agency Doyle Dane Bernbach. The campaign featured celebrities such as Joan Collins and Ian Botham. Vodafone rapidly took up battle in its fight with Cellnet for dominance in the UK mobile telephone market. It launched a £2 million TV campaign through Saatchi and Saatchi just two weeks after Cellnet's release. Interestingly Vodafone used its new campaign to push the other services it offered, besides the mobile telephone network. The move may have enhanced the image of Racal-Vodafone in terms of its size, reliability, experience in communications and its overall capability to build and sustain a mobile network. This drive to promote Racal-Vodafone's overall product offering was set to balance Cellnet's strong corporate image as a subsidiary of British Telecom.

Once Vodafone gained the position of the largest network in 1986 (Figure 3), Cellnet slipped into second place and remained there for the next twelve years. Orange challenged both Cellnet and Vodafone's positions in the year 2001 when it rapidly gained market share and became the largest mobile communications network. In July 2001 Vodafone's market share was seen to trail that of Cellnet and Orange. Vodafone slipped behind the two companies to become Britain's third largest mobile phone operator.

[iv] Racal and Vodafone demerged in September 1991.

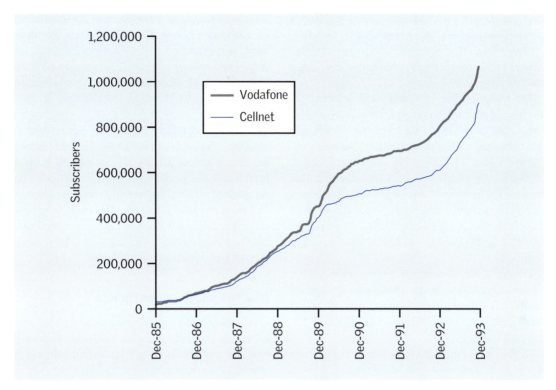

Figure 3 Cellnet and Vodafone network performance

Orange was the last operator to enter the industry yet it grew rapidly to become the largest network to date. Orange's story defies all notions of first mover advantage as it challenged One2One, Cellnet, and finally Vodafone in its race for the largest portion of market share. Orange overtook One2One in 1996. Its strategy to overtake competitors started prior to the date it switched on its network. Its main strategies were: to set off with a network which had a larger coverage than its closest competitor; to offer better handsets; to offer simplified pricing structures.

When Mercury launched One2One in September 1993, Hutchison was close to launching Orange. However, research had showed 50% coverage of the UK population to be the minimum level acceptable to customers. While Mercury had a strong proposition, with new phones and cheaper calls, its 30% coverage of the UK market was not enough to challenge large operators. After the launch of One2One both Vodafone and Cellnet initially resisted calls to cut

their prices. One2One felt the pressure to reduce its tariffs because it did not offer national coverage like its competitors. In view of the price cuts, Orange's launch was delayed further.

Hutchison felt that it was important to have a minimum of 50% coverage on entry into the UK market and to rapidly achieve over 90% coverage. An investment of £450 million was allocated for 1994 when the service was to reach 70% of the population. This commitment required considerable capital outlay by Hutchison, the owner of Orange. Commitment of capital outlay on this scale made the challenge of Orange to Vodafone and Cellnet of a different order to that of Mercury. It allowed Orange to take the process of change in the mobile telephone market forward, benefiting from the effect One2One had as an earlier catalyst of change.

The Orange network was attractive to consumers from the outset. Since it covered the main UK metropolitan areas and the connection motorways at launch, it immediately had a significant advantage over its closest rival One2One. From its launch period, Orange offered more benefits than One2One. Its Nokia handsets doubled as radio pagers, and had screens that could display voicemail and caller identification.

The target market for Orange was described by the head of product marketing Graeme Oxby as: 'Not those right at the top of the corporate market, but the remaining 90% of the populace.' Business customers were initially the principal target, predominantly middle managers and small business owners. The new target was largely ABC1 customers and predominantly younger age groups attracted by the possibilities of digital technology. Orange was to benefit from the larger population of the new target segment.

In July 2001, Orange's network grew to 3.4 million subscribers, which challenged Vodafone's position as industry leader. Orange was attracting more customers on both the subscription and the pre-paid tariffs.

At the beginning of 2002, Orange and Vodafone were in dispute over market leadership claims. Orange claimed a lead over Vodafone, while calling for the industry to use the same definitions for 'active' customers. Orange did not include 'inactive' users in its calculations and was pressing for a common, industry-wide definition of active customers. It said that if it used the industry's current definition of an active customer it could add another 656,000 users to its 12.4 million UK customer base. Graham Howe, Orange's deputy chief executive and finance director, said: 'I thought about using the industry definition but it just didn't make sense because you add in customers you know are inactive. I'm not saying the Orange definition is the perfect one but I think we need to get a group together to figure out what the industry definition should be.'

The debate saw the rise in popularity of a most important acronym in the mobile industry: average revenue per user ARPU. Operators in developed mobile markets were struggling to push up ARPU, even at the expense of growth in terms of subscriber numbers. Vodafone said it was still the UK's biggest mobile phone operator in terms of both revenue and profits and noted that the industry was now more focused on ARPU. Vodafone, which had

99.9 million customers worldwide in 2002, reported an ARPU of £274 in 2001. Orange, on the other hand, was reporting revenues alongside customer data. The company reported 2001 revenue up 25% at £8.3 billion. It added 8.8 million customers in that year, to take the total to 39.3 million, a 29% increase.

In the period under analysis there is no overall industry leader in the mobile communications industry. Vodafone is seen to have held the longest lead, from 1986 to 2001, yet Orange's meteoric rise is equally significant. The industry shows evidence of shifting patterns of leadership. This implies that the growth of MNOs is not a result of positive feedback from previous subscribers, but a result of other factors such as network externalities.

Market share convergence

Figure 4 provides an interesting picture of the trends in market share of Cellnet, Vodafone, One2One and Orange. Cellnet started out with a high market share, relinquishing it to Vodafone over a period of 2 years. Vodafone and Cellnet held their positions at a stable level, until the entry of One2One and Orange in 1993 and 1994. At that point the market share of the older companies diminished as the new companies rapidly increased their hold on the market.

Cellnet held the highest market share from the start of the industry up to August 1985. Vodafone held the longest lead, from 1985 to 2001. Orange's dramatic growth moved it to the top position in 2001. The change in industry leadership clearly shows that winner-takes-all strategies were not, or could not be, exploited in this industry.

At the time when Orange overtook Vodafone, Cellnet's subscriber base dropped for the first time ever. Cellnet's subscriber base fell by 268,000 in accounting terms over the quarter to settle at 10.9 million in July 2001. The operator also saw a decline of 20,000 in its post-paid base. This decline was due to a move towards a three-month accounting standard similar to Vodafone. At this point Cellnet started to count only those customers who had used the phone at any point in the last three months. The new accounting measure reduced the bias on over-inflation of subscriber figures.

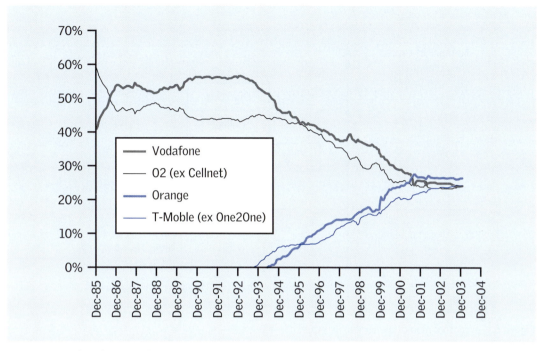

Figure 4 Market shares in the UK Mobile communications industry

Orange had the fastest growth rate in the industry. Orange saw its contract base increase by 222,000 net new customers to 3.4 million in the three months to the end of June, compared with 89,000 in the first quarter and with Vodafone's overall growth of 269,000. Orange, which allowed for 1 million inactive prepaid customers in its accounting, was outperforming Vodafone, even in the battle for more valuable postpaid customers.

Brand consistency

Figure 5 shows the number of times the companies changed ownership and brand names. It can be assumed that change in ownership does not have a direct effect on network growth. Orange underwent three ownership changes and it grew into the largest network. Vodafone had one change in ownership, when it separated from Racal and floated its stocks in 1991. Cellnet and One2One changed ownership twice. Orange was originally owned by Hutchison Whompoa and BAE, which shed its ownership

in 1998. Mannesmann bought Orange in 1999. Orange was bought out again by France Telecom in 2000, when Vodafone took over Mannesmann. Vodafone was the only network operator that was not bought out by third parties. Cellnet was originally owned by British Telecom and Securicor. It became wholly owned by British Telecom in 1999. Cellnet was demerged from British Telecom in the same year and floated on the stock exchange in 2001. One2One was originally owned by Cable and Wireless and US West Media Group. It was partly floated in 1997, and bought out by Deutsche Telekom in 1999.

From the four companies there is some indication that consistent branding can be linked to performance. Brand name consistency is the common characteristic of Orange and Vodafone, which have the highest brand equity in our research sample. They kept their brand name unchanged for the duration of their life span in mobile communications. Orange and Vodafone are almost equally successful. On the other hand, One2One was rebranded twice from Mercury One2One to One2One to T-Mobile.

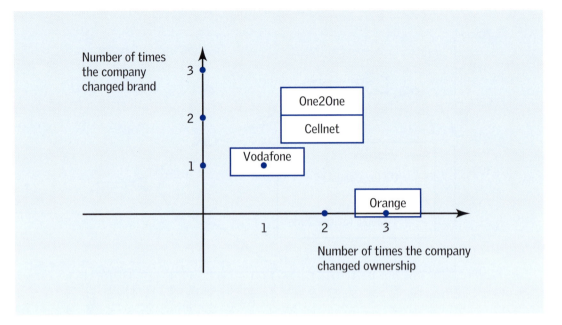

Figure 5 Perceptual map of ownership vs brand consistency

Cellnet was rebranded from BT Cellnet to Cellnet to 02.

Critical mass and market growth

In the early days of the mobile communications industry, the achievement of a critical mass was a clearly stated goal. Vodafone and Cellnet, the pioneers in the industry, invested substantially to set the 'watershed' of subscribers in motion. The industry was striving to gain enough subscribers to move into an area of the demand function where it would be easier to attain more subscribers. In its objectives, the industry was verbalising the characteristics of a positive feedback system to reach a hyperactive state of development. Figure 6 illustrates important turning points in the mobile industry's market development.

Critical mass may be evaluated in terms of inflection points on the demand function of mobile telephone subscribers. An inflection point occurs when the rate of change, or the gradient of the curve, changes in magnitude and direction. A typical diffusion of innovation curve has an S-shape with a first-order inflection and two second-order inflection points.[1]

♦ The first-order inflection point (Point B) occurs when the increase in the adoption rate is the fastest for the entire diffusion. By and large, the first-order inflection point occurs when 50% of the population has adopted the innovation.

♦ The two other second-order inflection points occur when the rate of adoption switches from a slow rate to a faster one, and vice versa. The standard deviation of subscribers, gives the values of the second-order inflection points before and after the first-order inflection point.

Inflection Point A (co-ordinates: 9.8 million subscribers, mid 1998) represents the most important turning point for the industry. The coefficient of determination for network externalities at that point was around 65%.[v] At the same time, important changes were taking place in pricing and

---

[v] The correlation between number of new customers and network size was R = 0.8. The coefficient of determination $R^2 = 0.65$ is a rough indication that 65% of the new subscriber data is attributed to network size. The value is a relative rule of thumb measure for the strength of network externalities.

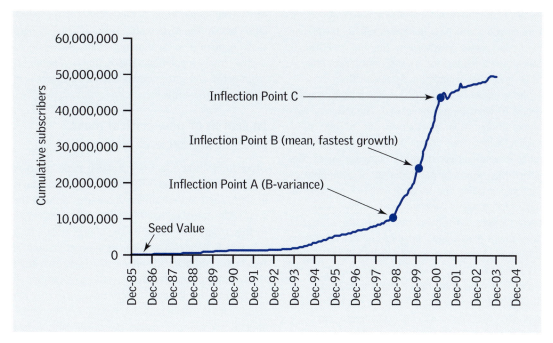

Figure 6 Inflection points

distribution policies, which were to transform the industry's landscape. The mobile phone networks started to sell handsets in supermarkets nationwide. Furthermore, pre-paid phone cards were introduced which addressed potential users' apprehension of the subscription system.

Critical mass acts on the adoption of the MNO platforms in a similar manner for all companies. The deviations in the occurrences of critical mass are limited to a maximum of eighteen months, notwithstanding that the second set of MNOs entered the market a decade after the first set. The individual MNO network size has a small effect on the date of attainment of critical mass. The dates registered for Point A, the lower second-order inflection point, are in the order of the network size: Vodafone being the largest followed by Cellnet, Orange and One2One. The lag in the dates, however, has no relationship to the date of entry. The lag in attainment of inflection points diminishes through Point B and Point C, as the networks grow similar in size and market shares converge.

The exponential rise in demand was combined with a rapid reduction in cost of sales effort

per subscriber. At Point A, the demand exceeds supply[vi] by a wide margin and the marketing strategies changed from a 'push' strategy to one of distribution efficiency. Prior to the critical mass point, the companies had aggressive direct sales forces which sold mobile telephones on a door-to-door basis. In 1999, both Vodafone and Cellnet changed their sales strategy significantly. Post critical mass, the sales forces were transformed to support high street and supermarket distributors, where most of the sales were occurring on a cash and carry basis.

Marketing practitioners can readily identify when inflection Point A has been reached, but mathematical models and statistical techniques are required to forecast the other two inflection points.

Inflection Point B (co-ordinates: 23.5 million subscribers, end 1999) was less apparent to marketers when it occurred. It showed a very small decline in the rate of increase of demand.

[vi] The demand exceeds supply only temporarily, because supply was increased as a response to demand.

However, in statistical terms it was a very important turning point, which could have predicted the arrival of the industry's downturn by the end of 2000. It takes the same increase in subscribers from Point A to B, as it takes from Point B to Point C.[2]

The occurrence of the first-order inflection point (Point B) went largely unnoticed. The industry was going through the spectacular rise of text messaging, which rose from 11 million to over 100 million messages per month in just one year.[3] The UK's SMS explosion is attributed to a number of factors, including the service's ease of use and its value for money. Another main factor was the breakthrough agreement on network interoperability, which was announced by the country's four operators at the beginning of April 1999.[4]

Furthermore, by the end of 1999, when the first signs of decline were noticeable, the industry was anticipating major upheaval with the impending government auctions of 3G licences and the announcement of Vodafone Airtouch's takeover of Mannesmann. The 3G auctions were to determine the future survival or lack thereof of Cellnet, Vodafone, One2One and Orange. The takeover was to affect two out of these network operators, as Mannesmann owned Orange at the time.

There was no reference to the small decrease in growth in a sample of 400 articles from industry publications and the general business media from November 1999 to October 2000. Even up to October 2000, just a few months prior to the slow down, the industry was still reporting signs of a growing market and record sales.

Inflection Point C (co-ordinates: 37.1 million subscribers, end 2000) marked the start of the decline in growth of the UK mobile communications industry. The demise was not apparent for over two years, when clear signs of saturation started to emerge. The decline in sales growth was picked up by the stock market. In May 2002, Vodafone shares closed below 100p, the lowest since February 1988. The weakness in mobile stocks spread across the sector. Analysts said investors were concerned about the short-term outlook for revenue growth, and the delays in bringing out commercial products and services related to GPRS and 3G.[5]

Another factor that affected the decline in the industry's growth was the population threshold at the current price level. A percentage of the population would never use mobile phones, which implies that the point of saturation occurs below the figure of the total population. The demand function is asymmetric and settles down faster at the later part of the industry's history.

In search of new critical mass – product life cycle extension

Other forces that affect demand will come into play in the future of the UK mobile communications industry, and indeed similar industries around the world. The actual demand function will be dislodged further from an S-shape, as the characteristic of a subscriber changes. These changes are attributed to two factors: first, mobile phone users may own more than one telephone. The mathematical calculation of the S-curve would thus have to be adjusted, as the figure for the total population is no longer the upper limit of the demand curve. The upper limit would shift above the population threshold. Second, the mobile phone industry will expand its product life cycle by promoting subscriptions on automated equipment, which will relay consumption information through a mobile connection. The industry would thus push out the population threshold even further, and extend its full potential to encompass individuals as well as machinery.

As the statistical total population for the industry is pushed beyond the national population, the total potential population becomes less finite and more extendable. For example, a household with two adults has the potential to provide the mobile industry with a minimum of two subscriptions. The same household could also provide a number of additional mobile subscriptions for energy and water meters, feedback channels for satellite television channels, and remote operation of domestic appliances. M-commerce, which is commerce conducted via mobile telephony, has the potential to boost the sales figures even further. Wireless shopping, travel information, ticketing, mapping, banking and trading are some of the applications that will see m-commerce revenues rise.

Copycat strategies

Isomorphism is a form of mimetic behaviour or strategic herding that is in vogue in some of the most dynamic industries of the new information economy. The copycat strategies between among Cellnet, Vodafone, One2One and Orange are a good example. Strategic isomorphism has strong appeal because of its risk reduction properties, which ensures the survival of more firms in the industry. However, there are some serious caveats. Industry profit margins are likely to decline, as shown in a study of the German mobile market.[6]

Deutsche Telekom's D1 and Mannesmann's D2 joined the incumbent C-Tel in 1992. Herding effectively removed divergence among the MNOs' services, tariffs and customer niches. When another MNO, E-Plus, emerged in 1994, it differentiated itself with pricing packages for low-volume private users, including students, families and senior citizens. Within a few months, the other networks copied E-Plus's strategy, destroying its brave effort to increase differentiation in the industry. Nattermann's (1999) analysis of the impact of such crowding shows that a 10% decline in the wireless industry's SDI[vii] resulted in an 11.2% decline in profit margins. Between 1992 and 1998 the SDI fell by 83%, taking margins down 50% from their maximum point. The reduction in strategic differentiation created by the incumbent operators was responsible for the lost earnings, which amounted to more than £495 million in 1998 alone. As strategic differentiation and margins decline, companies anxiously endeavour to reintroduce differentiation from competitors, typically by expensive brand enhancement campaigns and higher marketing spending.

A study by the Federal Reserve Bank in 2000 shows that the US personal-computer industry is another field which suffered a lowering in margins due to isomorphism.[viii] From 1976 to 1988 the PC industry's SDI went down by over 37% as companies copied the now dominant IBM-clone model. As a result of the decline, margins fell by 56%, representing £1.8 billion in destroyed margins by 1988. The increased herding effect in product design diminished 'brand' effects, which would have been developed over time from the firms' distinguishing characteristics. Brand effects, including such intangibles as reputation and image, are the drivers of price differentiation, which creates premium pricing margins. If isomorphism erodes distinctive brand characteristic, it will also erode the opportunity to charge for intangible factors.

Industry landscape and structure

The mobile communications industry can be divided into five interacting levels. Each of the levels in our framework has its own economic dynamics and each contributes to the overall network, with technology and regulation in the background (Figure 7).

Regulatory background

In the UK, mobile communications companies fall under the UK Wireless Telegraphy Acts 1948–1967 and the UK Telecommunications Act 1984. The Radio Communications Agency has the authority to grant licences under the Wireless Telegraphy Act. The Department of Trade and Industry is responsible for the sector under the Telecommunications Act. The Office of Communications (Ofcom) is responsible for the enforcement of the licences' issues.

The regulatory institutions' main concern was to encourage and preserve competition. In order to stimulate the growth of a new supply chain, Cellnet and Vodafone were not allowed to market their services directly to the consumer from 1985 to the mid 1990s. The direct sales restriction was lifted when the third and fourth licences came into operation. Orange and One2One were not subject to such restrictions as they were viewed to be at a disadvantage compared to earlier entrants.

The regulation of the UK MNOs has a balancing effect on how the mobile networks develop and on competition. Regulation is starting to match the demands of complex dynamic markets. Regulation is creating new forms of control that fall under the definition of self-organising systems. In this case the regulatory objective is to create self-correcting mechanisms that preserve competition. Although the original objective is maintained, the way of doing it is novel as the outcomes are not entirely predictable.

A classic example would be the 3G spectrum auctions in the UK and across the globe (see Figure 8).

---

vii Strategic Differentiation Index. See Nattermann (1999).[7]
viii The findings are summarised by Nattermann in *McKinsey Quarterly* (2000) Number 2, pp. 22–31.

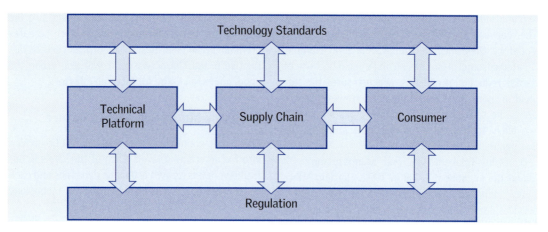

Figure 7 The multilevel dynamics of the mobile communications industry
Source: Sammut-Bonnici and McGee, 2002.[8]

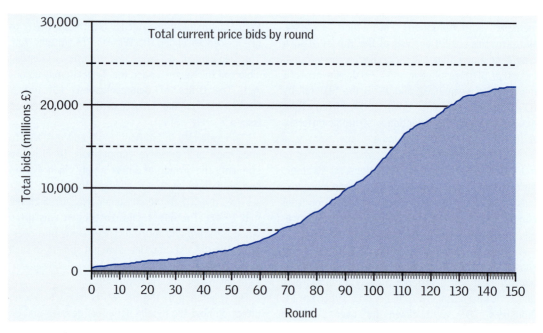

Figure 8 The UK 3G auctions
Source: DTI.

The auctions were designed to match the industry's predicted profitability of the introduction of a new generation of technology. The idea was that firms would bid to the maximum of the technology's feasibility. Thus governments found a way of introducing a licensing system that generated a self-correcting form of revenue, which gauged future profitability.

However, as with all complex systems, the outcome was unpredictable and other factors took hold of the system. The auctions were essentially a taxation procedure on an infant industry, and a key factor to allow MNOs to continue operating. Prospective MNOs faced the situation of having to bid for their future existence, or give up their operation once and for all. Thus the bidding did not stop at the profitability limits, but moved into the limits of what the companies could borrow from their banks. The mobile spectrum in Europe generated £200 billion, with Britain and Germany raising £22.5 and £60 billion respectively. The result was the depletion of cash flow, a delay in third-generation launches and uncertainty in the stock markets.

Another form of self-correcting regulation is the concept of 'market influence' inbuilt into the licence agreements of the MNOs. The definition set in the Telecommunications Act licences implies that MNOs should not exploit price inelasticity that may arise for the demand-side of the market. Market influence behaves as a self-regulatory measure whereby MNOs keep their market strength in check, in order to preserve their licence agreements. As competition in the industry grew, the need for market influence mechanisms diminished and this form of regulatory control was reduced substantially throughout Europe.

Technology standards

Mobile communications technology has evolved along a logical path, from the simple first-generation analogue products designed for business use to second-generation digital wireless telecommunications systems being used in B2B, B2C and C2C markets.

TACS (Total Access Communication System) and ETACS (the extended version) formed the first generation of mobile systems in Europe. The GSM (Global System for Mobile) standard is the second generation of mobile communication systems in Europe, supporting digital voice telephony, SMS text messaging and, more recently WAP and GPRS. Throughout the 1990s, every country in Europe implemented cellular networks based on the GSM specification.

Third-generation (3G) technologies are coming in two versions: CDMA2000 and WCDMA. The technology promises the introduction of video over and above what is already provided by second-generation technologies: images, Internet, voice and data services. Japan was the first to launch 3G in October 2001. The UK followed in 2003. Europe and the US are following slowly. The launch of 3G has been delayed by major regulatory, technical and commercial barriers. This uncertainty about 3G occurred at a time when GSM penetration was approaching saturation in many European countries and when regulators were increasing pressure on operators to reduce excessive profits.

The licence for CDMA technology worldwide is owned by Qualcom. The company is facing an exceptional situation. Every operator in the word that uses 3G technology will have to pay licence fees to Qualcom. (As the names of the standards imply, both CDMA2000 in the US and WCDMA in Europe and Asia use CDMA technology.)

The telecommunications standards we have today are a product of protracted market strife. Mobile technology has become widespread and practical only after going through a period of struggle between competing standards. The process is reminiscent of VHS vs Betamax, and Microsoft vs everyone else. As the wireless industry moves into 3G, it is going through the same arduous process.

The mobile telecommunications industry has also experienced hybrid standard setting. This type of standardisation emerges as private firms adopt strategies to undercut collaborative decisions taken in negotiated standardisation. They introduce new products which not only initiate unprecedented developments, but also create incompatibilities, lock-in effects and pockets of market power. Mobile Internet is a typical example, where companies, standards organisations and governments create a hybrid standard setting environment.[9]

Standards organisations are playing an increasingly important role in the strategy for versioning standards. The GSM Association is guiding the evolution of the mobile industry through a family of wireless technology standards from today's standard through to GPRS (General Packet Radio Service), EDGE (Enhanced Data Rated of GSM Evolution) and 3GSM. Each subsequent standard offers a higher level of service. GPRS provides open Internet. EDGE facilitates faster data streaming, and 3GSM will provide video streaming.

Switching costs are minimised when standards are designed to evolve from one another. The introduction of revolutionary standards would be costly. The pay-off is superior performance against the high cost of switching standards. The example is the price paid by mobile telephone operators to switch to third-generation licences. Mobile spectrum auctions earned European governments £200 billion. The mobile operators had to bid. To renounce third-generation spectrum was to sign their own death warrant. The outcome of these auctions left mobile operators no option but to increase debt to survive. The result was the depletion of cash flow, a delay in third-generation launches and uncertainty in the stock markets.

Physical platforms

Physical platforms in mobile communications are the technical networks connecting mobile phones, base stations, mobile exchanges and landline exchanges. The system extends from a national to an international level. Telecommunications platforms have had to cope with the complexity of interoperability among different systems, and to master the agility required to shift rapidly to newer standards.

Interoperability As in the supply chain case discussed earlier, companies divided their platform structure into separate modules, each with some degree of autonomy.[10] Each module is designed with the flexibility for rapid change, such as the shift from ETACS to GSM. The complexity feature is retained because each module is interoperable with other modules to form a weblike complex system. The modules are therefore interdependent through the nodes, or joints between the modules. Interoperability between modules creates value for the user, as we observe in the ability to call overseas on a mobile telephone. Roaming of mobile telephones from country to country is another example.

Interoperability exists between platforms of different MNOs[ix] in the same country, or different platforms in different countries. Physical platforms have evolved from the simple structures, such as the older regional railway system, to a complex structure of interconnected sub-platforms.

For this reason, the joints between the sub-networks become the strength of the whole structure, or conversely it could be its Achilles heel. It is therefore vital to define standards for joints. The

standards that govern how a system and its modules interact are called the network's architecture (Morris and Ferguson, 1993).[11] Henderson and Clark (1990)[12] review two kinds of dynamic processes in modular systems: modular innovation and architectural innovation.

The former type retains the architecture of the network including its joints, but modifies the modules. By preserving the basic architecture of a system, MNOs offer users enough compatibility to shift from one product generation to the next. The changes occur in the innovations and improvements of the modular components. They are fitted into the system when required, and will be removed when obsolete. The result is a hybrid dynamic of change that preserved the platform's architecture, while creating innovations within the module structure. A series of minor incremental modular changes can lead to an overall network platform that is radically new.

Capacity

A further aspect of network platforms concerns communication capacity and its expansion over time. Valletti and Cave (1998, p. 112)[13] make some observations on how this is addressed in the UK industry:

On the one hand, there is the obvious investment decision of firms. As more cells are added, more subscribers can be supported by a network. Such a decision can be made by a firm on the ground of the optimal choice of coverage and capacity of its network. However, the choice is constrained by the regulatory requirement of 90% of the population being served by a certain date, assuming that there are no regulatory flaws. On the other hand, capacity has also increased over time, for technological reasons. Continuous improvements have allowed for a more efficient use of the existing spectrum so that more people can be handled by the same number of base stations. Finally, and equally importantly, the Government can decide to release significant amounts of additional radio spectrum for the mobile communications sectors.

Telecommunications networks fall under an 'integrative class' of complex networks, because of their tendency to integrate information from a large

---

[ix] Vodafone, Cellnet, Orange and One2One are mobile network operators (MNOs).

number of sources. Other networks that form part of this class are air traffic control and management systems, military command and control systems and electricity network sharing. The integrative class is characterised by: a large number of diverse information sources; the need to interoperate and integrate both equipment and information; the need to detect events in a complex network of connections; the need to operate across techno-socio barriers; and the need to operate as an open system which includes interoperability, portability, scalability; and the need to evolve.

The interconnectivity in mobile communications hinges on two important factors: the interconnections in the networks and the sharing of call revenue. The original objective of operating an open platform determined the survival of all the competing mobile platforms, which could evolve from one generation of transmission standards to the next in a concerted effort. Call revenue sharing ensured that the interconnectivity was kept at a high level of reliability across all the networks, in order to preserve revenue streams.

Interconnectivity in the information economy leads to the concept of 'co-evolution'. Evolving to meet the needs of other members in the value chain is becoming a more effective strategy than satisfying the company's own needs. Adapting to meet other companies' need leads to more business. Riding the new wave of co-evolution, companies are avoiding costly races against each other, in favour of a strategy to joining forces to gain more customers. We are observing this effect in NEC and Siemens, which have joined forces to supply the networks for Hutchison 3G, which will be a key network provider for third-generation telecommunications in Europe.

Co-evolution and collaboration are even more relevant in industries where network externalities are a vital part of corporate success. The more customers join a network, such as a telecommunications service, the higher is the incentive for other customers to join. This effect is causing companies to collaborate on issues of compatibility. With 3G mobile phones on the horizon for Europe and the US, the standards war for a mobile Internet operating system has begun. Microsoft, Linux, Symbian and Openwave are in the race to establish a widely accepted standard. This is an example of old-style competition, but it has caused a wave of co-evolution in another layer of competitors.

The issue of standards has motivated Nokia and Siemens, Europe's largest manufacturers of mobile phones, to collaborate. They have teamed up to accelerate the introduction of third-generation mobile services. The collaboration of the companies will guarantee that Nokia and Siemens handsets can communicate with each other seamlessly. In this way the two companies, which have a combined global market share of 45%, will benefit from network externalities and the positive feedback generated from a larger compatible technology platform. Nokia and Siemens anticipate that other equipment vendors will link up with them to minimise industry fragmentation.[14]

Image phones gave the Japanese market a boost similar to when DoCoMo introduced I-Mode wireless web service. DoCoMo, which had planned to concentrate on the introduction of 3G system with video capabilities, still bolstered its line of second-generation phones with a camera phone called the I-shot. DoCoMo President Keiji Tachikawa said: 'we recognise there is strong demand for cellular phones with cameras, so we will increase the number of current-generation camera models.' Companies saw their revenue from basic voice phone services decline, while sales of those equipped with cameras and related services were bringing in more money. The new models were reinvigorating a market that was becoming sluggish.

In Figure 12 the x and y-axes are normalised to reflect the penetration of the population by the UK and the Japanese mobile networks. The S-shape pattern of diffusion remains largely similar. This time UK's superior population diffusion rates are seen to be much higher than Japan's, although the comparison is not entirely on the same level as larger populations would have different economic demographics.

Japan was one of the first countries in the world to introduce the 3G standard, almost two years before it appeared in Europe. DoCoMo led the world in starting 3G services in October 2001, followed by KDDI in April 2002, and J-Phone in December 2002, so all three have a 3G presence. The European market gradually saw 3G services coming online in 2003 and 2004.

Supply chain

The mobile communications industry occupies an important position in the information economy. The structure is built on layers of communication network companies, hardware and software manufacturers, Internet service providers, e-commerce transaction companies, media and content companies, and myriad service companies (Figure 9).

The network infrastructure suppliers are companies such as Alcatel, Nortel Networks, Motorola and Ericsson that provide communications networking equipment. Intel and 3Com form a subset of companies in this category, which supply interfacing hardware and software.

The network operators provide the basis of the exchange of information between companies and

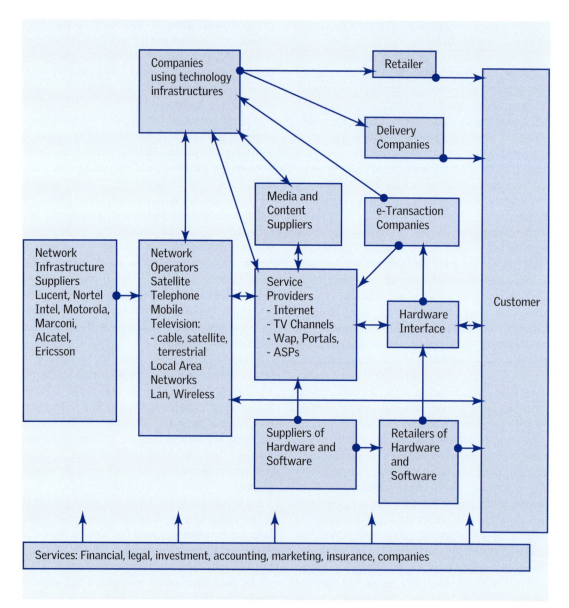

Figure 9 Mobile communication industry in the information economy

their customers. The medium they operate could be based on satellite, telephone, mobile, television or area networks. British Telecom, AT&T, Vodafone and T-Mobile offer landline and mobile telecommunications networks. The operation of these companies is interconnected with other companies. For example, Vodafone uses BT's network. Credit card companies use Vodafone's mobile network for offsite credit verification. Vodafone has sold fixed-line telephone services from Energis and Racal Telecom networks. The interoperability of different telecom networks has become a complex business operation.

The 3G telephone, which will become the new customer interface, would dictate a change in Internet transmission management and the nature of media content, all the way down the supply chain. The supply chain in the information economy shown in Figure 9 takes the form of a weblike network where each member may have to collaborate with all the other members. Inter-collaboration is necessary partly because of software and hardware compatibility. An example of this weblike structure is the relationship between e-transaction companies, ISPs, media content providers, and the companies that own the web pages.

The nature of the supply chain of the UK mobile communications industry changed dramatically as the network operators became more powerful.

When the UK mobile licences were granted, Cellnet and Vodafone were not allowed to sell direct to the customer. The regulators posed this restriction to create two tiers of firms in the industry that would balance each other's power. The first tier was the network operators (Cellnet and Vodafone) that were to have an engineering orientation and would focus on the technical platform. The second tier of firms consisted of distributors and service providers, which would market the product to the public. In spite of the regulators' intention to equalise power in the supply chain, the network operators grew more and more powerful. They progressed to the top of a hierarchical distribution pyramid in just a few years, through a deliberate strategy of controlling the supply chain population. This was achieved through the three stages described below.

1   Buyouts and mergers of distributors and service providers: By reducing or freezing prices,

Vodafone and Cellnet eroded the margins of hardware retailers. Survival of distributors and service providers became a direct function of market share. The larger companies were able to stay in business while the smaller ones were forced to merge or to sell-out. In the late 1980s we see the takeovers of National Radiophone, Advanced Car Telephone, and the sale of 40% in Air Call. Takeovers continued through the 1990s. The service provider arm of Robert Bosch, Hi-Time, MCP, and Excell were the next companies to be bought out of the supply chain, by competitors in their own tier.

2   Acquisition of suppliers by Vodafone and Cellnet: In the mid 1990s, acquisitions changed in nature. This time the MNOs started to buy into the supplier tier, further strengthening their power in the supply chain. Vodafone bought Hawthorn Leslie and Peoples Phones. It acquired shares in Astec Communications, Martin Dawes, and Talkland. By the end of 1996, Vodafone had direct control of 70% of the customers connected to its network. Cellnet joined the acquisitions game in the late 1990s. In 1997, it bought shares in The Link and acquired Martin Dawes, and DX Communications in 1999. It bought the Mobile Phone Store in 2000.

3   Supply chain control strategies: In the history of mobile communications, we see repeated evidence of the mobile operators determining the prices of phones and tariffs, even though the regulator intended that service providers would have some market power.

In 1992, the Federation of Communications Services (FCS), the mobile communications industry criticised Vodafone for quoting prices in its advertising. At the time, Vodafone was not allowed to sell its service direct to the customer. Oftel issued a report on unfair practices by Vodafone and Cellnet against independent providers. The companies were cross-subsidised by BT Mobile Communications, Securicor Cellular Services and Vodac, which were daughter companies. The regulator concluded that cross-subsidies were in contravention of the Cellnet and Vodafone licences.

Over the years, in spite of Oftel's efforts to moderate market power, the market share of the

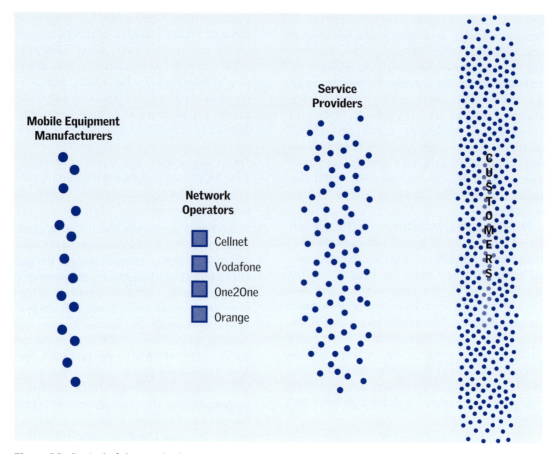

Figure 10 Control of the supply chain

independent cellular service suppliers continued to diminish. By 1996, the network operators owned 10 service providers that captured 77.5% of the market.

A determining factor of the power of the network operators was that they controlled the bottleneck of the supply chain (Figure 10). The number of network operators that could enter the market was determined by government licences and limited to four firms. On the other hand, the suppliers to the left and the right of the network operators in the figure operate in a competitive market with no controls on entry and exit.

Consumer networks

The consumer network is the final level of interacting dynamics in the mobile communications industry. The behaviour of consumers is affected by regulation (choice and pricing), technology standards (service offering), physical platforms (reliability) and the supply chain (retail access). Nonetheless, the consumer network exhibits strong characteristics of its own, such as network externalities.[x] Consumers affect each other's buying behaviour in a positive feedback loop, resulting in critical mass effects and exponential growth.

Network externalities are a powerful force in the

---

[x] Network externalities are observed in products where the possession of a product by one consumer affects the value of product for some other consumer. Telecommunications is a classic example where the value of the telephone for any individual depends on the number of colleagues, friends and relatives in possession of a telephone.

UK mobile communications industry. The correlation between number of new customers and network size was R = 0.8. The coefficient of determination R^2 = 0.65 is a rough indication that 65% of the new subscriber data is attributed to network size. The value is a relative rule of thumb measure for the strength of network externalities.

Network externalities affect the individual firms from the industry's total installed base and not the individual network platforms. This is the main difference between competing platforms that are independent (VHS and Betamax) and communications platforms that are typically interconnected (telecommunications). This effect shows us how and why market shares converge in the presence of strong network externalities and how market shares become similar for the four companies over the long run.

The increase in subscribers is interdependent with the utility of the whole network as well as with the utility of competing networks. The utility of other networks has a similar stronger effect on new subscribers to a company's own utility. Thus we can start to understand why market shares converge even in the presence of strong network externalities.

Comparison of UK and Japanese market development

The model of development for the UK mobile market is replicable in other environments. The UK's demand curve exhibits the characteristics of an S curve with a mixed influence model of diffusion. The diffusion of the product is determined by external and internal influences. The external influences are derived from the demand side characterised by network externalities and critical mass. Internal influences in the UK market are marketing effects determined by product, price, distribution and promotion policies.

The internal and external influences are present in mobile industries around the world. Network interconnectivity, technology and regulation are experienced to varying degrees in all countries. As a consequence marketing strategies are similar to the UK scenario, and internal influences on consumer demand are also similar. External influences, largely driven by network externalities, are a mathematical function of network adoption and operate irrespective of geographical location.

Japan's population is 122 million, just over double that of the UK. The market for mobile phones in its current state is nearly saturated, as in the UK industry. There are still possibilities for growth in automated mobile commerce, and in the new 3G technology that will allow video transmission. With 60% of the Japanese population (around 73 million subscribers) using mobile phones by 2003, companies can no longer expect rapid growth of the overall market. Towards the end of our data collection period, competition had started to show signs of recovery with the introduction of 3G.

The main difference between the UK and the Japanese diffusion processes is that Japan's industry started in 1980, five years earlier, and that 3G was introduced in 2001 two years earlier than the UK. We shall discuss the implications of these differences and whether they affect the similarity in the diffusion processes of the two countries. Figure 11 illustrates the UK and Japan adoption curves, normalised by the number of years of operation of the industry.

In the figure we see the UK and Japanese diffusion functions following an S curve shape, typical of mixed influence models of diffusion. Interestingly critical mass is reached at the same period within thirteen years from the date of introduction of the mobile industry. Although this means that Japan approached critical mass in 1993, five years before the UK, it is striking that the market dynamics retained the same time frame to move into exponential growth.

While the two countries' diffusion models are similar in their general trend and nature, earlier technological adoption on the part of the Japanese introduces interesting differences. While Europe and the US were experiencing a downturn in sales in 2000, Japan's market was undergoing an upturn. The growth in e-mail photo services started with J-Phone's launch in November 2000 of its Sha-mail model. KDDI followed in April 2001, followed by NTT DoCoMo in June 2001. Image telephones were so fashionable during the year that demand exceeded supply. The demand for the phones even outstripped the production of digital cameras. The industry sold 15 million camera phones by the end of 2002. Figure 12 illustrates the UK and Japan adoption curves, normalised by the number of years in operation and penetration.

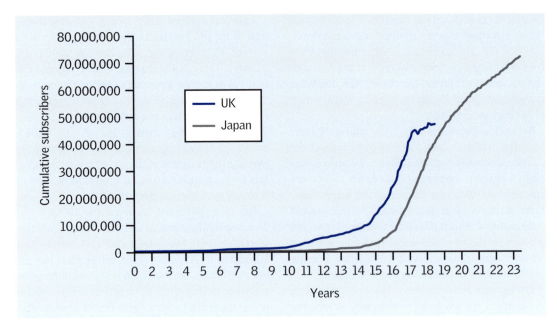

Figure 11 UK and Japan adoption curves – normalised by years in operation

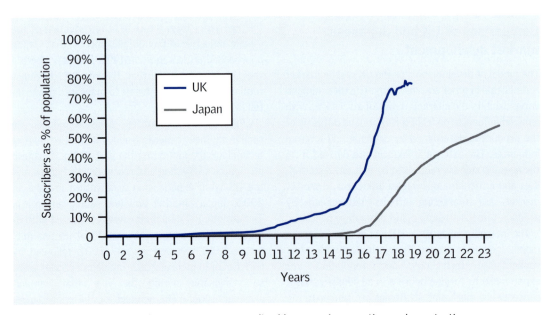

Figure 12 UK and Japan adoption curves – normalised by years in operation and penetration

The future of the mobile communications industry

The future of mobile telephony lies beyond picture and video transmission promised by third-generation technology. It will depend on the development of technical capability that generates a personal transaction environment that supports identity and payment.

Digital money transacted through electronic cash payments and billing will have a revolutionary impact on the industry. The industry is moving towards multi-application SIM cards integrated with network services. The technology opens up opportunities for non-telecom applications whereby a mobile phone would act as a bank payment card. New technologies will sustain electronic identity through public key infrastructure (PKI) and biometrics. Identification of users will be integral to ordering and paying through a mobile phone. Data transmission of wireless will increase dramatically and information exchange protocols such as XML are expected to evolve accordingly.

Voice recognition and synthesis technologies are expected to create the next wave of usage in mobile communications. The lack of space for a keyboard on a mobile handset has limited its range of use. Voice recognition would open up new possibilities for the mobile industry as the capability of a mobile phone moves closer to that of a personal computer. The impact of voice technologies is expected to increase mobile usage dramatically, as it opens the channels for people to speak directly to machines, without a keyboard interface.

Mobile network operators, such as Vodafone, T-Mobile, O2 and Orange, will need to adapt as they move from a model based on the economics of utilities to a model that is rooted in the wireless economy.

Strategic challenges

The challenge for future mobile phone products and services lies in the significance of interdependence between consumers and networks. Network externalities need to be addressed directly rather than tacitly as the evolution from one technological generation to another will follow in rapid success. New products face the challenge of having to replace older platforms. Each new product faces the gradual climb towards critical mass, a period of exponential growth and the limitation of market size. The strategies to be adopted are wide and varied. Should the strategy of open platforms be retained? When is the best time for a network operator to introduce a new service? What is the role of innovation and process efficiency in the quest for new subscribers? Would the current copycat strategies lead to a reduction in innovation, or would the equipment providers balance out this factor?

References

1   Valente, T (1995) *Network Models of the Diffusion of Innovations*, Hampton, VA: Hampton Press Communication Series.
2   Valente, ibid p. 9.
3   *Mobile Communications*, Nov 11, 1999.
4   *Mobile Communications*, 261/3.
5   *Financial Times*, May 4, 2002
6   Nattermann, PM (2000) 'The German Cellular Market: A Case of Involuntary Competition?' *McKinsey Quarterly*, 2, pp. 22–31.
7   Nattermann, PM (1999) 'The German Cellular Market: A Case of Involuntary Competition?' *McKinsey Quarterly*, 1(4) August.
8   Sammut-Bonnici T. and McGee I (2002) 'Emerging Strategies for New Industry Structures', *European Business Journal*, December pp. 174–185.
9   Vercoulen, F and Wegberg, M (1998) 'Standard Selection Modes in Dynamic, Complex Industries: Creating Hybrids Between Market Selection and Negotiated Selection of Standards', Maastricht: Nibor Working Paper, Nib98006.
10 Langlois, RN and Robertson, PL (1992) 'Networks and Innovation in A Modular System: Lessons from the Microcomputer and Stereo Component Industries', *Research Policy*, 21(4), pp. 297–313.
11 Morris, CR and Ferguson, CH (1993) 'How Architecture Wins Technology Wars', *Harvard Business Review*, 71(2), pp. 86–96.
12 Henderson, RM and Clark (KB) (1990) 'Architectural Innovation: The Reconfiguration of Existing Product Technologies and the Failure of Established Firms', *Administrative Science Quarterly*, 35, pp. 9–30.
13 Valetti, TM and Cave M (1998) 'Competition in UK Mobile Communications', *Telecommunications Policy*, 22, pp. 109–131.
14 Sammut-Bonnici, T and Wensley, R (2002) 'Darwinism, Probability and Complexity – Transformation and Change Explained through the Theories of Evolution,' *International Journal of Management Reviews*, 4, pp. 291–315.

WARWICK
BUSINESS SCHOOL

Case 19 The low-cost airline industry in Europe

After 31 years and several economic downturns, Southwest continues to validate its founding philosophy: maintaining permanent low-costs as a basis for permanently low fares is the only way to run a permanently profitable airline. Air Transport World, 22nd July 2002

History

The European low-cost airlines copied the format from Southwest Airlines, based in Texas. After 31 years of operations, Southwest has proved that the business model is sustainable. In 2003 Southwest's pre-tax profits of $483 million were more than all the other US airlines combined. In the same year American Airlines (the worlds largest carrier) posted a loss of $1.2 billion, while another of the US major carriers – Delta – lost $773 million Furthermore, in May of the same year Southwest boarded 6.54 million domestic passengers, which was more than Delta (6.34 million) and American Airlines (6.22 million). For the first time in aviation history a low-cost airline was the market leader.

Southwest offers a low-fare, high-frequency, point-to-point no-frills service that is in marked contrast to the established market offering from the US major carriers that provide a hub-based network (meaning that customers will often fly via an intermediate point in order to reach their destination), which incurs greater costs and results in higher fares for passengers. The relative success can be seen through Southwest's financial results (see Appendix 1 for a full details), the year-end results for 2003 marked Southwest's 31st consecutive year of profitability. During the same year, United Airlines lost $47 on every passenger that boarded one of its aircraft. In the USA the low-cost airlines now account for 32% of all domestic passenger traffic, and JP

Morgan's market forecasts show this could reach 40% by 2006.[1]

Considering the financial success of Southwest, it comes as little surprise that the majors are fighting back with a low-cost formula of their own. Early in 2004 both United Airlines and Delta Airlines started to operate with a low-cost subsidiary airline. Delta's discount airline is branded separately as 'Song', United's as 'Ted'. The perennial problem for the majors operating offshoot airlines is the ability to reduce their cost base to competitive levels. Often the subsidiary will be penalized by legacy contracts in place at the parent company (for example with the unions or suppliers). Moreover, segmenting the market between the full service and low-frills service offerings is complex. This makes the sustainability of dual operations extremely difficult to achieve in the long term.

The market is also attracting a new breed of airline that has many characteristics of the low-cost model, including point-to-point services and single aircraft type but with superior in-flight service. JetBlue, which started operations in 2000, is the leader of this group, having worked hard to reduce their operating costs to 7 cents per mile, which is 0.5 cents less than Southwest.[2] To date, however, JetBlue has studiously avoided head-to-head competition with Southwest and consequently downward pressure on yields for both airlines has not occurred. Notwithstanding, JetBlue harbours ambitious expansion plans (intending to spend $7 billion to take the fleet size to 290 by 2011), so ultimately direct competition in an overcrowded market is likely to occur.

The key attributes of Southwest's success

Southwest was the first airline to consider going back-to-basics with air travel. It determined that a basic product offering could strip away unnecessary operating expenses. First to be discarded was the assignment of seats and the provision of in-flight meals. Not only did this save on catering and cleaning costs, but it also allowed for an alternative cabin configuration that eliminated the on-board galley, thus freeing up space for more seats to generate more revenue.

Stephen Hodge prepared this case under the supervision of John McGee as a basis for class discussion rather than to illustrate either effective or ineffective handling of a business situation.

---

[1] 'Trouble in low fare land', *Wall Street Journal*, 13 February 2004.

[2] *Smart Money*, June 2002, pp. 102–106.

Operational efficiency is achieved via the utilization of a single aircraft type (Southwest started with three B737s in 1971; at the end of 2003 it operated 398). This simplifies scheduling and flight operations, reduces maintenance cost by decreasing spare parts inventory and rationalizes training of both engineers and crew. Another critical benefit of operating a single aircraft type is the potential to negotiate favourable terms with the aircraft manufacturers; Southwest was the launch customer for three versions of the B737 – the 300, 500 and 700 series. Moreover, Southwest quickly realized that aircraft make no money when they are sitting on the ground, so it pioneered the concept of a quick turnaround. The average amount of time spent at the gate is 20 minutes. For an industry characterized by high fixed cost high asset utilization is the key to success; by reducing the time aircraft spend on the ground Southwest are able to offer more services with fewer aircraft – Southwest's fleet of B737s are in the air 11.09 hours per day, more than any other major airline.[3]

Further efficiency is achieved through employee productivity. The US airline industry has a long history of having poor labour relations. However, Southwest's employees, which are non-unionized, are considered an integral part of their success; the pilots fly 80 hours per month in comparison to 50 hours at United Airlines, while flight attendants work 150 hours per month compared to 80 hours at many rival airlines. Herb Kelleher, Southwest's charismatic founder, is quoted as saying, 'We are not a company of planes; we are company of people'.[4] By placing staff at the centre of the business Southwest is able to find employees willing to complete multiple tasks, for example flight attendants assist with the aircraft cabin cleaning, enabling the quick turnaround. Although the Southwest employees work longer and smarter they are still employed by one of the top 10 businesses to work for in the US, as recognized by *Fortune* magazine.[5]

Employee productivity has been achieved without sacrificing service to customers; in 2002, the *Wall Street Journal* ranked Southwest first among airlines for customer satisfaction, according to a survey by the American Customer Satisfaction Index. The unique culture instilled by Herb Kelleher has had a large part to play in the employee and customer relations. 'If the employees are happy, satisfied, dedicated, and energetic, they'll take good care of the customers. When the customers are happy, they come back. And that makes the shareholders happy.'[6] From the beginning, the employees of Southwest Airlines created a family atmosphere that fostered creativity, independence and friendliness between employees. As Southwest grew larger it interviewed the top employees in each job function; this enabled them to identify their common strengths and create 'job profiles'. These profiles were then used for training and development of existing employees. Furthermore, consistency in new recruits was maintained by the instigation of peer interviews – pilots hired pilots, and gate agents hired gate agents

Another key facet of Southwest's business model is to operate from secondary airports. Not only are these less congested, thus preserving the quick aircraft turnaround time, but they also offer convenience to passengers with locations closer to city centres than principal hub airports (e.g. Houston Hobby, Chicago Midway). By avoiding the major hub airports Southwest are able to select markets which are underserved in terms of frequency and have high fares. The strategy of choosing to compete in these markets means that Southwest avoids head-to-head competition with other low-fare airlines, instead choosing to attack the domain of the major carriers. Consequently it is common for fares to drop by much as 70% once Southwest enters the market. This strategy has proved to be so successful that Southwest has a 69% market share on their top 100 city-pair markets.[7]

Deregulation of the European airline industry

One of the catalysts for Southwest's growth was the deregulation of the US domestic market for air travel in 1978. Within Europe complete liberalization of the air transport industry was not completed until 1993. Until this time the industry was highly regulated, mostly because of the protectionism offered by countries whose objective was to promote their

[3] Southwest Annual Report, 2003.
[4] Southwest Annual Report, 2003.
[5] Southwest Annual Report, 2003.

[6] Jon Magratta, *What Management is: How it works and why it's everyone's business*, The Free Press, 2002, p. 199.
[7] Southwest Annual Report, 2002.

own national carriers. The industry was characterized by government interference, over capacity, poor management, large-scale losses and state aid. The effect of liberalization was to reduce the barriers to entry for new airlines and open up routes for competition. Prior to liberalization, most routes within Europe were operated solely by the (mostly state-owned) national flag carriers. As a result, competition was limited and consumers had little choice except to pay high fares. However, in spite of there being a highly regulated market most nationalized airlines contrived to mount up large losses, often requiring national government subsidies in order to maintain the prestige associated with airline operations. Paradoxically the liberalization of European air transport services initially increased the level of state aid for European airlines as they undertook massive restructuring programmes in order to become more competitive in the future. SAS – the Scandinavian-based airline – reported that European airlines were granted $12.5 billion during the period 1991–1997.[8] See Appendix 2 for a full breakdown.

In theory, liberalization allowed EU-based airlines to operate on routes between member states but, in practice, this proved difficult to execute; in order to fly between two points an airline needs take-off and landing permission (known as a slot) from the relevant airport authorities. For historical reasons the national flag carriers control a large percentage of the slots at the principal hub airports of London Heathrow, Paris Charles De Gaulle and Frankfurt, thus creating a barrier to entry. Increasingly, the flag carriers are realizing the value of these slots and a grey market in slot trading has now opened up – in 2003 BA paid SN Brussels (the airline created from the bankruptcy of Sabena) £30 million for eight daily slot pairs.[9]

The low-cost airlines have been attracted by new market opportunities away from these principal airports. However, most ventures have proved to be short-lived. Of the 80 carriers that began operations after 1992, 60 were bankrupt by 1996.[10] Of the starts-ups born in the 1990s two airlines have successfully exploited market opportunities: Ryanair and easyJet. Although deregulation reduced the barriers to entry, a review of low-cost airline industry over the past few years indicates that a good deal more than access to financial capital and a couple of leased B737s is required in order to set up a profitable airline. Excluding Ryanair and easyJet, the European low-cost segment accumulated losses of almost $300 million between 1996 and 2001.[11] Casualties of these losses included Debonair, AB Airlines and ColorAir. easyJet and Ryanair have also seen off potential competitors through acquisition (easyJet purchased GO in 2002, while Ryanair acquired Buzz), and between them they account for 88%[12] of the scheduled low-cost market in Europe. Considering that Southwest Airlines has a market share of 50% of the US low-cost market, the advantage of entering the market early, building brand recognition and establishing a route network is clear. Later entrants have difficulty in matching the cost base, providing sufficiently low fares and building up traffic. Although the low-cost airlines now account for 7% of intra-European air travel as measured by the number of passengers flown, many forecasts predict that penetration rates have the potential to reach 25%.[13] The winners in capturing this growth will be, as per Southwest's model, those with the greatest cost advantage.

Ryanair

We want to be the Wal-Mart of the Airline business. No one will beat us on price. Ever. (Michael O'Leary, Ryanair CEO, Ryanair Annual Report 2002)

Ryanair began operating in 1985 with small fifteen-seater aircraft on point-to-point routes between England and Ireland. By 1990 Ryanair was serving

---

[8] 'Air France aid attacked', *Air Transport World*, August 1998, Vol. 35 Issue 8, p. 9.

[9] 'Swiss Slots', *Financial Times*, London, 24 September 2003, p. 20.

[10] Thomas Lawton, *Cleared for takeoff: Structure and strategy in the low fare airline business*, Ashgate Publishing.

[11] Ibid.

[12] Bingelli and Pompeo, *The McKinsey Quarterly*, 'Hyped hopes for Europe's low-cost airlines', 2002, No. 4.

[13] Ibid.

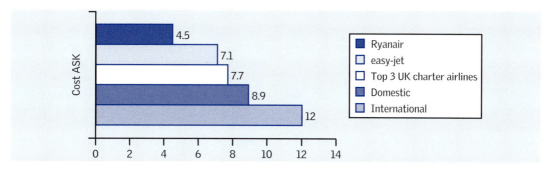

Figure 1 Cost comparison: Ryanair versus other airlines (costs are quoted per available seat kilometre (ASK) 2001 in cents)
Source: Bingelli and Pompeo, *The McKinsey Quarterly*, 'Hyped hopes for Europe's low-cost airlines', 2002, No. 4.

26 city pairs and carrying 700,000 passengers but it was in financial difficulties.[14] The reincarnation of Ryanair began when Michael O'Leary was sent to Texas to examine Southwest's operations. Consequently the Ryanair business model is a clone of Southwest's and O'Leary is now the CEO of Ryanair. O'Leary has many traits in common with Southwest's Herb Kelleher. O'Leary is a fiercely competitive character who relishes a fight and has spurred Ryanair on to become Europe's most successful, most profitable and highly valued airline. By 2002 Ryanair had a market capitalization of €4.9 billion, some 45% larger than British Airways.

Ryanair's growth has been based on defining the market for low-cost travel. New routes have provided a low-cost alternative to the flag carriers with the average price of a one-way ticket on an international intra-European route of €50–€85,

Table 1 Breakdown of Ryanair cost advantage versus top 3 major international flag carriers (all costs are per ASK and quoted in cents)

Cost item	Cost advantage	Ryanair's advantage per ASK
Overhead	Lower general, administration cost	0.5
Distribution	Internet sales account for 94% of bookings. No travel agents' commission paid	1.7
Passenger services	No catering costs	0.8
Crew costs	Higher crew productivity, pilots paid according to hours worked. Commonality due to single aircraft type	0.6
Airport charges, ground handling	Lower charges due to use of secondary airports. Negotiated better ground handling charges	2.6
Seat density	15% more seats per aircraft	1.3
Total		7.5

Source: adapted from Bingelli and Pompeo, *The McKinsey Quarterly*, 'Hyped hopes for Europe's low-cost airlines' 2002, No. 4.

[14] Thomas Lawton, *Cleared for takeoff: Structure and strategy in the low fare airline business*, Ashgate Publishing, p. 91.

compared to €180–€200 on British Airways or Lufthansa. Moreover, Ryanair has provided consumers with an alternative transport means – some of their routes compete directly with rail or possible car journeys e.g. Stansted–Newquay. By making air travel affordable Ryanair has fuelled their own growth, as passenger numbers increase it is able to benefit from operating efficiencies, thus creating a multiplier effect of ever decreasing costs and fares. However, at the same time, profits have continued to rise from 2000 to 2003 profits grew by 44%, 44% and 59%, with the highest operating margins in the industry. Appendix 3 contains more detailed information on Ryanair's financial performance.

The basis for Ryanair's success has been the cloning of Southwest Airlines efficient operations with low fares made possible by lower operating costs. Figure 1 and Table 1 provide a cost comparison between Ryanair and other European airlines.

As Table 1 indicates, a part of Ryanair's cost advantage comes from the way that O'Leary has also cleverly exploited his suppliers. Away from the congested hub airports there is a vast amount overcapacity in secondary airports across Europe. O'Leary took advantage of this by exploiting local regeneration efforts – in Charleroi, Belgium, Ryanair received €15 million as a sweetener from the regional government. However, in February 2004 the European Commission ruled that this amounted to state aid (the regional government provided the funds as a spur for economic regeneration) and Ryanair were forced to pay back €4 million of the subsidy. The implication of this ruling for Ryanair is that future route development will become more difficult. Subsidies from regional governments enabled them to slowly build the critical mass of passengers required for profitable operations. Without the subsidy it is likely that some of Ryanair's thin routes will be cancelled. Furthermore, it also sends a signal to airports competing for Ryanair's business that the balance of power may shift back in their favour.

With an operating model of ruthless cost control, quick aircraft turn time (Ryanair match Southwest's 20-minute average) and servicing secondary airports, Ryanair is able to stimulate the demand for air travel by providing a cost-effective alternative to other transport modes. All of these factors are a mirror image of Southwest's operations. However, one area that Ryanair has conspicuously chosen not to copy Southwest is in customer care. O'Leary's mantra is low fares, not customer service. In contrast to Herb Kelleher, O'Leary views the two as being mutually exclusive. Customer service is seen as an additional expense and a barrier to keeping fares low. One of O'Leary's politer quotes regarding customers is 'What part of no refund don't they understand?'[15] His mission is to re-educate customers that flying should be akin 'to taking a bus' and that low fares can only be achieved through cutting of costs across the board. Unlike easyJet there is no compensation for delayed flights and customer complaints are given only cursory attention.

easyJet

If you create the right expectations and you meet or exceed those expectations, then you will have happy customers. (Stelios Haji-Ioannou, easyJet's founder, IMD Case Study easyJet 'The Web's Favorite Airline')

Around the same time that Ryanair were copying the Southwest model, Stelios Haji-Ioannou (who likes to be known as just Stelios) was developing his own version of a low-cost airline, based out of London's Luton airport. Stelios is the son of a Greek shipping magnate and persuaded his father to invest £5 million in his start-up airline. Stelios started operations at the end of 1995 with two leased B737s and, in order to keep costs down, acted as a virtual airline by contracting-in everything required from pilots to check-in staff.

easyJet's inaugural flights were from Luton to Edinburgh and Glasgow, which were promoted via innovative advertising on the side of the aircraft 'Fly to Scotland for the price of a pair of Jeans'. In the early days easyJet used aggressive marketing techniques in order to build up brand recognition and attack the competitors. easyJet has probably been the most successful low-cost airline at attacking the market space traditionally occupied by the full service airlines, especially British Airways and BMI

---

[15] 'Ryanair talks of disaster, but the low-cost revolution flies on', *Financial Times*, 7 February 2004.

in the UK and Swiss in Switzerland. Until now, as in the US, direct competition between the low-cost airlines is rare.

Stelios became famous for high-profile media battles with competitors, for example when British Airways launched it's own low-cost subsidiary GO, which ironically was later purchased by easyJet; with suppliers, when Luton airport wanted to raise landing charges associated with easyJet's operations; or with government as Stelios successfully lobbied for fairness on air passenger duty (airport tax). All of these stunts were orchestrated in order to educate the general public on the true costs of air travel and to promote the benefits of a low-cost alternative. The spin-off was that customers saw that there was a real benefit to flying on a low-cost carrier, while companies with large travel budgets also recognized that low-cost provided a real alternative to full service airlines. In October 1999, readers of *Business Traveller* magazine voted 'Best Low-cost Airline' easyJet.

easyJet increased profits during the 5-year period 1999–2003 from £21.1 million to £138.6 million, however, the pre-tax profit margin remained unchanged at 15% (see Appendix 4). A part of easyJet's success is attributed to the unique working culture that Stelios instilled in the airline. In common with Southwest Airlines, the objective was to build a strong, inclusive employee-led culture at easyLand – the airline's headquarters. The culture was determined to a large extent by the easyJet Culture Committee, an elected group drawn from company staff, whose remit was to establish company policy on the working environment and management communications, as well as organize the social calendar. Stelios's belief was that 'work should be fun' and even went as far as to make the position of 'party animal' an official one. The objective was to instil a sense of pride in the staff, which would enable superior customer service.

The confidence that Stelios had in his staff was portrayed in January 1999 when he allowed ITV to provide a fly-on-the-wall documentary of life for both the passengers and staff at easyJet. By the end of the year the programme had become ITV's most successful docu-soap with 9 million viewers. For easyJet it provided priceless publicity. However, without a strong culture of customer service this

venture may well have proved to be a spectacular own goal. In contrast to O'Leary, Stelios took customer satisfaction extremely seriously, often taking easyJet flights in order to interact with the passengers. Stelios believed that this was the best form of market research possible. easyJet's approach to customer service was acknowledged in March 2001 when it was the only low-cost airline to be ranked in the first division of a customer satisfaction table in a *Holiday Which?* survey. All of easyJet's core values are summarized in their mission statement.

easyJet's mission statement

To provide our customers with safe, low-cost, good-value, point-to-point air services. To offer a consistent and reliable product at fares appealing to leisure and business markets from our bases to a range of domestic and European destinations. To achieve this we will develop our people and establish long lasting partnerships with our suppliers.

Source: www.easyjet.com.

easyJet's business model is based on direct sale to the end customer. Unlike Southwest Airlines it does not pay travel agents for even a small proportion of their business and it estimates this saves them 25% on distribution costs. Since April 1998 easyJet has been encouraging customers to book online and within 18 months had achieved one million sales via the Internet. In order to encourage online sales easyJet were the first to provide a discount for seats booked via the web. Furthermore, it amended their online booking policy so that seats purchased more than two months in advance could only be booked online. Moreover, web bookings provided customers with complete control over their itinerary; they could quickly compare the costs of alternative travel dates and times, which was aided by the one-way fares on offer. The flexibility over fares offered was extended to cover changes to existing bookings – for £10 plus the difference between the two fares, easyJet provided full flexibility on time of travel. This was in marked contrast to the traditional full service airlines which placed a large number of restrictions on their 'economy' tickets. Because easyJet had transparent and flexible pricing it quickly started to attract business travellers eager to find cost-effective travel solutions. On some routes business travellers soon accounted for 50% of the passengers.

In contrast to Ryanair, easyJet's expansion has been based around operations from Europe's principal cities – easyJet now have bases in Geneva, Amsterdam, London Gatwick, Paris and Berlin to support Luton. In this context easyJet has drifted away from the original low-cost model of operations to secondary airports in order to preserve the quick aircraft turnaround times and efficient asset utilization required for low-cost airline operations. However, the focus is still very much on filling as many seats as possible. The objective is to maximize the revenue per passenger. This is achieved through a yield management system – as demand for a flight increased then so does the fare. The system is designed to ensure the optimal balance between available capacity, the number of seats sold and the revenue each passenger contributes. Appendix 4 contains detailed load factor data from 1999–2003.

Another golden rule of low-cost airline operations has also been breached by easyJet. After a yearlong head-to-head battle between the two principal aircraft manufacturers easyJet announced in October 2002 its intention to appoint Airbus as its preferred aircraft supplier. As part of the deal easyJet placed a firm order for 120 Airbus A319 aircraft for delivery over 5 years from September 2003, with an option to purchase a further 120 with protected prices. By turning to Airbus, easyJet has lost the efficiencies in training, maintenance and the lower operating costs that are associated with single fleet operations. Despite the additional complexities of operating another type of aircraft easyJet maintain that the financial benefits of the deal far outweigh the integration costs. Sir Colin Chandler, easyJet's Chairman, stated that the Airbus deal was 'significantly better value than the offer made by Boeing'.[16] Moreover, easyJet expects that the Airbus will offer a cost decrease of 10% against their current B737 fleet. However, it should be noted that Ryanair has chosen the B737-800 as the basis for their fleet, which provides 28 more seats than the A319.

Appendix 9 contains data on the number of seats by aircraft type.

easyJet's strategy of serving Europe's primary airports, targeting the business traveller and mixing the fleet, creates an impression of a conventional airline business model, when compared with Ryanair. This would provide an explanation of, as per Figure 1, easyJet's cost disadvantage of 2.6 cents per ASK versus Ryanair. In the long run this may prove to be a critical source of competitive advantage for Ryanair.

Competition

The response from British Airways

The effect of the low-cost airlines targeting passengers from the traditional full service airlines has been catastrophic on the profitability of British Airways (BA) (see Appendix 5), the response to which was to announce the 'future size and shape' programme in February 2002. BA's CEO Rod Eddington described the programme as being 'based on three simple tenets: to reduce cost, restructure the short-haul operations, and remove complexity from the business'. The target is to deliver £650 million in annualized saving by March 2004,[17] the majority of which comes from manpower savings. In essence BA are playing catch-up with the low-cost carriers; it is applying elements of the low-cost business model to a full service airline. These include increasing the number of Internet bookings, price flexibility and rationalizing operations.

After flirting with their own low-cost airline operation (GO) BA was one of the first to realize that the market for short-haul traffic was undergoing a structural change as a result of low-cost airlines rather than a cyclical change. BA sold GO in June 2001 to a venture capital backed management buy-out led by Barbara Cassani. At the time of the sale Eddington was quoted as saying that the £110 million. BA received for GO represented a good return on the initial investment of £25 million made three years earlier.[18] The sale of GO was one of

---

[16] easyJet letter to shareholders, 24 February 2003. Available on www.easyjet.com.

[17] 'BA keeps taking the medicine', *Financial Times*, 10 Feb. 2004.

[18] BA press release, 14 June 2001, available on www. britishairways.com.

Eddington's first acts when he took the helm at BA, the rationale being that operating a no-frills service alongside a full service strategy was not sustainable in the long term. More specifically BA were finding it difficult to justify a substantial price premium for the full service offering, effectively it was eating into its own profits. Subsequently, in August 2002, easyJet acquired GO for £374 million, creating Europe's largest low-cost airline.

Although BA is not yet breaking even on short-haul operations, previous losses have been greatly reduced. As a result of adjusting their business model full service airlines are now able to offer an alternative to low-cost travel. Having finally realized that in the post deregulation age supply of capacity is not tightly controlled and price-sensitive customers' demand can be manipulated, the full service airlines are now able to sell the benefits of additional product features. For customers that value convenience, i.e. being flown directly to their destination, as opposed to a satellite airport up to 100km away, and the level of service associated with a traditional airline including assigned seating and onboard meal service, the established airlines have started to provide an affordable alternative to the low-cost carriers. Indeed, much of BA's current advertising is explicit in promoting the benefits of travel with a full service airline. However, as Willie Walsh of Aer Lingus points out, the size of the premium charged for additional service features has shrunk forever.

BMI

As the UK's second largest airline after BA, BMI has proved vulnerable to the growth of low-cost carriers. BMI's main base is at London Heathrow, where it holds 14% of the available landing slots. BMI operates around 2000 flights per week with a fleet of 53 aircraft. Although the primary focus has been on domestic and short-haul travel, BMI, as a member of the Star Alliance, is attempting to break into the more lucrative intercontinental market. As a medium-sized carrier with a relatively high fixed operating cost base BMI has lost market share to easyJet and Ryanair. See Appendix 7 for summary financial data on BMI.

BMI's response to the threat posed by the low-cost airlines has been to open its own low-cost subsidiary – bmibaby, which now has three operational bases at East Midlands, Cardiff and London Gatwick, effectively making it the third-largest low-cost operator in the UK. However, the rationale behind operations appear to be stuck somewhere in the middle between the true low-cost model and the full service airline. Some of BMI's old habits such as express check-in for business travellers, allocated seats and in-flight service have proved hard to give up. Moreover, it would appear that BMI has not heeded the warnings apparent when BA gave up trying to run a full service and a low-cost airline in tandem. In particular there is evidence that bmibaby is cannibalizing some of BMI's business by operating head-to-head on certain routes. From summer 2004 both airlines will serve Prague: BMI from London Heathrow and bmibaby from London Gatwick.

The global perspective

The low-cost revolution is now becoming a global phenomenon. In Australia, Virgin Blue, founded by Sir Richard Branson, started operations and has precipitated a vicious price war in the Australian domestic market. From mid 2004 Quantas will be fighting back with a low-cost format of their own, flying under the brand Jetstar. A similar success story can be found in Malaysia. Air Asia, formed in December 2001, now operates 15 B737-300s on point-to-point routes between Indonesia, Malaysia, Thailand and Singapore. With some one-way fares as low as $13, stimulating demand from the 500 million people who live within three hours of Air Asia's bases in Kuala Lumpur, Bangkok and Singapore is not proving to be problematic.[19] The success of these low-cost airlines is creating political pressure for further liberalization of air transport services within Asia, and at the end of 2003 Singapore Airlines (SIA), one of the world's most profitable airlines and second in terms of market capitalization, announced a joint venture in a low-cost subsidiary Tiger Airways. In some respects this a defensive move against the plans of former SIA executives to open a third low-cost carrier in Singapore during 2004, ValuAir.[20]

---

[19] 'Having fun and flying high', *The Economist*, 13 March 2004, Vol. 370, Issue 8366, p. 63.

[20] 'SIA to release Tiger in Asia low-cost airlines', *Financial Times*, p. 32, 10 December 2003.

Sustainability

As the UK market for low-cost travel becomes more saturated fewer new routes are becoming viable. As a consequence the low-cost airlines have turned their attention towards Europe in order to provide growth. easyJet and Ryanair have opened new bases in markets that are poorly served by the national airlines; seven out of the ten routes operated by Ryanair from Frankfurt Hahn were not served by Lufthansa, while easyJet's success in Geneva coincided with the decline of the Swiss national carrier Swissair. In May 2003 easyJet revealed that it was the number one carrier at Geneva airport with 26% of passengers, ahead of Swiss, Air France and BA.[21] easyJet's success in Switzerland has been a major factor in the reborn national carrier Swiss, which emerged from the high-profile bankruptcy of Swiss Air, continuing to mount losses. As witnessed in the US, in selected markets the low-cost airlines are now starting to replace the traditional flag carriers.

The advantage of this expansion strategy is that in the medium term direct competition between the low-cost carriers is avoided. However, new entrants are continuously being encouraged to fight the low-cost market. In Germany, Air Berlin has remodelled itself from being a charter carrier into a flight-only seller with operations from eight German airports to London, Milan, Vienna, Barcelona and Zurich as well as operating domestic flights within Spain from its Malaga hub. Air Berlin, with 9.6 million passengers in 2003 is now Germany's second-largest airline after Lufthansa[22] and Europe's third-largest low-cost carrier. Appendix 8 provides a comparison between Air Berlin, Ryanair and easyJet.

Outside Germany and the UK, however, the low-cost carriers may experience difficulties stimulating enough demand. Other transport modes provide greater competition, for example the high-speed rail network in France, and the propensity to travel great distances for holiday and leisure activities is much reduced. In the long run it's likely that low-cost airlines will need to compete more on a head-to-head basis, something that has largely been avoided until now. Another market segment that could come under attack from the low-cost carriers is Europe's €45 billion package-tour market. Presently the charter airline industry accounts for 21% of intra-European travel – some 45% of flights for German holidays are purchased as part of a package, a figure that has remained constant for the past five years.[23] However, as demand for package tours stagnate the vertically integrated tour companies are looking to spin off their airline operations and compete in the low-cost segment. Thompson holidays are now following My Travel's lead in starting up its own low-cost airline operation.

Any fool can grow in the airline industry whilst losing money and we are surrounded by many fine examples of this in Europe at present. The difference with Ryanair is that we achieve consistent growth, but deliver equally consistent profit growth at high margins despite offering the lowest air fares in Europe. The challenge facing us over the coming years will be to maintain our growth, whilst improving customer service, upgrading the fleet with the new Boeing B737 aircraft, but continuing to lower our unit costs and maintaining industry leading margins. (Michael O'Leary – Ryanair Annual Report 2003)

The low-cost airlines are also susceptible to cost pressure from their suppliers. The deal for landing and passenger charges at Ryanair's biggest base – London Stansted – expires in 2006, when the airport operator BAA is commencing work on a £2 billion second runway. As the expansion must be paid for by the airlines using the airport this will force higher charges for the incumbents. At the same time, existing airport deals between secondary airports and the low-cost airlines are coming under close scrutiny from the European Commission, which is eager to stamp out any cross-subsidization. Moreover, as the industry matures the opportunities for manufacturing large cost savings become scarcer, for example switching sales on to the Internet lowered costs sharply; however,

---

[21] Source: www.easyjet.com

[22] 'An old hand at low fares', *Air Transport World*, January 2003.

[23] 'Bingelli and Pompeo, *The McKinsey Quarterly*, 'Hyped hopes for Europe's low-cost airlines', 2002, No. 4.

with easyJet and Ryanair selling about 95% of sales via the web the scope for further cost-cutting becomes limited.

As the competition increases and the established airlines start to realize operating efficiencies that allow them to compete on price with low-cost airlines, the low-cost airlines have started to experience growing pains. There is likely to be some turbulence ahead if Ryanair are to achieve their forecast of carrying 50 million passengers per year by 2009 with a fleet of 149 aircraft; recent experience has shown that as capacity has increased the yield per passenger has declined. Much of the recent growth in passenger numbers has been achieved by special promotions and giveaways to passengers with the flexibility to fly at off-peak times. In February 2004 Ryanair announced a profit warning for the first time, the root cause for which was an average year on year decline in fares of 30%. This was matched by a corresponding fall in the load factor from 81% to 77%.[24]

As the industry matures, easyJet's culture has also been evolving. In 2003 Stelios stepped down as chairman of easyJet – a sure sign that the entrepreneurial spirit required to set up the airline was less relevant in the running of a maturing business. Sir Colin Chandler, who has a long list of directorships to his name, replaced Stelios. Nonetheless, easyJet has been subjected to the same pressures on yield as Ryanair; in the six-month trading period to the end of March 2004 easyJet lost £18.5 million, which created nervousness for investors as the share price dropped by 25%.[25] The result of these financial pressures on easyJet and Ryanair is a decline in their price earnings ratios. (The price earnings (PE) ratio is generally accepted as an indicator of future profitability.) Although easyJet is presently trading at a PE ratio of 35, Ryanair's is down to 15, as compared with 35 four years ago.[26] The suggestion from analysts is that the declining revenue per passenger could be symptomatic of ambitious expansion plans (see Appendix 10 for share price data). On a more positive note, however, there is still a substantial difference between the pre-tax profit margins for the established carriers and the low-cost carriers, despite both easyJet and Southwest experiencing diminishing returns in the past couple of years.

One of the consequences of this evolution is that Ryanair entered negotiations with Boeing to reschedule the new aircraft delivery. For the next few years Ryanair are looking to maintain capacity growth at no more than 20–25%. Considering that easyJet and Ryanair have between them placed orders for 245 new aircraft there is likely to be a shakeout across the industry, particularly once head-to-head competition commences.

---

[24] 'Source: www.ryanair.com.

[25] 'easyJet takes brunt of airline sector woes', *Financial Times*, London, 6 May 2004.

[26] Data from http://finance.yahoo.com.

Appendix 1 Southwest Airlines load factor and financial data

	1999	2000	2001	2002	2003
Turnover $bn	4.735	5.649	5.555	5.521	5.937
Pre-tax profit $m	474	625	631	417	483
Pre-tax profit margin	10%	11.1%	11.4%	7.6%	8.1%
Passengers m	57.5	63.7	64.4	63	65.5
Load factor	69%	70.5%	68.1%	65.9%	6.8%
Fleet size (B737)	312	344	355	375	398

Source: company reports.

Appendix 2 State aid to European airlines 1991–1997

Air France	1991	$570
Sabena	1991	$970
Iberia	1992	$1300
Aer Lingus	1994	$250
Air France	1994	$3700
Olympic	1994	$2300
TAP	1994	$1100
Iberia	1996	$710
Alitalia	1997	$1600

Source: SAS as reported in 'Air France aid attacked', *Air Transport World*, August 1998, Vol. 35, Issue 8, p. 9.

Appendix 3 Ryanair load factor and financial data

	1999	2000	2001	2002	2003
Turnover €m	295.8	370.1	487.4	624.1	842
Pre-tax profit €m	57.5	72.5	104.5	150.1	239.4
Pre-tax profit margin	19.4%	19.5%	21.4%	24%	28.4%
Passengers m	5.3	6.1	8.1	11.1	15.7
Load factor	71%	n/a	n/a	82%	81%

Source: company reports.

Appendix 4 easyJet load factor and financial data

	1999	2000	2001	2002	2003
Turnover £m	139.8	258.9	354.9	551.8	931.8
Pre-tax profit £m	21.1	47.0	63.0	156.8	138.6
Pre-tax profit margin	15.1%	18.2%	17.8%	28.4%	14.8%
Passengers m	3.1	5.6	7.1	11.4	20.3
Load factor	75.9%	80.8%	83.0%	84.8%	84.1%

Source: company reports.
Note: Ryanair's financial data are published in €, easyJet in £.

Appendix 5 British Airways load factor and financial data

	1999	2000	2001	2002	2003
Turnover £m	8915	8940	9278	8340	7688
Pre-tax profit (loss) £m	225	5	150	(200)	135
Pre-tax profit (loss) margin	2.5%	0.5%	1.6%	(2.4%)	1.7%
Passengers m	45.0	46.6	44.4	40.0	38.0
Load factor	70.7%	69.8%	71.7%	70.4%	71.9%

Source: company reports.

Appendix 6 American Airlines load factor and financial data

	1999	2000	2001	2002	2003
Turnover $m	17730	19703	18969	17420	17440
Pre-tax profit (loss) $m	985	813	(1762)	(3511)	(1228)
Pre-tax profit (loss) margin	5.5%	4.1%	(9.2%)	(20%)	(7%)
Passengers m	n/a	n/a	n/a	94.1	88.8
Load factor	69.5%	72.4%	69.0%	70.7%	72.8%

Source: company reports.

Appendix 7 BMI selected statistics

	2000	2001	2002	2003
Turnover £m	739.2	756.9	723.8	772
Pre-tax profit (loss) £m	8.2	12.4	(19.6)	(9.8)
Pre-tax profit margin	1.1%	1.6%	(2.7%)	(1.3%)
Passengers m	7.1	6.7	7.5	9.4

Source: www.flybmi.com.

Appendix 8   Summary Table 2003 data

	easyJet	Ryanair	Air Berlin	British Airways
Profit	€76.4 m.[1]	€239.4 m.	€30 m.[2]	€198[3]
Turnover	€1370 m.	€842 m.	€880 m.	€11301
Passengers	20.3 m.	22.4 m.	9.6 m.	38.0 m.
Load factor	84.1%	81%	79.3%	71.9%
Routes	151	127	N/a	170
Aircraft				
B737	67	68	42	19
A319	5			21
BAE146		6		5
Other			3	171
Total	72	74	45	216[4]
Confirmed aircraft orders	120 (A319)	125 (B737)	n/a	20[4]

[1] The easyJet results have been converted from £ to € at the exchange rate £1 = €1.47 (http://uk.finance.yahoo.com, 4 May 2004).
[2] The Air Berlin figures are an estimate from *Air Transport World*. The company publishes no financial data.
[3] The British Airways results have also been converted from £ to € at the exchange rate £1 = €1.47.
[4] As at 31 December 2002. Source: www.bashares.com.

Appendix 9   Aircraft type and seat numbers

Aircraft	Maximum no. seats
A319	156
B737-700	149
B737-400	167
B737-800	189
BAE 146	110

Notes: easyJet is the launch customer for the A319 in a single-class cabin configuration. The maximum number of seats available on the aircraft is 156.
Ryanair inherited the BAE146 following the acquisition of Buzz in 2003. This aircraft type will be phased out and replaced by the B737-800.
Both Ryanair and Air Berlin operate the B737-800; however, Ryanair squeeze an additional 5 seats into their version (189 vs 184).
Source: Company websites.

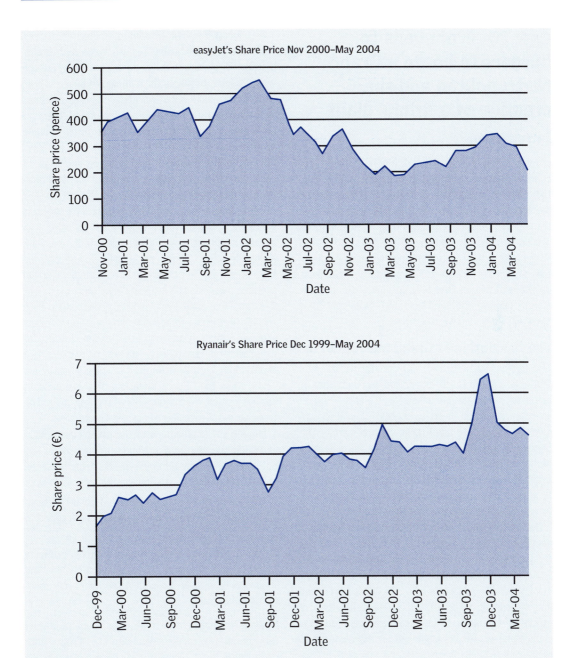

Appendix 10 Ryanair and easyJet share prices
Source: adapted from data published on http://uk.finance.yahoo.com.

Case 20 **From beds to burgers to booze – Grand Metropolitan and the creation of a drinks giant**

Introduction

Diageo is the world's largest alcoholic beverages company and was formed in December 1997 from the merger of its two predecessor firms, Grand Metropolitan and Guinness. This case examines the transformation of Grand Metropolitan from its origins as a hotel company in post Second World War London, through the various changes of direction it experienced prior to the merger with Guinness in 1997 and follows the story through to the present day to analyse the problems and challenges that have and continue to face Diageo.

The foundation of Grand Metropolitan

The foundation of Grand Metropolitan in the late 1940s was down to the entrepreneurial activities of one man – Max Joseph. Joseph was a career entrepreneur, who had been a successful real estate investor and estate agent prior to the start of the Second World War. He began purchasing a serious of hotels from 1947 onwards. These hotels were originally focused on London but gradually expanded to cover various overseas locations including Paris, Amsterdam, Monte Carlo and New York.

During this initial period of Grand Metropolitan's development and expansion, the culture of the organisation remained relaxed and non-bureaucratic. For example, the purchase of hotels was undertaken quickly, based on Joseph's innate business judgement and without the aid of detailed business analysis. The growth of the business, however, gradually forced a change and introduced a demand for more advanced management control systems and resulted in the hiring of Stanley Grinstead, a future CEO of the business, as its Chief Accountant in 1960. This move was quickly followed by the firm's IPO in 1961.

Robert Salter prepared this case under the supervision of John McGee as a basis for class discussion rather than to illustrate either effective or ineffective handling of a business situation.

© Robert Salter, Warwick Business School, 2004.

Although Grand Metropolitan started to acquire various non-hotel businesses from the mid 1960s, during this period of the company's history, Joseph was still keen to follow the same basic business concepts and ideas that had worked with his acquisitions in the hotel trade. Throughout this period, the core principle was that the business acquired 'trading property assets', with the idea being that the cash flow from the business needed to be sufficient to cover the costs of servicing any debts that had been built up to acquire the properties concerned.

While Joseph focused on only acquiring those assets which he believed would innately rise in value (e.g. because of the increasing demand for hotels), his management style didn't specifically focus on the subsequent ongoing control and management of the acquired business. The focus of Grand Metropolitan at this time was based on 'making deals' rather than specifically looking to add shareholder value from the acquired entities. It was therefore standard practice for Grand Metropolitan to leave the existing management of an acquired organisation in place following an acquisition, while the CEO or Chairman of any significant businesses that were acquired was typically invited on to the Grand Metropolitan board of directors.[1]

Though the acquisitions of the mid to late 1960s extended the company's original management and business philosophy into new areas, Jospeh insisted that all acquisitions satisfied the following criteria:

1 the companies acquired needed to be in businesses that were in some generic sense related to the hotel trade; and

2 the businesses were required to be property intensive – this was an extension of the 'trading property assets' concept that has been mentioned above.

Among the businesses that were acquired during this period were several catering firms, pub-restaurants and a chain of off-licences. However, by the late 1960s, the firm's requirements regarding its future acquisitions were gradually relaxing and the early 1970s saw a move into less related industries and segments. This period saw the acquisition of

---

[1] The practice of inviting the Chairman/CEO of acquired businesses on to the Grand Metropolitan board resulted in the company's board growing to 18 at one stage.

Express Dairies in 1969,[2] and Mecca, a dance hall, bingo hall and casino group, in 1970.

Most acquisitions until this stage had been undertaken on a friendly basis (Express Dairies was the one notable exception). However, this focus on friendly acquisitions changed with the takeover of the brewer Truman, Hanbury and Buxton (THB) in 1972 after an acquisition process that lasted 9 months. The eventual price paid (£48 million) was the most paid by Grand Metropolitan for any acquisition up to that date and was approximately 50% more than the price for Express Dairies only 3 years earlier.

The acquisition of THB subsequently led to the the acquisition of British brewer, Watney Mann, later in 1972. Watney Mann was a significantly bigger brewer than THB and also included its own distillery subsidiary, IDV. As with the THB acquisition, the takeover process was drawn out and Grand Metropolitan was required to make three separate offers for the company before a bid of £435 million was eventually agreed upon. This price was the most ever paid for an acquisition in Britain up to that date and left Grand Metropolitan with significant debt levels, just as economic conditions in Britain began to deteriorate significantly.

The years of struggle

From 1973, Britain was racked with a serious of economic problems, caused by the effects of international oil price rises and intensive industrial action by Britain's coal miners, which resulted in a 3-day working week being introduced by the British government due to serious energy shortages. At the same time, Grand Metropolitan was being seriously squeezed because of its high debt levels and these problems were being compounded by the following circumstances:

1   Its failure to successfully divest the spirits division (IDV) of Watney Mann, as had originally

been planned when the acquisition was undertaken.

2   A significant fall in UK property values, which threatened to undermine the strength of Grand Metropolitan's balance sheet.

The pressures faced by the company during this period resulted in it having to announce its first fall in trading profits in 1974, and resulted in the firm focusing on trying to improve the trading performance of its various divisions to avoid a genuine threat of bankruptcy. As part of the focus on improving the group's trading performance, Allen Sheppard was recruited by Joseph to specifically head up the brewing division of Grand Metropolitan. At the same time, the group's spirits division, IDV, was separated from the brewing division and placed under the leadership of Anthony Tennant.

Sheppard and Tennant both set about improving the performance of their respective divisions aggressively, but did this in very different styles. While Sheppard successfully revitalised and strengthened the sales of Watney Mann's regional beers, his core focus during this period was on reducing head count within the division and on cutting costs. In contrast, the focus at IDV was very much on improving the marketing and promotion of IDV's brands and there was no significant focus during this period on product or cost rationalisation.

Despite the very different business philosophies that had been followed by Sheppard and Tennant, both approaches proved highly successful. By the late 1970s, Grand Metropolitan's profits and cash flows had significantly improved and the firm was once again in a strong financial position – this was the result of both the improvement in the firm's trading income and the revitalised UK property market which helped increase the value of the assets shown on the company's balance sheet.

US diversification

Joseph and Grinstead were aware that Grand Metropolitan had been on the edge of bankruptcy during the mid 1970s and took from this experience a determination that the firm should never again be as dependant purely on the UK economy as it had been at that stage. Therefore, as the company's

---

[2]   Although the Express Dairies business did include hotel and restaurant subsidiaries, the door-to-door milk delivery business was at the core of its operations. At this time, the firm controlled approximately 25% of all door-to-door milk deliveries in the UK.

financial position improved in the late 1970s, they became increasingly receptive to the idea of international expansion.

The first serious opportunity for international expansion resulted in the acquisition of the US-based Liggett Group in 1981. While the Liggett Group included the distributor of IDV's products in the US, the firm was involved in a wide range of other products (e.g. pet food, cigarettes and fitness equipment), and had only a limited focus on property. Although Joseph was unconvinced about the merits of this acquisition, it was pushed through by Grinstead who had by this stage replaced Joseph as Chairman of Grand Metropolitan, despite the fact that it brought the company into areas of business in which they had little or no experience.

Following the acquisition of the Liggett Group, Grand Metropolitan acquired Intercontinental Hotels from Pan-Am Airlines. As with many of the acquisitions of the 1950s and 1960s, the Intercontinental Hotels acquisition was completed quickly (within one week). However, while the Intercontinental deal offered Grant Metropolitan the 'comfort' of being in a business which it new well, this acquisition did at the same time represent a step away from the focus on acquiring 'trading property assets'. In reality, few of the Intercontinental hotels were actually directly owned – rather, they were typically operated by the group under management contract and franchise arrangements.

Following Joseph's death in the early 1980s, Grinstead continued to focus on acquiring further companies in the US. During this period, Grinstead's principles when considering potential purchases and acquisitions were based around the following:

1 Acquiring service companies in general, on the basis that he believed the service sector in general would expand more quickly over the coming years than manufacturing.

2 Looking to continue diversifying away the risks associated with only doing most of Grand Metropolitan's business purely in the UK.

During the period up until the mid 1980s, the span of acquisitions undertaken by Grand Metropolitan under Grinstead's chairmanship was wide ranging and diverse. The companies acquired provided services ranging from childcare, home-based healthcare and optical retailing.

While Grinstead was focused on the US acquisitions policy during the early to mid 1980s, the company also became increasingly focused on trying to increase the operational performance of its business units, in contrast to the very 'hands-off' management style that had traditionally been a feature of Grand Metropolitan's philosophy. The process of focusing on operational improvement was, in many respects, led by Sheppard, and his team pursued an aggressive policy of rationalising the business units for which they were responsible. The 'Sheppard approach' to operational improvement focused on the divestment of underperforming or peripheral facilities or business units, but also tried to combine this rationalisation focus with improved marketing performance and a decentralised management policy that provided operational managers with real autonomy.

The Sheppard approach worked very effectively in the areas under his responsibility (basically the UK brewing and food businesses). However, Tennant at IDV continued to pursue a very different policy and was in some respects even more successful. IDV gradually became Grand Metropolitan's largest profit source, based on a strategy that focused heavily on trying to control the distribution channels, so that IDV could get as close as possible to the end-customers of its products, and an ongoing heavy investment in product marketing and branding. During this period under Tennant, IDV also successfully focused on the development of a range of new alcoholic beverages.[3] Under Tennant, throughout this period there continued to be no specific focus at IDV on cost control and product rationalisation.

However, despite the successes of Tennant and Sheppard, by 1986, the investors in the City of London had begun to lose confidence in Grinstead's emphasis on expansion. Grand Metropolitan's earnings per share growth had ceased by 1986 (although the company remained profitable), and around this

---

[3] Among the products that were developed by IDV during this period was Bailey's Irish Cream, which became the best selling product in its market segment worldwide. During the 1980s, IDV introduced 32% of all the new products of the world's 7 biggest alcoholic beverages companies.

time, the Grand Metropolitan's shares were being downgraded by the City. By the time that Grinstead stepped down in 1987, to be replaced by Sheppard as CEO and Chairman, there were strong rumours and suggestions in the City that a corporate raider might try to take over Grand Metropolitan with the aim of selling off the individual divisions of the firm.

The Sheppard years

Despite the City's dissatisfaction with the acquisitions policy that had been pursued by Grand Metropolitan during the early to mid 1980s, acquisitions continued under Sheppard's leadership. The two key acquisitions during the Sheppard years were Heublein from RJR Nabisco in 1987 (a move which doubled the size of IDV's spirits business) and Pillsbury in 1989. The acquisition of Pillsbury enabled Grand Metropolitan to expand its food business on an international scale,[4] while also providing it with significant rationalisation opportunities in accordance with Sheppard's tried and tested approach to business.

The Grand Metropolitan team that moved into Pillsbury's operations after its acquisition was led by Ian Martin, one of Sheppard's key disciples. This team removed about one-third of Pillsbury's existing management within 12 months of the acquisition as part of its stated policy of cutting the division's operating costs, improving the impact of the well-known Pillsbury brands and developing new products and/or markets.

While Sheppard oversaw the acquisition of these two businesses, there was a simultaneous focus on divesting unwanted or unnecessary Grand Metropolitan businesses in a move that became known as 'Operation De-cluster'. The strategic focus under Sheppard was for Grand Metropolitan to increasingly focus on food, drinks and retailing, with all businesses that remained in the group needing to show that they could satisfy the following three criteria:

1 a good brand image;

2 good market shares; and

3 an international scope.

The decision to focus on only the food, drinks and retail businesses was based on the idea that it was better to be a leader in a few areas than a real 'jack-of-all-trades' with no specific strengths. As part of this policy of greater specialisation, Grand Metropolitan did consider the possibility of focusing on purely one market area, but at the end of the day, the company was not at this stage willing to 'put all of its eggs in one basket'. This was despite the fact that Sheppard was aware that the highly focused approach would provide Grand Metropolitan with the opportunity to benefit from the maximum amount of specialist knowledge and focus.

In addition to the big acquisitions and the wide ranging series of corporate disposals, the Sheppard years were characterised by a significant focus on trying to change the overall management philosophy and corporate culture within Grand Metropolitan. Many of Sheppard's key management team from his time in charge of the UK food and brewing businesses replaced the existing central Grand Metropolitan management teams in areas such as personnel and finance. At IDV, where George Bull had replaced Anthony Tennant,[5] the influence of Sheppard and his management policies was slightly more muted than elsewhere within Grand Metropolitan, because of IDV's long history of closely guarded independence and overall level of profitability relative to other areas of the business. However, even so, IDV saw a greater emphasis on cost reduction and rationalisation during these years than had previously been the case.

At the same time, under Sheppard, Grand Metropolitan placed a great deal of emphasis on the training of managers – e.g. via an organised policy of internal transfers throughout the group, in an attempt to spread best practices as widely as possible. Per Sheppard, the role of the corporate centre during this period encompassed the following factors:

1 It was responsible for providing a 'tough and challenging culture' for top management that

---

[4] Among the businesses owned by Pillsbury were Burger King, Pillsbury Doughboy, Haagen Dazs Ice Cream and Green Giant.

[5] Tennant left IDV in 1990 to become CEO of Guinness.

was focused on demanding superior operational performance and cost leadership.

2 It focused on spotting and nurturing management talent within the various Grand Metropolitan business units.

3 It should focus simultaneously on improving operational performance with the business units and improving the branding and promotion of Grand Metropolitan's products.

The post-Sheppard years

Sheppard retired as Chairman and CEO of Grand Metropolitan in 1993. Although he had originally proposed that he should be replaced by Ian Martin, who had been responsible for overseeing the rationalisation and turnaround of the Pillsbury acquisition, Sheppard's recommendation in this respect was ignored by Grand Metropolitan's board of directors. They argued that George Bull's experience in successful brand building at IDV was more appropriate for the CEO role of a consumer products company in the 1990s than Martin's traditional focus on cost cutting and rationalisation. Therefore, Bull replaced Sheppard as CEO in 1993, while Martin subsequently left the company to pursue other interests.

Under Bull's leadership, the period from 1993 to 1996 was characterised by a continuous focus on the divestment of Grand Metropolitan's non-branded businesses, combined with ongoing attempts to acquire strong brands and to widen the international scope of the business. While the focus on cost control and restructuring remained from Sheppard's era, under Bull the group was also keen on maximising its international strengths, opportunities and alliances as he believed that Grand Metropolitan's growth potential depended on its ability to successfully access the high growth potential offered by the alcoholic drinks market in the world's emerging economies. However, while it remained a profitable company under Bull, it was also recognised by commentators and analysts that Grand Metropolitan struggled to effectively manage the demands of trying to build up an international business with far-flung operations.[6]

Furthermore, the group's share price continued to 'underperform' on the London Stock Exchange.[7] This continued underperformance, combined with the desire to strengthen Grand Metropolitan's international access, provided the background for the decision to merge Grand Metropolitan and Guinness in 1997. The new group was originally led by Bull and Tony Greener of Guinness, until Bull's retirement in 1998, when Greener took over sole responsibility. At the time of the merger, Diageo (as the merged group was called), consisted of the following core businesses:

1 Guinness Brewing; this included a wide range of brewing businesses around the world, including Spain's biggest brewer (Cruz Campo) and Desnoes & Geddes in the West Indies.

2 Pillsbury.

3 United Distillers and Vintners (this was the merged name for the combination of Guinness's United Distillers subsidiary and Grand Metropolitan's IDV division).

4 Burger King.

Diageo: the early years

The merger of Grand Metropolitan and Guinness created the world's sixth largest food and drinks business and was initially well regarded by City analysts, who saw genuine opportunities for the new business. At the time of the merger, it was claimed that the merged entity would be able to 'cut costs and exploit marketing synergies, while building global economies of scale.'[8] The perceived attractiveness of the merged company can be found by comparing the pre- and post-merger share prices. Immediately prior to the merger announcement, Grand Metropolitan and Guinness stock had been trading at 516 and 515 pence respectively; after the formal merger went through in December, the market price of the combined group was 590 pence per share.

At the time of the merger, the idea had been for the combined entity to continue operating and growing in all of the two predecessor firms' existing

6 Ernest Beck, Wall *Street Journal*, 19–01–98.

7 Ernest Beck, *Wall Street Journal*, 19–01–98.
8 Article in the *Wall Street Journal*, 20–05–00.

business units. In both the brewing and food divisions, it had famous and popular brands, while in the spirits area it had, through the merger, become the world's biggest spirits company. Nine of the world's top 25 global spirits brands, including such famous names as Smirnoff, Johnnie Walker and Bailey's, were owned by the group.

At the time of the merger announcement, there was, despite the general City approval of the alleged benefits that would arise from the fusion, some criticism of the proposal for the merged entity to continue operating in both the food and alcoholic beverages markets. Perhaps the strongest critic of the proposed strategy was Bernaud Arnaut, a non-executive director of Guinness at the time and Chairman of the French drinks company LVMH Moet Hennessy, which was a major shareholder in Guinness at this time. Arnaut strongly argued for the benefits that would arise from his alternative proposal to merge the alcoholic drinks divisions of LVMH, Guinness and Grand Metropolitan while selling off Grand Metropolitan's Pillsbury and Burger King divisions. Despite Arnaut's proposals to the contrary, the merger of Grand Metropolitan and Guinness went through as originally proposed in December 1997, after a delay of approximately seven months.

The early months of Diageo appeared to be well regarded by the City and in July 1998, the Diageo share price reached a high of over 700 pence per share – a rise of over 18% in the seven months since the merger of Grand Metropolitan and Guinness was finalised and the shares started trading on the London Stock Exchange. At this time, Diageo was already able to announce that the anticipated annual savings of £195 million that were due to arise as a result of the merger would be reached and analysts were suggesting that annual savings from the merger would actually be approximately £50 million greater than originally estimated.[9]

However, despite the fact that Diageo shares were still well regarded by the City in 1998, the merged entity was experiencing a range of problems at this stage. In 1998, John McGrath, the CEO of Diageo, admitted that the group's performance was actually

destroying shareholder value – while its weighted average cost of capital was 10.5%, its actual return on total invested capital was during this period, only 9.5%.[10] While Diageo was one of the few British companies in this period to publicly focus on shareholder value creation as a core aim of the business, the fact that the business was, at least initially, undermining real shareholder value creation shows that there was plenty of work to do in improving the performance of the business as a whole.

Throughout 1998 and 1999, despite relatively moderate overall financial results, Diageo continued to argue that there was nothing wrong with the Diageo business model. Paul Walsh, who led Diageo's Pillsbury division at the time of the merger and who would go on to replace McGrath as CEO on the latter's retirement in 2000, publicly stated in 1998 that 'Pillsbury will be a principal contributor in achieving Diageo's aims of doubling total shareholder returns every four years.'[11]

In an attempt to improve Diageo's performance and support the combined food and drinks business model, McGrath announced plans for the formal sharing of best practice throughout the Diageo group. These plans focused on having the executives of the various Diageo divisions take responsibility for 'looking at each other's patches to transfer best practice across the group'.[12] In addition, in January 1999, Diageo set up a cross-divisional marketing excellence team with members from Burger King, Guinness, UDV and Pillsbury in order to try to achieve marketing and promotional synergies and best practice across its various business divisions. However, while Diageo was able to develop and exploit minor marketing synergies (e.g. Burger King was able to utilise Pillsbury products in some of its restaurant promotions), by 2000 Diageo was admitting that the marketing synergies and benefits of the merger were negligible and journalists and commentators were pointing out that Diageo's shares had under-performed the market by 31% between January 1999 and September 2000.[13]

---

[9] *Financial Times*, 07–07–98.

[10] Report of interview with John McGrath, *Financial Times*, 18–03–98.

[11] Paul Walsh reported in the *Financial Times* by Maggie Urry, 21–10–02.

[12] John McGrath quoted in the *Financial Times*, 18–03–98.

[13] John Thornhill, *Financial Times*, 08–09–00.

At the same time that Diageo had been struggling to make the merger a clear success in its core business areas, the policy of sell-off and disposal continued as it had at Grand Metropolitan throughout much of the 1980s and the first half of the 1990s. While the disposal of many of the group's minor spirit brands was often because of the need to satisfy the various regulatory bodies around the world, other disposals (e.g. the disposal of the Spanish brewer Cruz Campo in 1999) were undertaken because of the perceived need to dispose of underperforming units and could be compared to the disposals that had been undertaken by Grand Metropolitan under Sheppard and Bull's leadership.

Diageo: the Paul Walsh era

At the time of McGrath's retirement as CEO of Diageo in 2000 and his replacement by Paul Walsh, a long-time Grand Metropolitan employee who had been partially responsible for the turnaround at Pillsbury, the company still faced a difficult post-merger future. The promised marketing synergies had largely failed to materialise while the performance of Burger King and Pillsbury was perceived by analysts to be undermining the success of the group's drinks divisions. In addition, franchisee holders at Burger King had become increasingly restless at what they perceived to be the failure of Diageo to manage the fast-food restaurant business effectively,[14] and had begun to publicly call for the Burger King business to be spun off as a separate entity.

The problems facing the company during this period resulted in Diageo agreeing to merge its Pillsbury division with General Mills, Inc., in 2000 (as part of the agreement, Diageo took a substantial minority stake in the expanded General Mills, Inc.). This development followed the announcement of Diageo's plans to put up 20% of Burger King for sale via an Initial Public Offering. Although Diageo under Walsh was clearly keen to dispose of Burger King in its entirety, US capital gains tax rules worked against the idea of initially offering more than 20% of Burger King for sale.

While the disposal of Pillsbury to General Mills went through without any significant problems, the planned partial disposal of Burger King was a much more drawn out and convoluted process. The initial plan to offer 20% of Burger King to the public via an IPO was eventually dropped because of stock market problems in 2000 and 2001 and Diageo didn't manage to dispose of Burger King until 2002, when it agreed to sell the business to a private equity consortium. Even then, Diageo had to accept getting only $1.5 billion for the business (when the original IPO plan had been launched, the business had been valued at $2.5–3.0 billion), while also having to provide the buying consortium with a wide range of financial assistance and guarantees.[15]

At the same time that Diageo was disposing (or trying to dispose) of Burger King and Pillsbury, it focused on trying to acquire some of the brands held by the spirits division of the Canadian drinks company Seagram, in an association with the French company Pernod Ricard. Diageo entered into a consortium with Pernod to acquire them, because it was keen to stop major rivals from acquiring them and it was not in a position to acquire the Seagram spirits brands in their totality, because of regulatory constraints in various countries. Although the acquisition process was long-drawn-out and convoluted, Diageo eventually agreed to pay $5.3 billion to obtain famous Seagram brands such as Crown Royal and Captain Morgan Rum. However, while Walsh called the deal a success, some commentators argued that Diageo's partner did better from the Seagram deal. In addition, despite having entered into the alliance with Pernod to specifically avoid getting into problems with the competition regulators around the world, this move was only partially successful, as US regulators insisted that Diageo needed to sell off either its newly acquired Captain Morgan Rum brand or its existing Malibu brand.[16]

---

[14] For example, during the 1990s under Grand Metropolitan and Diageo, Burger King was led by four separate Chief Executives.

[15] According to Newspaper reports (e.g. *Financial Times*, 20-02-04), Diageo's financial guarantees in respect of the Burger King sale amounted to $1.05 billion.

[16] Diageo eventually disposed of Malibu to Allied Domecq in 2002.

Diageo: what does the future hold?

Following the generally successful integration of Seagram's spirit brands and the disposals of Pillsbury and Burger King, the divisions that had been holding back Diageo's growth since the merger, one would perhaps imagine that the company's future is assured. However, while Diageo's stated goal for the future is now based clearly 'on delivering high quality growth in premium drinks',[17] there are still significant problems and issues which the company needs to address if it is going to enjoy significant growth over the coming years.

The volume growth in the alcoholic beverages market is limited (typically 1–2% per annum),[18] and this means that the innate future growth prospects for Diageo are also limited. In addition, while being the largest alcoholic beverages company in the world may be an attractive position to be in, it does also bring potential disadvantages in Diageo's case, as it would appear that the pure size of the company and the dominant position that it enjoys in many areas of the drinks markets may limit its ability to undertake any further significant acquisitions. Furthermore, Diageo in general (and Guinness in particular) is struggling in the core UK and Irish markets, as drinkers increasingly move away from going to pubs and prefer to buy their drinks in supermarket to enjoy at home. This development could result in Diageo facing thinner profit margins on its products, as they become increasingly squeezed by the powerful supermarkets.

Given the above problems and issues, future profit increases may therefore have to be achieved by one (or more) of the following methods:

1 Focusing on continually cutting the company's costs.

2 Stealing market share away from other firms and types of alcoholic beverage (e.g. from wine).

3 Continuing to successfully develop new alcoholic products that can help attract new drinkers.

4 Improving marketing and getting closer to the customer than any of the competition.

While Diageo (and previously Grand Metropolitan) have shown that they have been able to successfully develop new alcoholic beverages over an extended period of time, some commentators have questioned the long-term viability and/or stability of such a tactic. In this regard, one should note that some of Diageo's more recent innovations have only met with limited market success, while serious concerns have also been raised about the long-term market sustainability of some of Diageo's more successful, recent introductions such as Captain Morgan Spiced Rum in the US which, although produced like a beer (to benefit from lower US tax duties), is specifically designed to taste like a spirit (these types of drink are called malternatives). Overall, critics argue that too many of Diageo's new products are akin to brand extensions rather than the introduction of genuinely new products that help steal market shares from rivals.

Some commentators have also pointed out that the aggressive way in which Diageo has tried to change the 'rules of the game' in respect to the boundaries that apply to the alcoholic drinks industry has not always been successful. For example, Diageo has tried to persuade the major US TV broadcasters to remove their voluntary ban on the advertising of spirits without long-term success.[19] Additionally, the aggressive way that Diageo exploited the brewing rules in the US when developing the 'malternative' drinks concept resulted in heavy government lobbying from the influential US brewing industry. This lobbying has provisionally succeeded in that the US government agreed to change the rules so that 'malternative'-style drinks can only qualify for the reduced beer tax rates if they actually 'taste more like beer'. As one journalist has said, it has often appeared 'one step forward and two steps back for Diageo'.[20]

In addition, some commentators have raised question marks about the long-term future of Guinness within the Diageo empire. Although Diageo publicly remained committed to the Guinness brand, sales of

---

[17] Chief Executive's Review, Diageo Annual Report, 2003.
[18] *Business Week*, May 2003.

[19] Although Diageo was initially successful in persuading NBC to drop its advertising ban on spirits, NBC backed down under pressure and never screened the advertisements.
[20] Gerry Khermouth and Kerry Capell, *Business Week*, 19–05–03.

the stout are falling in both the UK and Ireland and Diageo have recently announced plans to close the Guinness brewery and Park Royal in London and centralise all European and North American Guinness production in Dublin. One also needs to ask whether the values associated with a traditional beer or stout are actually closely linked with the various spirits brands with which Diageo is most closely associated and whether there are genuine and significant marketing and distribution synergies between spirits and beers for the company.

However, despite the above concerns, it is clear that under Walsh's leadership Diageo will aggressively challenge the status quo in its markets and is keen to try new products and to challenge old market assumptions. Walsh remains publicly committed to ensuring that Diageo grows by more than the 1–2% market average growth rates, and it is clear that Diageo is willing to copy the successful practices of potential rivals to help achieve this growth. In this respect, Diageo in the US has started to use it power in the spirits sector to follow the example of Anheuser-Busch in the US beer market by increasingly centralising its US distribution network (with one distributor now taking responsibility for one whole state). As part of this pattern of increased centralisation, Diageo have started to simultaneously demand that each distributor appoints a specialist team to look after the whole of the Diageo account in their region as one of the requirements for being awarded the account.

Despite possible concerns about the company's long-term growth prospects, during the first part of the 21st century Diageo shares have outperformed the overall London Stock Exchange and its shares are continuing to trade at a premium compared to some of its major rivals such as Allied Domecq, while it remains well regarded by City analysts. The company has also shown that it has a strong cash flow stream over a period of several years and has shown itself over the past few years to be happy to return excess cash to shareholders. Perhaps the real question is, however, whether Diageo can continue to satisfy and exceed stock market expectations in the longer term with its present format and focus, or whether it will need to reinvent and redefine its strategic direction to maintain this favoured position with investors.

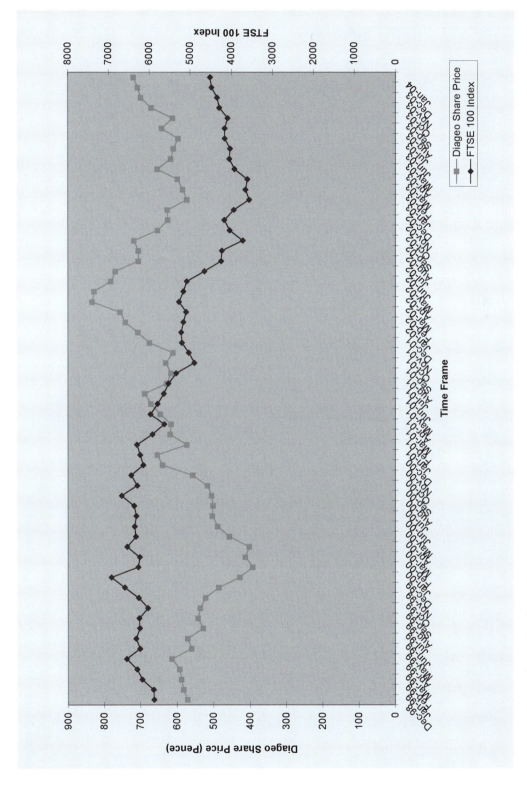

Exhibit 1 Diageo share price fluctuations

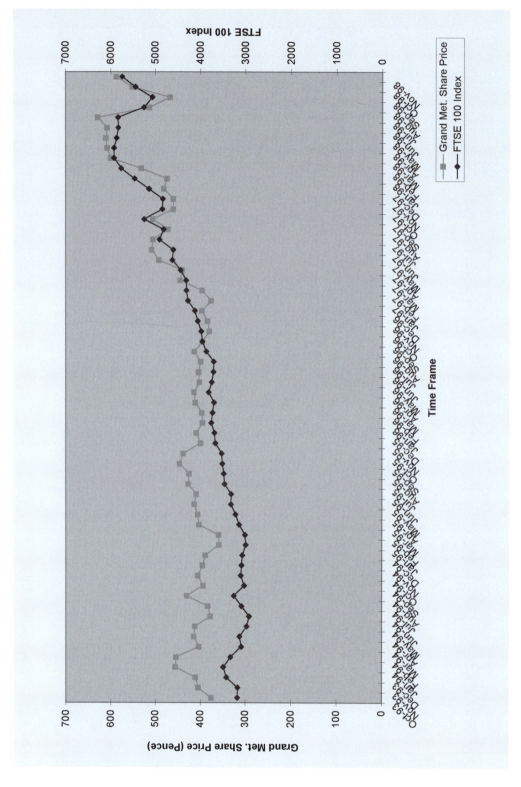

Exhibit 2 Grand Metropolitan share price fluctuations

Appendix 1 Diageo profit figures

	30 Dec 1996	30 June 1998	30 June 1999	30 June 2000	30 June 2001	30 June 2002	30 June 2003
Turnover – continuing activities	12,753	17,596	11,795	11,870	8,622	9,254	8,961
Turnover – disposals	687	106			4,199	1,455	479
Turnover – acquisition						573	
Group turnover	13,440	17,698	11,795	11,870	12,821	11,282	9,440
Profit on ordinary activities before tax	1,332	2,368	1,467	1,451	1,722	2,336	654

Notes:
1 The accounting period ended 30 June 1998 covers a period of 18 months. All other accounting periods cover a period of 12 months.
2 The accounts for the period ended 30 June 2003 include a special provision of £1.5 billion in respect of the disposal of Burger King.
3 Accounts have not been adjusted to reflect any changes to UK Generally Accepted Accounting Principles (GAAP) during the above periods.

Appendix 2 The core Diageo brands as at July 2003

Smirnoff – The world's best selling premium vodka.
Johnnie Walker – The world's best selling Scotch whisky.
Captain Morgan – The world's number two selling rum.
Bailey's – The world's number one cream liqueur.
J&B – The number two selling Scotch whisky in the world.
Cuervo – The number one selling tequila in the world.
Tanqueray – The number one selling premium gin in the US market.
Guinness – The world's best selling (and best known) stout.

Appendix 3 A summary of major acquisitions and disposals within Grand Metropolitan and Diageo between 1988 and 2002

2002 calendar year
– Sale of Burger King to a private equity consortium is finalised.
– Sale of the Malibu brand to Allied Domecq is finalised.

2001 calendar year
– Acquisition of Seagram spirit and wine business (in association with Pernod Ricard) is finalised.
– Disposal of Pillsbury via a combination with General Mills, Inc., is finalised.

2000 calendar year
– Diageo initially decides on the partial flotation of Burger King (subsequently not executed).

1999 calendar year
– Sale of Cruz Campo (Spain's largest brewer) to Heineken.
– Disposal of a range of 'minor' spirit brands including Cinzano Vermouth (to Campari).

1998 calendar year
– Acquisition by Pillsbury of the bakery products business of Heinz.
– Disposal of Dewar's whisky and Bombey gin to Bacardi.

1996 calendar year
– Sale of Pearle Vision Optical Retailers to the Cole National Corporation.

1995 calendar year
– Purchase by Pillsbury of Old El Paso Mexican-style food products.

1993 calendar year
– Disposal of Chef & Brewer pub-restaurant chain to Scottish & Newcastle brewers.

1992 calendar year
– Sale of Express Dairy and Eden Vale businesses to Northern Foods.
– Purchase of Cinzano Vermouth.
– Sale of Burger King's distribution services arm.

1991 calendar year
– Disposal of Grand Metropolitan's brewing interests.
– Sale of Wienerwald (a German/central European restaurant chain).

1990 calendar year
– Disposal of Wimpy table service restaurants.
– Disposal of Berni pub-restaurants.

1989 calendar year
– Grand Metropolitan acquires the Pillsbury food chain (including its Burger King subsidiary).
– Purchase of UB chain of fast-food restaurants.
– Purchase of Eyelab optical retailers in the US.
– Sale of UK casino interests.

1988 calendar year
– Sale of Intercontinental hotel chain.
– Purchase of various US optical retail firms including Vision Express and Eye & Tech.
– Disposal of Grand Metropolitan's soft drink bottling facilities.

This case study was prepared for this textbook by faculty members at Warwick Business School, University of Warwick, UK. This case study may not be reproduced in any form without prior permission. For more information, visit www.wbs.ac.uk.

Case 21 **The hostile bid for Blue Circle**

Introduction

Early summer 1999, Rick Haythornthwaite, the CEO of Blue Circle PLC, became aware that one of its largest rivals, Lafarge, under its Chairman and CEO Bertrand Collomb, was considering a takeover bid. In fact, Lafarge had started planning for the acquisition in June 1997, some two years earlier. Both companies were leading global players in the world cement industry: Blue Circle, a FTSE 250 PLC, was capitalised at £2.752 billion,[1] while Lafarge, a French giant, was capitalised at FFR76.591 billion. The takeover, launched on 31 January 2000 was an all-cash hostile bid, which valued Blue Circle at £3.4 billion. If the takeover bid succeeded, Lafarge would become the largest cement company in the world.

Blue Circle and its advisers started work on updating its defence plan, which consisted of valuations on several bases together with expected lines of attack and potential responses to these issues.

Industry background

World demand for cement is approximately 1.5 billion tonnes per annum, and between 1990 and

....

This case is intended as a basis for class discussion rather than to illustrate either effective or ineffective handling of a business situation.

© Duncan Angwin, Philip Stern, Sarah Bradley, Warwick Business School, 2004.

....

[1] 1999 estimate.

1997 demand grew at a compound rate of 5.5% compared with population growth of 1.5% over the same period. Production and consumption data are shown in Appendix 1. Regional differences can be significant and consumption is increasing in the developing world much more than in the developed world. Since 1990 per capita consumption grew by 7.1% in Asia whereas in Europe it fell by 1.4%, although this latter figure partly reflects the fall in consumption in former Eastern Bloc countries. Regional cement trends are shown in Appendix 2.

Per capita cement consumption varies between regions, with the North American and European markets consuming approximately four times as much cement per person as Africa. Regional consumption per capita is shown in Appendix 3. Regional averages can, however, mask country differences, and within Europe Portugal consumes nearly 1000kg per person while the UK only uses 210kg, largely because of different construction methods for residential and infrastructure work.

Industry consolidation

The main players in the cement industry can be divided into four strategic categories, as shown in Figure 1.

International producers have a strong home base, which has supported limited investment overseas. The businesses remain largely independent and there is limited sharing of skills and expertise. Multinational producers are larger groups that have been investing internationally for some years. Production decisions remain largely domestic although some trading of cement takes place.

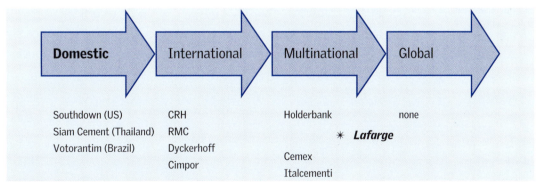

Figure 1 Cement industry value chain
Source: *European Cement Review*, January 2000, HSBC.

Trading and operational synergies increase as the groups expand and returns are therefore generally higher than those for international producers. Global producers are currently a theoretical category where production and capacity decisions are taken on a global basis. The advantage would be the erosion of price discrepancies and the rising of average prices as a result of less competition (*European Cement Review*, January 2000, HSBC).

The last few years have seen large-scale consolidation of the cement industry with nearly 80 million tonnes capacity acquired by the leading producers in the four years to the end of 1999 (see Appendix 4). This represents over 8% of global cement capacity, excluding China. The top six multinational producers have 30% of global capacity at the end of 1999 compared with 11% in 1988.

Appendix 5 shows major deals entered into in the last three years, and Table 1 gives the capacities of the largest companies.

Key expansion opportunities lie in the regions where national players still dominate. The percentage of regional markets controlled by international and domestic producers are shown in Table 2.

Blue Circle

In 1999, Blue Circle was the sixth largest cement producer in the world with a total kiln capacity of 40.6 million tonnes. Blue Circle was the parent company of an international group of companies whose core businesses were cement, aggregates and ready-mix concrete. Cement contributed the majority of group sales and operating profit. It was quoted on the London stock exchange and its market capitalisation at 31 December 1999 was €4.7 billion.

Blue Circle had market leader positions in the UK, Malaysia, Greece, Nigeria, Denmark and Kenya and was number five in the US. The Group's market share and major competitors by country are shown in Appendix 8. Although some way behind Holderbank and Lafarge in size, Blue Circle doubled its cement capacity between 1997 and 1999 with acquisitions in Asia and Greece. In addition, during 1999, the non-core heating and bathrooms divisions were disposed of. (Selected financial information is shown in Appendix 6.)

Lafarge

In 1999, Lafarge, the French heavy building materials group, was the second largest cement pro-

Table 1 Cement kiln capacity by largest companies and by region

	Total kiln capacity (millions tonnes)							
	Western Europe	Eastern Europe	Africa	Asia	Oceania	North America	C & S America	Total
Holderbank	16.4	6.6	5.7	17.4	1.2	15.3	21.3	83.9
Lafarge	24.7	12.0	12.0	6.0		13.2	8.2	76.1
Cemex	10.4		4.0	10.2		1.1	41.1	66.8
Italcementi	30.2	2.6	3.6	3.9		5.4	0.7	46.3
Heidelberger	33.8	12.5	1.2	3.0		10.5		61.0
Blue Circle	16.7		4.1	12.3		6.7	0.9	40.6
CRH	5.8							5.8
RMC	8.9	6.5			3.1	1.0		19.5
Dyckerhoff	10.7	2.6				4.7		18.1
Cimpor	7.1		2.4				2.8	12.3

Source: *European Cement Review*, January 2000, HSBC.

Table 2 Regional markets controlled by international and domestic producers

Region	National players market share (%)	International majors market share (%)
Asia (excluding China)	90	10
Middle East	84	16
Eastern Europe	73	27
Africa	71	29
Latin America	70	30
Western Europe	37	63
North America	37	63
Total (excluding China)	70	30

Source: *European Cement Review*, January 2000, HSBC.

ducer in the world, with total kiln capacity of 76.1 million tonnes (see Table 1), behind Holderbank of Switzerland. Lafarge was also the world's largest producer of roof tiles and the third largest ready-mix concrete producer. Lafarge was quoted in Paris and London and its market capitalisation at 31 December 1999 was €12.1 billion. Lafarge's other building materials activities include aggregates, plasterboard and speciality materials.

Lafarge has market leader positions in France, Poland, Morocco and Canada, is number two in Venezuela and Turkey, and is number three in the US, Brazil and Spain. Lafarge's market share and major competitors by country are shown in Appendix 9. Cement contributes approximately one-third of sales but more than half of operating profit. (Selected financial information is shown in Appendix 10.)

Haythornthwaite: Blue Circle's new CEO

Rick Haythornthwaite, CEO of Blue Circle at the time of the hostile takeover, had previously held a number of positions at BP and had been a director of Premier Oil plc. He joined Blue Circle in October 1997 and had initial responsibility for Heavy Building Materials in Asia where he was the architect of Blue Circle's strategy for investing in Malaysia. He later took responsibility for Europe. He became Chief Executive designate in December 1998 and finally CEO in July

1999 on a salary of £390,000; a discount of 20% of the median level to reflect his lack of experience in such a role.

The first rumours that Blue Circle might be a potential bid target occurred in October 1999, after the Group issued a profits warning. This came only six weeks after the announcement of the half-year results and severely undermined the credibility of the new Chief Executive. The following month it was reported that Lafarge had engaged an investment bank to assist them in preparing a bid. Little further was heard until 30 January 2000 when the *Sunday Telegraph* reported that a bid was imminent.

Bertrand Collomb, the Chairman and Chief Executive of Lafarge, telephoned Rick Haythornthwaite that weekend to discuss a possible takeover. The price of £4.30 per share was mentioned, but this was dismissed by Haythornthwaite.

The hostile bid

On 1 February 2000 Lafarge announced a pre-conditional offer for Blue Circle of £4.20 per share. The offer represented a premium of only 1.4% over Blue Circle's closing middle market price of £4.14 on 31 January, although it was a premium of 33.6% over the closing middle market price of £3.1425 on Thursday 27 January, the day before there was significant speculation in the market concerning a possible bid for Blue Circle. It was acknowledged by analysts that the two groups were strategically a good fit, but the consensus was that the price would have to be close to £5.00 per share for the bid to succeed.

Lafarge attacked Blue Circle primarily for mistakes made in the past, including the diversification strategy of the 1980s and early 1990s. By diversifying, Blue Circle had fallen behind its international competitors and it was now heavily dependent on 'too few countries'. Lafarge asserted that 'this "over-dependence" on a small number of operating territories means that Blue Circle's profitability is inherently volatile'.

Defence plan

Blue Circle's financial advisers at the time of the bid were the merchant bank Lazards. They had been heavily involved in producing the defence plan in 1999. They now steered the conduct of the defence itself. The first critical issue was what value to put on Blue Circle? The valuations prepared by City analysts (see Table 3) were all based on information in the public domain and on the analysts' expectations of future growth in the various markets.

The analysts' valuations were generally around 500 pence, with some exceptions, namely Oddo Equities[2] (25 January 2000) and Credit Suisse First

Table 3 Analysts' valuations of Blue Circle

Date	Source	Nature of valuation	Pence per share
March 1999	Lazard Brothers for BCI	DCF	433
September 1999	Warburg Dillon Read	Target price	500
January 2000	HSBC	Target price	430
13 January 2000	Lazard Brothers for BCI	DCF mid-point	486
25 January 2000	Oddo Equities	Stand alone value Discounted free cash flow	390
31 January 2000	Warburg Dillon Read	Target price	500
22 February 2000	Goldman Sachs	Target price	471
	HSBC	Target price	500
	Warburg Dillon Read	Target price	500
24 February 2000	Credit Suisse First Boston	Stand alone value Discounted free cash flow	390
24 February 2000	Teather & Greenwood	Exit price	500
3 March 2000	Commerzbank	Break up value, before premium for control	446
7 March 2000	Robert Fleming & Co	Target price	500
12 April 2000	Oddo Equities	Take out price	519
20 April 2000	Robert Fleming & Co	Target price (post Asia and OIP announcements)	550
1 December 2000	Schroder Salomon Smith Barney	Take out price	490–495

Note: BCI is Blue Circle Industries.

2 Oddo Equities later increased their valuation to in excess of 500 pence towards the end on the bid process and after the release of the OIP and Asia documents.

Table 4 Blue Circle forecasts against actual results

Date prepared	Source	Operating profits 2001 forecast £m
November 1999	2000–2002 Business Plan	560
November 2000	2001–2003 Business Plan	519
June 2001	Full year forecast	491
September 2001	Full year forecast *	385

Note: *£33 million of the reduction between the June and September 2001 forecasts is due to the sale of Blue Circle's Canadian cement business.

Boston (24 February 2000). Lazards had access to Blue Circle financial information including management accounts, forecasts and budgets. Their valuation presented to the board in January 2000 was prepared based on the 2000–2002 business plan. This valuation seemed a reasonable estimate provided the profit forecasts in the Business Plan were considered achievable. Blue Circle, however, tended to achieve actual results lower than plan, and profit projections were sometimes wildly optimistic (see Table 4).

Lazards were instructed to reduce the profit forecasts in the 2000–2002 plan to bring them down to more achievable levels. Their discounted cash flow analysis prepared for the board of Blue Circle valued the business at 486 pence, which was seen as relatively conservative. This valuation provided support for the claims of management that the Lafarge bid of 430 pence undervalued the group.

Blue Circle's response

The initial response of Blue Circle to the Lafarge approach was to dismiss the bid as significantly undervaluing the company. There was then a delay until Lafarge issued its offer document on 10 February 2000. Blue Circle's response to this document was to reiterate the earlier assertion that the offer undervalued the company, but also to claim that the Lafarge bid was a 'quest for our Asian assets' and that this 'validates the investment strategy' of the group.

The first significant document issued by Blue Circle was the early release of the group's 1999 results on 21 February 2000. The publication date was brought forward by five weeks, partly because the original date would have been after day 39, the latest date on which Blue Circle could issue new information, and partly to provide a solid base from which to launch the defence in which management attempted to justify their current strategy. The document stated that:

Lafarge's chairman has congratulated our management for 'doing all the right things'. He is right to.

- *We have a business that is fundamentally changed, refocused on our strengths in cement, aggregates and concrete.*
- *We have invested carefully, building leading positions in our chosen markets.*
- *We have exciting growth prospects.*
- *We will deliver substantial performance improvement and cost savings in the near term.*

The document also showed that the final dividend for 1999 would be 10.95 pence per share, which was an increase compared with internal plans (see Table 5).

On 23 March 2000 Blue Circle issued a document setting out the open market value and development value of the group's land holdings in Kent and elsewhere. The open market value was estimated at £227 million and the development value at £546 million.

On 28 March 2000 Blue Circle issued a profit forecast for its Asian businesses where it had been investing heavily. Indeed, this heavy investment had been at a time when profits in Asia were falling and these difficult trading conditions had been

Table 5 Dividends declared and paid for the years 1994 to 1999

	Interim dividend (pence per share)	Final dividend (pence per share)
1994	3.75	8.0
1995	4.0	8.5
1996	4.25	9.0
1997	4.65	9.85
1998	4.85	10.35
1999	5.05	10.95

responsible for the profits warning. Under the rules of the Takeover Code, the group would not normally have been permitted to issue such a forecast, but because Lafarge had itself issued forecasts for the prospects in Asia, Blue Circle was permitted to respond.

The document set out forecasts for profits for Asia for 2000–2002 to convince shareholders that the investments in Asia would pay off in the short term. In defending management's strategy the document stated that *'Blue Circle has followed a deliberate strategy of increasing investment in Asia in anticipation of what is now a strong and sustainable recovery.'*

On 6 April, Blue Circle announced its operational improvements programme (OIP). The document announced details of the projected benefits arising from such cost savings and included forecasts of the benefits to be achieved to be of the order of £116 million per annum by 2002. The document also reiterated that the Lafarge bid undervalued the company.

The final salvo in Blue Circle's defence was launched on 11 April 2000. Blue Circle was so confident it would deliver on the promises in the property, Asia and OIP documents that it would return £800 million to shareholders in advance. The first tranche of £400 million was to take place by way of a tender offer for Blue Circle's shares, although the form of the second tranche was left open.

The return of capital was in effect a down payment to shareholders, demonstrating the confidence of management in delivering the promises they had made. It had the consequence of increasing Blue Circle's gearing significantly from 17.2% (end of 1999) to 107.7% (end of 2000), and of dramatically reducing the free cash flow available for future projects.

The return of capital document issued on 11 April summarised the main defence themes of property, performance improvement, Asia, and strong market positions, under the headline *'Blue Circle is a business with renewed momentum'.*

Other options

At the same time as these actions were being taken, Blue Circle considered a number of other options.

Management buy-out

An MBO team was put together, headed up by Operations Director David Lovett and staffed by the Finance Director and other managers from Blue Circle's North American operations. The MBO would have been the eighth largest ever and work needed to start early if it was to have any chance of success. The then Head of Mergers and Acquisitions at Blue Circle stated in interview that he believed that Lazards had effectively sabotaged any chance of success with an MBO as they had advised Haythornthwaite that the financing could be arranged in a short period of time. This opinion was not voiced by the Strategy Director, although he agreed that work on the MBO started too late in the defence process to have any chance of success.

The Blue Circle Strategy Director stated that he believed that the process of preparing the MBO case was very divisive within the organisation and that it distracted attention from the main fight. Within the organisation the MBO was unpopular as it would have been a North America takeover of the group and would have required significant disposals of operations to be feasible. Externally the Strategy Director believed that it did create noise in the markets and therefore may have unsettled Lafarge. The MBO option was examined but not pursued.

Acquisitions by target

Prior to Lafarge's bid, Blue Circle had started talks with Southdown, a US cement manufacturer, in 1999 with a view to agreeing a takeover. The two parties were close to agreeing a deal in early 2000 when the bid by Lafarge was launched, and indeed the bid may have been precipitated by leaks of the talks. If Blue Circle had acquired Southdown, the combined group would have been too large for Lafarge to afford.

Blue Circle remained in contact with Southdown during the defence process, although Southdown were not prepared to contemplate a deal until such time as Blue Circle had defeated Lafarge.

White squire defence

In this instance Votorantim would invest in new equity to enable Blue Circle to acquire Southdown. Some discussions were held with Votorantim but this option was not pursued further.

White knights

Management examined the possibility of a merger with a number of parties including Italcementi, Cemex, Holderbank, Hanson, RMC and Aggregate Industries. White knight deals failed on several fronts. Haythornthwaite commented that the potential white knight deals failed to provide the cash that the shareholders seemed to want and the potential white knights were also reluctant to become involved. The Strategy Director stated that Collomb had spoken to the other majors and effectively warned them against becoming involved in the bid.

Dawn raid

On 19 April, day 46 under the City Takeover Code, Lafarge launched a dawn raid and picked up 19.9% of Blue Circle directly and a further 9.6% through its bankers. Lafarge then increased its offer to £4.50 per share. Lafarge was confident of victory.

There were very few legal or regulatory defences available to Blue Circle at this point. Competition clearance from the European Commission was a formality, and the only areas where there were competition issues were the United States and Canada, so the scope for action by Blue Circle was limited.

Blue Circle appealed to the Canadian regulatory authorities following Lafarge's dawn raid. Under Canadian law, Lafarge was only permitted to acquire up to 20% of Blue Circle before receiving clearance, but the stake held by Lafarge's bankers meant that Lafarge effectively controlled nearly 30% of Blue Circle. Lafarge claimed it had agreed to make divestitures as required by the relevant authorities and that it had received prior approval from the Canadians. However, the Canadian authorities denied this. Even so, the authorities declined to take action against Lafarge.

The hostile bid fails

Early on in the defence process shareholders did not want to talk to Blue Circle. Investors were not prepared to sit down and talk to management until the final offer had been made by Lafarge and no further information could be released. During the last ten days of the offer period Haythornthwaite and James Loudon, Blue Circle's Finance Director, held a number of meetings with institutional investors in an attempt to persuade them to back management and reject the bid.

As day 60 approached, the lobbying of shareholders paid off when Schroeder's publicly backed the incumbent management on 26 April. This was followed by other shareholders and the bid was rejected. On 3 May Lafarge announced that it had received acceptances that, together with its holdings amounted to 44.5% of Blue Circle. The bid therefore lapsed. This was the first all-cash bid for a FTSE 100 company to fail for fifteen years.

Lafarge's reaction

Collomb and Lafarge had been severely shaken when the 2000 bid failed, particularly as they already controlled nearly 30% of Blue Circle following the dawn raid in April 2000. Collomb was very heavily involved with the hostile bid and the defeat was seen by many as a personal failure, particularly as it was rumoured that Lafarge's advisers recommended a revised offer in the range 460–470 pence in April 2000, and Collomb had ignored this advice by only increasing the bid to 450 pence. It is highly unlikely that Collomb would have launched another hostile bid for Blue Circle in 2001 as he would not have been prepared to risk failure again.

Blue Circle's reaction

Immediately following the successful defence in 2000 the remuneration committee of the board met and agreed that Haythornthwaite's package should be reviewed. His base to salary was increased to £490,000 per annum, being the median for a Chief Executive in the industrial sector. In addition, Haythornthwaite was granted a large number of executive share options and stock appreciation rights to take his entitlement up to the maximum four times salary that was permitted. It would normally have taken four years to build up to the full holding. It should be noted that Haythornthwaite's options were granted outside the normal timetable for such options, and that other directors were not granted additional options at this time.

At the time of the first bid in 2000 Haythornthwaite held options and SARs over a total of 431,166 shares. This would have realised a profit of approximately £340,000 at the original offer price of £4.20 and £469,000 at the revised price of £4.50. The recommended bid in 2001 gave rise to a potential profit on Haythornthwaite's share options and SARs of approximately £1.1 million.

The stated motivation of the remuneration committee was retention. The committee was aware of Haythornthwaite's increased profile in the market following the successful defence of Blue Circle, and felt that it was important for the group that he continued in office to ensure delivery of the defence promises. The additional salary and options were designed to prevent Haythornthwaite from leaving Blue Circle.

Post-deal options for Blue Circle

Blue Circle was left with a major competitor effectively owning 29.5% of its shares, and this increased to 32.2% after the first tranche of the return of capital, by way of tender offer, was completed. To be able to remain independent Blue Circle needed to undertake a major acquisition or merger, but potential partners were unwilling to participate while Lafarge owned more than 30% of the Group.

Late in June 2000 a two-day board meeting was held to review strategy. It was acknowledged that Lafarge had few strategic growth options as attractive to it as Blue Circle, and it was considered that a price of £5.00 to £5.50 could be justified. Delivery on the defence promises was vital, but the directors also considered that step-change acquisitions should also be pursued.

At the time of the announcement of the group's interim 2000 results in September, Haythornthwaite wrote to Collomb, offering to brief him, in his capacity of major shareholder, on the results. The two Chief Executives met and agreed that they would not allow pride to get in the way of achieving the best deal for the shareholders of both groups. Haythornthwaite said that he was not ready to sell yet, but that if a deal were to be done the price would have to be 'a long way north' of what was previously offered. This was followed by a meeting in a London hotel where Haythornthwaite and Collomb discussed a possible link-up.

At the October board meeting Haythornthwaite explained to the board the difficulties facing the group in the current operating environment and also reported that the first draft of the 2001–2003 business plan was forecasting operating profits for 2001 of £511 million, significantly below brokers' consensus of £539 million. Haythornthwaite presented three strategy options to the board, which dealt with the relative short-term strength but medium-term weakness of the group. These included achieving an early deal with Lafarge; an acquisition to move out of Lafarge's reach; and a merger with another party. Considerable time and resources had been devoted to evaluating acquisitions of or mergers with various parties following the strategy meeting in June. The board decided that negotiations should begin with Lafarge, but that the other options should remain open to avoid undermining the current position of strength.

Haythornthwaite's approach to Lafarge was timed to maximise his negotiating position. The OIP was expected to achieve results in 2000 in excess of those promised during the defence. Total operating profits for 2000 were forecast to meet market consensus, although the quality of earnings was relatively poor, with higher than consensus profits from property disposals and a number of one-off accounting adjustments. Profits for Asia were forecast marginally below market consensus but in line with defence promises. However, the forecasts for 2001 and 2002 showed operating profit below market consensus, and it was considered that these forecasts were challenging, with more potential for downside than upside.

At Lafarge, Collomb's confidence was dented and he may not have been prepared to risk failure again. Even so, under takeover regulations he would not have been able to bid again until May 2001. Haythornthwaite took advantage of this by initiating negotiations well before that time.

Haythornthwaite met Collomb again to start the negotiations. By early December 2000 it was clear that a deal could be done with Lafarge or else a dignified exit. It was in the interests of both groups to resolve the position and it was known that Collomb was unwilling to risk another hostile takeover. Both sides were extremely anxious that there should be no leaks, and had there been any Haythornthwaite would have walked away.

Lafarge started at £4.70 with no dividend but Haythornthwaite had been adamant that he needed to be able to present the deal as being worth over £5.00 per share in order to recommend it to shareholders. However, the Blue Circle board agreed privately that they would accept an offer price less than the discounted cash flow valuation of £5.00 per share as management credibility would be lost if they rejected a 'reasonable value'. The reasonable value they agreed upon was £4.70 to £4.75 per share. The advisers to both sides worked in the period up to and over Christmas, finally agreeing a deal at £4.95 per share plus a final dividend.

A board meeting was held on Sunday 7 January 2001 to decide whether to recommend the Lafarge offer to shareholders. A revised discounted cash flow valuation had been prepared by Lazards based on the 2001–2003 business plan forecasts, and by coincidence this gave a value for the group of £4.95 per share. The directors therefore had no hesitation in recommending the offer to shareholders.

The vast majority of Blue Circle's shareholders were institutions and they readily agreed to the bid. However, many individual shareholders, who were mainly ex-employees with an emotional attachment, voted against the takeover, as they saw Blue Circle as a 'British Institution'.

The agreed takeover at £4.95 per share was described in February 2001 as 'a sensibly priced deal' by analysts at HSBC. Lafarge's shares responded favourably, rising sharply immediately after announcement and remained relatively stable at this higher level.

After the completion of the takeover

Haythornthwaite left Blue Circle on 11 July 2001 following completion. On 24 July 2001, it was announced that he would be appointed CEO of Invensys with effect from 1 October.

Case Questions

1 Why was Blue Circle bid for?

2 Was it in the interests of Blue Circle's shareholders for the hostile bid to fail?

3 Were the defence strategies adopted by Blue Circle consistent with reducing the chance of takeover but not prejudicial towards its shareholders?

4 Did Hawthornthwaite act in his own best interests or his shareholders'?

Appendices; Financial Information

Appendix 1 Global cement market (including China)

	1990	1991	1992	1993	1994	1995	1996	1997	1998e	1999e	Av. growth rate 1990–99e	Av. growth rate 1990–97
Production (millions tonnes)	1008	1042	1130	1206	1308	1388	1440	1473	1449	1494	4.5%	5.6%
% change		3.4%	8.4%	6.6%	8.5%	6.1%	3.7%	2.3%	−1.7%	3.1%		
Imports (millions tonnes)	71	72	76	78	90	100	102	102	101	102	4.1%	5.3%
% change		0.8%	6.6%	2.7%	15.5%	10.8%	1.9%	−0.4%	−0.6%	0.5%		
Exports (millions tonnes)	70	72	75	81	93	101	105	105	105	110	5.1%	6.0%
% change		2.0%	4.9%	7.2%	15.0%	9.3%	3.9%	0.2%	−0.1%	4.1%		
Consumption (millions tonnes)	1006	1037	1127	1197	1296	1376	1427	1458	1440	1483	4.4%	5.5%
% change		3.1%	8.7%	6.2%	8.3%	6.2%	3.7%	2.1%	−1.2%	3.0%		
Population (millions)	4972	5075	5179	5226	5276	5360	5443	5518	5589	5663	1.5%	1.5%
Kg per capital	202	204	218	229	246	257	262	264	258	262	2.9%	3.9%
% change		1.0%	6.5%	5.2%	7.3%	4.5%	2.1%	0.8%	−2.5%	1.6%		

Source: *European Cement Review*, January 2000, HSBC

Appendix 2 Regional cement trends

1990–97 growth	Consumption	Production	Population growth	Per capita growth
Europe	−0.9%	−0.4%	0.5%	−1.4%
N. America	2.1%	2.7%	1.1%	1.0%
Asia	8.9%	8.9%	1.6%	7.1%
S & C America	3.3%	3.2%	0.3%	3.0%
Africa	2.6%	2.6%	2.6%	–
Oceania	2.9%	2.1%	2.0%	0.9%
Total	5.5%	5.6%	1.5%	3.9%

Source: *European Cement Review*, January 2000, HSBC

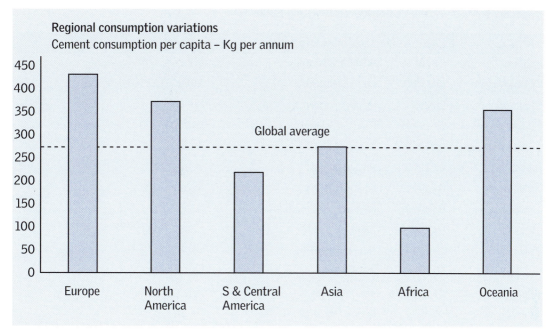

Appendix 3 Cement consumption per capita by region

Appendix 4 Acquisitions by large cement producers 1996–1999

Area	Tonnage (m)
Eastern Europe	22.3
Asia (excluding China)	20.3
Western Europe	11.5
Latin and South America	8.8
Africa	7.1
North America	6.6
Middle East	3.1
Total	79.7

Source: *European Cement Review*, January 2000, HSBC

Appendix 5 Major cement deals between 1998 and 2000

Acquirer	Date	Target/Country	Price $m	Price per tonne
Lafarge	Q1 2001	Blue Circle/various	7050	179
Cemex	Q4 2000	Southdown/USA	2850	225
Hanson	Q4 1999	Pioneer/various	2600	na
Heidelberger	Q2 1999	Scancem/various	2400	200
Anglo American	Q4 1999	Tarmac/UK, USA	2000	na
RMC	Q4 1999	Rugby/various	1400	176
Dyckerhoff	Q4 1999	Lonestar/USA	1200	294
Heidelberger	Q4 1999	CBR minorities/various	1100	175
Blue Circle	Q4 1999	Heracles & Halkis/Greece	680	124
Cimpor	Q3 1999	Brennand/Brazil	594	212
Cimpor	Q2 2000	Ameriyah/Egypt	550	187
Suez Cement	Q1 2000	Tourah/Egypt	523	108
Blue Circle	Q2 1999	Kedah/Malaysia	499	130
CRH	Q2 1999	Finnsementti/Finland	440	210
Blue Circle	Q4 1998	APMC/Malaysia	421	125
CRH	Q3 1999	Thompson McCulley/USA	420	na
Cemex	Q1 1999	Apo/Philippines	400	166
Italcementi	Q1 1998	24% Ciments Français/various	400	125
Cemex	Q4 1999	Assiut/Egypt	373	104
CRH	Q1 2000	Shelly/USA	362	na
Lafarge	Q1 1999	Beni Suef/Egypt	358	265
Valderrivas	Q4 1999	Giant/USA	343	202
RMC	Q2 1998	Wulfrather/Germany	280	90
CRH	Q4 2000	Jura/Switzerland	265	na
Valderrivas	Q4 1998	Atlantico/Spain	260	190
Semapa	Q1 2000	Gabes/Tunisia	250	220
Lafarge	Q3 1998	BC South Africa/South Africa	248	92
Cimpor	Q4 1998	Ciments de jebl Oust/Tunisia	243	200
Holderbank	Q4 1999	Siam City Cement/Thailand	228	100
Holderbank	Q3 1998	Phinma/Philippines	287	105
Blue Circle	Q4 1999	Alexandria/Egypt	200	130
Uniland	Q4 1998	Cements d'enfidha/Tunisia	168	159
Holderbank	Q3 1998	Siam City Cement/Thailand	153	100
Total			$29.5bn	

Source: *European Cement Review*, February 2001, HSBC

Appendix 6 Selected financial information on Blue Circle

Blue Circle Industries PLC	Selected financial data *£millions*				
	1995	1996	1997	1998	1999E
Group turnover	1,775	1,815	1,939	2,021	2,301
Operating profit (before exceptional items)	290	309	360	349	330
Operating margin	16.3%	17.0%	18.6%	17.3%	14.3%
Profit before tax (before exceptional items)	273	298	342	318	267
Earnings per share (before exceptional items) (pence)	21.4p	23.5p	29.0p	28.0p	23.5p
Net dividend (pence)	12.5p	13.25p	14.5p	15.2p	16.0p
Net assets	1,235	1,275	1,293	1,457	1,520
Net debt	36	1	245	565	596
Gearing (%)	2.9%	0.1%	18.9%	38.8%	39.2%
Market capitalisation at 31 December	2,510	2,625	2,586	2,414	2,752

Source: 1995–1998 actuals – Blue Circle Industries PLC 1995–1998 annual accounts
        1999 estimates – *European Cement Review*, January 2000, HSBC

Appendix 7 Blue Circle's share price performance

Appendix 8 Blue Circle's market share and competitors by country

Country	Market share	Competitors
UK	47%	Heidelberger (24%), RMC (20%)
USA	6%	Holderbank (12%), Southdown (10%), Heidelberger (7%), Lafarge (9%), Ash Grove (6%), Dyckerhoff (5%), Ciments Français (5%)
Malaysia	47%	CIMA (9%), Perak Hanjoong (6%), Pahang (6%), CMS (8%), Tasek (7%), Holderbank (5%)
Chile	40%	Holderbank (34%), Cemex (22%)
Philippines	20%	Holderbank (34%), Cemex (20%), Lafarge (15%), Northern (5%)
Denmark	90%	Imports
Greece	53%	Titan (40%), Ciments Français (6%)
Canada	13%	Lafarge (42%), Holderbank (17%), Heidelberger (18%), Ciments Français (7%)
Singapore	24%	Jurong (14%), National (14%), Ssangyong (13%), Sin Heng Chang (11%), Singapore Cement (8%), Asia Cement (6%)
Egypt	c2%	Holderbank (7%), Lafarge/Titan (5%), Cemex (12%), other domestics (10% each)
Nigeria	c30%	3 state owned companies
Kenya	c90%	1 domestic company

Source: *European Cement Review*, January 2000, HSBC

Appendix 9 Lafarge's market share and competitors by country

Country	Market share	Competitors
France	33%	Ciments Français (30%), Holderbank (14%), Vicat (Heidelberger) (14%)
Germany	7%	RMC (16%), Dyckerhoff (23%), Schwenk (15%), Heidelberger (14%), Holderbank (7%)
Italy	3%	Italcementi (32%), Unicem (20%), Cementir (10%), Holderbank (7%)
Poland	20%	Heidelberger (20%), CRH (20%), RMC (15%), Dyckerhoff (8%)
Czech Republic	15%	Heidelberger (47%), Dyckerhoff (19%), Holderbank (19%)
Turkey	12%	Heidelberger (15%), Ciments Français (7%), locals (66%)
Morocco	30%	Ciments Français (30%), Cimpor (9%)
Philippines	15%	Holderbank (34%), Cemex (20%), Blue Circle (20%), Northern (5%)
Indonesia	4%	Cemex (35%)
Egypt	4%	Suez (12%), Tourah (12%), Cemex (12%), Helwan (11%), National (11%), Amreyah (8%), Holderbank (7%), Blue Circle (2%)
Canada	33%	Holderbank (18%), Heidelberger (12%), Blue Circle (16%), Ciments Français (7%)
Spain	14%	Cemex (23%), Valderrivas (17%), Ciments Français (6%), Holderbank (8%), Cimpor (5%),
Venezuela	30%	Cemex (50%), Holderbank (20%)
Brazil	10%	Votorantim (40%), Jao Santos (11%), Holderbank (9%), Cimpor (9%)
USA	9%	Holderbank (12%), Southdown (10%), Heidelberger (7%), Blue Circle (6%), Ash Grove (6%), Dyckerhoff (5%), Ciments Français (5%)

Source: *European Cement Review*, January 2000, HSBC

Appendix 10 Selected financial information on Lafarge

	FF millions 1995	1996	1997	1998	1999E
Group turnover	33,218	35,262	42,066	64,294	68,500
Operating profit	4,110	3,755	5,178	8,238	9,725
Operating margin	12.4%	10.6%	12.3%	12.8%	14.2%
Profit before tax	3,720	3,333	4,647	6,714	8,075
Earnings per share (FF)	26.6	20.4	27.2	31.3	37.2
Net dividend (FF)	10.0	10.0	11.0	12.0	13.0
Net assets	23,204	24,160	26,121	29,521	31,776
Net debt	4,446	10,912	33,884	36,553	40,284
Gearing (%)	12.9%	37.0%	97.1%	93.3%	93.4%
Market capitalisation	30,332	29,226	35,512	51,528	76,591

Source: 1999 estimates – *European Cement Review*, January 2000, HSBC

Figures and tables

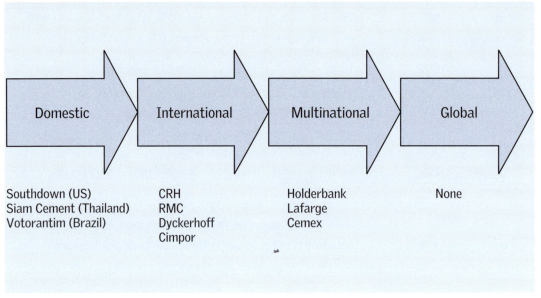

Figure 1 Cement firm evolution
Source: *European Cement Review*, January 2000, HSBC

Table 1 Cement kiln capacity by largest companies and by region

Total kiln capacity (millions tonnes)								
	Western Europe	Eastern Europe	Africa	Asia	Oceania	North America	C & S America	Total
Holderbank	16.4	6.6	5.7	17.4	1.2	15.3	21.3	83.9
Lafarge	24.7	12.0	12.0	6.0		13.2	8.2	76.1
Cemex	10.4		4.0	10.2		1.1	41.1	66.8
Heidelberger	33.8	12.5	1.2	3.0		10.5		61.0
Italcementi	30.2	2.6	3.6	3.9		5.4	0.7	46.3
Blue Circle	16.7		4.1	12.3		6.7	0.9	40.6
RMC	8.9	6.5			3.1	1.0		19.5
Dyckerhoff	10.7	2.6				4.7		18.1
Cimpor	7.1		2.4				2.8	12.3
CRH	5.8							5.8

Source: *European Cement Review*, January 2000, HSBC

Table 2 Regional markets controlled by international and domestic producers

Region	National players market share (%)	International majors market share (%)
Asia – (excluding China)	90	10
Middle East	84	16
Eastern Europe	73	27
Africa	71	29
Latin America	70	30
Western Europe	37	63
North America	37	63
Total (excluding China)	70	30

Source: *European Cement Review*, January 2000, HSBC

Table 3 Blue Circle's acquisition history 1979–2000

Company acquired	Acquisition year	Comments
Cemento Melon	1979	Chilean cement manufacturer
Armitage Shanks	1980	UK sanitaryware manufacturer Sold at a profit 1999
Tulsa cement works	1984	Oklahoma, USA
Ravena limestone quarry	1988	New York, USA
Birmid Qualcast	1988	Included Potterton heating boilers, Qualcast, Atzo and Webb lawnmowers, New World cookers, foundries, Qualitas bathroom products, Wrighton and Elizabeth Ann kitchen furniture, • Foundries and kitchen furniture businesses sold 1990 • Garden products sold at a loss in 1992 • New World cookers sold at a loss in 1994
Blue Circle Aggregates	1989	US aggregates operations
Ockley Brick Company	1990	UK based brick manufacturer Sold at a loss in 1997
Myson	1989	Radiators, heating pumps
Georgia Marble	1989	US aggregates company
Ceramica Dolomite, Italy	1990	Italian sanitaryware manufacturer Sold at a profit 1999
Aalborg	1990	50% share in Danish cement producer Sold at a loss in 2000
Harleyville cement works	1991	South Carolina, USA
Basic Energy	1991	Small clinical incineration business Sold at a loss 1998
Thermopanel	1991	Swedish heating group – radiators, valves, towel warmers
Celsius, France	1992	Heating equipment manufacturer and suppliers in France and Germany Sold at a loss in 1999
Total losses on acquisitions for period		Estimated at £235m
	1992	Keith Orrell-Jones takes over as Chief Executive Autumn 1992
St Marys Canada	1997	Canadian cement company
Needler Group Ltd	1998	Canadian aggregates and concrete block manufacturer
Philippines	1998–9	Various cement manufacturers in Philippines
APMC	1998	50% of Malaysian cement group
Kedah Cement	1999	Malaysian cement manufacturer
	1999	Rick Haythornthwaite takes over as Chief Executive July 1999
Alexandria Portland Cement	2000	Egyptian cement manufacturer
Heracles Cement Company	2000	Greek cement manufacturer
West African Portland Cement Company and Ashaka Cement	2000	Controlling interests in Nigerian cement manufacturers

Table 4 Analysts valuations of Blue Circle

Date	Source	Nature of valuation	Pence per share
March 1999	Lazard Brothers for BCI	DCF	433
September 1999	Warburg Dillon Read	Target price	500
January 2000	HSBC	Target price	430
13 January 2000	Lazard Brothers for BCI	DCF mid-point	486
25 January 2000	Oddo Equities	Stand alone value Discounted free cash flow	390
31 January 2000	Warburg Dillon Read	Target price	500
22 February 2000	Goldman Sachs HSBC Warburg Dillon Read	Target price Target price Target price	471 500 500
24 February 2000	Credit Suisse First Boston	Stand alone value Discounted free cash flow	390
24 February 2000	Teather & Greenwood	Exit price	500
3 March 2000	Commerzbank	Break up value, before premium for control	446
7 March 2000	Robert Fleming & Co	Target price	500
12 April 2000	Oddo Equities	Take out price	519
20 April 2000	Robert Fleming & Co	Target price (post Asia and OIP announcements)	550
1 December 2000	Schroder Salomon Smith Barney	Take out price	490–495

Note: BCI is Blue Circle Industries

Table 5 Blue Circle forecasts against actual results

Date prepared	Source	Operating profits 2001 forecast £m
November 1999	2000–2002 Business Plan	560
November 2000	2001–2003 Business Plan	519
June 2001	Full year forecast	491
September 2001	Full year forecast *	385

*£33 million of the reduction between the June and September 2001 forecasts is due to the sale of Blue Circle's Canadian cement business

Table 6 Dividends declared and paid for the years 1994 to 1999

	Interim dividend (pence per share)	Final dividend (pence per share)
1994	3.75	8.0
1995	4.0	8.5
1996	4.25	9.0
1997	4.65	9.85
1998	4.85	10.35
1999	5.05	10.95

Case 22 **BA profits in flight**

To be the undisputed leader in world travel (BA Mission, 1997)

The Chairman of BA was sitting at his desk in 'The Hub', located on the top floor of Waterside, the new British Airways HQ, observing BA planes taking off from Heathrow. He was trying to take stock and detemine how successful (or otherwise) the implementation of the global strategy had been at both a domestic and international level. He was reflecting upon whether this had been an appropriate strategy at this time and if it had been effective in fortifying the airline in an increasingly competitive context.

Company background

We have the skills, style, spirit and financial strength that are the envy of our competitors. (Lord King, Chairman 1992)

The airline sector is still a highly regulated industry, constrained by national and international operating laws and conventions; however, this has not prevented many international airlines from promoting themselves as 'global airlines'. In the UK airline sector, historically there have been only a few major players, including British Airways, the original national carrier, which was privatised and inherited prime locations at all major UK airports, including Heathrow, and is still perceived by many as the national carrier.

British Airways plc (BA), is a public company listed on the London Stock Exchange and based near London's Heathrow Airport. BA's history can be traced back to the early days of the aviation industry from 1919 to the birth of the package holiday mass market and the expansion of international travel which began in the late 1960s and 1970s. BA formed as the result of a merger in 1972 between British Overseas Airline Corporation (BOAC) and British

European Airways (BEA). In 1987, BA was privatised from being a state-owned national carrier.

BA has undergone significant structural and cultural changes since being privatised. To cope with increasing competition both domestically and internationally, management at BA has had to adjust the culture and structure of the airline in an effort to make it more competitive and customer focused. This posed several key challenges for senior managers. A brief summary of the airline's recent history follows.

Preparing to privatise (1980–1987)

Lord King was appointed Chairman, charged with restoring the Group to profitability and preparing for privatisation. With an overall deficit of £544m declared for 1981/82 including special provisions to pay for an extensive 'survival plan', which included staff cuts, suspension of unprofitable routes and disposal of surplus assets, the task of re-establishing the company as the world's leading airline began in April 1983. In 1982 a new CEO, Sir Colin Marshall, was appointed. This heralded a period of change of image, change of culture and a focus on increasing profitability, including repositioning of the carrier as the *World's Favourite Airline*, introducing a new corporate identity for the airline called 'Manhattan' and, in 1983, a corporate training programme called 'Putting People First' when 40,000 employees attended a two-day training programme.

During this phase, attempts were made to reposition the organisation within the changing environment, with the goal of making BA more competitive in the new 'global' marketplace and for the company to embrace the concept of the 'customer is king'. However, the culture at the time remained operationally focused:

> *At this time British Airways was a classical transport bureaucracy, somewhat analogous to the railways, whose primary agenda was to keep the aircraft flying safely. This operational orientation had been inherited after the War from the RAF. It was a viable approach in the highly regulated and stable market of the 60s and 70s. The systems were rule bound designed to operate on the assumption that people could not be really trusted.* (Management Communications Report 1988)

In the early 1980s, the airline was facing large financial losses and the public opinion of the airline was in decline. Market research found that the

---

By Dr Bridgette Sullivan-Taylor, Warwick Business School.

The material in this case is taken from original research conducted by the author and from a selection of working papers.

© All material is copyright of the author and cannot be used without prior permission.

service provided by BA was seen as 'cool, aloof, professional and impersonal' and that passengers were dissatisfied if their basic needs were not being met. The results suggested that: 'Passengers wanted to be treated as individuals whose problems, cares and anxieties were responded to in a personal and caring way rather than a piece of cargo to be shipped from A to B' (Management Report 1988).

Management realised that if BA wanted to become a people-oriented organisation, responsive to the needs of its customers, both management behaviours and the wider corporate culture had to change. In response, BA attempted to rebrand itself as the 'World's Favourite Airline' and adopted a new corporate identity known as 'Manhattan':

> Changing the culture was much more difficult than revamping the image. Staff were focused on our customers. But research revealed significant gaps between customers' expectations of what 'good service' was and those of our staff. Our staff concentrated on getting the routines right, the operational aspects of the job and the mechanics of service. Customers took that for granted; they were more interested in human aspects of service-spontaneity, warmth, concern, friendliness and attention to individual needs.
> (Gurassa, Head of World Sales, 1997)

Internally, a number of new programmes were initiated in an attempt to change the organisation's values and belief systems. These programmes used a variety of innovative people-management practices. One such programme was known as 'Putting People First', when 40,000 employees attended a two-day workshop, aimed at instilling a heightened focus on both the internal and external customer.

Privatisation (1987–1995)

King and Marshall began to turn the airline into 'one of the world's most successful' (Harper, 2000:42). During this period, significant changes occurred within the organisation in the early to mid 1980s. These included a rationalisation of almost 24,000 jobs down to 36,000; the significant reduction in the number of routes serviced and the introduction of a new corporate mission with the objective of the company becoming the best airline in its class: 'to be the best and most successful company in the airline industry'.

Once privatisation was completed, the airline faced a different business climate within the industry. Changes in legislation enabled BA to develop alliances with a variety of other carriers. BA also differentiated its service offering through the launch of new products and services, which culminated in a new corporate identity. At the same time, the airline underwent a period of rationalisation and restructuring with non-core activities being outsourced, leading to redundancies and labour disputes.

However, the characteristics of a state-owned organisation continued to permeate BA's culture. The company had been a government institution and a civil service culture, characteristically bureaucratic, hierarchical and status oriented, was endemic. These characteristics were reflected in the norms, behaviours and attitudes of employees (Bruce, BA Management Report, 1998:7).

As the UK's national airline, BA had operated within a monopolistic context and had become operationally focused. For example, it had a propensity to invest in state of the art engineering development and maintenance programmes. The Concorde project required a level of R&D investment that was far above that which any private sector airline could afford.

The merger with British Caledonian in 1987 resulted in an industrial dispute between the airline and the stewards and stewardesses association (BASSA). After the dispute was resolved, a period of significant investment occurred which led to the development of new brands and new cabin services features as detailed in Table 1.

In 1991, the Gulf War began. This resulted in a decrease in traffic which had a significant impact on the airline's profitability. BA reduced its network activity in response to a decrease in demand for flights by consumers, who felt unsure about travelling at this time. During this retrenchment phase 4,600 employees were offered redundancy packages and early retirement and another 2,000 employees were asked to work half-time until demand had returned to normal levels. Simultaneously, in an attempt to boost demand, the airline began an innovative marketing campaign called the 'World's Biggest Offer' in an effort to increase consumer confidence and recover from the downturn in traffic.

Table 1 1987–1991 (*BA Fact Book*, 1997)

		The 1987–1991 Period
Dec 1987	Brands	BA and United Airlines announced a worldwide marketing partnership.
1988	Profit	$300 million [profitable for the first time].
Jan 1988	Brands	New Club World and Club Europe Brands introduced. Investment of over $100 million on upgrading and improving business class products.
March 1989	Brands	New First Class service introduced.
May 1990	Network	At BA's initiative, the world's airlines set up an Infrastructure Action Group based in Geneva and operating under IATA, to work for the elimination of restraints which threatened to stifle the growth of the aviation industry. BA carried 25 million people.
Jan 1991	Brands	World Traveller and Euro Traveller brands were introduced.

The 1990s were also significant due to the change of leadership and a refocusing of the organisational philosophy, as Sir Colin Marshall succeeded Lord King as Chairman. This period is summarised in Table 2. At this time, the organisation's initials, BA, were still often taken to stand for *'Bloody Awful'* due to the inconsistent standard of service being delivered. Marshall stated that in the 1990s, however, *'customer service had joined "motherhood" as one of the unassailable virtues of our time, and consequently there is growing pressure to improve the responsiveness of organisations to those whose interests they exist to serve'* (Bruce, 1998:2). Marshall was pivotal in introducing a customer-focused vision for the organisation and supported the 'Managing Winners' programme, aimed at renewing the airline's commitment to delivering internal and external quality customer service. The challenges, which followed, are summarised by the Head of World Sales:

Our first challenge for the rest of the 1990s is growth. The second challenge is cost. The third challenge is management style. The outdated style of managing by control, setting standards and targets, dictating work designs and schedules and operating through bureaucracies and structure has to be replaced. The demand from employees today is for more participation and involvement in decision making, less bureaucracy and paternalistic care, and more respect and value as individuals. If this is what drives employee satisfaction in the 1990s, this is what we intend to provide.' (Head of BA World Sales, *BA Fact Book*, 1997:10)

During the remainder of the early 1990s, the airline enjoyed stable growth, achieved through an expansion of the route network and through the introduction of innovative products and services. This is summarised in Table 3.

The 'Ayling' era: Ayling as CEO (1995–2000)

In 1995 there was a key change in leadership in 1995, when Robert Ayling was promoted from Managing Director to the position of CEO. This marked the beginning of the 'Ayling' era. At this time BA was regarded as one of Britain's blue-ribbon companies, as both a prestige private company and a privatised national organisation. BA's performance results was also strong during this period:

- 1995 The airline announced record Group pre-tax profits of £430m for the six months that ended 30 Sept 1995, up 23.2% on the previous year. The interim dividend is up by 10% to 3.85 pence a share.

- 1996 BA announced pre-tax profits of £104m for the three months ended 31 Dec 1995, up 30% compared with the previous year.

- 1996 BA announced record pre-tax profits of £585m, up 29.4% on the £452m (before the US Air provision) achieved in the previous year. Basic earnings per share increased (before US

Table 2 1992–1993 (*BA Fact Book* 1997)

		The 1992–1993 Period
April 1992	Corporate Culture Programme	A renewed commitment to keep BA ahead in quality passenger service was pledged by the airline with the launch of 'Managing Winners', the new management programme and 'Winners', the new corporate event.
July 1992	Leadership change	Lord King announced he was to step down as Chairman in July 1993 after 12 years. Sir Colin Marshall, later Lord Marshall, takes over full executive management responsibility for the airline with immediate effect.
Sept 1992	Market	BA was assigned one of the highest credit ratings in the world.
Oct 1992	Global strategy	The airline unveiled its first fully integrated global advertising campaign called 'Feeling Good'.
Dec 1992	Network: Partnership Investment	US and UK governments did not approve of BA's attempt to invest in US Air due to a bilateral air services agreement.
Jan 1993	Alliance Investment	BA and US Air alliance, e.g. code-sharing opportunities.
Jan 1993	Legal case	BA paid £610,000 in settlement of a libel action brought by Richard Branson and Virgin Atlantic Airways.
Feb 1993	Leadership change	Lord King retired as chairman. The board of BA appointed Sir Colin Marshall as Chairman and Robert Ayling as Group Managing Director. Sir Michael Angus continued as non-executive Deputy Chairman. BA also intended to increase the non-executive representation on the Board. Lord King is invited by the Board to become the first President of British Airways.

Table 3 1993–1995 (*BA Factbook* 1997)

		The 1993–1995 Period
1993	Industrial dispute	Strike between management and BASSA.
March 1993–94	Network Devpt	Extension of global network.
1994	Industrial dispute	Strike between management and BASSA.
August 1995	Profits	BA announced pre-tax profits of £135m for the three months ended 30 June 1995 an increase of 57% in comparison to the same period last year. The result set a new first quarter record for the airline, ignoring asset disposals.
Sept 1995	Campaign	BA announced a £500m 3-year plan that intended to revolutionise air travel. The programme was called 'Insight' and began with the relaunch of Club World and Executive Club frequent flyer programmes. A completely new First Class service was launched in the winter and the other cabins were relaunched later.

Air provision) by 25.7% with dividends per share up by 10.1%.

As part of this key leadership change the global strategy was adopted including a handful of decisions including introducing the BEP programme (which involved restructuring, outsourcing and downsizing), as well as introducing a new corporate identity and developing the global network through joining an alliance.

BA had implemented international strategies in the past. These had been either operational, through ongoing extensions to the network into new market destinations, through mergers (BOAC and BEA in 1972–1974), through product extensions such as providing charter airlines when mass package holidays became the vogue in the 1970s, as well as through new innovations such as developing Concorde with Air France in 1976. Then, in the 1980s, during the privatisation process the airline was repositioned as the 'World's Favourite Airline' and the new mission introduced in 1987 was for BA 'To be the Best and Most Successful Company in the Airline Industry'. Through most of the late 1980s and 1990s BA continued to extend its products and services offering to its broad range of customers in order to grow its market share.

Then in 1995 BA introduced the 'Insight' programme intended to 'revolutionise air travel' and began to relaunch its brands. As part of this overhaul, in 1996 the Business Efficiency Programme (BEP) was introduced, aimed to save the airline £1 billion in costs by 2000. The programme involved both the reallocation of current investment into new initiatives and the restructuring and centralisation of activities.

Ayling recognised that one of BA's strengths was its identity as an upmarket international airline, but he also recognised the need to balance the aspiration to globalise and compete internationally with the desire to achieve greater efficiency through cost cutting:

Our job is to find ways of reducing expenditure while increasing the value for money that our customers get. If the customers value something and you want to keep their business, you don't take it away and say, 'Will you please pay the same fare', or worse still, 'Will you please pay more'. They will go somewhere else. (Ayling, 1999:66)

The manifestations of the BEP are illustrated in Table 4.

Although BA had implemented a variety of international initiatives to create a more outward focused airline, it was not until 1997 that it decided to adopt a strategy of becoming a global airline, when the new mission was introduced 'To be the undisputed leader in world travel' which included an integrated approach to globalising the airline's service and product offering under the new corporate mission – to become 'truly global' – and a new identity, 'Utopia,' was introduced as part of BA's new 'global' focus.

The corporate strategy was intended to globalise the airline through achieving scale and scope efficiencies. However, implementing many of these decisions involved managing the fine balance between investing in the launch of new products to improve customer service, developing a global network and simultaneously reducing overall operating costs, within the context of a highly competitive industry and a highly unionised workforce, each providing specific challenges for management and for the execution of a global strategy.

However, at the same time that this new corporate strategic intent was launched, Ayling had also decided that in order for the airline to maintain its position in such a competitive context, £1 billion in costs needed to be removed from across the airline by 2000. This created an internal tension which resulted in conflict. During the summer of 1997, in response to the introduction of the aggressive cost-cutting programme (called BEP), a major industrial dispute occurred. This dispute was a critical event in the airline's history and affected future management-worker relations.[1] This dispute was a reaction by the cabin crew community who had perceived that the

---

[1] BA has a long history of industrial disputes. In the recent past there had been several major strikes with various unions including in 1972 during the merger between BEA and BOAC; 1987 with BASSA over the merger with British Caledonian; 1993–1994 with BASSA; in 1996 a potential strike by BALPA was averted.

Table 4 1996–1997 (*BA Fact Book*, 1999)

		The 1996–1997 Period
	Network development	BA continued to code-share with American and Canadian carriers.
July 1996	Labour dispute	A threatened strike by members of the pilots union, BALPA, was averted.
	Alliance	The proposed alliance between BA and AA received approval from the House of Commons Transport Select Committee.
August 1996	Profit	BA announced a record pre-tax profit of £150m for the 3 months to 30 June 1996, up 11.1% on the £135m achieved in the same period last year.
Sept 1996	Restructuring	BA unveiled plans for a transformation of the group for the year 2000. The plans aimed to meet new market and customer needs, and included the restructuring of the workforce to ensure the company had the right skills in place to achieve £1B of efficiencies. To ensure it had the right people with the right skills in the right jobs for the new millennium, the airline carried out an extensive programme of redeployment and retraining. Severance and early retirement was offered to 5,000 volunteers and around the same number of new staff, skilled in customer services and languages, were recruited.
November 1996	Restructuring	The airline announced a restructuring of its Passenger Revenue Accounting Dept, which resulted in a reduction of around 600 UK jobs. Half of these jobs became obsolete through automation, while another third were contracted to World Network Services, a new development based in India.
February 1997	Restructuring	BA announced a £250m investment in a new World Cargo Centre at Heathrow. The significant increase in automation led to a reduction of almost 400 jobs from the current workforce.
February 1997	Restructuring	BA announced that it was combining its general accounting activities at a new Global Accounting Centre in London. The result was a reduction of around 290 posts over three years.
March 1997	Restructuring	BA announced an agreement with 2,800 ground services staff in its Aircraft Services department at Heathrow. The agreement included a two-year pay freeze, best practice throughout the department and lower starter rates for new recruits.
March 1997	Restructuring	Outsourced: BA transferred its Ground Fleet Services business, which provided vehicle management and maintenance services at Heathrow and Gatwick for 5 years.
March 1997	Investment in route	BA announced it was investing US$100 million to improve facilities for passengers travelling to and from New York. The project included the expansion of the airline's own terminal at John F. Kennedy International Airport, major new road access to the building, and new premium passenger facilities at Newark International Airport.
April 1997	Restructuring	The airline announced a streamlining of its Engineering department including outsourcing arrangements.
May 1997	Mission	New Mission 'To be the undisputed leader in world travel'.
May 1997	Restructuring	Staff at the BA World Cargo Centre voted for a proposal that included a two-year pay freeze, changes to working practices and simplified grading structure.

Table 5 May 1997–Sept 1997 (*BA Fact Book*, 1999)

		The May 1997–September 1997 Period
May 1997	Restructuring	BA members of Cabin Crew 89 union voted overwhelmingly in favour of proposals, which included pay restructuring and lower starter rates.
June 1997	Brand	Utopia. BA unveiled its new corporate identity designed to help establish the company as the undisputed leader in world travel. Changes included the new tailfin designs.
July 1997	CEO	First calls were made for Ayling to be sacked at AGM.
August 1997	Restructuring	BA Engineering announced a strengthened focus on maintaining and servicing BA's own aircraft. It continued to sell services to other operators, but on a more selective basis. This policy enabled the department to streamline its organisation and resulted in a reduction of 450 managerial and support jobs.
July 1997	Labour Dispute	Some of the cabin crew workforce at the airline held a three-day strike. Talks progressed between BA, the Transport and General Workers Union and the BA Stewards and Stewardesses Association (BASSA) and aimed to resolve the industrial dispute.
Sept 1997	Labour Dispute	Settlement of the issues central to the cabin crew dispute. The agreement, which came into immediate effect, secured the £42 million annual savings targeted from cabin crew as part of the Business Efficiency Programme. It also paved the way for a new relationship between airlines and the unions that represented cabin crew.

BEP programme would have a detrimental impact upon their working practices. Although the strike lasted for only three days, it was estimated to have cost the airline £125 million. The dispute led to a loss of morale by employees and a loss of confidence in the CEO by shareholders, who called for his dismissal at the AGM.[2] This period is summarised in Table 5.

In the continued pursuit of the BEP cost savings target, management continued to downsize and outsource large departments within the airline, such as catering, landing gear business and other non-core functions, despite ongoing resistance from internal stakeholders affected by these changes. This period is summarised in Table 6.

Table 6 Sept 1997–August 1998 (*BA Fact Book*, 1999)

		The September 1997–August 1998 Period
Sept 1997	Downsize	BA announced the sales of its Landing Gear business.
Dec 1997	Outsource	BA completed the sale of its Heathrow catering production units to Gate Gourmet. The 1200 staff transferred to Gate Gourmet.
May 1998	Profits	BA announced its preliminary results for the full year 1997/98. Driven by the BEP which delivered £250 million of cost efficiencies, pre-tax profits for the year were down just 9.4% to £580 million compared to the previous year's record levels. The result was achieved despite the industrial dispute, which cost £125m and the strength of sterling, which at the pre-tax level cost the group £180 million.
Aug 1998	Route	BA announced that it will suspend services to Osaka as a result of worsening passenger demand and the continued fall in the value of the Japanese Yen.

---

[2] However, it was not until January 2000 that the board requested that Ayling relinquish acting as CEO.

The Asian economic crises occurred in 1997–98, affecting capacity on major passenger routes in the Asian region. In 1999, the BA Chief Economist wrote a report entitled 'Globalisation: expanding our horizons' that discussed the implications of these global trends for the airline:

This year, we have been provided with a painful reminder of the increasing interdependence of the global economy. The shock waves from the economic and financial crisis in East Asia have spread far and wide. Financial instability has spread to Russia and South America. Banks have lost money and multinational companies are reporting reduced profits – hitting stock markets. Jobs are being lost in the financial sector and in the manufacturing industry. Globalisation is no longer a gleam in the eye of business school theorists. It is an established part of business life. And the fact that a downturn in Asia is now causing job losses in the Northeast of England and Scotland provides us with stark and graphic illustration of the new realities of the global marketplace ... The service sector also needs to brace itself for a period of restructuring, particularly as information technology opens up new markets and revolutionises traditional ways of delivering existing activities. We see this happening in our own industry as video-conferencing and other forms of business communication offer alternatives to business travel. (Sentence, BA Economics Department Report, BA Intranet, 1999)

Many airlines, including BA, had realised that due to sheer cost considerations and the highly regulated air transport environment, they were unable to provide a global network which covered every possible destination. To overcome these factors, BA began to forge alliances with other airlines in a move to provide a 'single global network':

I think people who stop and think certainly understand that this industry has to participate in the global situation that is taking place in all industries. Unfortunately we are so hamstrung with regulations that we have to operate under bilateral agreements, formed in 1944 before the industry really existed, so we can't do it like other industries and so we can't go in, take over countries, able to operate their licences out of their countries at least outside of the EU. The only way we can participate in globalisation as an organisation is by striking these alliances or relationships with other carriers. Yes there are some problems felt over the franchise programme that we are operating essentially in this country, where there is a degree of overlap and a degree of concern that is created, but our first partnership we entered into in 1987 – I think it was with United Airlines – this sort of thing has been around for quite some time. (Lord Marshall, Chairman)

In September 1998, the oneworld™[3] alliance was launched. This was an attempt by a variety of airlines to 'globalise' their service offering, within the industry constraints, through marketing alliances with other carriers, who operated within specific disparate regions. Details of the oneworld™ alliance are in Table 7.

Throughout 1998 and 1999, considerable investment continued into a variety of brand relaunches to align the airline's strategic focus with the business travel market. This narrowing of strategic focus altered the way BA serviced its main premium markets, operated its flight schedules,

Table 7 September 1998 (*BA Factbook*)

		The September 1998 Period
Sept 1998	Alliance	oneworld – American Airlines, British Airways, Canadian Airlines, Cathay Pacific Airways and Qantas Airways announced the new oneworld global alliance. Combined total of 220,000 employees in 138 countries. 600 destinations are served and access to over 200 lounges was provided.

[3] A profile of the oneworld alliance can be seen on page 374.

Table 8 1998–1999 (*BA Factbook*, 2001)

		The 1998–1999 Period
Nov 1998	Brands	BA launched a range of new services and benefits for 'World Traveller' passengers.
April 1999	Strategy	BA took delivery of its last Boeing 747-400 aircraft in keeping with the airline's new global strategy geared towards focusing on the most profitable segments of business and thereby improving returns.
May 1999	Brands	BA announced that it would be developing radical new products, which would redefine long-haul business travel and set new benchmarks in comfort and design. The plans included improvements to Club World featuring completely flat beds, a new state of the art entertainment system with bigger screens, in-seat power for lap top computers, email, phones and fax.
	Products	BA launched BA Global Financial Services and products.
	New Centre	New World Cargo Centre opened.
	Profits	BA reported pre-tax profits of £225 million for the year ended 31 March 1999, including Business Efficiency Programme benefits of £610 million.
June 1999	Downsizing	In line with its strategy of reducing the rate of its capacity growth, the airline announced that it will terminate the lease on one Boeing 767-300, as permitted under the lease agreement. BA sells its shares to Galileo International Inc (a travel agency reservation company) releasing a profit before tax of £149 million. BA sells its in-flight catering facility at Gatwick for £14 million.
August 1999	Restructuring	BA announces its intention to accelerate its reduction in capacity. The airline plans to reduce its mainline scheduled capacity by 12% over the next 3–4 years. BA announces its intention to save a further £225 million (excluding one-off severance costs) in the current financial year to support profitability in a challenging trading environment. The main focus of the actions will be on improving efficiency in support areas of the company. Plans include the deferral of some non-fleet capital expenditure, an acceleration of other cost saving plans and reduction of 300 managers (a 10% cut) is targeted. Staff reductions are expected to be managed by voluntary means, the cost of which is expected to be in the region of £40 million. The airline will continue to invest in its new strategy and in innovative products. More code-sharing plans announced and upgrade of Concorde.

and configured its fleet and the associated manpower planning. The various initiatives are detailed in Table 8.

One of the results of the new strategic focus on the premium market was the increased investment in new innovations for the business club brands and the purchase of smaller aircraft with a larger number of business class seats which were scheduled to operate more frequently on the core business routes. These developments are detailed in Table 9.

Despite the investment in new products and services, such as the launch of new premium cabin related brand features and the aggressive cost cutting of the BEP, profits continued to decline over this period and BA became known in the press as *'the ailing airline'*. The board of BA dismissed Robert Ayling in March of 2000. Lord Marshall stood in as acting CEO and was succeeded by the new CEO, Rod Eddington, in May 2000.

The next section details the content of the global strategic intent.

Table 9 1999–2000 (*BA Factbook*, 2001)

		The 1999–2000 Period
Sept 1999	Brands	The airline announced a £50 million programme of improvements to Club Europe.
Oct 1999	Fleet	BA ordered 12 new 100-seat Airbus 318s with options to purchase 12 more aircraft. The move to the new, smaller A318 was a further step in the airline's fleet strategy, which aimed to modernise the fleet, increase average yields and reduce capacity.
Nov 1999	Global alliance	BA and AA file an application with the US Department of Transportation to code-share on flights serving 75 destinations in the UK, USA, Europe and Africa, as part of their plans to develop a global marketing alliance.
Dec 1999	Brands	London Eye opened by Prime Minister – Ayling on Board of BA-sponsored London Eye. Millennium Dome opened New Year's Eve – Ayling on Board of Millennium Dome.
Jan 2000	Chain relationships	BA announced plans for fundamental change to the way the airline works with UK travel agents.
Jan 2000	Brands	BA presented its new products and announced the introduction of a new cabin class. 'Lounge in the Sky' concept set for rollout in both Club World and World Traveller Plus.
Jan 2000	Strategy	BA took delivery of its first two Boeing 777 Extended Range aircraft. This signalled the next stage of the strategy implementation that focused on smaller, more profitable aircraft.
Jan 2000	E-commerce	World's first commercial interactive TV travel section on a UK cable company. Will be developed for on-line bookings.

The global strategic intent – why 'go global'?

Global network, global outlook: recognised everywhere for superior value in world travel. (BA Global Goal, BA Factbook, 1997:13)

In the late 1990s management had decided to reposition the airline as *'the world's favourite airline'* focusing on being both 'global and caring'. This change in focus had been driven by an awareness during the mid-1990s that British Airways was facing increasing competition from both domestic and international carriers. In order to increase market share, management felt that BA needed to differentiate the offering to appeal to the diverse needs of the 60% of its passengers whose journey originated from outside the UK. Prior to this the focus had been mainly on meeting the needs of the 40% of domestic customers, who also travelled internationally.

This view was further supported by market research undertaken during the early 1990s which indicated that BA was considered by passengers from overseas markets as providing service which

Table 10 2000 (*BA Fact Book*, 2001)

		The 2000 Period
March 2000	Change in Leadership	Robert Ayling resigned and Lord Marshall acted as CEO and as Chairman of BA until a new CEO could be found.
May 2000	Change in Leadership	Rod Eddington appointed as CEO

was 'too cool and aloof' and therefore too British oriented. In late 1995, senior management then commissioned a large market research study across several of its key target markets. BA customers were carefully selected to represent a cross-section of travellers in terms of: age, gender, reasons for travel and frequency of travel. The research indicated that the traditional BA corporate identity, known as the 'Landor' image, was seen by the public as *distinctly British, masculine, catering more for business travellers, arrogant, traditional and old-fashioned.*

The research also found that the notion of being 'British' was perceived by these customers to have changed. Results from this research are found in Table 11.

On the basis of these results regarding the change in 'Britishness', management commissioned further market research to determine whether the airline should also change its corporate identity to align with the new corporate mission, vision and values. Table 12 provides an overview of the market research findings in regard to the shift in perception of 'Britishness' and the perceived positive and negative associations.

The market research also indicated that in the worldwide context, societal values had significantly changed from the 1980s to the 1990s. The changes are detailed in Table 13. It was found that across all major markets researched, a backlash against the customer values of the 1980s had occurred.

The research suggested that the BA brand should be repositioned to reflect the changing values of the 'new' world. It should be seen as bringing people together, a world 'glue', a network, a web making the connection at both the macro and micro levels.[4] The new identity would embrace the notions of a global and caring world, fragmentation, a shift in gender balance, tolerance, individuality and corporate responsibility and would be executed through initiatives that were tangible and grounded in reality. In the light of the research, BA was seen to need to reposition itself in the global marketplace, with a new corporate mission, vision and values, and to take the *'opportunity to take a moral stance, which was visible, tangible and experienced at ground level'* (Research International Report, 1995).

Thus, by adopting a globally focused strategy the Chairman considered that the CEO was appropriately responding to changes in the competitive airline industry:

> Over the last few years we have changed our strategy quite a lot because the market has fundamentally changed. The pound has become much stronger and our competitors in Europe have got much better too, and we used to have the market to ourselves. (Chairman)

In order to implement a *'Think Global, Act Local'* strategy, however, a significant number of operational decisions needed to be made regarding the

Table 11 Changing notions of 'Britishness'

The traditional Britain	The modern Britain
Britain as a theme park; with the monarch, heritage, mother of parliaments, leader of democracy, a nation of integrity	A multiracial society living in harmony. International 'mecca' (esp. London). Fun, quirky, eccentric. Leaders in style, fashion, music. Youth influencing other parts of the world. Centre of world communication, manufacturing excellence

Source: adapted from Curtis, 1997:19, BA market research report, 1997.

----

[4] The new youth generation also brought new views and perspectives relating to gender, greater tolerance, post-materialism, individuality/autonomy, freedom institutions and hierarchy. The implications of these societal changes meant that British Airways needed a new identity to reflect the changing values.

Table 12 Views of 'Britishness'

Negative Associations		Positive Associations		Areas in which Britain excels
Tradition	Proud	Creativity	Independent	Scientific research
Conservativeness	Stubborn	Ingenuity	Self-confident	Fashion
Insularity	Rigid, formal	Individualism	Traditional	Software
Exclusivity	Inflexible, dogmatic	Invention	Integrity	Design
Stiff	Not open-minded	Classy	Tolerant	Media
Distant	Insular	Gentlemanly	Harmonious	
Square	Exuberant and	Polite, courteous	Humorous	
Arrogant	Eccentric	Reliable	Sociable	

Source: adapted from Curtis, 1997:19, BA market research report, 1997.

extent to which the organisation needed to appeal directly to the vast number of different customer groups and regarding what competencies needed to be developed in order for the customer service delivery platform to deploy the global strategy. Decisions needed to be made as to how to implement this strategy in practice and how far the organisation should go in localising such a service offering on a global scale in order differentiate BA further from its global competitors.

Components of the global strategy

This section describes the nature of the corporate mission, vision and values of the airline at the time the global strategic intent was formulated, as well as how the strategic intent was translated into product and service propositions, which were then interpreted into service specifications for the strategy to be operationalised.

The emergence of the global strategy arose from these market research activities and management perceptions. BA responded by adopting themes and values from this new world, with goals such as becoming a '*global and caring*' airline. One of the four goals, therefore, was to become '*Truly Global*', which was also defined by these research activities.

The 'Truly Global' goal reflected the changing competitive structure in our industry. It recognises the new ways customers can be served

Table 13 Changes in wider society

1980s	1990s
– 'yuppie' consumerism	– a focus on individual; time for self, rather than work
– curbing of excesses	– respect for individuals rather than companies/organisations
– greater restraint	– time for community and family; looking after each other, 'traditional values (individualism also can be seen as a threat)
– a move back to 'traditional values'	
– a greater self-awareness of 'others', especially the 'have-nots'	– safety and security (risk aversion)
	– moving from material to spiritual values; quality of life, rather than success, soul searching, moral and ethical questioning (e.g. nuclear testing)
	– environmental consciousness

Source adapted from Curtis, 1997:19, BA market research report, 1997.

Table 14 Global goals

FACTORS	ACTIVITIES
Global Passenger Benefit	Consistency of customer satisfaction across markets and partners
Global Travel Network	Relative quality of connections offered between the projected top 40 international business cities
Brand Recognition	Spontaneous recognition of BA as international airline compared with other carriers in key markets
Multicultural	Fit between customer contact staff/management nationalities and those of BA's customer base

by effective international alliances. The major airlines and, more importantly, their most frequent customers, are beginning to see the attractions in such alliances.

For British Airways to succeed as these changes take effect we need to concentrate on how customers can be better served by a global alliance network, based on seamlessness and consistent standards. We also need to be a company with a positive global outlook, through developing the competitive strength of our alliance network and the global impact of our brands; we will also be seeking profitable new ways of meeting customer needs for travel-related products worldwide.

We must commit to our value of being 'global and caring', recognising the culturally diverse nature of our customers and aiming to serve them with a high level of awareness and sensitivity. This will be measured by asking customers of different cultures about how well their needs are met when they travel with us. Overall we must aim to be truly global, with a truly global network and a truly global outlook. (BA Goals, BA Intranet 1999)

The goals of becoming a 'Global network, global outlook: recognised everywhere for superior value in world travel' and of having a 'Share of worldwide air passengers who provide income to BA or its alliances' was broken down further into sub-goals, as described in Table 14. The goals of developing a global network and outlook and to be known for superior value were underpinned by four key factors, namely providing global customer benefits, a global travel network, brand recognition and being multicultural.

The strategic intent of the airline was to become 'the undisputed leader in world travel'. The corporate 'Strategy Plan' further detailed the specific nature of this new focus:

British Airways has adopted a focused strategy for the 21st Century. It encompasses four main elements: offering our customers the industry's leading premium brands, with world beating customer service delivered by inspired people, while building an airline, with alliances, that can truly serve the world, all contributing to a renewed drive towards greater profitability and shareholder value. Focused on the world, focused on our customers, focused on our people and, focused on profitability. As the world industry faces fundamental change, British Airways is undergoing its fourth strategic evolution since privatisation. In this year's annual report, while reviewing the past 12 months, we also focus on our vision for the future. We outline the steps we are taking to ensure we fly into the new millennium firmly on track to become the undisputed leader in world travel. (BA Annual Report 1998–99:2)

The corporate strategic plan was then further translated into several strategic elements. These four strategic elements show where the global strategic intent was to fit in to the strategic agenda of the organisation. The 'official' description of each of the four strategic elements and the associated specific functional initiatives used to deploy the corporate strategy are detailed in Table 15.

The mission, vision and goals

At the time of privatisation, the mission, values and goals of the airline were redesigned to align the

Table 15 The four strategic elements

Strategic Element	Overall Focus	Initiatives	Directors' Comment
1. Focused on profitability	Our new fleet and network refinement strategies are building on our business efficiency programmes, enabling us to concentrate on strong profitability into the future.	New fleet and network strategies New World Cargo Centre (May 99) Business Efficiency Programme Premium Focus	'Our fleet and network refinement programmes will enable us to deliver real benefits to the business – and to our customers.' Director of Strategy.
2. Focused on customers	Customers remain at the heart of everything we do and exceeding our customers' expectations is of paramount importance to our future.	World Traveller (economy) relaunch New Club World business in the wings Smoother service on the ground	'We are completely committed to customer service and innovation. We will continue to invest in providing our customers with ground-breaking products and services into the future, whenever and wherever it makes good commercial sense.' Director of Marketing.
3. Focused on the world	We are using our worldwide network and our new alliance relationships to offer customers the best choice and flexibility and to enable us to concentrate on the most profitable markets.	oneworld™ takes off A growing world network Alliance partnerships strengthened More franchises and partners	'With oneworld™ British Airways is at the centre of a world-leading alliance that more than matches any competitor.' Director of Alliances.
4. Focused on our people	Our people are the key to our success. We are investing in providing the best possible working environments to inspire our people all over the world.	State of the art workplaces – Waterside, World Cargo Centre, 'hot desking', cyber surfing. Putting People First Again Share ownership Good people management and In Touch programmes Changes to union agreements (pilots)	'People who feel good about their working world deliver the best results. That is the philosophy that lies behind British Airways' approach to its employees.' Director of Human Resources.

Source: BA Annual Report 1998-1999:30.

organisation more closely with the expectations of the airline's customers:

In 1986, Sir Colin Marshall, then its Chief Executive, set out the Mission for British Airways – 'To be The Best and Most Successful Company in the Airline Industry'. Then it seemed an impossible dream for a BA dubbed 'Bloody Awful' by customers. But by improving customer service and by redefining its marketing, sales and managerial approach ready for life in the private sector, the company transformed its reputation and its finances. Customers were impressed by a new-found focus on service.

Figure 1 Mission, values and goals
Source: *BA Fact Book*, 1997:13.

Investors, including most employees, also bene-fited from the growth in the value of its shares. (BA Fact Book, 1997:13)

The TMT redefined the mission, values and goals, towards better customer services, achievement of financial and operational targets and improved ways of working between employees and management. The new mission, values and goals are detailed in Figure 2. Four areas that needed to be addressed were identified: the global economic climate, the challenge of competition, what customers were asking for and what employees wanted.

The new mission statement became *'to be the undisputed leader in world travel'*. The new values included being *safe and secure, honest and respon-sible, innovative and team-spirited, global and caring, a good neighbour*. The new goals became cus-tomers' choice (airline of first choice in key markets), *strong profitability* (meeting investors' expectations and securing the future), truly global (global network, global outlook recognised everywhere for superior value in world travel), *inspired people* (building on success and delighting customers), as detailed in Figures 3 to 5 (*BA Fact Book*, 1997:13).

These diagrams indicate the linkages between the mission, vision, values and associated goals and detail the objectives of each of the goals. This overview illustrates where the 'Truly Global' goal was positioned within the overall corporate vision.

The global strategic implementation initiatives

Many different organisation-wide change initiatives were introduced to execute the 'truly global'

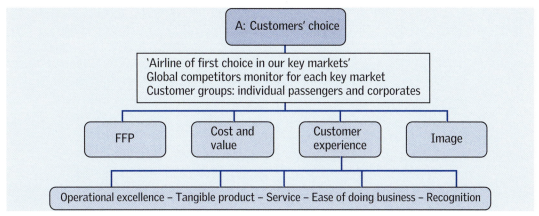

Figure 2 Goal A
Source: *BA Fact Book*, 1997:13)

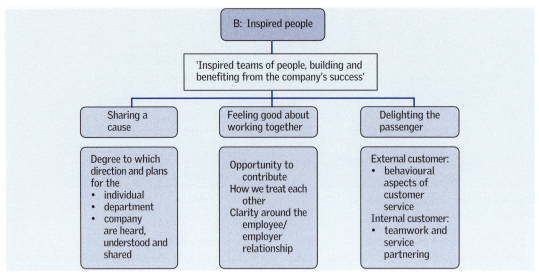

Figure 3 Goal B
Source: *BA Fact Book*, 1997:13)

strategic intent. The following section provides an overview of the nature and extent of these initiatives specifically designed to deploy the new global strategy into practice. These included a highly visible corporate identity change, the launch of a global alliance, a new flagship HQ and a new corporate communication programme. These organisation-wide initiatives are listed in Table 16.

Utopia

In 1997, Ayling declared that the new corporate image on the aircraft was *'the physical manifestation of a fundamental review of our mission. No longer will the airline be just a UK carrier but a global airline based in Britain'*. The changes to the image of the airline required the repainting of over 300 aircraft at an estimated cost of £60 million (*BA News*, 2000:10).

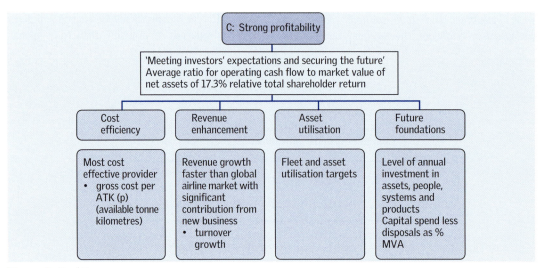

Figure 4 Goal C
Source: *BA Fact Book*, 1997:13)

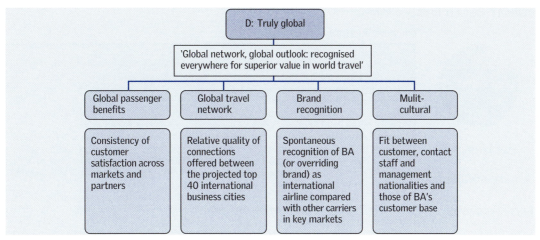

Figure 5 Goal D.
Source: *BA Fact Book*, 1997:13)

The most visual symbol of the change in strategic emphasis was the attempt to change the airline's corporate identity. It was believed that such a change would help to communicate the new mission, vision and values:

One of the issues faced was the question of how to interpret and deliver the positioning identified in the Masterbrand Research – 'Global and Caring'. Reflected in the metaphor 'nothing is too big and nothing is too small'. The positioning was expressed as: 'an airline of its world and for that world, born and based in Britain – citizen of the world' (global); 'a passionate commitment of the British Airways community to serving the communities of the world' (caring). The change in identity is to reflect that British Airways is building from British to global; from premium/business to all people who place value on the travel experience; from long-haul, to both
short and long-haul; from masculine and upright to warmth and humanity. (The Research Business International Report: 1995)

BA developed a new marketing campaign, called Utopia, based around the use of global images. The market research indicated that this new identity would help convey BA's aspirations for the future, by appealing to travellers worldwide and indicating that the airline was a 'British' airline. BA wanted to be both a British airline and also a 'global' airline. Using images from five different continents BA hoped to convey values of cultural sympathy and diversity.[5] In June 1997, the new BA corporate identity was launched. Another marketing campaign attempting to create the perception that the organisation was a global operator was the oneworld™ alliance. The logo that represented the alliance was then added to any visual representations of the airline, as part of the corporate identity.

Table 16 Corporate level initiatives

Year	Initiative
1997	Utopia, the new corporate identity
1997	The Waterside building and its particular design features
1999	oneworld™
1999	Putting People First Again, corporate communications event

5 Market Research Department Reports 1997 and 1998.

Table 17 Benefits to oneworld Members

oneworld **Features**

Aer Lingus

American Airlines

BRITISH AIRWAYS

CATHAY PACIFIC

FINNAIR

IBERIA

LAN

QANTAS

More people to support you
- Together we employ over 260,000 people in over 130 countries. Our employees will be there to help you, on the ground and in the air, wherever your journey takes you in the oneworld network of over 550 destinations around the globe.

Greater rewards for frequent flyers
- If you are a member of the American Airlines Advantage, British Airways Executive Club, Cathay Pacific Marco Polo Club, Finnair Plus, Iberia Plus, Qantas Frequent Flyer, LanChile LanPass or Aer Lingus TAB you will find that the rewards and privileges of membership have been greatly enhanced. You will earn miles in your particular program whenever you travel on eligible flights and fares of the oneworld alliance airways. Qualifying flights will also count towards the maintenance or advancement of your tier status. 2 And, when you are ready to redeem your miles, you can do so to over 550 destinations worldwide.

  Because our eight frequent flyer programs have different names for their various membership tiers, we have created a set of oneworld symbols: oneworld Emerald, Sapphire and Ruby.

Smoother transfers
- We place great emphasis on the service we provide, in flight and on the ground, especially to passengers with onward connections. We hope to make your transfers between oneworld member airlines as smooth as possible.

More value
- oneworld Global Products bring a new simplicity to planning both regional and around-the-world itineraries to your choice of over 550 destinations.

Access to airline lounges
- The oneworld alliance airlines provide over 400 lounges across the globe. If you are a top-tier member of one of our frequent flyer programs, you will have access to our lounges prior to departure.

  At peak periods, access to certain lounges may be restricted due to capacity constraints. Access is available on the day of departure when your next onward flight is with a oneworld member airline. Access may not apply at a limited number of third-party-operated lounges.

Source: www.BA.com

Waterside

Another attempt by management to change the culture of the airline was to move the functional managers into one custom-built, open-plan environment known as 'Waterside'. This transition into the new 21st-century working mode (which included 'hot desking') was another of Ayling's high-profile changes.

The move to Waterside was a further attempt to create culture change by bringing together many departments in one location and to reinforce the 'global and caring' strategic intent.

The design was such that each wing of the building was named after a region of the world and each workspace, meeting and training room was named after particular cities within that region. The idea was to provide a global perspective to daily work.

oneworld™

The oneworld alliance was launched in 1998 and embraced 220,000 employees in over 138 countries,

serving 600 destinations and providing access to over 200 lounges. Table 17 lists features of oneworld including the various airline partners involved in the oneworld alliance and the benefits offered to oneworld members.

Putting People First Again (PPFA)

To give effect to this strategic intent, the external image and customer perception of the airline needed to be aligned with the internal image, culture and behaviours of the employees. At the corporate level, initiatives such as corporate training programmes were introduced in an attempt to change the internal culture. One of these programmes, '*Putting People First Again*' (PPFA), attempted to broaden attitudes, to promote a more outward-looking perspective and to increase the focus on customer service. PPFA emphasised the importance of meeting individuals' needs through an increased understanding of different cultural needs. Employees from all levels across the network were flown to the

UK HQ to attend this one-day training event. This programme followed on from the previous PPF programme that had been introduced by Sir Colin Marshall in 1983 when the organisation had first been privatised and which was designed to reinforce a more customer-driven organisational culture. The PPFA communication programme revolved around a common charter that was communicated to all those who attended the training programme. The charter is described in Figure 6 below.

<u>Putting People First Again</u>
Charter
'So, what's it all about?'
'Honest, direct communication'
You told us in the Employee Opinion Survey that you wanted more. This is your chance to get it!
'Our Customers'
They are critical to our profitability. We'll be discussing what they want and how we deliver those needs.
'Today's business'
An honest picture of what's going on in the company at the moment.
'Tomorrow's World'
A glimpse of what the future holds for our business and what we need to do to secure that future.
'So, what do we want from you?'
'Involvement'
Your expertise, your knowledge.
'An open mind'
Listen and respect the contributions of colleagues.

Figure 6 BA PPFA Charter 1999

This case study was prepared for this textbook by faculty members at Warwick Business School, University of Warwick, UK. This case study may not be reproduced in any form without prior permission. For more information, visit www.wbs.ac.uk.

Case 23 House of Townend Limited

Wine Online: new competition in the UK wine trade

Introduction

Throughout the late 1990s unprecedented growth in e-commerce had a profound effect on many industries, yet the fine wine trade was surprisingly slow to react to the changes brought about by this new technology. Towards the close of the decade a handful of traditional wine merchants cautiously entered the market, faced with new competition from dedicated Internet operators. Although wine would seem to be a product perfectly suited to selling online, many long-established wine businesses have found that they did not have the skills or resources to compete effectively in this new medium. This case examines the position at the end of 2000 for a company approaching its 100th anniversary: Yorkshire-based *House of Townend*.

House of Townend Limited

The company is a wholly owned subsidiary of J. Townend & Sons (Hull) Limited, a holding company controlled by J.E. Townend and his immediate family. House of Townend Limited ('*Townend*') is an importer, wholesaler and retailer of high-quality wine. These three trading activities generate three discrete revenue streams through various trading divisions.

Overseas agency agreements, foreign market purchases and imports are managed by the agency division *Cachet Wine*. This relates purely to quality wines sourced directly with the producers, for which a sole supply agency is in place. Foreign currency transactions are carried out through the main

Townend operation, which remains responsible for all wholesale activity.

The wholesale division is the core business, supplying quality hotels and restaurants and a limited number of resellers. A team of 10 experienced salespeople is supported by a permanent telesales operation and own-fleet distribution. A cash-and-carry operation has recently been launched, at the main site in Hull, serving regional pubs and off-licences.

The retail arm operates 11 shops under separately branded *House of Townend* wine shops and *Booz Brothers* off-licences. Only one is a fine wine shop, attached to the *Willerby Manor Hotel*, a related Townend Group undertaking. Three further shops are wine-led, although positioned further downmarket. The seven Booz Brothers shops are downmarket off-licences selling a range of beers, spirits and CTN lines, with wine taking a secondary role.

Case background

In preliminary interviews, the Managing Director suggested that the firm was under-utilising its assets. He was keen to investigate the possibility of launching an online operation.

Within the retail division a small mail-order business had been operating on a low-key basis since 1995. It used essentially the same wine list as the wholesale supply list, with different pricing and VAT presentation, and contributed approximately £200k in revenues. This operation was recently used as the vehicle to test a pilot e-commerce project. A Website was constructed, which was effectively little more than a price list published on the Web. This operated under the domain name www.houseoftownend.co.uk.

The commercial effect of the pilot project was negligible and the site was aborted to allow a refocusing of the strategy. The domain names remain active and new site formats are being considered for a relaunch in 2001.

The UK wine market

The UK wine trade is almost exclusively an import business, with exports (mainly consisting of re-exports) amounting to less than 1% of total revenues. The wine sector is only one element of the booming alcoholic beverages market, in which the

---

This case was prepared by Andrew Bramley, Warwick Business School.

The material in this case is taken from the original research conducted by the author. This case is intended as a basis for class discussion and is not intended to illustrate either ineffective or effective handling of a business situation.

UK is one of the most important European consumers with a total market value of £32 billion.

Britain has traditionally played an important role in shaping the European and global wine market. British wine merchants are greatly respected, exerting considerable influence over prices and the ratings of wines in each new vintage. It is significant that France's biggest market is the UK, accounting for 18% of French wine exported. The UK is also the most important market for Germany, Australia and New Zealand.

The supply side of the global wine market is dominated by geographically fixed factors of production. The locus of primary production cannot shift, since wine nomenclature is strictly controlled and linked to geography, vineyard site and grape variety, along with a host of contingent factors such as the age and provenance of vines, mandatory vinification techniques and the quantifiable chemical composition of the wine itself.

Although larger operators from both Europe and the New World are continually seeking new foreign vineyard sites to establish a physical position and production base in their respective export markets, the market remains highly fragmented in terms of both supply and distribution. Of particular relevance to wine merchants contemplating e-commerce supported by outsourced logistics and distribution is the particular deficiency the UK market has in its physical distribution channels. The haulage and freight service infrastructure is poor, especially in provincial areas. This remains a problem for traditional wine merchants dependent on carriers for deliveries.

The world's best classic wines are scarce and demand far exceeds supply. Many of the better producers and well-established estates strictly limit the quantities sold to any one merchant, and allocation levels tend to be set in direct proportion to the length of the trading relationship and perceived prestige of the intended destination or sale point. Many top French winemakers, for example, like to see their wines sold in internationally renowned restaurants and perceive that an association with a celebrated chef enhances the credibility of their wine.

For this reason a key factor in the supply-side economics is the need to maintain sources of rare wines, establish new ones, or seek out the rising stars of the future and secure consistent supply through working closely with growers in product development. It is in this area that New World producers have the greatest impact on the changing market.

For example, although Australian wine only accounts for 2.3% of world production, Australia generates around 25% of the world's leading scientific papers on oenology and viticulture. Californian vinification expertise is similarly sought after, and 'flying winemakers' from Australia, New Zealand and the Americas are advising vineyards and winemakers in all areas of the world, even in the classic French heartlands of Bordeaux and Burgundy.

In the late 1980s circa 85% of all the wine exported in the world came from just four Western European countries (France, Italy, Portugal and Spain). By 1997 this had fallen to 72%. The current figure is 69%, yet New World exports have grown at an astonishing rate over the past decade. To take just two examples, Australia has grown by 350% and Chile by 400%.

Excessive fragmentation and over-regulation are undermining the fine wine producers of the Old World. *The Economist* has called this a global market-wide battle, fought between 'Terroir' and 'Technology'. The desire to protect regional identity and the integrity of famous vineyards has produced a plethora of legislation, such as the French *Appellation Contrôlée* (AC). The strictness of AC confines core production methods and means the French vignerons are less able to react to changing consumer tastes or adapt to new technology. The new breed of winemaker is less constrained by such legislation and this is driving greater innovation in vinification.

Further down the value chain at the wholesale level, which primarily concerns Townend, the market is characterised by high asset specificity, coupled with potential labour mobility. In this context, human capital specificity arises because skills are uniquely specific to the area of expert knowledge surrounding fine wine, to precise knowledge of certain rare wines from growers in their portfolio, and to knowledge of the regional peculiarities of the hotel and restaurant business.

Buyers in that industry view their wine suppliers as valued and trusted advisers. Having invested time and learning in the relationship, and time in under-standing the range of wines and their growers, they are likely to consider that sales relationships on a personal level are of equal importance to the corporate trading history. This is a market of considerable and growing importance for the specialist merchant. Between 1995 and 1999 the UK hotel trade grew 25% in value terms, followed by the restaurant sector at 20%.

Hence, specificity also extends into complementary markets and, unfortunately for merchants such as Townend, the people acquiring special skills, contacts and knowledge may easily move from one organisation to another without any significant retraining.

Sales of all alcoholic drinks are sensitive to price and, therefore, to changes in tax and duties. The anticipated introduction of the euro is expected to bring greater pan-European fiscal alignment although, to date, there has been limited harmonisation in duties since the formation of the Single European Market in 1993. At a retail level there has been a significant growth in cross-border shopping to take advantage of EU tax differentials.

This has also affected the hotel and restaurant trade. For those restaurateurs or hotel groups willing to outlay larger sums, parallel imports are an increasingly attractive option, especially in premium product sectors, in which UK agencies typically set significantly higher prices relative to those in the country of origin. The clearest example of this was in the sales of champagne during the build-up to the millennium celebrations. Many hotel operators went directly to the producers, anticipating both scarcity and high prices in the UK. In reality, however, the expected boom did not arrive, leaving high stocks within the hospitality industry and causing a further slowing down of champagne sales through legitimate agency channels.

In recent years domestic demand for local wines in producing countries has declined, while wine consumption in traditionally strong beer-drinking countries is on the increase. Major wine producers have been forced to pay attention to their export markets to compensate for falling domestic sales of even their generic wines. The rise in wine consumption in the UK has been especially strong, making this an increasingly important market (see Figure 1).

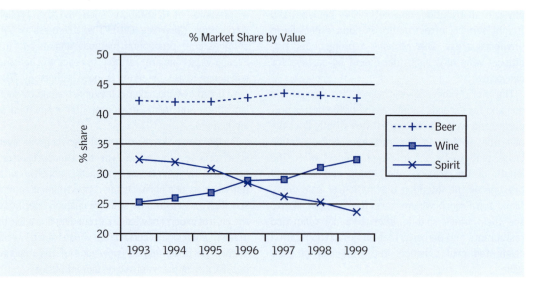

Figure 1 Shift in UK market shares of alcoholic drinks, 1993 to 1999
Source: Mintel/ACNielsen.

The major retailers and supermarket chains have been instrumental in developing the profile of the wine market and lately have done much to assist the specialist merchant. By bringing good quality wine to the shelves, they encourage its purchase as a regular weekly item, and a high information content in their marketing strips away the traditional mystique and cultural barriers that may have previously inhibited buyers.

Now high-street multiples are engaging in sophisticated micro-segmentation and strategic marketing to better understand the UK wine drinker, and most have their own expert tasters, buyers and consultants – previously the domain of the specialist wine merchant. This has been one of the main factors underpinning the increase in popularity of New World wines and in the sheer range and global representation of wines on the shelves of major supermarkets and off-licences.

The changing UK market shares of the key wine-producing countries are shown in Figure 2.

Bringing better wine into mainstream domestic consumption has had a spin-off effect in increased media exposure, which plays a key role in educating consumers. An example of this is the wider appreciation of different grape varieties today, in contrast to 10 years ago, when consumers who might buy wine on the basis of region or AC had no idea which grapes were used in its make-up. High-profile media coverage promotes the idea that wine is fashionable and knowledge of wine is a desirable social skill; an image also perpetuated by positive television exposure. At a higher level of consumer knowledge, media such as *The Wine Advocate*, *The Wine Spectator*, *Decanter* and various independent Web-based commentators such as www.wine-pages.com do much to increase consumer awareness.

Research by Mintel into UK wine buyers' changing preferences, carried out by survey between 1994 and 1998, showed definite trends suggesting increasing acceptance of higher-quality wine:

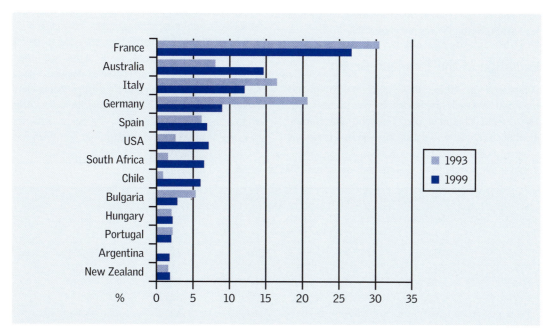

Figure 2 Patterns in UK wine consumption, % share by country of origin[a]
[a]Aggregate % changes by volume.
Source: *The Economist* Intelligence Unit.

- A willingness to experiment with higher-priced wines from new areas
- Greater awareness of differing wine 'styles' based on grape variety
- Greater reliance placed on advice and information at point of sale
- Increasing purchases of different wines to match food

The value of the overall market has increased faster than volume as customers have traded-up in quality to more costly wines. Between 1993 and 1999 the UK market's value increased by 67%, or 43% in real terms (see Table 1).

The slight decline in 1995 was due in part to falling production after poor harvests in Australia, California, Italy and Spain. The resultant pressure on supply and pricing, allied to shortfalls in the production intended for domestic use in these markets, meant that UK retailers found difficulty in sourcing wines at lower price points, which are vital for bringing new consumers into the market.

The upper levels of the trade, however, were not greatly affected and overall values continued to rise, suggesting that this is a surprisingly resilient segment of the market incorporating consumers who are increasingly less price-sensitive.

Evolution of the Townend Group

Established in 1906, the Townend Group has remained in family ownership to the present day. The present Chairman, J.E. Townend, was fundamentally a retailer and during his previous tenure as MD the scale of the business grew to 35 retail outlets. Gradually the emphasis has shifted in favour of wholesale activity with a commensurate reduction in the number of shops throughout the past 20 years.

Under the leadership of the current MD, John Charles Townend, the profile of the business has been substantially changed. At the time of his joining the company in 1988, the portfolio of retail shops numbered 14, with wholesale turnover relatively static and in the region of £0.5m annually. The majority of that revenue consisted of low margin fast-moving lines, sold into supermarkets and grocery multiples. A significant boost to wholesale turnover came in 1992 when Townend won the national supply contract to the TUCO university purchasing group, worth £0.5m per year for 3 years.

From this point onwards the focus of the business development was almost exclusively on wholesale supply, mainly to hotels and restaurants, and between 1997 and 2000 the retail portfolio has diminished at the rate of one shop per year.

The direction of this expansion was aided by the judicious recruitment of specialists in the field of wholesale supply to the on-trade, and in the acquisition of smaller businesses already in this field. The demise of two key competitors, *Yorkshire Fine Wines* and *Chennell & Armstrong*, provided scope for the recruitment of several high-calibre sales personnel. Both these businesses enjoyed good reputations in the region and their sales teams were highly respected. The current Sales Director, Alan Whitehead, was employed in the same role for Yorkshire Fine Wines. He was recruited in 1994 and

Table 1 UK market for still wine of fresh grape 1993 to 1999[a]

	Volume Sales	Index	Value Sales	Index	Inflation adj.
	M litres		£m		£m
1993	617	100	3,500	100	3,500
1994	651	106	3,800	109	3,714
1995	645	105	4,000	114	3,787
1996	678	110	4,400	126	4,074
1997	740	120	4,930	141	4,437
1998	794	129	5,410	155	4,724
1999	839	136	5,850	167	5,038

[a]excludes champagne, sparkling wine and fortified wine.
Source: Mintel/ONS/HM Customs & Excise.

several members of his old team have since joined Townend, most notably Mike Luke, a specialist in wholesale on-trade accounts.

Acquisitions and divestments

This changing profile has been underpinned by a series of divestments and acquisitions.

A major divestment took place in 1986, when 18 retail shops were sold to Blayneys. The proceeds of this sale were invested into the Willerby Manor Hotel, now a wholly owned subsidiary of the holding company J. Townend and Sons (Hull) Ltd. The hotel currently turns over circa £2.3m p.a. and sources its wet purchases, worth around £200k, through Townend.

The continued expansion of the wine division has reflected the relative significance in the industry of human capital and intangible assets. The refined skills and expertise of the people selling the wine, allied to their personal contacts and network of loyal customers are of equal importance to factor inputs, tangibles and capital assets. John Charles Townend set about recruiting several key people through acquisition of their businesses and assets.

The purchase of *Cachet Wine* in 1995 is a case in point. This was a small business run by Graham Coverdale in York, turning over circa £500k p.a. Essentially the trading assets and stock were bought along with the intangible assets and network of contacts associated with Mr. Coverdale. A similar deal took place in 1999 with the absorption of *Phil Parrish Wines*, a local business with revenues of circa £200k.

The attractive aspect of these deals was in the acquisition of new customer accounts and revenues in the hotel and restaurant on-trade, and both these people are now important members of the sales team. Immediately following its purchase, Cachet Wine was used as the platform to develop Townend's agency wines division, which effectively came on stream in and around 1997.

Group restructuring

Significant group restructuring took place between 1995 and 1999. At the start of this period, the majority of the principal wine and spirits trading activity, at circa £4.5m, remained in the holding company. Various smaller operating companies came within this umbrella and the group structure was characterised by close divisional interrelationships, with several reciprocal participating-interest holdings and extensive cross-billing between divisions. There are also unlimited multilateral guarantees and cross-guarantees within the group, between group undertakings, and between companies in which the holding parent has participating interests. The controlling family has historically viewed the group as one complete entity, inseparable by divisions. In addition to the sales made between Townend and the hotel, substantial management charges are levied between divisions.

In 1998 there was a reported change of trade in J. Townend and Sons, from wine merchants to a holding company with property letting interests. There were a number of transactions between divisions, including transfers of assets, write-back on taxable-event disposals, and revaluation of investments to reflect the underlying net assets of wholly owned subsidiaries. At the height of this reorganisation there were nine separate entities within the group activities.

The reorganisation was phased in to bring alignment and coherency to the group trading activities, since all the wine revenues and trading assets at wholesale and retail levels have gradually been subsumed within House of Townend Ltd. In the 1998–1999 period freehold and leasehold land and buildings with net book values of £2,072,680 and £300,620 were transferred to the holding company from Willerby Manor and House of Townend respectively. The above restructuring has culminated in a streamlining of the group into three key areas as at the end of 1999:

◆ **J. Townend and Sons (Hull) Ltd:** Holding company controlling all group property

◆ **House of Townend Ltd:** All wine and spirit importing, wholesaling and retailing

◆ **Willerby Manor Hotels Ltd:** All hotel and catering activities

Consolidated wholesale and retail wine trading figures for 1995 to 1999 are shown in the 5-year financial performance analysis (see Figure 3).

In calculating the aggregate sector performance the accounts of 117 companies engaged in the same area of the wine trade were analysed and a control group of 66 extracted from the total sample. This control group was chosen on the basis of similar size, operating parameters and customer profile to Townend.

Systems and processes

I spend as much time placating irate customers and sorting out incorrect deliveries as I do selling wine ... either the customer has got someone else's wine, or the vintages are wrong, or they only get half the stock they ordered because the warehouse couldn't find everything. The problem is this Dickensian warehouse system and the fact that nobody talks to anyone else in the different departments. (Mike Luke, Sales Executive)

The company has grown up within a range of Victorian canal-side warehouses, each with its own warren of offices and interconnecting staircases. Mike Luke felt that this in itself contributed to poor communication throughout the company and reduced the accountability of individuals for errors by limiting regular face-to-face contact.

As an importer, Townend has a Customs-bonded warehouse registered with HM Customs & Excise, with a strictly licensed record system for import stock based on an old UNIX platform. The company's main information system is similarly built on UNIX, which has been gradually upgraded and expanded over the past 15 years. There is no interface between the two systems.

The bonded warehouse stock is scrupulously monitored at the time of delivery, due to mandatory Customs compliance and audit procedures. Any incorrect deliveries are notified and records amended before the wines go into storage. However, through regular observation in the warehouse it became clear that there are no formal locations in the bonded section and no layout or plan of the wines in long-term and short-term storage. The process is entirely dependent on the memory of the bondsman, one of the company's longest-serving employees.

In the main warehouse serving the daily deliveries, staff turnover is high and errors are frequent. The orders office generates a manual picking list, which is taken around the warehouse by staff compiling the orders. Each boxed order is given a dispatch note in duplicate, the carbon copy of which is eventually used for compiling the customer invoice. It takes between 7 and 10 days to generate the invoice, which is then mailed to the customer.

All the retail shops are equipped with proprietary DOS-based EPOS systems. The hardware in each shop is basically a till with bar code scanner. Each unit relies on remote dial-up to interface with the management system at head office, which is by text file exchange. This system frequently leads to stock errors. The calibre of shop staff was acknowledged as a weak link in the process. Wine product knowledge is scarce and very little training is carried out, or requested by staff. Notably, the viability of some of the remote shop sites, as stand-alone units, was questioned by the Sales Director and most were not viewed as complementary to the core wholesale fine wine business.

Sales and marketing

Alan Whitehead believes his team of salespeople to be unrivalled in terms of their maturity and the respect they command in the trade. Most have been in the wine business all their lives, and since many have run their own businesses they are extremely profit-aware and have a good range of personal contacts at all levels in the supply chain.

The relatively recent telesales operation is primarily an order-collecting function, since the salesforce is responsible for the selling-in of new lines. All the relationship building is done at the client premises face-to-face, and it is here that long-standing trust is built between client and sales force. The convivial nature of both hospitality business and wine trade means that this may often take place in a semi-social context.

John Townend has developed notable wine tasting and buying skills over the years, and works closely with Alan Whitehead on the development of the trade list and the range of suppliers in the portfolio. The trade list represents a unique range of products, since the 94-year history of Townend has influenced the willingness of better vignerons to supply limited allocation wines in realistic quantities. Hence, the classic regions such as Burgundy and Bordeaux are well represented by top producers. The addition of

Consolidated wholesale and retail trading activities 1995 to 1999

Year Ending	1995	1996	1997	1998	1999	key changes
						1995–1999%
Turnover	6,613,288	6,875,942	7,278,226	7,855,466	8,529,966	28.97
Gross profit	1,186,008	1,217,030	1,482,777	1,645,102	1,896,166	59.87
PBIT	36,193	3,497	72,256	108,111	142,146	292.74
Interest	27,999	11,146	26,349	41,833	42,264	
Taxation	4,655	807	3,775	4,979	6,635	
PAIT	3,539	−37,458	42,132	61,299	133,182	
Dividend	-	-	-	-	-	
Retained Earnings	3,311	−37,458	42,132	61,299	133,182	3922.41
Fixed Assets	966,367	846,790	854,158	933,349	1,268,249	31.23
Current Assets	2,747,292	3,392,840	3,320,667	3,765,864	3,240,077	17.94
Stocks	1,223,491	1,196,934	1,402,944	1,635,626	1,880,860	
Trade Debtors	674,090	716,678	870,792	953,267	1,018,882	
Cash	3,665	2,859	2,857	3,200	2,721	
Total Assets	3,713,659	4,239,630	4,174,825	4,699,213	4,508,326	21.39
Current Liabilities	2,233,873	2,791,154	2,681,271	3,205,727	3,092,196	38.42
Trade Creditors+accruals	751,597	1,003,555	1,030,789	1,202,219	1,435,751	91.02
STL [Bank Overdraft]	705,215	1,115,956	1,080,291	1,200,753	1,312,810	86.16
Capital Employed	1,479,786	1,448,476	1,493,554	1,493,486	1,416,130	−4.3
LTL {debt > 1 yr}	-	6,148	9,094	2,878	240,836	
ShareHolders' Funds	1,479,786	1,442,328	1,484,460	1,490,608	1,175,294	−20.57

Ratio Analysis	note	1995	1996	1997	1998	1999	sector avg
							1999
Performance							
ROCE [PBIT / CE]	a	2.45%	0.24%	4.84%	7.24%	10.04%	22.21%
ROI [PBIT / TA]	b	0.97%	0.08%	1.73%	2.30%	3.15%	6.61%
Gross margin		17.93%	17.70%	20.37%	20.94%	22.23%	22.15%
[~ Movement yr-on-yr]		datum	−1.30%	15.10%	2.79%	6.15%	0.82%
Net margin	aⁱ bⁱ	0.55%	0.05%	0.99%	1.38%	1.67%	2.60%
[~ Movement yr-on-yr]		datum	−90.71%	1852.02%	38.63%	21.08%	0.12%
EVA	c	−£123,433	−£150,425	−£88,270	−£78,118	£24,310	
Efficiency							
Sales: Capital Employed	aⁱⁱ	4.47	4.75	4.87	5.26	6.02	8.54
Asset Turnover	bⁱⁱ	1.78	1.62	1.74	1.67	1.89	2.54
(Debtors*365) / Sales		37.20	38.04	43.67	44.29	43.60	49.37
(Creditors*365) / Sales		41.48	53.27	51.69	55.86	61.44	61.72
Sales : Stocks		5.41	5.74	5.19	4.80	4.54	7.29
Liquidity							
Current Ratio		1.23	1.22	1.24	1.17	1.05	1.20
Acid Test		0.68	0.79	0.72	0.66	0.44	0.91
Stability							
Gearing [on total debt]		47.66%	77.47%	72.94%	80.59%	109.71%	84.52%
Interest Cover		1.29	0.31	2.74	2.58	3.36	5.98
Growth							
Sales growth yr-on-yr		datum	3.97%	5.85%	7.93%	8.59%	8.94%
[~ Inflation-adjusted]		datum	3.88%	5.67%	7.67%	8.44%	8.79%
PBIT Growth yr-on-yr		datum	−90.34%	1966.23%	49.62%	31.48%	1.25%
[~ Inflation-adjusted]		datum	−88.22%	1907.11%	47.99%	30.96%	1.23%

Economic Indicators		1995	1996	1997	1998	1999	1995–1999%
RPI % change yr-on-yr	d	3.54	2.43	3.12	3.42	1.67	11.11
GDP % change yr-on-yr	e	2.83	2.63	3.52	2.21	2.14	10.86
Interest rates %	f	6.57	5.79	6.73	7.34	5.69	−13.39

ab Component elements of ROCE and ROI may not agree due to rounding
c   An EVA cost-of-capital substitute rate was estimated from LIBOR +2%
d   RPI from aggregate quarterly RPIX underlying rate. Index: 1995=100
e   GDP seasonally adjusted, at constant market prices. Index 1995=100
f   Annualised rate calculated from LIBOR expressed as weighted daily averages. Source: Bank of England

Figure 3 Townend Group: 5-Year Financial Performance Analysis specialist wines from some of the foremost growers in the New World through agency agreements with Cachet Wine means it is feasible for Townend to supply all the needs of quality hotels and restaurants.

Sales meetings are held in a 4–6 week cycle and while these are performance-based and target-led there is very little exchange of information or training relating to the actual products and the portfolio of specialist producers. More importantly, the unique knowledge that has been built up within the team is not disseminated, exploited or added to.

> Strategy? I think if you ask all ten of us you'll get ten different answers ... we are not really told anything about marketing, or the planned Website, or any new things coming up. It would be helpful if we could have a bit more information passed around – sometimes our sales meetings seem more like a collection of strangers who occasionally sit in the same room together. We don't really talk about promotion, marketing, new brands or suchlike. (Graham Coverdale, Sales Executive)

The issue of brand proposition in this specialised sector is complex. Wine trade marketing tends to be concerned with, for example, 'The Wines of Australia' or 'Fine Wines of Chablis' as general concepts, and the exposure of specific wines, and certainly of their agents or wholesalers, is limited. Due to a fragmented supply market there are no major world-class brands to speak of and, with the exception of the top champagne houses, the concept of mainstream 'branded wine' is anathema to the high-quality specialist merchant.

Branding in the upper reaches of the market is subtle, and may best be described as a nested hierarchy, ranging down from country level, to regional Appellation, to the grower or négociant-éleveur and then, on a micro level, to the estate or vineyard site. The difficulty for wholesalers like Townend is that they get little exposure in this branding hierarchy.

New competition in e-commerce

In the 12 months to the end of 2000, competition in wine e-commerce intensified. The evolution of this relatively new sector has followed similar trends seen in the US market during its own growth period some two years earlier. In the USA, the more advanced state of development may be attributed to the generally earlier public acceptance of Internet technology and the fact that the majority of USA consumer demand is for domestic wines.

In the UK, several key players have emerged, with a small number of highly resourced Internet-focused operators establishing a first-mover advantage in the upper reaches of the market. These same trends in changing structure were apparent in the US market, when just a few significant players such as Virtual Vineyards established an early lead.

However, there is evidence from both sides of the Atlantic that e-commerce may not yet destroy the established business model of the traditional wine merchant, since both US and UK markets are afflicted with similar problems of physical distribution. While in the US this is due to restrictive distribution laws still remaining from the Prohibition era, the net result is the same: wine e-tailers are experiencing a boom in sales, yet these are not necessarily at the expense of revenues in existing channels.

Important UK merchants with a mix of both wholesale and retail revenues are reporting differing customer reactions to e-commerce. Bibendum and its close rival, 300-year-old Berry Brothers & Rudd, were two of the first London merchants to launch Websites in 1998.

Bibendum completely closed down its retail shops in favour of an Internet operation in 1999. In-company research showed that 60% of existing Bibendum customers had Internet access and the majority generally supported the company's e-commerce initiative. However, while the core of its £20m operation is in wholesale revenues, its retail operation is positioned quite differently to Townend, being based purely on minimum 1-case order quantities for home delivery within the M25 boundary. Despite widespread use by the company's retail customers, the online operation generated little increase in total retail sales.

Berry Brothers took a different approach, offering to deliver any quantity to any UK address. It did not have a major retail presence at this time, with no dedicated retail shops. The majority of existing retail mail-order customers did not use the new Website.

The Berry Brothers site still only accounts for 5% of total sales, although recent e-commerce compound growth is significant, with 60% of purchases each month from first-time visitors.

The most significant entrant this year is *Virgin Wines*, a pure online operation headed by Virgin Direct founder Rowan Gormley. Although it has no history in the wine trade, as a highly capitalised business prepared to withstand losses for three years, with the backing of the Virgin group, at face value it poses a serious threat. Many new start-ups have underestimated the time and capital needed to build an Internet-compatible brand and a core of loyal customers. Virgin Wines has a marketing director with a background in pure e-commerce rather than the wine trade, and a loyal captive audience of over 1 million online Virgin customers. It has quickly gained market share from other online operations, even those of long-established merchants such as Bibendum and Berry Brothers.

A new breed of virtual intermediary is emerging, following the model of info-mediary 'navigator': in the US a first-mover was winesearcher.com, essentially an intermediary/search facility representing the list content of wine sellers. Although represented as a source of advice, price comparison and impartial recommendation, its revenues clearly came from commission paid by the merchants. Once more, UK market development is emulating that of its American counterpart, although since it is now two years further on in technological terms, the solutions are more creative.

One such example is uvine.com, the first 'stock exchange' for fine wine. Headed by Christopher Burr, former head of wine at Christie's, uvine.com is an Internet-only business offering investment advice and managed transactions between trade and private wine buyers and sellers. They are able to emulate the advice and expertise element in the package offered by a wine merchant, broker or auctioneer, yet their reach and audience is far wider. This effectively disintermediates traditional businesses through competing on information content, quality of advice, speed and timeliness of response, yet allied to commission rates of only 3.5% as against 10–15% with the major auction players, or the typical wholesale trade gross margins of between 20 and 25%.

A way of fighting this type of disintermediation is through inimitability of product and Internet-enabled introduction and dynamic visual promotion of channel-specific products. The US market again provides the best and earliest examples of this strategy, exemplified by the specific labelling and visual product differentiation adopted by the Mondavi Corporation for some of its premium Californian wines offered over the Web. Berry Brothers are already evaluating a number of specific wines for this treatment, for example a small range of specialised late-harvested Gewürztraminer and Tokay wines from a little-known grower in Alsace, in unusual bottle sizes and with avant-garde one-off painted label designs.

Interactive survey: WWWine Focus Group

The current state of the competition and the relative Internet presence of competitors' Websites was assessed through an interactive focus group of private and professional wine buyers and food and wine writers in Britain and the USA. Entitled the *WWWine Focus Group*, the two-stage survey was based on an interactive online survey instrument disseminated by e-mail to 41 participants.[†]

The group first provided an assessment of the desirable qualities of wine Websites, and generated a list of the keywords, search engines and portals most likely to be used in any speculative Web-search. From the list of key words suggested by participants, a detailed Web-search was made using 10 different search engines, 5 food and wine-related portals and links from leading sites serving the food and wine industry. In total, 114 search or link permutations were executed. The results from part 1 of the survey are summarised in Table 2.

In phase 2, sites with the greatest exposure in the Web-search were then graded by the focus group. Participants provided a critique of those sites on various levels, which generated a ranking of each operator according to the perceptions of more discerning consumers.

In the survey section providing contextual comments, most criticism was levelled at the juvenile

† The survey was conducted by the author during research at Harvard Business School. The guidance offered during this project by Professor Stephen Greyser of Harvard is gratefully acknowledged.

Table 2 Focus group ratings of Website attributes and content

Critical Dimensions of Websites	Other Web Services Requested	
Rated 1–6 in order of importance	*Rated as Essential*	*Rated as Desirable*
1 Information Content	Declared stock levels	Wine recommendations
2 Fast Download Time	Tasting notes	Discussion forum
3 Ease of Navigation	Rating of vintages	Technical information
4 Range/Quantity Offered	Search facility	Tailored Q&A service
5 Price of Wines	Private access by PIN	Market reports
6 Presentation and Graphics	Secure transactions	Profiles of producers

nature of much of the general material and advertising throughout the Internet. It was considered extremely important to be able to avoid this type of material, get to the target site quickly, navigate it efficiently and place an order as simply as possible. In addition to the major evaluation criteria set out in Table 2, the following points were consistently raised:

♦ It is not desirable to have specialised and detailed oenological information or scarce, unusual or limited-allocation wines listed for the general public to see.

♦ Buyers are likely to spend more on unique or sole-supply wines if *genuine* expert comment and technical information are available.

♦ The simplistic language used on the Internet, the basic level of advertising and the technologically led 'jargon' are detrimental to serious wine buying.[‡]

Table 3 shows the results of part 2 of the survey. Essentially this suggests the likely competitors to Townend's future online operation.

Websites of competitors

The site drawing the most favourable comments was Berry Brothers'. Extracts from the site Webpages are shown at Exhibits 1 and 2.

Exhibit 1 shows a buying window, with a profile of *Jean-Paul Droin*, a small grower in Chablis, along with a description of his wines. Exhibit 2 demonstrates the

Table 3 Focus group results: ratings of top 10 UK wine Websites

Rank	Company	Profile of Main Business [a]	URL
1	Berry Bros. & Rudd	Traditional London merchant	http://www.bbr.com
2	Bibendum	Modern wholesaler	http://www.bibendum-wine.co.uk
3	Oddbins	High-street off-licences	http://www.oddbins.co.uk
4	Chateau Online	Internet operation	http://www.chateauonline.co.uk
5	Wine Planet	Internet operation	http://www.wineplanet.co.uk
6	Majestic Online	Wine cash & carry warehouse	http://www.majestic.co.uk
7	Virgin Wines	Part of diversified brand group	http://www.virginwines.com
8	Uvine	Fine wine 'stock exchange'	http://www.uvine.com
9	Bordeaux Direct	Mail order/wine club model	http://www.bordeauxdirect.co.uk
10	Lindbury Wines	Ex mail order – now all www	http://www.itswine.com

[a] Where different – note certain operators are Internet-only and, in the case of uvine.com, while this is not strictly speaking a merchant, it is nonetheless taking revenues from the traditional merchants' market.

[‡] Particular criticism was reserved for terms such as 'shopping trolley', cartoon images of supermarket baskets and splash screen 'stings' or animated banners on click buttons such as 'Buy It Now' or 'Add To Shopping Basket'.

considerable time and expense involved in updating and maintaining the site content. The underlying technology of the page construction is exploited with the 'recommended wine' window, which changes at random, suggesting different wines to the visitor as the click-stream increases. The site's search facility was the most highly rated of all, and it was noted that the buying section of the site also allows the customer to screen searches on the basis of style of wines, advice content, producer profile or growing regions. It also incorporates a 'bypass' mode to go straight to the ordering facility.

Surprisingly, the site most criticised was Virgin. Over 70% of the group commented that, while there were some good wines listed, finding them was too difficult. Virgin scored lowest on 'ease of navigation' and 'information content'. Criticisms centred on illogical layout, with too many questions put before wine could be bought, and the site's reliance on adolescent humour and oversimplification of the subject matter. As well as causing annoyance it was felt this prevented the search facility from working adequately, and resulted in the 'wine wizard' recommendations falling short of expectations. By way of example, if Australian Shiraz was not noted as a preference in a 'wine wizard' search, the list of recommended wines excluded all Rhône such as Hermitage or Côte Rôtie, classic Italian reds such as Barolo or Amarone, and all Spanish red wines apart from Rioja. The site structure is clearly conceived by technical designers and e-commerce mass retailers rather than wine specialists. Since the search facility works on case-based reasoning it is apparent that the wines have been inappropriately classified from the outset, based on an oversimplified model and limited understanding of the wine consumer.

Exhibit 3 provides an example from uvine.com. The e-mail shown was actuated by a contemporaneous transaction on the site. Although it is automatically activated, it imparts elements of 'news' and 'information', allied to tailored recommendations based on past buying patterns. This proactive approach has effectively 'hijacked' recent information from static media (such as the *Wine Spectator* ratings) and reprocessed it, although the mode of delivery gives it a feeling of timeliness and spontaneity. This system combines proactive and reactive customer contact, with some overlap between personal telephone contact, Internet-enabled CRM and automated transaction processing offered in multiple foreign currencies. The focus group commented widely that the sort of tailored personal recommendations made show a deep understanding of the product, matching the type of advice normally expected from a high-quality wine merchant.

Summary

This case has shown that protected supply chains and inimitable products are important success factors in establishing a sustainable and resilient e-commerce model. New online operators deploying new types of resources threaten the established skills of traditional wine merchants in maintaining and protecting their unique product knowledge.

A key element in Townend's future strategy, therefore, must be to concentrate on high information content and differentiated or preferably unique and non-comparable wines. John Charles Townend has already declared that further expansion into the area of sole agency wines is his preferred route. Such a move would also protect key elements of a difficult supply market plagued by scarcity and vagaries of price, weather and economic uncertainty.

While there is an ever-present threat of disintermediation without exclusive supply contracts in place, important personal relationships with trade customers must also be strengthened and protected. Retail consumers have negligible switching costs and hence their loyalty is transient. However, in the wholesale on-trade sector, merchants have the opportunity to create more permanent associations.

This is an industry driven by people. Townend's future success depends on its relationships with leading producers, a deep knowledge of their unique wines, and the cumulative experience of its salespeople. There is an underlying caveat to this case: the successful integration of a wholly effective online operation requires skills, resources and specialised knowledge that may, at present, be unattainable for Townend without significant investment.

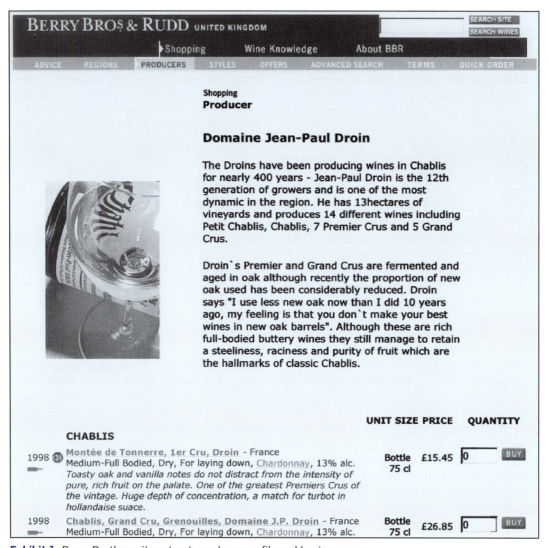

Exhibit 1 Berry Brothers site extract: producer profile and buying screen
Source: http://www.bbr.com.

Exhibit 2 Berry Brothers site extract: interactive news board in wine knowledge section
Source: http://www.bbr.com.

```
From:      enquiries@uvine.com
To:        a.bramley@Bradford.ac.uk
Subject:   uvine - good offers on the uvine exchange
Date:      8 Sept 2000 12:56:59 +0100
```

Reply	Reply All	Forward	Previous	Next	Close

Dear Mr Bramley

uvine.com has now changed the way that wine is bought and sold - with the world's first fully functional exchange for quality wines.

In a further ground-breaking step, uvine now gives you the opportunity to:

- Open an account in any one of a wide range of currencies
- Trade wines in a variety of locations around the world

This will enable online wine trading within and between different areas of the world while settling balances in the currency of your choice.

The service is open to everyone, free to join and the quality and provenance of all the wine is guaranteed. All this with the lowest commission rates in the world* - just 3.5% on either side.

Find out more about the new service, at http://www.uvine.com

As you know, we offer the latest in wine information, investment advice and wine trading strategies for your own p ortfolio. Up-to-the-minute market reports and expert appraisals are available for network members. Here are some more recommendations and hot tips selected from the wines on the exchange today, based on the sort of trades and investments you have been making lately...........................

Ch. Duhart-Milon-Rothschild 1995
Best offer GBP 190

Ch. Pavie 1999 (En Primeur)
Best offer GBP 640

Charles Heidsieck Brut Millésime Champagne 1990
Best offer GBP 145 per 6x75cl bottles: rated 97 by Wine Spectator magazine

Barolo, E Pira 1990
Best offer GBP 375

Tirecul Lagravière Cuvée Madame 1996
Best offer GBP 520 per case of 12x50cl bottles

Offers are per case of 12x75cl bottles in b ond unless otherwise stated and are correct at time of writing.

If you have any questions about the wines in these offers, the trading process or about uvine, please do not hesitate to contact us. We would be happy to recommend further wines if these do not match you current requirements. You can reach us by e-mail at enquiries@uvine.com or by telephone on 0800 328 8448, or, if calling from outside the UK, +44 20 7518 1555.

Yours sincerely,

uvine.com

If you do not wish to be contacted with details of further good offers on the uvine exchange, please send an email to unsubscribe@uvine.com

*As at September 2000

Exhibit 3 uvine.com automated message: low cost services and personalised offers

This case study was prepared for this textbook by faculty members at Warwick Business School, University of Warwick, UK. This case study may not be reproduced in any form without prior permission. For more information, visit www.wbs.ac.uk.

Case 24 **Shell shock: why do good companies do bad things?**

Introduction

On 9 January 2004 the Royal Dutch/Shell Group became involved in Britain's biggest business scandal since the Guinness Affair of 1986, after it emerged that the company had overstated its proven reserves of oil and gas. This concerns 'a reduction of 4.47 billion barrels (23%) from the previously reported end–2002 figures of 19.5 billion barrels' (Malcolm Brinded, Managing Director of Shell Transport).[1]

'Proved reserves'

Royal Dutch/Shell define proved reserves as follows:

> Proved reserves are the estimated quantities of oil and gas which geological and engineering data demonstrate with reasonable certainty to be recoverable in future years from known reservoirs under existing economic and operating conditions ... Oil and gas reserves cannot be measured exactly since estimation of reserves involves subjective judgment and arbitrary determinations. All estimates are subject to revision.[2]

During January 2004, relative to the FTSE World Oil & Gas Index, shares in Shell Transport & Trading fell by 17% and shares in Royal Dutch Petroleum fell by 10%.[3]

Britain's most admired company

Shell 2001: Britain's most admired company

Shell is one of Britain's most admired companies. Each year *Management Today* asks the chief executives of Britain's ten largest companies in 24 sectors to rate each company in their sector on a scale of one to ten against nine criteria. In December 2001 these 240 chief executives rated Shell Transport & Trading Britain's 'most admired' company with a score of 73.72 out of 100. The citation said: 'Chairman Philip Watts exemplifies the good sense that made Shell this year's winning company.' One of the academic researchers, Dr Michael Brown of Nottingham Business School, explained the choice as a reaction to 11 September and the economic recession: 'When it's raining and the landscape is flooding, people cluster around the strongest mountains – they go where they feel safest' (*Management Today*, December 2001).

> Pragmatic Shell headed by the anonymous Philip Watts since Sir Mark Moody Stuart retired in the summer, was seen as a secure haven. Shell's marketing success is often overlooked. It is one of the few companies in the world (Mercedes and Nike are others) and possibly the only one in the UK that can advertise its products merely by showing its logo minus a name. In uncertain times, such reassurance, built up over the years with campaigns like 'You can be sure of Shell' supplies a warm comfort blanket.
>
> Shell's drive to the summit may have been helped by the sector's advanced knowledge of a smart deal in the offing. Soon after the deadline for voting passed, Shell disclosed that it had become the largest US petrol retailer after concluding a deal worth £2.5bn with a Saudi partner to take over Texaco service stations. That left Shell with 22,000 retail sites in the US. Even so, if analysts and fund managers had

This case was written by Professor Bernard Taylor, Executive Director, Centre for Board Effectiveness, Henley Management College. It is intended to be used as the basis for class discussion rather than to illustrate either effective or ineffective handling of a business situation. The case was compiled from published sources.

© 2004 Professor Bernard Taylor, Henley Management College, UK, 24 August 2004.

1 The Shell Transport & Trading Company plc Annual Report and Accounts 2003, p.3.
2 *Meeting the Energy Challenge: The Shell Report 2002*, 5 March 2003, p.26.
3 Source: Thomson Datastream, quoted in 'Shell Accounts Get Signed off at Last', *Financial Times*, Tuesday 25 May 2004, p.21.

been voting, Shell would not have topped the rankings.[4]

In the summer Shell took a pasting, with analysts accusing it of offering the market inconsistencies, vagueness and contradictions. The outcry was sparked by a presentation to analysts by the company's exploration and production division, in which Shell admitted it was downgrading its annual growth target from 5% to 3%.

In the *Fortune* Global Hundred published in July 2001, Royal Dutch/Shell Group was ranked sixth among 'the world's largest corporations' and second to DaimlerChrysler in 'Europe's Top 25'. As the editors pointed out, 'higher crude-oil prices meant that oil producers were able to turn black gold into black ink' and 'on average petroleum refiners' revenues grew 39% and their profits increased 124%, an earnings jump bigger than in any other industry.'[5] According to *Fortune* in the fiscal year 2000/2001 Shell reported revenues of $149bn, up 42% on 1999/2000, and profits were $13bn, an increase of 48% over the previous year. At this time Shell had 90,000 employees.

Corporate social responsibility

In the Shell Annual Report for 2001 Philip Watts wrote a personal message as Chairman of the Committee of Managing Directors:

> In a troubled and unsettled world, we delivered our second best ever earnings in 2001. Our returns were among the best in the industry and we have met the challenging promises we made to our shareholders three years ago. We continue to focus on delivering robust profitability, while leveraging our competitive edge to grow value.
>
> At the same time we are striving to fulfil our commitments to society based on our strong Business Principles. This included using the principles of sustainable development in all our operations – taking account of their social and

environmental consequences as well as the economic dimension. We believe long-term competitive success depends on being trusted to meet society's expectations.[6]

The Shell Report 2001 provided a comprehensive analysis of Shell's economic, social and environmental performance, and many of the results were independently verified.

Alois Flatz, Head of Research at Sustainable Asset Management, an independent consultant to companies on social and environmental reporting, was favourably impressed by the Report:

> Shell's commitment to sustainability has increasingly gained credibility as key strategic decisions have been made to back up their high profile communication on this subject. Moreover, the clear links between business principles and performance indicators establishes Shell's reporting on sustainability as being best in the class.[7]

'Our business principles'

Shell's business principles are communicated to management, employees and all stakeholders. They can also be found in Shell's Annual Report to Shareholders. They recognise the company's responsibilities to its shareholders, customers, business partners and the societies in which they operate. Shell wishes to make a contribution to social and economic development, to safeguard the environment and to mitigate the risks to their investments.

They also stress the need for Shell's people 'to compete fairly and ethically', to maintain safe and healthy operations and 'to provide full relevant information about their activities to legitimately interested parties subject to any overriding consideration of business confidentiality and costs'.

Business integrity is a core value: 'Shell companies insist on honesty, integrity and fairness in all aspects of their business and expect the same in their relationships with all those with whom they do business.' Also, 'all business transactions on behalf of a Shell company must be reflected accurately and fairly in the accounts of the company in accordance

---

4 Chris Blackhurst, '2001: Britain's Most Admired Companies', *Management Today*, December 2001.

5 Jeremy Kahn, 'The World's Largest Corporations', *Fortune*, 23 July 2001, p. 96.

6 Philip Watts, 'Message from the Chairman', *People, Planet and Profits: The Shell Report 2001*, p.1.

7 Quoted in *The Shell Report 2001*, p.9.

with established procedures and be subject to audit'.[8]

Implementing business principles

The Shell Report had a special feature on 'Doing Business with Integrity', which was in two parts: bribery and whistleblowing.

Bribery On the subject of bribery the company reported that:

> Shell companies seek to compete fairly and ethically – no bribes, no political payments and fair competition. In 2001, 13 cases were reported in which bribes were offered to Shell staff or they were detected soliciting and/or accepting bribes directly or indirectly. In nine of these cases, employees refused the bribes and the cases were reported. In three cases employees were dismissed. The remaining case is under investigation. We report only the number of proven cases, but investigate many more suspected incidents; even when not proven thorough investigations make it clear that we mean what we say with 'no bribes'.[9]

The Report includes a table indicating the number of bribes offered and the dollar values involved for the years 1998 to 2001.

Whistleblowing The Report also included a whistleblowing case study:

> Increasingly Shell companies are providing means for employees to raise concerns in confidence and without risk of reprisal, using mechanisms such as hotline numbers or whistleblowing schemes.
>
> In the USA a 24-hour, seven-days-a-week Ethics and Compliance Helpline is open to Shell people who have a query on legal and ethical conduct or who want to report concerns or violations ... The US helpline is part of a programme to ensure that all employees are aware of the Group's Business Principles and Code of Conduct in the USA which includes key

policies unique to the USA. A Corporate Ethics and Compliance Officer supports this effort.[10]

In 2000, Shell companies in Nigeria also introduced a policy encouraging staff to report unethical behaviour (anonymously if necessary) and as a result of this policy nine employees were dismissed and eight contractors were removed from Shell's suppliers' list.

The present oil crisis

The oil crisis

On Friday 30 July 2004 oil prices surged to a 21-year high, reaching $43.80 a barrel on the New York Mercantile Exchange. In London Brent crude climbed to $41.74, a 15-year high.[11] On the other hand, despite high oil prices the largest oil companies have in recent years replaced only three-quarters of their production. The result of growing demand and companies' unwillingness to plough more resources into finding oil is a tight supply situation. Add to this the continuous threat to oil supplies in Iraq and Saudi Arabia and the likelihood of government restrictions on oil supplies in Russia.

So what is the future prospect? Experts are forecasting that the demand will rise by more that 50% in the next 20 years. Yet there is little prospect of a significant increase in supplies. According to the International Energy Agency, demand will grow at 'a breakneck pace' but investment is unlikely to follow suit. This means higher prices for the foreseeable future.[12]

The high prices are having a magical effect on the profits of the international oil companies. In the last week of July 2004 Exxon Mobil reported that the company had earned almost $6bn in the second quarter of the year, an all-time record for any US company in a three-month period.

> But the major oil companies are not responding to higher prices and earnings by increasing their

---

[8] *The Shell Report 2001,* p.25.
[9] *The Shell Report 2001,* p.9.
[10] *The Shell Report 2001,* p.8.
[11] 'Oil prices keep gushing upwards', *The Sunday Times,* 1 August 2004.
[12] Irwin Stelzer, Director of Economic Policy Studies, Hudson Institute, 'Soaring oil price lubricates the advance of Kerry', *The Sunday Times,* 1 August 2004.

search for oil. Exclude Russia and BP's output is declining. So are Shell's and Chevron Texaco's. Production at Exxon Mobil is more or less flat. Only Total with its commitment to Africa and Asia seems to be stepping up production.[13]

The new chairman/chief executive

Philip Watts was appointed Chairman and Managing Director of Shell Transport and Trading plc in August 2001 at the age of 56. He had had an outstanding career with Shell spanning 30 years, which had taken him to South East Asia, Africa, the Middle East and Continental Europe. He had worked on virtually every job in Exploration and Production – from seismologist and geophysicist to Exploration Manager before being appointed Chief Executive of Exploration and Production in 1997.

During the 1990s he moved into general management, first as Managing Director, Nigeria, next as Coordinator of Regulatory Affairs, Europe; and then as Director for Planning, the Environment and External Affairs in London. His abilities were also recognised outside Shell. He was elected to the Executive Committee of the World Business Council for Sustainable Development and at around the same time he became Chairman of the UK's governing body of the International Chamber of Commerce (ICC).

The overbooking of reserves

Philip Watts was no doubt chosen to be Chairman and Chief Executive of Shell because of his successful track record in Exploration and Production.

From 1991 to 1994 he was Managing Director of the Shell Petroleum Development Corporation in Nigeria. Shell has extracted an estimated $30bn worth of oil from Nigeria but at a huge environmental cost, particularly in the region of Ogoni. When Ken Saro-Wiwa started a popular protest movement that threatened to disrupt oil production, the Nigerian government, which receives a substantial income from oil revenues, reacted quickly by sending troops into the protesters' villages.

Eventually Ken Saro-Wawa was arrested and hanged. Shell formed a crisis group to rebuild its reputation with environmentalists and the task force was led by Philip Watts. Another factor that clinched his promotion was his unflinching determination to deliver results for the company. Unfortunately the record shows that he may have been too optimistic in forecasting the performance which might be achieved from the Nigerian and other fields that he knew well.

An independent report by Davis Polk, a US law firm, states that by early 2000 it was clear to Shell's exploration and production unit, of which Philip Watts was then Group Managing Director, that the Nigerian reserves 'could not be produced as originally projected or within its current licence periods'.[14]

Leaked company memos also show that production from the Yibal field in Oman began to decline in 1997, but Watts believed that a new technology called 'horizontal drilling' might enable the company to 'extract more from such mature fields' and that year the proven oil reserves figures for Oman were mistakenly increased as a result.

In Australia too, Shell had celebrated the discovery of half a billion barrels of oil, equivalent in the Gorgon gas field. But it was going to be very hard to exploit these reserves. Although Shell had a small exploration base there, the company would need to build a large gas liquification plant on Barrow Island, which was a Class A protected nature reserve. So the gas plant would be subject to environmental impact studies and the Australian government would be under intense pressure to protect the unique wildlife. Shell's partners in the Gorgan project, Exxon Mobil and Chevron, have not included the Gorgon field in their lists of proven reserves.[15]

On the other hand, in 2003 Sir Philip Watts and Walter van de Vijver, working together, scored a major success. By a spate of shuttle diplomacy involving many flights to Russia, they convinced President Putin to allow Shell to have access to 'the world's next big oil province'.[16]

[13] Irwin Stelzer, *The Sunday Times*, 1 August 2004 (op cit).

[14] Paul Durman and Lucinda Kemeny, 'Another brutal week for Shell as report makes Watts the fall guy', *The Sunday Times*, 25 April 2004. pp. 3.8 and 3.9.

[15] Rajan Datar, *Shell Shock*, BBC2 programme, 21.50–22.30, Thursday 15 July 2004.

[16] Lucinda Kemeny "Ready to Blow", *The Sunday Times*, 18 April 2004, p.5.

Enron, WorldCom and Sarbanes-Oxley

Enron

Philip Watts became Chairman and Chief Executive of Shell Transport and Trading in the summer of 2001 and in the autumn of the same year the world business community was rocked by the Enron Affair, the first of a series of high-profile corporate scandals and failures that led to a radical reform of company law and regulation in the USA.

In mid October 2001, Enron, the Houston oil and gas company, reported a third-quarter loss of $638m and disclosed a $1.2bn reduction in shareholder equity, partly related to off-balance-sheet partnerships which had falsified the company's results. This was the largest corporate bankruptcy in American history and the consequences were appalling. Their auditors, Arthur Andersen, one of the world's leading accountancy firms, was convicted of obstruction, fined $500,000 and the Andersen partnership was dissolved. Chairman/CEO Kenneth Lay and the Chief Financial Officer (CFO) Andrew Fastow resigned and they were prosecuted for fraud. Investors lost billions of dollars on their shares and Enron's employees also lost their pensions and thousands of them lost their jobs.[17]

WorldCom

After the Enron debacle, President Bush was asked to tighten up the regulation of corporations and auditors. He refused saying that he did not want to punish the majority of company executives who were acting properly because of what seemed to be the bad behaviour of 'a few bad apples'. Then came the WorldCom scandal. On 25 June 2002 the board of WorldCom, America's second largest mobile phone operator, revealed that their top executives had inflated the company's profits by $3.8bn. (This number has since grown to $9bn.) During 2002 alone, WorldCom's shareholders lost $3bn; many thousands of employees lost their jobs and the company was put up for sale. WorldCom's auditor was Arthur Andersen and, as at Enron, it had turned a blind eye to the fraud in which the company's

accountants had categorised billions of dollars of annual operating costs as capital expenditures, so that the expenses could be stretched out over a number of years. In the financial year 2001 this allowed the company to turn an annual operating loss of $662m into a $2.4bn profit.[18]

After this revelation the FBI and the Securities and Exchange Commission (SEC) indicted WorldCom's top executives and CalPERS, the US's largest state pension fund launched a suit to regain some of the $580m which the fund had lost on its WorldCom shares.

Other restatements

In the summer of 2002 Xerox Corporation also revealed that their accounts for 2001 had overstated their operating earning by $1.4bn. In fact, during 2002, 240 companies notified the SEC that they wished to re-state their accounts. This was four times the number of restatements that was recorded only 5 years earlier in 1997.[19]

The Sarbanes-Oxley Act

After Enron, WorldCom, Xerox and a spate of other accounting scandals, the US Congress and business leaders urged the President to take action to reassure investors, to restore confidence in the integrity of US corporations and financial markets and to discourage fraudulent corporate behaviour.[20]

On 30 July 2002 President Bush signed the Sarbanes-Oxley Act, which established a new, much tougher regime of regulations to control the actions of boards of directors, corporate executives, accountants and auditors. The Act included the following arrangements:

◆ *Tougher penalties for corporate fraud* The legislation creates penalties for corporate fraud of up to 20 years for destroying or altering documents sought in federal investigations.

---

[17] Richard Lacay and Amanda Ripley, 'Persons of the Year: The Whistleblowers', *Time*, 30 December 2002, pp. 18–43.

[18] Richard Lacay and Amanda Ripley, op. cit.

[19] John A Byrne, 'Let's really clean up those numbers – Now', *Business Week*, 15 July 2002, p.73.

[20] Doug Cameron, Andrew Hill and Tally Goldstein, 'New Set of Controls on Corporate America', *Financial Times*, 12 August 2002. Also Louis Lavelle and Mike McNamee, 'Will Overseas Boards Play by American Rules', *Business Week*, 16 December 2002, p.38.

Also chief executives who certify false financial reports will face prison terms of 10–20 years and fines of $1m to $5m.

- *An Independent Accounting Oversight Board* The new law creates a new (independent) five-member private sector board to oversee the accounting industry – with subpoena authority and disciplinary powers.

- *Restrictions on auditors' consulting* The law would restrict consulting and other non-auditing services that accounting firms could provide to clients.

- *Curbs on financial analysts* The SEC is empowered to impose new rules on financial analysts to prevent conflicts of interest.

- *Facilitation of investors' lawsuits* The Act also extends the period of time in which defrauded investors might bring lawsuits against companies.

- *Form 6K filing* The requirements on Form 6k filing came into force on 29 August 2002 – a more detailed and onerous reporting system.

- *Empowering the audit committee* The audit committee of the board, consisting of independent directors should have the authority to propose external auditors to the shareholders.

- *Loans to top executives* The Act placed a ban on subsidised personal loans to top executives and required prompt disclosure of share dealings to repay company loans.

- *Vouching for financial statements* Separately, 700 companies with annual revenues of more that $1.2bn must meet an SEC deadline to confirm that their Chief Executives and Chief Financial Officers will vouch for the veracity of their companies' accounts.

- *Dual listings* Shortly afterwards the SEC made it clear that European and Asian companies with US listings would be covered by the Sarbanes-Oxley Act but the application of certain provisions would be negotiable.

In the summer of 2002 the impact of the Sarbanes-Oxley Act was reinforced by the new listing requirements issued by the New York Stock Exchange and NASDAQ which require firms

- to get shareholder approval for all stock-option plans;

- to have a majority of independent directors on their boards;

- to have only independent directors on the audit committee and the committees that select chief executives and deal with executive compensation.[21]

Corporate governance in the UK

The corporate scandals in the USA and the Sarbanes-Oxley Act prompted a review of regulation across the European Union and particularly in the UK. In Britain there was a traditional bias in favour of self-regulation – for Codes of Practice rather than new laws, and reliance on professions to set standards and discipline their own members.

Ever since the bankruptcy of Enron, British accountants had been quietly congratulating themselves that 'it couldn't happen here'. But, particularly after the Sarbanes-Oxley Act the regulation of British auditors and accountants seemed inadequate. In the last five years the US SEC has required 1,200 companies to correct their audited accounts. By comparison Britain's Financial Reporting Review Panel – with only one full-time accountant – acted as a kind of ombudsman. The Panel only investigated if there was a complaint. In 12 years the Panel had made only 67 inquiries and had requested 15 restatements, and in most cases the companies had been let off with a caution.[22]

However, behind the scenes the British government was planning to establish an independent regulator along the lines of the US Accounting Oversight Board and early in 2004 they announced the establishment of the Financial Reporting Council, which incorporates the Financial Reporting Review Panel and is also responsible for regulating the accounting profession and the inspection of audits.[23]

[21] 'Reforming Corporate Governance: In search of honesty', *The Economist*, 17 August 2002.

[22] 'Accounting: Holier than Thou', *The Economist*, 8 February 2003, p.85.

[23] Lucinda Kemeny, 'Watchdog with real bite for number crunchers', *Sunday Times,* 28 March 2004.

After the publication of the Cadbury Report in 1992, Britain became a pioneer in corporate governance and the Cadbury Code became a model for the self-regulation of quoted company boards in other countries. The past decade saw over a dozen inquiries advocating:

◆ an expanded role for non-executive directors;

◆ tighter control of executive remuneration;

◆ fuller disclosure and transparent financial reporting;

◆ the active engagement of institutional shareholders; and

◆ independent regulation of accountants and auditors.

These recommendations were brought together in a New Combined Code, which took effect in July 2003 and was intended to make boards more independent and more effective in controlling chief executives and their management teams.

At the same time, the Netherlands and other Continental countries were reviewing their company laws and developing their own corporate governance codes. Particularly relevant to Shell was the Tabaksblat Committee Code, which was also published in 2003. So Philip Watts's watch from July 2001 to March 2004 coincided with a period of intense activity that led to the reform of laws, regulations and codes of practice aimed at imposing tighter controls on executive teams, their accountants and auditors.

Corporate governance at Shell

Shell was founded in 1907 through a merger between a Dutch oil company, which was partly owned by the Dutch royal family, and Shell, which was an international trading company. However, instead of forming one company with one set of shareholders they established the Royal Dutch/Shell Group as a joint venture between two companies and two groups of shareholders. The Royal Dutch Petroleum Company, which is based in The Hague and listed on the Dutch stock exchange, has a 60% interest in the Group. Shell Transport and Trading plc has its headquarters in London, is listed on the London stock exchange and owns a 40% interest in the Group. For this reason, Shell has two boards of directors. Under Dutch law, Royal Dutch has a two-tier structure with a supervisory board and a management board and Shell Transport operates under the British system with a unitary board.

These two 'parent company' boards are responsible for appointing the directors to the two 'holding companies': Shell Petroleum NV and the Shell Petroleum Company Ltd. The Group Managing Directors of these companies form the Committee of Managing Directors – the top management team which runs the Royal Dutch Shell Group which consists of Service Companies, Operating Companies and Regions (see Figure 1). One or two of these Group Managing Directors also sit on the parent company boards, i.e. on the management board in the Netherlands and on the unitary board in Britain.

In practice the Royal Dutch supervisory board and the Shell Transport board do a great deal of work together. For example, their three main committees – Group Audit, Social Responsibility and Remuneration and Succession – have members from both boards but Shell Transport has a separate Nomination Committee (see Figure 2).

From 2001 to 2003 Sir Philip Watts was both Chairman of the Board and Managing Director of Shell Transport. He was also Chairman of the Committee of Managing Directors (CMD) and the other members of the CMD were the other Group Managing Directors Jeroen van den Veer, Chief Executive of Chemicals, and Walter van de Vijver, Chief Executive of Exploration and Production.

Under Sir Philip Watts's chairmanship, the board of Shell Transport included a number of eminent and experienced non-executive directors:

◆ Sir Mark Moody-Stuart KCMG (UK), Managing Director and Chairman of Shell Transport from 1997 to 2001.

◆ Lord Oxburgh KBE, FRS (UK), former Chief Scientific Advisor to the Ministry of Defence.

◆ Nina Henderson (US), previously Corporate Vice President of Bestfoods, a major US foods company.

◆ Luis Giusti (Venezuela), fomerly Chairman/CEO of Petroleos de Venezuela.

◆ Sir Peter Job KBE (UK), previously Chief Executive of Reuters.

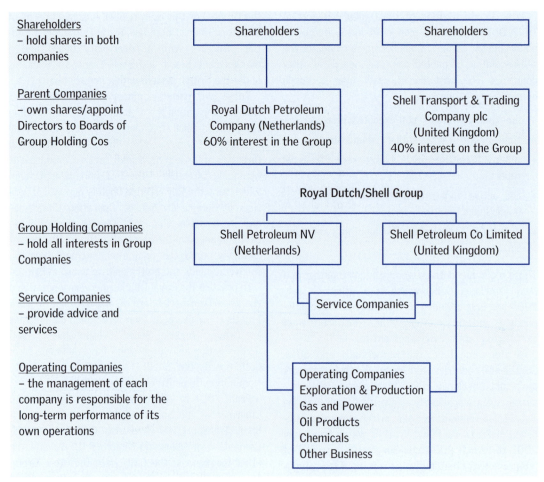

Figure 1 Royal Dutch Shell Group structure
Source: The Shell Transport & Trading Company plc, Annual Report & Accounts 2003, p.6.

◆ Sir John Kerr GCMG (UK), previously Head of the Diplomatic Service and Principal Private Secretary to the Chancellor of the Exchequer.

◆ Teymour Alireza (Saudi Arabia), Chairman of the National Pipe Company, Saudi Arabia.

◆ Sir Peter Burt FRSE (UK), Executive Deputy Chairman of HBOS plc and former Governor of the Bank of Scotland.

◆ Dr Eileen Buttle (UK), former government scientist. Trustee of environmental non-governmental organisations.

During 2003 there were a total of 17 board meetings and they were well attended. Judith Boynton,

the Group Chief Financial Officer was appointed a Group Managing Director and Executive Director of Shell Transport in July 2003 and she regularly attended the board meetings until she resigned on 18 April 2004.

The Group Audit Committee

The Royal Dutch Petroleum Company also had an impressive supervisory board and some of the directors were members of the Group Audit Committee (GAC).

◆ Aad Jacobs (Netherlands), Chairman of the Committee, a former Chairman of the Board of Management of ING Group, a major Dutch financial services company.

	Royal Dutch	Shell Transport
Group Audit	Aad Jacobs Lawrence Ricciardi Henny de Ruiter	Sir Peter Burt Luis Giusti Nina Henderson
Social Responsibility	Jonkeer Aarout Loudon Maarten van den Bergh Wim Kolc	Lord Oxburgh Teymour Alireza Dr Eileen Buttle
Remuneration and Succession	Jonkeer Aarout Loudon Lawrence Ricciardi Henny de Ruiter Prof. Hubert Markl	Sir Peter Job Nina Henderson Sir John Kerr
Shell Transport Nomination	Lord Oxburgh Sir Peter Burt Sir Peter Job Sir John Kerr	

Figure 2 Royal Dutch Shell Group board committees
Source: The Shell Transport & Trading Company plc Annual Report & Accounts 2003, p.9

- Lawrence Ricciardi (USA), previously President of RJR Nabisco Inc.

- Henry de Ruiter, Managing Director of Royal Dutch 1983–1994.

The other committee members were: Sir Stephen Burt, Luis Giusti and Nina Henderson – all directors on the Shell Transport Board.

During 2003 there were a total of six meeting of the GAC and the members attended virtually all the meetings.

In the 2003 Annual Report and Accounts the Shell Transport & Trading Company plc reviewed its corporate governance arrangements against the requirements of the New Combined Code. The key points from this review are listed below:-

- *Independent directors* Of the nine non-executive directors on the Shell Transport Board, seven are wholly independent of any personal business connection with the companies of the Royal Dutch/Shell Group. Accordingly, the structure of the board during the year observed the New Combined Code provision that it should have a majority of 'independent non-executive directors'.

- *The Chairman* Sir Philip Watts was Chairman of the Board and Group Managing Director of Shell Transport throughout 2003.

- *The Chairman's other commitments* Sir Philip Watts's other commitments during the year included mambership of the World Business Council for Sustainable Development and Chairman of the International Chamber of Commerce's UK governing body.[24]

- *Performance evaluation* During 2003 the Shell Transport board carried out a series of evaluations of

  – the board as a whole;

  – individual members;

  – the Chairman, and;

  – board committees.

The Chairman evaluated the directors individually. For the collective appraisal they used a questionnaire. The Chairman was evaluated by the Senior Independent Director, Lord Oxburgh, and the non-executive directors.[25]

- *Dialogue with shareholders* The dialogue with institutional shareholders was maintained through an investor relations programme agreed by the board. In 2002 the board nominated Lord

---

[24] Shell Transport & Trading Company plc Annual Report & Accounts 2003, p.121.
[25] 2003 Annual Report, p.121.

Oxburgh as Senior Independent Director and arranged for him and other directors to attend quarterly institutional investors' presentations when appropriate.

- *Auditor's remuneration*   Audit fees for Shell Transport amounted to £129,000 in 2003 – up from £31,000 in 2002. The fees payable to PriceWaterhouseCoopers LLP for non-audit servcies in the UK were £31,600 in 2003.

'Unbooking' the reserves

- *9 January 2004* a Shell public relations executive told journalists and investors that the company had carried out a review of its 'proved' oil and gas reserves. As a consequence the figures would be reduced by 20%. This revision would cut the value of the reserves by 3.9bn barrels of oil equivalent (boe) from 19.5bn to 15.6bn.

  Shell shareholders were shocked by this surprise announcement and in a few days they saw the price of their shares fall by over 10%. The institutional investors also complained about the way they had been treated – that this important announcement had been made by a middle manager – and not by Sir Philip Watts himself.

- *5 February*   Sir Philip Watts apologised on television for his absence from the presentation of the revised figures. However, he was being overtaken by events.

- *19 February*   The US SEC launched an investigation into the downgrading of the reserves.

- *3 March*   Sir Philip Watts, the Chairman/Chief Executive, and Walter van de Vijver, the Chief Executive of Exploration were forced to resign.

- *17 March*   The US Department of Justice opened a criminal investigation into Shell's unbooking of reserves.

- *18 March*   The company reduced its estimate of reserves for a second time by a further 250m barrels and postponed the publication of the Annual Report and Accounts, and the Annual Meeting with the shareholders.

- *22 March*   There was a meeting between Shell's directors and their institutional shareholders.

- *19 April*   The company announced a third cut in oil reserves and Judy Boynton the Chief Financial Officer, resigned.

- *24 May*   Shell's proved oil reserves were reduced for a fourth time to 14.35bn barrels of oil equivalent. This represented a reduction of 23% on the initial figure. Shell's Annual Report was finally published and the two Annual General Meetings were scheduled for 28 June.[26]

Estimating reserves

These revelations about the company's reserves have left many former executives puzzled. Shell's internal processes for checking the state of its reserves were thought to be as safe as Fort Knox. Each year in The Hague around 30 of the company's most senior staff, including Philip Watts, would hear evidence from the exploration and production people in the field. The annual 'programme discussions' could take three hours – starting with technicalities and moving on to detailed explanations by staff about their estimates of reserves.[27]

The process started in the field. Teams of technical staff would regularly review the data coming in from the wells. If they found any indications that underground reserves were greater or lower than expected, the new information had to be reported immediately to the head office of Shell's Dutch business in The Hague. If the adjustment was significant – more than 5% – a team would arrive from head office. But at some stage in the past three years something had started to go wrong. As early as 2002 Shell's management realised that the company was not finding enough oil to replace production – a key measure of an oil company's future profitability. Years of opportunistic investments had left Shell with a legacy of small fields which did not match the company's production requirements. To remedy this, it would require a major new initiative – an acquisition or an entry into a new field.

It is alleged that a decision was made to relax the rules by which the company accounted for proven reserves – a measure used by the SEC to determine

26 Clay Harris, 'Shell accounts get signed off at last', *Financial Times*, 25 May 2004.
27 Lucinda Kemeny, 'Ready to Blow', *Sunday Tines*, 18 April 1004, pp.3–5.

whether oil and gas can be produced with 'reasonable certainty' using current technology. Shell's decentralised management – which is often cited as a strength – became, in this case, a weakness. Some units were run as small kingdoms with different practices adopted in different subsidiaries and divisions.

The dam broke in January 2004 when Shell admitted the 20% overstatement of reserves. The reclassification was blamed largely on the overbooking of developments in Nigeria and at Ormen Lange, a gasfield off the Norwegian coast.

The issue now is, 'who knew what and when?' Company documents from late in 2003 which were leaked to the *New York Times*, said that Shell's top management had concluded that 1.5bn barrels, 60% of its Nigerian reserves, did not meet the SEC's accounting standards for proven reserves. However, the management were reluctant to change the figures for fear of damaging the relationship with the Nigerian government.

Philip Watts and Walter van de Vijver may have been forced to take the blame for the overbooking of the reserves. But it seemed unlikely that they, and Judy Boynton, Shell's CFO, were the only senior executives who knew about the 'cover-up'. In early April, Walter van de Vijver issued a public statement making this clear:

> From the inception of my tenure as head of Exploration and Production I worked diligently to diagnose and improve the health of the business. I regularly communicated to the Committee of Managing Directors the nature and quantity of the potentially non-compliant reserves and our efforts to assess the magnitude of the problem, prevent recurrence and implement off-setting measures.

Analysts and investors hoped that the company would not merely blame the three senior managers but would offer some broader proposals to improve corporate governance and internal control in the Shell Group. Eric Knight, who represents CalPERS, the largest US public sector pension fund, said: 'The question is who is running the group and who is responsible when there is a problem. The truth of the matter is that it is everybody and nobody.'[28]

What went wrong?

Press reports show that Shell was not the only oil company that had to recalculate and restate its estimates of proved reserves. On 29 June 2004, Norsk Hydro had cut its global reserves figure by 6.6%. Also, differing interpretations of the SEC rules have led to different companies booking different estimates for the same field. For example, for the Ormen Lange gas field in the North Sea the companies booked the following proved reserves: BP: 80%; Norsk Hydro: 49%; Exxon Mobil: 35%; Statoil: 25%; Shell: 20%.

On 29 June 2004 BP also restated its proved reserves to bring them in line with the SEC's definition. BP raised its proved reserves by 23m barrels to 18.36bn. This was because, in deciding whether a project is a sound investment, BP uses its own planning price of $20 per barrel to determine its reserve levels and the SEC used the end-of-year price, which was $30.10. As BP explained, 'An investment is made for 20–25 years, therefore we wouldn't make an investment decision based on one day's price'.[29]

How Shell's management came to overestimate their reserves of oil and gas is unclear. A number of possibilities have been advanced:

1 *Over-optimistic forecasting* In their forward planning, senior executives of oil and gas companies must rely on the estimates which they receive from geophysicists and exploration managers. The estimation of reserves is not an exact science. Both technologists and executives need to make assumptions about the volume and quality of the reserves, their accessibility and the rate at which they can be extracted etc. Shell's managers might well have believed that there were more reserves in the ground or that a higher proportion of the oil could be extracted using modern technologies.

2 *Decentralisation* Shell's organisation is highly decentralised. National organisations were semi-autonomous and their executives might have overestimated their production e.g. in Australia and Nigeria.

---

28 Lucinda Kemeny, 'Ready to Blow', *The Sunday Times*, 18 April 2004, p.5.

29 James Boxall, 'BP surprises with upward adjustment' and Nicholas George, 'Norsk Hydro restates reserves', *Financial Times*, 30 June 2004, p.29.

3 *The executive bonus*   In the late 1990s Shell's management had been encouraged to aim for 'stretch targets' and these numbers were linked to an incentive bonus. This too could have motivated them to inflate their estimates of reserves.

4 *Philip Watts's drive for success*   Philip Watts was highly motivated and willing to take risks. He had worked his way up the levels of the organisation, finding and producing oil in Indonesia, Sierra Leone, Malaysia and Brunei. In Nigeria he had continued to produce the oil despite the opposition of local protesters and international pressure groups. Clearly, he thought he could do it again.

5 *The Securities and Exchange Commission (SEC)* It is conceivable that the regulators in London and The Hague would not have investigated Shell's estimates of their oil and gas reserves. In the event it was the US SEC that queried the figures; the British and Dutch authorities took action only after the SEC had started their formal investigation.

The internal investigation

In early February 2004 the Group Audit Committee (GAC) commissioned an internal investigation into how the overbooking had occurred. The investigation was carried out by the US law firm Davis, Polk & Wordwell and they were given access to the internal memos and the minutes of the Committee of Managing Directors (CMD). When their report was published on Monday 19 April, Lord Oxburgh, the non-executive director who took over Sir Philip Watts's role as Chairman said the company sought to limit the blame for what went wrong at Shell to 'the human failings' of a few individuals.

Jeroen Van der Veer, the new Chief Executive of Shell and Chairman of the CMD, promised 'behavioural and cultural change' at the company to ensure its reserving policy was accurate and to create a clear line of command at the top of the company. He stated: 'We want to foster a culture where bad news can be passed up the line without fear of reprisal'. Malcolm Brinded, who had taken over as head of Exploration and Production at Shell, attempted to reassure the financial markets that there would be no more bad news. He said the company had carried out a 'painstaking and thorough' review that would 'draw a line' under Shell's difficulties.[30]

The Davis Polk Report published the in-company emails which passed between Walter van de Vijver and Sir Philip Watts from the time when Mr van de Vijver had taken over from Sir Philip Watts in August 2001. From the start Mr van de Vijver felt they were 'caught in a box' 'due to aggressive booking of reserves in 1997–2000'.[31]

As early as 11 February 2002, van de Vijver told the CMD that the company might have overstated its reserves by 2.3bn barrels because they were ignoring SEC guidelines.[32] He wrote, 'Recently the SEC issued clarifications that make it apparent that the Group guidelines for booking reserves are no longer fully aligned with the SEC Rules' – because of 'potential environmental and commercial showstoppers'.[33]

Under the SEC definition reserves are called 'proven' if thay can be extracted economically and sold for profit. If reserves are not 'proven' in this way oil companies are required to admit that and say that the reserves are only 'probable'.[34] In van de Vijver's opinion the 'showstoppers', i.e. factors that were preventing Shell from getting these reserves to market, were being ignored. He pointed to overbookings in Australia, Norway, the Middle East and, most of all, Nigeria, where there was political unrest and environmental damage.

On 28 May 2002, Philip Watts wrote to van de Vijver, emphasising that it was vital not to unbook the unproven reserves until new reserves had been found to replace them. He should consider 'the whole spectrum of possibilities … leaving no stone unturned'.

30 Katherine Griffiths, 'Shell looks to draw a line under reserves fiasco with shake-up of board structure', *The Independent,* 25 April 2004, p.19.
31 Paul Durman and Lucinda Kemeny, 'Another brutal week for Shell as report makes Watts the fall guy', *The Sunday Times*, 25 April 2004, pp. 9–10.
32 Jeremy Warner, 'Shell's convoluted whodunit script is worthy of fiction', *The Independent*, 20 April 2004.
33 Rajan Datar, 'Shell Shock', *The Money Programme*, BBC2, 15 July 2004, 21.50 to 22.30.
34 Rajan Datar, op. cit.

On 2 September 2002, Van de Vijver sent a note to the CMD with a copy to Judith Boynton, Shell's finance director, emphasising the difficulty Shell would have in achieving 100% reserves replacement ratio (RRR) for 2002 – the target which had been set. 'Unfortunately we are struggling on all key criteria ... RRR remains below 100% due to aggressive overbooking in 1997–2000.'[35] (Shell is replacing only between 50% and 60% of the oil it produces. BP and other big rivals manage 100% to 150%.)

The whistleblower

Eventually it was through Walter van de Vijver that the issue was made public. In the autumn of 2003 he asked Frank Coopman, the Chief Financial Officer of the Exploration and Production unit to make an assessment of Shell's proved reserves. Coopman made his analysis and reported that the figures for 'proved reserves in Shell's 2002 financial statement were materially wrong'.[36] He wrote that to hide this fact would 'constitute a violation of US Securities law and the multiple listing requirements'.

Walter van de Vijver replied in no uncertain terms: 'This is absolute dynamite, not at all what I expected and needs to be destroyed'. Walter van de Vijver said he wanted a report with some positive suggestions that he could present to the CMD. However, Frank Coopman, like some other whistleblowers, lost his job and has since left the company. Judith Boynton, Shell's Chief Financial Officer, complained that she had not been consulted about the report on the reserves position that had been prepared by Frank Coopman. She had somehow been cut out of the loop and she also resigned from her position in April 2004.

In the autumn of 2003 van de Vijver could see the writing on the wall. On 9 November he wrote to Sir Philip Watts in some desperation: 'I am becoming sick and tired about lying about the extent of our reserves and the downward revisions which need to be done because of far too aggressive/optimistic bookings.' Then in December he wrote to a colleague: 'We are heading towards a watershed reputational disaster ... The problem was created in the 90s and foremost in 1997–00. I will not accept cover-up

stories that it was OK then but not OK with the better understanding of SEC rules now, and it took us two and a half years to come to the right answer.'[37]

On 8 December van de Vijver submitted a 42-page report to the CMD. A comprehensive audit of reserves had just been completed and this showed the reserves had been overstated by 3.6bn barrels. With the SEC investigation in progress the CMD had no alternative but to inform shareholders and the public about the real situation and the announcement was planned for 9 January. Shortly afterwards a Dutch acquaintance of van de Vijver told a journalist, 'It's because he respected the company so much that he didn't want to blow the whistle but instead ordered an investigation and tried to remedy the problem through the company. He is a man who has invested his whole life in Shell and believed its ethos of looking after its employees fairly and for life. He was the archetypal company man who was on course to take over the company.'[38]

The fines and the court cases

On 15 July 2004 the BBC *Money Programme* interviewed investors, regulators and lawyers to discover what their reactions had been to the 'Shell Affair'. US oil analyst Fadel Gheit said, 'Most investors and analysts had almost blind faith in the company and its management. Unfortunately all this came to a screeching halt after this disclosure.' Peter Montagnon of the Association of British Insurers said, 'Most people will have a stake in this, if they have a pension; Shell is such a large company that, if you have a pension pot, some of it is in Shell. So when you have an announcement like this, the value of your pension pot is reduced accordingly.'

Within a few days of the Shell announcement, the price of Shell Transport shares fell by 8% and the market value of the company fell by 8%. The video reporter concluded, 'Millions and millions of people had investments either directly in Shell or through their pension plans. They may not have known they

[35] Damian Reece, 'Revealed: bitter power battle that put Shell in the firing line', *The Independent,* 20 April 2004, p.4.
[36] 'Blowing the Whistle', *CFO Europe*, May 2004, p.46.

[37] Damian Reece, op. cit.
[38] Paul Durman and Lucinda Kemeny, *The Sunday Times*, op. cit.

were investors in Shell, but now they know that Shell lied to them and cost them money.'

Stanley Bernstein, a New York lawyer also contributed to the programme. He is leading a class action against Shell on behalf of a group of shareholders, based on the false declaration that Shell's CMD signed and submitted to the SEC in March 2003. This booked 19.3bn barrels of oil reserves, whereas the corrected figure agreed on 24 May 2004 was only 14.35bn barrels. He said, 'Shell had lied intentionally and had deceived the public about how much oil it had in the ground and how certain it was that the oil could be brought to market. Once the truth came out the stock price dropped precipitously to reflect the fact that the company was not as valuable as its competitors were.' He also spoke of the reactions of the regulators: 'When you have a fraud perpetrated over a long period of time. When you have a fraud perpetrated by the very heads of the company with specific responsibility for this core issue, the regulators are going to get their teeth into this and make sure there is appropriate punishment for the individuals involved.'

Executive payoffs and bonuses

Shareholders were concerned that the executives who were responsible for exaggerating the estimates of Shell's proved reserves were given large grants of salaries and pensions. For example, Sir Philip Watts received a final payoff of £1m and an annual pension of over £580,000.[39] Newspaper reports suggested that both Walter van de Vijver and Judith Boynton also received payoffs of around £1m each.[40]

Shareholders also suggested that the executive bonus system might have encouraged managers to overbook the reserves. However, a Shell spokesperson replied that this measure of operational peformance accounted for only 6% of annual bonus payments.[41]

The fines

On Friday 30 July 2004 Shell paid £83m ($151m) in fines to draw a line under its disputes with the US SEC and UK's Financial Services Authority (FSA). The SEC had accused the company of having breached fraud, internal control and reporting requirements. The FSA said the Group had committed 'market abuse'.[42] Press reports stated that there was still a strong chance that Shell will face a criminal prosecution before the US Department of Justice. There was also a possibility that individuals might face civil and criminal cases.

How did Shell respond?

Jeroen van der Veer, who as Chairman of the Committee of Managing Directors (CMD) replaced Sir Philip Watts when he resigned in March 2004, is working with the new non-executive Chairman of Shell Transport & Trading, Lord Oxburgh, to clarify Shell's complex governance structure and to install a stronger and more independent system of financial reporting and control. All the time, Shell management is under intense scrutiny from shareholders and the media. Jeroen van der Veer said, 'It is by far the most difficult part of my career. There is huge pressure all the time and you are living absolutely in a glass house with magnifying glasses on top wherever you go.'[43]

In the Annual Report & Accounts for 2003 Shell described the measures which had been taken to strengthen their corporate governance and financial control systems:

1 *An independent Chairman*   After the departure of Sir Philip Watts, who was both Chairman and Chief Executive of Shell Transport the two roles have been separated and Lord Oxburgh, a non-executive director has been appointed to the job of non-executive Chairman.

2 *The internal inquiry* The Group Audit Committee (GAC) commissioned an independent review by US lawyers Davis Polk of the the overbooking of the reserves. They also sanctioned the publication of a summary of the report and accepted its recommendations.

---

[39] Rajan Datar op. cit.
[40] Katherine Griffiths, *The Independent,* 25 April 2004, op. cit.
[41] Michael Harrison, *The Independent,* 16 July 2004.

[42] Carola Hoyos *et al,* 'Shell pays $15m in fines to Watchdogs', *The Financial Times,* 30 July 2004.
[43] Deborah Hargreaves, 'Shell fighter begins the big clean-up', *Financial Times,* 30 July 2004.

3 *Booking of reserves* In future, the CMD and the GAC will take a formal role in reviewing the booking of reserves and there will be a 'systematic use of external reserves' expertise to provide challenge and assurance at critical points in the reserves booking and reporting process'.[44]

4 *Corporate governance codes* The Annual Report & Accounts and the board's processes had been adapted to ensure that they conformed to the UK Combined Code, the Sarbanes-Oxley Act and the rules of the New York Stock Exchange. In the Netherlands the company would take account of the Tabaksblat Committee's Code.

5 *The overbooking of reserves and compliance with regulations* The investigation and report to the GAC by Davis Polk & Wordwell listed the deficiencies which had led to the overbooking of reserves:

- the Group's guidelines for booking proved reserves were inadequate;

- the Group's CMD and the Parent Company Boards were not provided with appropriate information to form disclosure judgements;

- the Chief Financial Officers of the businesses did not have direct reporting responsibility to the Group Chief Financial Officer;

- there was a lack of understanding of the meaning and importance of the SEC rules; and

- there was a control environment that did not emphasise the paramount importance of the compliance element of proved reserves decisions.[45]

All these issues had been addressed to strengthen and clarify reporting procedures. Also to emphasise the importance of compliance with the requirements of regulators, in future the company's lawyers would be involved at every stage and the Group Legal Director would attend meetings of the CMD and the parent company boards.[46]

6 *Unifying the two boards and a possible merger?* In response to further pressure from institutional investors, Shell formed a steering committee of Shell board members to look at alternatives to the present dual board structure and commissioned Citigroup and NM Rothchild to act as financial advisers to the steering committee on corporate restructuring. On 11 August 2004 the company announced that it had reached a 'preliminary agreement' to unify its two boards and had asked its financial advisers to assess the feasibility of merging its Dutch and British holding companies.

What further action is required?

So what went wrong and what should be done to prevent it happening again?

1 'A few individuals'?

The Davis Polk Report and Lord Oxburgh, the Chairman of Shell, suggested that the overbooking was the fault of 'a few individuals'. Hopefully, these individuals could be asked to resign, the control systems would be improved and it would be possible to draw a line under the whole sequence of events. But Walter van de Vijver made it clear, in his opinion, that he had told everybody who counted at Shell, certainly the CMD and the board of directors, about his concerns over the state of the company's reserves.[47]

2 A simpler organisation structure?

Some of Shell's institutional investors thought the problems could be much broader. Eric Knight who represents CalPERS, said 'the question is who is running the group and who is responsible when there is a problem. The truth of the matter is that it is everybody and nobody.'[48]

The company is a joint venture between two companies that are subject to different laws and

---

[44] Malcolm Brinded, Managing Director of Shell Transport, *Shell Transport & Trading Company Annual Report: 2003,* 23 May 2004, p.3.

[45] *The Shell Transport & Trading plc Annual Report 2003,* pp.40 and 41.

[46] *The Shell Transport & Trading plc Annual Report 2003,* pp.41 and 42.

[47] Lucinda Kemeny, 'Ready to Blow', op. cit.

[48] Lucinda Kemeny, op. cit.

different governance codes. There are two sets of boards and a 'Conference', where the Dutch supervisory board and the British unitary board meet to discuss strategy. At the executive level the Group is coordinated by three Group Managing Directors meeting in a Committee of Managing Directors. It is not surprising that some investors called the present structure Byzantine.

3 Big-hitting non-executive directors?

Other investors are asking for 'the injection of some senior big-hitting independent directors who will take an unjaundiced view of Shell's predicament'.

4 Tighter controls?

Certainly the SEC will demand a reorganisation of Shell's internal processes for checking the state of its reserves and its accounts generally – including the internal audit and the relationship with the external auditors – where were the external auditors?

5 Finding new reserves

A gulf still separates Shell from BP and Exxon Mobil. Last year Shell replaced its oil and gas at 63% of the production rate. So at the current rate of production Shell has 10.2 years of oil left in the ground. BP and Exxon have between 13.5 and 14 years, so Shell is starting from a base 30% lower than its rivals.

As Sir Philip Watts insisted, the first objective must be to raise the replacement rate from 63% to 100% – so that the reserves in the ground will be maintained. This will involve routine development work to rebook the downgraded barrels by bringing them up to SEC criteria. According to Clay Smith of Commerzbank, Shell expects that of the 4.7bn downgraded reserves, 85% will be reclassified as 'proven reserves' over the next ten years.[49]

6 Increased investment or acquisitions

To get access to new fields, for example in Iraq, Iran, Libya or China, Shell will probably have to spend more money and take more risks. Shell is planning to increase its capital expenditure from an average of $13bn a year to $14.5bn for future years – the majority of which will be spent on exploration and development.

BP has spent $14bn a year over the past two years – including some fairly risky deals in Russia In addition BP has acquired reserves through acquisitions and mergers with Amoco, Atlantic Richfield and Burmah Castrol. To quote one analyst, 'You have to ask whether Shell can do it by itself, or whether it is going to do it like BP – by acquisition.'[50] This also raises the question whether Shell could manage a merger or acquisition with a corporate structure in two countries.

7 Loss of trust

Finally, Shell's leadership faces a deeper problem. Shell, once regarded by many as a paragon of honesty and fair dealing has had its reputation spoiled by the actions of its top management team. Thousands of Shell's employees around the world will feel that they too have lost something valuable – the pride of working for a company that has an unblemished reputation for integrity and ethical behaviour.

It took Shell many decades to build this reputation. How can this reputation be rebuilt? And how is it possible to prevent Shell executives, at the top level, from risking the company's reputation in the future?

---

[49] Oliver Morgan, 'Shell's Ground Zero', *The Observer,* 30 May 2004, p.5.
[50] Oliver Morgan, op. cit.

Case 25 Abrakebabra: surviving the franchisee revolt

A brief history of Abrakebabra

In 1982 two brothers, Wyn and Graeme Beere, founded what in 20 years' time would become Ireland's largest Irish-owned fast food franchise. In the early 1980s Graeme was selling fast food at the front of an off-licence (Deveney's) in the Rathmines area of central Dublin. Wyn was working as a chartered surveyor in a prestigious international property firm. Dublin lacked the restaurant culture of other European cities. Instead Dublin's social life centred on its vibrant pub culture, with bars focusing on drink sales, rather than offering a variety of food to customers. All pubs closed simultaneously at 11pm nightly. Graeme noticed an important gap in the market – where do people go for food after a night out?

The entrepreneurial solution was to create a fast food restaurant that specifically catered for this market. The offering would be new for Dublin: a product mix of kebabs, burgers and chips, popular in London at the time, and late opening until 4am. Searching for a name for this venture, Graeme chose a play on words: a mix of the name of a Steve Miller number one record in 1982 'Abracadabra' and the kebab as the central product. In 1982 the newly named 'Abrakebabra' opened, a 'licence to print money', as one of the founders put it.

The two brothers went from one owner-operated, small fast food restaurant in 1982 to a peak of 59 franchised outlets in the late 1990s. Through entrepreneurial leadership they survived two recessions and a franchisee revolt. This partnership was unbroken until 2001 when one of the brothers, Wyn, decided to retire from the business. His 50% stake was bought out by Gaiety Investments Ltd, the venture capital vehicle of leading Irish entrepreneur Denis Desmond. The exit of Wyn and the entry of Gaiety Investments Ltd present both a challenge and an opportunity to the company. The challenge is how to move from an entrepreneurial mode of control to a more formal managerial control system. The opportunity is that a fresh equity injection by Denis Desmond can help fuel the expansionary strategy of Abrakebabra.

The franchisee revolt

They [the franchisees] forgot the help that they got. They forgot about the brand and they started thinking that they could do it themselves. We had a little bit of a revolution there in the last couple of years, but all the guys went out of business.[1] (Managing Director of Abrakebabra)

By 1997 Abrakebabra ran 11 company-owned restaurants. These restaurants had delivered powerful advantages to the brothers in the past. They had been an important source of cash flow during the development of the business-franchising model. Company owned restaurants were also an important learning mechanism. By 1997, however, these company-owned units were consuming the majority of the brothers' management time.

This case was written by **Rosalind Beere**, Trinity College Dublin, and **Peter McNamara**, University College Dublin, UCD Business Schools, Department of Business Administration, Belfield, Dublin 4, Ireland. Financial support of a grant from **Davy Stockbrokers** to undertake a series of teaching case studies is gratefully acknowledged. This case study is a reprint which was originally published by the European Case Clearing House. Copyright remains the property of UCD Business Schools.

We wish to also acknowledge the help of Abrakebabra Limited who have co-operated in this research by giving access to management, staff, franchisees and company documents. In particular we wish to thank the 13 interviewees for their time and insights into the company.

Disclaimer: This case is intended to be used as a basis for class discussion rather than to illustrate either effective or ineffective handling of an administrative situation.

---

[1] Interview with Graeme Beere, founder and Managing Director.

Resources spent on these restaurants meant less managerial attention could be given to the running of their franchising system, which at that time represented over 80% of the company's restaurants.

A decision needed to be made about the long-term strategy of the firm as to whether it could continue to function effectively with such a split focus, between being a franchiser and a restaurateur. In response to the strategy crisis the decision was made to franchise out all company-owned restaurants. Graeme Beere recently summarized the strategic logic of moving to a franchise-only management system as follows:

> The success of Abrakebabra is all about location, location, location. It is a hands-on cash business and we don't want investors, we want owner-occupiers. ... We found the key was to franchise out the outlets and concentrate on the brand. The wake-up came when our accountant told us that 80 per cent of our income came from franchising, but that 80 per cent of our time was spent on the 11 stores. We put franchisees into all of our stores and turnover increased immediately. All our head office time is now spent looking after the brand and franchisees who need help.[2]

However, trouble was on the horizon in the form of a group of franchisees who expressed concerns over the management of the Abrakebabra franchising network. Some of them claimed they were unhappy with the lack of management focus. It became apparent that a number of franchisees were arranging secret meetings to which the Abrakebabra management team were not invited. The brothers decided to confront this possible revolt head on. They called individual meetings with the franchisees. During these meetings the benefits of being an Abrakebabra franchisee were clearly communicated. Any franchisee that was not clearly committed to the Abrakebabra ethos was then released from their contract.

The experience of the franchisee revolt highlighted issues faced by the partners and their control mechanisms. The Abrakebabra management team created a new identity centred on an exclusively franchise driven business growth model. This case explores the extent of goal alignment between the franchisees and the franchiser and the management control systems that the brothers installed to maximize value creation for both parties.

Performance of Abrakebabra

By 2003 Abrakebabra's new managerial control system had yielded considerable dividends. Abrakebabra had maintained its position as the largest Irish-owned franchise network in its business domain – with 55 franchises. Only McDonald's, with 66 franchise outlets was larger (see Table 1 for size of main competitors). This success had also facilitated the exit of one of the founding brothers, Wyn and a fresh injection of capital with the entry of by Gaiety Investments as a major shareholder. Gaiety Investment's 50% stake cost a reported €3.8 million, valuing Abrakebabra at €7.6 million by the end of 2002.[3]

In 2003 Abrakebabra had sales of €33 million, with the typical franchisee restaurant generating individual sales of €300,000 to €380,000. Franchisees pay a fee of 6% on gross sales, after Value Added Tax, with a further 1% advertising levy. The set-up costs for a franchisee are estimated to be €50,000 (all financial figures from www.Abrakebabra.net). These charges grant franchisees use of the Abrakebabra brand name, purchasing systems and franchisee supports, as outlined below. Profit margins for franchisees are estimated to be as high as 20%.[4] The *Sunday Business Post* indicated that expected profits for the year ended December 2002 were €1.1 million[5] for the Abrakebabra group, while actual profits were later reported to be over €900,000, up 350% on 2001 profits.[6]

---

[2] McMahon, S. (2003) 'Franchising for the Future', *Sunday Business Post*, 25 May 2003.

[3] 'Desmond Invest €3.8 million in AbraKebabra,' *Business and Finance,* 11 April 2002.

[4] O'Halloran, B. (2002) Abrakebabra to Take a Bigger Bite of Fast Food Market', *Business and Finance,* 11 April 2002.

[5] McMahon, S. (2003) 'Franchising for the Future', *Sunday Business Post,* 25 May 2003.

[6] Business News (2004) 'Abrakebabra works its magic', *Sunday Business Post,* 22 February 2004.

Table 1 Main franchise restaurant outlets operating Ireland in 2003[7]

Name	Seating availability	Number of restaurants	Ownership
Abrakebabra	Seating	55	Irish
Supermacs	Seating	45	Irish
McDonald's	Seating	66	US
Burger King	Seating	22	UK
Four Star Pizza	No Seating	26	US
Domino's Pizza	No Seating	17	US

The exact profitability of both the franchising network and individual franchisees are difficult for external third parties to independently confirm. This is because the size of Abrakebabra means that full profit and loss accounts do not need to be made publicly available by the Irish Companies Registration Office (CRO). An analysis of the abridged accounts (primarily balance sheet information) that are publicly available from the CRO is complicated by changes in the structure of the organization. Over the last ten years Abrakebabra operations have encompassed a number of companies including Abrakebabra Holdings, Abrakebabra Limited, Abrakebabra Franchising, and Abrakebabra Meats, among others. An analysis of the abridged accounts of these firms does not offer significant insights into the underlying profitability of the franchiser.[8] These firms are not required to publish sales figures through the CRO, thus external parties cannot observe the amount of levies raised from franchisees.

What lies behind the valuation of Abrakebabra itself, and the profits generated by individual franchisees, is the franchise lead growth strategy and managerial control systems installed in the wake of the 1997 franchisee revolt. It is to these that we now turn our attention.

Goal alignment and value added from the franchising model

We went through a phase where the franchisees were controlling the business ... we reversed the whole process and are now far stronger ... I'd know exactly how to deal with them [the franchisees]. I've learnt.[9] (Managing Director of Abrakebabra)

From 1997, emphasis was to be placed on running Abrakebabra as a core franchising support system. With no company-owned restaurants to manage, the two brothers were able to formulate a new strategy that focused exclusively on a franchising business model. A number of unsuitable franchisees did not adhere to the Abrakebabra ethos and exited the franchising system. The process of franchising out company-owned restaurants, the experience of the franchisee revolt, and exit of unsuitable franchisees led management to a realization that the quality of their franchisees was just as important as the total number of franchisees in the network. Thus, management looked at the franchising system with a new perspective.

The franchiser

The single most important thing in a franchise chain is the franchisee.[10] (Abrakebabra Financial Accountant)

The Abrakebabra management team, having franchised out the remaining company-owned

---

[7] All competitor information was obtained by contact with each company's head office.

[8] As part of this case study the authors undertook an analysis of the abridged accounts of Abrakebabra Holdings and Abrakebabra Limited using the published accounts from the CRO (www.cro.ie) in February 2004. Abrakebabra Franchising and Abrakebabra Meats were not in operation in 2004.

[9] Interview with Graeme Beere, Founder and Managing Director.

[10] Interview with Dominic Kelly, Company Financial Accountant.

restaurants, to began seriously reassess their role as a franchiser. In the aftermath of the franchisee revolt the management sought clarification of the value Abrakebabra Ltd created for its franchisees, both in its role as the strategic centre and as operational services provider. At this time, Abrakebabra decided to reconsider their key objectives as a franchiser. The financial accountant, Dominic Kelly, noted that:

> Your average Managing Director's role in life is to increase his shareholders wealth. Ultimately that means [getting] rich. Shareholder value is [created] in two ways ... You either create profits which generate dividends or you create a business that is worth money even if it's not necessarily paying dividends.[11]

The firm sought to maximize long-term shareholder value through a twin focus on profit maximization and sustainable growth of its franchising network. These goals were achieved by delivering and capturing value for the franchisees. Abrakebabra now saw their core competencies as being divided into four domains. The first domain was brand identity. Second, new product development. Third, centralized purchasing to attain economies of scale. Fourth, training, mentoring and franchisee management. Additionally the franchiser would provide support services to the franchisees such as legal services, capital acquisition, and property management advice. Do franchisees believe that these benefits accrue from membership of the Abrakebabra franchisee network? Seven franchisees' perspectives on why they are members of Abrakebabra are provided in Appendix 1. This evidence indicates that in general franchisees concur with management on the benefits of being a franchisee.

The management team could see the obvious benefits of franchising as a system of growth and they redefined and reasserted the advantages of such a structure. The company had achieved rapid expansion and market penetration with relatively low capital investment. Abrakebabra had been able to expand the number of outlets, increase market coverage, market share and brand equity with limited

financial exposure. In addition, individual restaurant operational duties were delegated to franchisees, and profits increased through the enhanced motivation of these individual operators; attributed to the fact that individual franchisees have made significant financial investments in their business and are thus more likely to be motivated to maximize sales and minimize costs, when compared with hired managers in the same position. Furthermore, Abrakebabra also benefits from a positive cash flow and risk is transferred away from the company because the franchisees accept all financial, human resource and business risk themselves, limiting the financial liability of Abrakebabra should an individual franchise fail.

However, after identifying the positives, to achieve their new focus the Abrakebabra team set about looking at the disadvantages of franchising and the potential problem areas needing to be addressed. Key problems were the control and monitoring of the franchisees' performance in terms of financial performance and restaurant standards. The management team acknowledged the difficulty in exercising tight controls over the franchisees, due to the nature of the relationship as stipulated in the franchise agreement. Indeed, a crucial problem faced by the management team is to ensure that franchisees declare their true level of business activity. Another challenge is to verify that franchisees are achieving and maintaining the highest standards in their restaurants. The Abrakebabra management team knew that they needed to readdress these key areas. In doing this they also needed to define their franchisees' objectives and try to further align both parties' goals and priorities.

The franchisee

> Why did you want to become an Abrakebabra franchisee? I thought it was going to make loads of money. (Abrakebabra Franchisee)

An important goal of a franchisee is the maximization of wealth. How can Abrakebabra help maximize wealth? What benefits should the franchisees be receiving from Abrakebabra?

The Abrakebabra website points to three benefits of becoming a franchise, namely, that it is easier to

---

[11] Interview with Dominic Kelly, Company Financial Accountant.

raise finance, the risk of failure is lower, and franchisees can use a product of proven appeal (www.abrakebabra.net). The management team recognized that Abrakebabra's proven track record and success with earlier franchisees had provided new franchisees with a tried and tested business formula. Dominic Kelly points out:

> The franchisee will pay his money to join the chain, we say here's your store opening manual, here's your shop fitting manual, here's your sandwich or kebab making manual, so that literally they can sit down and read it and from day one and have a 95 per cent chance of making money … because that's why he is paying his money.[12]

He also links the financial goals of the franchisee with the success of the franchiser:

> When a franchise chain succeed, you get at least 95% of your franchisees making money, profitable and happy and once that happens then they are quite happy to pay the franchise fee.

Other benefits experienced by the franchisee are as follows. First, access to Abrakebabra's investment in new product development and large marketing programmes. Second, the opportunity to be their own boss, while having access to the Abrakebabra experience through supervision and consultation. Third, economies of scale in purchasing, advertising, and staff training and reducing operating costs. These advantages lie beyond the reach of a sole trader, but are available to a franchisee.

However, possible shortcomings of Abrakebabra as a franchiser needed to be considered by the management team. Franchisees may find the restrictions of the non-negotiable franchise agreement unattractive. Abrakebabra may not live up to a franchisee's expectations. Brand mismanagement by Abrakebabra might harm the whole system. The franchisee may not be able to avail themself of new supply opportunities because they are locked into buying from a designated supplier of Abrakebabra. So the management team needed to ensure that such problem issues were avoided.

The contract: The franchise agreement

A comprehensive document it deals with everything … right down to termination.[13]

In looking at the relationship between Abrakebabra and its franchisees, the management team needed to assess the most critical document governing this relationship: the franchise agreement. This defines each party's legally binding obligations, duties and rights. Abrakebabra writes the contract; the terms are non-negotiable because the company is the owner of the brand and its associated trademarks. The agreement grants the franchisee exclusive rights to operate an Abrakebabra restaurant at an approved location and to use Abrakebabra's trademarks and other rights of the company in conjunction with the operation of the restaurant. The rights and responsibilities associated with an Abrakebabra franchise agreement require that all franchisees pay an initial fee for a single restaurant, a 6% franchise royalty fee and 1% for group advertising. In order to calculate this figure franchisees are required to submit to the company weekly sales reports for their respective restaurant.

In return for the initial fee and royalty payments, Abrakebabra helps to set up a franchisee's restaurant, with provision of training and general assistance in central services such as: brand awareness, bulk buying, health and safety training and standards maintenance. The Abrakebabra management also lend their expertise in property selection and the fitting out of a new restaurant. In addition franchisees receive continuous supervisory support from head office and have an assigned area supervisor who carries out regular visits. A quarterly newsletter is also produced at head office and distributed to all franchisees, describing operational changes, current food prices, management advice and assistance and so on. If a franchisee has any issues, they contact head office or their area supervisor via telephone and assistance is immediate.

After assessment the management team considered that the contract was not the central issue which needed to be addressed. In their view the key

---

[12] Interview with Dominic Kelly, Company Financial Account.

[13] Interview with Wyn Beere, founder and retired Director and Company Secretary.

problems were ones that could arise after the contract is signed, such as ongoing monitoring of operational and financial performance of a franchisee. Careful selection of franchisees could assist in minimizing both performance problems and the risk of a future franchisee revolt.

Franchisee selection

If the franchisee isn't making money, he can't pay you. So if you have a franchise that doesn't work you are not going to get your franchise fee ... and the thing collapses ... so your number one priority is to pick the right franchisee.[14]

Abrakebabra realized that the success of their franchising system was highly dependent upon the quality of their franchisees and so an important issue facing them was how to ascertain a potential franchisee's level of quality. The problems that Abrakebabra faced in selecting a new franchisee was that potential candidates could appear to be suitable at first glance but over time be deemed unsuitable.

Originally, first franchisees had been chosen on the basis that they had the financial resources and background necessary to run a successful franchise restaurant. Abrakebabra's management quickly made themselves acquainted with the background of franchising laws and issues. As a result of the success experienced by the company during 1982–1990, Abrakebabra was inundated with interested candidates. Consequently Abrakebabra was able to be more selective in choosing its franchisees. However, the recruitment process had remained relatively informal. Dominic Kelly states:

The stronger your brand gets the easier that [franchisee selection] gets because if you have a good brand then people [franchisees] get attracted to it.[15]

However, after the franchisee revolt the management team decided to make the process more formal. They set about formulating a selection system to help identify suitable franchisees. The process is as follows: first of all potential franchisees have to fill out a formal application form, providing basic personal details and capital available for investment. If chosen, they are interviewed in a first round of interviews by David Zebedee, the Franchise Director. He evaluates each franchisee's ambitions, intentions and personal characteristics. The initial steps of franchisee selection are described by David as follows:

Firstly they would read our brochure, they would fill out the application form and sign a confidentiality form and then we would move to the preliminary interview phase ...[16]

Abrakebabra looks for commitment to the company, because each new franchisee signs a ten-year contract. They do not want investors who only give monetary investments and fail to run the restaurant properly.

Educational and business background

Abrakebabra wants people with experience in management and entrepreneurship. They want people with ambition and passion to run a restaurant full time, serving customers to the best of their ability. People with ideas and drive and with a strong sense of responsibility to the franchiser, their customers and community. Previous education is not as important as previous experience in business, especially in the food business, or any business dealing with customers and staff. Franchisees vary from those who have completed primary education through to university graduates. The best combination is experience and education.

Training of a franchisee

Before the shop opens we'll send them [franchisees] off to a local shop [Abrakebabra restaurant] to be trained ... we'll pick out a shop which is near enough to them, and Karen [an Abrakebabra trainer] will oversee how they are trained.[17]

When a franchisee is selected and deemed suitable to run and operate an Abrakebabra franchise,

---

[14] Interview with Graeme Beere, Founder and Managing Director.
[15] Interview with Dominic Kelly, Company Financial Accountant.

[16] Interview with David Zebedee, Franchise Director.
[17] Interview with Sinead Reid, Operations Manager.

official training begins. The company has found that over the years the best possible form of training is on the job with another franchisee. A new recruit is assigned to an established franchisee and works up through the ranks in a restaurant until they are capable of operating and managing it. This form of training can take from two weeks to three months.

The trainee must have a thorough knowledge of the restaurant and all its internal procedures and activities. At this point, if both Abrakebabra and the new recruit are still committed they both sign the franchise contract. Dominic Kelly describes the extensive training process for new franchisees as follows:

> *The training programme is set up for them [franchisees], Sinead who is here will go and work with them building the store ... Then Karen will come on board. Karen will help them recruit their staff and look after operational procedures in the store ... Then Natalia who is here [in Abrakebabra headquarters], she stays on for a period of 4–5 weeks with that franchisee giving them full back-up. She works in the store for 4–5 weeks so it is quite intensive. At the end of the actual training ... they should know the A–Z of Abra.*[18]

The franchisee must be competent in all tasks needed to run a successful Abrakebabra franchise restaurant such as: cooking techniques, till operation, financial management and reporting, supplier management, stock control, health and safety requirements, human resource management and customer management, among other skills and competencies. Once selected and trained as a franchisee, they enter a long-term ten-year contract with Abrakebabra. The ongoing management of this relationship is described below.

Managing the relationship between franchisee and franchiser

Wyn Beere described the affiliation Abrakebabra had with its franchisees as being of a maternal nature:

> *I look upon a franchisee as someone ... when they are with us for the first year ... they are like a baby ... they need everything ... you're like the mother ... they take everything from you ... Then after about five years they learn to read and write, and they start to do their own thing. Then they become a teenager and they think they know everything ... more than you. When they get ... say to about ten years with us they actually want to do their own thing. That's what we found ... If you keep them for ten years you are doing very well ...*[19]

Abrakebabra the franchiser makes its profits from each individual franchisee's entry fee (lump sum) and an ongoing 6% levy on all franchisees' gross revenues (excluding the 1% advertising levy). For this fee Abrakebabra needs to ensure that all franchisees deliver consistent product and service quality levels to the end customer. In return Abrakebabra provides good support infrastructure for their franchisees.

> *I think the main thing is support, that there is someone at the end of the phone ... who can help them deal in any aspects ... [from] suppliers, staffing ... to the business end of things – [preparing and selling] the food. ... Support is our main end of things – guidance and leading them.*[20]

Franchisees make their profit by efficient management of operations and attraction of customers into their restaurant in preference to rival operations. Dominic Kelly states:

> *So if you consider that your food is costing you say 35% for an average week ... your wages are costing you 25%; that's 60% of your turnover gone. Now out of that you've got 40% left to pay all the rest of your overheads, including financing costs, so really you can see where all of a sudden that 5% of your gross profit becomes critical because the difference between having 40% or 45% left, that might be the difference between*

---

[18] Interview with Dominic Kelly, Company Financial Accountant.

[19] Interview with Wyn Beere, founder and retired Director and Company Secretary.

[20] Interview with Sinead Reid, Operations Manager.

make or break. With the franchising system, profits are maximized.[21]

Franchisees pay the franchiser for their expertise in operational issues, access to economies of scale, supply chain management, bulk buying, marketing and branding. All of these benefits make the franchisee more cost efficient than if they acted as a sole trader. One example of the benefits that access to bulk purchasing is the supply deal with C&C for soft drinks. In return for exclusive supply of soft drinks C&C (distributors of Pepsi and Club orange) contributes about half of the total marketing budget of Abrakebabra.[22] This enables the network to keep the advertising levy at 1% of franchisee sales. Abrakebabra management have suggested that 'bulk buying offers Abrakebabra operators an extra 10 per cent profit margin over and above the industry norm of 60 per cent'.[23]

Broadly speaking the franchisees appear to concur with Abrakebabra's perspective on the royalty fee. As one franchisee put it:

The franchiser effectively makes income from the franchisees, so it's very hard to have a paternal attitude towards someone you're trying to make money from. Theoretically it works very well and in actual fact I've a very good relationship with the franchiser in this respect because of the way we evolved together ... So long as the individual unit is successful and it falls into that category that there is a division of a third or two thirds ... in terms of the actual net profit ... and they're helping. If your net profit drops ... they come in and say you know we'll help you ... to develop, to fight for your profit ... On a bad day you know we'll split the difference.[24]

However, Abrakebabra needs to ensure that franchisees maximize their gross revenue and maintain high levels of product and service quality. Maximization of revenues means increased profit for

---

[21] Interview with Dominic Kelly, Company Financial Accountant.

[22] O'Halloran, B. (2002) 'Abrakebabra to Take Bigger Bite of Fast Food Market', *Business and Finance,* 11 April 2002.

[23] McMahon, S. (2003) 'Franchising for the Future', *Sunday Business Post,* 25 May 2003.

[24] Interview with an Abrakebabra franchisee.

Abrakebabra through the franchisee royalty fee levied on each franchisee's operation. Maintenance of high levels of product and service quality ensures that Abrakebabra will be successful as a franchising system in both end-consumer markets and in the attraction of future franchisees. Thus, Abrakebabra needs to ensure that franchisees are consistent in the following: use of the brand, restaurant design and maintenance, health and safety, product quality, and customer service. Franchisees face a difficulty in that maintenance of these standards may suppress their profits. The central question is how can Abrakebabra ensure that on the one hand these standards (costs) are maintained equally by all franchisees and on the other hand that franchisees accurately report weekly gross revenues to head office (thus attracting a total 7% levy; 6% for royalty fee and 1% for advertising budget)? Over the years Abrakebabra have installed and modernized a series of monitoring and control systems to manage these two key issues.

Monitoring: operational controls

The challenge faced by Abrakebabra is the large cost involved in monitoring these standards, all of which must be absorbed from the revenues that it derives from the 6% levy on franchisee's revenues (excluding the 1% advertising levy). In relation to franchising, the quality of service at individual outlets needs to be consistent and must meet a pre-ordained minimum standard. The franchisee's quality of effort and meeting of contractual requirements needs to be continuously monitored.

The Abrakebabra management team looked at a number of contractual clauses in the franchise agreement, which stipulated how the franchisees should operate their outlets. The clauses specify and regulate how the business should be run on a daily basis and shape its long-term development. These control systems fall into two categories: monitoring of operational tasks and attainment of strategic goals.

The first category is designed to regulate day-to-day business. Detailed in the operations manual, it includes hours of operation, prices, product quality, accounting systems, layout, décor and Abrakebabra's right to inspect the premises and make changes unilaterally. These contractual clauses allow the company to control their franchisees' daily operations and ensure that the franchisees uniformly follow the 'ideal' business format model.

The second category involves more strategic controls that shape the longer-term business trajectory. This group of controls include sales targets and objectives, expansion triggers, contract duration, contract renewal and a contract termination option. Abrakebabra creates operational controls to establish, maintain and increase the business's turnover (upon which it received percentage fees), whereas franchisees are more interested in maximizing profit.

The Abrakebabra management team then turned to how they physically monitored franchisees. The first of these methods is via financial monitoring. Every Monday, franchisees must call in their previous week's sales figures to head office. These figures are then checked off the previous year's, with profit and loss assessments being checked and maintained over time. To improve both the accuracy and efficiency of monitoring revenues the franchiser's management team have begun to put modems in every Abrakebabra franchisee till. This means that all sales information from a till is immediately relayed to head office, ensuring that Abrakebabra maintains direct contact with a franchisee's sales status. The modems not only allow the management to monitor sales figures but in addition give vital information on the success of their product mix, and whether certain products are increasing in popularity. If on the other hand certain products are underperforming, promotional campaigns can be targeted at these products. In addition, the sales information helps the company monitor year-on-year sales progress. This use of technology is an important monitoring asset for the management team. As the Franchise Director states:

> Now we are introducing modem systems whereby we can read their [franchisees] tills from head office; we have four shops currently online and the plan for the rest of this year is to get the whole group. The till-monitoring system would give us the exact turnover of what the shop did ... What we had in the past – we were taking the franchisees' word on his turnover, so now its automatic.[25]

The benefits of this new system would at first appear to be weighted in favour of the franchiser. However, the weekly chore that every franchisee faces on a Friday and a Monday of calculating their weekly turnover and relaying this information to head office will be eliminated, thus benefiting them in saving time and effort.

The second and equally important method of monitoring for the Abrakebabra management team is the use of standards checking. Abrakebabra has a team who are divided into four areas in Ireland: north, south, east and west. Regional team supervisors visit their respective franchisees on a systematic and regular basis. As Franchise Director David Zebedee states:

> It's ongoing monitoring. Each franchisee will be visited at least twice a month by somebody from head office ... [who] check standards ... [A] hygiene audit is done at least every six weeks in every store ... [as well as] ongoing monitoring ... In addition to this, Abrakebabra has a health and safety officer who also must check and maintain records of each restaurant's standard. All of the above monitoring checks are recorded in report form and delivered to head office. Any problems are dealt with immediately.[26]

Ian Beere, Health and Safety Officer confirms:

> There are four of us, geographically, north, south, east and west. We have our own fourteen or so [shops]; we are in there every month, that gives us another continuous contact with the franchisees.[27]

Customers are also a great source of monitoring. Customer comment cards are available in all restaurants. Customers can (and do) phone Abrakebabra headquarters directly if they wish to make a complaint about service provision in an individual franchise restaurant. The information received from this form of direct consumer response monitoring is essential for the management team. Ian Beere states:

> ... we are watching their turnovers ... we get customer complaints, [which] are good indicators of what is going wrong ... If you get a

---

25 Interview with David Zebedee, Franchise Director.

26 Interview with David Zebedee, Franchise Director.
27 Interview with Ian Beere, Health & Safety Officer.

number of complaints you know there is something going wrong. [There is] one good monitor
and that's the customer . . . .[28]

Finally, mystery shoppers are also employed by the Abrakebabra management. The feedback received from this method of monitoring is a great way of surveying franchisee standards and competence levels.

The mystery shopper idea was to find out how the food was going ... and we paid the mystery shoppers so they wouldn't go in with a voucher and say we are from head office ... Ian organised that. It works ... and is monitored closely.[29]

Conclusion

From a franchisee's perspective it is clear that the changes in strategy, post 1997, have delivered increased value for them. As one franchisee put it:

I'd say that the brand has really improved in the last couple of years ... I think they have taken a far more professional approach – to the business ... You know, when I was setting up they did everything they could for me.[30]

From the perspective of the franchiser, the changes post 1997 have also been successful. From a difficult position in 1997, with franchisees in open revolt, the management have turned the firm around. Franchisees now see the value that the franchiser creates. New franchisees are being attracted to the venture and opportunities to attract fresh capital have arisen.

The question for the management team at Abrakebabra now is how far and how long can the growth model be sustained?

---

[28] Interview with Ian Beere, Health & Safety Officer.
[29] Interview with Wyn Beere, founder and retired Director and Company Secretary.

[30] Interview with an Abrakebabra franchisee.

Appendix 1 **The franchisee's perspective of Abrakebabra membership.**

Franchisee 1: 'Why Abra? Well at the time I looked at others. McDonald's, Supermacs, Abrakebabra, the whole package, you know. I'd met every one of them and I'd just found them [Abrakebabra] to be the most attractive package out of the whole lot.' We [franchisees] are part of a big, bigger picture [in terms of] marketing and branding … more than independent outlets. And also from a financial point of view we are better off because we are purchasing at least 12–13% cheaper than the small independent body would be doing.'

Franchisee 2: 'Why did I decide to franchise? I saw a strong name, with a strong product in a strong location and I went for it. Why did I decide to go Abra? Very strong and powerful product range, innovative [and] different.'

Franchisee 3: 'I was already in the business … and I knew that somebody would open up in [my area] if I didn't … so I got in there first! Why Abra? Because it was … how would you say … size basically. They had a presence … and [their design specifications] fitted the site … It wasn't big enough for McDonald's.'

Franchisee 4: 'We owned our own restaurant and McDonald's came to town. It [Abrakebabra] was something to do battle with McDonald's because it affected our business up to about a third of our trade dropped … because of that … I looked around at other franchises … I remember that I ate in Abrakebabra before and loved the food and so I made inquiries [about becoming a franchisee] and as a consequence we went for it.'

'Yes, advertising and bulk buying would be the two main benefits … their back-up services are pretty good as well.'

Franchisee 5: 'I had looked around and McDonald's and Burger King had come to [my area] and I had seen Abra [also]. I thought it would be good. I had gone along to a show in O'Reilly Hall in UCD and there was an Abra stand, a Pizza Hut stand … I went away and I didn't really know what to do. Then a while later I saw an ad in the paper and made the call to Abra and went from there.'

'Advertising, and bulk buying, yes … they would be the biggest benefit … and of course they [Abrakebabra] help to solve problems with suppliers if a delivery hasn't been made or other stuff. Oh and the name is the biggest benefit of course.'

Franchisee 6: 'Advertising and bulk buying …'

Franchisee 7: 'Advertising, bulk buying, and legal [expertise] … Wyn has a huge amount of experience in relation to landlords, dealing with neighbours, rights of way, all this sort of thing. So that's always been a big, big help; they have a huge expertise which they accumulate …'

INSEAD

Case 26 Creyf's (Solvus Resource Group): David against Goliath in the European temping industry

This case received the 2003 European Foundation for Management Development Case of the Year Award in the category 'International Business'

Prologue

The board meeting scheduled for Wednesday, 28 March 2001 was looking set to be one of the most challenging for Creyf's CEO Michel Van Hemele in his attempt to gain support for acquiring the IT consulting group, Bureau Van Dijk Computer Services (BvD).[1]

Creyf's, a Belgian company that provided a wide range of staffing services and solutions at local, national and European level, was present in nine different countries and consisted of four main business units: general temping, specialized temping, secondment and projects, and other HR services and consulting. On a European scale the company was ranked fifth after Adecco, Manpower, Vedior and Randstad.

Since 1988, Bureau Van Dijk CS had helped customers to build high-value solutions in information technology. The company designed the solutions, implemented them and assumed responsibility for the continuous management and execution of the process. It offered a wide range of competencies but mainly focused on four core domains: enterprise resource planning solutions (mostly SAP), e-consulting, infrastructure management and information and communication technology. (Exhibit 9 shows more detailed information on BvD).

Van Hemele felt that this acquisition would fit perfectly into his most recent strategic plan to expand Creyf's specialized divisions and reduce the focus on general temping as it was both very expensive and nearly impossible to remain profitable in all the different domains in which the company was involved.

However, others in the company felt that the existing dual strategy, which was both profitable and in line with customers' needs, should not yet be abandoned. Moreover, BvD, capitalizing on the expected growth potential in its sector, was asking an astronomical price. Several members of the board feared that the acquisition might be 'a bridge too far' for a company that had hitherto been successful in rather small-scale acquisitions. In addition, the financial markets were sceptical about the potential investment and the risk that management was prepared to take for something that was not even Creyf's core business.

Nonetheless, Van Hemele was convinced that the takeover was the logical, necessary step in developing a clearer, more profitable strategy in the future. He entered the meeting room ready to take up the challenge, confident that he could prove his many opponents wrong. The board was prepared for a lively debate.

This case was written by Eline Van Poeck, Research Assistant, Katholieke Universiteit Leuven, with Paul Verdin, Affiliate Professor at INSEAD and Professor at Solvay Business School (ULB) and Katholieke Universiteit Leuven. Constructive comments by Nick Van Heck of Executive Learning Partnership, and Steve Nysten, Research Assistant at Solvay Business School (ULB), are gratefully acknowledged. It is intended to be used as a basis for class discussion rather than to illustrate either effective or ineffective handling of an administrative situation.

[1] Although only the computer division of Bureau Van Dijk ('Computer Services') was for sale, we will nevertheless simply refer to this acquisition as 'Bureau Van Dijk' and abbreviate it to 'BvD'.

Temporary labour services: in the grip of globalisation

The early 1990s had changed the temporary work services industry ('temping' for short)[2] dramatically. The diminishing role of national legislation in the unified labor market, the liberalization in some European countries of temporary work contracts, and the growing trend in cross-border contracts between European multinationals with temporary work businesses (TWBs) were all factors that explained the industry's evolution.

Consequently, a group of European (some global) TWBs had formed competing on a more international level. In 1994 the most successful players in terms of market share were: Manpower (10%), Ecco (8.8%), Randstad (6.9%), Bis (4.3%), Adia (4.3%) and Vedior (3%).

Given the clear trend towards internationalization, the temping industry was dominated by European rather than local business at the beginning of the 90s. Ironically, it was then that Creyf's decided to reverse its internationalization strategy and refocus on the traditional Belgian market.

Restructuring at Creyf's in the early 90s: 'back to local'

When, in April 1992, Michel Van Hemele traded in his career at the Generale Bank, (Belgium's largest bank at that time) for the position of CEO at Creyf's Interim, he found a company in serious trouble. Latterly, the small temporary staffing company established by Herman Creyf in 1963 had got 'carried away' creating a European dimension. This had become particularly pressing in view of the advent of the Single Market which was expected to significantly change the landscape as a result of the ambitious Internal Market Program (IMP) or 'Europe 1992' as it was called, launched by the

European authorities. According to Herman Creyf, *'You need to establish Europe 1992 yourself. It's eat or be eaten.'*[3]

It was an ambitious dream, but one which ended up in a nightmare of loss-making and even fraudulent agencies, acquired across Great Britain, France, Spain and Portugal (see Exhibit 3).

Creyf had left his company after an IPO on the Brussels stock exchange a year earlier and had sold most of his shares to the Antwerp holding Ackermans & Van Haaren (AvH). Van Hemele was invited by this new 'reference shareholder' (which owned 40.57% of the shares) to help the recently hired CFO, Bart Gonnissen, put the company back on its feet.

Van Hemele and Gonnissen would soon become an inseparable and largely effective team, complementing each other in many ways. While Van Hemele turned out to be the more charismatic and prominent leader of the two, Gonnissen was the wizard at figures who, often behind the scenes, took care of all the financial and fiscal aspects of the CEO's decisions. Their critical analysis of the company's situation very soon led to the conclusion that *'The end is near. The foreign adventure of Creyf's is over. The group will concentrate again on the familiar Belgian market.'*

In no time the company was drastically reorganized leading to the liquidation of the French agencies, closure of the Spanish activities and a management buy-out in Portugal. The disastrous British agencies had been sold to Herman Creyf a couple of years before. Indeed, it had been one of the major conditions of AvH when agreeing to purchase Creyf's shares.

At the same time, Creyf's had managed to hold an honorable third position in its home market, trailing two Dutch temporary services companies: Gregg Interim (the number two) and Interlabor (the number one). From then on, Creyf's would focus purely on growth in the Belgian market. After all *'Interim work is rather local. You can only create limited added value across borders.'*[4]

---

[2] We will concentrate on the notion of temporary work in the sense of *travail intérimaire*. It involves a tripartite relation between a temporary work business (TWB), a temporary worker and a user-firm (client). More details on the temporary service industry can be found in the Industry Note: '*The European Temporary Work Services in 1994*', Nick Van Heck and Paul Verdin, INSEAD/K.U.Leuven, 1999.

[3] Herman Creyf, FET 27/04/1990 (Financieel Economische Tijd, a leading local newspaper).

[4] The two previous quotes of Michel Van Hemele can be found in FET 31/10/2002 and FET 29/12/1992.

Two important decisions were taken. Firstly, the main goal was to eliminate Creyf's disadvantage with regard to coverage of the home market (c.f. its main competitors). The number of agencies was expanded and some important blind spots on the Belgian map got filled up. By 1995, the Belgian network consisted of 60 offices.

Secondly, cost management and profitability became the core of Van Hemele's strategy. In 1993 this led to the disposal of the Acmé Group, a small, unprofitable temporary services group from Liège acquired by Creyf's in 1990 (see Exhibit 3).

Henceforth, Creyf's reverted to being a profitable local company. However, many analysts started wondering whether it would continue to buck the trend in the temping industry or get on board the internationalization train that was passing through the European landscape. This question became increasingly pressing when things started to get rough in the Belgian temping market.

Renewed growth in the mid-90s

In very little time the Belgian general temping sector fell victim to the keen price competition between Gregg and Interlabor, resulting in a significant reduction of profit margins. Van Hemele realised that, despite Creyf's present comfortable situation on the Belgian market, its narrow focus on general temping in one small European market made the company too vulnerable in the future: 'Big international companies start to purchase on a European scale. Besides, Creyf's has become the ideal prey for foreign groups wanting to buy market share in Belgium.'[5]

His concerns resulted in a 'dual strategy' from the mid-90s which acknowledged that it was important to be present in more than one market (regionalization), while offering more than one product (diversification). Van Hemele had clearly heard the whistle of the passing internationalization train.

Diversification in services

Herman Creyf had resisted a diversification strategy for his company and concentrated purely on general temping. This refers to the temporary recruitment and dispatching of workers in all kinds of industries, with emphasis on quality and flexibility. While generally high volumes can be generated in this segment of the market, profit margins tend to be rather low. His successors were convinced that only by diversification could the company be successful. Specialized temping was the first new activity to be developed. It also refers to the temporary recruitment and dispatching of workers, yet in very specific industries where higher profit margins can still be found.

By 1994 the company thus consisted of four specialized divisions,[6] with Express Medical Interim, acquired in April 1994, being the most important and most profitable.

In 1997 the company acquired ADV Consult (see Exhibit 5), resulting in the development of a third activity for Creyf's, dubbed other HR services, which refers to complete recruitment services – plus selection programs, training programs, career advice, job search training and mobility programs.

Regionalization strategy

The first move towards regionalization was made in the business of general temping. In November 1994 the company acquired Lux Conseil International, the third largest temporary services company in Luxembourg. Over the period 1996–1997 the company rode this trend and acquired Pro Consultant and SFI in France, Van Den Boom in The Netherlands and BGT Personalservice in Germany (see Exhibit 5). All were markets with considerably higher profit margins in general temping than Belgium.

> We have no intention of becoming a European group, but our economic territory does not end at the country's borders. In the long term we would like to be active, where our clients are.[7]

In 1998 the acquisition of Draft Engineering in the Netherlands marked the beginning of its regional expansion with regard to a fourth new segment, secondment and projects. This refers to the provision

---

[5] Michel Van Hemele, Trends 03/10/1996.

[6] Creyf's Data, Creyf's Engineering, Creyf's Maritime, Creyf's Express Medical Interim.

[7] Michel Van Hemele, FET 02/11/1994.

and outsourcing of engineering and IT managers to fulfill certain projects in other companies. It was regarded as a profitable activity.

In less than a year the company had expanded in this segment in the Dutch market by buying Promates, Beaver Software and the Done Group (see Exhibit 5).

The take-over of the large Dutch group, Content, in 1999, could be seen as the perfect illustration of the dual strategy followed by the company since the mid-90s. On the one hand, the acquisition signified an important expansion of its segmentation strategy. The group's specialised temping services were enlarged with Content, StarJob and Carrière (all elements of the Content Group) and its other services segment could benefit from the integration of Schroevers, SBO and Info Opleiders (see Exhibit 5). On the other, it also strengthened the group's international presence: from then on 75% of the group's turnover was realized outside Belgium (nearly half of it in the Netherlands).

By the end of 1999 Creyf's was clearly an international company once more, despite the memories of its hapless foreign adventures in the early years. Commenting on the U-turn, Hamele said, *'From a strategic perspective, Herman's [Creyf] choice to internationalise was definitely the right one. However, one can question the way it was done.'* [8]

An acquisition-based strategy

Van Hemele's internationalization strategy was clearly based on some key characteristics as most acquisitions followed a similar pattern with regard to the selection of new markets and targets, the financing of the operations, and the integration of the acquired units.

The selection of new markets and targets

It was on the basis of the 'pigeon' strategy, the 'oil slick' strategy[9] or the 'euroregio' strategy that the international market penetration of the group took shape. As staffing was in essence a local business, Creyf's focused mainly on markets with similar culture, language or legislation. This meant that the company sought potential targets within a limited perimeter around the head office in Antwerp. Thus it first tried to build up a dominant position in Northern France, the Benelux, and West Germany. (Exhibit 6 shows the geographically expansion of the group from 1993 until 1998.)

Moreover, the proximity of the acquired units made it possible for the CEO/CFO management duo, Michel Van Hemele and Bart Gonnissen, to regularly visit their local businesses to make sure that everybody remained on the same wavelength at all times. After all, it was the personal fit with the local company's management that had determined the deal in the first place:

> *Before we buy a company, we pay them a couple of visits to check if they are on the same wavelength. It has happened that we decided not to buy an excellent company only because it didn't match. Conversely, we have already bought companies with poor results simply because we believed in its management.* [10]

Suitable local managers were typically open-minded entrepreneurs, ready to take initiative and to improve business. They believed in the group's mission and were keen to pursue the company's interest at all times. As one local manager put it: *'You always try to do what's best for the company because you know that, in the end, it will be the best for you too.'* [11]

Financing the operations

A second characteristic of Creyf's internationalization strategy had to do with the financing of the acquisitions. Local management was never paid in shares. All transactions were effected in cash to avoid dilution of Creyf's stock. Consequently, Creyf's had to seek a couple of capital increases to raise its own funds and to make possible the financing of the internationalization strategy (see Exhibit 7). AvH, the reference shareholder, contributed to those capital increases in accordance with its participation.

Moreover, Creyf's would rarely buy an entire company at once, preferring to acquire only a part of

---

[8] Michel Van Hemele, FET 24/11/1999.

[9] 'Pigeon' refers to the limited distance a pigeon can fly. 'Oil slick' refers to the way an oil slick expands over the water surface.

---

[10] Bart Gonnissen, FET 10/11/2001.

[11] Gé Geurts, General Manager, Creyf's Netherlands.

it at first. According to the operational results of the company after the acquisition, local management would receive either more or less for the remaining shares:

> *The local managers are of course super motivated because of this earn-out construction. We have already carried out different deals in which the management received more for the last 30% of the shares than for the first 70%.*[12]

Integration of the acquired units

> *You need to buy the right target at an acceptable price and integrate it afterwards in a correct way. The real work always started after the deal was done.*[13]

A high level of decentralization characterized the organizational structure of Creyf's. The acquired businesses would be managed as a network of autonomous business units in which maximum flexibility around a strategic design was guaranteed. In the belief that temping was in essence a local business, the acquired companies were allowed to keep their autonomy after the deal was done.

Thereafter, coordination within the Creyf's group mainly consisted of the financial reports, the IT system and regular visits by the management team. The holding staff in Antwerp consisted of only 15 people, a number that was still too high according to Van Hemele.

The company's flat structure and its short decision lines made it possible to take quick decisions and to act promptly. Creyf's also benefited in that this unique operational structure meant that it could regularly buy a company at a lower price than its competitors. As Gé Geurts, general manager of Creyf's Netherlands, put it at the moment of the acquisition: *'A take-over by a larger Dutch agency had no added value for us. We wanted to maintain our autonomy.'*

Entering the new millennium

Continuing acquisitions

From the end of the 90s, Creyf's dual strategy speeded up. In the year 2000, it started to take over

companies at an average speed of one company per month, resulting in the tremendous expansion of its product and geographical scope (see Exhibit 4a/b).

The end of the 90s brought the long overdue legalization of the Spanish and Italian temporary staffing industry (see Exhibit 2). Creyf's immediately focused on further expansion of its general temping segment in those markets to capitalize on all possible growth potential. In Italy, Interiman was bought (July 2000). In Spain, Verticce Business (October 2000) was taken over. The general temping segment also expanded into France with the acquisition of SPIA (October 1999) and IPS (November 1999). The Dutch general temping business would benefit from the purchase of VDN Group (August 2000). Creyf's also penetrated two new general temping markets. Firstly, in June 2000, it acquired Alpha Personal Service in Austria. Secondly, in October 2000, a start-up of Creyf's Interim was launched in Switzerland.

The secondment and projects segment expanded into Luxembourg with the acquisition of World Fiduce (June 1999), into the Netherlands by acquiring Applicon Group (January 2000), and into Belgium with the takeover of Wevecos (December 2000). Specialized staffing was further developed in Belgium with the acquisition of Orange Consult (July 2000), and in Spain with the acquisition of Verticce Business Consulting (October 2000).

Creyf's and its European market position

Over six years Creyf's had developed from a virtually unknown Belgian general staffing agency into a major European provider of HR services. The key to this unique track record had been its decentralized structure in combination with a strong entrepreneurial spirit. The current management had carried out complementary and mostly small-scale acquisitions, building Creyf's into one of the most important players in Belgium, the Netherlands and France (see Exhibit 4b). The company had over 30 brands, offered four different services, and was present in nine different countries (see Exhibit 4a)

In the year 2000 Creyf's consolidated turnover was €1.27 billion. Its consolidated operating profit was €66 million. (Exhibit 4c shows in detail how Creyf's turnover and operational result was divided over its international network, and its different services.)

---

[12] Bart Gonnissen, De Standaard 10/11/2001
[13] Michel Van Hemele, FET 24/11/1999.

On a European scale, Creyf's was ranked number five after Adecco, Manpower, Vedior and Randstad. Adecco, the outcome of the mega merger between Adia and Ecco in 1996, had clearly become the world's leading Goliath: it was No. 1 or 2 in 12 of the top 13 staffing markets and its market position conferred important unit cost advantages, resulting in higher EBITDA margins than its peers despite similar capital intensity. (More information on these key players can be found in Exhibit 1.)

As a huge gap existed between the industry Goliaths (with a European market share of about 10–15%) and Creyf's (with a European market share of only a few percent), one might wonder whether David could ever win this battle.

The fear of 'getting stuck in the middle'

Although the company had clearly done well with its dual strategy, Van Hemele and Gonnissen started to fear that the same approach could no longer be maintained in the new millennium.

In the six year period, the company had developed a fragmented portfolio on the basis of national and international small-scale acquisitions. They felt that its scope of activities had become too large to guarantee maximum productivity. After all, nobody could be good at everything.

Moreover, as the international network of Creyf's had grown tremendously, Michel Van Hemele was no longer able to visit all subsidiaries on a regular basis. This raised some concern as his 'management by travelling' had always been a key factor in the coordination and supervision of the group's activities.

Therefore, Creyf's management duo believed that time had come to narrow down the company's strategy and focus on a specific activity as the basis for further expansion. As general temping was differently positioned than the three other segments of the group, the feeling was that in the future the emphasis should either be more on general temping, or on the rest.

General temping had increasingly become a commodity market, weighed down by keen price competition and low profit margins (see Exhibit 4c). Only an overall cost-leader could still make money in this segment. From the start, Adecco had clearly focused on this business. The company's relatively high-market share and its heavy up-front investments and aggressive pricing had resulted in a low-cost position and an above-average return in general temping. For Creyf's it was too late to follow this strategic line. It would require huge capital investments without any realistic hope of ever catching up on Adecco's international coverage.

Of our four activities, only one is concentrated on general temping. This activity is very cyclical and generates low profit margins: although it contributes 70% to our turnover, it only generates 49% of our operational results. I'm not convinced we should go for a volume increase in general temping.[14]

It was clear therefore that a debate – if not a fight – was shaping up between the successful small players like Creyf's and the big four industry Goliaths.

David against Goliath

Van Hemele felt that the David vs. Goliath battle could not be won by 'doing what the competition does' – a 'me too' strategy would not bring prosperity. Hence, the strategic aim was to focus attention and investments on the other three activities of the company, i.e., specialized temping, detachment and projects, and other HR services. The idea was to realize a unique, high-quality service. For the detachment and projects segment, this implied a development from simple 'manpower provision' into 'total solutions provision', i.e., instead of merely offering flexible employment to a client, Creyf's wanted to provide total solutions with regard to IT and engineering. The subsidiaries Draft and Cluster were already solution providers for engineering, while Beaver Software was mainly a capacity provider for IT.

So when in March 2001 the IT consulting group, Bureau Van Dijk Computer Services (BvD), was put up for sale, Michel Van Hemele was more than interested to buy in order to establish the solution approach in the IT segment. But not all stakeholders of Creyf's seemed to be supportive of the CEO/CFO duo's intended strategic shift.

---

[14] Michel Van Hemele, De Standaard 08/05/2001.

First of all, several members of the board were not convinced that the current strategy had to be abandoned, particularly as the company's financial results (see Exhibit 4e) and its share price (see Exhibit 4d) had showed a positive evolution over the last few years. They wondered why Creyf's would change a strategy which was clearly rated positively by its key clients and shareholders.

Some of Creyf's key clients (Bosch, Nike, Daikin) were all large users of Creyf's general temping services but made only sporadic use of its other services. The main added value of working with Creyf's was founded in the stability of the relationship and the pro-activity and the willingness of the company to invest in their general temping services. One could wonder how far the company would be able to continue pampering its key clients if the strategy was merely focused on specialized services. Moreover, if future investments in general temping were at risk, would then a key client like Nike, who had a purchasing contract with Adecco on a European basis but did work with Creyf's in Belgium, maintain this exclusive partnership?

Thus board members feared that the CEO/CFO duo had overlooked the opportunity cost of the potential acquisition of BvD, which would definitely seal the intended strategic shift. Furthermore, convinced of the growth potential in its segment, BvD was asking more than €69 million – a huge amount of money for Creyf's, whose profits from ordinary business operations stood at €66 million at that time.

Clearly such an investment in specialized services would lock out similar investments in general temping in the future. Although low profit margins were common in the Belgian general temping industry, higher margins were still to be found in some European countries. By focusing purely on specialized services Creyf's would miss out on these opportunities. Italy, for example, which had only legalized its temporary staffing industry in 1999, still carried considerable growth potential. However, Adecco was clearly taking advantage of the Italian market's liberalization and had opened more than 150 offices in the last year. If Creyf's wanted to become a dominant player in this high-growth market, they would be forced to quickly expand their Italian network. However, to do so they

needed money – money which now risked being spent on a non-core segment.

Secondly, the financial world was also sceptical about Creyf's intention to acquire BvD. Although it had always been successful in small-scale acquisitions (with lower P/E), Creyf's was now planning to take over a company with a higher P/E ratio (see Exhibit 8). Many analysts wondered why the company would be willing to pay such a high premium for the expected future earnings of BvD. Was it indeed realistic to expect continuous growth for the IT company? Hadn't the latest financial results of BvD shown signs of the negative pattern which had affected so many technology shares? What if this expected growth failed to materialize? They also questioned the way the company intended to finance the operation, i.e., by issuing converted Creyf's bonds in exchange for BVD shares. Would this not increase Creyf's debt ratio and threaten the financial balance of the company?

For Michel Van Hemele, however, further growth in the IT sector could be anticipated. BvD's high price incorporated a large amount of goodwill. As the founder and director of BvD, Jean-Paul De Nys, explained, further growth potential in his segment was only to be expected: 'IT people are like undertakers. They will always be necessary.' De Nys was particularly attracted by Creyf's established international network on which he hoped to be able to further BvD's international expansion.

Thirdly, for Ackermans & Van Haaren, Creyf's reference shareholder, temping was clearly a local business. For them the key to success would be *being better than the competition in every single location/business you are in'. So* the real question was not which segment Creyf's had to focus on, but how to create critical mass in every segment they were active in.

The proposed acquisition: a unique opportunity or a bridge too far?

The board meeting was scheduled on the night of Wednesday 28 March to decide on this highly contentious takeover of BvD. Michel Van Hemele was ready to convince the other board members of the strategic importance of the acquisition. He feared that without an urgent strategic focus, the company risked getting stuck in the middle – not able to continue the positive results of the past nor keep up with the Goliaths in the future. But would the board be supportive of his arguments?

Would they regard it as reasonable to significantly change the approach and put at risk what had been built up carefully over the years? Would they feel time had come to get rid of the dual focus and start concentrating on where the money was? Would they consider BvD as the best catch the company could go for? Did they believe in its growth potential, which Michel Van Hemele clearly saw? Or would they listen to the needs of the key clients and the concerns of the financial world and continue the safe path that had turned the company into a successful European player? Which future strategy would guarantee David winning the coming battles against the Goliaths of the temping industry? Could the acquisition of BvD be the crucial 'stone in the sling' leading to victory?

Exhibit 1 Competitive analyses
a. Ranking of European Staffing Companies
Market Shares in Continental Europe (2000)

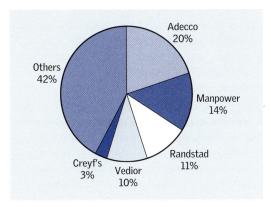

Source: ING Barings.

b. Financial Overview of Top Five European Staffing Companies

In EUR billion	Group Revenue		Group EBITDA		Group EBITDA/Revenue	
	1999	**2000**	**1999**	**2000**	**1999**	**2000**
1. Adecco SA	11,515	17,506	580	929	5%	5,30%
2. Manpower Inc	9,702	11,55	292	402	3%	3,50%
3. Vedior NV	4,057	6,584	185	344	4,60%	5,20%
4. Randstad Holding NV	5,565	6,168	350	305	6,30%	4,90%
5. Creyf's	929	1,273	67	93	7,20%	7,30%

Source: Sector Analysis 'The Dutch Staffing Sector', NIB Capital Bank.

c. The Key Players
Adecco SA (Headquarter: Chéserex, Switzerland)
Adecco was formed in August 1996 from the mega merger of Adia and Ecco. Since 1996 the business had grown to become the industry Goliath. In 2000 it generated nearly €18 billion, making it 75% larger than its nearest competitor, Manpower. Adecco had over 6,000 branches in 58 countries and had 700,000 temporary staff working for 250,000 clients per day. Adecco had

a global market share of 12% and a very strong global market position – it was No.1 or 2 in 12 of the top 13 staffing markets, which collectively accounted for 90% of the total market. The only market where Adecco was below No.2 was the Netherlands. France and the US were Adecco's most important markets.

Therefore, Adecco positioned itself as being the global leader. According to some analysts, however, prudence was in order. Adecco consisted of three different divisions.

Adecco Staffing was its mainstream staffing division which offered light industrial and clerical temporary staffing on a global scale and generated the bulk (74%) of the group EBITDA. Ajilon was its specialist division. It was mainly US focused and operated in the IT and telecom markets (70% of sales) but also had a small finance business. Ajilon generated 15% of EBITDA. The third division was Career Services, which mainly covered its outplacement business, Lee Hecht Harrison, and contributed 11% of EBITDA.

Adecco's market position conferred important unit cost advantages, given the economies of scale in staffing, and partly explained why Adecco had higher EBITDA margins than its peers despite similar capital intensity.

Manpower Inc (Headquarter: Milwaukee, USA)

In 1955 Manpower was established in Canada. The first European offices opened in 1956 in the United Kingdom. Manpower France was established in 1957. In 2000 it was the second largest employment service organization with group revenue of nearly €12 billion. It was engaged in delivering high-value staffing and workforce management solutions worldwide. The company consisted of a network of 3,900 offices in 63 countries. Its largest operations, based on revenues, were located in the United States, France and the United Kingdom. Manpower was organized and managed primarily on a geographic basis. The company's operating countries were United States, France and EMEA (Europe, Middle East and Africa, excluding France). The firm provided employment to more than 2.7 million people worldwide and was the industry leader in employee assessment and training. Manpower also provided a range of staffing solutions, engagement and consulting services worldwide under the subsidiary brands of Brook Street, Elan, The Empower Group and Jefferson Wells.

Vedior NV (Headquarter: Amsterdam, The Netherlands)[15]

After the acquisition of Bis in 1997 and Select in 1999, Vedior became the world's third-largest temporary staffing company after Adecco and Manpower. In 2000, the company had over 2,000 branches in 29 countries and 10,500 temporary staff working for one million clients. It generated revenues of €6.58 billion and had a global market share of 4%. Vedior had greater exposure to specialist staffing than Adecco and Manpower. Specialist staffing accounted for 58% of EBITDA in 2001, compared to 15% at Adecco and 10% at Manpower. Vedior consisted of three divisions: Select, VediorBis and Vedior Europe. Select was its global specialist staffing business and its largest division. Select earned the highest EBITDA margins in the group. Select's revenues were evenly split between the US, UK and Europe, with some minor exposure to both Asia-Pacific and Latin American markets. VediorBis was the third-largest French general staffing business. Vedior's smallest division was Vedior Europe which operated across Europe (with the exception of France) but whose operations were mainly focused in the Netherlands, where it was No.3, and Belgium, where it was No.2.

Randstad Holding NV (Headquarter: Diemen, The Netherlands)

Randstad was the fourth largest in the world after Adecco, Manpower and Vedior, having group revenues of over €6 billion. It was only one third of the size of Adecco and half the size of Manpower. It had only minimal permanent placement exposure and only 5% of its revenues were generated from specialist staffing. 77% of Randstad's revenue, and all of its EBITDA were generated in Europe. Randstad focused on the SME[16] segment, major accounts represented only 5-10% of Randstad's revenue.

---

[15] More background information on Vedior can be found in the following case: 'Vedior International's European Strategy: The French Revolution', Nick Van Heck and Paul Verdin, INSEAD/K.U.Leuven, 1999.

[16] Small and Medium Enterprises.

Its business was split evenly between clerical and industrial staffing. Benelux (48% of gross profit), the US (21% of gross profit) and Germany (10% gross profit) were Randstad's three largest markets. Randstad had the leading market position in the Netherlands with a 35% market share, and to an extent in Germany, where it was the No.1 but with only 7% market share. It also had strong market positions in two of the minor European markets: Spain (16% share) and Denmark (13% share). However, Randstad had a weak position in the US, with less than 2% market share. It also had weak market positions in France, the UK and Italy and Switzerland. Randstad had five divisions. Its three general temping divisions (Randstad Europe, Randstad North-America and Tempo Team), a small specialist division, Yacht, and a low cost bulk staffing division, Capac.

Exhibit 2 Changes in regulation (1989–1997)

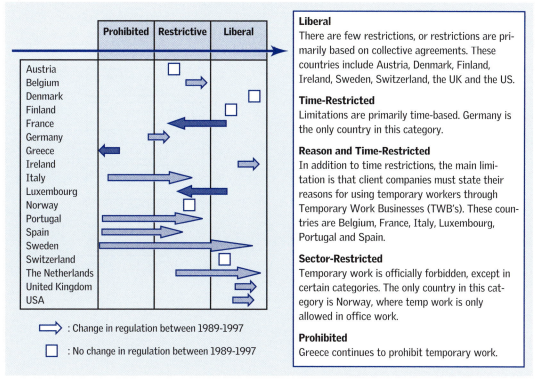

Liberal
There are few restrictions, or restrictions are primarily based on collective agreements. These countries include Austria, Denmark, Finland, Ireland, Sweden, Switzerland, the UK and the US.

Time-Restricted
Limitations are primarily time-based. Germany is the only country in this category.

Reason and Time-Restricted
In addition to time restrictions, the main limitation is that client companies must state their reasons for using temporary workers through Temporary Work Businesses (TWB's). These countries are Belgium, France, Italy, Luxembourg, Portugal and Spain.

Sector-Restricted
Temporary work is officially forbidden, except in certain categories. The only country in this category is Norway, where temp work is only allowed in office work.

Prohibited
Greece continues to prohibit temporary work.

Source: 'European Temporary Work Business Gaining Ground', Staffing Industry Report, 1999.

Exhibit 3 The results and organigram of Creyf's International BV (31/12/1990, €)[17]

	Great Britain	France	Spain	Portugal	Crey's International BV
Turnover	547,200	17,848,433	1,377,346	95,860	19,868,840
Operating Profit	−428,236	65,320	51,339	−83,664	−393,928
Profit to be distributed	−524,171	−51,934	41,844	−13,386	−595,713

Source: Annual Report 1991 Creyf's Interim.

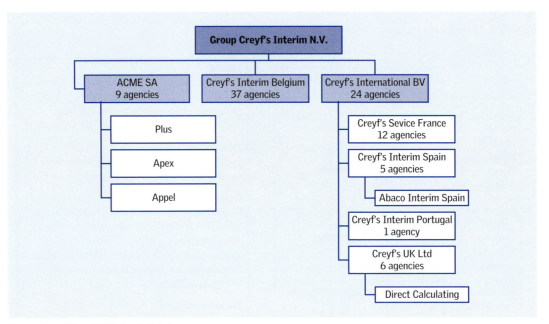

Source: Annual Report 1991 Creyf's Interim.

....

[17] Local currencies have been converted into Euro in order to enhance comparison.

Exhibit 4 The Creyf's Group (2000)
Leading Brands

		Belgium	Netherlands	Luxembourg	France	Spain	Italy	Germany	Austria	Switzerland
General Temporary Employment	Creyf's Interim	●	●	●	●	●	●			●
	BGT							●	●	
	VDN		●							
	BBB		●							
	Intersales		●							
	ASA		●							
	APS								●	
	Nord West Personal							●		
Specialized Temporary Employment	Content	●	●							
	Carrière		●							
	StarJob		●							
	ASA		●							
	Alter Ego			●						
	Express Medical	●								
	Prolink	●								
	Technitemps	●								
Secondment and Projects	Beaver	●	●	●						
	Orange	●								
	Wevecos	●								
	Draft		●							
	Done	●	●						●	
	Promates		●							
	Cluster		●							
Other HRM Services	SBO		●							
	Schoevers		●							
	Creyf's Select	●	●				●			
	BGT Select								●	
	ADV	●								
	Info Opleiders		●							
	BCR		●							
	Qualibre		●							
	BGT Outsourcing							●		

Source: Annual Report Creyf's 2000.

International Network

Country	Number of Agencies	Market Position
The Netherlands	220 agencies	4
France	160 agencies	6
Belgium	92 agencies	3
Germany	22 agencies	15
Luxembourg	6 agencies	1
Austria	4 agencies	/
Spain	5 agencies	/

Source: Presentation Michel Van Hemele: 'Value Creation through growth Commitment', 21/06/2000.

Turnover and Operational Results

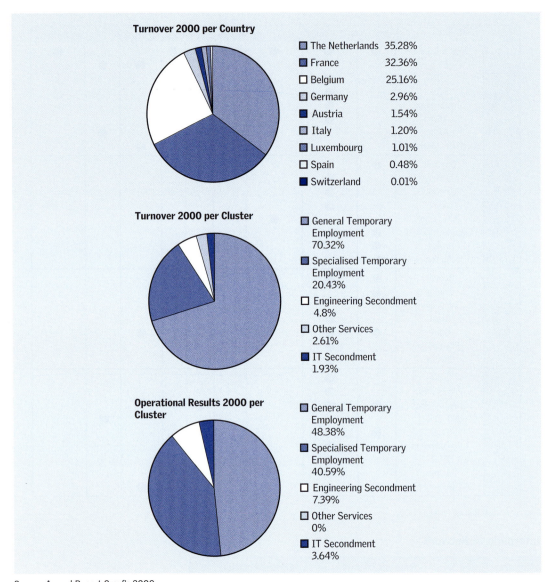

Turnover 2000 per Country

- ■ The Netherlands 35.28%
- ■ France 32.36%
- □ Belgium 25.16%
- □ Germany 2.96%
- ■ Austria 1.54%
- □ Italy 1.20%
- ■ Luxembourg 1.01%
- □ Spain 0.48%
- ■ Switzerland 0.01%

Turnover 2000 per Cluster

- ■ General Temporary Employment 70.32%
- ■ Specialised Temporary Employment 20.43%
- □ Engineering Secondment 4.8%
- □ Other Services 2.61%
- ■ IT Secondment 1.93%

Operational Results 2000 per Cluster

- ■ General Temporary Employment 48.38%
- ■ Specialised Temporary Employment 40.59%
- □ Engineering Secondment 7.39%
- □ Other Services 0%
- ■ IT Secondment 3.64%

Source: Annual Report Creyf's 2000.

Historical Share Price Information Creyf's Group

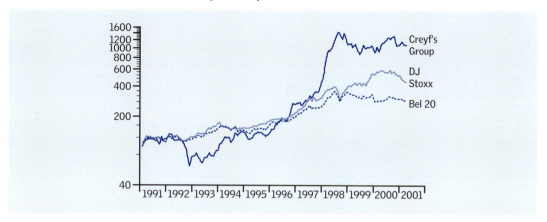

Financial Results Creyf's Group (1999–2000)

X €1000	2000	1999	Δ
Turnover	1,221,971	1,037,515	+17.78%
Operating Result	78,303	58,822	+33.12%
Profit on Ordinary Activities	70,133	54,380	+28.79%
Net Result	41,248	28,492	+44.77%

Source: Annual Report Creyf's 2000.

Exhibit 5 List of major acquisitions 1994–2001

1994			
April	100%	Express Medical	Belgium (Specialized Temping)
November	60%	Lux Conseil International	Luxembourg (General Temping)
1996			
January	80%	Pro Consultant	France (General Temping)
May	100%	SFI/SFB	France/Belgium (General Temping)
October	90%	Van Den Boom	The Netherlands (General Temping)
1997			
April	100%	ADV	Belgium (Other Services/Consulting)
September	80%	BGT Personalservice	Germany (General Temping)
1998			
March	100%	Draft	The Netherlands (Second/Projects)
April	100%	Alter Ego	Luxembourg (Specialized Temping)
April	N/A	Partner/Iso	France (General Temping)
November	100%	Innotiv	The Netherlands (Second/Projects)
December	100%	Beaver Software	The Netherlands (Second/Projects)
1999			
January	100%	Done Group	The Netherlands (Second/Projects)
September	100%	Content Beheer*	The Netherlands
October	100%	SPIA	France (General Temping)
June	100%	World Fiduce	Luxembourg (Second/Projects)
November	75%	IPS	France (General Temping)
2000			
January	100%	Applicon Group	The Netherlands (Second/Projects)
June	100%	Alpha Personal Service	Austria (General Temping)
July	100%	Orange Consul	Belgium (Specialized Temping)
July	60%	Interiman	Italy (General Temping)
August	100%	VDN Group	The Netherlands (General Temping)
October	100%	Verticce	Spain (General Temping)
October		Start-up Creyf's Switzerland	Switzerland (General Temping)
December	100%	Wevecos	Belgium (Specialized Temping)
December	100%	Cluster	The Netherlands (Specialized Temp)
2001			
January	100%	Technitemps	Belgium (Other Services)
February	100%	BBB Uitzendorganisatie	The Netherlands (General Temping)
February	90%	Nord West Personal AG	Switzerland (General Temping)
March	100%	Lestor Group	Spain (General Temping)
March	100%	Mentor Group	Spain (General Temping)

*Content, StarJob, Carrière (Specialized Temping); ASA Studenren Uitzendbureau, InterSales (General Temping); Schroevers, SBO, Info Opleiders (Other Services)

Exhibit 6 Geographical expansion on the basis of the 'Oil Slick'-Strategy

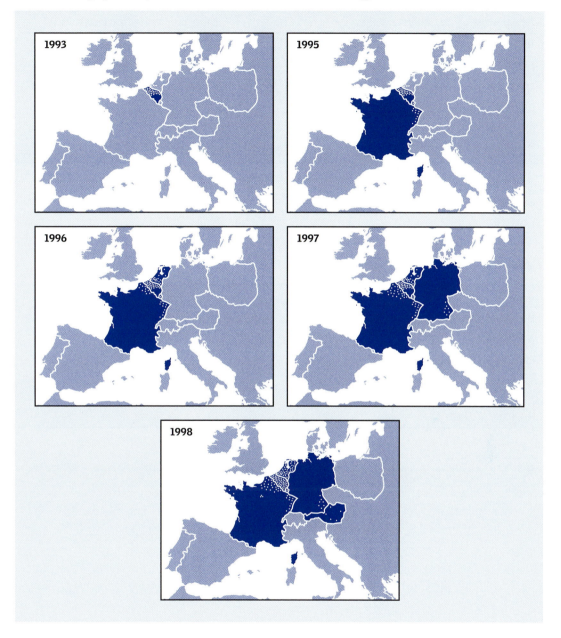

Exhibit 7 Capital increases of Creyf's

Date of Deed	Total Capital ([E]) after Transaction	Number of Shares after Transaction*
16/12/1998	16,991,950	1,408,292
24/12/1998	17,198,455	1,425,407
29/06/1999	67,968,817	21,727,033
03/08/1999	69,683,679	22,275,209
22/06/01	172,149,643	24,735,894
04/07/01	174,576,769	25,084,644

*For comparison purposes, the number of shares was calculated taking into account the stock-split of '99, i.e. 1 share was split into 10 shares.
Source: Annual Report Creyf's 2001.

Exhibit 8 Key financial data on acquisition and target

X €1000	Creyf's	BvD
Number of Shares	25,084,644	2,660,719
Net Profit	43,927,000	2,022,146
Earnings Per Share (EPS)	1.75	0.76
Share Price (P) (End of March '01)	25.5	18.6
P/E Ratio (P/EPS)	14.75	24.47

Exhibit 9 Financial information on Bureau Van Dijk

Evolution of Turnover (1997–2000)

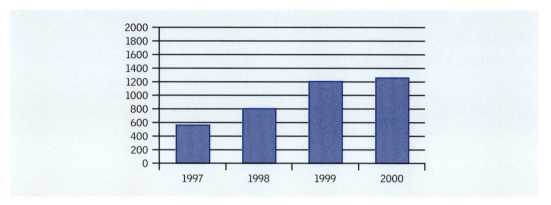

Breakdown of Turnover by Activity (1997–2000)

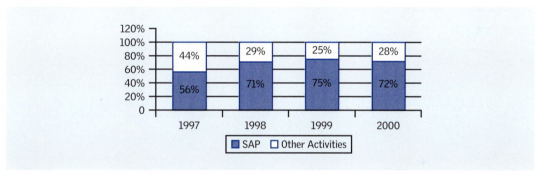

Breakdown of Turnover by Country (1997–2000)

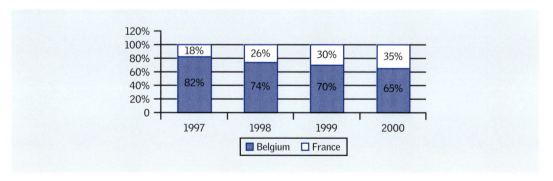

Financial Results (1999–2000)

X €1000	2000	1999	Δ
Turnover	31,320	29,870	+4.85%
Operating Result	4,070	5,980	−31.9%
Profit on Ordinary Activities	3,990	5,860	−31.9%
Net Result	2,310	2,920	−20.89%

Source: Annual Report Bureau Van Dijk CS 2000.

INSEAD

Case 27 **Strategy and performance management at DSM**

It was April 2003, and Hans Dijkman, Business Group Director of DSM Melamine, had just attended a Business Strategy Dialogue (BSD) meeting. DSM Melamine was the global leader in the manufacture and marketing of melamine, a chemical compound used to make highly resistant surfaces, supplying almost one third of world demand. However, Dijkman and his team faced significant challenges in terms of cost competitiveness, aggressive competition, market maturity in Europe and the US, and emerging growth, particularly in China.

Business Strategy Dialogues had been introduced at DSM in the mid-90s to help structure the firm's strategy development process. The BSD process consisted of five distinct phases resulting in a thorough review of the industry, market trends, customer needs, competition and the position of the relevant business group. In 2001, as part of its new

This case was written by Marjolein Bloemhof, Research Associate at INSEAD, under the supervision of Philippe Haspeslagh, Professor of Strategy and Management, and Regine Slagmulder, Associate Professor of Accounting and Control, both at INSEAD. It is intended to be used as a basis for class discussion rather than to illustrate either effective or ineffective handling of an administrative situation. Support from DSM in assembling the information presented in the case is gratefully acknowledged. Some case facts have been disguised for confidentiality reasons.

The authors gratefully acknowledge the financial support provided by the ABN AMRO Research Initiative in Managing for Value.

01/2004-5165

Value Based Business Steering (VBBS) system, DSM had also started to align its strategic planning and financial management processes by introducing Strategic Value Contracts. These contracts contained both performance indicators to monitor the implementation of strategy, and value drivers to measure economic value-creation.

BSDs were initiated whenever either the business or corporate felt the need, on average every three years. DSM Melamine was currently performing its fourth BSD at the request of Dijkman who felt that the current 'actively maintain' strategy would soon fail to achieve the financial performance targeted in his Strategic Value Contract.

Management of DSM Melamine had been discussing the possibility of pursuing a 'grow and build' strategy. They felt that they had reached the limits of cost reduction and that the only way to grow for DSM Melamine was by investing in new melamine plants. Dijkman, however, doubted whether corporate management would agree with this change. Would they emphasize the corporate strategy of becoming a specialties company and thus be reluctant to invest heavily in a commodity such as melamine, or would they let VBBS principles prevail and let themselves be swayed by Melamine's financial track record?

From state mines to specialty company

DSM origins go back to 1902 when the Dutch government founded Dutch State Mines (DSM) as a state-owned coal-mining company. In the 100 years of its existence DSM reinvented itself several times from what was originally a coal mining company, first, as a petrochemicals business, then a commodity chemicals business, and more recently a specialties company.

DSM became a public company in 1989. In 1993, Simon de Bree was appointed CEO and under his leadership DSM continued working on a portfolio shift towards advanced chemical and biotechnical products for the life sciences industry and performance materials. These activities were characterized by good earnings, quality, and strong growth. When de Bree stepped down in July 1999 he was hailed for having reduced the company's exposure to cyclicality and improved its structure by shifting towards a larger share of value-added products. He left the company in good shape both financially and portfolio-wise. Peter Elverding, the board member in charge of integrating Gist Brocades at that time, succeeded de Bree as CEO. Under his guidance, DSM was able to complete its strategic transformation into a specialty chemical company.

By 2003, the company had more than 20,000 employees spread across 200 offices and production sites in 40 countries. It was the leading producer of life science products, performance materials and industrial chemicals, and had a turnover of €6 billion in 2002 (see Exhibit 1 for key figures). Its headquarters were located in Heerlen, in the south of the Netherlands, close to the site of the former coal-mines. In 2002, on the 100th anniversary of its foundation, DSM was given royal status and re-named Royal DSM.

Vision 2005: 'Focus and Value strategy'

One year after his appointment, Elverding announced the outcome of the Corporate Strategy Dialogue conducted in 2000 and labeled 'Vision 2005: Focus and Value'. With the implementation of Vision 2005, DSM would complete its strategic transformation into a specialty chemicals company. Elverding announced that DSM was planning to spin off its petrochemical business. This decision was not without emotion as the petrochemicals business was regarded by many as the 'roots' of the chemical company.

In addition, Elverding announced ambitious targets of increasing annual sales by approximately 60% to €10 billion by 2005, despite the planned withdrawal from the petrochemicals business, which provided one-third of the company's turnover in 2000. At least 80% of sales would have to be generated by specialty products; the rest would come from industrial chemicals, such as melamine and caprolactam, where DSM was already the global leader. Acquisitions would account for half of the sales increase and the remainder would be achieved through organic growth, roughly 6% per year.

Besides focusing on a global leadership position in the specialties business, Vision 2005 also addressed DSM's desire to increase its market capitalization as management felt that the company's stock was undervalued. There were several reasons for this underperformance, including concerns about DSM's portfolio breadth relative to the size of the company, but management believed that the main reason was the market's perception that DSM still was a cyclical stock with predominantly a commodity profile. Management hoped that the implementation of Vision 2005 would turn DSM into a real specialties company, leading to a re-rating and appreciation of its market capitalization. A major part of the Vision 2005 strategy was accomplished when DSM successfully sold its petrochemicals business to Saudi Arabian Basic Industry Corp (SABIC) in June 2002. With a total net consideration of €2.25 billion, this transaction was the largest single deal in DSM's history. In a separate transaction, DSM sold its entitlement to an annual portion of the net profits of EBN[1] to the Dutch government in December 2001. These transactions created a solid cash cushion of over €3 billion to fund the expansion of the specialty portfolio targeted in Vision 2005. To protect its cash trove from unwanted parties, and to keep the funds and transformation process transparent, DSM took the unusual step of placing the revenues from the disposals of EBN and the petrochemicals business into a new subsidiary, DSM Vision 2005 BV. The use of these resources required approval by the governing board of the foundation, which consisted of three members of DSM's managing board and three members of the supervisory board. After the divestment of petrochemicals, DSM had become a substantially smaller company, but with a portfolio that matched the desired profile. Specialties now represented well over two-thirds of total sales, justifying a reclassification from 'bulk commodity player' to 'specialty player'.

In February 2003, Elverding was able to announce the next step in implementing Vision 2005 as DSM

---

[1] EBN: Energie Beheer Nederland, the entity controlling the state participations in the exploration, production and marketing of natural gas in the Netherlands, the management of which was entrusted by the State to DSM.

signed a contract to acquire Hoffman-La Roche's vitamins, carotenoids and fine chemicals business for €1.75 billion, the largest acquisition it had ever made.[2] The acquisition would help restore its total sales, which had been reduced to less than €6 billion as a result of the divestment of petrochemicals, to over €8 billion. More importantly, it would boost the specialty part of DSM's portfolio and help achieve the goal of 80% of sales in specialties two years ahead of the scheduled date (2005). Various analysts were skeptical about the acquisition, however, because of the price pressure and the low growth prospects of the business.

The DSM organization

DSM had a decentralized organizational structure built around 15 business groups (consisting of various business units) that were empowered to execute all business functions. The business groups were grouped into three strategic clusters, mainly for reporting purposes (see Exhibit 2). DSM believed that this structure ensured a flexible, efficient and fast response to market changes. The business group directors reported directly to the managing board of directors. Staff departments at corporate level supported the managing board and the business groups. The business groups contracted the services of a number of shared service departments, DSM Research, and intergroup product supplies at market prices.

The managing board of directors was a collegial board with five members. It was responsible for making decisions about the company's strategy, its portfolio policy, and the deployment of resources. Most board members were 'board delegates' for various business groups. The top management team consisted of the 15 business group directors and the corporate vice-presidents reporting to the board. The third layer of management consisted of 300 senior executives. The top 300 were considered 'corporate property'; they were on one central payroll

and Corporate had the authority to relocate these executives within DSM if they felt the need to do so.

DSM's corporate culture was traditionally informal and consensus-oriented, as is the case in many Dutch companies. Long-standing careers at DSM were encouraged. However, because DSM had been a cyclical company where 90% of the business results were the outcome of external circumstances that could not be influenced, DSM historically did not have a strong accountability culture.

The strategic planning process at DSM

Until the early 1990s, DSM had operated a traditional strategic planning process with planning and budget cycles taking place throughout the year However, DSM management was no longer satisfied with this process. They felt that Corporate Planning owned the strategic planning process and that it served too many different purposes (corporate, divisional, business and functional strategy, internal and external). The process had become routine over time and had degenerated into a 'numbers exercise'. The link between strategy and performance was not clear, but more importantly, top management felt that the quality of strategy development was poor. Most of the strategies focused mainly on cost reduction. The primary beneficiary of such strategies was not the company but its customers, since most of the cost savings were typically passed on to them through price reductions. To enhance the quality of the strategy development process, a new approach called the Business Strategy Dialogue (BSD) was introduced in 1992. These BSDs led to Corporate Strategy Dialogues (CSDs) which were intended to improve the corporate strategy development process.

Corporate strategy dialogue

DSM's strategy development process started with an extensive study of the current situation and the outlook for the company for the next few years. The Corporate Strategy Dialogue was held every three years with a team of 40-50 company-wide executives. It was aimed at developing a long-term corporate strategy, with evaluations and choices being made about portfolio composition,

[2] The deal was closed in September 2003, after the final approval of the anti-trust authorities was obtained. Roche's Vitamins & Fine Chemicals business was renamed DSM Nutritional Products (DNP).

investment priorities and geographical spread. The whole process took six to nine months and was wide-ranging, involving intensive discussions in DSM Corporate top meetings, with the supervisory board and the Central Works Council. The end product was a shortlist of corporate top priorities.

The first CSD was performed in 1994, followed by another in 1997 and a third in 2000. Besides new themes that were defined in each CSD, a number of common themes had consistently been part of the CSD, such as profitable growth, leadership position, coherent portfolio, reduction of cyclicality, growth markets, reduction of dollar-sensitivity, geographical spread, and being an attractive employer.

Once the priorities were set, the corporate strategic plan was to be implemented over the next two to three years. Focusing all energy on realizing its corporate priorities had allowed DSM to achieve most of them before their target dates.

Business strategy dialogue

The businesses were responsible for developing and implementing their (approved) Business Strategy Dialogues (BSDs). The purpose of a BSD was to provide a consistent method and terminology to help structure the strategy development process and improve its quality. BSDs were mostly initiated by the business groups themselves, but were sometimes requested by corporate. They occurred at regular intervals of three years on average.

The BSD process consisted of five phases with several steps within each phase. The five phases were: Characterizing the Business Situation; Analyzing the Business System at Macro Level; Analyzing the Business System at Micro Level; Options and Strategic Choice and Action Planning and Performance Measurement (see Exhibit 3). But before a BSD could be started, some preparatory work had to be done.

Starting up   One of the first things to be done was to identify a facilitator and a challenger. To facilitate the implementation of the BSDs, Corporate had trained around 30 'facilitators' to support the business teams in its creative thinking process. They were selected from the top 350 executives and asked by the Chairman of DSM to become a facilitator. The task of a facilitator was to prepare the strategy development process with the business group director by defining the scope of the exercise, discussing the composition of the core team, examining the time schedule, drafting a list of important strategic issues, and appointing a project manager who was responsible for the operational part of the strategy development process. The most important role of the facilitator, however, was to make sure that the BSD led to real strategic options and a real choice, as expressed by Marthijn Jansen, facilitator:

The role of the facilitator is to make sure that the BSD focuses on the right issues, that in the 'options phase' the conversation diverges, and that in the defining of the KPIs phase, everything converges to a clear path and a clear view of the implications of the choices made.

In addition to a facilitator, a 'challenger' was selected. The challenger had an important role as he/she had to question the BSD team about the assumptions, analyses and conclusions it made. Challengers were chosen from the top 100 managers within DSM. In addition to the internal challenger, a business group could also ask 'outsiders' to challenge them on specific issues. These outsiders – often (technology) specialists – also shared their knowledge.

The core team in the BSD typically consisted of the complete business management team supported by specialists from further down the organization. They were advised not to have more than 10 to 12 people as management felt that larger groups did not allow for effective discussion and hampered the creativity of the process. In large or complicated businesses sub-groups were formed to address specific questions. The BSD process consisted of workshops and discussion sessions led by the facilitator. Input and participation by all concerned was considered very important.

Characterizing the business situation   The objective of this phase was to collect and structure the necessary information to be used as input to the BSD. The Group provided the businesses with a strategic data checklist of the information that might be useful for the BSD such as environmental and market analysis, competitor assessments and analysis of manufacturing, R&D, HRM, finance and processes. Data were supplied by functional discipline. In addition to data gathering, the checklist offered a useful format for summarizing and presenting the information. The data set was structured in accordance with questions such as:

◆ What business are you competing in?

◆ Which other businesses and products are you competing with?

◆ How attractive is the industry in terms of growth and profitability?

◆ What is your competitive position (benchmarks)?

◆ What are the dynamics? What trends can be expected in your business system?

Practice showed that this phase could take two to four months. Corporate management emphasized that the businesses should not view this information-gathering phase as a checklist exercise but rather approach it from an 'issue-driven' angle.

Analyzing the business system at macro level

In this phase, which took approximately two days, the industry in which the business unit competed was analyzed from the outside in, based on Porter's Five Forces model. The discussion focused on the examination of the value added in the business chain, the customers, the competitors, the business dynamics and the drivers of the industry. An important step was the analysis of the different generic strategies followed by key competitors. Understanding generic strategies forced the businesses to categorize the different ways in which a business could compete in the industry. A strategic group was defined as a cluster of companies following the same generic strategy. The outcome of this phase included a basic understanding of the 'rules of the game', i.e. the strategic groups in which the business might compete and a preliminary view of the key success factors (KSFs) that must be met in order to compete successfully within a certain strategic group.

Analyzing the business system at micro level

In this phase the organization was analyzed from the inside out, by looking at the internal process. Important tools for the analysis of the internal value chain were market segmentation, activity-based costing, internal or (preferably) external benchmarking of functions, and assessment of the technological position. The conclusions of the micro-discussion included an analysis of the business unit's capabilities – both strengths and weaknesses – to compete in its strategic group. This phase took on average two days.

Options and strategic choice

After having assessed the competitive environment and the business unit's capabilities to compete successfully in its environment, the outcome of both steps were compared, i.e. internal capabilities were compared with the list of KSFs (see Exhibit 4 for an example of DSM Melamine). This allowed the business to make a choice as to the strategic group in which it wanted to compete. Furthermore, it allowed the business to verify whether it really could serve the selected market segments and determine what steps were necessary to achieve or sustain leadership within the strategic group.

Action planning and performance measurement

Once the strategic choice had been made, the strategy had to be translated into an action plan and linked to performance measurement. Based on the strategic mission and objectives of the business unit a limited number of performance indicators that were important to the corresponding KSFs were selected. Performance indicators monitored the implementation of the strategy and were the measurable part of the KSFs, allowing comparisons with competitors and performance monitoring over time. Examples of performance indicators included market share, pipeline of products, quality, customer satisfaction, and cost per unit. The objective of performance measurement was to provide periodic information on the progress made toward the defined targets for each performance indicator. Furthermore, it helped management set objectives and target levels for the next period.

Annual strategic review (ASR)

The Annual Strategic Review (ASR) was performed by each business group, and comprised a progress report on the implementation of the BSD, an update or reassessment of major business risks, an updated sensitivity analysis and updated financial projections. The ASRs of the business groups constituted the building blocks of the corporate ASR whose purpose was to monitor the execution of the Corporate Strategy Dialogue. An important element in the review was the confirmation that the chosen strategy in the BSD was still valid and that the implementation was on track. Therefore, the validity of the main assumptions on which the strategy was based had to be checked and the consequences of changes in the business environment for the strategy evaluated.

Benefits and challenges of the BSD system

Benefits In 2000, six years after its implementation, the BSD had become an accepted system for developing business strategy. DSM management was pleased with the improved quality of strategy formulation and the team-building aspects. One business group director coming from outside DSM commented:

> The strategic planning process is very good at DSM. It is a robust and effective process. And it is a living system, contrary to many other companies where people just 'feed' the system.

Many people valued the 'challenger' part of the BSD, where someone from outside the business group challenged the assumptions and outcomes of the BSD. One business group director recalled:

> Corporate said to us: 'The BSD is nice but not rigorous enough. Come back when you have really looked at the intrinsic value of each market segment. Not at macro level, but at market segment level.' This was very good because it forced us to get a real grounding in segments.

People agreed that the BSD process greatly enhanced the insights and understanding of the business. In addition, it forced alignment, both across functions in the business unit and with respect to the strategy. Furthermore, people felt that the BSD gave legitimacy to initiate changes later on when the business got to the implementation phase. Another big advantage of the process was that strategy development became a three-yearly process with just an annual update. One top executive of corporate planning commented:

> Performing a BSD is a lot of work. But once you are done, you are done for two to three years.

Challenges The final phase of the BSD – translating strategy into performance measurement – remained a challenge. Hein Schreuder, Corporate Vice President Strategy & Development, expressed his concern:

> DSM invests heavily in a good strategic diagnosis, but the ultimate focus should be on delivery.

Although DSM had improved the quality of strategic thinking in the planning process, the question remained indeed how to link it with execution.

Value based business steering

In 2000, Henk van Dalen, Director of the DSM Polyethylenes business group, was appointed to the managing board. He believed that the necessary step to implement Vision 2005 and its promise for performance was a more intense focus on value-creation in the businesses. According to the newly introduced Value-Based-Business Steering (VBBS) concept, the overall target for DSM was to create value for all of its stakeholders, i.e. shareholders, employees, customers, and society.

DSM approached VBBS from three different angles. The first was accountability as the basis for financial control. The second was alignment of DSM's strategic business planning processes to materialize its promise for performance. The third was the introduction of new financial operating metrics that translated Vision 2005 and BSDs into economic value terms. DSM decided to start with the third angle because it had the biggest impact on the organization and was a first step in aligning strategy with performance measurement. As a result, VBBS was strongly driven by the finance department – at least initially.

New financial business steering metrics

A new set of performance metrics was developed for internally measuring and managing financial performance in terms of value-creation (see Appendix 1). Cash Flow Return on Investment (CFROI) became DSM's new yardstick for measuring the performance of its businesses. Contrary to other value-based management companies, DSM decided to use CFROI only for internal reporting and financial performance measurement, while ROI remained the performance measure for external reporting. A reason for this decision was that DSM felt that the complex CFROI calculations were difficult to explain to investors. Furthermore, DSM first wanted to see if the new metrics would work.

Total Shareholder Return was an important external performance indicator related to value-creation for DSM as a whole, but could not be directly linked to the performance of individual business groups. DSM chose to introduce Cash Value Added (CVA) to translate value-creation from a capital market point of view into an objective internal DSM measure. CVA represented the cash surplus generated ('value realized') by a business once all capital providers had been compensated. To determine the 'value created' by a business, DSM measured the increase in value (delta CVA) from year to year. Because DSM was a decentralized company, the group did not impose delta CVA targets; instead, target setting was done in a bottom-up fashion. To achieve a positive delta CVA and thus create value, a business could work on two key value drivers: by improving CFROI or by investing in profitable projects.

Investments were evaluated against the Internal Rate of Return (IRR) hurdle, i.e. the before-tax weighted average cost of capital (WACC). If an investment met the WACC hurdle, it created value. However, DSM imposed an additional performance standard by plotting the current business position and the historical performance of a business group on a so-called 'C-curve' (see Exhibit 5).

The C-curve provided a clear indication of the preferred route to value-creation for a business depending on its current return. Three basic scenarios could be distinguished. For businesses that generated returns below the WACC, restructuring and improving the return was priority number one. Businesses that had returns around the WACC needed to improve their performance and were encouraged to explore methods to increase CFROI. Finally, businesses that had returns well above the WACC found themselves in a position that was profitable; the way to create value for this kind of businesses was to grow while improving or maintaining CFROI.

Operationalizing VBBS Value-creation for DSM as a whole was translated into the internal value-creation measure delta CVA. This measure could be applied at the business group level, but also at lower levels such as business units or product/market combinations. The next step in the VBBS process was to translate the abstract concept of value-creation into operational actions using the concept of value drivers. DSM defined a value driver as an 'operational variable which can be influenced by acts of management and which has a direct link with value-creation.' Examples of value drivers included: working capital as a percentage of sales, raw material costs per ton, production costs per ton, and sales price per ton.

At this stage, the difference between value drivers and performance indicators became clear. Performance indicators were developed during the BSD and monitored the implementation of the strategy. Value drivers were developed during the VBBS analyses and monitored how the implemented strategy resulted in economic value-creation. Performance indicators applied to the strategic and tactical level and provided early warning signs ('leading indicators'). In contrast, value drivers applied to the operational level of the organization and were financial and often results-based and therefore 'lagging indicators'.

Value drivers and performance indicators did not necessarily have a one-to-one relationship. One performance indicator (e.g. market share) could influence multiple value drivers (e.g., volume, margin, cost), and vice versa, one value driver could be affected by several performance indicators. For the commodity businesses, value drivers and performance indicators often covered the same variables. For example, a value driver could be cost per ton, while the corresponding performance indicator would be a relative measure – costs compared to competitors. However, the link was much less clear for the specialty activities where factors such as the management of the innovation pipeline would be decisive for success. There could be a significant time lag between the filling of the pipeline with new products and the value-creation caused by higher sales volume resulting from these new products.

Once the metrics were defined and the concept of VBBS was clear, DSM started with the strategic assessment of its various businesses. These assessments yielded valuable new insights into the positioning of specific businesses. For example, some businesses that accounting wise (i.e., based on ROI) looked like diamonds in the portfolio, turned out to be value-destroying businesses from a CFROI perspective. Loek Radix, Director of Corporate Finance, explained:

I was almost physically attacked when I delivered that message. But the strategic assessments were a huge eye-opener about how we should manage a certain type of business. Before, there was an atmosphere of complacency in successful businesses. There was no mindset at all about delta value. However, it is not important what today's value is; it is important what the evolution in value is.

Although people got excited about the results from the VBBS assessments, implementing the new metrics and coming up with value drivers turned out to be a technically difficult and time consuming process. Although the consultants were able to explain the concept of CFROI and CVA, translating this into specific measures was extremely complex. According to Radix:

The sweaty part starts when you really have to develop the metrics in detail. Questions like: 'What do I do with foreign investment?' or 'What is the percentage of economic depreciation?' were difficult to answer. We had to re-define items during the process. That was not really helping us in the introduction of VBBS and we got pushback from the operating managers.

In early 2002, the general knowledge of the VBBS system in the DSM organization was still limited. Although top management understood the big picture, a survey testing more detailed knowledge showed that even at the executive level a lot still had to be learned. One corporate manager estimated that it would take three to five years for people to really understand and work with the new system. However, at corporate level, VBBS thinking had already significantly changed the strategic approach vis-à-vis the businesses. Whereas previously corporate finance used to strive for consensus, the department was now more able to challenge the businesses, helped by the C-curve. According to Radix:

Before we had a culture of managing conflict in our department. Now we are able to say, 'No, we don't agree, we oppose this investment.' We now challenge businesses whose CFROI is above the WACC to grow, and we refuse to give additional investment money to businesses whose CFROI is below WACC. We now say 'If you don't have 8% CFROI, then your first task is to get that CFROI before you get money for investments.' As a business unit manager you can no longer say: 'I will grow out of the misery.' VBBS and the C-curve really helped to challenge in a different way.

More than new metrics: creating strategic alignment through strategic value contracts

Although VBBS within DSM was still very much metrics oriented, right from the early days DSM was aware that it was much more than just adopting new metrics: DSM management felt that it gave them the tools and insights to align the business strategies to performance measurement. The connection between strategy and performance measurement was made by elaborating the BSD into Strategic Value Contracts (SVCs).

From 2001 on, each new BSD had to result in a SVC. A SVC was a summary of the main conclusions of a BSD translated into measurable targets for the next three years. It contained two main sections which had to be explicitly approved by the managing board: 1) bottom line results focusing on CFROI and CVA and the breakdown thereof in controllable value drivers, and 2) strategic goals laid down in the strategic mission and the implementation specified in terms of key success factors, performance indicators and strategic milestones. Thus, both performance indicators for monitoring strategy implementation, and value-based measures for monitoring value-creation were incorporated into the contract. Future performance of the business would be monitored against the agreed-upon SVC.

DSM felt that the SVC was a strong communication tool and helped the implementation of strategy and VBBS at the business group levels. It explained the steps of how businesses were planning to execute their strategy. This led to more transparency and helped the management board ask the right questions and challenge the business groups. One management board member explained:

What always had frustrated me about the BSD was that a strategy was developed, but monitoring the implementation of this strategy was difficult. I am very pleased with the Strategic Value Contract because people are now forced to implement the strategy. Now, people really have to finish the BSD. That is much clearer.

The SVC was signed by the business group director and the business group referee in the managing board, who signed on behalf of the entire managing board. A successor taking over responsibility for someone's business also had to take over the existing SVC. Proposals for substantial modifications to the contract could only result from major changes in the business environment and had to be approved by the managing board. In early 2002, two business groups had their SVC and five other contracts were in progress. By 2003, nearly all business groups had their SVC.

Compensation

In the past, not meeting targets was widely tolerated at DSM, largely as a result of the fact that DSM had been a cyclical company where 90% of the businesses results were beyond the firm's control. DSM management felt that it had to change this 'culture of excuse' and high level of 'cyclicality tolerance' as DSM transformed into a specialties company. The implementation of SVCs supported this change in culture.

DSM felt that the next step in the implementation of VBBS was to link it with the managers' performance evaluation system. In 2002, it rolled out a new performance appraisal system for its executives which evaluated managers based on their ability to develop sustainable strategies and get them approved (BSD), the achievement of targets set in the SVC, and a number of enabling factors, such as having the right processes and workforce in place. The management board evaluated the top 30 executives, who in turn appraised the managers below them. This appraisal was used to determine managers' salary evolution.

The second element of the compensation system was a short-term incentive program which ranged from 20% to 30% on top of the base salary. This incentive scheme was linked to VBBS by replacing

ROI with delta CVA and calculating bonuses based on the current year's delta CVA. Thus, executive compensation was linked both to personal targets and to financial performance measures, such as CFROI, delta CVA and CVA. Lower management was held responsible for the relevant value drivers. Finally, DSM introduced a personnel share option scheme alongside the existing management option scheme in 2001.

When SVCs and the new performance appraisal system were first introduced, managers felt uncomfortable as the pressure on them gradually mounted. On the other hand, the contracts made it clear what was expected of them and improved communication both between the business groups and Corporate and within the business group itself. SVCs also led to a demand from the business group directors with respect to key individuals in their organization. Previously, corporate HR had the authority to move people around and managers typically changed jobs every 18 months to two years. Under the new system, however, some business group directors claimed that they were unable to achieve their SVC targets if they could not keep their key managers. DSM management therefore decided that employees would not move around for a period of three years, but also stated that business group directors had 'corporate' responsibilities in terms of training and follow up of people.

In 2002, DSM was unable to meet its ambitious profitability targets due to unfavorable economic developments. However, a number of corporate improvement targets relating to safety, health and the environment, and a number of targets linked to the Group's strategy were realized. The overall realization was 20%. Moreover, the Supervisory Board had used its discretionary powers to grant an additional bonus to the members of the Managing Board amounting to 10% of their fixed annual salary, in recognition of their extraordinary efforts in strategically repositioning the company.[3]

The BSD and VBBS process at work at DSM Melamine

The DSM Melamine business group was part of the 'Industrial Chemicals' cluster. It was the global

---

[3] Source: DSM Annual Report 2002, page 43.

leader in the manufacturing and marketing of melamine, supplying almost one third of global demand. Melamine is a heat- and scratch-resistant plastic mainly used in impregnating resins and adhesive resins for laminated flooring and panels in the wood-processing industry. It is also used in car paints, durable plastic tableware, euro bank notes, and flame-retardants. The gas-phase production technology that DSM Melamine used to produce melamine was a proprietary technology developed in 1967 and was a highly sophisticated process technology. The raw materials for the production of melamine were natural gas, ammonia, carbon dioxide, and urea. Since ammonia and carbon dioxide were by-products of melamine production, melamine plants had to be built close to a urea plant.

In 2001, world consumption of melamine was nearly 700,000 metric tons, valued at approximately $700 million. DSM Melamine was well established with advanced production plants on three continents and a sophisticated technical support system in place for its customers. In 2002, DSM Melamine's image was one of a global reliable supplier of 'hassle-free' product in Europe, Americas, and Asia Pacific. It earned more than half of its sales from long-term contracts with large customers who considered melamine a strategic purchase item and valued security of supply.

The melamine market was subject to high volatility. Demand for most downstream markets for melamine was greatly influenced by general economic conditions. Consequently, demand followed the fortunes of the leading world economies. Furthermore, demand and capacity had not always been in balance, leading to significant price fluctuations. In 1998, for example, the melamine market was characterized by supply shortages caused by technical problems at several melamine producers worldwide. High imports from overseas by melamine consumers via traders raised spot prices to levels of €3,500/ton. In 1999, however, prices collapsed to €800–900/ton. One of the major challenges for melamine producers was therefore to balance supply and demand.

Forecasting demand was not sufficient, however. An accurate estimate of global melamine supply was also needed to avoid major under- or over-supply. This was hard to predict because of the many unplanned maintenance shutdowns at several melamine producers worldwide. The management of DSM Melamine had worked hard to improve its estimates of capacity utilization vis-à-vis global nameplate capacity.

The early BSDs

DSM Melamine started in 1992 with its first BSD, followed by others in 1995 and 1999. The BSD process proved to be very helpful in addressing the problems and challenges the business group was facing and dramatically changed its performance (see Exhibit 6 for the C-curve for DSM Melamine for the period 1992–1997).

BSD 1992 The main outcome of the 1992 BSD was the final approval of a US$80 million project to dismantle a relatively new melamine plant at Geleen in the Netherlands, and reconstruct it in Indonesia. DSM Melamine had made the decision to build the plant in Geleen in 1989 when it predicted a 5% annual growth in melamine in Europe. However, since then melamine sales and prices in Western Europe had declined as demand in key markets in the former Soviet Union stagnated and exports to Eastern Europe slumped. The management team of DSM Melamine had to decide whether to close, sell, or relocate the plant that had been built only in 1992. Management decided to rebuild it in Indonesia where its Jakarta-based business Joint Venture, DSM Kaltim Melamine, in which it had a 60% stake, would own and operate the plant. DSM had wanted to build a Southeast Asian melamine plant for some time as the Asia/Pacific region was a fairly new market that was developing at a fast pace, especially in countries with major wood-processing industries. The Geleen plant was dismantled in 1994 and rebuilt in Indonesia in 1997, thereby reducing the company's worldwide melamine capacity for three to four years. The plant was the largest melamine plant in the Far East and the first to be built in Southeast Asia.

BSD 1995 In 1995, the second BSD led to a major strategic breakthrough in the eyes of management. The strategy was to 'actively maintain' its global leadership position in terms of market share, technology, cost and customer image. Competition was based on 'price over volume' and DSM Melamine wanted to grow at the prevailing market rate. A breakthrough in the BSD process occurred when DSM Melamine woke up to the fact that it did not have the right technology to grow with the market. Instead of continuing to build large plants with gas-phase production technology – which would cover the growth of the market for the next four to five years – management decided to acquire Shortened Liquid Phase (SLP) technology in 1997. This technology, which required fewer production steps to produce high-quality melamine, would enable DSM Melamine to build smaller plants while still being cost competitive with the traditional gas-phase plants. However, to achieve the same quality level as the melamine obtained in DSM's gas-phase process, the SLP technology had to be upgraded.

BSD 1999 In 1999, a third BSD was performed. The project motivated by the new review was to build a fourth Melamine plant in Geleen based on the new liquid phase technology, which required an investment of €90 million. A portion of that investment would be used to expand urea production at the site. The melamine plant was expected to come on-stream by end 2003.

The strategy that followed the 1999 BSD was to continue the 'actively maintain' strategy. Management of DSM Melamine expected worldwide consumption of melamine to grow by 5–6% per annum. This growth was concentrated in Europe and to a lesser extent Asia (China) and the Americas. Accordingly, DSM Melamine planned to expand its global capacity by 30kt every two to three years in addition to de-bottlenecking the existing plants.

Key success factors for the actively maintain strategy were 'lowest cost delivered' by de-bottlenecking existing gas-phase plants and new low cost technology, and 'security of sales'. The latter could be achieved by negotiating long-term contracts with global key customers, meeting the requirements for strategic customer alliances, and differentiating service levels.

The strategic value contract

In 2001, the first SVC was drafted for DSM Melamine. Since it was DSM's first experience with these contracts, it was primarily viewed as a learning experience. The subsequent 2003 contract, signed in September 2002, was considered the first 'real' contract. It was based on the 1999 BSD and would be revised at the end of 2003, once the 2003 BSD was finished. (Exhibit 7 shows an extract of the SVC for the period 1999–2003.)

The 2003 BSD process

The 2003 BSD was initiated by the management of DSM Melamine (DMM), as the Annual Strategic Review of 2002 had shown that its current strategy would not enable the business group to achieve the ambitious targets set forth in the SVC. Projections by DMM showed that the group would have a zero or negative delta CVA from 2004 onwards and reach a major negative delta CVA in 2007. These calculations were based on assumptions from the corporate planning group which had predicted a major economic slowdown for 2007.

In addition, the environment had changed considerably. After experiencing strong demand in 1998 and most of 2000, melamine markets declined or remained stagnant in most regions in 2001. High natural gas costs, lower margins, depressed demand, and significant capacity additions during 1998–2001 forced many melamine producers to curtail production in 2001. Producers such as Melamine Chemicals and Namhae Chemical exited the market. However, industry experts expected the demand for melamine in the US and Western Europe to recover and grow at nearly 3% per year from 2001 to 2006. Demand in Southeast Asia, particularly in China, was expected to experience much higher growth rates because of increasing production of laminates for both domestic use and exports. In the 1999 BSD, DMM had not actively looked into China, as the main investment opportunities were seen to be in Europe (see Exhibit 8 for regional growth forecasts and realization). However, because of the impressive annual growth rate (15%) of the Chinese melamine market, the management of DMM wanted to investigate the impact of China on its current strategy.

Kick-off The BSD 2003 of DMM started with a kick-off meeting in September 2002 with the BSD global management team, including the management team from Sittard, the general manager of America, the general manager of Indonesia, and the facilitator. Although the facilitator typically came from outside the business group, DMM decided to ask its own Director of Planning and Projects, Marthijn Jansen, to act as facilitator. In his former function at corporate planning, Mr. Jansen had been facilitator for various business groups and was therefore perceived as very experienced in this role. He was expected to spend half of his time on the BSD process for a period of six months. The challenger, Jos Goessens, Business Group Director of Plastic and Engineering, was asked to join the BSD team in January 2003.

One of the criticisms of previous BSDs was that people felt that they were used to 'sell' a project to top management. The BSD team wanted to prevent this from happening again in 2003 and therefore stressed the importance of challenging each other during the whole process and making a serious effort at identifying alternatives.

As DMM wanted to perform an 'issue-driven' BSD, the BSD team started with identifying the subjects on which they thought decisions were needed. A total of 35 issues were identified ranging from subjects such as marketing & sales, operations, R&D, personnel & organization, and finance, to regional issues related to DMM Indonesia, America, Europe, and China. The next step was to decide which information was needed on these issues to make decisions and who should provide it.

Value teams The BSD team decided to create so-called 'value teams' for each issue, who were responsible for gathering information (i.e. phase I of the BSD – characterizing the business situation) and performing phase II (i.e., analyzing the business system at macro level). By implementing value teams DMM wanted to involve as many people as possible in the BSD process, thereby creating a large platform for the BSD. The value teams presented the results of phase I and II to the BSD team in December 2002. The micro analysis was finalized in February 2003. The next phase was options and strategic choice (phase IV).

Options and strategic choice A main point of discussion in the BSD 2003 was DSM Melamine's position in the US, Indonesia and China. Its 50-50 joint venture with Cytec was the largest player in

the US with the highest prices. However, the business was not profitable because of high raw material costs. DSM Melamine had the best plant in the world located in Indonesia, but profits there were unsatisfactory due to unstable raw material supply and the negative impact on demand of the Asian crisis. Consequently, it was unable to realize the low cost production necessary. Furthermore, DSM Melamine did not yet have a position in China, which the marketing managers viewed as the fastest growing market.

Management felt that the existing 'actively maintain' strategy may no longer be the best, especially since VBBS required businesses to deliver a positive delta CVA every year. According to one of the managers at DMM:

> VBBS has its limits. It is nice for a start-up business but for a mature business it is very difficult to produce a positive delta CVA year after year. It is not easy to create value within a three-year contract in a business like melamine where it takes two to four years for a plant to be operational. So VBBS can lead to short-termism. You have the choice to either increase CFROI on the existing asset base by cutting costs or raising prices, or you can increase the asset base. However, the latter takes more time and involves greater risk.
>
> If DSM did not have VBBS, we would probably continue with our current 'actively maintain' strategy.

In February, after the macro and micro session, management felt that it should present Corporate with the basic choice to either grow the business – as Dijkman and his team felt that they had reached the limits of cost reduction – or otherwise divest.

Growing the business

In the ASR 2002, it was concluded that DSM Melamine could grow faster than was currently the case but that it lacked the capacity to do so. Management wondered if it should be more aggressive and investigated growth opportunities in, for example, Trinidad, a Caribbean island with natural gas production, the Middle East, Europe, and China (see Exhibit 10 for the choice on growth ambitions, ranging from 'give up market share' to 'aggressive growth'). In Europe, DMM's main competitors, such as Agrolinz, were following 'grow/build' scenarios in response to growing worldwide demand. Leon Halders, Vice-President Marketing & Sales DSM Melamine, noted:

Our two main competitors in Europe are growing heavily, one is tripling and the other is doubling. They are not part of a large company like DSM, but part of a company where melamine is the most attractive business. Melamine is profitable, but because we are part of DSM with a certain strategic mission, we are not the spearhead of DSM strategy.

Although DMM had looked into several growth options, China still seemed the most natural and promising market because of its high growth rates. However, questions remained. First of all there was the question of how DMM, which positioned itself as a main supplier, should enter the Chinese market which was currently a spot market. Another issue was the fact that DMM's existing customers had no significant production base yet in China, which meant that it would have to build a customer base. Finally, a wave of capacity expansion in 2004–2006 was expected to result in oversupply. According to industry analysts, approximately 210 thousand metric tons of melamine was added between 1998–2001, with China accounting for nearly half of new capacity. If all announced capacity expansions were completed, global capacity utilization was expected to fall to approximately 80% in 2006 from 86% in 1998. Some anticipated melamine projects were likely to be postponed or cancelled as a result. But, despite the above challenges, the BSD team still believed in major growth opportunities in China.

As DSM Melamine's financial performance exceeded the WACC, requests for investment to build new melamine plants were justifiable from a VBBS point of view. Dijkman, however, wondered if corporate management would agree with this new strategy, as it was not in line with DSM's corporate strategy of becoming a specialties company. Furthermore, investments in melamine plants always involved large amounts of money (between 50 and 100 million euro), which in the first few years would significantly lower DMM's CFROI.

The corporate perspective on DSM Melamine

At corporate level, DSM management faced a dilemma. From a financial perspective and in line with VBBS principles, investments in DSM Melamine would make perfect sense. On the other hand, following the corporate strategy of becoming a specialty company, one could question how much more to invest in the remaining commodities business such as melamine. It was also important to think through how investors and analysts would react if DSM were to invest further in its melamine business. Earlier in 2003, the management board had already committed to a €50 million proposal of Caprolactam, its other remaining commodity business.

Another issue confronting the management board was the permanent challenge of balancing short-term requirements and long-term value. Big investments would significantly lower DMM's CFROI and only increase CVA in the long-term.

While debating the dilemma on the growth opportunities for DSM Melamine, however, Corporate was also challenging the business on the cost side. It agreed that DSM Melamine had a good low cost position, but as one corporate executive explained:

We push DSM Melamine. The business has excellent low costs but we are not interested in costs per ton. We would like DSM Melamine to benchmark itself against competitors in its BSD 2003 so that they can see their relative cost position.

The broader issues In addition to the strategic issues facing DSM Melamine, Corporate also had to tackle the remaining challenges of the BSD and VBBS processes. First, VBBS implementation was heavily centralized in the sense that the corporate center, as opposed to the business groups, was driving the change. Although the corporate center had trained facilitators and provided tools to support the implementation, the process was complex and somewhat slow, with significant differences in progress on implementation between the various business groups. The question was how DSM could speed up the process. Top management hoped that the new appraisal system would help the implementation move forward.

Another concern related to how BSDs and SVCs could be effectively translated into specific actions and program management. Thus far, it had been entirely up to the business groups whether and how to operationalize the chosen strategy in terms of value drivers, or how to integrate the SVC with the performance measurement system such as the balanced scorecard. Business groups chose their own way to resolve these issues, with the outcome often being dependent on the consultant that had been hired.

The real test for the future was 'consequence management'. What should DSM do if a business group did not meet its contract, given DSM's historical culture of tolerance for mediocre performance?

Finally, there were some more fundamental questions. Implementing the new financial metrics had led to greater emphasis on short-term performance. DSM felt that this short-term focus could be hazardous for a specialty company that heavily depended on innovation and R&D. For example, in 2000 one of DSM's most successful and profitable products was Stanyl, a product which had been 10 years in development, with negative EPs throughout all those years. How would these kinds of investment projects be handled under the new approach?

Exhibit 1 Key figures on DSM

Balance Sheet (€million)	2002	2001
Fixed assets	3,639	4,442
Current assets	5,357	4,133
Total assets	8,996	8,575
Capital employed	4,570	5,763
Group equity	5,186	4,298
Provisions	682	809
Net debt	−1,038	867
Total group equity and liabilities	8,996	8,575

Income Statement (€million)	2002	2001
Ongoing Activities		
Net sales Life Science Products	2,168	2,237
Net sales Performance Materials	1,767	1,855
Net sales Polymers & Industrial Chemicals	1,268	1,302
Net sales Other Activities	433	357
Total, ongoing activities	5,636	5,751
Operating profit plus depreciation and amortization (EBITDA)	767	741
Operating profit (EBIT)	383	336
Capital expenditure (including acquisitions)	496	561
Discontinued activities		
Net sales	1,029	2,219
Operating profit plus depreciation and amortization (EBITDA)	125	301
Operating profit (EBIT)	67	185
Total		
Net sales	6,665	7,790
Operating profit plus depreciation and amortization (EBITDA)	892	1,042
Operating profit (EBIT)	450	521
Capital expenditure (including acquisitions)	536	652
Profit on ordinary activities after taxation	349	369
Net profit	1,188	1,415
Dividend	199	199
Depreciation and amortization	442	521
Cash flow	1,630	1,936
Workforce at 31 December	18,375	21,504

Exhibit 2 Organizational structure, as of March 2003

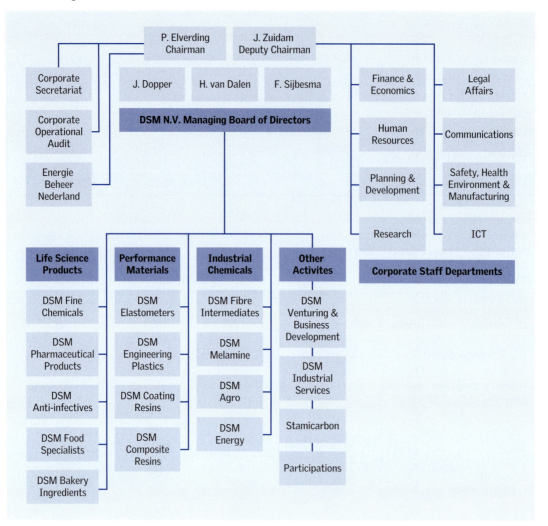

Exhibit 3 The strategy development process

Phase	I Business Situation	II Macro Business System	III MicroBusiness System	IV Options/ Strategic Choice	V Actions & Performance Measurement
Tools	Strategic data checklist	Facilitators	Facilitators	Facilitators	Management reporting format
Duration	2–4 months	2 days	2 days	1–2 days	Continuous
Objective	Gather basic information for BSD	Analyze business dynamics, drivers and strategic groups	Understand own capabilities, analyze strength/ weaknesses	Understand options, select performance indicators and targets	Continuously measure progress
Tasks	• Environmental and market analysis • Competitor assessment • Analysis of manufacturing, R&D, technology, HRM, finance, processes	• Discuss business chain • Analyze dynamics • Determine industry drivers • Characterize strategic groups	• Formulation and evaluation of options • Detailed KSF analysis • Qualifiers • Differentiators • Formulation of indicators • Targets from competitive benchmarking		• Progress control • Action plan • Target setting • Continuous improvement program
Output	• Document with required information • Strategy support database	• Strategic groups • Industry drivers	• Capabilities • Organizational/ HR assessment	• Strategic plan outline • Strategic mission • KSFs • Indicators • Targets	• Strategic contract versus targets

Exhibit 4 DSM Melamine: strategic groups, BSD 1999

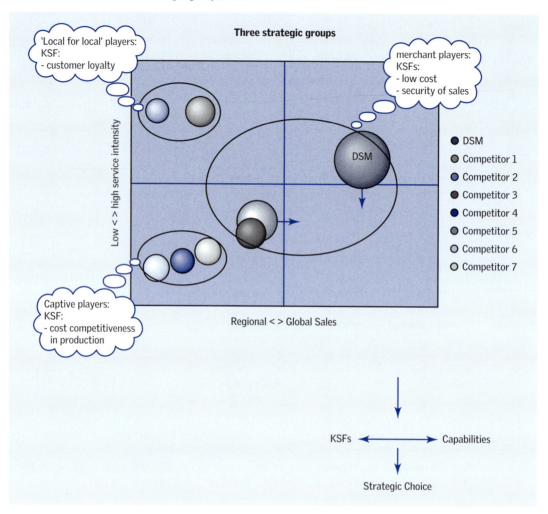

Exhibit 5 C-curve

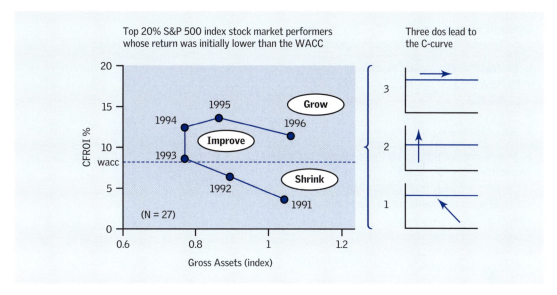

Exhibit 6 C-curve for DSM Melamine 1992–1997

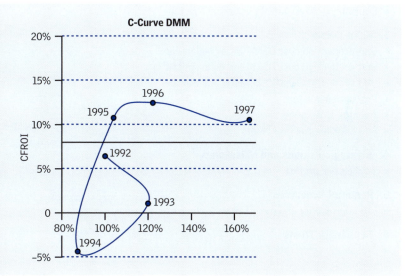

Gross Assets (Index: 1992 = 100)

Exhibit 7 Extract of the strategic value contract for DSM Melamine 1999–2003

Strategic mission.
Actively maintain global leadership in market share, technology, cost, and customer image.

1. Financial Performance Measures:
- EBITDA (m€)
- CFROI (%)
- CVA (m€)
- Delta CVA (m€)

2. Key Success Factors and Performance Indicators
Security of sales
- Long-term contract with global key-customers
- Meet the requirements for strategic customer alliances
- Differentiate service levels
- Volume sold under contract
- Share of Integrated Panel Producers
- Share global customers

Lower cost
- De-bottlenecking existing gas-phase plants
- New low cost technology
- Capability to Produce (CTP)
- Controllable fixed out of pocket cost/m ton

3. Value Drivers:
- Unit production cost DSM Kaltim Melamine
- Unit production cost DSM Melamine Americas
- Unit production cost DSM Melamine Europe
- Production volume
- Average sales price
- Sales volume existing plants

4. Strategic Actions and Milestones
- Defined per project

5. Required Resources
- Pre-approval for the next 3 years

6. Sensitivity Items
- Global utilization rate
- USD/EUR currency rate

Exhibit 8 BSD 1999 regional growth rates: forecasts versus realization

	1999 Forecast	1998–2002 Realization
Europe	4.0%	4.5%
Americas	5.4%	0.0%
Asia Pacific (APAC)	5.9%	2.9%
China	7.7%	33%

Exhibit 9 DSM Melamine choice on growth ambitions

Market Share Target			
20%	25%		30%
Give up market share	Organic growth	Active growth	Aggressive growth

• Price over volume
• 'Europe only'
• Lose market leadership
• Max short term cash
• Irreversible:
  – give up China
  – lose scale economies
  – technology standstill
  – competitors build
	• Organic growth with existing customer base
	• China as opportunity market only
	• No new production capacity
	• Accept gradual loss of market share
		• Gain market share
		• Access to new Integrated Panel Producers customers
		• Significant market share in China
		• Build lowest cost plant, leave high cost plant
		• Signal commitment to leadership
			• 'volume over price' policy for plant load
			• Secure lowest cost position worldwide
			• Acquisition may bring growth without price erosion

Appendix 1 Definition of Metrics

CFROI: The Cash Flow Return on Investment is a return measure that is the ratio of the Sustainable Cash Flow divided by the Gross Assets.

CVA: Cash Value Added is the Sustainable Cash Flow remaining after a reservation has been made for the capital charge. Formula: (CFROI − WACC) * Gross Assets.

EBITDA: Earnings Before Interest & Tax, Depreciation & Amortization. EBITDA equals the Revenue minus the Cost of Sales.

Gross Assets: The sum of all historical costs of the assets that are being used by a business plus Working Capital and Economic Goodwill paid for any acquired company.

IRR: Internal Rate of Return. Discounting of future cash flows to the year in which the planned investment is made.

ROI: Return on Investment. This is a return measure expressed as the ratio of the Operating Profit of a business and the Capital Employed.

Sustainable Cash Flow (SCF): EBITDA − Tax − Economic Depreciation + Other SCF from non-consolidated companies.

Total Shareholder Return (TSR): Dividend + stock value increase.

WACC: Weighted Average Cost of Capital is the average return on invested capital (debt and/or equity) that capital providers demand from a business. In the case of DSM, the WACC equals 8%.

INSEAD

Case 28 **Opening the gate on gatetrade.net: The making of the first Nordic B2B Marketplace (A)**

To be or not to be in the marketplace: September 2000

Gerda Norstrand, the number three executive at Post Danmark (PDK) the Danish postal service, looked back on the brief trimester that had passed since Carsten Lind, director of IT services, had come to her with a major piece of news. Three companies representing a significant share of the national economy – Danske Bank, TDC and Maersk Data – were en route to establishing the first online B2B marketplace in Denmark. Could and would PDK join their alliance?

From the start, Norstrand and her CEO, Helge Israelsen, were convinced that the online marketplace did fit with PDK's core business of logistics – a term which, for them, covered more than the traditional letters and parcels. It could also be an important strategic development for PDK in a new domain. PDK's board of directors and executive board agreed to proceed and Norstrand took PDK into the alliance that was forming.

....

This case was prepared by Dr. Mark Hunter, Senior Research Fellow at INSEAD, under the supervision of Dr. Yves L. Doz, The Timken Chaired Professor of Global Technology and Innovation and Professor of Business Policy. It is intended to be used as a basis for class discussion rather than to illustrate either effective or ineffective handling of an administrative situation.

Copyright © 2002 INSEAD, Fontainebleau, France.

12/2002-4986

Staying in the alliance, however, required the final approval of the board of directors. The timing of board meetings meant that by September 2000, PDK was the only alliance member that had not yet signed its shareholder agreement. As the crucial meeting approached when Norstrand and Israelsen would have to carry the board with them, victory seemed far from guaranteed. How could she and her boss persuade the board that this venture offered new markets for PDK's core businesses? And what other benefits could they point to?

Delta, Tango, and Coffee: Spring 2000

In the first months of 2000, Den Danske Bank's new senior vice-president for e-finance, John Andersen, wondered how his company could expand in the New Economy. The trick was to turn 'a threat into an opportunity,' he said.[1] Danske Bank needed more online products for its corporate clients, and its competitors were developing them too. Although it was the biggest bank in Denmark and the second-largest in the 'Nordic-plus' countries (Denmark, Sweden, Norway and Finland),[2] it needed to grow beyond that base – virtually, if not physically.

There was top-level commitment behind Andersen's search. In 1999, Danske Bank announced that 'internet distribution [would] compete with and partly replace' its traditional outlets, such as retail branches.[3] By the end of 2000, one quarter of all securities transactions through the bank would be done via the Internet.[4] A major part of the bank's future was online – yet for the moment it was overwhelmingly a bricks-and-mortar company. The Danske Securities division, its online leader, had a

....

[1] Mr. Andersen was interviewed by David Midgley, Professor of Marketing at INSEAD, in May 2001. We gratefully acknowledge his permission to use his notes.

[2] By year-end 2000, following a merger with RealDanmark, Danske Bank disposed of 626 branches in Denmark, 67 in Norway, 42 in Sweden, plus branches in the U.K., U.S., and Germany, and subsidiary banks in Luxembourg and Poland. Ibid., p. 6.

[3] Den Danske Bank Annual Report 1999, p. 9.

[4] Danske Bank Annual Report 2000, pp. 6, 24.

turnover of just 242 million Danish kroner (Dkr)[5] in 2000 – a sliver compared to the 3.5 billion Dkr of the traditional retail banking sector and overall income of 18 billion Dkr.[6]

Andersen knew that some of Danske Bank's competencies – in areas like electronic transaction systems, databases, and call centers – would be valuable assets in any online project, but those core skills would not suffice for some of the opportunities Andersen had begun studying during a visit to the United States. On his return, he began meeting regularly with executives from two other Danish blue-chip companies, looking for an idea they could develop together.

They called themselves the 'Delta Tango' group, but because they were still working on an informal basis one member dubbed them 'the coffee group'. Danske Bank was already a partner with one player – Maersk Data, the information technology (IT) subsidiary of the A.P. Moller group, the most powerful industrial and shipping conglomerate in Denmark.[7]

Maersk Data, a group in itself, owned all or part of eleven New Economy firms, including the data warehousing company DMdata, a 50-50 joint venture with Danske Bank. The bank was also DMdata's biggest customer. Though Maersk Data was still relatively small, with net revenues of 125 million Dkr on turnover of 1.68 billion Dkr in 1999, CEO Steen H. Knudsen aimed at nothing less than making his company 'world-class' by providing clients with 'any IT service they require.'[8]

The group was completed by Frank Olesen, senior vice-president for corporate strategy at Tele Danmark (soon to be renamed TDC)[9], the recently privatized Danish national telecoms company for which Andersen had previously worked. A giant in the Danish economy, TDC's market capitalization of 119 billion Dkr – twice the value of its shares only two years earlier – represented over one-fifth of all the capital on the Danish KFX stock exchange. But Olesen felt the company had to exploit the Internet more or risk seeing its annual growth rate of nearly 16% fall.

For him, Internet technologies were a 'game changer' that would soon transform entire industries and value chains. Communications, transactions and content would become a single industry, based on data moving via Internet protocols. There were powerful signs in his own company that the shift was underway. TDC's core businesses in mobile and fixed telephones and networks were reaching maturity. In stark contrast, Internet services and traffic had increased by 79% in 1999, along with a 114% burst in revenues from high-speed ISDN lines.[10] And while voice traffic on TDC's network grew only 3% annually, data traffic was exploding at the rate of 5-10% *per month*.[11] In Internet lingo, TDC needed 'more like this.'

Olesen thought TDC's best chance in the New Economy lay in 'alliances focussed on strategic assets that each partner can bring, and how these assets fertilize each other.'[12] The other options – like intensifying product development in-house, or outsourcing it – didn't seem as promising to him. The problem wasn't just developing new products but getting them to market, he said: 'The list of products that the market can hold is larger than what we can do alone.' But in fact, TDC had barely any experience with alliances. It was time, thought Olesen, 'to learn to operate in an environment where partnerships and alliances are part of daily life.'

The members of Delta Tango were part of a homogenous culture whose corporate elite is a small club. In that circle, violations of the 'Jante Law,' a national tradition that bans boasting or American-style shows of affluence, are frowned upon; so are attempts to build independent networks outside

---

[5] The exchange rate for the kroner versus the U.S. dollar on May 22, 2001 was 8.61 Dkr = 1 $US.

[6] Op. cit., Danske Bank Annual Report 2000, pp. 7, 21.

[7] The A.P. Moller Group's 1999 revenues were over 49 billion Dkr. Source: Preliminary accounts 2000, A/S Dampskibsselskabet Svendbord, Dampskisselskabet AF 1912 A/S.

[8] 'About the Maersk Data Group – business principles.' Via www.maerskdata.com/mdw/en/business.nsf/nval/$First.

[9] On April 26, 2001, Tele Danmark A/S officially changed its name to TDC A/S.

[10] Ibid., p. 29.

[11] Private communication, May 2001.

[12] Interviewed May 1, 2001. All quotes from interview, unless otherwise specified.

the club. Steeped in those values, the group quickly found common ground, said Olesen:

> In terms of corporate culture and values, the three companies do have some similarities – a relatively conservative approach, a thorough approach … not the habit of undertaking very risky projects. Not a high degree of risk aversion but prudence as to what we go into. … [So] we sit together, discuss opportunities, and find we think similarly and have the same picture of the future. But where should we start?

The first list: February–March 2000

By February, the Delta Tango group had narrowed its focus to four areas: Wireless (WAP) applications for portable telephones (such as an Internet portal, plus consumer and business services), e-commerce, systems integration services, and standardized workstations.

The latter two offered big markets that already existed: systems integration services alone were already worth over 10 billion Dkr annually in Scandinavia and the market was expected to double within three years. But there was tough competition from established providers. Likewise, computer and electronics industry heavyweights were fighting over the hardware side of the workstation market, while pushing their own software solutions. Though Delta Tango were confident that they could develop attractive services in both markets, they reckoned that earnings would be low.

WAP applications and e-commerce offered new and far larger fields. Of the two, WAP seemed more interesting. International Data Corporation, a respected New Economy research company, estimated that WAP applications would generate 40 billion Dkr in turnover across Scandinavia within eight years. Delta Tango thought they could capture one quarter of that revenue. Only another alliance could provide all the assets and skills that were required to get in the game – and none had yet appeared. Delta Tango's large existing customer base might be enticed onto a WAP portal. And the first-mover advantage would be worth 15% of the market.

But the risks included development costs that were hard to predict – a problem that applied

equally to e-commerce. The major cost for WAP was developing 'content' – information, services and a portal. That would absorb half of revenues for at least three years, while Delta Tango's members confronted a steep learning curve. Notwithstanding, the group favoured higher risks and higher returns, and recommended going for WAP applications. E-commerce was consigned to fourth place on the list.

Listening to the Oracle: Spring 2000

Back in January 2000, product manager Stig Brandt of Oracle Denmark – a subsidiary of the California-based Oracle Corporation, the world's leading supplier of information management software[13] – had noticed that Danske Bank was expanding online. He made a cold call on the bank to pitch Oracle's solutions for financial services. In the next meeting, he recalled:

> We talked about how Danske Bank could achieve higher customer retention by establishing a B2B marketplace – a list of things like order services and financial services, hosting, trade validation online, escrow services on the Internet. These were the services we could offer through our platform.[14]

B2B marketplaces – Internet-based exchanges of goods and services among companies – were the hottest topic in the New Economy. They represented 'simply the next generation of productivity growth for the United States economy,' said a participant in a landmark Federal Trade Commission conference in June 2000.[15]

The reasoning behind that claim looked rock-solid: In the U.S. alone, B2B transactions accounted for 85% of the $20 trillion in annual exchanges of goods and services, according to the Federal Department

---

[13] Oracle's revenues in 2000 were $US10.1 billion. See www.oracle.com/corporate/overview/.

[14] Interviewed May 1, 2001. All quotations from interview, unless otherwise specified.

[15] Staff of the Federal Trade Commission, 'Entering the 21st Century: Competition Policy in the World of B2B Electronic Marketplaces.' Washington, Oct. 2000, p. 7. Despite a tone of unrelenting optimism among participants, this report can be considered essential reading for anyone interested in this subject.

of Commerce. Moving those deals online promised to shave up to 90% off transaction costs by streamlining or eliminating paperwork, handling and other processes.

And the shift seemed to be underway. In 1999, Forrester Research estimated that $109 billion worth of B2B deals were done through the Internet and predicted that the figure would grow to $1.3 trillion by 2003. The IT advisory firm Gartner Group was even more optimistic: it said the turnover would be no less than $7.2 trillion and that 7,500 B2B marketplaces would be competing for that action.[16] At the time, there were only 300 B2B marketplaces worldwide. If the pundits were right, this was a gigantic opportunity for new players.

But Andersen felt that the idea made sense only if there were partners. He brought it to the Delta Tango group, which had considered e-commerce before choosing WAP applications. Danske Bank changed the situation, said Olesen: 'E-commerce and B2B became number one of the priorities.' A meeting was set to begin drawing up detailed plans in June.

The Post gets the message: June 2000

At Post Danmark, IT director Carsten Lind was implementing an unrelated project with Oracle. He heard about the meeting and got himself invited. As it happened, he said, 'I was doing the identical business case for a hypothetical B2B marketplace with the Post as a major player, or the only player.'[17] He concluded that the Post couldn't do it alone – nor, he said, could any of the eventual gatetrade.net owners: 'What is a B2B exchange? A financial flow, a physical flow, and an information flow. None of these companies on their own can supply that skill set.'

Unlike the others in the group, PDK is a public service company – in legal terms, an 'independent public company' whose sole shareholder is the Danish Ministry of Transportation. But it had already declared its intention to become a limited liability company with its capital open to the private sector.[18] Since 1995, PDK it had been operating like

a private company in some ways, publicly reporting net profit of 285 million Dkr on turnover of 10.8 billion in 1999.[19] Yet in the public mind it remained a government bureaucracy. 'I say we're like a private company, but who knows it?' commented Gerda Norstrand, Lind's boss.

Like other state-owned companies in the European Union, market liberalisation exposed PDK to new threats, including a price war with delivery companies like Federal Express,[20] not to mention the Deutsche Post and Royal Mail. PDK responded by diversifying into internet, warehousing, international and remail operations but with mixed success: by 1999 it owned between 25% and 100% of six subsidiaries with combined losses of 29 million Dkr.[21] Nonetheless, sales dropped in parcel delivery, PDK's second most important revenue stream.[22] An inside position in a B2B marketplace could change that trend, thought Norstrand: 'Being part of the marketplace, we would see what kind of new services are needed, so we're better able to meet demands in our core business.'

Norstrand believed that the Internet would change PDK's core business in any case: 'We think in two years all our parcels will be IT parcels – registered electronically in one way or another.' PDK had just introduced its WebPack service, offering electronic track-and-trace of parcels to small businesses. It wanted to turn its offline PFS service (the Danish acronym for 'the Post's dispatch system') into an

---

16 Op. cit., 'B2B Marketplaces in the New Economy', p. 2.

17 Currently CEO of Transynergy. Interviewed May 2, 2001.

18 Post Danmark, 'Annual Report and Accounts 2000', p. 12.

19 Post Danmark, 'Annual Report and Accounts 1999', p. 12.

20 'All Post Danmark's important competitors in Denmark are now attached to international networks which have sufficient strength to create a large competitive power and consequently cause a price war in the Danish market.' Op. cit., 'Annual Report and Accounts 2000', p. 15.

21 These ventures included the remail companies Belgian Mailhouse BV, Scandinavian Distribution and Postal Service A/S, and Nordic Mail AB; the courrier company Budstikken Transport A/S; Pan Nordic Logistics AB, a parcel distribution service; Weblogistics A/S, a distribution and warehousing service for e-commerce companies; and Billetnet A/S, an online ticket service. PDK owned between 33 and 100% of each. See Post Danmark, 'Annual Report and Accounts 2000', p. 38.

22 While PDK's turnover in parcels increased by 1.9% in 1999, sales fell 3.4%, partly because of an increase in the weight limit for letters to 2kg. Ibid., p. 13.

online product for major corporations, too. Joining the new marketplace in the 'fine company' of Denmark's biggest companies could speed up that move, said Lind: 'You'd be branded with those people and their customers.'

Behind their thoughts was the fact that there wasn't room for many B2B marketplaces in Denmark. If only one could succeed, Norstrand wanted PDK's logistics infrastructure to be part of it. At the June meeting, Lind argued that without a ready-to-go logistics wing, a marketplace would never fly:

> My card was, with all the problems dot-coms had with fulfilment [of online orders], I said, 'Why not build an exchange that differs in that we have end-to-end control for the users? They can get all logistics services from one point integrated into the engine.'

Lind came back with a first victory: PDK was admitted into a project team that would make the business case for a B2B marketplace. Said Lind, 'We wrote a memo of understanding so no partners would get married to someone else. We had it a month but nobody signed it. But there was trust that nobody would exit.'

Backing out would carry invisible but high costs for whoever tried it. In Denmark, a small country that has historically faced expansionist threats from its neighbors Germany and Sweden, keeping one's word and sticking together are ingrained survival traits. They are also crucial to business reputations. 'We have a saying: "A man is a man and a word is a word," ' noted Andersen. 'A lot of deals have been closed on that phrase.' And with four of the biggest companies in Denmark at the table, no one wanted to break his word to the others.

The key word in everyone's mind was 'speed.' Said Brandt, 'It was very important to close down other initiatives, so that nobody came in from outside [Denmark]. That was my argument: "Close the market, be the first mover, and expand." '

A matter of goals: June 2000

The Delta Tango group became a project team of 15, with members from all four companies, plus Oracle. Said Lind, 'In that period of constructing, TDC,

PDK and Danske Bank were putting in lots of hours. Danske Bank was the strongest player because they're financially very strong. Maersk Data was not as present.'

Some of the others sensed that Maersk Data might not need them as much as they needed Maersk Data. Its in-house expertise covered logistics, retail and other IT systems, as well as Web development. And Maersk Data belonged to a group that owned massive logistics capabilities, plus immense financial resources. In short, it could assemble most of the necessary assets for a marketplace itself. Moreover, only Maersk Data already had the hot New Economy image that the others – all known as conservative, traditional companies – wanted for themselves.

When conflict emerged, however, it was on other grounds. Some members didn't understand that Oracle was providing a standard platform and thought they would have to underwrite a major development project. Once Oracle had walked the group through the technical solutions, another difference appeared. Said Brandt:

> It depends on what kind of people you put in. Danske Bank put in business people – they did not focus on functions, they focussed on business value. PDK put in IT people. If you talk to IT people, they look at problems. The business people look at opportunities. . . . If you're four different players from different areas, they don't have a common knowledge of the main goal.

Unlike PDK or TDC, the alliance was 'not strategic to us as such,' said Kenn Herskind Jorgensen, president of Maersk Data's subsidiary Venture IT, who represented his group on the project committee. 'It's not part of our core business,' he explained. 'One of the challenges in that alliance is we're a venture company. We make money on dividends or exits. And we don't want to get trapped by not being able to exit.'

As Herskind – and to some extent, Danske Bank – saw it, the point was to profit from the marketplace, even if that meant giving it up someday:

> A likely scenario is that, if successful, we would be approached by one or more internationals – other online marketplaces – to make an alliance

or an acquisition. What's going to happen is a smaller number of online marketplaces, international consolidation. If we're buying paper, why not link to other marketplaces to source internationally? The technology supports that. It won't happen overnight but we'll see consolidation. And I would go for having it acquired.

Maersk Data also had a major interest in the IT that would be developed and implemented here. Much of its revenue came from consulting, and a win here would enhance its reputation in a hot sector of the Web. Oracle, too, wanted that prize, said Brandt: 'Marketplace operations are very new, and they're secretive about their experiences. Maybe because their experiences are not so good – or because their knowledge is valuable. If you have a success, the elements will be very valuable to sell.'

Olesen, too, was looking far down the road: 'At the time of decision-making, I don't think TDC considered the amount of profit.' One of his concerns was keeping an eye on Maersk Data, whom Olesen considered 'a potential competitor'. Someday soon, he thought, Maersk Data might move from IT services to telecoms infrastructures, which was TDC's core business:

One of the more forward elements of the value chain is applications. Our competitors are moving to these elements and using them to gain customer relationships. When they have customer relationships in the forward parts of the value chain, they use that to work back to the infrastructure. I see that constantly with our competitors: very often it's IT companies, with systems integration and applications expertise. In that sense, Maersk Data is a competitor of TDC. I think it was an underlying understanding of both parties.

Olesen hoped the marketplace could lead to future collaborations with Maersk Data – a vision he considered 'quite compelling.' Herskind saw it, too: 'TDC and us could have done this alone, strategy- and tech-wise.' But TDC was aware that an alliance with Maersk Data could be even more risky than outright competition. The close relations between Maersk and Danske Bank might put TDC at a permanent disadvantage.

Danske Bank saw the venture as a way to extend its leadership in cash management solutions throughout the Nordic countries. Cash management involves sophisticated methods of routing cash, netting balances and computing interest, plus some IT integration between a bank and its clients. The integration increases customer retention because access to the cash flows of large companies opens doors to additional banking business. Likewise, a B2B marketplace could begin with online procurement, then push for IT systems integration between its customers and Danske Bank's financial services. The bank would grow closer to its major clients.

Moreover, the marketplace would provide 'a new product in the basket' when Danske Bank called on potential customers, said Andersen. He was thinking of new value-added services like digital certificates, payment guarantees, online credit evaluation, credit scoring and invoice handling. Finally, as Brandt suggested, it might offer the bank an opportunity to do more business with the public sector, which was looking for ways to cut its procurement costs – exactly the benefits a B2B marketplace could provide.

Making the business model: June–July 2000

Oracle now took the lead in writing the business case, with Lind and Maersk Data closely involved. Olesen recalled: 'A key strategic decision – the founding decision – was that the marketplace is a process improvement company.' Unlike many online marketplaces, this one would not only function as an auction platform whose main benefit is to knock a few points off prices, Olesen explained:

Our vision was improving processes for buyers and sellers. Auctions [alone] won't facilitate that. It is trading, where the integration of the ERP [enterprise resource planning] systems of the buyer and seller are key – into the warehousing, distribution, and financial systems of buyer and seller. You improve the processes throughout the full value chain, removing costs for both buyer and seller. We are not in the price game.... The price will be lower, but that's a secondary effect. The real benefit is in the processes.

That idea appealed to PDK's purchasing director, Holger B. Nielsen, who wanted to see 'hard benefits' from the marketplace. Nielsen had already used online procurement to reduce the Post's grocery supply transaction costs by 90%. He estimated that an overall online procurement system at the Post would pay for itself in a year 'if people use it for every transaction. Even at 50% [of all transactions], it's a winning proposition.'

A second crucial decision was led by Danske Bank, recalled Brandt. This would be a 'horizontal' marketplace offering goods from different sectors, not a 'vertical' exchange serving one industry. A vertical marketplace carried the risk that a minority of suppliers would quickly establish dominance, thus scaring away new vendors. And it would be far harder to scale up into new industries or new territories.

However, a horizontal marketplace requires a catalogue structure – the only means by which buyers can compare multiple sources and specifications for similar products on a computer screen. The decision of whether they should create their own catalogues, or simply 'aggregate' suppliers' existing catalogues, remained open.

The catalogue issue raised a concern for Post Danmark, which as a public entity is subject to European Union government procurement rules. These rules dictate that purchases over a minimum level be made through tenders.[23] They were written before online marketplaces existed and made no provision for the supply chain integration processes that were at the heart of the exchange's future development. Thus PDK might find it legally impossible to fully profit from the marketplace, a fact that was acknowledged in the business case but not resolved.

The business case called on the owners to build liquidity quickly by channeling a maximum of their non-strategic procurement (goods that are not essential to production) through the marketplace. Ultimately, the goal was for each owner to put all their non-strategic purchasing on the marketplace, but they formally committed to putting in a 20–25% share of these purchases.

It wasn't an equal load for each partner, noted Olesen: 'There is a clear indication of who will be doing the most purchasing on the marketplace – us, because we have the most non-strategic buying.' A rough calculation[24] shows that TDC could put a maximum of about 1.5 billion Dkr of purchases on the marketplace, followed by the Post, at about 1 billion. Maersk Data, in contrast, could not approach those figures. 'We weren't expected to compensate,' said Herskind. 'At the time we were the drivers – that's a significant contribution, to get the thing off the ground.'

The allies' best guess was that value-added services (VAS) could generate between one quarter and half the venture's revenues after a year. The business plan mentioned logistics and financial services such as payment, billing and collection, or credit rating and approval. Supply-chain management through integration between the marketplace and its customers' back-end systems was also evoked. But it could not be predicted which VAS would be feasible, technically or commercially. Marketplaces around the world were still trying to discover the answer to that question.

Left unsaid was that each partner could provide services that could also be provided by another partner, or by the marketplace itself. For example, TDC offered electronic signature certification. PDK had created a similar service, then dropped it. The marketplace might be a chance for PDK to try again. However, there was a real possibility that the value-added services would be captured primarily by Maersk Data.

What *was* spelled out was that any deals between the marketplace and its owners had to be conducted on an 'arm's length' basis, according to 'sound commercial principles'. No owner could be compelled to purchase anything in gatetrade.net (as the marketplace would be called) that it could buy cheaper elsewhere, and no owner could force services upon the marketplace.

But, Herskind wondered, what if one of the owners had the choice between passing a deal to gatetrade.net and getting 25% of the revenue, or keeping it in-house?

---

[23] The limit is 1.6 million Dkr, or about $US200,000.

[24] Approximately one-third of all business purchases are non-strategic goods, and in 2000, TDC reported 4.6 billion Dkr in purchases of goods and services.

If a Norwegian marketplace comes to us to host it, and gatetrade.net could do it, do we put it in there or do it ourselves? A similar case came up – two, in fact – one for us, the other at TDC. Small cases. They came up during the formation period, before the launch. That was a danger. Our CEO saw that and said, 'I'll give that up, put it in gatetrade.net. But I expect if that happens for you guys, you'll do the same.' TDC did the same. [But] if this were a $1 billion order, what would you do? Keep it, or share it with your partners?

Oracle in question: August 2000

As the business case neared completion, Oracle was threatened by a counter-proposal from IBM, which the founders seriously considered for several weeks. Despite its driving role from the start, Oracle was perceived by some as 'a partner without financial commitment,' in Holger Nielsen's phrase. Its risks were limited to the licensing fees it would lose if the project failed. And Maersk Data believed that the price Oracle charged for its software license and consulting was too high.

Brandt countered that Oracle was making a strategic commitment: under no circumstances would it work with another marketplace in Scandinavia. Moreover, he pointed out that under Oracle's deal with gatetrade.net, 'The more liquidity and trade on the marketplace, the more license fees we get. So we will do whatever we have to do to make gatetrade.net successful.'

Oracle's supporters within the alliance raised the following points, summarized by Herskind, who led the re-negotiations with Oracle:

We not only needed the solution – we needed an international brand. Everything associated with this platform had to be associated with quality and professionalism. People are very dubious about going online. Some of the suppliers are really small – 100, 200 people. We had to be sure that everything they saw was something they recognized. That was part of the marketing strategy. And the business case still works.

But the debate remained unresolved as the allies drew up a shareholder agreement. Oracle or not, they were going ahead.

The core of the business: September 2000

Gerda Norstrand considered the shareholder agreement's terms. Each of the four founders put in 25 million Dkr for a 25% share of the capital. Any one of the founders could exit, but the others retained a right of first refusal on the shares and a right of approval of new investors. PDK had joined exclusive company as an equal.

But to move forward, the change represented by gatetrade.net must now be accepted by both the board and employees. The investment was minimal for a company of PDK's size and Norstrand had no doubt it would pay off in the short and long term. She believed gatetrade.net would be profitable and that it would reinforce PDK's existing investments in online procurement. It would also complement PDK's portfolio of ventures in parcel distribution and warehousing. The experience gained, in terms of making alliances work and exploring a new industry, would be very valuable. And if the core letter and parcel businesses were indeed going online, like everything else, PDK had to be there or watch its business migrate elsewhere.

Was she right? Was the business case strong enough to prove her point? And were these the allies PDK needed to take her company into new markets and synergies?

Exhibit 1 Gatetrade co-founder portraits

Maersk Data: The Importance of Being Somebody

In Denmark, the name 'Maersk' denotes the heart of the A.P. Moller Group, the country's most powerful industrial and shipping conglomerate. Maersk Sealand, Maersk Air, Maersk Olie og Gas and Maersk Data contributed some 30 billion Dkr to A.P. Moller's total 84 billion Dkr (about 10.5 billion $US) of revenue in 2000.

The Maersk corporate culture takes careful groundwork and execution as a given, and disdains publicity. In the latter regard Maersk Data is an exception within the group. It was originally created in 1970 to service the information technology (IT) needs of A.P. Moller. By the end of the 1980s, Maersk Data graduated from an internal division to a separate corporation with subsidiaries in the US and Japan. A decade later, it owned all or part of 28 companies in seven different countries, including 11 New Economy ventures spanning a range from B2C e-commerce to data warehousing and web design. And it began to seek wider recognition, arguing that if it weren't known to other venture capital players, it wouldn't get invited to the table when major deals went down.

In keeping with Maersk style, however, the shift was anything but impulsive. With the approval of its parent, Maersk Data was running a real-world experiment in the benefits of getting attention from the media – a strategy that included gatetrade.net. The New Economy was growing within A.P. Moller in more ways than one.

Den Danske Bank: Straining at the Seams of Denmark

How big can you get in Denmark? In 2000, following a merger with its competitor RealDenmark, Danske Bank had 626 branches on Danish soil, about four-fifths of its worldwide presence. Its 3 million retail customers were equivalent to about 60% of the Danish population. If Dansk bank wanted to grow, it had to move further and faster abroad and into new business sectors.

It was moving from a solid, profitable base. At the end of 2000, the bank held assets of over 1.3 trillion Dkr. Its activities were divided into six core sectors – mortgages, retail banking, wholesale banking, insurance and pensions, investment banking, and investment management. In 2000, every one of those sectors showed significant earnings growth – in the case of retail banking, 86%. Income was 26 billion Dkr (up from 22 billion Dkr the previous year), and net profit was over 6 billion Dkr. For shareholders, Danske Bank had provided an annual 27% return on capital (including dividends) since 1995.

Could Danske Bank keep it up? Pressure was growing from competitors like Nordea, the largest financial conglomerate in Scandinavia, with 10 million retail customers. By no coincidence, Nordea announced, as gatetrade.net got underway, that it was keeping a close watch on the venture. Danske Bank had to move fast and well.

TDC: How Far Can You Spread on Your Own?

Following its privatization in 1995, the former Tele Danmark placed foreign acquisitions at the core of its strategy. By the end of 2000, nearly half of its 47 billion Dkr in annual revenues – twice its revenues in 1996 – came from TDC's subsidiaries abroad. And between 1997 and 2000 the company's customer base nearly doubled to 11.5 million accounts by adding mobile and landline subscribers in Switzerland, Poland, Lithuania, the Czech Republic, Hungary, Austria, Belgium, the Netherlands and Germany.

However, TDC's domestic revenues were nearly flat in 2000, growing slightly from 21 to 22 billion Dkr, as its traditional core telephony business reached maturity. Competition abroad was fierce, notably in Switzerland, where the newly-renamed TDC captured 13% of the mobile telephone market, and 26% of the landline business from the established operator, Swisscom, by the end of 2000.

TDC Switzerland was one of seven business divisions around which the company reorganized in 2000. The others included a broadband and communications solutions provider, a mobile operator, an Internet division, a directories publisher, a cable-TV operator, and TDC Services, which mainly supported the other divisions. While they shared common expertise in network technologies, each division had a different geographic focus: the Internet branch concentrated mainly on Denmark and Switzerland, the directories branch aimed at the Nordic region, and the mobile operator bought third-generation UMTS licenses from the Netherlands to Poland.

TDC was fighting on numerous industrial, service and territorial fronts. Could it secure its gains without allies?

Post Danmark: Beyond Letters and Parcels

In 2000, Post Danmark (PDK) faced changes in its business and culture that could fairly be called revolutionary. The European Union's goal of 'liberalizing' public service monopolies forced PDK to confront the likelihood that, in the near future, its exclusive rights to carry letters and parcels would apply only to the smallest and least profitable. Meanwhile, as PDK's annual report predicted, 'Competition will intensify from other countries' postal operators', not to mention the likes of Federal Express.

The Post's executives argued that PDK would ultimately have to 'be converted into a limited liability company' with capital open to the private sector. But consensus on this goal, let alone how to achieve it, was limited. Public service employees, who represented some 40% of PDK's workforce of 30,000, were reluctant to change their status and privileges. Nor was it clear that PDK would be a great success as a listed corporation: Only once in the years 1996-2000 did either its growth or its operating profit margin exceed 5%.

In this context, PDK's strategy of investing in acquisitions or start-ups on the edges of its core logistics business – including an online ticket service, software for electronic parcel services, and e-commerce warehousing – revealed not only its ambitions, but the human and financial constraints on them. PDK, too, had to move toward the future, but not too far or fast at once.

Exhibit 2 The promise and trials of B2B marketplaces

Online B2B marketplaces can be simply defined as Internet-driven exchanges, in which buyers and sellers are brought together through auction or catalogue sales.

The added value of the concept resides in cost reductions. By exchanging information electronically, both buyers and sellers can streamline paperwork and handling of orders. Comparing multiple vendor offerings online makes it possible for buyers to negotiate better prices. Conversely, sellers can find new customers through an exchange at less expense than through tradeshow exhibits or in-person calls.

There are currently about 1,000 e-marketplaces in operation. 'Vertical' operations service a single industry, while 'horizontal' marketplaces span several sectors. Within those broad categories, marketplaces are mainly distinguished by their business models. 'Buyer-driven' marketplaces are exemplified by Covisint, founded by General Motors, Ford, and DaimlerChrysler in 2000 to rationalize supply processes and prices across the automobile industry.[25] 'Seller-driven' marketplaces like PlasticsNet.com, which deliver qualified leads to buyers, often represent a defensive response to the power of buyers. There are

---

[25] See www.covisint.com for the exchange's own view of its operations and ambitions.

specialists in B2B auctions, like the used equipment marketplace Tradeout.com. 'Reverse auctioneers' such as Freemarkets.com are used by buyers to post offers, with sellers bidding down the price until a deal is made. Catalogue aggregators offer comparisons of different list prices (which may then be negotiated) and specifications across product categories.[26]

Whatever the type, marketplaces generally derive revenues from membership fees, transaction fees, or services (such as logistics and industry information). Their greatest current appeal is that they help drive down prices, by putting suppliers in competition. Ford says that it saved $US70 million over one year in process costs and price reductions through Covisint, and that these savings 'easily' covered its investment in the exchange (which Ford did not disclose).[27]

The future benefits of e-marketplaces, it is promised, will be far greater – maybe even 'the next generation of productivity growth for [the] economy.'[28] Once users' enterprise resource planning (ERP) systems are linked to an exchange, control of manufacturing, inventory, logistics and warehousing can be streamlined. Managers can clamp down on 'maverick' buying – purchases made outside company procurement guidelines, which have been estimated to account for between 30% and 50% of corporate procurement.[29] Ultimately, buyers and sellers might jointly develop products and services, using data from the exchange to model future needs.

There is a precedent for these claims in the decade-old creation of electronic data interchange (EDI) systems, private networks designed to foster supply chain integration between a large company and its suppliers. The retail giant Wal-Mart, a pioneer in this domain, reportedly used EDI to lower costs by up to 95% and to stay in close touch with consumer demand. But as equities analyst Todd C. Weller noted, 'EDI has never achieved critical mass due to its proprietary nature, lack of flexibility, and significant investment requirements.'[30]

E-marketplaces promise many of the benefits of such private systems at a far lower cost – plus a stupefying business opportunity. The U.S. Department of Commerce estimates that B2B transactions account for 85% of the $20 trillion in annual exchanges of goods and services in that country. For some observers, the question is when – not if – a giant share of those B2B transactions will migrate online.

In a now-famous prediction, the IT advisory company Gartner Group said that by 2003 the turnover on B2B exchanges would be no less than $7.2 trillion, and that 7,500 marketplaces would be competing for the action.[31] Software application providers like Ariba predicted a dire fate for those who resisted the trend: 'Ultimately, all businesses will buy on a marketplace, sell on a marketplace, host a marketplace, or be marginalized by a marketplace.'[32]

[26] These categories are partially adapted from a glossary published by NetMarkets.com at http://www.nmm.com/nm101-b2basics/index.asp, which has the merit of categorizing e-marketplaces or 'net exchanges' by their functions. A standard nomenclature for this industry, like the industry itself, is still under development.

[27] See Carlos Grande, 'Ford recoups investment in Covisint web exchange.' *Financial Times*, July 1, 2001 (via www.ft.com).

[28] Staff of the Federal Trade Commission, 'Entering the 21st Century: Competition Policy in the World of B2B Electronic Marketplaces.' Washington, Oct. 2000, p. 7. The document summarizes a landmark FTC-sponsored conference. Though the quote reflects the often uncritical optimism among participants, this report can be considered essential reading on the subject.

[29] The lower figure is drawn from 'Entering the 21st Century', p. 25. Consultants such as Carsten Sennov, a vice president of Cap Gemini Denmark, consider 50 percent a more likely figure for maverick buying, noting that 'the larger and more dispersed the organization, the more maverick buying there is.'

[30] Todd C. Weller, 'B to B Commerce: The Rise of Marketplaces', Legg Mason Equity Research, Spring 2000, p. 4.

[31] Ariba, 'B2B Marketplaces in the New Economy', Mountain View, CA, March 7, 2000, p. 2.

[32] Ibid.

Perhaps – but meanwhile software providers have discovered that creating stable and highly functional marketplace platforms is a daunting task.[33] 'Suppliers remain leery of the pressure [exchanges] will put on prices,' notes the *Washington Post*.[34] And after the energy marketplace Pepmarket.com shut down in March 2001 with losses of $1.4 million, president Jay Demarest commented that buyers and sellers alike were 'just not ready to adopt that technology in daily business processes yet.'[35]

As the U.S. Federal Trade Commission noted, 'The most important requisite for the survival of a B2B marketplace is to have sufficient transaction volume.'[36] The same could be said for the industry as a whole. Once e-marketplaces become a standard way of doing business, and can deliver on their promises, the sector will surely explode. At the same time, it will very likely see intense consolidation (as is already happening in the online logistics market). But as with dot-coms, it is taking longer and proving more difficult than the New Economy prophets foresaw.

Exhibit 3 The pricing of Gatetrade.net

Devising the pricing model for gatetrade.net was 'one of the key issues – and coming up with it was a difficult exercise,' said Kenn Herskind Jorgensen, president of Maersk Data subsidiary Venture IT and a gatetrade.net board member. In fact, it is still ongoing, especially where value-added services are concerned, as we'll see shortly.

1. Buying and Selling: the Basic Fee Structure

The guiding principles behind gatetrade.net's fee structure were two-fold: encourage customers to enter by reducing up-front costs, and discourage them from exiting by increasing their investment in the marketplace over time. But the founders realized that there was no ideal, ready-made way to set the fees, said Herskind:

> Oracle did a lot of numbers, we looked at the market prices, then we did the groundwork in groups. The fine-tuning was done [later on] by the management. We didn't go out and do models, scenarios, downside protection analysis. We threw the numbers on the table, had discussions and said, 'This is it.' We could've done it a million ways. We thought, focus on kroner, like the customers. Look at what any purchasing person is looking for: 'If I buy 100 kroner's worth on gatetrade.net, what does it cost me to buy?'

The first cost to the customer is a one-time registration fee of 10,000 Dkr, plus an annual subscription fee of 1,000 Dkr per user. (In other words, a corporation with 10 purchasing agents using gatetrade.net pays 10,000 Dkr annually, in addition to the registration fee.)

Placing a tender offer or auction on gatetrade.net costs 2,500 Dkr. The marketplace also takes a commission fee of up to 100,000 Dkr on each completed auction from the seller, based on a sliding rate of 0.5%–2% (the bigger the deal, the less the percentage). For example, a 'lot' of computers auctioned through gatetrade.net for 10 million Dkr will cost the seller 2,500 Dkr to place the auction, and 20,000 Dkr in commissions – a total of 22,500 Dkr (assuming that the seller has already registered with the marketplace).

Catalogue users pay no commissions on their purchases through gatetrade.net; instead, they pay 6 Dkr for each 'document', or catalogue search. Suppliers, however, pay a commission of between 1% and 0.2%

---

[33] For example, in May 2001, a promotional event sponsored by Ariba at Las Vegas became the occasion for public criticism of the company. See Mark Jones, 'Ariba Strives to Prove it's Still in the Game', www.infoworld.com, May 4, 2001.

[34] 'Business-to-business e-commerce arena faces shakeout', Washington Post, May 7, 2001 (via Internet).

[35] Erich Luening and Margaret Kane, 'Why B2B went bust', CNET News.com , May 7, 2001 (via Internet).

[36] Op. cit., 'Entering the 21st Century', p. 20.

based on their average number and volume of transactions annually: the greater the size of both, the less the commission.

Thus a supplier who does 25 million Dkr of business on gatetrade.net, but with an average transaction value under 1000 Dkr, will pay 200,000 Dkr in commissions – a rate of 0.8%. A supplier with the same overall volume, but whose average transaction value is 50,000 Dkr, pays 137,500 Dkr in commissions, or 0.55%. This raises a customer relations issue: if you were the first supplier, would you try to negotiate a better rate?

Suppliers also absorb catalogue costs, starting with 5 Dkr per 'stock keeping unit' (SKU), or separate item hosted. Use of the Requisite Corporation's 'e-merge' catalogue creation tool costs between 3 and 5 Dkr per item, depending on volume (and may be negotiated). Gatetrade.net will create catalogues for the customer at approximately 16 Dkr per item – its own cost for making this content. In other words, catalogue costs – the most significant upfront expense by far – are kept to a minimum, though gatetrade.net passes them on to the customer.

2. What Price for Value-added Services (VAS)?

Recall that gatetrade.net's business case foresaw that value-added services would generate between 25% and 50% of revenues within a year. The founders also realized that VAS create an exit barrier for customers because each service deepens the customer's dependence on the marketplace. But which services should a marketplace provide, and what can it charge for them?

The first VAS for gatetrade.net were planned to be online by the end of 2001 – financial services such as certification, payment guarantees, online credit evaluation, credit scoring and invoice handling, plus supply chain management and logistics. Billing and revenue collection would follow. (Gatetrade.net hoped to capture interest revenue, based on the time elapsed between collecting payments from buyers and disbursing the monies to sellers.)

Eventually, gatetrade.net could also look at ways of packaging and selling data from transactions as 'marketplace intelligence' (in other words, 'whom buys what from whom'). However, respecting clients' confidentiality would impose certain limits. For example, gatetrade.net could not reveal the transactions of specific customers, only movements within industry segments.

In an address to the Oracle Postal Forum at Brussels on 11 December 2000, Gerda Norstrand of Post Danmark noted that a major VAS domain would involve integration between gatetrade.net and customers' back-end systems. 'This entails a range of solutions,' she said, 'spanning from very individualized ones to big businesses, to almost 'plug-in' solutions to smaller businesses.' Creating those solutions would lead to implementation and other IT services, as well as what Norstrand called 'an educational process to make such companies understand the real rationale' behind the marketplace. That process, too, would be a billable service.

But it remains unknown what price gatetrade.net or its partners will charge for such services; in September 2001, no standard fees for VAS appeared on its site. This discretion – or in some cases, secrecy – is typical of e-marketplaces in general. Quite simply, there are no benchmark prices for VAS in the industry. This reflects the ferocious competition among exchanges to capture and keep customers, which entails that fees for services be quietly negotiated rather than published. It also reflects the fact that until more marketplaces get past the start-up phase and begin to deliver measurable benefits, no one can specify the real worth to their customers of specific services.

What this means is that gatetrade.net, like other e-marketplaces, will have to rely partly on trial-and-error to learn what its VAS are worth to clients. And it will have to do so quickly because, as its management is aware, over time value-added services are increasingly regarded by customers as basic services whose delivery should be included in the registration fee.

Case 29 **The consulting industry in the new world of information**

Does the internet change everything? The impact of the internet on consulting has been widely reported (Brown, Colvin, Moran, Stepanek). The main thrust of these reports is that the old guard just doesn't get it, leading to the influx of a new breed of firms with a different consulting model for an e-services market estimated to grow from $12.9 billion in 1999 to $80 billion in 2003 (Stepanek). There are a number of important differences from the traditional approach and assumptions in the consulting industry.

First, e-business demands consulting at much faster speed. First-mover advantage and high levels of uncertainty make it more important for companies to iterate, learn and reiterate:

> There is no time for separate advice, the situation demands an approach of do, learn and adjust. (Financial Times, July 2000)

This has led to a typical engagement of 90–180 days, compared to the many months or even years spent on enterprise resource planning (ERP), the mainstay of consulting revenues in the 1990s (Stepanek). Fees are more likely to be on a fixed project basis than the time-plus-costs model, which encourages overruns. The greater number of projects carried out in a year also accelerates learning.

Second, technology and strategy are now completely intertwined. Added to the need for speed, this demands an integrated approach that combines business strategy, creative design and technological implementation within the same cross-functional team. Teams tend to be smaller, comprising 12–18 consultants rather than the small armies of ERP projects (Sammer).

Third, the consultant-client relationship is changing; e-business firms are often much more intimately involved with the organisations they advise.

This case study is extracted from an MBA Projectal by Simon Kitchen 'Connections in the Wireless World', Warwick Business School September 2000.

© John McGee & Simon Kitchen, 2000, Warwick Business School.

Equity in exchange for consulting is a common practice and e-firms can take on the entire operational requirements or incubation of a dot.com start-up. This kind of *total immersion* is much closer to the behaviour of venture capitalists and represents a significant departure from the detached independence of the traditionalists (Colvin).

Fourth, given that talent is a key resource, e-firms have succeeded in attracting the brightest and the best from business schools (Hamel). This can be explained by differences in ownership structure and culture. Most e-firms are publicly quoted and offer stock options to all staff. This is in sharp contrast to structures in which up-or-out rules apply and only the partners at the apex of the organisation can hope to share in the greatest rewards (Milgrom and Roberts offer an explanation based on agency theory for this apparent disincentive). The culture of e-firms is much more relaxed, with no strict dress code, less travel and 'sexy' working environments (Sweeney 2000). They also have a compelling sense of vision, with Sapient, for example, claiming it is 'changing the way *the world* works' (Sapient). The combined effect of all these can be seen in staff attrition, with Scient claiming a rate of 11% versus an industry average of 25% (Scient). The skills shortage that exists in e-business is even more marked in the wireless arena where very few people have any experience of the complex blend of skills required.

How successful has been this new breed of e-firms? They have enjoyed triple-digit growth (Stepanek), with approximately 80% of their business coming from Fortune 1000 companies, the hunting ground of traditional consultants. According to a Forrester survey, 76% of companies do not look to their usual suppliers for advice on e-business, although the size of projects is typically much smaller at $1–3 million (Sweeney). E-firms may also be guilty of claiming more than they actually deliver: even the top performers in a survey of FTSE 500 clients earn unimpressive scores. No single provider offers an end-to-end service and there is a perceived need for firms to help structure complementary offerings (Forrester Research).

Response of the incumbents

Almost every firm has either repositioned itself as internet-savvy or set up a discrete e-business practice.

Andersen Consulting claims that 30–40% of its projects now have e-commerce content (Brown 1999), and IBM's e-business services were worth $3 billion last year (IBM 2000b). Andersen has created its own venture capital unit and McKinsey is taking a stake in some of its own clients for the first time. McKinsey are also adopting 'parallel processing', with strategic framing and implementation happening concurrently, and less data-driven analysis (Sweeney). Andersen, McKinsey and PricewaterhouseCoopers (PwC) are exploring the use of internal talent exchanges in an attempt to retain staff by giving them greater control over their own careers. Many firms are adopting new compensation models with greater risk-based elements, such as PwC's share unit plan (Sammer). Andersen has almost doubled its number of partners (Kennedy Information Research Group). All of this suggests that the incumbents recognise the need to remould themselves, if they are to provide picks and shovels for the internet Gold Rush. However, to replicate the capabilities of the upstarts, they need to realign themselves on many dimensions, not just one or two. Of course, that is much harder with a large organisation, with its embedded values and structure, than it is when starting from scratch.

Enter the vendors

The threat to consulting incumbents is not confined to the e-firms. Many hardware and software vendors are attempting to move up the food chain and emulate the success of IBM Global Services:

> All equipment vendors are moving towards a solution-selling focus that helps customers harness value from products more quickly. (Arnold et al.)

In the wireless space, almost every vendor claims to offer consulting as part of its end-to-end service. Some, like Ericsson Business Consulting created in January 1999 (Baladi), are quite explicit about their objectives:

> Ericsson is undergoing a fundamental shift from being a technology supplier to also becoming a leading consultancy. (www.ericsson.com August 2000)

There are several motivations for these moves. In the new economy, information is the most valuable element and consulting offers higher margins than selling boxes. Vendors also recognise that consultants wield considerable influence over the purchasing decision for hardware and software. By moving into that space, they can gain significant pull-through revenues. For example, IBM operates on the basis that for every $ in consulting fees, $3 will be generated for other services and products (IBM 2000a).

Scale and scope, mergers and acquisitions

Although the emergence of new competition is reshaping the consulting industry, its effects are only beginning to be felt on the incumbent oligopoly shown in Table 1. Taking O'Shea and Madigan's estimate of the total value of the global consulting market as $62 billion, the 10-firm concentration ratio is 78% and the five-firm ratio is 51%. As Segal-Horn predicted, economies of scale and scope mean that the largest multi-national firms enjoy a huge concentration of market power. Despite their rapid organic growth, the e-firms are still minnows by comparison – Sapient, one of the largest, has 2,800 employees and revenues of only $319 million.

Consolidation seems set to continue with a recent spate of mergers, acquisitions, alliances and joint ventures. Cap Gemini has acquired Ernst & Young for $5 billion (echoing the purchase of AT Kearney by EDS in 1995). Andersen and Microsoft have combined to form Avenade, which plans to have 5,000 consultants helping to sell Microsoft-based internet services (Colvin). From the vendor side, Hewlett-Packard has announced plans to buy PwC for £14 billion (Sunday Times, September 2000). Cisco has invested $835 million for a 5% stake in a joint venture with Cap Gemini, and taken a 20% stake in KPMG. This is indicative of its strategy to partner with services firms in ecosystems, rather than build up an internal consulting practice (Consulting Magazine, March 2000).

A separate driver at work is regulatory pressure by the SEC in the United States for accounting firms to divest their consulting arms, because of the potential for conflict of interest. This lies behind KPMG Consulting's planned partial flotation at $2.5 billion (Consulting Magazine, September 2000).

Table 1 Consulting firms by revenue

FIRM	REVENUE $m	CONSULTANTS	$REV per CONS
IBM (est)	8,043	65,000	123,738
ANDERSEN	7,514	53,248	141,113
PwC	7,170	40,560	176,775
DELOITTE	5,050	28,625	176,419
ERNST & YOUNG	4,050	17,348	233,456
CSC	3,640	22,000	165,455
KPMG	3,500	17,000	205,882
CAP GEMINI	3,161	25,337	124,758
McKINSEY	2,900	5,670	511,464
MERCER	1,950	14,100	138,298
ARTHUR ANDERSEN	1,400	9,810	142,712

Source: Colvin.

The telco view

The attitude of telcos to vendors may be critical for the relationship between consulting and the wireless world. As we have already noted, vendors favour deep relationships across global markets with one or two other key vendors, with perhaps occasional strategic input from a specialist. Other suppliers are regarded as point solution providers, to whom the primary vendor may decide to subcontract some elements (IBM 2000a). If telcos, rather than brands, portals or enterprises, are the key players in this space, these conservative attitudes will make it very difficult for consulting firms to gain a foothold without the aid of the telco equipment vendors.

Sense and respond?

To enjoy economies of scale and scope, consulting firms leverage their knowledge and offer services with minimum customisation to their clients. This underpins their business model, with large numbers of young inexperienced consultants charged at high hourly rates feeding the high income of a few senior consultants. At worst, this can result in projects where little more than the name is changed from one client to the next (O'Shea and Madigan). This model may prove inadequate in an environment characterised by high levels of instability. The challenge will be to develop a more dynamic approach that enables clients to feel they are getting a service tailored to their individual needs.

Strategic groups

One could group consulting firms based on any number of factors such as size, ownership structure, market segmentation and so on. Figure 1 shows a grouping along two dimensions: product/service focus and speed of response. Focus means the degree of specialisation in a particular area versus the offering of an integrated, end-to-end service to a wide variety of clients from different industries. Responsiveness means both how quickly a firm can move from analysis to execution (this could be quantified by average project length), and how swiftly it has adapted to environmental change. Clearly, it would take a variety of metrics to assess each dimension and one would then have to weight each one. Therefore, the assessment in Figure 1 is based on qualitative observations and subjective judgement. Naturally, the groups described below do not encompass all consulting firms and undoubtedly there are some hybrids, which have the characteristics of more than one group.

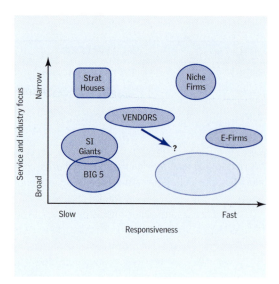

Figure 1 Strategic groups in the consulting industry

Big 5

This refers to the consulting arms of the large accounting firms of Ernst & Young, Pricewaterhouse Coopers, KPMG, Arthur Andersen, and Deloitte Touche. Their strengths lie in large-scale projects, long-term relationships and deep knowledge of vertical industries. Their entry point to consulting came with the introduction of information technology to accounting departments. While this bias remains today, they offer a wide range of services including business strategy, enterprise resource planning, IT consulting and outsourcing, and change and knowledge management. Their natural inclination is to extend assignments to as many layers over as long a time frame as possible. Combined with their size, this results in slow responsiveness.

SI giants

Systems integration is dominated by a few huge organisations: IBM, Andersen Consulting, CSC, EDS and Cap Gemini. Between them, they control most of the world's important databases. While they often compete with the Big 5, they are typically selected for their expertise in complex, large-scale IT assignments rather than business strategy. Their industry experience is broad, though perhaps not as deep as

that of the Big 5. Recently, Andersen and IBM have added services to create an integrated e-business offering. Size and history slow their response speeds.

Vendors

As we have already seen, hardware and software vendors are entering the consulting market. In the wireless world, key players include Nokia, Ericsson, Hewlett-Packard, Oracle, Cisco, Nortel, Lucent, Siemens and Unisys. In many ways, they are attempting to emulate IBM's successful reinvention of itself as a services provider. Their strengths are their technological understanding and monopoly on market access. Their weaknesses are the lack of independent consulting experience in many industries and across service lines. They are not a homogeneous group in terms of speed of response: while most are regarded as slow. Cisco is seen as one of the most dynamic companies in the fast-moving internet space.

Strat houses

These include McKinsey, Bain, Boston Consulting Group, Booze Allen Hamilton, Mercer, Monitor and numerous others. Typically organised as partnerships, they command fees of up to $500,000 per consultant per annum (four times that for the outsourcing of computer services). Weak on implementation, they provide an intellectual approach rooted in the design, planning and positioning schools of strategy. Their greatest asset is probably their access to clients at the CEO level via the old-boy network. While covering all industries, they focus exclusively on strategy and do not offer end-to-end integration. The pursuit of analytical rigour is often at the expense of speed: months of work can result in little more than a thick report.

Niche firms

These firms are even more tightly focused than the strat houses. There are a number that specialise in strategy and research in the digital arena, including Analysys, Decipher, Informed Sources, Ovum and Spectrum. They offer deep knowledge of the telco, media and internet industries, often advising regulators and government on strategic or business modelling issues. Their small size, independence and narrow focus make them nimble and able to punch beyond their weight in terms of influence.

E-firms

This group is highly fragmented, with many players including Viant, Scient, Sapient Proxicom, Razorfish, Agency.com, Organic, IXL, marchFIRST, Digitas and Cambridge Technology Partners. Although coming from diverse backgrounds (web design, advertising, systems integration, direct marketing and pure-plays), all have moved to offer an end-to-end integrated service focused on the internet. The enthusiasm of investors and favourable demand conditions has enabled these publicly traded companies to build global scale quickly, often through multiple acquisitions. With strong cultures and a sophisticated understanding of knowledge management, fast response seems embedded in e-firms. However, as well as coping with their own rapid growth, they now face a number of other challenges. The bursting of the e-bubble has resulted in plummeting stock prices (Viant's market capitalisation has fallen from $2 billion to $236 million during six months in 2000, for instance), which will restrict further expansion. A slowing in demand growth has made it imperative that they begin to differentiate from one another. The maturing of e-business means there is a growing need for vertical industry knowledge.

White spaces and other opportunities

Figure 1 throws an interesting light on current industry moves. Cap Gemini's acquisition of Ernst & Young appears to be designed to broaden the focus of the vendors and improve channel access. The partnership between IBM and the strategy house Mercer increases the ability of both parties to claim an end-to-end service. IBM's merger of its consulting and systems integration businesses into Business Innovation Services formalises the breadth of its offering. All of these moves ignore the dimension of speed of response.

One of the benefits of strategic group analysis is that it can highlight white spaces – areas not currently occupied by any group – that represent opportunities to extract future rents (McGee and Thomas). Thus, we can see a large space in the bottom right, 'broad and fast' quadrant. While this would represent the optimum strategy for the wireless world, it requires competencies that in some ways are juxtaposed – these constitute mobility barriers. What kind of organisation could offer complete breadth at the same time as being agile enough to respond quickly to environmental changes?

The strat houses and niche firms are pursuing narrow differentiation strategies and seem unlikely to want to compete in this space. Niche firms may be targets for those who want to buy some speed, although it is doubtful whether the qualities that make them successful can be preserved through the acquisition process. We believe that all but the most prestigious strat houses may find their position increasingly difficult unless they can provide a faster response. One solution could be to break firms into 'virtual niche firms', harnessing their reputational assets without the dead weight of organisational inertia.

Although the e-firms are currently best positioned to move into this space, to do so would require major investments in new capabilities. This will be hard to finance given current market conditions in 2000. Nevertheless, one might expect a few players such as Sapient and Scient to attempt this. The rest appear vulnerable to consolidation.

The Big 5 and SI Giants will have to struggle against legacy structures and thinking in order to reposition themselves. Some members of the Big 5 seem to lack any clear sense of direction.

The vendors are a mixed bunch but their lack of tenure as consultants may be an advantage: learning new skills can be easier than unlearning old ones. Cisco has proved itself adept at strategic acquisition and choreographing its entire business web in delivering value. Although its origins are in network equipment, Cisco describes its value proposition as 'advice and the intellectual property around it' (Tapscott et al.). This could be the firm most capable of success in this space.

References

Arnold *et al.* 'Wireless, not Profitless', *McKinsey Quarterly*, 2, 1998.

Baladi, P 'Knowledge and Competence Management: Ericsson Business Consulting', *Business Strategy Review*, Winter, 1999.

Brown, E 'The E-Consultants', *Fortune*, 12 April 1999.

Colvin, G 'Old Consultants Never Die: They Just Go E', *Fortune*, 12 June 2000.

Forrester Research, 'Scoring Europe's E-business Help', February 2000.

Hamel, G 'Waking up IBM', *Harvard Business Review*, Sept/Oct 1999.

IBM (2000a) 'Cheryl Altany Wireless Consulting Unit BIS North'.

IBM (2000b) 'IBM.com Annual Report 1999'.

Kennedy Information Research Group, 'E-services Report', April 2000.

McGee, J and Thomas, H (1992) 'Strategic Groups and Intra-Industry Competition', *International Review of Strategic Management*, 3.

Milgrom, P and Roberts, J (1992) *Economics, Organization and Management*, Prentice Hall.

Oran, N (2000) 'Impact on Consultancies', *Financial Times*, 5 July.

O'Shea, J and Madigan, C (1997) *Dangerous Company*, Nicholas Brealey Publishing.

Sammer, J (2000) 'Paying for Performance', *Consulting Magazine*, May.

Sapeint (2000) 'Architects for the New Economy', www.sapient.com, August.

Scient (2000) 'Annual Report'.

Segal-Horn, S (1993) 'The Internationalisation of Service Firms', in *Advances in Strategic Management*, 9, pp. 31–55.

Stepanek, M (2000) 'Clash of E-Consultants', *Business Week*, 19 June.

Sweeney, J (2000) 'McKinsey at the Crossroads', *Consulting Magazine*, January.

Tapscott, D, Ticoll, D and Lowy, A (2000) *Digital Capital: Harnessing the Power of Business Webs*, McGraw-Hill.

Case Study Section Index